AS LONG AS
THEY DON'T
MOVE
NEXT DOOR

Segregation and Racial Conflict
in American Neighborhoods

Stephen Grant Meyer

ROWMAN & LITTLEFIELD PUBLISHERS, INC.
Lanham • Boulder • New York • Oxford

ROWMAN & LITTLEFIELD PUBLISHERS, INC.

Published in the United States of America
by Rowman & Littlefield Publishers, Inc.
4720 Boston Way, Lanham, Maryland 20706
www.rowmanlittlefield.com

12 Hid's Copse Road
Cumnor Hill, Oxford OX2 9JJ, England

Copyright © 2000 by Rowman & Littlefield Publishers, Inc.
First paperback edition 2001.

British Library Cataloguing in Publication Information Available

Library of Congress Cataloging-in-Publication Data
The hardback copy of this book was catalogued by the Library of Congress as follows.

Meyer, Stephen Grant, 1962–
    As long as they don't move next door : segregation and racial
conflict in American neighborhoods / Stephen Grant Meyer.
      p.   cm.
    Includes bibliographical references and index.
    1.   Afro-Americans—Segregation. 2. Discrimination in housing—
United States. 3. United States—Race relations. I. Title
E185.61.M37 2000
363.5'1—dc21

            99-34669
            CIP

ISBN 0-8476-9700-2 (cloth : alk. paper)
ISBN 0-8476-9701-0 (pbk. : alk. paper)

Printed in the United States of America

♾™ The paper used in this publication meets the minimum requirements of American National Standard for Information Sciences—Permanence of Paper for Printed Library Materials, ANSI/NISO Z39.48-1992.

CONTENTS

PREFACE

"As long as they don't move next door." The title is inspired by Phil Ochs. Once considered a rival of Bob Dylan, Ochs wrote topical songs containing a mixture of satire and bile. Most of his venom was saved for the likes of Orval Faubus and Richard Nixon, but in "Love Me I'm a Liberal," he chides what he considered the hypocrisy of the typical liberal. In one verse, he castigates northern supporters of the civil rights movement who condemn Jim Crow and the racism of southern bigots but deny or dismiss the prejudice against blacks in the North. Given the discomforting accuracy of Ochs's observation, the song's lines, "I love Puerto Ricans and Negroes / As long as they don't move next door," hit an appropriate note of social criticism.[1]

A second inspiration for the title lacks the acerbity of the first but is equally telling. It comes from a critical analysis of American race relations at the end of the twentieth century. Profound and positive changes have occurred in race relations in the United States over the past half-century. One now sees blacks working alongside whites. African Americans are usually admitted as equals to theaters, hotels, restaurants, stores, and other privately owned public facilities. Legal restrictions on political and voting rights have been erased. The courts outlawed segregation in schools, yet segregation persists. The most significant hindrance to further improvement of race relations in the United States remains the tendency of the races to live separate lives in separate neighborhoods. Whites have accepted African American advancement toward equal citizenship rights as long as they don't move next door.

Finally, a word is necessary about the purpose of this book. Most American history textbooks contain extensive treatments of the civil rights movement as led by Martin Luther King Jr., of school desegregation and the *Brown* v. *Board of Education of Topeka* case, and of race relations in the South. Readers will also find discussions of the urban unrest in the North and West a generation ago. But perhaps with the exception of the Chicago riot of 1919 and a very brief treatment of King's move North after 1965, readers of textbooks will not find much discussion of race and housing or of the conflict over residential space in the United States. Numerous monographs exist that tell of ghettoization and other housing issues for African Americans in specific localities. Many of them are of high quality and have become extremely influential, but no new national study exists. My first purpose, therefore, is to extend the literature and tell a story that hitherto has not been told, one of great achievement as well as profound pain.

My second purpose is to amend the existing literature. The accepted truth on the issue is contained in *Forbidden Neighbors,* a book by Charles Abrams published more than forty years ago and one that, in my opinion, is fundamentally flawed. Abrams focused more on the premise that residential segregation was caused by government and industry than on the idea that it was an outgrowth of deep-seated racial prejudice. He did this, I speculate, because as a leader of the public housing and urban renewal movement, Abrams held out the hope that governments could solve the problems of injustice that faced African Americans and the poor, particularly if governments were seen to be the cause of such problems. Furthermore, Abrams was an active and dedicated player in the civil rights movement, and the movement needed to focus its resources on remedying the injustices of institutionally supported segregation in the South. And, I believe, Abrams and others feared that a true telling of the breadth and depth of racial conflict in the urban North and West in the 1950s might have led African Americans to respond as earlier generations had—with riotous retaliation.

Forty years later, I do not share that fear because I realize that most blacks, although not aware of the specifics of the incidents related herein, know this story. They have lived it and are living it. Therefore, the book will not come as a revelation to them. It may, however, come as a revelation to many white Americans. Moreover, I do not believe that it is the purpose of history to cover up disquieting events. At my most naïve, I believe that the "truth shall make us free." What follows, I contend, is the truth about race relations in the United States.

Derrick Bell, in *Faces at the Bottom of the Well,* talked about "the permanence of racism." Racism, sadly, is probably a permanent blight on the American community, particularly now because of the complacency or petty political badgering that most Americans have exhibited in response to questions of racial injustice. I, like Bell, hold out little hope that racial conflict will ever be eradicated completely. But I do hope that a more truthful remembering of events will lead to a more accurate diagnosis of the degree of the disease and may, in turn, enable us to come closer to a real and lasting cure.[2]

ACKNOWLEDGMENTS

So many people are involved in the completion of a book that it is hard to thank everyone and not have acknowledgments sound like an overlong Academy Awards acceptance speech. If I have omitted anyone as an oversight, then I want to apologize up front. I also want to note that any errors that may still exist in the text are entirely my responsibility.

This project began as a dissertation at the University of Alabama. First, I wish to thank the University of Alabama Graduate Research Council for two years of financial support through the research fellowship program. Because I was a foreigner with limited means of legal employment, the aid was essential to the completion of the dissertation.

I wish to acknowledge the help, critical comments, and suggestions of my committee and particularly those of Forrest McDonald, whose wide-ranging knowledge and understanding were absolutely integral to the completion of the project and who provided me with a model of the erudite yet approachable historian to which I aspire. I would also like to thank Jeff Norrell, who was involved in the early stages of the work by helping to shape the scale and scope of the thesis and who has kept a continued interest in its ultimate publication.

My profound appreciation goes to the long list of colleagues who have given advice and encouragement over the more than six years that it has taken to complete this book, particularly Glenn Crothers, Robert McFarland, Mark Rose, Jerrell Shofner, Tom DiBacco, Guy Hubbs, Bob England, Rich Megraw, Mel McKiven, Jim Martin, and Don Critchlow. Thank you to Steve Wrinn and the dedicated editors at Rowman & Littlefield for their excellent and detailed copy-editing and for their heartening encouragement. My thanks also go to my professors at the University of Alabama and the University of Toronto, most notably Bill Berman, who showed me what thinking critically was all about. And to the librarians and archivists who rendered expert and congenial aid during the research of this piece, especially those at Amelia Gayle Gorgas Library at the University of Alabama, the Wayne State University Archives of Labor and Urban Affairs, the University of Louisville Archives, the Atlanta University Center and Emory University, and the exceptionally knowledgeable staff of the Manuscripts Division of the Library of Congress. I also wish to thank Mary Johnson of the *Milwaukee Journal-Sentinel* for helping with some of the pictures and The Crisis Publishing Co., Inc., the publisher of the magazine of the National Association for the Advancement of Colored People, for authorizing the use of photographs and art work.

Personal thanks go to my Canadian friends who have given me unfailing support over the years and particularly to Brad and Nancy for not only showing interest in the project, but also for offering a bed to me while on road trips. My sincere thanks to Jan and Allen and Julia, who gave me great advice and a job in a down market. Finally, to my family go my deepest thanks: to my wife, Lori, who is always encouraging and who offered useful insights and timely critical commentary; to her family, now mine as well, for their support and encouragement; and, finally, to my family in Canada, to whom I dedicate this book, for providing me with the solid foundation on which to build this different kind of housing project.

INTRODUCTION

"Keep This Neighborhood White"

Probably the chief force maintaining residential segregation of Negroes has been *informal* social pressure from whites.[1]

This study springs from the simple observation that racial tension persists in the United States. It observes American race relations from the undervalued vantage point of the conflict over residential space to gain a new perspective on the nature of prejudice and intolerance.

Although tremendous advances have been made against racial injustice during the past half-century, segregation endures. It continues in the neighborhoods of the nation. What is more, many Americans of both races have come to accept racial separation as appropriate. To live among people of similar culture and condition, to enjoy the support of that community and its services, is natural. If that were the only basis for the segregation that exists, then there would be no reason to question the condition of race relations in the United States today. But the reality of the situation differs considerably. A century of discrimination, obstruction, intimidation, and violence underlies the current circumstance of residential racial separation.

The twentieth century has seen a tremendous racial battle over the right to buy and occupy housing. The scale and persistence of that conflict demonstrate that despite advances in other areas of interaction, many whites remain reluctant to accept African Americans as social equals. They refuse to accept blacks as neighbors. Significant elements in the black community, meanwhile, have resigned themselves to the enduring prejudice. They have accepted spatial and social separation; some even volunteer to segregate themselves from white communities in the hope of gaining peace and strength.

Looking through the prism of the conflict over residential space also gives a new

dimension to the civil rights movement. Contrary to the best hopes and good intentions of civil rights activists, racial tension did not end with the implementation of
anti-discrimination laws. The lack of resolution exposes the fact that some of the
historical and theoretical premises on which the National Association for the Advancement of Colored People (NAACP) and other civil rights groups based their
movement were faulty. The lawyers of the NAACP's Legal Defense and Education
Fund (LDF) and the academics who inspired them pursued a strategy of legal reform. They believed that distinctions between de jure and de facto race discrimination in the United States were significant. They believed that the Jim Crow system
of the South reflected a deeper and qualitatively different type of racism than the
customary discrimination practiced throughout the rest of the nation. But as the
conflict over residential space demonstrates, racial prejudice, as a form of xenophobia, runs deep in the nation's culture. Legislation and public policy did not create it,
and they alone cannot rectify it. Furthermore, the conflict shows that racism is a
national, not regional, phenomenon. Until whites outside the South honestly and
openly confront their own history of prejudice, violence, and discrimination, race
relations in the United States will continue to be a source of instability and potential
calamity.

I

The homestead and neighborhood possess tremendous significance in American
culture. Clichés regarding the importance of "hearth and home" abound in the
language. Sayings such as "Home Sweet Home" and "There's no place like home"
conjure images of warmth and security. "A man's home is his castle" denotes control
over one's domain. "Good fences make good neighbors" and "not in my back yard"
signify the importance that issues of household security and dominion can hold
when intertwined with community and social relationships.

On the basic economic level, the homestead is real property. As such, it is protected under common and constitutional law. One's home cannot be taken without
due process of law. It cannot be entered without permission or a judicial warrant.
Buying a house, meanwhile, is the largest single investment that most Americans
will make. Appreciation of the property's value can lead to economic security. Its
depreciation, however, can lead to personal economic ruin and its attendant anxiety
and tension.

The size of the investment causes home ownership to have yet a more specific
value and meaning in American culture. Home ownership represents the goal in the
pursuit of happiness. Its attainment marks the realization of the American Dream.[2]

Beyond its economic value, to many people home ownership can symbolize
social commitment. "A home owner," a Missouri court observed in 1944, "becomes a solid citizen with a stake in the community." When the average person
purchases a house, he or she accepts the responsibility of a mortgage—promising to

make steady payments and stay put. Understanding the importance of home ownership to the nation, President Franklin D. Roosevelt told Congress during the Great Depression: "The broad interests of the Nation [require] that special safeguards . . . be thrown around home ownership as a guarantee of social and economic stability." Not surprisingly, a comprehensive program of legislative protection and incentives has become central to government's contract with the middle class. Mortgage insurance, a one-time reprieve from the federal capital gains tax for the sale of one's home, and the mortgage deduction from the federal income tax evince the importance citizens and government place on home ownership.[3]

The homestead, paradoxically, also symbolizes independence. It has come to represent individual rights and freedom from outside interference. Robert N. Bellah and his colleagues describe it well in *The Good Society:* "Home ownership, that most intensely personal form of private property, reinforces the equation of the good life with individual security and private happiness."[4]

Persons across the political spectrum have embraced the homestead as a symbol of liberty. Advocates of a constitutional right of privacy, for example, use the homestead as the line across which government cannot pass to regulate personal behavior. Meanwhile, the defense of one's home has become an integral part of the campaign against gun control. Many Americans even insist that they have a right to use violence to protect their home. In the late 1960s, according to one study, 58 percent of male respondents believed that "a man has a right to kill a person to defend his house." Legal supports of those who do use violence to defend their property have become stronger in recent years. In the late 1980s, the state of Colorado, for example, passed a so-called make my day law that provided home owners with special protection from prosecution should they employ deadly force against a burglar or other intruder.[5]

The homestead holds the same significance for African Americans as it does for whites. Blacks similarly strive to enjoy the benefits of home ownership, the stability, and the potential for economic security. But it may also have an even deeper meaning for many African Americans. Joe R. Feagin and Melvin P. Sikes contend, "Home is for African Americans the one place that is theirs to control and that can give them refuge from racial maltreatment in the outside world."[6]

Because of the importance of the homestead, neighborhoods transcend other points of social contact. "The physical proximity of home and dwelling-places, the way in which neighborhoods group themselves, and [their] contiguity," the African American sociologist W. E. B. Du Bois observed, make neighborhoods the first line of communication and social interaction. Because of this fundamental position in culture and community, the neighborhood can provide a superior vantage point from which to assess preference and prejudice in interpersonal relations, one more basic to an individual's living condition than the job site, market, or school. The composition of neighborhoods therefore offers particular value in the study of the importance of race in the United States.[7]

II

The recent historical discussion of American race relations follows two lines. One school of thought focuses on the white supremacist behavior practiced in the southern states. It considers the South as an especially, possibly even a uniquely, racist society. It does acknowledge that discrimination in political and civil rights existed in the North but insists that northern forms of white supremacy never reached the character of the racial subjugation practiced in the South. Even the most refined form of this thesis, as articulated by C. Vann Woodward in later editions of *The Strange Career of Jim Crow*, draws the South as a singularly racist society. The South was exceptional because southern whites exercised racial oppression through legislated segregation and disfranchisement. The legal restrictions adopted by southern states, this school maintains, were qualitatively different and more oppressive than the customary limitations that may have faced African Americans in the North.

This school tends to take an optimistic view of race relations generally, emphasizing adaptability and change over entrenchment and continuity. It contends that racial discrimination was less entrenched and therefore less significant outside the South because those regions did not codify white supremacy. Moreover, because it contends that the system of discrimination was imposed from above by a southern power elite, this school even holds out hope for racial justice in the former Confederacy. The Woodward thesis, for example, contends that race relations in the South were in flux during the last third of the nineteenth century. Then, during the 1890s, relations shifted radically from a fluid and random exercise of white supremacy to a fixed system of racial subjugation and separation. It is possible but insignificant that southern whites felt prejudice against blacks during the whole of the period. They did not establish a system of racial discrimination and separation until politically opportunistic elites moved to reconcile the "estranged white classes" and to reunite "the Solid South."[8]

Followers of this interpretation of southern history and American race relations contend that racial discrimination is a learned behavior. As such, they surmise, it can also be unlearned. They suggest that increasing contact between the races will improve relations. When the races come to understand each other better, they will start to assess each other as individuals and appreciate their mutual interests. Tolerance will increase; racial tension will decrease. To create an environment in which tolerance can thrive, this school believes that governments must enact laws that support integration and racial contact. Legislation imposed segregation and discrimination on a reconstructed South. Changing the laws will reverse the process.[9]

The second, more despairing view of American race relations can be found in the works of John W. Cell, Howard N. Rabinowitz, Derrick Bell, Joel Williamson, and Leon F. Litwack. This argument holds that racism runs deep in the American mind, in Cell's words, having "been imported in the minds and psyches of the earliest European settlers." This school further contends that the differences in race relations in the North and South constitute differences of degree, not kind. The South has proved to be more overtly racist than the other regions, but an insidious bigotry permeates the whole nation. This second position does not make a strong distinction between discrimination in law and discrimination in behavior. Racial discrimination and prejudice therefore seem more constant, running through the entirety of American history. Charles S. Johnson, the African American sociologist and housing expert, made this point plain when he called a chapter of his study of de jure segregation, "the development of legislation to reinforce customs."[10]

On the question of continuity or change, I offer a synthesis of the two tracks. From the pessimistic viewpoint, this study shows that racism, as an innate form of xenophobia, does run through American society. Some degree of conflict has arisen in almost every instance in which blacks have breached the walls of traditionally white areas. And although governments and institutions played a role in upholding discrimination in housing, they were not responsible for the original racial conflict. Indeed, segregation laws were often seen as progressive developments enacted to restore peace and order to neighborhoods or to protect the public health. Meanwhile, as the optimists had contended, the changes that have occurred in race relations and in the living conditions of African Americans during this century demonstrate that with time and effort racial prejudice can diminish. Governmental intervention and social engineering—changes in the law to encourage interracial contact and refinements in democratic expectations of society—can ameliorate racial tension. The benefit of hindsight, however, enables us to understand that this change occurs at an evolutionary, not a revolutionary, pace. It will take generations for the policies to bear fruit.[11]

On the question of southern distinctiveness, the evidence demonstrates that racial discrimination is a national dilemma. The emphasis that many academics and civil rights activists have placed on southern racism, therefore, has distorted the reality of race relations in the United States. Race relations in the South did differ from those in the rest of the country. Owing to the size of the black population in the region, the South developed as a bicultural rather than a multicultural society. To maintain racial supremacy, whites built a structure of institutional and legal oppression. Residential areas, however, differed from the other venues of social contact. Most southern cities actually evinced a lower degree of residential segregation than did northern cities. Moreover, during much of the twentieth century, racial conflict and violence over housing were less common in the South. The Jim Crow system eliminated the possibility of blacks achieving equality with whites: southern whites had no need to fear any threat to their status. Residential segregation also proved inconvenient to whites who preferred to have black servants close at hand. Racial conflict in southern neighborhoods did not reach a significant scale until the Jim Crow system of oppression fell apart in the years following World War II. Southern practices did differ from the rest of the country, but white supremacy and racial discrimination are national phenomena.

III

Historically, African American migration into new neighborhoods has followed a pattern. T. J. Woofter long ago likened it to that of an advancing army. "A small outpost," he suggested, would be "thrown out ahead, and, if the terrain [was] favorable for occupancy by larger numbers, [then] the mass [would] advance." The rhetoric of invasion has come to dominate interpretations of the migration. Most blacks did not intend to lead assaults on white areas; they only sought better housing, but many whites interpreted the rhetoric literally. They blocked the penetration as if defending against a foreign enemy, using any means at their disposal to deter the migration. Throughout the country, the black point-men found the terrain tough slogging and the natives hostile. Early on, muckraking journalist Ray Stannard Baker observed another general principle: "the more Negroes the sharper the expression of [white] prejudice."[12]

Although the racial conflict over living space has long been a subject of investigation, most observers have tended to misjudge the extent, character, and significance of the resistance perpetrated against African American in-migrants. They have focused on the largest housing conflicts—riots in Chicago in 1919 and 1966, Detroit in 1942, and Cicero, Illinois, in 1951. Observers from Woofter in the 1920s to Douglas S. Massey and Nancy A. Denton in a recent study, have claimed that violence occurred only during the initial penetration of a neighborhood, that it happened once and then subsided, and that it "crested during the 1920s," recurring only sporadically thereafter. Even Charles Abrams in *Forbidden Neighbors*, still the most influential study of housing discrimination, errs by underrepresenting the extent of the violence in northern cities. Resistance against African Americans moving into white districts occurred more commonly as thousands of small acts of terrorism. And this study shows that, rather than cresting in the 1920s, resistance persisted throughout the century, the most vicious and extensive violence occurring in the North during the two decades following World War II.[13]

Closer historical examination of the issue unearths other weaknesses with the literature. Observers have tended to view the conflict over living space and housing from the top down. Adopting a Woodwardian worldview, they stress the institutional means by which residential segregation was "imposed" or "maintained." "During the war years and the 1920s," contends the eminent sociologist Karl Taeuber, for example, "the whites who controlled the shelter industry devised and implemented ways to contain the black population." Taeuber and others blame the real estate, lending, and construction industries for creating and perpetuating discrimination. Realtors, they maintain, convinced white home owners that property values would decline if African Americans moved in next door. Lenders refused to grant mortgage loans to blacks desiring to move into white areas. Such observers also emphasize the role that government has played in sustaining racial discrimination in housing. Government, they insist, gave legal sanction to discrimination through legislation, execution, and adjudication. As Taeuber puts it, "lending agencies, developers, sales and rental agents, public zoning agencies, school districts, police and other governmental agencies collaborated to confine blacks to existing areas of concentration, to channel expanding black populations to limited additional areas, and to steer whites elsewhere.[14]

The real estate industry did play a part in arousing concerns about property values and integration. Beginning in 1913, the National Association of Real Estate Boards (NAREB) instructed its members not to contribute to residential race mixing. It adopted racial criteria for appraising property in the 1920s. A textbook on real estate practice published in 1923 instructed prospective brokers that it was "a matter of common observation that the purchase of property by certain racial types is very likely to diminish the value of other property in the section." The *Appraisal Journal*, published by the American Institute of Real Estate Appraisers, echoed these sentiments. In a 1938 article, the appraisers advised, "ratings of location will be impaired where protection from adverse influences is inadequate to the extent that it is likely that lower racial and social groups will be attracted to the area." They continued: "If the present and prospective market is tolerant of such conditions, [then] their effect is of little importance," but "where the presence of nuisance tends to accelerate the rate of transition to lower racial or social occupancy, proper recognition of these conditions is obligatory." Even as late as 1957, a NAREB teaching manual counseled against introducing "undesirable influences" onto a block. Included among the undesirable influences cited were bootleggers, gangsters, or "a colored man of means who was giving his children a college education and thought they were entitled to live among whites."[15]

Governments did enact race-restrictive zoning ordinances, and federal agencies did refuse to integrate public housing projects and denied mortgage insurance to blacks intending to move into white areas. The Federal Housing Administration (FHA), for example, agreed that an African American invasion caused property values to fall and led to racial conflict. The agency actively upheld deed restrictions against African Americans. It furnished a model race-restrictive clause in its guidelines for builders and subdivision contractors from 1935 to 1937 and insisted that such provision be utilized. And in the 1940s, the FHA administrator even fought inclusion of anti-discrimination language in proposed housing legislation. Meanwhile, other sections of the housing bureaucracy, such as the United States Housing Authority (USHA), may not have intended to discriminate, but even they fell into a pattern of discrimination because of local laws and public opinion.[16]

It is essential to understand, however, that neither government nor realty, lending, and construction interests forged racial policies out of thin air. They did not act in a political and economic vacuum. To be sure, they did play a role in maintaining the dual housing market. But the weight of evidence demonstrates that they reflected a popular unwillingness on the part of whites to have African Americans living in their midst. Before the states and cities enacted restrictive zoning statutes and real estate boards and government agencies developed policies to maintain residential segregation, white home owners used violence and intimidation to scare blacks out of white neighborhoods. Although they have been justly criticized for perpetuating injustice, the policies and laws were created to keep the peace and maintain stability.

Numerous reasons underlay white resistance to residential integration, and protection of their investment resided high on the list. Whites believed that the coming of African Americans to the neighborhood heralded the decline of the living standard of the area. According to Robert C. Weaver, the noted African American expert on housing and first secretary of the Department of Housing and Urban Development, the charge that blacks "take over a good dwelling and let it run down was repeated so widely and so insistently that it . . . found general acceptance." When formerly white areas did deteriorate after racial transition, as often happened, whites saw their worst fears confirmed. Few, of course, took time to analyze the causes of the decay. They ignored the fact that discrimination in employment, in moneylending, and in choice of neighborhood often ensured that the only houses African Americans could afford would be older properties in already declining areas. Whites failed to understand that the higher finance costs that blacks were forced to pay often left them unable to pay for the upkeep of a dwelling.[17]

Trepidation and hostility at the prospect of having black neighbors derived from more than just economic issues. It grew out of stereotypes drawn from what whites believed characterized everyday life in the black community. When they viewed life in the ghetto, whites saw only crime, licentiousness, and people living in overcrowded, dilapidated dwellings. Stereotypically, life in the slum engaged "every kind of vice known to the demimonde"; life in the bottoms was "fecundmellow." Many whites, if they thought about it at all, believed that African Americans preferred this "uncivilized" life or, worse still, that they were racially predisposed to such a life. Concern over race mixing further fed white anxiety. Many whites felt, as did a woman in Baltimore, that if blacks and whites lived on the same block, then "the children of the two races [would] grow up together and intermarry and [that] such a thought [was] repellent to one who [had] the integrity of the white race at heart." Beyond the negative stereotypes, many whites also feared that integration would threaten their own social and economic status. The perceived threat became more real as large numbers of African Americans migrated from rural to urban areas and from the South to the North and West.[18]

To protect their status, their investments, and their living environment, white home owners resisted integration. The resistance began with sporadic acts of violence and vandalism against the property of the newcomers. To quell this trend and restore peace, local governments enacted restrictive zoning ordinances that ghettoized blacks. Neighborhood improvement associations, housing developers, and speculative builders, meanwhile, drew up private restrictive covenants, forcing home owners to pledge never to sell their property to blacks. Realtors and financial institutions joined in the discrimination, instructing brokers and lenders not to assist African Americans wanting to move into white districts. When the laws failed constitutionality tests or when covenants broke down, white home owners once again took the law into their own hands. In some instances, entire communities opposed blacks moving into white neighborhoods. Hundreds or thousands of demonstrators would gather to picket and heckle, throwing rocks or even bombs. The mobs included men, women, and children. Indeed, since pickets were usually maintained throughout the day, housewives would often lead demonstrations while their husbands were at work. Teenagers would join in after school, as much to keep themselves amused as to terrorize the new residents.[19]

IV

To fight the injustice, African Americans and civil rights organizations embarked on a "Campaign Against Residential Segregation." The crusade began in the courts but soon moved to all areas of politics and government. Legal histories, such as Mark V. Tushnet's *Making Civil Rights Law,* offer excellent treatments of the formation and evolution of the strategy of litigation employed by the civil rights movement. Tushnet views housing as a secondary issue, one important to the development of jurisprudence but not central to his analysis, which is the story of the fight against segregation in schools. One large study exists that does focus on housing. Clement E. Vose's *Caucasians Only* offers a narrative retelling of the fight against restrictive covenants. It neglects the other side of the legal battle and, though strong in many ways, suffers from many of the same assumptions that plague the work of Abrams. Furthermore, the Campaign Against Residential Segregation went on far beyond the courts.[20]

The NAACP led the crusade. Unlike many civil rights questions, discrimination in private housing was principally a middle-class issue, and the NAACP was primarily a middle-class organization. As the campaign progressed, nearly every other civil rights organization added its voice. The crusade initially challenged both public and private modes of discrimination through the judicial system and then moved to legislatures and the public forum.

Despite the established doctrine of "separate but equal," the NAACP hoped that the courts would be most sympathetic to its objectives and would strike down public and private discrimination. First challenging race-restrictive zoning ordinances, the organization argued that protection of private real property was too important a constitutional right to be circumscribed by state and local statutes. In 1917, the Supreme Court agreed, ruling a Louisville ordinance to be unconstitutional in the case of *Buchanan* v. *Warley.* The achievement of *Buchanan* took decades to bear fruit, however, because many southern cities ignored the ruling and dared the NAACP to sue.

The fight against restrictive covenants proved to be an even greater struggle. The LDF was forced to hone its legal arguments and convince the court that state enforcement of private acts of discrimination through court injunctions not only represented an abridgment of civil rights guaranteed by the U.S. Constitution but also could be remedied. Not until 1948, after decades of tactical developments, did the LDF succeed in its battle against race-restrictive covenants in the case of *Shelley* v. *Kraemer.*

After the court victories of the late 1940s, the NAACP and several other activist organizations united to form a more focused coordinated council, the National Committee Against Discrimination in Housing (NCDH), to lobby state and federal legislators to protect the housing rights of minorities. The NCDH, led by its first president, Charles Abrams, fought the discriminatory practices of government and the real estate industry and fashioned model anti-discrimination legislation for cities and states. The black clergy joined in the campaign, preaching on the immorality of racism and coordinating demonstrations to combat discrimination, and the black press and academics of all races further exposed the hypocrisy of the "American dilemma."[21]

During the 1950s, while most of the nation's attention was focused on the South's massive resistance to school integration, cities in the North and West witnessed almost constant strife over housing. Even the most celebrated blacks of the day— Jackie Robinson and Willie Mays—met with resistance. Segregation grew as many white home owners took advantage of federal home loan policies to flee to the suburbs, but the fight against housing discrimination forged ahead. The NCDH grew as a political force, especially in New York, which became a laboratory for anti-discrimination policies. The NAACP and NCDH also adopted some new tactics that they had learned from the grassroots civil rights movement.

The 1960s saw the culmination of the legal campaign against residential segregation. The proponents of open housing pressed President John F. Kennedy until he outlawed racial discrimination in certain categories of housing through an executive order in 1962. Four years later, one of their own was given a voice in the cabinet: President Lyndon B. Johnson appointed Robert Weaver as the first secretary of the Department of Housing and Urban Development. In 1968, as cities exploded in race war over housing and other issues, Congress took the final step, reversing nearly sixty years of injustice. Where the laws of the early part of the century had imposed racial restrictions and supported discrimination, the Civil Rights Act of 1968, better known as the Fair Housing Act, outlawed discrimination and sought to take affirmative action in winning better access to better housing for African Americans. The pursuers of racial justice had won, at least in law. The races reached a truce in 1968. The Fair Housing Act reduced racial violence in the streets by removing most of the conflict to the courts.

v

Race still matters in the United States. In the late 1970s, William Julius Wilson suggested that the significance of "race" was declining. "Fundamental economic and political changes" such as the emergence of a black middle class, desegregation of public schools, and the civil rights revolution, according to Wilson, had made "economic class affiliation more important than race in determining Negro prospects for occupational advancement." In this view, if an African American had enjoyed a middle-class upbringing, including a middle-class education and possibly a college degree, then he would enjoy favorable opportunities for employment and promotion. The person's race, Wilson asserts, would have less of an effect on the individual's "access to those opportunities that are centrally important for life survival" than it once had. Wilson is largely correct with respect to the focus of his study, the underclass, but he pays scant attention to the life experiences of the middle class. When one observes residential race relations, the weaknesses of Wilson's position become even clearer. Wilson had focused on the one element that he considered to be "centrally important to life survival," that is, employment. Shelter, however, is arguably equally important to survival. For the reasons mentioned above, the dwelling space is different from the workplace. Even those who seldom experience racism personally at work or school do meet discrimination when facing the issue of where to live. In spatial relations, race matters more than economic class. Those African Americans who have tried to move into traditionally white districts have tended to enjoy wealth and education at least equal to those of their white counterparts. They have usually belonged to what stands for the "occupational elite" of the race: doctors, lawyers, business leaders, and civil servants. They have even been wealthy celebrities.[22]

Observers of residential race relations have noted that when the black community encroaches on white areas it causes anxiety among the resident white population. According to Rose Helper, when whites even see African Americans in their neighborhoods, they often feel "'concerned,' . . . 'jittery,' 'disturbed,' . . . 'worried,' 'apprehensive,' and 'up in the air.'" And according to David L. Hamilton and George D. Bishop, any black family moving into the neighborhood "is a highly salient event" for whites. Whites, they found, notice new African American neighbors more than they do white newcomers. Cognizance of a black presence in the neighborhood does not always mean that conflict will ensue, but the record has shown that in most cases whites have responded unfavorably, at least initially, to African Americans moving into their neighborhood. And when conflict does occur, whites resist black newcomers because of their race, disregarding economic class altogether.[23]

Thirty years after its enactment, we can see that the Fair Housing Act has failed to integrate neighborhoods. As the urban historian Nathan Glazer notes, residential segregation has resisted policy intervention. It persists "despite the many state laws, and the national legislation, which make discrimination in rental and sales of housing illegal." It persists, despite the expanded political and economic opportunities for African Americans, the growth of the black middle class, and their increased movement into the suburbs. Indeed, over the past three decades significant numbers of middle-class blacks have chosen to move into exclusively African American suburban enclaves. Out of personal desire or surrender, they have segregated themselves.[24]

It has long been understood that segregation is a double-edged sword for the African American community. W. E. B. Du Bois explained the phenomenon in 1924, in an article entitled "The Dilemma of the Negro." Blacks initially fought Jim Crow when it first spread throughout the South. But then, according to Du Bois, the community "began to get a few educated Negro preachers, many trained Negro teachers, and some skilled Negro physicians." These "cultured individuals," Du Bois suggests, imparted "the elements of civilization . . . in much pleasanter and more effective ways than most white people" had. The community came to appreciate the value of these educators and artists and of the race. The black community discovered that segregation could have a positive effect on African American culture.[25]

The positive effects of racial separation created a dilemma for blacks. To paraphrase Du Bois, the dilemma runs as follows: as blacks enter American society, the distinctiveness of their culture is assimilated into the dominant white culture, but if they remain separate, if they voluntarily accept segregation to preserve their culture and identity, then that leads to permanent subordination to white society or worse, to race war because of what Du Bois called "race pride." James Weldon Johnson, the poet, writer, and executive secretary of the NAACP, made that last point more graphically. "If the antagonistic forces are destined to dominate and bar all forward movement," Johnson warned, then "there will be only one way of salvation for the race . . . and that will be through the making of its isolation into a religion and the cultivation of a hard, keen, relentless hatred for everything white."[26]

This century has witnessed the working out of "the dilemma of the Negro," traveling through Garveyism, the Harlem Renaissance, the civil rights movement, Black Power, the Black Aesthetic, the Nation of Islam, affirmative action, the Rainbow Coalition, Afrocentrism, and political correctness.[27] The dilemma now involves balancing "color-blindness" in law, industry, and residence with racial tolerance and the cultivation of cultural diversity. Blacks may justifiably prefer to reside in separate racial enclaves. They may prefer closer access to black institutions, churches, and businesses. And there is still white resistance to consider. Even if whites throw fewer bombs than they once did, white flight remains common, and social ostracism of black newcomers persists. Racially integrated neighborhoods are no panacea. But given the history of violence and intimidation over the century, the real question should be about whether African Americans have the opportunity to buy homes in whatever neighborhoods they choose to buy in and can afford and whether they will be protected if they so choose, not whether neighborhoods actually show racial balance. Progress has been made, but more needs to be done. As long as African Americans do not have free and equal access to property and the right to live wherever and amid whomever they choose, they do not enjoy full citizenship.

BORDER CONFLICT

The South doesn't care how close a Negro gets just so he doesn't get too high; the North doesn't care how high he gets just so he doesn't get too close.[1]

For three decades following the Civil War, race relations in the South were fluid. African Americans enjoyed a new status as freedmen. Many availed themselves of their newfound mobility by taking to the roadways, some aimlessly, others with great purpose. Although whites still reigned supreme, for some African Americans opportunities grew after emancipation as black entrepreneurs took advantage of segregated markets for goods and services and a thriving, if scanty, black middle class emerged in many cities. Most African Americans, however, remained impoverished, and many existed in peonage. White attitudes toward the freedmen had changed little over the years. Some whites employed violent means, notably the lynching rope, to keep blacks down. A few white academics and media propounded pseudo-scientific theories about the innate inferiority of the black race to justify oppression and exclusion. White politicians sought to accommodate this racial prejudice. In the 1890s, race relations began to stabilize. White majorities disenfranchised African Americans and codified segregation in schools, stores, hotels, public transportation, and other facilities. During this new era in white supremacy, many blacks chose to leave the South to try their luck elsewhere.[2]

When African Americans left the South for the urban mid-Atlantic and North at the turn of the century, they were huddled into ghettos, which quickly became overcrowded slums. When more prosperous blacks tried to escape the squalor by moving into white districts, they met resistance from white residents. Economic fears and a self-fulfilling prophecy that African American neighbors caused property values to decline gave foundation to the resistance. Anxiety over "race mixing"—the dilution and degeneration of the white race—and paranoia about the supposed licentiousness of blacks exacerbated it.

With their large and diverse citizenry, the larger centers of the Northeast, such as New York and Philadelphia, absorbed the newcomers. The African American migrants seemed, at first, just another immigrant group. Smaller cities, such as Baltimore, St. Louis, Kansas City, and Louisville, felt the influx of blacks differently. They lacked the housing and the facilities to accommodate the new population. Not only size but also the history of race relations in these cities determined the degree of white resistance. Blacks had never been totally excluded in these cities but had never enjoyed equal rights or status either. As the number of in-migrants grew, whites were forced to deal with the changing status of blacks. Many resented the prospect of having blacks live among them as equals and fought to preserve the status quo.

Anxious whites used violence and intimidation to keep African Americans off their blocks. Blacks saw their homes bombed or stoned. As tensions grew, cities tried to restore peace by trampling on the civil and property rights of African Americans. Cities enacted segregation zoning ordinances that prohibited blacks from moving into white neighborhoods. To satisfy the constitutional doctrine of "separate but equal," the laws also kept whites out of black sections. Whites, however, seldom chose to live in African American districts. Black leaders condemned the statutes, and the National Association for the Advancement of Colored People began the court battle to eliminate race-restrictive zoning ordinances that led all the way to the Supreme Court.

Racial residential segregation has existed in the United States at least since the first stages of urbanization. In eighteenth-century Boston, the African American community was relegated to "New Guinea" at the tip of the city's North End. In the early 1800s, blacks began moving to the river side of Beacon Hill to be nearer their jobs as domestics for the Brahmins. The area eventually won the appellation "Nigger Hill." During the colonial and revolutionary periods, New York City's African Americans were concentrated at the tip of Manhattan Island. Gradually they trekked uptown, following their employers first to what is now the financial district, then to "a fringe of nests to the west and south" of Washington Square, and then to Greenwich Village, always congregating on separate blocks.[3]

Slavery made the urban spatial distribution of the races distinct in the South. To maintain control over their property in the early nineteenth century, urban slaveholders quartered their bondsmen close to the main building. Later, according to historian Richard C. Wade, a pattern of "living out" developed. Slaves moved outside the master's compound, often converging in "the back parts" or the frontiers of cities. Residential separation of slave and master therefore increased over the course of the antebellum period.[4]

Free blacks in the cities of the Old South also tended to live closer to whites than they would have in the North. In Charleston, for instance, according to Ira Berlin, free blacks "resided on every major thoroughfare." The majority of African Americans did live in the poorer sections, in the bottoms near railroad yards or rivers, but even the slums usually were composed of "a melange of whites and blacks," Berlin asserts. Leonard P. Curry similarly notes that residential separation was not systematic and that the degree of segregation did not approach the levels of the twentieth century. He determines, however, that in most major cities "growing numbers of the free black residents lived in ever tighter residential concentrations which were pushed toward the periphery of the city." Using census data, Curry concludes that Louisville, Washington, D.C., and Charleston had insignificant levels of racial concentration before the Civil War, meaning that the races were scattered throughout the cities. New Orleans, however, showed a "high level of racial residential concentration." Curry adds that accurate estimates of the degree of segregation depend on the size of the census unit analyzed. Studies based on city wards rather than blocks, he contends, "conceal areas of high density Negro population within them." And regardless of how closely blacks resided to whites, proximity did not bring better living conditions. Curry shows that African Americans resided in small, poorly built and maintained structures that were "much more likely than the residences of whites . . . to be located in alleys and on closed courts, or crammed into the rear portion of narrow lots."[5]

Howard Rabinowitz, in his impressive examination of race relations in five southern cities during the postbellum era, shows that residential segregation grew as the South transformed a system of white racial control based on custom into a statutory and juridical strategy. He observes that areas of black settlement in Richmond, Virginia, for example, spread beyond the "antebellum nuclei" to create "the most famous concentration of blacks," the Jackson Ward. In Oberlin, North Carolina, a suburb of Raleigh, meanwhile, "almost all of the 750 inhabitants" were black. Likewise, Atlanta had several areas in which the black population was concentrated, such as Hell's Half Acre, Mechanicsville, Darktown, Peasville, and Pigtail Alley.[6]

Racial residential segregation had many sources. "Some of the housing segregation was voluntary," Rabinowitz contends, as blacks "welcomed the freedom from white surveillance, and enjoyed the company of other blacks." Racial separation also resulted from black poverty, white discrimination, the inadequate resources and policies of the Freedmen's Bureau, and opportunism on the part of white realtors and black businesspeople who sought to profit from a separate community and an inflated market demand. Consciously missing from Rabinowitz's list of causes is legislation because, he notes, "laws proscribing integrated blocks or entire sections of the community were a product of the twentieth century." Instead, he continues, "Southern whites sought to accomplish the same goals through a more subtle use of public and private power." Even in the newest southern city, Birmingham, Alabama, officials saw no need to legislate segregation of residences. So powerful was white domination and the social custom of separation that legal restrictions were redundant.[7]

Beginning in the 1890s and accelerating after the turn of the century, black migration restructured the urban residential distribution of the races. Huge numbers of African Americans moved from the rural South to cities in the North and mid-Atlantic. Washington, Baltimore, New York City, and Philadelphia saw dramatic increases in black population in this early wave of migration. Between 1890 and 1900, Manhattan's black population more than doubled, from 23,601 to more than 60,000. It rose by half again to more than 91,000 by 1910. Migrants clustered in the area known as San Juan Hill in the lower sixties on the West Side. To put this population increase in context, however, New York City experienced tremendous growth of all ethnic and racial groups during these years. The city's population quintupled to a total of 4,766,883 people between 1870 and 1910. Even with the tremendous influx of migrants from the South, African Americans constituted less than 3 percent of the city's total population. Philadelphia's African American population grew by nearly 20,000 to total 62,613 between 1890 and 1900 and by 20,000 more by 1910. Its size in proportion to the city's total population, however, remained almost constant. A ghetto formed in the southeastern part of the Seventh Ward and the adjoining Thirtieth Ward, along Lombard and South Streets, "with the worst black slum in the city at Seventh and Lombard." Middle-class blacks, perhaps 3,000 in number, lived in the same area but west of Eighth Street.[8]

New York and Philadelphia could absorb the black newcomers, at least before 1915, but migration had an immediate effect on Baltimore. Between 1865 and 1900, the city's population doubled to nearly 500,000. It grew by 50,000 more people between 1900 and 1910. Largely as a result of European immigration, more whites moved into Baltimore than blacks. Still, between 1880 and 1900, the black population grew from 54,000 to 79,000, giving the city the nation's second-largest black community after Washington, D.C. By 1910, Baltimore had dropped to third behind New York in total number of African American residents, but proportionally the new blacks had a greater impact on the Maryland city. The black population had swelled to nearly 85,000, 15.5 percent of the city's total.[9]

Its size offered Baltimore's black community some leverage in the local economy and in politics, but its continued expansion caused segments of the white power structure to view the migration as a threat. Democratic Party leaders tried to disenfranchise blacks. The politically weaker Republicans preferred that African Americans keep the vote, but they accommodated the new racial order by segregating party meetings. By 1901, the Grand Old Party required that African Americans be seated separately at party functions to ease the anxieties of white members. Baltimore's blacks tolerated their change in status because no other political home existed for them.[10]

Prior to the influx of migrants, African Americans had concentrated in Baltimore's central, southern, and eastern sections, but members of the race lived in clusters, usually along alleys and cul-de-sacs, in each of the city's twenty wards. No ghetto per se existed, but the migrants put tremendous pressure on the established black sections. Their poverty forced them into the cheapest housing. A ghetto called Pigtown developed in Southwest Baltimore. The continued rapid growth of the section and its impoverished condition meant the creation of Baltimore's first real slum. An 1892 account in the *Baltimore News* gave a disturbing picture of the ghetto: "Open drains, great lots filled with high weeds, ashes and garbage accumulated in the alley-ways, cellars filled with filthy water." The people in the slum, the *News* continued, were "villainous looking negroes who loiter and sleep around the street corners and never work." "Foul streets, foul people, in foul tenements filled with foul air," it concluded, "that's Pigtown." It is no wonder that those who could would try to escape the squalor.[11]

As early as the 1880s, members of Baltimore's black middle class, a group numbering about 250, began to "remove themselves from the 'disreputable and vicious neighborhoods of their own race.'" After 1898, the exodus increased when Sharp Street Memorial Methodist Episcopal Church, one of the city's largest black churches, moved to a site at Dolphin and Etting Streets. Within five years, the black high school and Union Baptist Church also moved to the area. Migration to the city's Northwest grew again when the Baltimore and Ohio (B&O) Railroad condemned blocks of dwellings in South Baltimore to make way for expansion of its yards. Most members of this last group posed no real threat to white areas because of their poverty, but their movement still struck fear in whites of a broader black "invasion."[12]

White behavior accelerated the racial transition. According to W. Ashbie Hawkins, whites fled the old neighborhoods, thereby throwing "great blocks of handsome houses on the market, [houses that] had to be disposed of to anybody, and often on any terms." Hawkins, a lawyer and community leader, a fixture in the Niagara Movement and later the president of the NAACP branch, would eventually take the city to court over residential segregation. By 1910, with whites fleeing to outlying new suburbs, blacks began buying property in the Druid Hill section of the city. The number who would actually own their homes remained minute—933 out of the city's nearly 85,000 blacks in 1910—but that did not lessen the concern of white home owners. Neither did the fact that the newcomers were from what Hawkins identified as the "upper strata of the city's entire black population"—doctors, dentists, lawyers, pharmacists, and entrepreneurs.[13]

When African Americans "invaded" a block in the Druid Hill section, conflict arose. Whites broke windows and committed various other property crimes against black-owned homes. In one instance, whites tarred the marble steps in front of a home. On Stricker Street, whites attacked a black family and stoned their house. Mobs forced one family from their new home on West Lanvale Street and threatened another when they moved into the 1100 block of Myrtle Street. Sometimes the intimidation worked, and blacks moved off the block, but the tide ran against the white home owners. As Hawkins describes it, "after a short time the excitement wore off," and whites either moved or resigned themselves to their fate. To try to restore peace, the realty market set aside about ten square blocks for black residents.

Nothing was officially said, but there existed "a tacit understanding that this section belonged to the Negro." As long as blacks contented themselves with the established blocks, peace would reign.[14]

In June 1910, George W. F. McMechen, a black lawyer, moved with his family into a house on McCulloh Street. The Yale University graduate had purchased the home in celebration of his professional success. The home was located in the fashionable Eutaw Place neighborhood, east of the Druid Hill Avenue boundary line of the black section. Residents of McCulloh Street protested the move. Neighborhood teenagers harassed the newcomers, but a police presence easily quelled the demonstrations. White home owners held a mass meeting to draw up a petition requesting that Mayor J. Barry Mahool "take some measures to restrain the colored people from locating in a white community, and proscribe a limit beyond which it shall be unlawful for them to go."[15]

Milton Dashiell took up the cause against the McMechens. An underemployed white lawyer and an avowed racist, Dashiell lived at 1110 McCulloh, only a block away from Biddle Alley, the repository of the poorest blacks displaced by the B&O expansion and the city's newest slum. Together with Councilman George W. West, Dashiell conceived the West Segregation Law, which stipulated that no black could "move into, or attempt to occupy, a house in a block where 51 percent or more of the houses therein were occupied by whites, or vice versa." An exception was made for black servants. Prominent African Americans protested the bill in public hearings, and black Councilman Harry Sythe Cummings voted against it, but to no avail. The bill passed both branches of the council by strict party vote; Democrats voted in favor and Republicans voted against. City Solicitor Edgar Allan Poe declared the law to be constitutional, residing well within the state's power to regulate for the peace, health, and morals of citizens, and Mayor Mahool signed it in mid-December. The city gave Dashiell one of the pens used in the signing; he declared it a "favor" he would "treasure."[16]

It is not hard to explain the city council's willingness to enact a segregation ordinance. The growth of the black community and the economic progress of a small segment of the race had rendered ineffective the customary restrictions on African American advancement. The decline of black sections into squalor provoked fear among whites that crime and disease would spread as ghetto walls broke down. The unrest caused by the movement of middle-class blacks into white districts forced the city to take some action to restore stability. The Democrats on the council saw a legislative solution as necessary, popular among the white electorate, and entirely consistent with the court-approved apartheid in effect across the South. Politically impotent, the African American community could not fight it.

Baltimore's lawmakers insisted that residential segregation was even more essential to maintenance of stability than racial separation on public conveyances and in schools. In a 1917 law review article, then City Solicitor S. S. Field explained the thinking behind the legislation. "If considerations of peace and good order justify [keeping] the races from meeting occasionally and for a short time in railway coaches," Field declared, "[then] is there not far greater danger of clashes between the races from families, white and black, living side by side, with their front doors within a few feet of each other every day?" He continued: "If the natural feeling between the races, or the danger of conflict between children is sufficient justification for separate schools, where children would be brought into contact only part of the time and under the supervision of teachers, [then] do not the same reasons apply with greater force to a measure which is intended to prevent the children from meeting in daily contact in front of their homes, and much of the time without any older person present to maintain order?" Finally, Field added an antimiscegenetic element to the apology. He insisted that concern over "cross-breeding between the races" made intermarriage and sexual intercourse between the races a crime, and "this same reason sustain[ed] provisions for preventing black and white children from growing up side by side with front door steps either adjoining or within a few feet of each other."[17]

Dashiell's ordinance had a short life despite the popular appeal. Riddled with technical flaws, it proved difficult to enforce and led to considerable confusion. In one instance, a white man living on a mixed block temporarily vacated his home during renovations and thereby shifted the racial composition of the block to a black majority. He apparently could not move back into his own house without breaking the law. Within a month of its enactment, twenty-six cases were prepared for prosecution. Hawkins and future Councilman Warner T. McGuinn argued on behalf of the defendants. When the first case came up, the court declared the ordinance void. It called the law inaccurately drawn and overly vague but did not question whether the law impinged on the property rights of African Americans.[18]

Undeterred, Dashiell and West undertook to draw up a new ordinance. They elicited the aid of William L. Marbury, the lawyer who had led the Democrat's disfranchisement movement. The new law was voted on in April 1911, passing easily along the same party lines as the first one had. A month later, however, the city council repealed the new segregation ordinance when it discovered a technical flaw in the April enactment process and then immediately enacted a replacement law. With the term "block" more clearly defined and the restriction now extended to include the construction of schools and churches in sections inhabited by a majority of the opposite race, the segregationists hoped that the new law would satisfy constitutional muster, but it too would fail in court.[19]

The questions of constitutionality left Baltimore's zoning law in limbo and created a void that whites filled with terrorism. In late 1913, after the third law failed in court and before a fourth attempt at drawing an ordinance stabilized the city, whites stoned and threatened several homes of blacks moving onto white blocks. In November, four homes were bombarded. Later, a group calling itself the "Committee of Decent White Citizens Against Negro Invasion" threatened to blow up another black family's house. In yet another episode, George Howe, the owner of a house at 95 Hartford Avenue, met a white mob with gunshots. He injured four and was sentenced to six months in jail. His conviction was eventually overturned.[20]

Baltimore's laws were only the first of several race-based zoning restrictions enacted across the country. Within a year of the enactment of Baltimore's first residential segregation law in December 1910, Winston-Salem and Mooresville, North Carolina, and Greenville, South Carolina, had enacted similar laws, and North Carolina's General Assembly was considering a bill requiring racial separation throughout the state, even in rural areas. In 1912, Virginia enacted legislation giving communities the right to restrict neighborhoods. A year later, Ashland, Norfolk, Portsmouth, Richmond, and Roanoke had taken advantage of the power. In that same year, Birmingham, Atlanta, Asheville, North Carolina, and Madisonville, Kentucky, followed suit. Louisville enacted a segregation ordinance in 1914. The following year, whites in Harlem did not win the enactment of a law but did pressure the New York City government to remove blacks from the area in order "to restore land values." By the end of 1916, Dallas, New Orleans, Oklahoma City, Miami, and many smaller cities had enacted or were considering restrictive zoning laws.[21]

Even in the Rocky Mountain and Far West regions, cities imposed or studied race-restrictive zoning ordinances. In 1911, whites in Denver had tried to block construction of the home of a black doctor named McLain. They pressured the white contractor to halt construction, suggesting that he would lose business otherwise. A threatening letter to the physician warned, "the American people, when aroused, are not to be trifled with, and while I am not predicting violence to either yourself or property, you certainly are aware that either or both might occur." McLain heeded the threat and moved elsewhere. Demonstrating that racism also ran high on the West Coast, twelve residents of East Hollywood, California, burst into the home of a black family and ordered them out. Denver and Los Angeles enacted segregation ordinances, and other cities considered such laws. Jim Crow had reached American neighborhoods.[22]

The two largest cities in Missouri also faced the question of residential segregation. In Kansas City, bombers damaged or destroyed seven homes owned or occupied by blacks on Montgall Avenue between April 1910 and November 1911. Five and a half years later, the dynamiting of "the better class of Negro homes" continued as terrorists twice bombed the home of Benjamin Williams, 2914 Woodland Avenue. Politics, however, prevented enactment of a racial zoning ordinance. The lower chamber of the city council passed a restrictive zoning law, but the legislation was tabled in the upper chamber. The small size of the black population—23,570, or 9.4 percent—and their economic ties to the dominant Pendergast machine made them no threat to the white power structure. St. Louis was another matter.[23]

In 1860, the African American population of St. Louis, both free and slave, was small, totaling just 3,297. Over the next decade, however, it grew by nearly 570 percent, to total 22,088, and it continued to grow. By 1910, blacks comprised 6.4 percent of the total population, numbering 43,960. Although the community was smaller, its economic circumstances closely resembled those of Baltimore's. It did enjoy more white support politically than in Baltimore because white elites maintained a paternalistic sympathy for blacks. But this did not keep white society from segregating schools and neighborhoods. The majority of blacks lived in a segregated district bounded by Lucas Avenue on the south and Cass Avenue on the north, between Eighteenth Avenue and the Mississippi River.[24]

As its population grew, conditions in the ghetto deteriorated. In 1908, a Civic League survey deemed more than 50 percent of the dwellings "unfit for human habitation." St. Louis's black middle class tried to escape by moving into white residential districts. At the first entry of an African American family into a neighborhood, whites fled, and formerly white neighborhoods became black neighborhoods. In 1909, the area around the white St. James Episcopal Church, for example, had transformed into a black enclave, causing the church to sell its rectory to a black undertaker. The priest explained the sale, saying, "More than fifty negro families have moved into the block . . . and an equal number of white families, many of them parishioners . . . have moved out of the parish."[25]

After 1910, white St. Louis changed its response and adopted a course of action that led to legislated segregation. Whites no longer fled at the onset of black migration—they resisted. Like Baltimore, St. Louis witnessed several incidents of violent resistance. Whites bombarded and smashed windows of homes in the 4000 block of Cook Avenue when African Americans tried to take occupancy. In 1911, twenty white block improvement organizations collaborated with real estate concerns to found the United Welfare Association (UWA), which would oppose African American migration and lobby for a segregation ordinance. Its president considered "Negro invasion . . . a danger . . . greater even than fire, or flood, or tornado—far greater."[26]

St. Louis elites were deeply divided over the restrictive zoning ordinance. Democrats supported it. Some local Republicans worked for the restriction, but others opposed it. The city's newspapers likewise were split over the issue. Labor interests opposed it, as did the Citizens' Committee, headed by the Rev. John W. Day of the Unitarian Church and including several of the city's top lawyers. The local branch of the NAACP and the Knights of Pythias lodge held mass meetings to voice their own opposition. They also lobbied the board of aldermen against its passage. Their efforts proved so successful that twenty-one of the twenty-eight aldermen and Mayor Henry Kiel voted against the legislation.[27]

The forces in favor of segregation refused to acquiesce. Capitalizing on Progressive-era reforms to the city charter that allowed the public to initiate referenda, the segregationists forced a referendum on the issue in early 1916. Fewer than half of the city's registered voters actually cast ballots, but of the 70,000 who did vote, more than 50,000 favored racial separation. The plebiscite passed, and at the end of February

1916, the city enacted the "Ordinance to Prevent Ill Feeling, Conflict and Colli-sions Between the White and Colored Races, and to Preserve the Public Peace." In April, the city building commissioner began what became known as the "ghetto census," mapping every city block to determine which streets were open and which were closed to blacks.[28]

Blacks across the country opposed segregation ordinances on several grounds. Booker T. Washington, perhaps the most influential African American of the time, called the ordinances unnecessary. "Colored and whites," he contended, "are likely to select a section of the city where they will be surrounded by congenial neighbors." He suggested that the matter of residence "is one which naturally settles itself." Washington insisted further that opposition to the segregation laws derived not from a desire "to mix with the white man socially." Rather, blacks objected to the "inferior accommodations in return for the taxes" they paid that invariably resulted from the restrictions. Washington opined that under segregation, streets and side-walks in black sections would be neglected; sewers would be inferior; street lighting would be poor; and there would be inadequate policing. A statement by Atlanta Mayor William B. Hartsfield in the 1930s affirmed Washington's prediction. "You could always tell where the Negro sections started," he confessed, "lights stopped, streets, sidewalks stopped."[29]

The NAACP led the challenges against race-based zoning laws. Local branches were the first to enter the fray, often with the support of nonmember whites. Baltimore's third attempt at an ordinance came under fire in 1913 in *State of Mary-land* v. *Gurry*. In Baltimore City Criminal Court, Hawkins convinced the bench of the law's impracticality. Judge Elliot ruled that it could only end in the depopulation of racially mixed blocks because the statute prevented both races from moving in and upsetting the racial status quo. He declared the law was unreasonable and void. On appeal, William Marbury convinced the State Appeals Court that Elliot had misinterpreted the law. The higher court understood the law only to mean that the majority race on each block would determine which race could enter. But the appeal still lost. The court declared the law unconstitutional on grounds that it prevented a property owner from occupying and enjoying his own property. Elsewhere, similar zoning laws failed for similar reasons. North Carolina's Supreme Court declared the Winston-Salem statute void because it interfered with the "right of a person to dispose as he pleases of his own." In 1915, Georgia's Supreme Court declared that Atlanta's law did not just regulate business, as the defense claimed; it "destroy[ed] the right of the individual to acquire, enjoy, and dispose of his property." After county and state courts upheld the St. Louis law, the Federal Circuit Court enjoined the city from taking action, insisting that "the Negro is entitled to the same rights as is a white man."[30]

As the issue developed, the national NAACP became involved. It established a legal defense fund with which to fight the laws, and in its Sixth Annual Report in 1915, it presented a manifesto condemning segregation ordinances. "Colored people, [while] increasing in thrift and wealth," the resolution observed, "have been trying in the last decade to move out of the slums and unhealthy places . . . into more desirable residential districts." But they have been "met by the plea that they [were] undesirable neighbors and that they [would] depress real estate values." "Hatred, riot, and even bloodshed," the NAACP observed, "[had] been the result . . . and [some] endeavor[ed] to prescribe the bounds of habitation by law." The organization therefore resolved to fight for "justice in all courts, and equality of opportunity everywhere."[31]

Louisville, Kentucky, had experienced the same increase in population at the turn of the century that the other cities had. Between 1880 and 1900, the total population grew by almost two-thirds, from 123,758 to 204,731. The black community grew even more dramatically over the same period: nearly doubling, to number 39,139, or about 20 percent of the total population. African Americans dwelled throughout the city. If they did live next to whites, however, then they did so not as neighbors and equals but as employees, tending to live off alleys and in inadequate dwellings. Little expansion in the black population occurred after 1900, but spatially the community changed significantly. By 1910, distinct black districts began to form in Smoketown, the city's slum, and in the west end. More prosperous African Americans lived along Chestnut Street in homes ranging from the finest in the city to pleasant, small cottages. They created an economic and cultural oasis. The Colored Branch of the Louisville Free Public Library, for example, was established on Chestnut in 1905 to serve the segregated population.[32]

After 1910, the expansion of the middle-class black community west along Chestnut Street raised concerns among whites. In November 1913, W. D. Binford, a mechanic employed by a city newspaper, spoke before the Louisville Real Estate Exchange to proclaim the dangers of integration. If whites were not wary, Binford warned, "one morning they [would awaken] to find that a Negro family had purchased and was snugly ensconced . . . in one of the best and most exclusive white squares in the city." He admonished whites for their passivity, warning that if they passed up this opportunity to protect their investments, then "the time [would] come when race disturbances [would] spur [them] to action." Within a month of Binford's speech, the city began the process of drafting the segregation ordinance.[33]

Whites in Louisville did not engage in violent intimidation to the degree they did elsewhere. According to available reports, "the only breach of the peace . . . arose from white people stoning a house in which an unoffending negro had hired two rooms." City officials, however, evidently feared greater conflict. The law, they claimed, sought to prevent the races from "overstepping the racial barriers which Providence and not human law [had] erected, and which, whenever they are overstepped, result inevitably in most serious clashes, and often bloodshed."[34]

Louisville's white press, particularly the *Kentucky Irish-American*, proclaimed racist support for a residential segregation law. The *Irish-American's* vehemence exposes the underlying racial tension in the city and provides insight into what passed for economic opportunity for blacks. The paper maintained "the only possible objectors to [the] ordinance [were] the high-toned darkies, composed of letter carriers, chauffeurs, waiters, and bell hops, who are not content to mingle with their own race."[35]

Not all whites concurred with the segregationists' reading of the situation. J. D. Wright, the president of the Real Estate Exchange, called for moderation. He suggested that the issue was still too new in Louisville and that the exchange should wait until the public had made up its mind. He warned that a Baltimore-style ordinance in Louisville might serve to stir up racial tensions and, in his words, "make the negro rebellious." Wright's reticence derived from racial paternalism and civic pride as much as from fear of conflict. He exclaimed that Louisville and Washington, D.C., were the "only two American cities in which the negro has ample chance to elevate himself." But Wright proved to be in the minority. Other exchange officials decried the harm black migration had done to property values.[36]

Louisville's African American community vehemently opposed any restriction on home ownership. The newly established NAACP chapter, organized for the purpose of fighting the ordinance, distributed 3,000 copies of a circular denouncing the bill. Church leaders, such as Charles H. Parrish of Calvary Baptist and others from Knox Presbyterian and Simmons Bible College, formed a steering committee to lobby the mayor's office. The church leaders, members of the NAACP, west-side home owners, and other civic leaders attended public hearings, making impassioned pleas against the statute. They argued that the law would confine blacks, who comprised one-fifth of the city's population, to just one-eighth of its land. They insisted that race prejudice constituted "the sole reason for this ordinance," a prejudice, they maintained, "that would keep Booker Washington, [a man] received by the Queen of England, . . . from living on the same street with any white man in Louisville."[37]

The General Council passed the new zoning ordinance unanimously in April 1914, and Louisville mayor John Buschmeyer signed it in May. The law "to prevent conflict and ill-feeling between the white and colored races . . . and preserve the public peace and promote the general welfare" prohibited African Americans from occupying property on blocks that had a white majority and vice versa.[38]

The city's blacks resolved to challenge the statute. A local attorney, Clayton B. Blakey, advised them that the ordinance was unconstitutional. The NAACP searched for a way to test Blakey's conclusion. William Warley, the branch president, and a white realtor, Charles Buchanan, contrived a plan. Warley proposed to buy property in a white block from Buchanan. The contract of sale would include a proviso declaring that Warley would not be required to accept a deed or to pay for the property unless he had the right "to occupy [it] as a residence." Knowing that the deal would run afoul of the segregation ordinance, Warley would refuse to pay Buchanan. The realtor would then sue, saying that the ordinance had deprived him of his livelihood. The plan came to fruition in October 1914. Warley bought the lot for $250 and then withheld $100 of the purchase price from Buchanan, and

Buchanan sued. With help from the local NAACP, Buchanan hired Blakey to represent him. Warley, following Blakey's advice, hired the Louisville city attorneys, Stuart Chevalier and Pendleton Beckley, to represent him. Blakey believed that a vigorous defense would enable Buchanan and Warley to escape the serious charge of collusion—that they had conspired to test the ordinance.[39]

The case of *Buchanan* v. *Warley* worked its way through county and state courts before reaching the Supreme Court in April 1916. As the case progressed, the NAACP's national office took notice, and the association's president, Moorfield Storey, volunteered his services in aid of Buchanan. As early as 1911, Storey had called residential segregation laws a "most inauspicious" interference with the property rights of African Americans. Other advocates offered their help as well. Baltimore's Hawkins, for example, filed one of seven amicus curiae briefs on Buchanan's behalf. The case was first argued before six justices in April 1916. Because of its importance in civil rights law, the High Court decided to rehear the case during its next session so that a full bench "might be present and take part in [its] determination." The Court reheard arguments in April 1917.[40]

As the NAACP had hoped, Louisville's city attorneys put on a strong defense. In a 121-page brief, Chevalier and Beckley offered numerous precedents in property law and the police power. They asserted that the statute did not differ from other zoning laws. "All rights, certainly all rights of property," they declared, "are relative[:] . . . when a man voluntarily chooses to live in a city, in close proximity to other men, he submits his rights to a great number of limitations." Residential segregation, they maintained, was but another legitimate limitation. They stressed the potential occurrence of racial violence without the law. "If there is a danger of conflict . . . where there is merely the brief and temporary and almost casual association in the schools and in the vehicles of public travel," they suggested to the court, then "how much greater must be the same danger where the relation is the fixed and permanent and uninterrupted one of immediate neighbors." Chevalier and Beckley even intimated that the potential for violent confrontations over housing required that Louisville enact the ordinance. "Upon the police power," they insisted, "depends the comfort of an existence in a thickly populated community, the enjoyment of private and social life, and the beneficial use of property." The ordinance, they concluded, was a "reasonable, . . . constitutional and valid" method by which to protect the peace and property of the people of Louisville.[41]

Attorneys Blakey and Storey composed an almost-too-clever challenge to the statute. On the surface, they were hired to defend a white man's property rights. They therefore stressed the significance of the injury caused to Buchanan's livelihood. The bulk of their complaint, however, argued that the zoning restrictions made blacks second-class citizens. The ordinances, they contended, deprived African Americans "of the rights which belong to every citizen simply because white men consider [them] inferior." They asserted that Congress had passed the Fourteenth Amendment to protect blacks "against precisely such consequences of race prejudice." They also refuted the defense's contention that the laws were needed to keep the peace and insisted that the police power did not include "preservation of property values." They ended by telling the Court that the statute had "no real or substantial relation" to the protection of public health, morals, or safety and was "a palpable invasion of rights secured by fundamental law. . . . It was invalid . . . unreasonable, [and] unequal in its application."[42]

In November 1917, the Court unanimously declared the ordinance to be unconstitutional. Associate Justice William Day rendered the Court's decision, calling the law an illegitimate exercise of state police power and focusing on the infringement on Buchanan's property rights. According to Day, the doctrine of "separate but equal" did not entitle the state to limit the free alienation of property. "Property," Day declared, "cannot be taken without due process of law." The issue before the Court was whether the state could restrict occupancy, purchase, and sale of property "solely because of the color of the proposed occupant." And on that question, it ruled, "all citizens . . . have the same right to purchase property." Although the "feeling of race hostility" presented "a serious and difficult problem," the Court decided that the problem could not be solved "by depriving citizens of their constitutional rights and privileges." The Court admitted the desirability of the ends, but it considered the means too drastic.[43]

Behind the Court's veil of unanimity hid serious concerns about collusion and the expansion of property rights implicit in the decision. Benno C. Schmidt Jr., a legal scholar of the Jim Crow era, has unearthed an unpublished dissent written by Justice Oliver Wendell Holmes in which the jurist questioned the validity of the initial purchase agreement between Warley and Buchanan, particularly given that Warley was head of an organization founded for the specific purpose of defeating the statute. But despite his reservations, Holmes did not publish the dissent.[44]

Unaware of the unpublished dissent, the NAACP and blacks across the nation exulted in the *Buchanan* ruling. The NAACP declared that with the decision the "practice of establishing . . . ghettos on a basis of race and color had been killed." The organization made much of the fact that the decision was unanimous. "When it is recalled that the Chief Justice is from Louisiana and that Mr. Justice McReynolds is a Tennessean," Storey remarked, not realizing the irony, "the significance of the unanimity of the Court is apparent." In Louisville, 400 African Americans gathered to celebrate the victory, hearing testimonials from Warley and Blakey and singing patriotic songs. The *Louisville Leader*'s city editor, Joe Cole Jr., waxed poetic when he learned of the decision. "One of Negro blood," he rejoiced, "feels very keenly his limitations when he attempts to record coherently his emotions when such a racial consummation . . . as the annulment of the obnoxious segregation ordinance comes to pass." "Can we not expect to see the day when our other disabilities shall be removed," he asked; "can we not feel that at least a little glimmer of this world-wide democracy shines for us?" The *Baltimore Afro-American Ledger* offered a restrained hope that the nullification would be "but a forerunner of the future decree which shall declare all discrimination between citizens as contrary to the principles of a free democracy."[45]

The *Buchanan* ruling did not open housing markets. White home owners and the real estate industry remained adamant about keeping blacks out of white neighborhoods. NAREB, for example, gave a narrow interpretation to the decision. It acknowledged that the ruling meant that government could not enact race-restrictive zoning policies but insisted that the court had not actually nullified the "separate but equal" doctrine. NAREB maintained that local housing organizations and individual home owners could exercise their right of private property by restricting occupancy on account of race. Because it believed that the "prevailing sentiment" favored racial separation, it declared that it would continue to caution its members against introducing minorities into white districts.[46]

Local governments did not move to open housing opportunities to blacks, either. Several cities in the South rejected the implications of the *Buchanan* decision. Richmond, Charlotte, Atlanta, and New Orleans enacted replacement ordinances that offered minor modifications to the one struck down by the Supreme Court. Some jurisdictions were more brazen still in their indifference to the High Court's decision. Alabama's legislature, for example, empowered Birmingham to establish a zoning board to classify inhabitants by race and pursue a new racial zoning strategy. The city's zoning board unveiled a new segregation law in 1926. Although its supporters claimed otherwise, the new law did not differ significantly from the Louisville ordinance. Thus, despite the 1917 *Buchanan* decision, the NAACP was forced to spend the next thirty-five years fighting race-restrictive zoning ordinances throughout the South.[47]

Cities that did not enact new restrictive ordinances found other ways to keep white districts intact. In Baltimore, for example, the demand for separate neighborhoods remained strong. The mayor's office was flooded with letters from whites demanding that segregation be preserved. "Cannot something be done to prevent the . . . absorption of the city by the negroes," one writer asked. At first, Mayor James H. Preston responded that he was "powerless to act." But after discussions with a friend in Chicago, he adopted a plan to maintain segregation as that city had done, through race-restrictive covenants and public pressure. Preston suggested that whites could impede integration "by putting [private] restrictions on their property. . . . If they all join in agreement not to sell or rent to negroes," he insisted, then "it would be effective and legal." To ensure the effectiveness of his plan, the mayor advised that there be improvement organizations in each city block to stop realtors from engaging in block-busting and to "prevent the rentals to undesirables." He also urged the "stimulation of a healthy public sentiment in the press. . . . A general condemnation by the public of a man who destroys another man's property whether he does it with an axe or by negroe [*sic*] incursions," he proclaimed, "will be efficient if it has the public behind it." To coordinate the effort, Preston organized a Committee on Segregation that included the city building inspector, health department officials, and representatives of the real estate board and improvement associations. Finally, to reduce the likelihood of blacks moving into white areas further, the city created a zoning commission to regulate types of structures and to establish height and size requirements that would restrict rowhouse construction and lock poorer residents into poor neighborhoods. St. Louis, Chicago, and even Minneapolis, with its tiny African American population, struck similar arrangements to keep districts intact.[48]

The changes in residential race relations during the first seventeen years of the twentieth century are instructive in many ways. One can see the push factors, such as crime, disease, and degraded physical surroundings, that caused middle-class blacks to move out of their traditional neighborhoods. Several pull factors are evident as well. Inexpensive, quality housing became available for purchase by African Americans as commuter routes enabled whites to move to the suburbs. Institutions and services, most notably churches, pulled black families with them.

Black communities did enjoy support from some white residents of border cities, but they could not keep segregationists from enacting restrictive zoning laws. The economic interests of the real estate industry, the political ambitions of white supremacists, and the paranoia of the white public over race mixing combined to limit the property rights of African Americans. In the absence of law or when legal authority was questioned, whites took the law into their own hands, employing intimidation to keep blacks out or harassing them once a move had occurred.

More positively, the housing conflict of the early century established the NAACP as a force for racial justice. The process of fighting the residential segregation cases taught the NAACP valuable lessons about the mechanics of fund-raising, community organization, and moral suasion. These tactics would be employed in subsequent operations. Although it is true that most cities circumvented the Supreme Court's ruling in *Buchanan*, at least the judicial precedent had been set: race-restrictive zoning ordinances were unconstitutional.

White resistance and discrimination had catastrophic results for the larger African American community, however. In the early stages of an area's racial transition, property values dropped as white flight opened up entire blocks. After the initial panic subsided, prices increased. The closed housing market caused a squeeze between the supply of homes and African American demand, forcing the cost of housing skyward. In St. Louis, for example, vacant lots available to blacks doubled in price. As land prices soared, it became harder for blacks to secure mortgages. The vandalism and destructiveness of white resistance made insurance too expensive for many African American home owners. Renters found the cost of accommodations rising beyond their means, too. In Baltimore, on average, African Americans paid one-third of their family income for rent, whereas the average in the white community was one-fifth. Barred from less expensive housing in white areas and unable to afford the upkeep of their homes, many blacks let their properties deteriorate. The fears of whites seemingly were proved valid: an African American presence on the block resulted in neighborhood decline. Furthermore, whites tended to make racial arguments for the declension. They blamed the victims. A black neighborhood's decline therefore served to sustain white fear and to perpetuate white resistance.[49]

As the next chapter shows, this first wave of conflict would be repeated as African American migration grew in the North. In retrospect, it would be but a ripple before the tsunami to come.

2

GREAT MIGRATION,
GREAT CONFLAGRATION

The mobs of a thousand men, women and children, lynch and burn one lone man in the South. In the North, the mobs gather under cover of night and threaten and intimidate and hurl stones upon a man and his family—COWARDS ALL![1]

The Great Migration started when the United States began gearing up for its entry into the Great War. African Americans had maintained a steady exodus from the South for decades, but in 1916 that stream became a flood. During the next three years, more than 500,000 African Americans caught what James Grossman called "Northern fever." During the next decade, nearly 1 million followed. The industrial centers of the North and Midwest received most of the migrants, but urban areas throughout the nation experienced a proportional rise in black population.

The African American in-migrants clustered into ghettos. Some cities maintained segregation by imposing zoning requirements on the size and quality of dwellings or by forcing blacks to get permission to move from the whites in the area. Where legal impediments did not exist, whites founded improvement associations and protective leagues that drew up race-restrictive covenants and made gentlemen's agreements. Government leaders and the courts countenanced the obstructions in the name of peace, order, and private property rights.

When covenants and agreements failed to maintain racial separation, whites used violence to keep blacks out. No northern city seemed able to escape racial tension. In New York City, numerous conflicts occurred over housing in suburban sections. Chicago saw the most extensive violence, including one of the most destructive race riots in the nation's history. Blacks in Detroit endured several bombings, and in 1925, they witnessed a mob scene, killing, and subsequent trial that kept African

Americans across the nation spellbound for nearly a year. Violence also occurred in such cities as Cleveland, Philadelphia, and Pittsburgh.

Segregation remained a double-edged sword for African Americans. Some communities flourished. Artists and writers exploited the separation to turn their attention inward and celebrate their community's unique culture. Entrepreneurs enjoyed an exclusive pool of consumers. The redrawing of city wards gave political leaders a voting base enabling them to win election to city councils. They used patronage to build even stronger power bases and to reap dividends for their constituents. But segregation also had negative consequences. African American enclaves became crime-ridden, overcrowded, and often impoverished. Uplift organizations, such as the National Urban League and the NAACP, built a social and economic safety network and helped newcomers find housing and employment, but the extent of the migration strained community resources. As had happened in the border states, blacks who could afford it tried to escape the slums by moving into traditionally white areas.

The NAACP persisted in the fight for access to better housing but with varying success. In *Harmon* v. *Tyler,* the NAACP challenged a race-restrictive zoning ordinance in New Orleans. In 1927, the Supreme Court confirmed the 1917 *Buchanan* v. *Warley* ruling forbidding such zoning laws. Persistent southern intransigence, however, forced the NAACP's Legal Defense Fund to continue to fight zoning laws on a state-by-state and city-by-city basis into the 1950s. Against restrictive covenants, the NAACP failed. That litigation culminated in 1926, when Louis Marshall and Moorfield Storey took the case of *Corrigan* v. *Buckley* before the Supreme Court. The Court held that restrictive covenants constituted private action and thus lay outside the reach of the due process clause of the Fourteenth Amendment. The decision enabled whites to maintain residential segregation without violence, thus leading to a brief period of equilibrium and relative calm in U.S. neighborhoods.

Between 1915 and the late 1920s, cities outside the South underwent a revolutionary reconfiguration. The Great War all but eliminated the flow of foreign newcomers that had flooded the urban North and West for a quarter-century. The rise of nativism in the 1920s halted the remaining immigration, with Congress officially closing the gates in 1924. The prospect of finding work in war production industries, however, induced the migration of southerners of both races to northern cities. Hundreds of thousands of southerners poured into New York City, Chicago, Detroit, and other industrial centers of the North.[2]

The decision to leave the South did not come easily for blacks. Although the region had meant white supremacist economic oppression, it was also their home. The North, meanwhile, was a mystery to many. African American newspapers and journals, usually published in Chicago or New York, provided prospective migrants with what information they got about the North. These reports painted pictures of economic prosperity, freedom from violence, and escape from segregation. They often exaggerated the opportunities available in the North. In reality, African Americans generally were relegated to the lowest-level industrial jobs—janitors and unskilled positions. Discrimination in housing pervaded the region. Yet blacks moved North, lured by the promise of better jobs, housing, and schools.[3]

Whatever the economic impetus, white violence and institutional discrimination played a significant part in causing the migration. *The Crisis* summed up the motivation to move out of the South in an editorial cartoon entitled, simply, "The Reason." It depicted a black man carrying a suitcase; a ribbon on his jacket displayed the words "To the North." He looked back upon the scene of a stereotypical plantation owner pointing at a lynched black man hanging from a tree. Those migrants who left oral records put it best when they said that they moved in hope of "bettering their position."[4]

African American populations in northern cities grew dramatically during the Great Migration. New York became the city with the largest black population in the country. Between 1910 and 1920, more than 60,000 blacks moved to New York City. Over the next decade, 175,000 followed, bringing the black population to 327,706 and nearly doubling the percentage of blacks in the city's total population (4.7 percent). Philadelphia saw an even more impressive rise. Between 1910 and 1930, the city's black community grew by more than two and a half times, reaching almost 220,000 people, or more than 11 percent of the population. In Cleveland, the black population, which numbered fewer than 8,000 in 1910, increased almost tenfold (to 8.0 percent). Detroit's 5,000 blacks in 1910 grew to 120,000 by 1930 (to 7.7 percent). And by 1930, Chicago had the second-largest black population of any city in the United States; nearly 200,000 more African Americans lived in Chicago in 1930 than in 1910 (representing 6.9 percent of the city's total population). Although much less profound, the African American population of Los Angeles increased more than fivefold; 38,894 blacks lived in Los Angeles in 1930 (3.1 percent of the population).[5]

As the Great Migration brought more blacks to New York, racial tensions over housing increased. The city had never had integrated neighborhoods, but after 1915 blacks became concentrated into a clearly defined area bordered by the Harlem River, Amsterdam Avenue, and Central Park. According to Gilbert Osofsky, New York real estate interests, confronted with rapidly deflating property values as a result of overbuilding around 1905–1906, "opened their houses to Negroes and collected the traditionally high rents that colored people paid." As the blacks moved in, whites recoiled in opposition. Initially, the backlash was reserved to coalitions of property owners organized in neighborhood improvement associations, but as the flood of African Americans into Harlem grew, white people chose to flee. Whites accepted Harlem as a black enclave, and as long as African Americans stayed within Harlem's borders, race relations remained tranquil.[6]

Harlem was the heart of black America. As the area developed, fraternal and social organizations such as the NAACP and Urban League moved their offices there to be closer to their community. As in the segregated districts of cities in the southern and border states, exclusion in Harlem allowed black entrepreneurs to prosper, and professionals flourished amid the ready-made clientele. Black politicians and activists such as Marcus Garvey, the leader of the Universal Negro Improvement Association (UNIA) and the "pan-African movement," came to Harlem to uplift the race. Religious innovators such as Father Divine, the "originator of religion on the chain-store plan," also came to Harlem. And musicians, intellectuals, and artists, including Duke Ellington, W. E. B. Du Bois, Zora Neal Hurston, and Langston Hughes, gathered with such energy as to create the Harlem Renaissance.[7]

Despite Harlem's energy, not all black New Yorkers wanted to stay in the ghetto. With the invigorated population came overcrowding, crime, and disease. Cheryl Lynn Greenberg insists that economic and artistic progress did not "dislodge entrenched racial discrimination or lessen Harlem's wide-spread poverty." Osofsky adds, "Within the space of a single decade," Harlem became "a neighborhood with manifold social and economic problems." Middle-class blacks consequently sought more healthful surroundings in the suburbs. Brooklyn's African American population, for example, more than doubled to almost 69,000 between 1920 and 1930 (to 3.4 percent).[8]

African Americans who ventured outside the accepted enclave of Harlem met with resistance. In 1921, when Robert E. Waddell moved into the Hills section of Brooklyn, his white neighbors protested to the Brooklyn Real Estate Board. They tried to block the sale, and when that did not work, they tried to intimidate Waddell into moving. In one instance, they sent a threatening note in the mail. "Unless you vacate and move," it warned, "you and members of your black family will be killed." It was signed, "The Committee." When Waddell sought help from the NAACP, Executive Secretary James Weldon Johnson wrote to the police commissioner to request surveillance. No violence followed the threats, and the situation subsided. The exercise was repeated in 1924, however, when another black family moving into a white area of Brooklyn received death threats from a group purporting to be the Ku Klux Klan. Over the next several years, other Brooklyn neighborhoods organized to keep blacks out, but the prompt action of the NAACP and the police department kept white resistance from resulting in actual violence.[9]

When Samuel Browne and his family moved into a white area on Staten Island, they fared less well. Resistance began slowly, eventually rising to violence. Between February and July 1924, Browne, a mailman, tried repeatedly to move into a home at West Brighton Avenue, but his fire insurance kept getting canceled. Insurance companies insisted that he posed a bad risk. The Glens Falls Fire Insurance Company, for example, refused to insure the home after it learned from another company that whites had threatened to burn the house down should Browne take occupancy. "Keep off risk (Negroes)," a memo from the Palatine Insurance Company warned.[10]

The Brownes received several threatening letters. "If you move into that house," one warned, "it will be the worst days [sic] work that you ever did. . . . You should know better than to move where you are not wanted." It was signed, "Yours in the flaming cross, K.K.K.," but it seems that the Klan had no part in it. Another letter, it seems, really did come from the Klan. "You sure are in for it," the letter menaced. "You have started something you will not be able to finish. . . . What has happen [sic] to you so far has been the work of a novice." The writers suggested that they had "very effective methods of handling people of [Browne's] calibre." They told Browne not to rely on the police for help. "The little protection you have now," they promised, "will prove a huge joke. . . . There are five of us for each Nigger on Staten Island." The terrorists informed Browne that this was his first and only warning. "We have never written you before, nor have we done anything thus far to harm you[;] a word to the wise is usually sufficient," they insisted. The letter was signed, "Are You Wise? K.K.K."[11]

Despite the threats and other problems, Browne started to move in on August 29, 1924. Two days later, in the middle of the night, vandals smashed the windows of the house. Despite the terror, Browne was determined to stay. He turned down an offer from the block association to buy the house back from him at a $1,500 profit. After vandals did more damage to the home in July 1925, the NAACP recommended that Browne take the perpetrators to court. Trying to influence public opinion against the violence, the association issued reports of the incidents to the New York press. It arranged counsel and, with the help of the congregation of Harlem's Abyssinian Baptist Church, raised money to help fight Browne's case. In August, a Kings County grand jury indicted ten whites for conspiracy and intimidation. The criminal case ended when Browne reached an out-of-court settlement with the whites and dropped the charges. A civil suit ended without a settlement, but Browne, now unmolested, remained in the house. The NAACP concluded that the situation could have reached a much higher level of violence, particularly once the Klan became involved, had it not been that "New York gave the Brownes adequate police protection."[12]

Chicago witnessed episodes of conflict more destructive than those in New York. The city had tried to keep racial divisions intact by informally striking an agreement with realtors and individual home owners not to facilitate the sale or rental of homes in white areas to African Americans. Because of population pressures, however, blacks continued to push against the frontiers of white districts. With neither a statute nor an informal arrangement to keep blacks out, whites took the law into their own hands. Fifty-eight bombings occurred over a span of forty-five months between 1917 and 1921, an average of one every twenty days. The bombings caused the deaths of two blacks, injured several persons of both races, and destroyed property. The tension reached its ugliest in July 1919, when a fracas between blacks and whites swimming and sunning at the beach grew into a riot that lasted thirteen days and left thirty-eight people dead, 537 injured, entire blocks of the Black Belt in ruins, and more than 1,000 people homeless.[13]

Prior to the Great Migration, several African Americans lived in white Chicago neighborhoods without causing alarm, but after 1915 resistance increased. An African American family moved onto an all-white block of Vernon Avenue in 1911, for instance, and lived there without conflict for five years before another black family moved into the area. African Americans on other streets shared similar experiences. As the black population grew, however, racial tension increased. African Americans pushed south into blocks in the low fifties—51st–55th Streets—prompting a white backlash. Residents reported "considerable friction" and "intense hostility." In one instance, a black family had bought a home in 1913 and had occupied it for four years without incident; then one day in July 1917, without warning or threat, a bomb blew away the front of the house.[14]

Most of the violent resistance occurred in the Kenwood–Hyde Park district on the South Side. Prior to the Great War, the construction of new luxury apartments along Lake Michigan had prompted many whites to leave their older homes in the area. Housing prices fell to a range that African Americans could afford, and the section began a racial transition. When the war came, however, new construction ceased, and property values skyrocketed. The large homes were partitioned into smaller apartments, and a steady increase in black population ensued. Neighboring whites, fearing the deterioration of their environs, organized to turn back the stream of blacks and to "make Hyde Park white." They began publishing the *Property Owners' Journal*, a newsletter agitating against black "invasion." When verbal intimidation failed, they used dynamite. Thirty-two of Chicago's fifty-eight bombings occurred in the district bounded by 41st and 60th Streets, Cottage Grove Avenue, and State Street.[15]

After 1921, racial violence diminished in Chicago. Several factors caused this calm. After the riot of 1919, Governor Frank Lowden formed the Commission on Race Relations, which met with representatives of the Chicago Real Estate Board and African American real estate and social organizations to find a solution to the tension. Two essential facts—that African Americans needed access to better housing and that whites opposed integration—narrowed its options. The commission therefore recommended the rehabilitation of existing black districts. It called for both communities to work to promote tolerance and to condemn violence. It also suggested that teaching migrants how to exhibit "appropriate" social behavior might lessen white concerns about crime, licentiousness, and neighborhood deterioration and lead to better relations. African American leaders seemed to agree. Black newspapers, for example, established beautification programs in the hope that "clean blocks" would make "good citizens." Finally, the race relations commission guardedly recommended that African Americans voluntarily accept segregation, and the black community's leaders went along. They sensed that a truce represented the best they could achieve, given the climate of racial hostility. Between 1920 and 1930, the proportion of African Americans living in almost exclusively black residential areas increased. More than half of Chicago's blacks lived in census tracts consisting of 90 percent black population or higher. Only one in ten lived in tracts where they constituted a racial minority. The promised housing rehabilitation, meanwhile, never materialized.[16]

Conditions in Cleveland replicated those of New York and Chicago on a smaller scale, but in Philadelphia residential racial conflict reached lethal proportions. Blacks already occupied two other houses in the area, but Mrs. Ardella Bond's move on to Ellsworth Street triggered violent opposition. On the night of July 26, 1918, a mob congregated. They threw stones and smashed windows. The incident escalated when Mrs. Bond fired shots over the heads of the crowd. It grew out of control after two white policemen were shot by a black man. Whites and blacks clashed throughout downtown Philadelphia for three days. When police finally restored peace, three whites, two of them policemen, and one African American man lay dead. Several others had suffered injuries. Whites had ransacked homes of blacks, and police had arrested some sixty blacks on weapons charges.[17]

Detroit, like the other cities, underwent a profound demographic and social change after 1915. Between 1910 and 1920, the city's black population grew by nearly seven times to number more than 40,000. By 1930, that number had risen to over 120,000. With the influx came a reorganization of housing patterns. Blacks who had hitherto been scattered among poorer ethnic immigrants became ghettoized. The caste system that, according to Olivier Zunz, had characterized Detroit's racial relations throughout the nineteenth century hardened as the black population grew. As elsewhere, whites repelled African American immigration into white districts by using restrictive covenants and physical intimidation: a mob of 200 whites, for instance, forced fifty blacks out of a rooming house on Harper Avenue in 1917.[18]

As in Harlem, the new conditions, in the words of David M. Katzman, created "a new community spirit, a sense of black community." Black entrepreneurs seized the opportunity to create businesses, and a black professional class developed. African American social and fraternal clubs likewise took their places within the community. The Urban League played an instrumental role in finding newcomers jobs in the war industries and automobile plants. The Detroit branch of the NAACP, established in 1913, assumed the usual strategy of fighting discrimination in the courts, city hall, and the state legislature. In its first year, it successfully lobbied the state to defeat a proposed antimiscegenation law. It also hosted the national conference in 1921. But mostly, the branch struggled less successfully to end police brutality and to achieve better access to schools and housing.[19]

In the early 1920s, race relations in the city became increasingly hostile. Interracial and police violence increased. Then in early 1922, the Ku Klux Klan began to win new support among Detroit's white residents. By the spring of 1923, Klan membership numbered as many as 22,000. The following year, the organization ventured with full force into city politics, backing Charles Bowles's campaign for mayor. On the Saturday night before the November election, Klansmen gathered in numbers approaching 50,000 for a mass meeting and cross burning in a field in Dearborn Township. But by slightly more than 10,000 of the more than 300,000 votes cast, John W. Smith, a Catholic who had the support of the black community, won the election.[20]

The deterioration of race relations in the city caused great concern among NAACP officials. As hostility and violence grew, the organization found itself unable to counteract the force of white prejudice. Robert W. Bagnall, director of the Michigan Branch Conference, feared that blacks would find "separate schools and Jim Crow cars in . . . northern cities" within twenty-five years unless the NAACP reformed and became "far stronger, far more closely-knit" and "far more united." As a result, the Detroit branch underwent an overhaul in early 1925. Under the leadership of the Rev. R. L. Bradby of the Second Baptist Church, the Detroit NAACP hoped to storm "the citadel of race prejudice and discrimination."[21]

Housing became the major concern after the NAACP's reorganization. The branch took two cases challenging restrictive covenants before Michigan courts but lost both. Walter White, disheartened by the judgments, held that the rulings would embolden "the mobbists who feel that the courts are with them." In April 1925, a mob of 5,000 whites threatened to burn down the home of a black man who had recently moved onto a block on Northfield Avenue. In June, Dr. Alexander L. Turner found a similar situation outside his home on Spokane Avenue a few blocks away. While black workmen painted the interior of the house, whites hurled bricks through the windows and ripped tiles from the roof. Police arrived but did little to stop the assault. The Tireman Avenue Improvement Association offered to buy the house back from Turner. When he accepted, the association loaded his furniture into a van and hauled it to the doctor's old house.[22]

Conflict continued throughout the summer as hostility grew among members of both races. Incidents of police violence against blacks sharpened fears of the imminence of race riots. Between January and September 1925, police shot fifty-five blacks, twenty of them fatally. In early July, a mob of about 1,000 whites gathered to taunt the family of John Fletcher, which had recently moved to a white block on Stoepel Avenue, on the city's west side. Demonstrators yelled, "Lynch him. Lynch him," and pelted the house with pieces of coal that had been left on the sidewalk for a neighbor. Someone from inside the house fired into the mob and hit a teenage boy in the leg. All the occupants were arrested, but because of Fletcher's connections with the police commissioner, the matter was dropped. On the night after the incident, the Fletchers moved, and the Klan celebrated; the nearly 10,000 present burned crosses and called for segregation laws. During the same week, another black home owner, Vollington Bristol, was "welcomed" to his new home by 2,000 whites. One of the women in the crowd taunted her male counterparts, saying, "If you call yourselves men and are afraid to move these niggers out, we women will move them out." Later in the month, an NAACP field secretary exclaimed in response to calls for peace, "the colored people of Detroit prefer a half-dozen race riots to the loss of any one right."[23]

After Labor Day, tensions in Detroit reached lethal proportions and became a national cause célèbre. On the morning of September 8, 1925, Dr. and Mrs. Ossian H. Sweet and their baby moved into their new home at the corner of Garland Avenue and Charlevoix. The Sweets were the first black family to move onto the white middle-class block, but at least six black families lived on the next street. They had purchased the house in the spring but delayed their occupancy because of the Turner and Bristol incidents and after receiving threats from the community.[24]

One of six children of tenant-farmer parents in Orlando, Florida, the thirty-one-year-old Dr. Sweet exemplified the upwardly mobile "New Negro." At fourteen, he won a scholarship to Wilberforce Academy in Ohio. When the scholarship fell through, Sweet worked shining shoes and sweeping snow, "doing all sorts of work in order to get an education." He spent his summers in Detroit working in hotels. Upon graduating from Wilberforce, he studied medicine at Howard University in Washington, D.C. In 1921, he returned to Detroit to practice medicine. There he met his wife, Gladys, a graduate of Detroit Teachers College. After two years of practice, Sweet had saved enough money to continue his studies abroad. The couple spent six months in Vienna and six months in Paris. While in Paris, they had their first child, a daughter. The doctor and his family returned to Detroit in 1924 to resume his medical practice.[25]

At the first rumor that blacks intended to move into the neighborhood, the Waterworks Park Improvement Association met to decide upon the best way to "maintain the high standard of the residential district." The throng heard a speech by the man who had led the mob against Dr. Turner. The association's chairman promised, "we'll throw no stones, fire no guns but we'll load this nigger's goods on the same van and send it back where it came from." Some of the assembled decided to terrorize the woman who had sold the house. If the Sweets moved in, they warned her, she would be killed and the house blown up.[26]

On the day of their move, the Sweets expected trouble. They had secured police protection, but except for some jeering from the neighbors, the move in was un-eventful. The Sweets brought in only a few pieces of furniture—a bed and a few tables and some chairs—but carried with them several guns and sufficient ammunition to protect themselves if violence erupted. By the next day, they had also stocked enough food to sustain them should the neighbors undertake a siege.[27]

On the night of Wednesday, September 9, the Sweets kept watch, joined by the doctor's brothers, Henry and Oscar, and several friends. Shortly after dinnertime, a crowd began to gather at the confectionery across from the house and in the schoolyard on the corner. By eight o'clock, when the first rock was thrown and the first window broken, the mob numbered as many as 1,000, by 8:30 P.M., about 2,000. The mob consisted mostly of blue-collar workers and merchants from the area, but it swelled to include the dangerous and the curious from nearby neighborhoods. Police later claimed that they had tried to control the mob by diverting traffic, but the effort was half-hearted if it occurred at all: four blacks were attacked when they unwittingly drove near the Sweet home.[28]

Shortly after 8:30, with stones smashing windows and gunshots apparently ringing from the mob outside the house, Sweet and the other men in the house started to fire into the crowd. According to a police witness, "a volley of from 15 to 20 shots . . . seemed to come from all sides of the house." One demonstrator, Leon Breiner, was hit and lay dead against the porch stairs of a house across the street, and another, Eric Hougberg, was seriously wounded. After the shooting stopped, police stormed the house. They arrested Sweet, his wife, his brothers, and the seven others and held them on charges of first-degree murder.[29]

Aware of the political ramifications of the shooting, city leaders condemned the violence. Mayor Smith, who, according to the Reverend R.L. Bradby, had been "very, very undecided" over the issue of African American migration, blamed the Klan for the violence. In a letter reprinted in the *Free Press*, he suggested that the Sweets had been hired by the Klan for the purpose of inciting a riot. He recommended that blacks forego the right to live where they chose. "To preserve the peace of the community," he asked them to "stop moving into white neighborhoods when they know that such action will cause trouble." Out-klanning the Klan, he exclaimed, "any colored person who endangers life and property simply to gratify his personal pride . . . is an enemy of his own race." The district attorney's office joined in the ridicule of the Sweets. Assistant Prosecutor Lester Moll told the press, "The evidence shows no act of violence or provocation on the part of the victims or any other persons, and the crime must be called premeditated murder." Police officials had lied to prosecutors about the circumstances of the incident in order to nullify their own culpability in its occurrence.[30]

Days after the arrests, Mayor Smith established an interracial committee of eight whites and eight blacks to investigate the Sweet episode. He charged the board with the task of prescribing ways of improving race relations in the city. "The rapid growth of Detroit, together with the consequential influx of hundreds of thousands of persons of different races," the mayor declared, "presented the city with a serious problem." He understood that it was "necessary that all persons have the facilities of housing and public service" and saw the disturbances as "symptoms of a dangerous civic condition." He felt it equally necessary, however, to denounce the Sweet incident as caused by the "prejudices existing between extreme members of the white and colored races." Neither Mayor Smith nor the committee members themselves expected much in the way of results.[31]

In the face of such condemnations from official Detroit, the black community and the NAACP prepared to defend the Sweets. On the day after the arraignment, the Detroit branch held a rally to raise money for a defense fund; later the organization's national office became involved. Walter White and James Weldon Johnson, the executive secretary, recognized the importance of the case in the context of the broader issue of housing discrimination. Johnson called it the "dramatic high point of [the] nation-wide issue of segregation" and declared that the issue comprised "a supreme test of the constitutional guarantees of American Negro citizens." A conviction of the Sweets, he worried, would give encouragement to the mobs "attacking homes of Negroes all over [the] country." Both men therefore insisted that they find the best defense team in the nation.[32]

Clarence Darrow, "the best criminal lawyer in America," accepted the NAACP's request that he lead the defense. "These colored people are entitled to a fair shake," he proclaimed with his inimitable gift for understatement. Fresh from his triumph in July in the "Scopes Monkey Trial," Darrow took the job and charged the NAACP only $5,000 for his services, about 10 percent of his usual fee. He recruited an accomplished colleague, Arthur Garfield Hays, to help him and asked that a "competent local white lawyer" be found to join the case. White agreed that a local white attorney might help win over an alienated white community "badly misinformed by the *Detroit Free Press* stories." Because of unfavorable press and the strength of the Klan, he suggested that the "first and most important step [was] to influence public opinion" and to win it "over to the defense prior to the trial." Several black lawyers who were already involved in the case filled out the panel.[33]

African Americans around the country expressed support for the Sweets in print. Black newspapers from Florida to Massachusetts to California ran stories on the trial. The *New York Amsterdam News* called it "the most important court case the Negro has ever figured in [during] all the history of the United States." "If a colored man is not secure in his own home, in [the North] where there is a semblance of civilization," the paper asked, then "where under Heaven in the United States is he secure?" The *Philadelphia Public Journal* exclaimed, "The heroic defense of their homes exhibited by those brave and fear[less] Detroiters . . . makes every Negro in this country their debtor." "Every Negro in the United States," the editors suggested, "should pay the debt we owe them." And the *Houston Informer* crowed, "great Negro newspapers, the Pittsburgh *Courier*, the *Chicago Defender*, the [Washington] *Afro-American*, the Detroit *Independent* are covering the trial with a thoroughness never before evinced."[34]

The national NAACP took advantage of the notoriety of the case to establish a $50,000 legal defense fund—the precursor to the Legal Defense and Education Fund. It would use the money not only to aid the Detroit eleven but also to fight cases challenging restrictive covenants and white primary laws. Johnson declared, "We want $50,000 as the munitions of war for such a fight in behalf of justice for the Negro as has not been fought since the Civil War. . . . It is now or never," he professed. NAACP branches around the country began fund-raising and found wide support. Students at Howard University, Sweet's alma mater, for example, pledged to give whatever they could. After only ten days, the association had already collected nearly $2,700.[35]

The Sweet trial began on October 30, 1925. Recorder's Court Judge Frank Murphy presided. It was widely known that Murphy harbored political ambitions. He saw the case as "the opportunity of a lifetime to demonstrate sincere liberalism and judicial integrity" and hoped that it might lead to the mayoralty. Walter White observed the trial for the NAACP and Joseph Pulitzer's *New York World*. He used his NAACP position to ingratiate himself with Judge Murphy and gain access to inside information throughout the trial. What he called his "flimsy connection" with the *World* helped him influence other journalists as to the validity of Sweet's defense. He later would recount that it made him "a somewhat important figure in the eyes of the local newspaper men [who would] listen with respect to [his] suggestions." White even won over the reporter for the *Detroit Free Press*, the paper that he considered most hostile to the Sweets; the *Free Press* reporter apparently "like[d White's] cigarettes." By the trial's third week, White's efforts had proven so successful that he wired Johnson that "full and fair reports by local newspapers [had] swung public opinion . . . so completely that acquittal of all eleven [was] being freely predicted."[36]

The prosecution was led by District Attorney Robert Toms, whom some in the black community alleged to be a member of the Klan. Toms argued that the Sweets had no reason to fear the white neighbors, let alone a right to shoot anyone. He based his case on the testimony of police witnesses, who claimed that no mob had assembled and neither stones nor gunshots had been directed at the house. The police insisted that the people on the street that night had acted as they would have any other night: they had strolled along the block, visiting friends and jovially conversing with neighbors on front stoops. Leon Breiner, they claimed, had just toured the street peacefully, smoking his pipe.[37]

Darrow adeptly dismantled the testimony. One prosecution witness, when asked by prosecutor Toms what he had seen on the night of the shooting, seemingly forgot his coaching. "Well," he replied, "there were—a great number of people and officers—I won't say a great number—there were a large—there were a few people there and the officers." On cross-examination Darrow asked him, "You kind of forgot you were to say a few people, didn't you when you started in?" "Yes, Sir," the witness admitted. Other witnesses broke down under cross-examination and admitted to seeing persons throwing stones at the Sweet home just before the shots rang out.[38]

The defense's case reached its most poignant phase when Ossian Sweet took the stand. The defense intended to show that Sweet's fear was justified. "When I opened the door and saw the mob," he told the jury, "I realized I was facing the same mob that had hounded my people through its entire history." He recalled for the jury his encounters with prejudice. He told them of an incident that had occurred in France. The Europeans had been unfailingly civil to him, but the American Hospital in Paris refused to admit Gladys when she was about to give birth to their daughter. He recalled an incident in Washington when a group of white men pulled a black man from a car and beat him senseless. He told of what he had read about racism across the United States: stories of riots in Arkansas, Tulsa, East St. Louis, and Chicago; of lynching in the South; and of incidents of police brutality in Detroit. He told of having read an article about the incident in Rosewood, Florida, in 1923, where African Americans were evicted from their homes, their homes destroyed, and their church burned. According to Walter White, Sweet made a "magnificent witness." He told "his story with restraint and simplicity." He "held [the] courtroom breathless." After hearing the litany of violence, according to Arthur Hays, "not only the jury, but [also] the city of Detroit had a different idea of what the Sweet Case was about."[39]

The trial culminated in Darrow's closing argument. Over the course of the trial, the renowned litigator studied history to educate himself about the issues involved in the case. In his summation, he traced black history through "the eons of evolution, [from] the Zambezi River . . . through the Gethsemane of slavery." He depicted the African American being tortured by the "Simon Legrees of Puritanism, [and] as the victim of mob violence." According to the *Detroit Times*, "Darrow's plea was marked by all the tense emotion, the deep pathos which won him his reputation." The report recounted that the "spectators kept a hushed silence, one or two dabbing at their eyes." Even Judge Murphy seemed overcome by Darrow's plea. "I had heard about lawyers making a judge cry," one lawyer observed, "but Darrow was the first man I actually saw do it." When Darrow finished, according to the *Times*, "he wiped an eye and sat down amid a hush shattered only as the judge found words and signaled the prosecutor to start his final plea."[40]

After the lawyers' final appeals, Judge Murphy charged the jury. Most importantly, he declared that the Sweets had the right to occupy the house. "Under the law," he instructed, "a man's house is his castle. It is his castle whether he is white or black." The jury began its deliberation on the afternoon of November 25. During the evening, bystanders heard shouting emanating from the jury room. Still deadlocked at midnight, the jurors requested that Judge Murphy instruct them in the law of self-defense and then returned to the jury room. The next day was Thanksgiving. Nevertheless, blacks flocked to the court. According to Walter White, they "remained waiting and watching, many of them going without Thanksgiving dinner in order to be on hand" when a verdict was announced. At midnight on the second day of deliberation, Murphy allowed the jury to retire. At 1:30 the following afternoon, after forty-six hours of deliberation, the jurors admitted that they could not agree on a verdict. Five jurors had stood for acquittal of all defendants; seven jurors voted to acquit all but Ossian and Henry Sweet and Leonard Morse, whom police had found holding shotguns when they entered the house. Judge Murphy declared a mistrial.[41]

Following the mistrial, the NAACP continued to exploit the Sweet case to raise money. In the words of Walter White, the case had "stirred Negro America as no other case has ever moved it." The *Washington Daily American* reported that local interest was growing every day, and to keep it that way the D.C. branch of the NAACP held special movie showings and raffles. In Los Angeles, the *California Eagle* commended the local branch of the NAACP, saying that it had "made a magnificent effort to raise its quota" and that the $1,000 "should be raised in jig time." The *Cleveland Call* told readers that they "should be willing to die fighting for the principles [of liberty]" but added that their deaths were not necessary: they could give to the defense fund instead. The principals in the case also joined the fundraising effort. After receiving permission from Murphy to leave the state, Ossian and Gladys Sweet made a tour of the East and Midwest. The defense attorneys also toured to raise the organization's profile. Hays spoke in Washington, D.C., and joined Sweet on the dais at the NAACP annual meeting in New York. Darrow himself made several appearances. The association met its goal of $50,000 just after Christmas; by March 1926, the total had reached $75,000.[42]

The second Sweet trial commenced in April 1926. This time the defendants were tried separately. The city, believing that it had the strongest case against Ossian's brother, Henry, tried him first. The junior at Wilberforce University apparently had fired the shot that killed Breiner. Several elements of the case had changed the second time around. The arguments of Darrow and Walter White had proven so successful in the first trial that public opinion had shifted in favor of the defense. Hardline racists demanded that attorney Toms continue the prosecution. Many more Detroit residents, however, wanted real justice to be achieved. The list of witnesses willing to testify that a mob not only had assembled but also had terrorized the eleven grew significantly. One thing had not changed, however. The defense again emphasized the Sweets' right to the home, their right to defend themselves, and the violent prejudice of the mob.[43]

On May 11, 1926, Darrow gave his second summation. He spoke for seven hours, having to break several times, overcome by emotion. James Weldon Johnson recalled that at times "Darrow's voice was as low as though he were coaxing a reluctant child," thus making listeners strain to catch his words, and then "his words came like flashes of lightning and crashes of thunder." Darrow finished with a personal appeal. "I do not believe in the law of hate," he plead; "I believe in the law of love. . . . I would like to see a time when man loves his fellow man, and will forget his color or his creed. . . . That is all, gentlemen," he concluded, "I ask you, in the name of progress and the understanding of the human race, to return a verdict of not guilty in this case." With those in attendance exhausted and overwhelmed, there was not a dry eye in the courtroom.[44]

Prosecutor Toms spoke the next day. He admitted that the case had taught him much about Detroit's race problem. He added, however, that it was not the jury's task to settle that problem. "Remember this courtroom is just a tiny speck in the world," he told the jurors, "we are not going to change anything here." The prosecutor denied coaching witnesses. He attacked Darrow for what he called "Darrow's pet prejudice," the idea that policemen are liars. He insisted that the Waterworks Park Improvement Association had acted responsibly and in the interest of the community, and he denounced the NAACP for "foisting colored people into white neighborhoods." Toms repeatedly played the race card, appealing to the jurors' prejudices and prompting many objections from the defense. He acknowledged that a person had the right to live wherever he could afford to live but insisted that "we all have many civil rights which we voluntarily waive in the name of public peace."[45]

On May 14, Judge Murphy instructed his second jury. He spoke to them for more than two hours, recalling the same elements of the case that he had in November. After lunch, the jury left to deliberate. Spectators expected a long wait and perhaps another hung jury. But after less than an hour of deliberation, the jury announced that it had reached a verdict of not guilty. Amid the pandemonium of sobs, sighs, applause, and shouts of praise, Henry Sweet, Ossian Sweet, and Gladys Sweet circled the courtroom, shaking every hand they could grasp—first the jurors', then their attorneys'—before finally breaking down in hugs and tears. James Weldon Johnson would call the Sweet case "the most dramatic court trial involving the fundamental rights of the Negro in American history."[46]

In the aftermath of the trial, race relations in Detroit seemed to improve, although how much is not clear. An article in *Current History Magazine* claimed that the acquittal had "no effect whatever in bettering conditions" and showed no "tendency [to] check residential segregation." Statements by local NAACP officials rebutted the magazine. Moses Walker observed that no further attacks on black home owners occurred and that even the "ordinary brutalities of the police department" had begun to subside. "The Sweet case has had a wonderful effect toward creating a better feeling between white and colored citizens in Detroit," Walker concluded. The prosecutors later told Darrow that they believed the Sweets had received a just verdict and that it had done a "great deal of good in Detroit."[47]

Mayor Smith recommissioned the Interracial Committee, renaming it the Committee on Race Relations and appointing Reinhold Niebhur as its chairman. The committee issued a report in 1926 and added to it a summary comment with recommendations in March 1927. According to *The Survey*, the report "produced a substantial contribution to [the] knowledge of the Negro in a northern industrial city." It proved "sufficiently comprehensive to make sure that there [were] not lurking somewhere unidentified major causes of trouble." The committee, however, did little more than survey conditions in an abstract manner, and it often seemed to ask the wrong questions. It inquired as to whether blacks moving into a neighborhood would depress property values but could find no evidence of actual depreciation. It assumed that housing policy and the condition of residential segregation depended on the "hysteria" of a few home owners and the opportunism of real estate interests. Because the committee did not ask whites specifically their opinions of African Americans, the subject of race relations had to be inferred from other evidence. White residents of Detroit claimed not to fear black competition in industry, nor did they mind having public contact with blacks, but they refused to keep social relations with them. The committee blamed that unwillingness on African Americans as much as on whites. It suggested that many African Americans had made an incomplete social adjustment to the urban industrial environment. On balance, however, the committee held that conditions remained stable in most areas of Detroit community life and had improved in some. It concluded, therefore, that race relations needed no substantial policy reform.[48]

Race relations had not improved as much as the committee or the NAACP believed. During the winter of 1927, arsonists set the deserted Sweet house ablaze. Luckily, the fire was put out before much damage occurred. In 1928, whites welcomed an African American into their neighborhood at Maybury Grand Avenue with threats, gunshots, and vandalism. Detroit police suggested that the blacks move out peaceably. Elsewhere, neighbors nailed a sign on the wall outside a house on Scotten Avenue, reading, "Nigger do not move in the building or we will blow it up." In October 1929, a bomb destroyed a black apartment house on Charlevoix within view of the Sweets' house. The nine families that had moved into the apartments during the summer were left homeless.[49]

The trial had a more positive effect on Darrow, Murphy, the NAACP, and even Toms and Moll. The prosecutors moved up through the legal system, eventually becoming judges. Judge Toms even joined the local NAACP, eventually sitting on its executive committee. In the summer of 1926, Darrow joined the NAACP Legal Committee, and in May 1927, he became a director of the national organization. To Frank Murphy, the trial brought the friendship, support, and admiration of the NAACP and the American Civil Liberties Union. Walter White wrote that Murphy had made to him a "rare gift[:] the experience of seeing a man preside over a trial who was not only completely free from the slightest suggestion of prejudice, but whose high moral character, ability, and learning surpassed that of anyone he had ever known." The friends won during the trial helped Murphy to move up the political ladder from mayor of Detroit through governor of Michigan, U.S. attorney general under Franklin D. Roosevelt, and finally to associate justice on the Supreme Court of the United States.[50]

For the Sweets, the future seemed to hold only more grief. Unwilling to move back into the hostile neighborhood, they rented the house out for a short while and moved in with Gladys's mother. Within a year, their daughter and then Gladys died from tuberculosis apparently contracted during Gladys's imprisonment. Henry Sweet completed his education and passed the Michigan bar. During the 1930s, he was an administrator in the Michigan State Conference of NAACP Branches, sitting as president in 1937. But in 1940, he too died of tuberculosis. Ossian Sweet moved back into the house on Garland after Gladys's death. During the next thirty years, he remarried and divorced twice and ran for public office four times, losing each time. Finally, on March 19, 1960, Sweet committed suicide, fatally shooting himself in the head.[51]

On the national level, the Sweet case had provided much needed publicity and money for the fight against housing discrimination, but just ten days after the trial ended, the black community met its most serious legal setback in the campaign against residential segregation when the Supreme Court upheld the legality of race-restrictive covenants in the Washington, D.C, case *Corrigan* v. *Buckley*. Lower courts had ruled that covenants constituted private action and therefore were beyond the reach of the Fifth and Fourteenth Amendments. As the hearing before the Supreme Court neared, however, Louis Marshall suggested that the NAACP argue that court injunctions enforcing the covenants constituted public action and that the enforcement was unconstitutional. If legislatures and municipalities could not segregate, he reasoned, then how could a court "by its mandate bring about segregation without running foul of the decision in *Buchanan?*" Marshall believed that it could not. But other NAACP lawyers lacked confidence in the idea. They decided to emphasize the argument that restrictive covenants violated the Civil Rights Act of 1866 and contributed to overcrowding, disease, and crime. The Court rejected all of the NAACP's arguments in the case. In its decision, the Court held that the Civil Rights Act and the constitutional amendments relied upon did not "prohibit or invalidate contracts entered into by private individuals in respect to the control and disposition of their own property." The Court insisted that restrictive covenants were a part of the common law of the District of Columbia. On the question of enforcement, the Court also denied Marshall's suggestion that injunctions equaled sufficiently intrusive governmental action.[52]

The *Corrigan* ruling caused a dramatic decrease in the access that African Americans had to adequate housing. White home owners and realty interests started to employ race-restrictive covenants more broadly. In Chicago, they became the basis of the truce in the race war. It was widely believed in the 1930s and early 1940s that as much as 80 percent of property in Chicago was indentured. Fisk University researchers counted some 222 covenants in place on Chicago's South Side in 1944. Significantly, 40 percent of them had been imposed between 1927 and 1929. Covenants were upheld by court rulings from Maryland to Missouri to California. Municipal zoning ordinances were no longer necessary to separate the races. The nation's courts forced African Americans to stay in racial ghettos.[53]

The Great Migration transformed the distribution of the races and thereby changed race relations in the United States forever. Whites across the country had to reevaluate their personal assumptions regarding African Americans. Those who had condemned Dixie's treatment of blacks since before the Civil War now had to confront their own prejudices. When faced with the choice, they chose segregation. African Americans had left the debt peonage and lynching of the South in search of a better job and a better life, but they found no promised land.

Inside the ghetto, some African Americans did have an opportunity to advance. Segregation allowed them to develop businesses that catered to the customs and needs of the separate African American market. But unlike earlier migrant groups, these more enterprising and prosperous blacks did not have the same opportunity to move out of the immigrant ghetto once they had achieved middle-class status. Instead, systematic and institutionalized discrimination continued to force them into separate enclaves. City officials conspired with private interests to maintain segregation. When informal agreements failed to keep blacks from entering white districts, conflict, violence, and intimidation resulted. Once courts gave tacit support to the covenants, however, whites used them to keep their blocks white. An unfortunate equilibrium developed, forcing blacks to remain in the ghetto.

Some observers of the migration contended that after brief episodes of tension and conflict, the races settled down into more regular patterns of behavior as they adjusted to the new conditions. A closer investigation of relations and activities in northern neighborhoods proves otherwise. The analysts made the mistake of emphasizing large-scale riots to the exclusion of more constant, smaller acts of terrorism. As this chapter demonstrates, conflict, violence, and intimidation were commonplace whenever and wherever African Americans tried to move into traditionally white enclaves. As the next chapter shows, racial violence over housing did not crest in the 1920s. It persisted during the Great Depression, but under different circumstances.

3

TOO DEPRESSED TO FIGHT, MUCH

Those immortal ballads, *Home Sweet Home, My Old Kentucky Home*, and *The Little Gray Home in the West*, were not written about tenements or apartments. . . . They were written about an individual abode, alive with the tender associations of childhood, the family life at the fireside, . . . the independence, the security, and the pride of possession of the family's own home—the very seat of its being.[1]

The Great Depression changed the dynamics of the racial conflict over housing. Many of the old pressures that pushed middle-class blacks out of the ghetto became less significant during the economic emergency. With no jobs to pull them North, most southern blacks stayed put. In-migration slowed, thus reducing the stress of overcrowding. Even middle-class blacks could not afford to move. The American dream of owning a house had to be put on hold. The 1926 *Corrigan* v. *Buckley* decision upholding restrictive covenants, meanwhile, made the question of moving into white neighborhoods moot to most African Americans. The conflict did not end, however. New, seemingly benevolent forces pushed the races together.

As a result of the Depression, governments began taking a conspicuous role in housing. National leaders realized the importance of adequate housing to the social fabric of the United States. They further understood that new home construction and home ownership could rejuvenate and stabilize the economy. President Herbert Hoover maintained that rationalization of mortgage-lending procedures and cessation of bank foreclosures were elemental to relief. Supporters of the New Deal likewise saw that the scale and scope of the housing industry made its revitalization essential to the resuscitation of the whole economy. The New Deal Congress installed in 1933 undertook to provide relief and induce recovery by clearing slums and building new housing.

Because relief from the economic emergency represented the primary purpose for its actions, the federal government often neglected social aspects of housing.

Planners did not always provide suitable replacement housing for persons displaced by slum clearance. This oversight hit African Americans hardest because they tended more often to live in blighted areas and dilapidated dwellings. When slum clearance efforts demolished their homes, they had to find shelter where they could afford it. Conflict arose when they looked for it in white neighborhoods.

The 1930s did bring some advances in the campaign against residential segregation. For the first time, blacks held positions in the federal housing bureaucracy. The influence of African American scholars grew, giving planning a new, more sympathetic perspective. The NAACP's Legal Defense and Education Fund persisted in its fight against race-restrictive zoning ordinances in the South, winning case after case until only the most intransigent holdouts maintained segregation by statute. It did not win the battle against restrictive covenants during these years, but the LDF used the court experience to refine arguments and legal tactics. Along with a growing network of activist groups such as the National Negro Congress, the NAACP took up the new challenge of protecting those displaced by slum clearance.

As this chapter illustrates, however, the Depression years proved frustrating for advocates of better housing for blacks. With some advances came many false steps and disappointments.

The Great Depression devastated African American communities. Even during flush times, blacks in the North tended to work as unskilled laborers in low-wage jobs. According to the Federal Emergency Relief Administration (FERA), nearly 30 percent of African Americans employed in 1930 worked as domestic servants. Another 20 percent were employed as unskilled laborers in manufacturing and mechanical industries. Despite their low status, even traditional "Negro jobs" were jeopardized when the Depression hit. White Americans, desperate for employment, took jobs as janitors and housekeepers, throwing blacks out of work. And even if they did hold on to their jobs, many blacks faced the prospect of decreased wages as employers, particularly in the South, proposed establishing a lower minimum wage for African Americans. In Manhattan, more than one out of every four black men was out of work in 1931, as compared to one in five white males. Unemployed black men in Chicago outnumbered white counterparts three to two. The same ratio existed in Philadelphia, where in 1932 some 56 percent of blacks were out of work. In Detroit, 60 percent of black men and three-quarters of black women were unemployed, as compared to one-third of white men and 17 percent of white women.[2]

Unemployment among working-class African Americans resounded throughout the entire community. African American businesses lost their consumer base. Shopkeepers, launderers, barbers, and beauticians struggled to stay afloat. Symbolizing the economic damage, the value of real property owned by African Americans, which had increased steadily since 1910, peaked in 1930 and then declined throughout the rest of the decade.[3]

Already on the lowest tier of national economy, African Americans were dispro-
portionately forced onto the relief rolls by the Depression. In 1933, according to
FERA, African Americans made up "only one-tenth of the total population of the
United States, [but] comprised an average of approximately one-sixth of the relief
population." The situation was even worse for urban blacks. According to a report
prepared by the National Urban League, in urban areas nearly 40 percent of blacks
were on federal relief in 1935, compared to less than 15 percent of whites. Some
cities had even higher percentages, and these figures still do not represent the full
extent of the problem. The Urban League found that African Americans were not
admitted to relief rolls as readily as whites. Moreover, when blacks did qualify for
work relief programs, they worked at wage levels lower than those of whites. Skilled
black workers, FERA concluded, "experienced difficulty in every section in secur-
ing classification and assignment at anything above unskilled work."[4]

The economic hardship caused by the Depression had a profoundly negative
effect on African American housing. The rate of in-migration of African Americans
to northern cities shrank dramatically. After tripling during the 1920s, the black
population of Detroit grew by only 24 percent during the 1930s. Chicago's African
American community increased by just 19 percent during the decade. Despite the
smaller rates of growth, restrictive covenants and other discriminatory practices
combined with the slowing of housing starts continued to force blacks to live in
decaying, overcrowded ghettos. In Chicago, the average number of occupants in a
black home was twice that of the rest of the population. The average African American home in Philadelphia had five times as many occupants as the average white
home.[5]

The scale and scope of the problem for blacks and whites prompted govern-
ments, for the first time, to make public housing a staple of their policy agendas.[6]
Hitherto, housing projects and urban redevelopment had tended to be sponsored
by private entrepreneurs and philanthropists. In 1925, for example, John D.
Rockefeller Jr., built a cooperative apartment in Harlem. Some 511 middle-class
African American "tenant-subscribers" and their families started moving into the
Paul Laurence Dunbar Apartments in 1928. In Chicago, Julius Rosenwald built
Michigan Boulevard Garden Apartments. The 421-unit development had rents
higher than the city's average but still showed an occupancy rate of 98 percent one
year after it opened. African Americans not only occupied the apartments but also
ran the building. Robert Taylor, later one of the leaders of the public housing movement in Chicago, managed the facility.[7]

Instead of building homes, government had provided funds for research into
housing issues. The Division of Building and Housing (DBH) was established in
1922 during Herbert Hoover's tenure as Commerce Department secretary. DBH
studied various aspects of housing, from zoning to construction to finance to maintenance. "When we started," Hoover would recall proudly, "there were only 48
municipalities with zoning laws; by 1928 there were 640." Although he opposed

direct federal involvement in the housing industry, Hoover did campaign to stimulate home ownership. He cofounded Better Homes in America, a volunteer organization that would lobby private industry to increase construction. DBH estimated that the country needed to build 400,000 to 500,000 units per annum to replace dilapidated dwellings and provide for increased population. By the time he became president, Hoover insisted that the government had met its objectives, commenting that "we had obviously replaced considerable bad housing."[8]

As president, Hoover used his position to expand the study of housing. In 1931, he convened the first national conference of experts on home building and home ownership. According to Hoover, the conference would study the "complex nature of modern housing [in] the hope of inspiring better organization" of government and industry. It sought to define "what housing ought to be" and to outline programs needed "to make it so."[9]

The conference concluded that the main problem with the government's housing policy was that no coherent program existed. "Improved construction of individual houses without consideration of the lot and street layout, or of protection by zoning," the housing experts argued, "resulted only in giving longer life to a slum." They recommended directed studies to improve understanding of how economic, social, and political forces intertwined in the field of housing. The experts called for more federal government involvement. They endorsed the president's plan to institute a system of home loan discount banks to stimulate construction and protect private ownership. They further advised Hoover to create "qualified official planning commissions," to groom programs to local needs, to facilitate the elimination of blighted areas, and to incorporate new technologies in construction. Only then, they concluded, would "suitable housing . . . be possible for every industrious American family."[10]

The question of African American housing occupied an entire committee. The experts surveyed the condition and quality of housing for blacks, the social and economic circumstances in black districts, home ownership and finance, housing projects, and the causes and results of residential segregation. Charles S. Johnson, director of the Social Science Department at Fisk University, acted as secretary for the committee and wrote its report. The committee noted that black home ownership in the urban North had doubled during the 1920s, but it added that the dwellings purchased tended to be "old and difficult to keep in repair." The committee also acknowledged the "special difficulties" that African Americans encountered in their search for financing and in the limited access they had to houses in certain districts. Although the committee did not uncover anything new, its report succeeded in organizing the data and presenting them in a more coherent and powerful form.[11]

The Committee on Negro Housing made few substantive recommendations, urging study and educational programs instead. It called for an investigation to settle the question of whether a black presence guaranteed depreciation of property values. As the Chicago Commission had done a decade earlier, the committee suggested that clubs in black districts educate the recently arrived in-migrants to develop in the newcomers a "better aesthetic taste within the home." It advised blacks to beautify their properties by planting grass and shrubs, painting exteriors, and generally cleaning up the homestead environment. This, the committee hoped, would offset the belief among whites that declension automatically followed integration. The committee recommended that states and municipalities establish permanent commissions mandated to investigate and resolve housing conflicts. Finally, it requested that the federal government encourage private industry to facilitate home ownership by blacks.[12]

The election of 1932 swept Franklin Delano Roosevelt into the White House and promised Americans a New Deal to solve the emergency. Roosevelt had long recognized the importance of housing to the economy and social life. As governor of New York, he had sponsored legislation demanding the improvement of housing conditions and adopted a strong rhetoric favoring government relief for residents of slums. In a speech in New York City in 1930, Roosevelt lamented the "squalid tenements that house the very poor" that lay clustered in the shadows of skyscrapers. He called the conditions a disgrace to modern civilization and demanded that housing interests cooperate to find "the solution of a big problem." He also called for increased regulation of tenements to reduce overcrowding, the potential for disease, and crime.[13]

Once in office, the Democratic administration developed housing relief programs through a process of experimentation. Stable home financing took a central place among the New Deal directives. Mortgages on single-family homes, Roosevelt proclaimed, were the "backbone of the American financial system." He insisted "that special safeguards should be thrown around home ownership as a guarantee of social and economic stability." To make it so, the Democrats created the Home Owners' Loan Corporation (HOLC). The HOLC provided advances to lenders and extended credit to home owners in default on mortgages.[14]

The New Deal for housing also involved the construction, repair, and improvement of dwellings through slum clearance and urban renewal. Job creation and work relief represented the primary motives behind the program, but in Mabel L. Walker's words, "the social conscience . . . with respect to substandard housing" also developed as the Depression persisted. Senator Robert F. Wagner of New York, for one, saw improvement of housing conditions and elimination of blight as important ancillary benefits from the policy. Shortly after the end of the "First 100 Days," Wagner guided through Congress a bill creating a Housing Division in the Public Works Administration (PWA).[15]

The PWA Housing Division existed for five years, and at best, it produced only mixed results. In its first two years, the agency spent more than $10 million dollars but provided only 3,401 new dwelling units. Reforms made in 1935 gave PWA greater control over administration of the program. Instead of relying on local and state governments to request aid, the reformed Housing Division would initiate, finance, and build projects itself. By the time it closed in the fall of 1937, it had begun fifty-one projects in thirty-six cities. Even at that rate, however, the number of dwelling units built represented only a tiny percentage of what the nation required.[16]

The legislation establishing the PWA Housing Division did not include specific protection for African Americans, but their interests were not totally ignored. Secretary of the Interior Harold L. Ickes insisted that blacks would find equal opportunity for employment in housing construction jobs. The agency, Ickes promised, would "take no note of creed or color" in hiring. The administration also created the Office of Advisor on Negro Affairs to the Public Works Administrator so that blacks could participate in the planning and management of projects. The cacophony of public and private interests tended to drown out the voices of African Americans, but the office did make some minor advances. African American social scientists found a place in the federal bureaucracy. They gathered data, refined the government's understanding of the special needs of the black community, and initiated objective criteria for defining employment discrimination in construction jobs.[17]

Although the division pledged not to allow discrimination in employment of construction workers, it could not overcome local opposition to integration of the housing itself. The first two slum clearance and public housing projects completed, for example, were built in Atlanta and were racially segregated. Techwood Homes, an apartment complex built for white occupants, opened in August 1936. The black project, University Homes Apartments, opened six months later. As with schools in the South, the facilities were separate but not equal. "When put side by side for comparison," a local historian observed, "it was clear that the 'lily white' Techwood project had superior construction, better design, extra social services, more activities, and greater media promotion." University Homes, according to Florence Fleming Corley, "had more people housed in less space, with construction costs and amenities at a minimum."[18]

A second bureaucracy of the early New Deal, the Federal Housing Administration, may actually have done more harm than good to the housing of the black population. Established in 1934 to coordinate the government's housing programs and insure mortgage loans, the FHA did lower and stabilize lending rates as well as underwrite the renovation and repair of private dwellings. The NAACP's Leslie S. Perry claimed, however, that FHA did "more than any other single instrumentality to force nonwhite citizens into substandard houses and neighborhoods."[19]

The FHA bolstered residential race segregation. Its *Underwriting Manual* used race as a basis for rejection of a loan if a black home buyer wanted to move into a white area, advising that if a project did not provide for protection against "adverse influences," then "the Valuator must not hesitate to make a reject rating." Adverse influences, according to the FHA, included "business and industrial uses, lower class occupancy, and inharmonious racial groups." "If a neighborhood [was] to retain stability," the manual opined, "[then it was] necessary that properties . . . continue to be occupied by the same social and racial classes."[20]

By early 1937, almost everyone agreed that the federal government's housing policies needed reform. Advocates of public housing clamored for expansion of the program to increase construction of low-cost rental housing. Urban planners believed that the government needed to fashion a permanent strategy to ensure attainment of housing goals. Private banking, real estate, and construction interests desired to keep government out of the home-building business beyond its role in guaranteeing mortgages. Several congressional leaders wanted the Housing Division rolled back and its authority dispersed to give states and cities more say in site selection, construction design, and occupancy. Others wanted urban renewal and public housing programs eliminated.[21]

Reform came by way of the United States Housing Act of 1937, better known as the Wagner Housing Act. Senator Wagner had first introduced his plan "for the elimination of unsafe and insanitary housing conditions, [and] for the development of decent, safe, and sanitary dwellings for families of low income" in 1935. At that time, Treasury Secretary Henry Morgenthau had opposed the idea, insisting that it would take a billion dollars to fund and would "shoot the government credit to hell." In Congress, representatives from rural and southern states had objected to it because it offered little benefit to their constituents. Wagner offered the bill again in 1937. This time, with the help of lobbying from the American Federation of Housing Authorities, the U.S. Conference of Mayors, and labor groups, it passed. The act established the U.S. Housing Authority in the Department of the Interior and authorized USHA to expend up to $500 million for slum clearance and low-income housing projects.[22]

The USHA recognized the need of improving race relations in housing. The agency therefore created the Office of Race Relations, superseding and expanding on the Office of the Advisor on Negro Affairs. The department reviewed applications for financial assistance submitted by local housing authorities and offered recommendations. Robert C. Weaver took the helm as its director. The son of a postal worker, Weaver was born in 1907 and grew up in the middle-class district of Brookland in Washington, D.C. The Weavers were one of only six black families among some 3,000 white households. Following in his grandfather's footsteps, Weaver was educated at Harvard University, becoming the school's first African American to earn a doctorate in economics. Weaver returned to Washington and entered the government in 1933, acting as associate adviser to Clark Foreman, the adviser to Interior Secretary Ickes on the economic status of Negroes. Weaver played an important role in several New Deal agencies and as a member of the "Black Cabinet" and would become among the nation's foremost experts on housing and urban issues. He also would have a noteworthy career as an integrator of the federal government. Shortly after his arrival in Washington, Weaver caused a stir in the lunchroom of the Interior Department. When he and a colleague went to eat at the whites' cafeteria, a group of women became so incensed that they raced to Ickes's office to ask him what he intended to do about it. Ickes retorted, "Not one damn thing!" and the cafeteria remained integrated. Weaver would gain more notoriety in the 1960s when he integrated the federal cabinet. With his appointment to USHA, Weaver offered the potential for African American interests to figure in urban planning. Indeed, according to the NAACP's *The Crisis*, the USHA pursued "a more fair and equitable racial policy . . . than in any other branch of the Federal Government."[23]

The NAACP's civil rights agenda during the 1930s focused on economic matters and its campaign to pass federal antilynching legislation, but the association also continued to work to eliminate discrimination in housing. It encouraged federal housing initiatives, believing that only a "national program of low cost housing" could save the urban black population from "inferior housing at exorbitant rents" and enable them "to develop wholesome, healthy community lives." During hearings in 1936, Walter White, the NAACP executive secretary since 1931, lobbied the Senate Education and Labor Committee on the issue. "Immediate aid," he argued, "should be given to those who are most underprivileged." He further urged that the legislation clearly state that the "housing projects shall be available to all Americans without regard to race, creed or color" and declared that government should "rise above racial, sectional or other prejudices."[24]

In the Wagner Housing Act, it looked as though Congress had heard the NAACP appeal, but the inadequacies of the new program soon became apparent. The NAACP had requested that specific provisions to protect blacks displaced by slum clearance be written into the legislation. The law did require that one unit of new housing be built for each slum unit demolished, but it did not guarantee that the new housing would be built on the cleared site or that the displaced persons would live in the new housing. African Americans living in areas targeted for demolition often found their homes razed only to make room for highways or parks. The replacement housing was built in other sections of a city, away from traditionally black districts. If a renewal project did include construction of new dwellings, then local administrators and private housing interests often cooperated to reclaim the site for white occupancy. And even when no obvious scheme to exclude the displaced blacks existed, the economy often conspired against them. The former residents of a cleared area rarely returned to live in the new project because it usually cost too much. The term "slum clearance" often really meant "Negro removal."[25]

The NAACP maintained that the Wagner Housing Act granted to local and state authorities too much control over site selection and project construction. It contended that, in view of the "traditional Southern attitude of ignoring the housing claims of Negroes," the new law would merely continue the type of segregation exemplified in the Atlanta projects. Local control, the NAACP insisted, would lead to more discrimination and further deterioration of black housing.[26]

Its failure to influence lawmakers caused the NAACP to redouble its efforts and sharpen its tactics in the fight against segregation and discriminatory housing practices. At its convention in 1937, the association gave the first tentative voice to its stance on housing. It acknowledged the efforts to provide low-cost housing for the poor and urged that the programs continue "with special reference to blighted areas in which black workers [were] forced to live." In slightly sterner language, the NAACP declared: "We protest any race discrimination in selecting the tenants or occupants of any low cost housing projects fostered or financed in whole or in part from public funds." In 1939, delegates again resolved to protest against discrimination, but this time they added a proviso urging the inclusion of at least one black on every local housing authority. By 1940, the NAACP position had matured sufficiently to demand that Congress pass "immediate legislation calculated to relieve this acute [housing] situation."[27]

The NAACP continued its pursuit of access to housing through litigation. It fought zoning ordinances in the South and continued its advance against race-restrictive covenants elsewhere. The association helped bring nearly twenty suits in Los Angeles, winning several of them on technical grounds. In 1929 it came close to winning the outright nullification of covenants in a West Virginia case when, in *White* v. *White,* the court decreed that such indentures placed an unreasonable restraint on the free alienation of property, suggesting that they cut off a large number of possible buyers and meant that property owners ceased to be in control of their own property. As their experience grew, the NAACP lawyers refined their courtroom tactics, and in 1939 the association created the Legal Defense and Education Fund, Inc., to help finance and coordinate litigation.[28]

In 1940 the LDF brought the case of *Hansberry* v. *Lee* before the U.S. Supreme Court, the first covenant case to reach the High Court since *Corrigan* in 1926. The case originated in Chicago, where African Americans had been hemmed in by covenants for more than a decade. Lamenting the situation, the NAACP claimed that an "Iron Ring" surrounded the city's Black Belt and locked African Americans into a ghetto of overcrowded substandard housing. In May 1937, Carl A. Hansberry bought and took occupancy of an apartment house on a white block of Rhodes Avenue. The property lay within a zone that had been restricted by the Woodlawn Property Owners' Association. In June, neighbors greeted the Hansberrys with a rock through a front window and a request to vacate the premises. They also sued Hansberry, claiming that the covenant protected their property. When the Illinois Supreme Court upheld the covenant, Hansberry appealed to the U.S. Supreme Court. In November 1940, the Court reversed the Illinois decision and ruled that Hansberry had a right to occupy the building.[29]

The *Hansberry* decision was not as monumental as it might first appear. The U.S. Supreme Court nullified the race-restrictive covenant on a technicality. The covenant had required 95 percent of the home owners on the block to sign on for it to take force. The Court ruled that because the vendor had not been a signatory to the original agreement and because the covenant had never acquired the requisite number of signatories, neither the seller nor the purchaser were subject to the covenant. Hansberry therefore got the property. The *Hansberry* ruling did not eliminate racial deed indentures, nor did it challenge the *Corrigan* precedent. But it did place race-restrictive covenants in Chicago and elsewhere in jeopardy if they did not fulfill the requirements of their implementation.[30]

Throughout the late 1930s, the NAACP also began developing grassroots organizations to influence local housing policy. It told members to assemble data on housing and "make the most earnest and persistent pleas to the local housing authorities for slum clearance in Negro residential districts." "The sooner Negro citizens get busy," the leadership suggested, "the sooner will Negroes begin to obtain some relief from the . . . paralyzing rents and congestion of the slums." By 1940, the effort bore fruit. With the aid of administrators sensitive to racial issues such as Robert Weaver, African Americans sat on twenty-two of the 300 city and county housing authorities across the nation. The liberal National Association of Housing Officials (NAHO) responded to the lobbying. Displaying an increased sensitivity to the issue, it suggested that local housing authorities should seek out minority group representatives in cases where the "housing of some racial group constitutes a distinct problem."[31]

The federal government's growing sensitivity to African American housing interests and the NAACP's advances in its lobbying effort were not paralleled by a seachange in the attitudes of most white Americans toward residential integration. The Depression and court support of race-restrictive covenants had slowed the stream of blacks into white neighborhoods, but when blacks did breach traditional racial boundaries, conflict still invariably ensued. Ironically, much of the violence derived from the slum clearance and renewal programs. Left homeless after the "federal bulldozers" had rolled through the slums, displaced blacks had to find other accommodations. In the highly restrictive dual housing market, their choices were limited to overpriced housing in an increasingly overcrowded ghetto or better homes in traditionally white areas. When they chose the latter, conflict and resistance erupted.[32]

The Atlanta renewal projects demonstrate how slum clearance could unwittingly make race relations and housing conditions worse for African Americans. The demolition of dwellings in the Tech Flats and Beaver's Slide sections surrounding the colleges of Atlanta University forced many blacks to find suitable housing elsewhere. When they tried to move into white areas, conflict resulted. In February 1937, an African American family moving onto Pine Street in the northeast section of Atlanta received several threats, and then whites tried to burn them out of the house. When the police arrived to investigate, they advised the blacks to move out. The blacks did so. In another episode, an African American physician purchased three lots in the all-white Mozley Park area of the city, received a building permit, and contracted to have a home constructed on one of the lots. White home owners protested. With the aid of a Klan cross-burning in a vacant lot in the West End and a Klan parade through the black district along Auburn Avenue, neighborhood whites drove the doctor out of Mozley Park. The opening of the University Homes project in April relieved much of the stress over housing and, coincidentally, the racial strife.[33]

The even more dramatic violence in Dallas in 1940 and 1941 provides further evidence that whites were still not prepared to have African Americans living next door. Dallas had imposed de jure racial segregation during the first wave of legislation in the 1910s, but blacks successfully challenged the ordinance in 1927. In *Liberty Annex Corp.* v. *City of Dallas*, the owner of a tract development from which African Americans would have been excluded under the zoning law brought suit against the city. A Dallas court dismissed the complaint, but the appellate court nullified the zoning ordinance following the precedent set in *Buchanan* v. *Warley* (1917). Afterward, the state legislature enacted a law empowering cities to create segregation laws, but Dallas did not take advantage of it.[34]

In 1939, the USHA selected an area in North Dallas for slum clearance. The site lay in the heart of the black community. Home owners there fought to get the site changed, but to no avail. When clearance began in the summer of 1940, nearly 400 families lost their homes. Because it was already overcrowded, few housing opportunities existed in the Black Belt. The blacks who could afford it therefore sought residences in the traditionally white blocks on the fringe of the ghetto. A few white home owners offered to sell their homes to African Americans. Knowing that the market had inflated property values and wanting to move away from the encroaching blacks, many whites were not just willing but actually anxious to sell out. Jumping at the chance to live in better housing, middle-class blacks began to move into the 3500 and 3600 blocks of Howell Street.[35]

The area bordering the ghetto seemed a logical site for middle-class black expansion. African Americans had lived in the 3400 block since 1909. New black migration in 1917 had caused violent resistance on the part of whites, but few expected significant white opposition in 1940. Those intending to move into the section viewed it as an area whose time as "a high-class white territory" had passed. According to one black home owner, it was "now time to make a first-class colored territory out of it." In a testament to the African American public's understanding of the reality of neighborhood racial transition, the observer added, "all the white people in the neighborhood should sell out their homes to colored people who are finding it necessary to move out of the area where the housing project is located."[36]

Many white home owners on Howell Street disagreed with the opinion of black Dallas about neighborhood transition and became determined to stay on the block. The *Dallas Express* reported that whites felt harassed by realtors and by the threats of neighbors to sell off their property. "The general opinion among white people," according to the *Express*, was that they did not want to have black neighbors and did not want to move but believed they would have to leave "if a large number of Negroes [moved] in." Whites said that they loved their homes and did not believe "they should be forced to move simply because the colored people have to vacate their homes on account of the housing project." Of course, no one actually forced the whites out. They could have stayed and abided black neighbors, but in Dallas in 1940, such a notion remained anathema. Beginning in August, whites in the area embarked on a scheme to keep African Americans out, a scheme that would eventually result in nearly twenty bombings over the next fifteen months.[37]

When the news broke that several of the homes along Howell Street had been sold to blacks, long-time white residents began a multifaceted program of resistance. Amid their threats of violence against the black newcomers and those whites who sold out, the objectors petitioned the Dallas City Council to designate the area for white occupancy only. City officials told them that such a declaration would be unconstitutional. So the petitioners filed a lawsuit to enjoin other whites from selling property to African Americans. The suit claimed that such sales caused the white home owners personal damage by depreciating property values in the entire neighborhood. When this tactic also failed, the whites posted signs in front of their houses reading, "Keep This Neighborhood White." They picketed the houses of those whites rumored to be willing to sell to blacks. They also tried to burn down a vacant house owned by blacks.[38]

In early September, the violent resistance began in earnest. The first outbreak occurred on September 4, 1940, when C. L. Walker and George Johnson tried to move into their homes. According to reports, while "a squadron of police patrolled the neighborhood," area housewives stoned Walker's house, breaking windows. Four days later, a house owned by Bush Jones, a black doctor, was burned to the ground. A policeman in the area reported that he had seen a car leave the house just after the explosion, but he did not give chase because his motorcycle would not start. On September 12, vandals made a bomb attempt on Johnson's home. On September 16, the garage behind the house owned by Earl Jones, Jones's son, was bombed.[39]

The conflict continued into October. On October 1, three unidentified whites bombed an unoccupied house on Lobdell Street, next door to a house into which a black family had moved that morning. Two days later, more than 100 white demonstrators visited the homes of blacks in the district to warn them that they had one day to vacate or be bombed. Earl Jones informed the NAACP of the march. He reported that the vigilantes had told him that they were "disgusted with [the] inaction of city officials" and that they had "more than 500 persons ready to act." He recounted that the leader of the gang had threatened him, warning, "You got to get out of here, as no niggers can live on this property." The man admitted to bombing Jones's garage, adding that it "should have been plenty of notice that we whites do not intend to let you niggers stay here." The next night, the gang, numbering over 500, returned to Jones's front yard. The protesters yelled abuse and threw rocks and brickbats, smashing windows and damaging dining room furniture and dishes. When the police arrived, according to Jones, they "respectfully requested these roughians [sic] not to throw any more rocks at the house." And "after a good deal of begging and persuasion," Jones remembered, "this bunch stopped throwing rocks and went away."[40]

The Dallas NAACP demanded protection for black home owners but got little help from city officials. Mayor Woodall Rodgers proposed creating an interracial housing committee to resolve the issue and consider plans for preventing a recurrence of violence. But the committee was interracial in name only. "It would be a mistake," its chairman contended, "to put any member of the negro race" on it. He insisted that the committee would "use every effort to work the matter out along correct lines" but told the NAACP that if the association should take part in negotiations, "it would merely arouse animosity." He doubted the organization's ability to comprehend the issue anyway because southerners, he reasoned, "feel that they better understand the colored people and know better how to get along with them on a fair and amicable basis than the members of [a] northern organization. . . . More than 95 per cent of the colored people," the chairman concluded, "prefer to live in communities in which white people do not live." The Dallas NAACP countered that a settlement meant more to African Americans than it did to whites and therefore African Americans needed to play a role in negotiations. Despite that plea, no blacks were appointed, and the committee ultimately designated the area for white residences.[41]

The NAACP blamed police and city officials for the continuing violence and eventually realized that they would not get satisfaction locally. Organization officials lobbied Governor W. Lee O'Daniel, requesting that he send Texas Rangers to protect black home owners. O'Daniel replied that he had "checked with Dallas Officials" and was satisfied that the local police were "competently handling [the] situation." NAACP Special Counsel Thurgood Marshall informed the U.S. Justice Department of the Dallas situation and requested that the Federal Bureau of Investigation (FBI) provide protection to blacks. The assistant attorney general, O. John Rogge, told Marshall that the FBI would investigate. Democratic Congressman Martin Dies of Texas had his House Committee on Un-American Activities (HUAC) look into the situation, too. Dies believed that communists or fascists, or maybe both, had infiltrated the NAACP and poisoned Dallas's black community, spurring blacks to challenge the status quo.[42]

Entering the second week of October, "things [were] still hot and getting hotter," according to the NAACP. A fire of unknown origin destroyed a house on Howell Street. City officials began to pressure blacks into vacating their homes. City Manager James Aston and City Planner Major Woods requested that Anna Wright not move into her newly purchased home on the all-white Bowser Street, a half-block from Howell. They visited the Walkers and Johnsons to ask them to leave, promising both home owners that they would get their money back for the sale and that the city would pay their moving expenses. Aston and Woods added that police protection would be withdrawn if they did not move. Both families informed the NAACP that they would remain in their homes regardless.[43]

On October 16, the mayor and council tried to settle the issue once and for all. With the housing committee's report before them, they resolved that the area surrounding Howell Street would be designated for white residence only. African Americans residing in the district would have to move. The city promised to help them find "satisfactory residences in Negro communities" and ensured them that they would "suffer no financial loss in doing so." The city council demanded that the planning board undertake to survey the entire city. The board would then create a general zoning plan that would allow for the expansion of a black community and would "accommodate additional residential demands where they arise." The city resolved to create a system of residential segregation. Because they had not legislated the separation, they hoped they had circumvented the *Buchanan* ruling.[44]

The next day, the city planner, the city manager, and the mayor visited C. L. Walker to pressure him into moving. To gain even more leverage, they brought along Walker's boss. The mayor told Walker that the city had arranged to give him back the $1,000 he had paid on his home, to pay the cost of moving and his rent for thirty days, and to help locate him in another home. Walker told the mayor that he did not want to sell. The visitors then told him that the police protection they could give him might not be sufficient to keep away the angry mob. But Walker remained firm. When Walker's boss told him not to worry about the situation affecting his job, the city officers left in a huff.[45]

For the next six weeks, the situation along Howell remained calm, but it reignited in December. The NAACP initiated a suit on behalf of Earl Jones. Jones claimed that the city had not met its responsibility in protecting black home owners and had illegally passed the resolution segregating the races. With the case about to come to trial, terrorists attempted to bomb a black's vacant house in the area. The court hearing was supposed to occur on the last day of the year, but sleight-of-hand by the city delayed it. Exposing the lengths to which it would go to obfuscate the issue, the city council surreptitiously inserted into the minutes of its October 30 meeting a notice rescinding the resolution of October 16. When the court did hear the case, the judge dismissed the complaint because the resolution no longer existed. He did offer his opinion of the resolution, however. He called it "unconstitutional, un-American, invalid, and insane."[46]

With the segregation resolution dead in the courts, with the city unable and unwilling to protect blacks, with state and federal officials essentially turning a blind eye, and with blacks adamant about defending property rights, Dallas stood at the brink of race warfare as 1941 began. In January, an explosion destroyed the home of Earl Jones. A month later, terrorists bombed the home of Dr. P. M. Sunday. When that failed to force the doctor out, they attacked two more times at the end of February. A bombing occurred in March and another in April. On May 8, in what the *Dallas Morning News* called the "heaviest bombing of the year," three sticks of dynamite shook the ground and wrecked the San Jacinto Village apartments. But still the violence had not ended. On May 22, whites dynamited the home of a black florist.[47]

Finally, after the May bombings, violence ebbed and the situation seemed to ease. The NAACP enlisted the aid of the American Civil Liberties Union to lobby the federal government to take action. Many in the public, meanwhile, charged that police had not done enough to stop the bombings. One white resident, although insisting that he was "no Negro-lover," intimated that had the bombings occurred in white areas, "there would [have been] plenty of arrests." The *Dallas Morning News*, with its tradition of enlightened racial reportage, also pressured the police. Police Chief James M. Welch doubled the force investigating the incidents, but no arrests came. Few suspects were even questioned. One man who was interrogated by police may have undergone scrutiny more for his German ancestry than for any actual involvement in race hate. The issue refused to go away. On November 29, terrorists set off what the *Dallas Express* called "undoubtedly the most damaging of any [bomb] which [had] rocked Dallas in the last fourteen months." The target again was the black florist. The bomb destroyed his house and the adjoining flowershop. The incident shocked the people of Dallas all the more because, according to the *Express*, "it had been an accepted fact that the city was through with such disturbances." Only World War II gave Dallas a real respite from the housing conflict.[48]

The years of the Great Depression often proved frustrating and destructive for African Americans. Because of discrimination and the soft foundation of their prosperity during the 1920s, blacks felt the hardship of the economic emergency of the 1930s even more profoundly than whites. Although migration had slowed, access to adequate housing in the urban centers remained a problem for many African Americans. Still hemmed in by restrictive covenants and discrimination in rental units and now with many more of them lacking the financial means with which to buy houses, African Americans were again forced into overcrowded and decaying ghettos. Despite the good intentions of government administrators and the few advances in civil rights law, government programs did much harm to the black community.

Many factors led to the negative effect of housing programs. African Americans felt the brunt of slum clearance most. Displaced by demolition of their homes, they were forced into the hostile environment of a discriminatory housing market. Inexperience in issues of housing and the decentralized structure of government exacerbated the damage, and a lack of trustworthy information about housing caused governments to get a slow start on correcting the problems. Real estate, construction, and financial interests guarded their territories against government encroachment. The federal government, moreover, had no history of public action. It was forced to experiment. And since the economic emergency gave motive to housing policy, the bureaucracy often overlooked the social aspects of the programs. Agencies, it seemed, took action to correct policies only after the damage was done.

White prejudice and violence played key roles in the persistence of housing discrimination and residential segregation. The FHA, influenced by the private housing industry, insisted that black migration into white neighborhoods would cause a decline in property values and likely engender white resistance. Unfortunately, private industry was right about the violence. Whites proved willing to go to almost any length to protect their neighborhoods from the perceived threat. Many supporters of the New Deal may have wanted to help blacks, but the governments closest to the people blocked their good intentions. Whites did not want their neighborhoods integrated. They rose up in protest, and government generally responded with expediency. To restore the peace, each branch and level of government perpetuated discrimination against African Americans.

Blacks did not lose everything during the Depression. In 1939, the NAACP's litigation wing, taking advantage of New Deal tax reforms, reorganized into a permanent Legal Defense and Education Fund. A number of African American lawyers became specialists in civil rights law. The LDF even undertook to train lawyers in civil rights litigation. The New Deal had also given many black social scientists the opportunity to enter government, and African Americans slowly gained a voice in policymaking. Robert Weaver was among the vanguard of this phenomenon. And black academics increasingly won respect with studies made from an African American perspective. Charles Johnson led this new class of researchers in the housing issue. As Harvard Sitkoff notes, Ira De A. Reid, J. G. St. Clair Drake, Horace R. Cayton, and E. Franklin Frazier added their expertise in the area of sociology.

The trials of the Great Depression laid the foundation for a consolidated and invigorated effort in the black struggle for justice in housing, but the climate of American race relations had not yet sufficiently changed for blacks to succeed in that effort. As the next chapter shows, the impact of World War II on the national economy, the distribution of the population, and the definition of racial justice forced further reform of American racial policy. That transition came slowly, however. In the area of black housing and home ownership and the spatial distribution of the races, it came even more slowly still.

4

HOUSING DURING WARTIME

Adequate housing is a morale builder and is essential to the speed and efficiency of national defense work.[1]

With World War II came a second Great Migration. The demand for the weapons and machinery with which to wage war ended the Great Depression and prompted a tremendous movement of workers of all races to centers of industrial production and shipping. African American migration started slowly, but after President Franklin D. Roosevelt established the Fair Employment Practices Committee (FEPC) in June 1941 and especially after the United States entered the war, it skyrocketed.

The explosion of war production in 1941 created economic opportunities for African Americans, but it also generated unrest. Some communities, such as Seattle, seemed to rally around the war effort and left prejudice aside. But others saw the war create new tensions or enflame long-simmering conflicts. Fear among whites about changes in their status and growing resentment among African Americans over the hypocrisy of the war rhetoric of the Atlantic Charter's "Four Freedoms" and the reality of their condition combined in a very combustible mixture. Between 1941 and 1945, race riots occurred in Los Angeles, Detroit, Newark, and New York City as well as Mobile, Alabama, and Beaumont, Texas.

Housing constituted a primary locus for racial conflict. Since centers of war production lacked adequate housing for the influx of workers, emergency construction of dwelling units to accommodate soldiers and workers became an essential part of the war effort. And although African Americans did not compose a large proportion of the early war migrants, any influx made an already desperate condition of overcrowding in the black districts more critical. Amid these new needs, old prejudices remained. Whites continued to refuse to live among African Americans, and where the races converged, conflict ensued. Whites at the Willow Run project near Detroit, in Baltimore, in Rockford, Illinois, and elsewhere blocked construction of temporary housing projects for African American workers. A riot in Detroit in February 1942 arose directly from the racial occupancy of Sojourner Truth Homes. Less dramatic but still destructive violence also resulted from black migration into white areas in Los Angeles and other cities.

The struggle for racial justice continued throughout the war. The NAACP and National Urban League were joined by A. Philip Randolph's March on Washington Movement, the Congress of Racial Equality (CORE), and other groups. They pursued a "Double V" campaign that, according to the *Chicago Defender*, stood for victory against Adolf Hitler and victory against "Adolph Jim Crow." The campaign entailed doing their "patriotic duty" to "observe scrupulously the basic requirements for the successful prosecution of the war," but it reserved "the right to expose and assail any malicious abridgment of the constitutional guarantees that [gave] meaning and substance to . . . citizenship." Like the Depression, the war enabled civil rights groups to fortify the foundation of a movement. This time, however, it gave them more numerous areas at which to attack. But as this chapter shows, the United States was still years away from granting African Americans their due.[2]

The Second Great Migration brought an even more dramatic shift of population than its earlier counterpart. Between December 1941 and March 1945, more than 15,000,000 Americans changed their county of residence and therefore were counted as migrants for census purposes. More than half the migrants moved to a different state, and of these, more than 3.5 million moved to a different region of the country. No comprehensive national census statistics exist measuring the migration of African Americans for the same period. A migration study executed by the Works Progress Administration, however, shows that blacks made up only 4.3 percent of the more than 2 million migrants in the twelve months following October 1940. African American migration remained slow until after the attack at Pearl Harbor, when white males left the factories for the segregated armed forces. During the three and a half years following U.S. entry into the war, an estimated 700,000 African Americans joined the stream of civilian migrants.[3]

The new migration derived from many of the same impulses as the earlier mass exodus from the rural South. Poverty and peonage continued to characterize the circumstances of many black sharecroppers. Although the number of lynchings reported had dropped since the mid-1930s, the prospect of mob violence continued to haunt southern blacks. But demographers have concluded that the new migration was "largely positive—a move with the expectation of steadier employment, better wages, or the acquisition of higher skill." That many African American migrants stayed in the region, moving from rural areas to southern cities, supports the idea that wartime migration represented a chase toward hoped-for opportunity more than a flight from injustice.[4]

The hope of finding work in the war plants lured southern blacks to Detroit, Baltimore, Los Angeles, and the San Francisco Bay area. An estimated 50,000

African Americans migrated from the Deep South to Chicago during the war. Detroit received approximately 65,000 black migrants from all regions between 1941 and 1945. The African American community of Baltimore grew, through migration and natural increase, by more than 20 percent between 1940 and 1943 to number about 200,000. Cities on the Pacific coast saw the greatest proportional increase in African American population. According to Census Bureau studies of five "Congested Production Areas of the West," black population in the urban West grew from 107,000 to an estimated 230,000 between 1940 and 1944. Just under 64,000 blacks lived in the city of Los Angeles in 1940, but four years later the population had nearly doubled. Between 1940 and 1944, the black population of the San Francisco Bay area more than tripled to number over 60,000.[5]

The migration to cities of persons of all races strained urban housing markets. Early in 1940, the federal government saw that housing shortages could hinder its war effort. By June, Congress had amended the Wagner Housing Act and authorized the U.S. Housing Authority to construct defense housing. In July, the National Defense Council created the Office of Defense Housing Coordinator (ODHC) and charged it with designing a policy for construction of defense housing and with coordinating private industry and public resources to achieve its objectives. To this end, a former assistant administrator at the Federal Housing Administration, Miles L. Colean, prepared a report entitled *Housing an Industrial Army*. He recommended restricting "nonessential migration" to reduce defense housing needs as well as to alleviate problems of readjustment after the war. The restriction of black migration, in particular, became a rallying cry for civic officials in the shipbuilding centers of the East Coast.[6]

In October, Congress passed the major housing legislation of the war era, the Lanham Act. Named for its sponsor, Representative Fritz G. Lanham, a Democrat from Texas, the act stipulated that war housing be inexpensive to build and use minimal construction materials. Most of the housing would be temporary and would be demolished after the war. In this way, Congress hoped to meet the needs of workers but not overtax resources or saturate the market with new housing and thereby irrevocably depress property values. The program was held up by haggling between real estate and financial interests on the one hand and advocates of public housing and slum removal on the other. But U.S. entry into the war made that debate moot by suspending slum clearance projects.[7]

Experimentation with housing policies continued as war neared. Because construction of defense housing lagged behind other preparedness efforts, President Roosevelt replaced ODHC with the Division of Defense Housing Coordination (DDHC) in January 1941. Recalling the bad experiences of the Great War, Roosevelt sought to meet the nation's housing needs in a more orderly fashion and to reduce the opportunity for landlords to capitalize on housing shortages by "gouging" renters. Legislation followed during the next months, but U.S. neutrality in the war slowed progress. Without an actual war emergency, Philip J. Funigiello insists, "greed, indolence, bureaucratic confusion, and the fear of federal usurpation of local au-thority" blocked the creation of "an integrated program coordinating housing with war production." Most Americans, according to Funigiello, remained "unwilling to make the individual sacrifices that a total commitment to national defense im-plied."[8]

After the Japanese attack on Pearl Harbor, most Americans became more willing to make the sacrifices necessary to win a war. In February 1942, Roosevelt created the National Housing Agency (NHA) to oversee government wartime housing policy and named John B. Blandford its director. The NHA would manage the FHA, the Federal Home Loan Bank Administration, and the Federal Public Housing Author-ity (FPHA). Blandford worked with the War Manpower Commission, the War Production Board, and the War and Navy Departments to coordinate construction of housing to meet the needs of war production workers while not diverting neces-sary resources. Only the construction of housing essential to the war effort was undertaken. When possible, existing buildings were converted into additional apart-ments. Over the course of the war, the government would make $2 billion available for emergency war housing and build 945,000 temporary dwellings.[9]

The status of African Americans under the new housing legislation remained unclear. Race relations services existed in the DDHC and in FPHA. The DDHC advisers were transferred to the Office of the NHA Administrator after Pearl Har-bor, but the war emergency muted the voices of these African American advisers. In August 1942, in one of his few clear statements of racial policy, Blandford declared, "in determining the need for war housing . . . no discrimination shall be made on account of race, creed, color, or national origin." The words sounded good, but federal administrators could not live up to the promise. Opposition from local white interests meant that federal officials repeatedly reversed occupancy and con-struction allotments, causing the *Chicago Defender* to remark that Blandford "had the backbone of a jellyfish." And resistance in other parts of the federal bureaucracy exacerbated the weaknesses of the declared policy of the NHA. The FHA, for ex-ample, refused to admit that it discriminated against African Americans. Its actions, however, repeatedly demonstrated the contrary. In 1943, FHA commissioner Abner H. Ferguson went so far as to lobby the Senate to keep it from putting an anti-discrimination clause into federal housing legislation. Even when government agen-cies did make clear statements against discrimination, the orders did not necessarily have the desired effect. In January 1941, the Federal Works Agency (FWA), which had taken over the USHA in a bureaucratic reorganization in 1939, issued an execu-tive order forbidding discrimination against black defense workers in emergency war housing. But discriminatory hiring practices meant that African Americans still had difficulty finding employment in war industries. Many found work only by filling the nondefense jobs abandoned by whites and therefore did not qualify for emergency war housing.[10]

White opposition to integration remained the most important factor obstructing access to defense housing. Housing, according to *The Monthly Summary of Events and Trends in Race Relations,* became "one of the most acute areas of racial tension." "The most significant fact about housing," the journal explained, "was the almost universally unsuccessful effort of builders with government subsidies to secure sites for dwellings for Negro defense workers." City after city witnessed resistance from local whites when federal officials proposed housing projects for blacks, and violence continued to be a potential consequence of that tension.[11]

In the spring of 1941, the DDHC recommended construction of 200 homes to accommodate African American defense workers in Detroit. Following the announcement, Detroit's housing commission proposed a site. Although they wanted the new housing, local blacks opposed the city's site because of its topography and proximity to heavy industry. Upon hearing of the opposition, the commission proposed a new site near the established black enclave of Conant Gardens. This location also met opposition. This time it came from property owners of both races who feared that a temporary housing project would adversely affect land values and community life. Emboldened by amendments to the Lanham Act that allowed federal administrators to select sites without local input, the FWA insisted on its choice. Administrators told the Detroit Housing Commission that they would "take full responsibility." They did make one concession: the housing would be permanent, not temporary in design.[12]

By autumn 1941, the community of neat, well-built, brick rowhouses neared completion. The Detroit Housing Commission named it Sojourner Truth Homes, after the emancipation leader. It invited African Americans to apply for occupancy. Conflict arose when local whites, who now supported the project, opposed its occupation by African Americans. At this point, the FWA switched its position. The administrator told whites that the question of the race of the occupants was still undecided. The Seven-Mile Fenelon Improvement Association led the protest against African American occupancy of Sojourner Truth Homes. It flooded Congressman Rudolph G. Tenerowicz's office with telegrams. Tenerowicz, a former mayor of Hamtramck, had initially pledged his support to the blacks in the controversy, but pressure from his Polish American constituents changed his mind. At Tenerowicz's behest, Congress threatened to rescind the project's funding rather than have the homes go to African Americans. When FWA Assistant Administrator Clark Foreman ignored the warning and authorized the homes for African American occupancy, pressure from Congress tightened, and Foreman resigned. Tenerowicz, meanwhile, had the House Un-American Activities Committee investigate groups that favored occupancy by African Americans. The probe, according to Tenerowicz, revealed that sixteen of the groups listed as supporters were "conspicuously and frequently mentioned in the records of [HUAC]." Venting his concern, the congressman declared that "unscrupulous, biased, [and] subversive . . . Negro and radical elements" were "bent on the destruction of human values and property values alike."[13]

In mid-January 1942, the federal agencies bowed to pressure from Congress.

Baird Snyder, the new FWA administrator, and C. F. Palmer of DDHC restricted Sojourner Truth Homes to white occupancy only. They also announced that the government would build housing for African American workers on the site origi-nally proposed by the Detroit Housing Commission, the one rejected by the NAACP and the Detroit Urban League. The regional coordinator of DDHC delivered the news. He told Walter White that he knew that the solution would disappoint local blacks. He insisted, however, that the decision was final. He also promised that in the future the policy would "tend in many ways to eliminate a repetition of the incident."[14]

Detroit's African American community and the NAACP refused to accept the decision as the last word. Walter White contended that the reversal "would make for the poorest kind of public relations and would be a direct attack upon civilian morale." To counter Tenerowicz, he won the support of Rep. Arthur W. Mitchell of Illinois, the first black Democrat elected to Congress. Detroit's black leadership, meanwhile, held a mass rally and picketed the mayor's office. With the help of the United Auto Workers (UAW), they won the support of Mayor Edward Jeffries and the Detroit City Council. At the end of January, the city requested that Sojourner Truth Homes be returned to African Americans. On February 2, Snyder and Palmer did another about-face. The black community celebrated what looked to be a great victory.[15]

On February 28, 1942, the first black families, having paid rent in advance, were set to begin to move into Sojourner Truth Homes. A mob of 700 armed white men and women had barricaded the entrance to the project. The police department had staked 200 officers at the scene in case of trouble. At about seven o'clock that morn-ing, a man driving his truck of furniture reached the barricade, halted, and asked police to help him through the mob. The policeman reportedly told the new resi-dent that he "had better turn around and go back." While the mover haggled with the police, a white man climbed onto the truck and menaced the driver. The white pickets began showering rocks on the caravan. Police informed the housing com-missioners that they did not have the resources to protect the tenants against the mob. The commissioners decided to defer occupancy until protection could be obtained.[16]

Within a few hours of the confrontation, a story had swept through the city that whites had formed a mob and that police had done nothing to stop them. In retali-ation, according to the NAACP's Roy Wilkins, local blacks "got their clubs, knives, [and other weapons,] and came out in their trucks. Then the police began to work on them." A riot raged throughout Detroit. Police arrested more than 100 rioters, fewer than five of whom were white. Explaining the discrepancy, a police inspector later told reporters that it would have been "suicide if we used our sticks on any of [the whites]." In the early rioting, two men were shot, and many more were injured by sticks and stones and bricks.[17]

For two days the situation at Sojourner Truth Homes remained critical. About

1,000 whites kept a vigil at the barricade. Elsewhere, a group of some thirty women carrying American flags and placards declaring "We Want White Neighbors" pick-eted the project's administration building. Mobs of whites also began terrorizing blacks in other neighborhoods. The city's blacks, meanwhile, demonstrated in the streets. Wilkins observed that they wanted to fight. "They are rapidly coming to the point," he reported, "where they do not believe or trust any white person or any government institution." One demonstrator proclaimed, while burning his draft card, "I will take my fighting and dying . . . right here on the streets of Detroit for some democracy for my own people."[18]

At city hall, Mayor Jeffries continued to support black occupancy, but both he and the NAACP realized that the decision would not be made in Detroit. Jeffries insisted that not giving African Americans occupancy would be equal to saying, "there is no place within Detroit where they can have new housing." The mayor admitted, however, that he felt "like MacArthur in the Philippines." He said that he was "responsible in the field, but [that] the decision [would be] made in Washington." To change that situation, the NAACP undertook a writing campaign with the hope of influencing federal administrators.[19]

On March 6, 1942, it seemed that a breakthrough had been reached. The FWA announced that black defense workers would occupy Sojourner Truth Homes. One reason for the step was that administrators had learned that the enemy was using the incident for propaganda purposes. The *Detroit Free Press*, for example, had reported that the Germans and Japanese used the riot to try to influence neutral countries in South America. But despite the pressure, the police department continued to block occupancy of the homes by African Americans. Police Commissioner Frank D. Eaman insisted that only with a force of several hundred police could he ensure the safety of black residents. A federal grand jury also refused to allow blacks to begin moving in until it had completed its investigation. U.S. Attorney General Francis Biddle had ordered the inquiry after it was alleged that the Ku Klux Klan may have encouraged its members to picket the development.[20]

The conflict continued unresolved for six more weeks. The NAACP, Detroit housing officials, and federal administrators met in Washington, D.C., to look for a solution to the impasse. It became increasingly assured that blacks would occupy the project. The only question was whether they could be protected. On April 15, the FWA and DDHC ordered the Detroit Housing Commission to begin admit-ting the African American defense workers. The next day, Police Commissioner Eaman resigned. The mayor claimed that the resignation had nothing to do with the riots, but the city's black community believed differently. They had held the police responsible for the riot. They accused them of siding with whites, of disarm-ing blacks but not whites, and of arresting blacks but not whites. The first African American tenants moved into Sojourner Truth Homes on April 29, 1942.[21]

In the aftermath of the riot, many Americans sought to cast blame. The grand jury indicted three of the riot's ringleaders for conspiracy and sedition. Two of the men indicted were officers in the National Workers League, an organization that HUAC had charged with disseminating Nazi propaganda. The third was an officer of the Seven-Mile Fenelon Improvement Association. The NAACP, meanwhile, blamed police for the extent of the riot and accused Tenerowicz of inciting it. The organization noted that just a day before the first clash, Tenerowicz had made a speech warning of the potential for violence if African Americans were admitted to the project. The NAACP demanded the congressman's resignation but did not get it. Tenerowicz, in turn, blamed the federal administrators. Many Detroiters agreed. Bureaucratic flip-flopping had weakened their trust. They did question the politicking by Tenerowicz, however. He would pay a price for his rabble-rousing by losing in the Democratic primary in September.[22]

With African Americans moving into Sojourner Truth Homes, the NAACP declared victory, but the triumph was incomplete. The project at times seemed like a militarized zone, with state police and soldiers posted to keep the peace, and greater access to housing had not been achieved. The Detroit Housing Commission maintained that any change in residential racial patterns would result in violent opposition to government housing and could endanger war production. Mayor Jeffries therefore announced that to avoid future conflicts, the city would "in no way change the racial characteristics of any neighborhood."[23]

Racial tensions continued to grow after the riot. The rapid influx of workers of both races fueled the discord. A series of wildcat strikes by whites trying to prevent the hiring and upgrade of black defense workers created a mood for conflict as workers walked out at the Hudson Naval Arsenal, U.S. Rubber, Hudson Motor Car, and Packard Motor Car companies in the spring of 1943. Whites also resisted the integration of emergency housing at the Ford aircraft plant at Willow Run west of Detroit. Several incidents of apparent police harassment of African Americans caused further friction. In June 1943, the city erupted. No housing incident triggered the violence. Rumors that African Americans had raped a white woman at Belle Isle Park and that white sailors had thrown a black woman and her baby into Lake St. Clair started the melee. Before federal troops could quell the riot, twenty-five African Americans and nine whites had died, and $2 million in property damage had occurred. As if paraphrasing Du Bois's "dilemma of the Negro," Walter White insisted, "the riot [proved] that segregation whether voluntary or involuntary produces separateness and friction."[24]

With tension still high after the second riot, the city tried to find ways to improve race relations. Immediately following the riot, Mayor Jeffries formed an emergency committee to study the source of the racial tensions. In March 1944, Jeffries established the more comprehensive Detroit Interracial Committee (DIC) to survey race relations and attitudes. The committee's first report offered few specific recommendations beyond suggesting that the city undertake an advertising campaign to promote racial tolerance. The DIC advertisements asked Detroiters to "Join the Fight Against Religious and Racial Hate" and to teach their children to be "Free from

Religious or Racial Prejudice." Although the scheme was well intentioned, one critic rightly noted, "the Committee [had] not yet come to grips with the basic causes of [the] tensions." The real cause of the conflict was competition over economic resources and living space. Racial tension would remain a concern in the city for the rest of the war.[25]

Events in Baltimore further demonstrate the tensions brought by war migration. In 1943, peace in Baltimore was imperiled by inadequate housing for the large population of African Americans who had come to the city in search of work. The Urban League estimated that the city's black population increased by nearly 40,000 between 1940 and July 1943, to 200,000. According to the Governor's Commission on Problems Affecting Colored People, blacks constituted 20 percent of the city's population but had access to 2 percent of the land. The Citizen's Planning and Housing Association sounded the alarm, noting that there were only 113 dwellings for each 1,000 blacks in Baltimore. "There are practically no habitable vacancies in areas of Baltimore accessible to war industries," it declared. "Negro residents," it added in a report to the mayor, were "inadequately housed and newcomers [had to] pile upon those who already [lived] in segregated sections of the city." The federal government understood the need for housing and allocated $8,000,000 for the construction of 2,000 temporary housing units for African Americans at sites in and around the city. Following established procedure, federal agencies chose as one of the sites a locale in Baltimore's east side suburbs near Herring Run Park. By April 1943, the city still had not approved the site and planned no action until after the municipal election in July.[26]

Whites in the Herring Run area organized in opposition to the project. The Eastern Confederation of Civic Associations held a mass meeting one Sunday in April to protest. A leader of the group, Rev. Luke Schmucker, a Lutheran minister, told the assembled that he opposed the project because his church had undergone a $100,000 renovation and would depreciate if the project were built. Other speakers maintained that the area was white and officials should not disrupt residential racial patterns. Some of the less openly bigoted speakers claimed that only the temporary character of the housing disturbed them. The homes, they contended, would amount to little more than shacks built at an expenditure of only $3,500 each. They added that the houses would not benefit African Americans native to Baltimore but were for in-migrants. At the end of April, the City Plan Commission finally confirmed the Herring Run site. The white challenge continued. Having won the support of Maryland Democrats, Congressman H. Street Baldwin and Senator Millard Tydings, opponents of the project convinced the FPHA to change the site.[27]

In May, the FPHA selected a location at Cherry Hill in South Baltimore for construction of 1,400 temporary housing units. This site met with opposition from African Americans because it was situated too far from the commuter railway and too close to a city garbage incinerator. Leaders of the black community lobbied the mayor to get the site changed back to Herring Run. Mayor Jackson refused, insisting that ultimate responsibility for site selection rested with federal agencies. Other pressure to return to the original site came from inside the federal executive branch. According to the *Baltimore Afro-American Ledger*, Undersecretary of State Sumner Welles lobbied the FPHA to insist on Herring Run because of the negative impression the conflict was making internationally. Meanwhile, according to the *Chicago Defender*, the FPHA continued to follow "an unfortunate tradition of vacillation," wavering back and forth between the different sites before finally devising a plan that administrators hoped would satisfy both parties. The agency announced that it would now build permanent housing on the Herring Run site. Whites could no longer hide behind the pretense that they opposed only the temporary character of the project. They had to admit that what they really feared was increased black migration and the possibility that the newcomers would become permanent denizens of Baltimore.[28]

During May and June, the FPHA and Baltimore city officials approved two smaller housing projects, but Herring Run remained in question. Whites continued to agitate against the site while blacks called for NHA Administrator Blandford's head. The National Negro Council demanded that Blandford be removed because of his "failure to provide needed housing for colored war workers." It denounced his inability to solve not just the housing problem in Baltimore, but a similar quarrel over the Willow Run project near Detroit and housing crises in Los Angeles, Philadelphia, Buffalo, and Chester, Pennsylvania. Unable to secure Blandford's dismissal, African Americans planned to meet with President Roosevelt to force the NHA administrator to make a decision. On July 10, 1943, the eve of the meeting with Roosevelt, Blandford announced that Herring Run had again been selected.[29]

Administrator Blandford's decision outraged Baltimore's white community. On July 20, 800 protesters, most of them women, marched on City Hall and ordered the new mayor, Theodore Roosevelt McKeldin, to block the project. Two Catholic priests, a Methodist minister, a rabbi, four councilmen, and a real estate broker spoke for the protesters. Father T. Vincent Fitzgerald of St. Anthony of Padua Catholic Church, located ten blocks from the site, called the project an "unwarranted intrusion in an area where there are no colored people." "People out here," he claimed, "would move away if the project was built." Father John J. Donlan of St. Dominic Catholic Church, twenty blocks north of site, put it more simply. "For many years," he asserted, "people in Maryland have known their place and have kept that place." Councilman Medio Waldt told the mayor that he had received 500 calls protesting the selection of the site, adding, "I understand they are bringing in the scum of the colored race." Another protester characterized the migrants as "shiftless, ignorant and totally undesirable."[30]

Mayor McKeldin listened to the protesters and reluctantly addressed the crowd. A Republican who had taken advantage of a split within the Democratic Party to win office, McKeldin insisted that he bore no responsibility for the decision. He had inherited the problem. "When I assumed the office of Mayor," he declared, "there was this problem of colored housing—not of my making, nor of yours, but whether we liked it or not, it was here." He informed them that he had appointed an interracial commission, composed of seven whites and two blacks, to inspect each of the sites. The commission had recommended the Cherry Hill location. The NHA, however, adamantly refused to accept that site. McKeldin insisted that he remained open to recommendations. He promised that the City Plan Commission would grant hearings to the protesters and then added to thunderous applause, "I am as much opposed to in-migrant colored people coming here as you are."[31]

The project was delayed again as the City Plan Commission held hearings on the Herring Run site. Congressman Baldwin spoke for those opposing the site. In a baldly racist statement, he insisted that the African Americans who would occupy the housing represented the worst laborers, those who work one day but not the next. He claimed that the war effort did not need such slackers and that when the war ended these black workers would be the first to be laid off and go on permanent relief. Baldwin added that constructing fine permanent war housing in Baltimore's suburbs would cause governments to stop funding slum clearance, thus making slums an immutable fixture in Baltimore. He declared, "the city is the proper place" for the housing and a temporary trailer park built on leased land was the proper format for the project. The congressman's suggestion amounted to little more than a thinly disguised proposal to make sure that the black in-migrants did not remain in Baltimore after the war. Despite the protestations, the commission affirmed its selection of the Herring Run site.[32]

Baltimore City Council took one last stab at killing the project. During the first week of August, while Mayor McKeldin enjoyed a fishing vacation in Maine, the council responded to a petition of 10,000 signatures demanding that the city stop the project. It enacted an ordinance prohibiting the construction of any housing project without first receiving authorization from the mayor, city council, or the board of estimates. The council then adjourned. Knowing that the law ran counter to federal legislation authorizing the NHA to select any site and build any project it chose, Baltimore threatened a protracted legal battle to find out which party held the constitutional position.[33]

Seeing that whites in Baltimore would never be happy with an African American project in the suburbs but realizing that the site best suited the black war workers' needs, the FPHA decided to return to its original plan—to build temporary housing on the Herring Run site. The acting FPHA commissioner, R. L. Cochrane, made the announcement. "It has been determined that there is a critical need in Baltimore for war housing for Negroes," Cochrane declared, "and we will now proceed with construction of temporary projects to meet this need." The FPHA began condemnation proceedings in September, and Baltimore sued. The actual filing of a suit seemed to surprise the FPHA. The agency suddenly seemed unsure of its position. Throughout October, the two sides discussed solutions to the impasse. Finally, in November, the FPHA gave in to the city's demands once and for all and announced that the Herring Run project would be scrapped. It would be replaced by four smaller projects. The new sites included Cherry Hill, already opposed by blacks; the boggy, mosquito-infested, low-lying ground at Turner Station; and a Holabird site, next to a polluted stream amid heavy industrial factories. Blacks protested, but the FPHA did not budge. Surveying began a week after the announcement. Baltimore's African American workers would get housing, but not the housing they wanted.[34]

An influx of migrants occurred with equal force in cities on the West Coast. Los Angeles became a boom town as a result of the war. Its location on the Pacific coast made the city tremendously important to national security in defense against Japanese attack. Its burgeoning shipbuilding and aircraft industries made Los Angeles an economic center as well. The shipyards had been quiet during the interwar period, but as war overtook Europe, they saw a rebirth. In 1939, the shipbuilding industry employed about 1,000 workers. On the eve of U.S. entry into the war two years later, that number had grown to more than 22,000. The aircraft industry underwent an even more dramatic surge. The nation's "Big Six" aircraft companies—Lockheed, Douglas, Northrup, Vega, Vultee, and North American—all had plants in the Los Angeles area. Just under 15,400 workers labored in the aircraft plants in 1938. More than 120,000 did so at the time of the Japanese raid, but few of these jobs went to African Americans. North American Aviation, for example, declared that hiring African Americans as machinists or aircraft workers ran against company policy. The company president offered only that there would be "jobs as janitors for Negroes."[35]

The Zoot Suit riot of 1943 demonstrated that large-scale racial conflict could occur on the West Coast, but that incident involved few blacks and had nothing to do with housing. Still, the City of Angels did not escape residential strife. African Americans had been among the founders of Los Angeles. For most of the first half of the twentieth century, however, they made up less than 4 percent of its denizens. Then, in the four years following 1940, the black population grew by nearly 200 percent and reached more than 7 percent of the city's total population.[36] As had been the case elsewhere, the influx stressed housing markets. *The Nation* reported that only 1,000 public housing units were built between 1941 and early 1945, and of the 120,000 private units constructed, only 1,300 were available to African Americans. One housing opportunity did open up to blacks in 1942, however, when African Americans took advantage of the abandoned homes of the relocated Japanese Americans in "Little Tokyo." According to Robert Weaver, 14,534 blacks lived in the tracts of "Little Tokyo" in 1946, whereas fewer than 2,500 had resided there prior to the war.[37]

For decades, whites in Los Angeles and its environs had been using race-restrictive covenants to keep the peace and to contain the small black community. The practice expanded during the war as home improvement associations, according to one local historian, "led vigorous campaigns to cover all standing residential structures with covenants." As a result, much of Pasadena County and the San Gabriel Valley was closed to African Americans in 1941. Deed restrictions in the western end of the San Fernando Valley, meanwhile, created what would become known as the "Cotton Curtain." In this way, whites effectively trapped black Los Angelenos into the central and southern sections of the city.[38]

The NAACP had led numerous challenges against the enforcement of covenants over the years, but not until World War II did the organization find lasting success. Perhaps the most significant case occurred in the Sugar Hill district of Beverly Hills. Between 1941 and 1943, black business leaders and actors had settled on Hobart and Harvard Streets. As their number grew, whites in the West Adams Improvements Association became fearful that the whole neighborhood would become black. They used an extant covenant to force the blacks out. The defendants in the case included film stars Hattie McDaniel, best known for her role as Mammy in *Gone with the Wind*, for which she became the first African American to win an Academy Award; Louise Beavers; and Ethel Waters. In 1944, a Los Angeles court ruled for the defense. In his decision, Judge Thurmond Clarke gave the clearest statement on the constitutionality of race-restrictive covenants of any court up to that time. "It is time," he insisted, that "members of the Negro race are accorded, without reservations or evasions, the full rights guaranteed them under the 14th Amendment." Incidentally, one of the white home owners who led the challenge to black occupancy in Beverly Hills was also an actor: the silent-screen comedian, Harold Lloyd.[39]

Covenants and the courts could not always contain racial conflict over housing because in many neighborhoods the indentures had expired. When African Americans breached the walls of formerly restricted sections, violence and intimidation often ensued. In 1941, tensions simmered in the Van Ness–Cimarron district. White harassment forced five African American families from their homes. In the West Slauson area, the Ku Klux Klan burned crosses on the lawns of homes owned by blacks as well as those owned by whites sympathetic to residential integration. In 1943, in the then-transitional district of Watts, the South Los Angeles Home Owners Association organized to block African Americans from moving into the area. Terrorists in Watts bombed at least one home. That same year in an unidentified white neighborhood, an engineer, William Maxwell, and his wife Frances, a teacher, faced months of harassment. Already refused delivery from milk and ice services, the Maxwells awoke one morning to find bills posted throughout the neighborhood calling for whites to resist black "invasion." "Protect Your Property!" the poster proclaimed. "If you don't sign up now," it warned, "more niggers will move in [and] they'll take over the district." The Maxwells moved back to the ghetto.[40]

Tensions also arose in suburban Los Angeles when two black families moved into Maywood, California, in 1942. The editor of the *Maywood-Bell Southwest Herald*, Eddie Salitor, led the campaign to force them out. Under the headline "KEEP MAYWOOD WHITE," Salitor declared that whites latterly had been fortunate in having time on their side: African American migration had not touched the small community. "Today, however," he asserted, "the situation is totally different." If whites wanted to keep "Maywood Caucasian and the type of community that [they could] be proud of raising [their] children in," then, Salitor warned, they must "get on the band wagon and help win the fight" against black invasion. The issue was made even more urgent for Salitor because the race restrictions on property in one section of the town were due to expire. He contended that blacks were "just waiting to move in [and] after they are in," he concluded, "it will take the moving of heaven and earth to remove them."[41]

The situation in Maywood became somewhat of a cause célèbre for African Americans in Los Angeles when the editors of the *California Eagle*, the black newspaper, "decided to beard the lion [of racism] in his den." Charlotte A. Bass and John S. Kinloch met with Maywood's mayor and attended a meeting of the Race-Restrictive Program. Bass and Kinloch found that race restrictions had broad support among whites in the town. They were shocked by some of the arguments against African American migration. The mayor, for example, admitted that his "only objection to Negroes moving in" was that they would "marry our women." The editors fled in disgust and disappointment, unable to convince the whites that blacks had a dire need for access to better housing. In an editorial in the *Eagle*, they asked whites to remember what the war with Hitler was about and how African Americans contributed to the war effort, but to no avail.[42]

The worst incident of racial violence against a black moving into a white district of Los Angeles occurred shortly after the war in the town of Fontana. The section had been one of the few in the Los Angeles area where African Americans enjoyed access to quality employment. Fontana's Richmond Shipyards was the largest employer of African Americans in the Los Angeles area. Housing, however, was another matter. African Americans found homes only in a segregated enclave on a rocky floodplain on the northern fringe. A black civil rights activist named O'Day Short decided to test the status quo by purchasing land in a white section in the fall of 1945. In early December, a small white mob threatened Short and ordered him to take his family and leave town. Short refused to leave. Instead, he reported the threats to the FBI and the county sheriff, and he informed the editors of the *California Eagle*. Next, the Fontana Chamber of Commerce offered to buy the property. Short refused. On December 16, terrorists attacked. The neighbors reported hearing an explosion and then seeing "blobs of fire" around the house. The Shorts were at home during the assault. They fled the home with their clothes ablaze. Short's wife and young children died almost immediately. Short lingered for two weeks, unaware of his family's deaths, before finally succumbing himself. No justice would come of the deaths of O'Day Short and his family. And racial tension in southern California would only worsen over the next two decades.[43]

The historian Richard Polenberg concluded that the Japanese attack on Pearl Harbor "marked more than the passing of a decade[:] it signified the end of an old era and the beginning of a new." As with similar suggestions of radical change in the process of history, the statement needs some qualification. Much of what transpired in the area of race relations and housing for blacks built upon the work undertaken during the 1930s. The greater awareness of the plight of African Americans and the greater desire to ameliorate those difficulties caused by the Depression persisted during the war. The good intentions, however, often faced insurmountable impediments. The devotion of resources to the war brought shortages to all the civilian population, but as in the Depression the bottom rung of American society, the African American community, felt the shortages most.[44]

Developments during World War II did provide many new opportunities for African Americans. Significant advances occurred in the area of employment. The fight against Nazi ideas of racial and ethnic inferiority caused many Americans to rethink their own biases and prejudice and laid the groundwork for future progress toward racial justice. Furthermore, the radical transmigration of blacks during the war spread the issue of race relations throughout the nation, created new concentrations of black population in the urban North, and gave blacks a greater political voice. Finally, a "heightened sensitivity" to discrimination engendered in blacks a more determined response to injustice and gave force to the grassroots civil rights movement that followed the war. Each of these elements and the growing sophistication of the organizations of racial uplift enabled African Americans to make headway in their legal struggle for equal rights and equal protection.

Just as during the Depression, African American advancement came slowly and met fierce resistance, particularly over the issue of housing. White Americans rose up in protest against changes in the status of blacks. They battled to keep neighborhoods lily-white. When they did not fight, they fled, allowing all-white blocks to become all-black. Governments, meanwhile, commonly responded to the violence and intimidation with expediency. To restore peace, they perpetuated discrimination. They refused to upset the racial status quo, offering only that the war effort demanded domestic tranquillity and that African Americans would find justice after the defeat of the Axis. But blacks still needed a place to live. Their desperation and their sense of insult led to greater belligerency. As relations became more strained, cities moved to contain conflict but not to solve the underlying causes of race tension.

World War II did not so much mark the beginning of a new era of race relations as it marked another stage in the struggle for racial justice and access to better housing. The conflict over space did not end with the war. Rather, despite significant advances in law, economic and political opportunity, and the philosophy of racial tolerance, in many ways the housing conflict grew worse during the postwar years.

5

A FAIR DEAL FOR BLACK AMERICANS

Lack of housing can lose a peace just as surely as it could help lose a war.[1]

In the years immediately following World War II, African Americans enjoyed some of the most substantive advances in housing since the 1917 decision in *Buchanan* v. *Warley*. Despite its horrors, the war had a tremendously positive effect on the status of blacks. The "strategic position" of African Americans, Gunnar Myrdal observed, had been "strengthened not only because of the desperate scarcity of labor, but also because of a revitalization of the democratic Creed." The war against Germany had included a fight against the racial theories of the Nazis. Images of Jesse Owens and Joe Louis defeating the Teutonic heroes merged with anti-Nazi rhetoric to make many Americans more sensitive to racial stereotypes, prejudice, and discrimination. The revelation of the atrocities of the Holocaust gave the propagation of racial tolerance the urgency of life or death. Social scientists successfully challenged theories of caste and racial hierarchies. As Myrdal notes, even whites who defended discrimination against blacks habitually described their actions as irrational and caused by prejudice. This change in the attitude of many white Americans created an environment somewhat more conducive to progress in civil rights.

The dramatic changes in urban populations caused by the Second Great Migration created a dire need for new housing and strained race relations. The influx of African Americans into cities did not end with the war. It grew. Net out-migration from the South amounted to more than 3 million persons between 1940 and 1960. The North and West saw a gain in black population of more than 85 percent during the 1940s.

As with earlier migrations, blacks were huddled into ghettos. This concentration of African Americans into a few districts offered some advantages. It gave many black political leaders greater clout in city governments and political machines, and it had repercussions on national politics, as the northern Democratic Party increasingly courted the African American vote. But it also led to overcrowding and the collateral problems of crime and disease.

Federal housing policy toward African Americans had been pulled in two directions during the war. Some agencies had accepted the fact that blacks needed adequate housing, but to win the war they ignored or postponed the execution of such housing programs. The Federal Housing Administration, however, continued to refuse to insure mortgages of blacks trying to move into white sections, thereby winning it a reputation as "the most serious government offender against racial equality." Many African Americans found their condition to be worse than that before the Japanese attack on Pearl Harbor. The near-moratorium on the construction of permanent housing, the inadequacy of emergency defense housing, and persistent discrimination left many displaced or ill-housed.

Social and political developments did afford some blacks better access to housing. New York, for example, became the first state to forbid racial discrimination in public housing. The NAACP continued to chip away at restrictive covenants until the campaign finally bore fruit in 1948, when the Supreme Court heard the case of *Shelley* v. *Kraemer*. The Court accepted the LDF's contention that enforcement of covenants constituted state action and violated the Fifth and Fourteenth Amendments. Furthermore, because of a persistent NAACP campaign, the FHA removed references to race and price stability from its *Underwriting Manual* and ultimately even refused to insure property on which race-restrictive covenants were recorded. Governmental pressure was even brought to bear against the National Association of Real Estate Boards. NAREB would eventually remove the racial language from its "Code of Ethics."

The change in the status of African Americans accelerated throughout the postwar years, and with it came racial tension. As middle-class blacks tried to escape slums by moving into white districts, once again whites rose up in resistance. As this chapter as well as Chapters 6 and 7 will demonstrate, racial conflict over space grew and developed into the most intense form of massive resistance by white communities throughout the country in the decade following the war.

The Second Great Migration did not end with the war. African Americans continued their exodus from the rural South throughout the postwar period and during the 1950s. Between 1940 and 1950, Detroit's black population more than doubled to number over 300,000, or 16.4 percent of the city's total population. The black communities of New York City and Chicago saw less growth in terms of percentage change, but in actual numbers the influx was immense. Some 230,000 more African Americans lived in Chicago in 1950 than in 1940. New York's African American citizenry grew by more than 317,000 persons, and the city's 775,516 blacks numbered almost 10 percent of the city's total population. African American populations in California also increased. Los Angeles already had a sizable black population in 1940, but it tripled during the next decade to total more than 211,000. San

Francisco's black community increased by more than 1,580 percent, and Oakland's increased by nearly 560 percent.[2]

During 1946, according to the National Housing Agency, "the demand for housing reached unprecedented levels." Along with the African American migration, the return of servicemen and women from overseas made housing construction a priority. Projects begun during the Great Depression had been shut down during the war because of the reallocation of resources. Most dwelling units built under the Lanham Act were inadequate, having been built only to meet the war emergency. The National Association of Housing Officials demanded the demolition of temporary housing, proclaiming that the nation had an obligation to its veterans to offer "the hope of something better than a return to the shacks and tenements and blighted neighborhoods from which many of them [had] come." To meet the crisis, the NHA estimated that 12,600,000 new dwelling units would have to be built by 1955.[3]

Working from a motto—No More Great Depressions—both social reform–minded and business-minded housing interests agreed that government must aid the private housing industry to invigorate the economy, boost new construction, and enable families to purchase adequate housing. They recommended that the federal government enact a "G.I. Housing Bill." Both groups also agreed that government should extend mortgage loan insurance through the FHA and encourage builders to construct more housing for middle-income families by providing "yield insurance," which would guarantee a "fair annual profit" on the private investment in housing.[4]

The urban crisis caused Harry S Truman to make housing a central plank in his reconversion plan for the postwar United States. The president's belief in decent housing for all Americans originated in New Deal progressive ideology, but his experience as a legislator increased his knowledge of housing conditions. In 1937, he had supported the Wagner Housing Act. As chairman of the Senate Special Committee to Investigate the National Defense Program during the war, he became aware of the importance of housing and the difficulties correlative to housing construction. During the 1944 vice presidential campaign, Truman had declared that housing was "the heart of a community" and contended that a federal construction program was necessary to "secure the greater welfare of the individual citizen." As president, Truman understood that much of his party's strength relied on urban voters, so policies needed to satisfy urban interests.[5]

Republicans also understood the importance of the housing issue but preferred a less direct role for the federal government. Senator Robert A. Taft of Ohio, for example, chaired the Special Subcommittee on Housing and Urban Redevelopment. A conservative who had opposed the New Deal as an unreasonable and costly extension of federal power, Taft still had voted for the Wagner Housing Act in 1937. According to historian Richard O. Davies, Taft's experiences in Cincinnati had caused him to appreciate that adequate housing was "a prerequisite to good citizenship." Taft also believed, however, that the best way to intervene was to assist the private housing industry, not to undertake a major federal construction program.[6]

Instead of creating a comprehensive housing plan, the government only tinkered with and consolidated existing programs. The Congress amended the Servicemen's Readjustment Act to make loans insured by the Veterans Administration (VA) more readily available to home buyers by raising the mortgage guaranty and extending the maximum term of amortization of loans. It renewed the Lanham Act to provide temporary housing to veterans. The only significant new development in housing policy in the immediate postwar years came with Reorganization Plan No. 3. The plan established the Housing and Home Finance Agency (HHFA), the nation's "first permanent peacetime coordinating housing agency."[7]

Laws and government policies designed to increase housing opportunities for blacks and to force open housing markets remained out of reach despite the growing influence and improved prosperity of African Americans generally. War production jobs, according to the NAACP, had provided "a significant number of Negroes with incomes attractive to the private housing market." The wartime ethos of conservation and investment in victory bonds had helped many to amass considerable savings: the National Association of Home Builders (NAHB) reported in 1944 that blacks held over $18 billion in savings and wanted to buy homes. The ability of African Americans to pay for better housing grew after the war. In 1947, according to Thurgood Marshall, veterans in Detroit reported an ability to pay $6,000 for a home; in Newark and Cleveland, they felt they could afford $7,000.[8]

Even NAREB started to see opportunities in serving the African American housing market; its open-mindedness, however, stopped short of supporting residential integration. In mid-1944, NAREB called for the construction of new segregated housing and declared that African Americans were "a good economic risk." But the organization instructed members that if blacks tried to buy a house in a white area, and "if the deal would instigate a form of blight, then certainly the well-meaning broker must work against its consummation."[9]

Truman sympathized with the plight of blacks but did not yet support integration in housing. As a member of the Pendergast machine in Kansas City in the 1920s, he had enjoyed the support of African Americans in local elections. He benefited from their vote again when he ran for the Senate in 1934. That political debt prompted him to back antilynching laws and an anti-discrimination amendment in the Selective Service Act. When he became president, he told the NAACP's Walter White that he had received "a great heritage" from his predecessor and promised to "strive to attain the ideals" for which Franklin Roosevelt had fought. But he did not believe in social equality for blacks. "I wish to make it clear," he told the National Colored Democratic Association, "that I am not appealing for social equality of the Negro." He contended that even black leaders preferred "the society of their own people." They wanted "justice, not social relations."[10]

Anti-discrimination housing programs met opposition from several different factions in Congress. Southern Democrats blocked civil rights legislation almost as a matter of course. The Taft wing of the Republican Party was receptive to the idea of racial fairness, but it opted for gradualism. "You can pass some legislation," Taft told the *Baltimore Afro-American Ledger*, "but if you go forward too quickly, reaction will set in." He warned that "when you pass some laws you are liable to run into race riots." The politics of the African American leadership, particularly the NAACP, further reduced Taft's willingness to move forward in civil rights. He accused blacks of having "sold themselves to the New Deal."[11]

Even when the federal government took seemingly positive actions, the policies tended to rest on precarious foundations. Blacks, for instance, had hoped to benefit from the creation of the Office of the Housing Expediter in 1945, which was to formulate plans that would encourage housing construction by private industry. African Americans were particularly heartened when the president named Wilson W. Wyatt, the liberal Democrat, former mayor of Louisville, and NHA administrator, to the post. Wyatt's actions soon quashed those hopes, however. His February 1946 report failed to recommend specific protection for African Americans in the more than 2 million units he said should be built. Then, although a coordinated racial relations service was created in July, Wyatt took two months to name a race relations adviser. In Wyatt's defense, the fault lay not in any reluctance to ease the housing problems of blacks but in his understanding of how political opposition would kill any housing programs that made mention of race. After Wyatt resigned in late 1946, African American housing advocates were given more cause for concern. HHFA Director Raymond M. Foley summarily terminated the employment of all race relations officers in an attempt to meet congressional budget cuts. The closing of the racial relations service aroused such opposition from civil rights advocates that Foley restored racial advisers to the housing bureaucracy in November 1947.[12]

The reorganized Race Relations Service was headed by Frank S. Horne and included five regional advisers in the Public Housing Authority and the FHA. Horne had been in Roosevelt's "Black Cabinet" as an adviser to Mary McLeod Bethune in the National Youth Administration. He was Robert Weaver's assistant at USHA and took over the Office of Racial Relations after Weaver resigned in 1940. Horne and his staff, including Deputy Assistant B. T. McGraw, functioned in an advisory and research capacity. They would formulate and execute policies "so as to assure equitable participation of minority groups in all programs." They would also head off potential racial disputes and recommend methods of alleviating conflicts when they arose. To achieve this end, the field assistants would work closely with local organizations and keep a close watch on race relations generally. The service was to forge policies guaranteeing the removal of barriers "obstructing full utilization of manpower in the construction industry." In a review of the history of race relations offices in the housing bureaucracy, Horne and McGraw contended, "these principles and procedures [were] pursued with vigor, persistence and skill." They admitted, however, that in the absence of legislative and judicial supports, "these administrative devices [were] impotent." [13]

A presidential election in 1948 provided a new opportunity for African Americans to pressure legislators to act because winning the black vote became central to Truman's election strategy. Opposition from the Progressive Party candidate, Henry Wallace, threatened to siphon off much of that vote, however. Thus, in an attempt to steal the thunder from the Progressive Party's strong statement on civil rights, the president, according to Truman scholar William C. Berman, issued two executive orders in late July 1948. The first directive authorized the creation of review boards in all executive departments and agencies to hear and adjudicate complaints of job-related discrimination and established the Fair Employment Board of the Civil Service Commission to oversee them. The second, even more symbolically significant order, declared "there shall be equality of treatment and opportunity for all persons in the armed services," thereby beginning the desegregation of the armed forces. Truman explained his actions to a gathering of 65,000 blacks during a campaign speech in Harlem a week before the election. Because he had been thwarted by the southern conservatives and the Republicans, he insisted, he "went ahead and did what the President can do, unaided by the Congress": he issued executive orders.[14]

Truman's stand on civil rights and his courting of the urban black vote lost him most of the vote from the Deep South. The Harlem speech was just the final nail in a coffin already sealed shut for many southern voters. They accused Truman of "out-Wallacing Henry Wallace," and charged him with trying to organize "mongrel minorities plotting to 'Harlemize'" the United States. Conservative segregationists in the southern wing of the party bolted to form the States' Rights Democratic Party, the Dixiecrat Party. Truman's wooing of the white liberal vote and black vote, however, paid off in key states in the Midwest and West. "Truman's plurality of Negro votes in California, Illinois, and Ohio," according to Harvard Sitkoff, "provided the margin of victory."[15]

After the election, with Democrats back in control of Congress, lawmakers embarked on a program to provide Americans with a fair deal from the government. Truman's Fair Deal included tax reform, a raise in the minimum wage, farm subsidies, expansion of Social Security, national health insurance, and civil rights objectives. It also included a comprehensive housing plan. In its final form, the housing bill provided more than $1.5 billion in loans and grants to cities over five years to assist in slum clearance, and it authorized construction of low-cost dwelling units. HHFA Administrator Raymond Foley insisted that the bill would begin the process whereby "the goal of a decent home and a suitable living environment for every American family," including those "who because of their income, race, or other circumstances . . . [hitherto were] forced to live under undesirable circumstances," would be realized.[16]

Despite the pronouncements, African Americans interested in greater access to housing had less to cheer about in the actual housing legislation. Both the House and Senate bills called for significant expansion of public low-cost housing programs, but neither of them offered civil rights protections for blacks displaced by slum clearance. Leslie S. Perry, head of the NAACP's District of Columbia branch, complained that African Americans living in slum areas had no place to go when dispossessed of their homes. He urged that some protection be put into the legislation "to assure the persons who are displaced . . . [have] a chance to get back in the houses on sites where they formerly lived." "Federal funds derived from the taxation of all the people," Perry asserted, could "no longer be used to subsidize the iniquitous practices of racial segregation and discrimination." Even staunch civil rights advocates insisted, however, that the issues of housing and civil rights had to be separated, lest neither program pass.[17]

Opponents of the housing bills did indeed try to link the issues of civil rights, integration, and housing. In the Senate, Ohio's junior senator, Republican John W. Bricker, and Senator Harry Pulliam Cain, a Republican from Washington, introduced an amendment to the bill with the intention of killing the legislation. The Bricker amendment, as it became known, prohibited racial discrimination or segregation in public housing projects. Bricker and Cain had designed the amendment to extract the support of southerners for public housing and thereby kill the bill. When offering the amendment, Bricker said that he knew "of no way of insuring equal rights to all our people except by writing a provision into the bill to that effect." Arguing that the amendment furnished senators with the perfect opportunity to vote their party platforms, Bricker asserted that the time had come for senators to cease "shadow-boxing" with the issue of civil rights. "If the bill with this amendment is defeated," Bricker concluded, "well and good."[18]

Many African Americans endorsed the Bricker amendment despite claims that it would kill the bill. In April, the NAACP's Washington, D.C., branch announced its support. The National Negro Council, headed by Edgar G. Brown, held that a housing bill without anti-discrimination protection constituted a "complete repudiation of the President's civil rights promises." Brown declared that African Americans had voted for the Democrat's platform and that Democrats had to live up to their promises. Blacks "in their old slums," Brown exclaimed, were at "a kind of desperate beach head. . . . In shacks and huts they [had] been free to live everywhere in the city," but private discrimination had forced them back into a ghetto since the end of the war. They could withstand the prejudice of private individuals, he insisted, because they were still freemen. "But against planned segregation by . . . congressional committees," African Americans were helpless. Because the "Dixie diehards" revealed that they would block the program, Brown maintained, the only alternative left was "to get as much equality as possible out of every [other] measure . . . by seeing to it that each bill enacted makes bias and discrimination" unlawful.[19]

The Bricker amendment met with opposition from housing advocates on both sides of the aisle in the Senate. Senator Homer E. Capehart, a Republican from Indiana, suggested that since the original bill made no mention of racial restrictions on applicants of federal aid, no anti-discrimination clause was needed in the act. Senator Taft said the amendment was unnecessary because equal opportunity was guaranteed in the location of projects: housing built in a black section of a city would be open to blacks. Forced integration of housing, moreover, had not always proved a productive idea. The Sojourner Truth riot, he suggested, "developed because those in charge were trying to do something which . . . should [not] have been done in the beginning. . . . A general statement that there should be no discrimination [was] all right," Taft added, "but circumstances might require a certain amount of segregation and a preference to one group or another."[20]

Democrats who supported the bill criticized the Bricker amendment more harshly. They impugned the Republican senator's motives, universally accusing him trying to kill the bill and contending that he would not vote for S.1070 even with his amendment in it. Senator Glen H. Taylor of Indiana contended that the housing bill was "not the proper place to fight out" the question of racial discrimination. Senator Paul H. Douglas of Illinois was a leading advocate of civil rights, but he also wanted the housing bill to pass. He insisted that the issue in S.1070 was housing, not discrimination. "We should not try to legislate on everything at once," he declared, "there [were] some problems which [the Senate] could leave to the future." The Bricker amendment failed by a vote of thirty-one for to forty-nine against. The housing bill passed in the Senate on April 21, 1949, by a vote of fifty-seven to thirteen. Two of the "no" votes belonged to Senators Bricker and Cain.[21]

Proponents of public housing found the challenge even more difficult in the House. The chairman of NAREB's Washington Committee called the proposal "socialized public housing" and "un-American." He insisted that it was "contrary to the Constitution" and "a menace to the American free-enterprise system." NAREB's newsletter called on every realtor to "be a Fanatic for Freedom" and to lobby his or her member of congress in opposition to what it called "the most dangerous piece of legislation of [the] generation." Truman lashed out at the lobbyists, calling them "the real enemy of the American home" and labeling their arguments "selfish propaganda at its worst." Congressmen actually came to blows over the bill. In an unlikely spectacle, Rules Committee chairman and octogenarian Adolph Sabath of Chicago challenged the opponents of the bill as an "unholy alliance and coalition." The sixty-nine-year-old Democrat from rural Georgia, E. E. Cox, called Sabath a liar and punched him in the mouth. Sabath's glasses crashed to the floor, but he flailed back at Cox, landing several blows before astonished House members could separate the ancient pugilists.[22]

As the House debated its bill, Congressman Vito Marcantonio introduced an amendment similar to Bricker's. The member of the American Labor Party representing New York City's Lower East Side did not want to quash the bill. He intended only to embarrass both parties and redress an oversight in the bill. He insisted that the time had come for Congress to meet "the question of race discrimination where it exists in ugly reality—in housing." Representative Adam

Clayton Powell, a Democrat from Harlem, supported Marcantonio in the symbolic action. The amendment did not pass, and the House scrapped its bill altogether, preferring to take up S.1070 in conference and amend it.[23]

Before it passed into law, advocates of better housing for African Americans made one last attempt to amend the bill. Representative Powell offered an amendment that granted to slum dwellers greater protection against displacement and greater control over the types of projects undertaken in the ghetto. The Powell amendment proposed that the government guarantee suitable low-cost replacement housing for each family displaced by slum clearance and urban renewal programs, instead of following the less specific 1937 requirement that for each unit of housing destroyed, a replacement had to be built. To generate public support for the measure, according to the *Atlanta Daily World,* Powell's allies claimed that without the amendment, blacks would be "evicted and not rehoused in the low-rent projects provided for [under] the act."[24]

Legislators and administrators remained unmoved. The new "general" of the HHFA, Berchmans T. Fitzpatrick, advised the congressional conferees to vote against the amendment. Alabama's representative at the conference, Senator John J. Sparkman, also spoke out against it. He contended that under the amendment blacks in the slums could block urban renewal projects, such as parks and highways, until they were assured of getting new housing. Sparkman insisted that the bill already provided for "a feasible method of temporary relocation" because it advised that project contractors and the government had to provide "decent, safe, and sanitary dwellings" in equal number to those demolished and "in the project area or in other areas not generally less desirable . . . and at rents or prices within the financial means of the families displaced." No specific protection against discrimination and no specific guarantee was necessary, the senator maintained. As with most of the House amendments, the Powell amendment did not make it into the final bill. Both chambers passed the Housing Act of 1949 in early July. President Truman signed it into law on July 15.[25]

African Americans did not get all the things they wanted in the Housing Act of 1949, but they still planned to take advantage of it. The Race Relations Office of FHA, which included Frank Horne, B. T. McGraw, and Corienne Robinson, gave black civic leaders advice on how to capitalize on the new legislation. They recommended that blacks work at the grassroots level to ensure that they were represented at the planning stage of clearance projects. They suggested that African Americans sit on land acquisition and redevelopment boards and insisted that black leaders had to take great care to ensure that displaced slum dwellers gained admission to new projects. "We must see to it," the officers asserted, "that slum clearance does not become Negro clearance."[26]

As politicians, analysts, and lobbyists tinkered, balked, and brawled their way throughout the 1940s, the housing situation for many African Americans in metropolitan areas festered. In Chicago, for example, the state of housing in the African

American community was "catastrophic," according to the executive director of the Mayor's Commission on Human Relations, Thomas H. Wright. In the decade preceding 1945, slum clearance projects had demolished 21,000 substandard housing units, about 7,000 of them occupied by blacks. The Ida B. Wells Homes project replaced only 1,662 of those dwellings when it finally opened in 1941. With an already dangerously low vacancy rate in the city, migration turned Chicago's housing situation into a housing crisis, particularly in the Black Belt. Emphasizing the point, the chairman of the Chicago Housing Authority (CHA) called the Black Belt "more crowded than the slums of Calcutta." Despite 18,000 housing starts in metropolitan Chicago in 1946, the number of dwelling units available actually shrank due to fire, decay, and disintegration. "And on top of those already living in unspeakably crowded conditions," Wright observed, "more people moved in." To solve the crisis, Wright suggested that the city planning commission "define the needs of all sections of the population as specifically and scientifically as possible" and then develop a coordinated program to meet those needs. "Regardless of good will or police power," he warned, racial conflict would be inevitable if more homes were not provided soon.[27]

Chicago's expanding black population pressed hard against the ghetto walls. The percentage of African Americans residing in predominantly black neighborhoods increased. More than half of the city's blacks (52.9 percent) lived in census tracts that were more than 97.5 percent African American. It happened that the number of nonblacks living in mixed-race tracts also increased. Arnold R. Hirsch makes clear, however, that those figures "revealed not a city undergoing desegregation but one in the process of redefining racial borders after a period of relative stability." Analysis of census tracts in the Oakwood–Cottage Grove area strikingly illustrates the racial transition. The four tracts abutting the Black Belt at Oakwood Avenue had a combined white population of 10,183 in 1940. Ten years later, only 4,305 whites remained. The area's black population, however, increased from 931 persons to 13,318 over the same period.[28]

Whites again tried to block the advance with race-restrictive covenants. A former president of NAREB, Newton C. Farr, led the fight. Farr lived in the house on Woodlawn Avenue in which he was born, just three blocks from the Black Belt. He claimed that if the covenants were dropped and "if a thousand Negroes" moved into white neighborhoods, "there'd be a war." The *Defender* claimed that Farr, "more than any single person," was to blame for keeping African Americans in the ghetto. When the covenants failed to stop the encroachment, whites found other methods to protect their neighborhoods.[29]

Population pressure, the slow reversal of deed restrictions after the decision in *Hansberry* v. *Lee* (1940), and the rise of African American incomes during the war had also increased black mobility and racial conflict in Chicago. The city had avoided a race riot during the war, but racial tensions did abound. The many incidents of violence and intimidation that occurred in 1944 signaled the beginning of a new cycle of racial housing strife, one that would grow even worse after the war. In

February, arsonists destroyed the house of a black on 37th Street, west of Wentworth Avenue. Four more attacks on homes occurred in the area over the next three months. A sixth attack ended most tragically. In May, terrorists firebombed a house on South Wentworth. Two children, ages seven and twelve, died in the blaze. In October, a home was stench-bombed, surprising the owner. He reported that he had bought the house "in good faith" from whites who were "quite willing to sell" to blacks, adding that the house had been advertised in a black newspaper. And when Virginia Dobbins bought a house two blocks beyond the ghetto, vandals tried to burn it down. She called the police, and they promised to send a squad car, but it never arrived. When Dobbins returned to the house the next day, she discovered it totally razed; even plumbing fixtures had been carted away, and little more than the foundation remained. In May 1945, the home of Rev. T. H. Dabney was bombed. Dabney's nearest black neighbors were only one block away, but the Oakland-Kenwood Property Owners' Association refused to permit any more blacks in the area. Bombings were reported in July, October, and November, too.[30]

In February 1946, the *Defender* reported that whites had begun a "full-scale attack" on African Americans. The campaign began when Farr's Oakland-Kenwood Property Owners' Association sued the city for damages caused by depreciation of property values. Next, a group called the White Independent Citizens' Committee formed to "do things [that] the Property Association [could not] afford to do officially." The committee's leader, Alton D. Baird, was remarkably candid about its goals and methods. While issuing "This Property NOT For Sale" signs to neighbors, he warned, "We're fighting in the front lines here in Kenwood. Those Jews better get wise; if we lose, their Hyde Park is next." When a reporter asked him his opinion of the bombing of a house in the neighborhood, Baird replied, "God, I thought that was great!" Baird's neighbor, Mabel Maddox, added, "I'd rather move out of Chicago if I have to live next to niggers."[31]

As the year 1946 progressed, opposition by the White Independent Citizens' Committee grew, and other vigilante groups joined in. The White Circle League and the National Association for the Advancement of White People began a Molotov cocktail campaign around Park Manor. In the words of a local minister, "the animosity of the community was at fever height." By July, twenty-seven bombings had occurred. An outrageous situation was becoming nonsensical, as Farr's organization tried to block the Seventh-day Adventist Church from moving into the neighborhood because it feared the church would admit African American worshippers and cause blacks to try to move into the area. In another incident, an unidentified group assaulted a white woman for merely entertaining African Americans in her house. The campaign even proved counterproductive. "By keeping the neighborhood in a constant state of tension, so that for nearly two years scarcely a night passed without the sound of . . . sirens shattering sleep," Rev. Philip A. Johnson concluded about the violence in his district, "they caused many a white person to decide reluctantly to sell out."[32]

Violence on an even larger scale occurred at Chicago's public housing projects. In January 1946, the CHA began a policy of nondiscrimination for admission to veterans' projects. The policy immediately met resistance from property owners' associations. In March, whites gathered to protest African American occupancy of a project northwest of the Black Belt. Police dispersed the crowd before a more serious incident occurred. During the summer, the CHA announced plans to build a new veterans' project at 60th Street and Karlov Avenue, 2 miles due west of the Black Belt near Chicago Midway Airport. By October, most of the apartments were occupied, all by white veterans. When the CHA invited applications to fill the remaining units, many of the new applicants were African American. Whites responded by taking over several of the unoccupied units as squatters. When the CHA began moving blacks into Airport Homes anyway, a white mob smashed windows and tipped over cars. For more than a month, the disturbance persisted. Only the removal of all African Americans from the project eventually brought peace. The Airport Homes riot, according to the *Defender*, constituted "the worst instance of race inspired violence in nearly 30 years." It was surpassed only eight months later when 5,000 whites demonstrated to keep African Americans out of the CHA's Fernwood Park Homes project in August 1947.[33]

The city of Detroit also experienced conflict over racial transition in its neighborhoods. During the war, only 2,000 units, 1,700 of them temporary in nature, had been built to house the 67,000 black workers who flocked to Detroit during the war. African Americans therefore faced tremendous difficulty in finding adequate housing as veterans returned from overseas. The conflict over space had exploded into the extensive violence of the riots of 1942 and 1943, but after the war, it could still be described as "Detroit's Time Bomb." The director of the city housing commission, Charles F. Edgecomb, told *Collier's* that the issue was so infused with tension that "discussing Negro housing in Detroit is like arguing religion. You've got to be loaded first."[34]

The reaction of some government officials in the city and the suburbs made the problem even more burdensome. City Councilmen William "Billy" Rogell, for example, pursued segregation as a solution to racial tensions. He even considered "taking an area and moving the whites the hell out—and moving the Negroes in." What African Americans needed, the popular former shortstop for the Detroit Tigers contended, was a city of their own. "We need a Harlem for them," he insisted. Dearborn's mayor, Orville L. Hubbard, campaigned on a platform of segregation. In 1948, Hubbard promised to "Keep Negroes out of Dearborn." He told voters: "If whites don't want to live with niggers, they sure as hell don't have to. Damn it, this is a free country. This is America." He also campaigned against black occupancy of a housing project for Ford Motor Company workers. It did not to matter to him that the developers never intended to admit blacks. The project was defeated, and Hubbard was reelected. Other suburban communities—Grosse Pointe, Bloomfield Hills, Birmingham—also excluded African Americans. Ironically, because of the covenants and gentlemen's agreements covering land in suburban Detroit and the unwillingness of realtors and politicians to challenge the status quo, the city's downtown became occupied almost exclusively by African Americans. Rogell got his wish.[35]

At the hint of encroachment, Detroit's whites fled to the suburbs, in numbers even more dramatic than Chicago's. Between 1940 and 1950, the white population of metropolitan Detroit grew by more than 350,000 persons. The city itself, however, saw only 5 percent of the increase, and those areas where white population did grow lay outside the downtown core. Hamtramck had a net decrease in population of 6,500 during that period as 7,854 whites fled. Highland Park watched nearly 7,100 whites leave between 1940 and 1950. Its black population nearly tripled over the same years. The downtown sections running along the east side of Woodward Avenue from the Detroit River to Highland Park and Hamtramck saw an even greater racial transition. Nearly 62,000 whites moved out, while more than 70,000 blacks moved in.[36]

Not all whites fled the city; some fought. In the wake of the 1943 riot, Mayor Jeffries had formed the Interracial Committee, headed by George Schermer, to track tensions in order to alleviate them before they could cause another riot. Schermer catalogued scores of incidents resulting from African American movement into white areas. They ranged in severity "from the use of warnings and threats to the crimes of malicious destruction of property and arson." One case testifies to the spite of the vandals. Having bought a vacant lot in a white district, the black man went to his property with his son to clear it in preparation for the laying of the foundation. When they arrived, the two found that someone had dumped a load of slag on the lot and scattered it around, rendering the property useless for a member of any race.[37]

Schermer kept a list of the leaders of the protests against black home owners. As in other cities, women tended to lead the picket lines. Interestingly, the same women often appeared at numerous demonstrations. Gertrude Murphy of Wabash Avenue, according to Schermer's records, led picket lines on Vermont Avenue in September 1945, on Sycamore Avenue in October 1945, and on Poplar Street in April 1946. At the Vermont Avenue protest, she warned that "almost anything might happen" if African Americans were allowed to occupy the home. "Some of the people in that neighborhood are hoodlums," she advised, "and you can never be sure of just how far they might go." Women also made threatening telephone calls. Leslie Matthews, a black realtor, reported that after selling a property, he received hundreds of phone calls that threatened personal harm and property damage, and all but one of them were from women.[38]

The memory of the race riots of 1942 and 1943 weighed so heavily on the minds of civic officials as to determine how they responded to any racial incident. In 1945, the city created a Special Investigation Unit to investigate racial incidents and to maintain peace. If an incident did occur, Schermer and his staff would work around the clock to contain the tension. In one instance, for example, two black families moved into homes in the Cass District and were met by more than 1,000 white protesters. The mob stoned the houses, but the riot squad soon contained and dispersed the crowd. Police then arrested four white men for disturbing the peace. When George Schermer of the Special Investigation Unit arrived, police informed him that they would control the immediate violence but insisted that the Interracial Committee had to restore stability. To ensure that African Americans did not hear exaggerated rumors of the incident and react violently, Schermer and his staff patrolled black sections of the city through the night. The next morning, Schermer called the city newspapers to determine how they would cover the story. He was relieved to find out that they did not intend to cover it at all. The African American weekly, the *Michigan Chronicle*, did run several stories about the ongoing incident, but the first was not reported until the following Saturday. Although a few minor incidents such as this did arise and access to housing remained a problem for Detroit's blacks, the Special Investigation Unit was able to make sure that housing conflict did not grow out of control.[39]

Amid the turmoil in Detroit, Chicago, and elsewhere, the campaign against residential segregation persisted in the courts. After the *Hansberry* victory, the NAACP brought more and more cases before state courts. By the mid-1940s, it was handling thirty cases arising from disputes in Chicago. In Michigan, the local NAACP headed ten suits against restrictive covenants and was determined to bring one of them before the U.S. Supreme Court, if necessary. Courts in Ohio, New York, New Jersey, Pennsylvania, and other states were hearing cases. California, according to the *Michigan Chronicle*, led the pack with some seventy cases involving disputes brought on behalf of blacks and Asian Americans.[40]

The Supreme Court finally decided the constitutional standing of public enforcement of race-restrictive covenants in 1948. The case of *Shelley* v. *Kraemer* originated in St. Louis in 1945. J. D. Shelley and his wife had bought and occupied a house on Labadie Avenue, a white enclave protected by a restrictive covenant. For breaking the covenant, the Marcus Avenue Improvement Association brought a suit against the Shelleys. It named Fern and Louis Kraemer as plaintiffs because Mrs. Kraemer's parents had signed the original covenant. According to the case's chronicler, Clement Vose, the NAACP, and other local black leaders wanted to force a final ruling on covenants. They compelled the Shelleys to take up the fight. In November 1945, the Circuit Court of St. Louis ruled that the covenant was unenforceable because the restriction had not received enough signatories and because the Shelleys had not received proper notice of its existence. The Kraemers appealed. At the end of 1946, the Supreme Court of Missouri reversed the lower court's decision. Leaders of the St. Louis African American community organized an appeal to the U.S. Supreme Court. Lawyers for the Shelleys petitioned for a writ of certiorari, and the Court agreed to hear the case, along with the Detroit case of *McGhee* v. *Sipes*. It also heard two suits originating in Washington, D.C.[41]

Justice Frank Murphy played a key role in bringing the cases before the High Court. The hero of the Sweet case had continued to advocate civil rights after leaving Detroit. As Roosevelt's attorney general, he created a Civil Rights Section in the Justice Department. While on the Supreme Court in 1945, he argued that the Court should hear a covenant case, *Mays* v. *Burgess*, but could not get the four votes needed to issue the writ of certiorari. He finally found success in 1947, convincing Justices Hugo L. Black and William O. Douglas and eventually Chief Justice Fred Vinson to approve the writ.[42]

The Legal Defense and Education Fund's lawyers refined their legal arguments and recruited allies in government to aid in the suits. They borrowed a strategy that had proved successful in the Supreme Court of Ontario, Canada, pointing out the fact that race-restrictive covenants ran counter to anti-discrimination principles that the United States had accepted in its approval of the United Nations Charter. As Mark V. Tushnet notes, the LDF also made use of a tactic that it would employ to great effect in the *Brown* v. *Board of Education* cases. They drew the court's attention to statistical and behavioral research into the social and economic consequences of discrimination. They contended correctly that the social ills wrought by overcrowding in the ghetto resulted in no small part from discrimination in housing and argued that the negative effects of a closed housing market provided a suitable basis for the court to invalidate state laws.[43]

Chief among the LDF's new allies was President Truman. Prodding from the NAACP and the Justice Department's Civil Rights Section prompted the president to provide aid where he could: in the courts. He authorized Attorney General Tom C. Clark to write an amicus brief in the pending covenant cases. The brief repeated arguments pertaining to the negative effects of covenants that LDF lawyers had been making since the 1920s. "This situation," the brief averred, "cannot be reconciled with the spirit of mutual tolerance and respect for the dignity and rights of the individual which give vitality to our democratic way of life." Another unlikely ally appeared in HHFA Director Foley, who added a supplementary statement to the brief. He argued that covenants limited the government's ability to effect slum clearance programs because they restricted the availability of property on which to relocate displaced blacks. Ernest A. Gross, a legal adviser in the State Department, added that the country had been "embarrassed in the conduct of foreign relations" by the acts of discrimination perpetrated by whites against blacks. Charles Abrams insisted later that without Truman's intervention, "it is doubtful that the Supreme Court would have accepted review."[44]

Six members of the Supreme Court heard the covenant cases in January 1948. Associate Justices Stanley F. Reed, Wiley B. Rutledge, and Robert H. Jackson did not take part, apparently because they owned land on which were placed racial deed restrictions. An overflow crowd witnessed the event. Solicitor General Philip B. Perlman opened the arguments on behalf of all the plaintiffs, insisting that covenants "should be relegated to the limbo of other things as dead as slavery." St. Louis attorneys George L. Vaughn and Herman Miller argued the case on behalf of the Shelleys, whereas Thurgood Marshall and Loren Miller represented the McGhees. Marshall, in particular, stressed the sociological data showing the debilitating effect that covenants had on African Americans' ability to purchase suitable housing.[45]

The Court's view on the subject remained a mystery even after the hearing. Privately, plaintiffs' attorneys believed that they had lost the case. The only thing that gave them hope was a discussion between Associate Justice Felix Frankfurter and the defense counsel in the *McGhee* case, James A. Crooks. Frankfurter asked Crooks whether he believed that judicial enforcement of restrictive covenants constituted government action that resulted in the use of state power to bring about results that private individuals could not achieve by themselves. Crooks admitted that Frankfurter's summary was accurate. He added, however, that the state's action was not itself an act of discrimination. He hoped to convince the Court to differentiate between the state's action and the result of that action.[46]

In May, the High Court issued a unanimous, if timid, decision written by Chief Justice Vinson. The panel held that covenants were private agreements and legal contracts among the signatories, thereby affirming the ruling in *Corrigan* v. *Buckley* (1926). The constitutionality of enforcement, Vinson recalled, had not been reviewed in the 1926 case because of want of jurisdiction. *Shelley* v. *Kraemer* and *McGhee* v. *Sipes,* however, directly addressed that question. Because they involved state laws and because the Court accepted the LDF's arguments regarding public action, the Court found race-restrictive covenants to be unconstitutional under the equal protection clause of the Fourteenth Amendment. The contracts, although legally written, could not be legally enforced. African American home buyers had won. Justice Murphy called the ruling "epoch marking" and as important as the decision in *Dred Scott* v. *Sandford* (1857). He told Vinson that the chief justice would "receive many blows" for the judgment but added, "with time the cases will make you immortal."[47]

The realty industry's response to the decision ranged from quiet disappointment to raucous reactionary opposition. The *Appraisal Journal* had expressed its view of the case in January 1948. "It does seem inconsistent to state that a court may not enforce a statute or ordinance providing for racial residential segregation and yet may constitutionally enforce an identical segregation arising from private contract," the editors observed, "yet this is an inconsistency which is explained by the fact that the terms of the constitutional limitations are framed so as to be applicable solely to governmental actions and not to those of private individuals." In this way, the National Association of Real Estate Appraisers, an adjunct of NAREB, declared its support for individual property rights. In July, it responded to the decision. The appraisers decried the ruling without specifically referencing race. Instead, they worried about the apparent expansion of the definition of government action and the instability that they believed would result from the negation of the restrictions. Having long held that penetration of white neighborhoods by blacks automatically led to the depreciation of property values, the appraisers speculated as to what new device could be created to maintain neighborhood integrity. They eventually proposed to undertake a large-scale construction program for African Americans on undeveloped lands. The journal's editors also dedicated realtors "to the job of educating Americans to live without strife."[48]

Some local real estate boards proposed more drastic measures. The Los Angeles Realty Board, for example, announced that it would start a campaign to amend the U.S. Constitution to guarantee enforcement of covenants. It insisted that the *Shelley* ruling had created "a most serious condition affecting home owners throughout [the] country" because the "practice of surrounding homes . . . with the security of such restrictions [had] become a traditional element of value in home ownership." Alleging that "the owners of comparatively modest homes" would suffer most under the decision because they had more of their wealth tied up in such properties and because the prices of such homes were "well within the purchasing power of vast numbers of Negroes," the board suggested that the "magnitude of the economic and social loss will necessarily create racial tensions and antagonisms and do much harm to [the] national social structure." "To avoid such consequences and to stabilize the values of home ownership," the board declared, it was essential to amend the Constitution. Nothing immediately came of the campaign, but real estate boards around the country would continue to push for a home owners' bill of rights.[49]

African Americans across the country celebrated the victory but did not delude themselves that the fight had ended. "For Negroes who have been hemmed into a relatively small area for years because of the covenants," the *Michigan Chronicle* proclaimed, "the decision was hailed as the equivalent of a second emancipation." The *Washington Post* similarly viewed the ruling as nearing "Abraham Lincoln's emancipation proclamation in the attainment of liberty by colored Americans." The NAACP's Walter White praised the work of the LDF and saw continued progress for the organization's civil rights campaign, but he added that it was "just a start." Michigan State Senator Joseph A. Brown, meanwhile, offered a particularly prescient interpretation of the ruling. "This is a definite and overwhelming victory," he asserted. "It has eliminated the underhanded signing business behind which white owners have hidden in order to enforce their prejudice. Now," he rightly concluded, "they will have to come out into the open without sanction of law."[50]

Several incidents came hard on the heels of the *Shelley* decision, but one occurring in Los Angeles suffices to prove Brown's fears correct. In August 1948, Nat King Cole purchased a $75,000 estate in the "fashionable" neighborhood of Hancock Park. Cole had recently become a major star in popular music with the hit recordings "Nature Boy" and "The Christmas Song (Chestnuts Roasting on an Open Fire)." He and his wife, Marie, had been looking for a grand new home and had been offered several, including one owned by the entertainer Mickey Rooney. But they fell in love with the home on Muirfield Road. The Hancock Park Property Owners Association opposed the move and held an emergency meeting to discuss a response. The group, according to the *California Eagle*, tried to purchase the home back, offering Cole an additional $25,000 to entice him away from the property. In communications with Cole and his representatives, the group revealed their concern and prejudice as well as their ignorance of the singer. "How would YOU like it," they reportedly asked Cole's manager, "if you had to come out of your home and see a Negro walking down the street wearing a big wide hat, a zoot suit, long chain and yellow shoes?" That image of the black musician did not in any way resemble Cole, and if they had taken up Cole's request to meet with them, then his neighbors would have found him to be a person who cultivated the opposite image—one of reserved sophistication.[51]

Cole refused the property association's offer and announced his determination to move into the home. He called the situation regrettable but declared, "I am an American citizen, and I feel that I am entitled to the same rights as any other citizen." With the backing of the Supreme Court, he asserted that he and his family intended to stay "the same as any other American citizens would."[52]

Cole, Marie, and their two daughters, Carol and Natalie, moved in on August 13, 1948. Since they could not buy Cole off, whites in the neighborhood tried to scare him away. First, someone placed a sign on the lawn reading "Nigger Heaven." Later, as Carol Cole recounted, "someone came in the night and on the front lawn they burned in the word 'Nigger.'" The second incident marked the end to the intimidation, but it had a lingering effect. "The shadow of that word," Carol remembered, "was always there."[53]

After the Second World War, Americans began to sort out what the conflagration had done to the nation's race relations. Among other things, the war had made plain the hypocrisy of white supremacy and egalitarian rhetoric. African Americans challenged governmental policies and demanded greater protection from white discrimination. They had fought for freedom. They had bought their war bonds and had paid their taxes. Now, many believed, blacks deserved to enjoy the equal protection of the laws ensured to them by the Constitution. Because it could afford to pay less attention to partisan politics, the Supreme Court led the way. It restored to African Americans their political rights by nullifying the white primary. The Court chipped away at "separate but equal" education practices, and it finally negated race-restrictive covenants. Walter White proclaimed the victory for blacks and the NAACP. "Thirty years of effort," he trumpeted, "was climaxed by the signal victory of the association before the Supreme Court" in *Shelley* v. *Kraemer*.

Politicians in the federal branch of government closest to the people moved the slowest to advance civil rights. Congress did not pass a single item of Truman's civil rights program. In housing, after years of stalling, it did relieve some of the pressure on blacks by instigating construction of low-cost housing. More importantly, when combined with reforms in the FHA and the negation in law of race-restrictive covenants, the passage of the Housing Act demonstrated to blacks that their energy had not been entirely wasted. But the 1949 act stopped short of guaranteeing that African Americans would have equal access to all housing. In ensuing years that oversight would cause many African Americans tremendous hardship.

As the 1940s ended, racial tensions and white resistance remained strong. Chicago and Detroit, in particular, became the sites of prolonged and one-sided race wars over neighborhoods. Despite bureaucratic and legal developments, racial discrimination persisted. The FHA did not insure a public housing project slated for mixed racial occupancy until 1949, and even into the 1950s the agency still ordered that housing cooperatives must build segregated dwellings or do without government mortgage insurance. Private discrimination persisted, as well. The American Council on Human Rights reported that race-restrictive covenants still found widespread use even though they were unenforceable in the courts. Private lending agencies remained unwilling to invest in property occupied by blacks or to accept mortgages on properties African Americans sought to build or purchase.

The demographic, economic, legal, and ideological developments in the wake of World War II did not just affect race relations in the North and West. As the next chapter shows, they also started to reverse the white supremacist and states' rights status quo that had defined race relations in the South for decades.

6

A SOUTHERN EXPOSURE

Damn the law! Down here we make our own law.[1]

Preceding chapters have focused on racial tensions in neighborhoods outside the South. This has not occurred because of oversight or distortion. Rather, white supremacy in southern cities, prior to World War II, proved so pervasive that it went almost unquestioned. White elites in many southern cities had ignored the dictate of the Supreme Court regarding housing. Cities in the South continued to use zoning laws to uphold residential segregation even after the second housing decision in 1927. It took decades before southern cities had to find new ways to restrict African American mobility. When zoning laws failed to contain blacks, as happened in Atlanta, whites did resort to violence. Generally, however, a combination of statute enforcement and paternalistic accommodation kept segregation intact. Black poverty provided an even greater assist to segregationists.

Southern violence against blacks prior to 1945 deviated from northern oppression. Lynchings occurred with sickening regularity. Such brutality dominated the worries of civil rights agents and black communities. Economic subjugation, moreover, meant that southern blacks posed little threat to whites. Social equality of African Americans was so remote that it did not matter where blacks lived. Residential segregation increased in southern cities between the Civil War and World War II, reflecting a desire for freedom and community among African Americans as much as white discrimination. The systematic, legal segregation of public conveyances, facilities, and schools meant that blacks faced more regular tyrannies than just where to live. The southern style of white supremacy, designed to keep African Americans "in their place," was so successful that little conflict over housing occurred.

The Great Depression and World War II significantly changed southern society. The South became increasingly urbanized after 1940. Because the region had not shared in the prosperity of the 1920s, the effect of the Depression was muted, but the economic calamity and agricultural blight forced crop prices below profitable values. Many southerners, including African Americans, fled the section in hope of finding greener pastures and fruit-filled orchards in California. African Americans also moved to southern cities in the hope of escaping poverty and destitution in the rural South.

The urban areas of the South did not rebound economically until the war. Whites benefited more from the new production jobs, but many African Americans did enjoy prosperity and opportunity. Many of them also found the strength to challenge the white supremacist status quo by agitating against segregation on streetcars and buses and at lunch counters. Although they often met with violence, African American servicemen stationed in the South became a symbol for civil rights activists and at times even led the resistance against white supremacy. "Southern whites," Pete Daniel notes, "had never before been assaulted on so many fronts of the color line."[2]

As their numbers grew and as their prosperity rose, blacks in southern cities faced the same pressures as had their northern counterparts. The housing market, though never open, became increasingly segregated. Even progressives, as represented by the Southern Regional Council (SRC), assumed that the races would live in separate districts. African American elites understood this as reality. Although many of them chafed at the circumstances, they abided by them, and some even benefited. But most African Americans, hemmed in by custom and statutes, lived in overcrowded and often blighted conditions. When they did try to take advantage of their new prosperity by moving out of the ghetto after the war, they met the same resistance as African Americans had elsewhere.

In the late 1940s and early 1950s, violence occurred throughout the South in response to the attempts of blacks to move into traditionally white sections. African Americans in Birmingham faced several bombings during their fight to eliminate the restrictive zoning law and throughout the 1950s when they moved into white areas. White resistance to the African American migration in Dallas reached a fevered pitch in 1950 and 1951. Violence occurred in Richmond, Chattanooga, Charlotte, and other southern cities. White block associations formed to restrict blacks through covenants and gentlemen's agreements. City planners designed highways and greenbelts to divide the races. Even Atlanta, the city that professed to be "too busy to hate," pursued segregationist policies as a matter of course and witnessed a series of bombings and mob scenes between 1946 and the mid-1950s.

Atlanta was a town of about 10,000, fewer than 2,000 of them African Americans, when the Yankees burned it down during the Civil War. By 1870, however, the city's black population had itself reached nearly 10,000. Even as other African Americans were moving north in the Great Migration, Atlanta's black community continued to grow, eclipsing 90,000 in 1930. Over the same span of years, residential segregation also grew. Blacks were pushed to the worst land, closest to railroad lines and industrial areas. In the 1890s, seven centers of African American concentration existed: two on the West Side, three on the South Side, and two more on the North Side. But according to local historian Michael James O'Connor, "at least one black household lived on nearly every street, and the city was honeycombed with all black alleyways . . . in otherwise white areas." As the city annexed more territory between 1900 and 1910, segregation increased. Whites moved to new sections, leaving older ones to blacks. The two areas on the West Side, for example, grew together to make one large enclave extending to Ashby Street. Migration to the West Side became more urgent after the Great Fire of 1917 raged through the black East Side around Auburn Avenue.[3]

In the 1910s and 1920s, as black Atlantans pressed against the ghetto walls, the city augmented de facto separation with zoning laws. Despite the ruling in *Buchanan* v. *Warley* (1917), the city used race-restrictive zoning ordinances until the early 1930s. City officials were aware of the illegality of the laws but pursued them regardless. In 1929, Atlanta prohibited a person from occupying a residence on a street where the majority of residences were occupied by persons whom they were forbidden by law to marry, thus demonstrating the link between residential integration and fear of "race mixing." The Atlanta City Council unanimously passed the new restriction over Mayor Isaac Ragsdale's veto. When that law fell, the city enacted another one in 1931. The Fulton County Superior Court eventually negated the ordinance.[4]

The zoning laws and customary segregation restricted mobility, but African Americans did try to find more adequate housing on the edges of white areas. The black entrepreneur Heman Perry began the move west across Ashby Street in the early 1920s. Perry's business empire collapsed in 1925, but he did succeed in selling a parcel of land to the city for the site of a black high school. Once Booker T. Washington High School was completed, African Americans built homes around it. By 1931, the National Benefit Life Insurance Company had paved many of the streets in the area and had constructed 511 new homes. Blacks from the Auburn Avenue area moved to the West End and "built fine brick homes in the division." The PWA public housing development on the West Side, University Homes, was completed in 1937, expanding housing opportunities. Another private development along the Hunter Street Corridor followed shortly thereafter.[5]

Whites did not leave the district happily, nor did they welcome the blacks into their neighborhoods. Throughout the 1920s, white supremacists held rallies or burned crosses and used violence to intimidate blacks. In 1922, the same year that Ku Klux Klan member Walter A. Sims was elected mayor, whites reacted to black "invasion" by setting Ashby Street School ablaze. They also bombed homes on Newport Street, Linden Street, and Jackson Street. In one incident at 333 Ashby Street, bombers were met with gunshots. In the 1930s, whites placed a sign at Kennedy Street reading, "This is the dividing line between white and colored." Despite the intimidation, African Americans flooded the West End because they had nowhere else to go. By 1940, 40 percent of Atlanta's black population resided in the district.[6]

As Atlanta entered the 1940s, race relations became a major issue. In 1942, Atlantans elected William B. Hartsfield mayor. He would still be the city's leader twenty years later. A consummate city booster, Hartsfield was able to negotiate with the black community and to keep the city's long-range interests in view. He generated a sense that Atlanta was truly different among southern cities. According to his biographer, it was often said of Hartsfield that he ran Atlanta "as if he owned the town." Atlanta gained a reputation for progress and came to epitomize the "New South." Much of the reputation was deserved. Atlantans did attempt to treat African Americans differently from the rigid white supremacist approach evident in Birmingham, for example. The black vote played no small role in this circumstance. African Americans constituted too important a bloc to be ignored by politicians.[7]

Hartsfield tried to reduce some of the political strength of African Americans by annexing white suburbs. He made a major push to annex Buckhead by playing on the race issue. "Our Negro population is growing by leaps and bounds," he explained. The out-migration of "good, white, home owning citizens" to the suburbs, meanwhile, was further tipping the electoral balance. With "the federal government insisting on political recognition of Negroes in local affairs," Hartsfield warned, "the time is not far distant when they will become a potent political force in Atlanta if our white citizens are just going to move out and give in to them." In grave tones, he asked, "do you want to hand them political control of Atlanta?" When Buckhead rejected annexation, Hartsfield turned to the African American community for electoral support. Always careful not to alienate white voters, Mayor Hartsfield slowly but successfully integrated the city's police force. He reputedly rid that force of Klansmen. He shrank signs demarcating segregated restrooms at the airport, and in a symbolic gesture of no small importance, Hartsfield made city clerks address blacks as "Mr." and "Mrs." instead of the condescending "Doctor" or "Professor." The mayor was proud of his accomplishments. "Georgians," he proclaimed, "have made great progress in social affairs, and will continue to do so." But he advised that they "would do it in a calm orderly way and within the framework of Southern wisdom and experience."[8]

Despite the official improvements, Atlanta seethed with the potential for racial conflict and housing became the flash point. In 1944, a potentially ugly incident was avoided when a booby trap failed. Whites had placed a bomb under the porch of a house owned by a black family in a white area. It was set to go off when someone stepped onto the porch but exploded prematurely when a newspaper tossed onto the porch set it off. Two houses were damaged, but no one was hurt. After the war, a white supremacist group called the Columbians patrolled the streets of the white West End to intimidate blacks. At the end of October 1946, they bombed one home. But during a rally a week later, Police Chief Marion Hornsby ordered the

Columbians arrested. Two were eventually convicted for inciting a riot and illegal possession of dynamite. In November, the state of Georgia sued the Columbians to revoke the organization's charter, and by May 1947 Fulton County solicitor Paul Webb declared, the "back of the Columbians [had] been broken."[9]

The police crackdown on the Columbians did not stop the intimidation. A series of apparent Klan bombings in May and July 1947 showed that the problem was not going to go away. In late October, two fires and a failed bombing within ten days of each other increased tensions even more. The owner of 831 North Avenue had a pipe bomb hurled through his window, but it did not explode. He told police that he had been living in the house for fifteen months and had been "annoyed constantly." The most serious incident was a fire at the home of Clifford Walton at 556 Chestnut Street. Walton was the first African American to breach the Kennedy Street divide. Whites crowded around Walton's house for more than a week. The Waltons finally were forced out of their home in the middle of the night after a white minister warned them that the mob had lost its patience and for the safety of the family they should leave.[10]

The increasingly grave housing situation in the West End forced African Americans to seek a remedy from the city. Forty-eight blacks owned property in the neighborhood but could not take occupancy for fear of being the target of terrorists. Since they could not move into their homes, they had to seek other accommodations and often found only inadequate space or exorbitant rents while they waited. The NAACP's C. L. Harper, chairman of the Atlanta General Housing Committee, insisted that Mayor Hartsfield and the police make it possible for blacks to occupy their homes. As it happened, a congressional committee on housing was holding hearings in Atlanta, and African Americans also used that forum to voice their complaints. Walter H. "Chief" Aiken, a leading local builder and the president of the National Builders Association, told the committee that the acts of vandalism were "examples of periodic eruptions which [could] be expected to flare-up until some type of systematic and planned solution [was] worked out."[11]

During October and November, black leaders met with city officials, including at times Mayor Hartsfield and Police Chief Herbert Jenkins, to discuss possible answers. Harper suggested that whites be given until April 1948 to move out of the disputed area. In return, African Americans would then agree to accept a new "imaginary borderline" across which they would not move. Representatives of the Atlanta Urban League, meanwhile, recommended that more dwellings be built for blacks to relieve the pressure. They submitted a plan to the Atlanta Housing Authority designating six possible areas that would be suitable for black residency. The plans were accepted. West View Drive would become the new dividing line between white and black neighborhoods in the West End, and new housing would be built on vacant land in the area.[12]

The Atlanta Housing Authority announced the agreement in late 1947. The deal had no standing in law because it could not be supported by a racially biased zoning ordinance. The council could only suggest that white and black residents comply. "It is hoped," the council propounded, "that business and civic groups alike will recognize and endorse the agreement." The sections reserved for blacks, it insisted, were "in fact, if not in law, the proper areas in which Negroes may build and live without racial or economic conflict to strive with all of us for a more prosperous and more democratic community." African Americans did agree not to move beyond West View Drive. In fact, for a time they did not expect to have to move below Hunter Street because the Urban League and the Life Insurance Company of Georgia planned to construct an all-black neighborhood called Fair Haven, above Hunter and west of Ashby. White residents in the area were less agreeable. Four white youths set fire to a house in January 1948, and several other incidents followed.[13]

Before the homes at Fair Haven could be built, slum clearance increased pressure for new African American housing and caused the situation to fester. Residents of the white neighborhood of Mozley Park became concerned when three homes were sold to African Americans. On February 13, 1948, whites swarmed the home of Rev. W. W. Weatherspool and ordered him to move. The next day some 200 whites marched on the Capitol to protest to Governor Eugene Talmadge. Talmadge told the demonstrators that he agreed with them, but he insisted that it was a municipal issue and sent the marchers on to City Hall. Mayor Hartsfield established a new interracial committee to negotiate a settlement. The African American minority contingent suggested a couple of options: blacks who already owned property in the section would hold on to it until it could be resold to whites, or, alternatively, a syndicate could buy the whole block of homes from the white owners at once, thereby ensuring property values would be maintained. Several days of negotiation brought no settlement. When a home on Ashby Street was bombed in early March, the Atlanta Chamber of Commerce blandly observed, "it appeared that the [1947] agreement . . . did not work out as planned."[14]

Whites in the neighborhood remained unhappy with the situation. They formed a real estate company called the West End Cooperative Corporation. Its president, Joseph M. Wallace, explained that investors would pay $100 per share in the company. The corporation intended to use the money to buy out whites who wanted to leave the West End and who might be willing to sell to African Americans. It would then hold and rent the property until a white buyer could be found. Wallace announced that the corporation also planned to use some of the money to finance lawsuits. To announce the plan, Wallace began publishing *The West End Eagle*. He filled the paper with raging antiblack stories that suggested conspiracies between Mayor Hartsfield, the communists, and northern agitators represented by the NAACP. Whites did eventually win a short-lived victory. African Americans sold their property. The Mayor's committee set the north-south line dividing the races at Chickamauga Avenue, and then city planners arranged it so that no roads ran directly from Mozley Park into the black area above Hunter Street.[15]

When the Fair Haven subdivision was opened in the summer of 1949, whites in

Mozley Park found themselves surrounded. Some of them tried to sell, but their section's proximity to the racial frontier dissuaded other whites from buying. They had to sell to African Americans. The cycle of violence began anew. Bombings occurred in 1950 and the spring of 1951. Following the pattern already set, the friction caused civic leaders again to seek a settlement. This time whites agreed to vacate Mozley Park. The white population of the census tract that included Mozley Park was 2,953 in 1950. By 1960, it had fallen to 895. The black population in the tract increased from 947 to 3,570. But during the transition period, still more violence occurred. Homes of African Americans were bombed during the summer of 1954 and in March and July 1956.[16]

Atlanta cultivated an image as a city of racial harmony, which observers of race relations seem to have accepted rather uncritically. Even a historian who looked "beneath the image" contends that Atlanta's negotiated settlements "created a peaceful . . . atmosphere in which racial reform could occur." According to the Taeuber and Taeuber indexes, however, residential segregation in Atlanta rose from 87.4 in 1940 to 93.6 in 1960. Some thirty race bombings occurred in the two decades following the war, more even than occurred in Birmingham over the same period. Even in the area of public housing, where observers have so favorably compared Atlanta to Birmingham, the Georgia city fell short of its nonracist reputation. The controversy over the placement of a black housing project along Forrest Road illustrates the point. In 1959, the City Planning Commission approved the construction of a housing project on the mostly vacant lands of the old Egleston Hospital to the north and east of Auburn Avenue. Blacks had lobbied for the housing as a way to relieve pressure on those who had been displaced by the construction of a new expressway and by industrial expansion. The Atlanta Housing Authority purchased the land, and a 350-unit facility was designed for the site. But before construction could begin, the city's board of aldermen had to rezone the section. White home owners in the area opposed the project, complaining that it would reduce property values and speed up black migration toward the Little Five Points and Druid Hills sections. Listening to the opposition, the city's aldermen rejected the rezoning petition, offering instead to pursue the clean-up of Buttermilk Bottom, a slum to the south of Auburn. The loss dealt a serious blow to the African American community. According to the *Atlanta Daily World*, it jeopardized the city's entire urban renewal program because federal housing officials cut off funding for other projects until the issue had been settled. The failure so alarmed the newspaper that it ran a front-page editorial, proclaiming that the housing was "essential to the preservation of the businesses and churches in the Auburn Avenue area. If the Auburn Avenue area shrinks up or dies," the paper asserted, "[then] the economic life of the entire Atlanta Negro community [will] be seriously impaired." Although the dire consequences did not come to pass, the incident, the persistent segregation, and the bombings demonstrated that white Atlantans may have been "too busy to hate," but only as long as blacks did not move next door.[17]

Prior to 1960, Birmingham had the third-largest black population in the South, and it represented all that was wrong with race relations in the United States. More than twenty bombings and countless floggings and cross-burnings were reported in the decade and a half following the war. A *New York Times* reporter, Harrison E. Salisbury, painted such a harsh portrait of the city that the Birmingham city government sued him for libel. "The water supply and the sewer system," Salisbury castigated, were "about the only public facilities [the races] shared." Called everything from the "capital of Jim Crowism" to the "Johannesburg of America," Birmingham was the last major city to enforce racial segregation by zoning ordinance. The city's fight to maintain these laws in the early 1950s, despite the fact that such laws had been ruled unconstitutional thirty-five years earlier, offered the first illustration of a policy of massive resistance to what they viewed as federal encroachment and interference with time-honored practices of white supremacy.[18]

From the time of its incorporation in 1871, Birmingham maintained racial separation by custom. It began regulating occupancy of property around World War I because white residents were disturbed by the high crime rate in the ghetto. In 1919, because of the *Buchanan* decision, the zoning law fell, but the city enacted a replacement ordinance in 1926. According to the zoning board, the new law promoted "health, safety, morals, and the general welfare" through a system of "equitable residential segregation," and, most importantly, it favored no race. The ordinance restricted occupancy but not ownership: blacks could and did own properties in white areas, but they could not occupy them. Despite the contention to the reverse, however, the new ordinance did not differ substantially from ones that had been found unconstitutional. And although whites were similarly circumscribed from occupying property in black districts, the plan was far from equitable. In 1926, African Americans made up about 40 percent of the population but had access to only 16 percent of the land. African Americans opposed the law, but they could not find a plaintiff willing to challenge it.[19]

Zoning in Birmingham remained fluid after 1926 despite the ordinance. The zoning board evaluated each case on its merit. If no whites were opposed, then the board transferred properties from white to black residential. The arbitrary nature of the zoning board's decisions meant that in some cases a single property would be zoned half black and half white. In frustration, Arthur D. Shores, Birmingham's delegate to the NAACP's National Legal Committee, told Thurgood Marshall that the law was impracticable and discriminatory. He proposed "to break this law down" even if it meant taking it to the Supreme Court. Shores had trained in civil rights litigation in the Legal Defense and Education Fund program at Howard University. He had led the court fight to enable black teachers to register to vote; he battled discrimination faced by African American railroad firemen; and he took on the local school boards and won equal pay for black teachers. But on the housing issue, he could not act until he found a plaintiff.[20]

African Americans finally brought pressure against Birmingham's zoning code after World War II. The war had had a significant effect on all areas of race relations in the city. Nearly 20,000 African Americans had migrated to Birmingham during the war. By 1946, blacks made up more than 43 percent of the population. The relative increase in wealth and the experience of fighting the Nazis prompted them to take a more aggressive stance against discrimination. These developments and the actions of Shores and the LDF, according to Robert J. Norrell, made whites "nervous . . . about a mounting black challenge to the caste system." After the gubernatorial campaign of 1946, race became the principal issue of reform politics. White supremacists struck increasingly racist poses, and the city was ripe for racial conflict.[21]

The increase in black population strained Birmingham's housing market. As in other cities, the war had slowed home construction, thereby removing an outlet for newcomers. A "steady industrial encroachment into . . . Negro zones" further reduced housing opportunities. Black neighborhoods decayed. The Birmingham District Housing Authority deemed housing substandard in every census tract where African Americans composed a clear popular majority. Dwellings were either overcrowded or in need of major repair or both. More than 97 percent of dwellings in "Old Birmingham," for example, were substandard. In 1938, the Smithfield Court project eased the situation somewhat, but still the Jefferson County Board of Health assessed all African American sections to be "blighted areas" of substandard housing.[22]

Housing tensions arose in late 1945 when Alice Allen bought a building on Center Street. The road divided African American and white sections in the city's west end: Smithfield lay to the east of Center Street, and the white district, Graymont–College Hills, lay to the west. Center Street itself was zoned as commercial property, but Allen intended to live in it. African Americans had found that they could circumvent the zoning code by occupying commercial buildings as dwellings. City officials usually ignored these transgressions. When whites in Graymont protested, however, the zoning board reclassified the property as white residential, thus blocking Allen's occupancy. Allen hired Arthur Shores to initiate a suit, but the city elected not to test the change in zoning. It returned the property to commercial status and refused to force Allen out. With Allen now able to occupy her property, Shores no longer had a case.[23]

Another prospective challenger to the city's zoning law appeared in 1947, when Samuel Matthews built a home just west of Center Street. When the building inspector informed Matthews that he could not occupy the dwelling because of the zoning restriction, Matthews sued. James H. Willis, the city attorney, told Shores that the city would rezone the property if they dropped the suit, but Shores rejected the offer. He did not want to have to go to court each time a case arose. He wanted to strike the law down once and for all. When the case went before the Federal District Court, Judge Clarence Mullins ruled the zoning code unconstitutional and enjoined the city from acting against Matthews. African Americans viewed the ruling as a major victory, but celebrations soon subsided. On August 18, dynamite destroyed the Matthews home. Because he was uninsured, he made no attempt to rebuild the house. City leaders condemned the bombing and called for local police to cooperate with state and federal law enforcement in an investigation, but the city did not act on the court's ruling. Though unconstitutional, the code remained.[24]

After the bombing, African Americans stayed on their side of Center Street, and calm returned to Graymont. The issue of inadequate housing did not disappear, however. In March 1949, the NAACP convened a housing conference. "Housing [was] bad for Negroes in Birmingham," guest speaker Chief Aiken announced, traveling from Atlanta only to tell the assembled what they already knew. "Bad practices, unenlightened traditions, unfair administration of the law, . . . [and] the failure of those in the field of real estate and construction to use vision," he contended, all contributed to the problem. The *Birmingham World* assessed the importance of the conference with unintended irony. The meeting, *World* editor Emory O. Jackson remarked, "kindl[ed] a new fire for better housing and greater home-owning."[25]

Just days after the conference, Bishop S. L. Greene of the AME Church moved into the disputed area. He had purchased two homes there in December 1948. The houses had been on the market for some time, but the white realtor had been unable to interest white prospects in them because they were too close to the black neighborhood. The Graymont–College Hills Civic Association (GCHCA) protested the move. Its spokesman, Clarence E. Henderson, told city commissioners to "move the Negroes out, or arrest everyone of them for violating the zoning ordinance."[26]

The renewed conflict in Graymont–College Hills left the City Commission in a quandary. The man in charge of enforcing the code, Public Improvements Commissioner James H. "Jimmy" Morgan, knew it was unenforceable. He called the code "weak and illegal" but insisted that neither he nor the city was ready for integration. In frustration, he puzzled to the rest of the commission, "I'm not in favor of them moving in with us, but where are they going [to live]?" Commissioner for Public Safety T. Eugene "Bull" Connor insisted that public sentiment was against integration and that any attempt to blend the races would result in "breaches of the peace, riots, and destruction of property and life." He added that it would be impossible for police to ensure safety in the neighborhood.[27]

Before the commission acted, vigilantes bombed the houses. In March, Greene's two houses and one owned by Johnnie Madison were dynamited. Shores held the city responsible, charging that officials conspired with white home owners to deprive African Americans of their rights. The NAACP likewise blamed the city. Enforcement of an illegal law encouraged lawlessness, insisted branch president A. C. Maclin. City officials condemned the bombings. Bull Connor promised police would "get to the bottom of this thing if they [had] to work around the clock," but no one was arrested. A Birmingham policeman later admitted that the bombings were not "truly adequately investigated because the detective division was unconcerned about crimes against black property."[28]

Over the next four months, the housing debate continued. The GCHCA held firm, telling the city that the ordinances had to be upheld. Short of that, they wanted the laws replaced with others that would maintain neighborhood integrity. Henderson assured the city that if nothing was done to keep the blacks out, then more violence would ensue. He actually knew more about the violence than he let on. A day prior to the bombings, he had received a telephone call from an unidentified man. The man visited Henderson that night and asked him to show him around the area. Henderson complied, showing him homes in which African Americans resided. On the day of the bombings, Henderson received another call. This caller informed him that they were "going to burn some wood up on the hill" that night. Henderson maintained that he did not know the callers, that he was not a member of the Klan, and that he did not know why the man wanted to see the homes of African Americans. Although these assertions strain belief, police did not have enough evidence against him to indict.[29]

The NAACP told blacks not to let threats "discourage their yearnings for better homes," but some did not listen. The city threatened Willie German with legal action when he tried to move into his house. He also received a threat from Klansman Robert Chambliss, a.k.a. "Dynamite Bob" Chambliss, the man convicted of the Sixteenth Street Baptist Church bombing. German would not fight. He rented the home to a black minister, the Rev. Milton Curry. When James Castor tried to move into a house on Center Street, police stopped him. Castor notified the NAACP, and branch leaders told him not to be intimidated by police. They sensed that victory would be assured if the local community could be persuaded to continue to fight. A. C. Maclin exposed the NAACP's predicament: All it could do "is call on law, invoke the protection of God, and urge [blacks] to be spiritually prepared for the ordeals and perils and risks involved in the cause of defending a democracy which is sure to fall unless they stand up for it." Castor moved in, and three days later he received a bomb threat.[30]

With pressure coming from all sides, the Birmingham City Commission tried to negotiate a settlement. The white blocks were nearly surrounded because African Americans had crossed 8th Avenue on the south, Center Street on the east, and 11th Court on the north. The City Commission sent Zoning Board chairman George R. Byrum to Atlanta to meet with officials to find out how they had solved the tensions over Mozley Park. Of course, they could not know that Atlanta's solution was only temporary. Jimmy Morgan asked race leaders to meet on the zoning problem. Morgan and Ben F. Ray, the chairman of the Alabama Democratic Party, drew up a list of thirteen blacks and five whites who would act as negotiators. Only five blacks, including Arthur Shores, took part. The negotiators thus became known as the "Committee of Five."[31]

Outright repeal of the code was off the table, but white and black moderates seemed willing to negotiate in good faith. The city contended that only by retaining the ordinances could Birmingham escape race war. Connor warned blacks that there would be "bloodshed in this town as sure as you're sitting here unless something is done." Byrum suggested that the city build a "buffer park" along Center Street between 9th Court and 11th Court. The proposal did not satisfy the committee, but the five did not completely oppose compromise. In the interest of peace, they were willing to let the law remain for the time being. They suggested that the new line be drawn a block west of Center Street.[32]

Birmingham's NAACP took a more extreme position. Maclin rejected the real estate board's contention that the code could be maintained and refused to negotiate as long as the city believed that the law could stand. He urged police to protect blacks living in the disputed area and solicited the aid of the U.S. District Attorney. Emory Jackson took an even more zealous line. He accused the "Committee of Five" of collusion and vowed to settle for nothing short of repeal. He also submitted his resignation as executive secretary of the NAACP's Birmingham branch to the national office in New York, saying that he could not stay "where [the] Negro leadership does not seem to be concerned in the fights for democracy." To keep pressure on the city and alternate black leadership, Jackson's editorials in the *World* rang out a call for "moral courage and democratic wisdom." He urged a solution that required that no one "sacrifice a fundamental right for a questionable custom," exclaiming, "Peace is not the absence of violence but the presence of justice."[33]

White extremists opposed the reform plan. Bull Connor vowed that he would never vote to change zoning regulations. "As long as I live," he told commissioners, "there will be separation in Birmingham." He had a different solution. Steeped in states' rights ideology and with an eye on the governor's chair, he pledged to fight the federal government. Connor also asserted that the city did not need to repeal the law. His "constitutional experts" assured him that the code would hold up even before the U.S. Supreme Court because the city would claim that without the law race war would result. City Attorney James Willis, Connor's expert, had actually warned Connor against testing the laws, but he did remark that the code had "a ten per cent chance of surviving if it were shown to be strictly nondiscriminatory." Because of Connor, there would be no negotiated solution. In August, the city voted to prosecute violators of the zoning code, making it a misdemeanor for African Americans to live in an area "generally and historically recognized . . . as an area for occupancy for members of the white race."[34]

In response to the city's decision, the NAACP embarked on a strategy to dispose of the zoning ordinance. African Americans would remain in the disputed area even if violence occurred, and the LDF would challenge the law in court, having found a new plaintiff, Mary Means Monk. To keep the issue in the public eye, the NAACP held rallies at churches and meeting halls. The first rally was the most significant. Nearly 2,000 blacks gathered at Smithfield Court. They collected $500 in small donations to aid bombing victims and passed the "Smithfield Court Resolution," declaring that they would fight the ordinance to its repeal. They also resolved to support Arthur Shores in answer to Connor's accusations. Whites proved equally unyielding. Terrorists dynamited the Center Street homes of two black ministers.[35]

Thurgood Marshall and his staff worked closely with the Birmingham NAACP and Arthur Shores in the Monk case. Marshall attended the Smithfield Court rally. As special counsel to the LDF, Marshall had won a tremendous reputation for intelligence and determination. His leadership in the most notable civil rights cases of the 1940s, moreover, earned him great respect among Birmingham's blacks. His interest in and acute knowledge of the housing problem had been proven throughout the decade. He had led the fight in the case of *Shelley* v. *Kraemer* in 1948. Marshall's message did not differ from the local NAACP's, but his presence had a special effect. He told the assembled that the NAACP would "fight until the right of every citizen to live where he chooses is guaranteed and protected."[36]

Shores and Marshall brought the *Monk* v. *City of Birmingham* case before Judge Mullins in November 1949. The outcome was a foregone conclusion, given that *Buchanan* had been the accepted precedent for thirty years and Mullins had already ruled favorably in the Matthews case, but Emory Jackson still wrote Roy Wilkins to make sure that Marshall attended the hearing. "No chances can be taken on this case," he told Wilkins. "Every error and setback will be exploited by our foes." Horace C. Wilkinson, a founder of the Dixiecrat Party, led the city's defense. He offered the arguments that defenders of racial restrictions always made, insisting that annulment would depreciate property values, lead to a breakdown of morals, increase miscegenation, and cause "race war." He concluded that the right of all citizens to peace and order, stable property values, and municipal services, "in short, their right to life, liberty and the pursuit of happiness in Birmingham," superseded the right of individuals to use or occupy property.[37]

The defense tried to use the violence in Birmingham as leverage in the case, but each time Wilkinson questioned city officials about peace and order, Marshall objected. He argued that the occurrence of violence was irrelevant to the question of Fourteenth Amendment due process. He refuted the city's argument, insisting instead that the illegal code created a climate of lawlessness. He even accused Connor of actually inciting violence "for the purpose of being able to argue later that segregation ordinances were necessary for peace." Judge Mullins sustained the plaintiff's objections, contending that the only question before the court was the law's constitutionality. In December 1949, Mullins ruled against the city.[38]

While the lawyers prepared appeals, blacks remained in the disputed area, and whites kept up the campaign of intimidation. In April, dynamite ripped the porch off Curry's home, and a bomb wrecked the half-finished house of Dr. Joel Boykins. Before buying the lot, Boykins had surveyed his white neighbors to measure their reaction to his moving into the area. When few of them opposed his plans, he petitioned the city to amend the zoning code to enable him to take occupancy. The commission did so unanimously. Another black home owner, Sam Hall, received several bomb threats in June 1950.[39]

The new rash of violence caused whites to take action. Governor James Folsom ordered an investigation into the bombings. White ministers called for federal aid to find the bombers. The U.S. Justice Department started its own investigation. White opinion had turned against the violence, but it had not changed regarding residential segregation. Many whites feared more for the city's reputation than for African Americans, believing that Birmingham was "getting a black eye over the nation" because of the bombings. They also worried that the inability of police to find the bombers would bring federal intervention. "We realize," the *News* editorialized, "that local and states' rights may be endangered by shortcomings in local law enforcement."[40]

The Court of the Fifth Circuit rendered its verdict on the appeal in the *Monk* case in December 1950. The city had again made the claim that the code was necessary to avoid "breaches of the peace, riots, [and] destruction of property and life." But the court ruled that such evidence, whether true or not, was "irrelevant and immaterial to [the] issue of constitutionality." "Police power, however broad and extensive," the court added, "is not above the Constitution." Given the precedents, the court could make no other ruling. Remarkably, the city did convince one judge: Robert L. Russell, the brother of Georgia Senator Richard Russell. Judge Russell dissented from the majority, contending that the ordinance was the only thing preventing a race war.[41]

On the surface, it was a major victory for Birmingham's black community. They had finally won their five-year struggle against the city's zoning laws. But whether whites would accept the judgment remained in question. Mayor Cooper Green warned that the "breakdown of the southern system of residential segregation [would] cause strife and turmoil." Three days before Christmas 1950, Green's warning proved correct when dynamite destroyed the home of Mary Means Monk. Weeks later, the city was denied a rehearing in January 1951. It appealed to the U.S. Supreme Court for a writ of certiorari, but that too was denied. The city gave up the fight.[42]

The question of whether blacks legally had a right to live where they pleased in Birmingham lingered for three more years. Not until December 1954 did city commissioners eliminate racial references in the code. In the new zoning ordinance, the parts that had contained the restrictions now insolently carried the phrase, "Deleted due to United States Court Decision on segregation." With the change in zoning, whites undertook an exodus to the suburban communities of Mountain Brook, Homewood, and Vestavia Hills. Although the black population of the transitional tracts of Graymont-Smithfield grew by fewer than 700 persons between 1950 and 1960, white population in the area shrank by more than 3,300. At least thirteen more racial bombings occurred between 1955 and 1963. Many of them grew out of the civil rights movement after the *Brown* v. *Board of Education* cases. The cycle of bombing did not end until four young African American girls were killed in the Sixteenth Street Baptist Church bombing of 1963.[43]

Other cities in the South and border states saw residential race relations become strained and violent in the postwar years. In the spring of 1949, the Ku Klux Klan burned a cross on the site of a proposed black housing project in Nashville. At the end of December, a dynamite bomb destroyed the unfinished development. In 1950, violence occurred in Charlotte after the construction of an expressway forced African Americans out of the ghetto. During the 1950s, other southern cities saw incidents of violence and intimidation. Norfolk and Chattanooga experienced several bombings. A black teacher in Richmond, J. W. Sweat, experienced months of harassment and intimidation when he moved into the Sugar Hill district in early 1949. A cross was burned on his lawn; bricks and pellets were fired at the house; and he received threatening letters: one, postmarked Richmond, included a bullet as a warning for him to get out. After a three-month probe, Richmond police arrested seven white youths for disorderly conduct and damaging property. During their hearing, the youths entered not-guilty pleas, insisting that they had fired at the house with the pellet gun but had not committed any of the other acts. The police investigator told the court that "anything the boys might have done was a boyish prank." The judge ordered a probation officer to make a further investigation, but the tensions in Sugar Hill had lessened, and three more black families had moved onto the block since mid-April. Nothing more came of the probes.[44]

Dallas, the half-southern and half-western city, experienced a new wave of racial violence in transitional neighborhoods in the early 1950s. The city had seen tremendous growth in population due to in-migration and annexation between 1940 and 1950. Its total population increased by nearly 140,000 in the decade to number more than 434,000. The African American population grew more modestly during the same period. In 1950 and 1951, however, the city embarked on a slum clearance venture and new construction of Love Field, the city airport. The projects caused the displacement of many African Americans living in West Dallas who sought relief in the older white sections of South Dallas.[45]

As blacks began moving onto blocks on the frontiers of the African American enclaves, the resident whites, like their counterparts a decade earlier, began a reign of terror. By July 1951, eleven bombings had been reported in the district; six more incidents involving "mysterious fires" had also occurred. After the eleventh bombing, the city established a special grand jury to run the investigation. With the aid of the FBI and the Texas Rangers, local police questioned a number of suspects, and in late summer 1951 the grand jury brought nearly a dozen indictments. Most of the vigilantes hailed from the blocks on which the violence occurred. Claude Thomas Wright, who confessed to three bombings and several other bombing attempts, lived next door to a house on Leland Street that twice had been the target of arsonists, and Pete Garcia resided next to the bombing site on Marburg Street. The grand jury failed to indict the presumed ringleader of the campaign, Charles O. Goff. As the chairman of the Exline Improvement Association and a city labor leader, Goff had represented white home owners on several occasions during the late 1940s and was suspected of planning the bombings. But the grand jury could find no direct link between Goff and the bombers, even though his name figured in Wright's confession. None of those brought to trial were convicted, but the violence subsided after the end of the year. Instead of employing terrorism, whites fled the district: 11,027 fewer whites lived in the tracts making up South Dallas in 1960 than in 1950.[46]

The white supremacist status quo in the South began to erode during the decade of the 1940s. African Americans slowly grew stronger politically after the demise of the white primary. The stationing of black servicemen in the South during the war, as well as the increased federal presence, brought changes in black status. The LDF challenges in education, the desegregation cases, and the quest for equal pay for black teachers signaled the change in the status of African Americans. Black migration to southern cities during and after the war, meanwhile, combined with urban blight to exacerbate the crisis in African American housing. As the traditional ghettoes became overcrowded, blacks were forced to seek new residences wherever they could find them; even if they were in all-white neighborhoods.

Although violence had never been absent from southern race relations, the post-war years brought new tensions to the region. The change in black legal status prompted white backlash. Politically, white southerners tried to impede African American advancement by withdrawing from the Democratic Party. The failure of the Dixiecrat movement marginalized the South nationally and forced white supremacists to take more extreme measures to maintain the status quo. They undertook a policy of massive and violent resistance to the civil rights movement. The policy became more pronounced after the *Brown* v. *Board of Education* decisions in the mid-1950s, but it had already shown its potential in the housing combat of the preceding decade.

Southern residential race relations became more like those of the rest of the nation in the postwar years. Southerners, ironically, were catching up to the rest of the United States in the way they maintained racial distance. The races were not as segregated in southern cities as elsewhere in 1940 because black servants commonly lived near their white employers. But this relationship changed between 1940 and 1960. De jure segregation, as evinced by Birmingham's zoning ordinance, had persisted in the region because of the long tradition of white supremacy. Where laws did not guarantee it, de facto segregation had been the expectation, and blacks had seldom challenged it. After the war, however, the changes in their legal and economic status gave African Americans the opportunity to challenge the status quo. The growth of black urban communities forced African Americans to fight for access to more housing. Many whites opposed the new black condition. They tried to intimidate blacks to keep their neighborhoods white. In lieu of violence, white southerners followed the example of their northern counterparts and fled to suburbs. Thus southern cities became more segregated.

Issues other than housing dominated southern race relations after 1954. The violence of whites and determination of blacks in the decade following the *Brown* decision would break down barriers to opportunity in almost all aspects of African American economic and political life in the South, except access to housing. As the next chapter attests, however, housing remained the central civil rights issue outside the South during the 1950s and early 1960s. The racial intimidation and violence over space in the rest of the country would equal, perhaps even surpass, anything the most ardent southern white supremacist would attempt.

7

"A RAISIN IN THE SUN"

Mrs. Johnson: Ain't it something how bad these here white folks is getting here in Chicago! Lord, getting so you think you right down in Mississippi![1]

The decade from 1949 to 1959 marked the era of the most significant upheaval in race housing. None of the issues or answers were new. But demographic, economic, legal, social, and intellectual forces merged to create a volatility not seen since the truce of the 1920s.

Turmoil crossed the nation. White leaders in urban areas of the South began facing substantial attacks—attacks they could not continue to ignore—from civil rights groups and segments of the federal government. In the cities of the North and West, the increased in-migration of blacks and out-migration of whites forced politicians to rethink the issue of race and housing. The demographic shifts prompted some civic leaders to make the necessary reforms to provide African Americans with better housing opportunities. Others used the perceived threat to white hegemony to build their political base and to close African Americans out of their municipalities. And some were paralyzed into inaction by the fear of race war and the further loss of a property tax base.

The 1950s witnessed a repetition of the racial conflagration seen after the Great War. Some things had changed, however. This time, social and political forces aligned against the white vigilantes. And thanks to government housing programs, flight to new suburbs offered a peaceful outlet to those whites still unwilling to have blacks live next door. It was only a matter of time before the white terrorists would lose, and violence and intimidation would cease to be a viable tactic to keep African Americans at bay. Still, Chicago, Detroit, Miami, Los Angeles, and numerous other cities saw tremendous conflict before vigilantism was defeated.

In 1957, *U.S. News & World Report* published a series of articles focusing on race relations outside the South. "It is in the North," the series declared, "that racial tensions [run] highest. . . . In Chicago, Detroit, [and] Los Angeles," it reported, "[blacks pressed] in on white neighborhoods with explosive results." The notorious battle over integration of Central High School in Little Rock, Arkansas, lay less than a month in the future, but the magazine was still not wrong. In Los Angeles, for example, the County Commission on Human Relations reported dozens of racial incidents over housing during the early 1950s, including six bombings.[2]

The Second Great Migration continued throughout the 1950s. Over the decade, net out-migration of nonwhites from the South numbered 1.5 million persons. Cities in the Midwest witnessed the largest influx of migrants. Approximately 558,000 blacks moved to Chicago, Detroit, and other industrial centers. Another half-million African American southerners moved to the Northeast, primarily to New York City, Philadelphia, and Newark, New Jersey. But even the West—Los Angeles, San Francisco, and Seattle—received more than 330,000 migrants. Chicago, by far, received the largest influx of new black population. More than 303,000 more African Americans lived in Chicago in 1960 than a decade earlier.[3]

"With the increase of Negro population," *U.S. News* reported, "a form of 'voluntary' segregation" developed: whites left the cities to the newcomers. Since the end of the war, the federal government had forged policies promoting private home ownership, principally through VA and FHA mortgage loan insurance. These programs, along with a rise in speculative housing construction and a growing economy after 1947, made private suburban housing affordable. The creation of transportation systems linking bedroom communities to the work place made living in the new suburban tracts more convenient. These new opportunities pulled whites out of urban areas. The steady influx of a new and usually poor African American population, meanwhile, provided the push. One white Philadelphian made the point most clearly: "It's like the black plague," he said, "everyone wants to escape."[4]

Many blacks entered the decade of the 1950s in a better economic position than ever before. Between 1940 and 1950, earnings of nonwhite workers trebled, bringing the median African American income near $1,300 per year. Furthermore, in 1939, according to *House and Home*, a negligible 0.1 percent of Negro households earned more than $5,000 a year, but that important "able-to-buy group" had grown to 5.4 percent by 1950. In another development, the FHA changed its policy in granting mortgage loans. It refused to guarantee loans on land covered by racially restrictive deed indentures. Few blacks were able to take advantage of the change, however, because the lending institutions remained reluctant to grant them mortgages, especially if they intended to move into a white neighborhood. The Urban League explained that lending institutions could evade the rule simply by not putting restrictions in writing because the judicial prohibition against race-restrictive covenants rested on "*the filing of a restriction and not on the actual imposition of restrictions by the mortgagor.*" In this way, landlords in New York City, for example, kept approximately 90 percent of the rental housing out of the reach of African

Americans. With new housing largely unavailable to them, African Americans, according to the Urban League, "in the majority of instances throughout the nation" were left with a "hand-me-down house."[5]

Racial transition in many communities was complete by 1960. In Chicago's South Side in 1940, for example, according to census figures, whites numbered more than 47,500, or 96 percent of the inhabitants of the thirteen tracts that bordered the Black Belt. By 1960, only about 1,600 whites remained. The African American population in the section, meanwhile, grew by a factor of forty during the two decades. More than 64,000 African Americans lived in the thirteen tracts in 1960.[6]

Conditions in Chicago's Hyde Park–Kenwood area illustrate how the migration affected residential race relations. The area had stabilized after the violence of the early 1920s. White block associations had stopped the African American advance at Cottage Grove Avenue. In 1940, the ghetto remained 1 mile west of the district. Blacks comprised only about 4 percent of the section's population. By 1950, in part because of continued resistance from neighborhood associations wanting to keep the area "racially pure," the percentage of blacks in the district had increased to only 6 percent. Over the next six years, however, racial transition occurred. In 1956, blacks made up 36 percent of the section's population. More than 20,000 whites had fled to lily-white suburbs, and some 23,000 blacks had moved into the quickly deteriorating district. Some of the white inhabitants of transitional areas chose not to leave, however. They fought.[7]

A number of incidents occurred in July 1949, marking the beginning of a new round of mob violence in Chicago. On July 25, a crowd of some 800 white demonstrators gathered in front of an apartment on St. Lawrence Avenue at 72nd Street into which Roscoe Johnson and his wife had just moved. People in the crowd began throwing stones, smashing out windows, and chanting, "Burn the black bastard out." About 10:00 P.M., someone threw a flaming rag into the building, and the fire nearly destroyed the structure. Chicago police were present throughout the episode, but they did nothing to stop it. Several other outbreaks occurred in the neighborhood over the next three days. The Mayor's Commission on Human Relations, which had observed the situation from the outset, compelled police to set up an effective patrol and restored calm to the neighborhood. Police also brought charges against the demonstrators for such crimes as disorderly conduct, vandalism, and inciting to riot. Most of those charged lived on adjoining blocks; their ages ranged from seventeen to forty-seven, but most of them were in their early twenties.[8]

In November 1949, the conflict over the Englewood district erupted into a full-fledged riot. The area had experienced violence before. In 1945, terrorist activity had included people throwing stones and bricks as well as firing a shotgun into a house on South LaSalle Street. No African Americans were actually moving into Englewood at the time of the riot in 1949. A black family had recently purchased a house in the district, but the riot began when a local labor organizer invited a few blacks to his house for an organizational meeting. A neighbor spied them entering the home, and she concluded that it too would be "sold to niggers." The rumor spread. Whites began gathering at the house. The mob eventually grew to about 10,000 persons, and for four days it wrought havoc, stoning property and beating bystanders. "That a false rumor that blacks were about to move into the area was enough to trigger the riot," Arnold Hirsch notes, "indicated the depth of the tension . . . in many white areas bordering the Black Belt."[9]

The violence persisted throughout Chicago during the next three years. In June 1951, after the attempted bombing of the home of Dr. Percy Julian in the Oak Park area, the third bombing in three months, the NAACP drafted a memo enumerating the incidents. Between 1949 and June 1951, there had been three bombings, ten incidents of arson, eleven incidents of attempted arson, and at least eighty-one other incidents of terrorism or intimidation. White Chicagoans, clearly, were not ready to allow blacks into their neighborhoods.[10]

A riot in Cicero outdid even the Englewood melee. The all-white Chicago suburb was inhabited mostly by second-generation Americans of Czechoslovakian, Polish, Italian, and Dutch descent. In May 1951, a black bus driver rented an apartment in the town. Harvey E. Clark represented the typical middle-class black existence at midcentury. A captain in the Army Air Corps during the war and a graduate of Fisk University, he had moved his family to Bronzeville on Chicago's South Side in 1949. There, Clark and his wife and their two small children were crammed into "one-half of a small two-room apartment," for which he paid $56 per month. A family of five lived in the other half. Once economically able to do so, Clark sought more space for his family. He chose Cicero because it was closer to the bus terminal. The apartment that he found was clean and modern, had five rooms, and cost only $60 per month.[11]

The Clarks tried to move their furniture into the apartment during the third week of June and were met by white protesters. When Cicero police arrived, they sided with the demonstrators. "Get out of Cicero," they told Clark, "and don't come back." The Cicero chief of police, Ervin Konovsky, forcibly turned Clark away. Clark sued the police department for discrimination and won. The federal judge enjoined the police from further interference with the move except "to exercise the same diligence to get this family into the apartment peaceably as [they had] to keep them out."[12]

The Clarks tried again to occupy the apartment on Wednesday, July 11, 1951. Some 100 housewives greeted them, heckling and picketing. During the afternoon, Cicero police did nothing to contain the growing mob. The Cook County sheriff did try to take control, but the situation only worsened: a policeman was injured when struck by a brick. Later, a mob of teenagers stormed the apartment and tossed furniture out of the third-story window to a cheering crowd below. "That's my boy," the mother of one of the hoodlums announced proudly, as she watched him throw a rock through a window. In about an hour, the youths destroyed what had taken nine years to acquire. They had even burned the Clarks' marriage license. But what hurt Harvey Clark most was the destruction of a piano. It had cost $800. He explained, "I remembered all the overtime I'd worked as a bus driver so that my daughter would have a good piano on which to develop her musical talents."[13]

On Thursday, the demonstrators became a legion of rioters. Neighborhood housewives kept a constant vigil during the day. In midafternoon, the crowd swelled as teenagers were let out of school. The men returned from work to find the streets filled. By early evening, a mob estimated at 4,000 voiced its opposition to the Clarks' presence, chanting "Go! Go! Go!" They firebombed the apartment house, gutting it and forcing its white residents to seek refuge. With the situation out of control, Governor Adlai E. Stevenson sent in the National Guard. The 450 guardsmen and 200 police battled for four hours before driving the mob back. It took until midday on July 13 for the soldiers and police to establish an eight-square-block perimeter and three more days to end the conflict.[14]

Local officials blamed the riot not on the mob but on those who had enabled Clark to rent the apartment. In September, the apartment's owner, the renting agent, Clark's attorney, and a man who allegedly had distributed communist literature after the riot were indicted for "unlawfully, and maliciously inciting, persuading and encouraging" a riot and for continuing "to riot, . . . injure and destroy . . . personal property, goods and chattels." The indictments were eventually dropped. With the exception of Konovsky, no rioters or officials were indicted by the county grand jury. A federal grand jury, however, indicted seven town officials, including Konovsky, for "conspiracy to prevent any Negro inhabitants from occupying and owning property in Cicero." Four of those indicted were convicted, but these convictions were reversed on appeal. As for the Clarks, they had determined "as a matter of principle to return to Cicero," but the racial tension ran too high. When the town of Norwalk, Connecticut, offered them a home, the Clarks accepted.[15]

Violence continued to occur in the Chicago area after the Cicero riot. One last example will show how whites also could be persistent in their resistance. Donald Howard was a twenty-five-year-old veteran and unemployed letter carrier. For years, he and his wife, Bettye Ann, and their children had lived in cramped quarters with relatives and had moved from place to place each time seeking a dwelling "a little larger and a little better" than the one before. Bettye Ann admitted that they "couldn't even imagine what it would be like to live in an apartment." Then, in July 1953, they moved into an all-white housing project in South Deering, a white lower-middle-class district situated between Lake Calumet and Lake Michigan. Trumbull Park Homes, and the Chicago Housing Authority (CHA) generally, followed a policy of segregation. A CHA official, however, mistook the light-skinned Mrs. Howard for white and accepted their application. At first, the Howards could not believe their luck. "When we first moved in," Bettye Ann exclaimed, "we could hardly believe it; we were so pleased." They did not know that they were about to live a year-long nightmare.[16]

As soon as the Howards moved in, neighbors assembled to demonstrate. They threw stones and menaced the blacks. Police tried to restore order and disperse the crowd, but the demonstrators, composed mostly of members of the South Deering Improvement Association and the White Circle League, remained. They picketed throughout the winter. Despite "the heavy cordon of police," large crowds continued to gather. They hurled bricks, fired pistol shots in the night, and propelled aerial bombs at point-blank range at the apartment. They also attacked and injured blacks passing near the project.[17]

In April 1954, nine months after the protests had begun, CBS Radio featured the conflict at Trumbull Park on its *The World Today* program. When the reporter asked one woman if she ever demonstrated against the Howards, she proudly responded, "Why certainly I picket. Every time I get a chance to, I'm out there. [I] come home from work, put on my slacks and [I am] out there, walking." Fear over deterioration of the neighborhood seemed to motivate the protesters. When the reporter asked a woman why she demonstrated, she exclaimed, "Every place that they've taken over, they've turned into a slum." Another told the reporter, "I just don't like to see anything happen to South Deering like it did to South Park," referring to the racial succession that occurred in Park Manor. That "was a beautiful neighborhood and [now it] is just a dump," she explained. A third claimed that she opposed having African Americans move into the area because "they'd throw papers all over the streets [and] they drive by with their cars and throw garbage out."[18]

The World Today also interviewed Bettye Ann Howard. In a poignant display, she gave the radio audience a tour of the apartment. The living room was "kept completely dark almost all the time," she revealed; "as you see, I have plywood up at the windows which is supported by two 2 × 4's." She explained that they had "it up at the window for [their] protection[;] so that the bricks [could not] come directly into the house to do us any harm." "The kitchen is much safer than the living room," Howard noted in the matter-of-fact tone of the war weary, "because up to now the people have not come into the project to molest us." Mrs. Howard also described her life at Trumbull Park. She got to work via a police patrol wagon that took them to and from the streetcar. She regularly faced verbal abuse from neighbors. And once, in a store, a woman threatened to throw a bottle of ammonia in her face. After the tour, the reporter finally asked the obvious question, "If it's so unpleasant, so unfriendly, why do you stay?" "Well," Bettye Ann replied, "because it's the first apartment that we have ever had." When asked, Donald Howard took a more prideful stance on that question. He told the reporter, "I'm not goin' to let someone say, well, you're not fit to live among me or among us, when they themselves are nothing but a bunch of poor trash."[19]

Throughout the struggle, the NAACP, the Mayor's Commission on Human Relations, and the Negro Chamber of Commerce pressured the mayor and CHA to protect blacks living at the project. When the protests began, the CHA announced that the Howards would remain, that other black families would be admitted, and that other housing projects would be integrated as soon as possible. Nine black families resided in Trumbull Park Homes by the spring. In March 1954, the Citizens Mobilization for Law Enforcement, organized by the NAACP and Negro Chamber of Commerce, held a march to protest what they considered an inadequate response. Mayor Martin H. Kennelly told them that from the outset of the problem he had instructed police to maintain order. He feebly assured the marchers that "the rights of individuals with respect to their homes and property must and will be protected." He appealed for calm, hoping that the races could "build better understanding" of each other's housing needs. The city council reaffirmed its policy that "public housing should be available to all eligible applicants without regard to race." Antiblack demonstrations continued, however. And the Howards moved.[20]

Starting in May 1954, the NAACP made a final push in Trumbull Park. It urged that a federal grand jury investigate and warned Kennelly that unless he ended the harassment, it would hold continuous demonstrations at City Hall. In July, U.S. Attorney General Herbert Brownell got involved, informing the NAACP that he would give the conflict "careful and continuous scrutiny." More importantly, Brownell also advised the NAACP on how to fight the protesters in court. The organization helped raise several damage suits in the name of the black residents of Trumbull Park in September. The antiblack protests withered in the face of the onslaught.[21]

Racial strife in Chicago continued to simmer after the truce at Trumbull Park Homes. In a March 1957 article in *U.S. News*, the Cook County sheriff called the situation "enormously explosive. . . . One incident," he suggested, "could blow the city up." More specifically, the U.S. Commission on Civil Rights heard testimony recounting the tensions in the metropolitan area. The commission found that between 1956 and 1958, some 256 incidents of racial violence were reported, including "Chicago's biggest race riot in years" in Calumet Park in July 1957. Not all of the episodes involved housing, and some involved black-on-white violence, but there were thirty-eight cases of arson, and the overwhelming majority of incidents occurred on the periphery of the Black Belt or other African American enclaves. The Chicago Urban League's agents told the commission that of the more than 160 incidents during 1956 and 1957, most occurred in Park Manor and Englewood. More than a dozen incidents occurred near Trumbull Park, where one African American witness maintained that racial violence had "become normal."[22]

Amid the conflict, racial transition in Chicago intensified. According to *U.S. News*, about 225 housing units changed from white occupancy to African American each week. The city's white population decreased by 300 persons every week because of flight to the suburbs. Its black population, meanwhile, grew by 600 per week, according to the civil rights commission. One witness quipped that integration in Chicago referred to "the period . . . that elapses between the appearance of the first Negro and the community's ultimate and total incorporation into the Negro ghetto." Resistance to the expansion of the African American community, some argued, made Chicago "one of the most segregated cities in the world."[23]

Like Chicago, Detroit underwent significant demographic shifts during the 1950s.

The black population continued to grow. More importantly, the ratio of African Americans to whites changed, and the spatial distribution of those communities became increasingly segregated, as white flight to the suburbs proceeded at a rapid rate. About 304,000 blacks lived in Detroit in 1950, or 16.4 percent of the population. By 1960, African Americans numbered more than 482,000, almost 29 percent of the total population. Suburban politicians were determined to maintain the monochromatic character of their municipalities. Orville Hubbard, mayor of Dearborn, continued the political tricks that had enabled him to win election in the 1940s. In 1956, he told the *Montgomery [Alabama] Advertiser* that Dearborn had grown as the result of an influx of whites "crowded out of Detroit by the colored people." "These people," the mayor insisted, "are so anti-colored, much more than you in Alabama." With some relish, the editor of the *Richmond Times-Dispatch* cited Hubbard as an example of racial intolerance in the North. "Negroes can't get in here," Hubbard was reported to have declared; "every time we hear of a Negro moving in we respond quicker than you do to a fire."[24]

With the new population came racial tension. Details surrounding the conflicts, however, remain sketchy. The Human Rights Department of the Commission of Community Relations (HRD-CCR), the heir to the Interracial Committee, followed George Schermer's strategy of suppressing information about incidents to forestall escalation into riot. No major riots occurred in Detroit during the 1950s, allowing city officials to claim that race relations were improving. But the HRD-CCR still investigated fifteen incidents in 1954 alone. In August 1955, two episodes included some 2,000 demonstrators and several nights of threatening protest. And these represent only the incidents that were reported. The NAACP insisted that many episodes went unreported.[25]

Although precise accounts of violence could not be found, it remains clear that significant conflict occurred. A handwritten chart prepared by HRD-CCR investigators recorded nineteen incidents occurring between June 1953 and September 1955. These do not include the fifteen from 1954 mentioned above. The conflict occurred on the periphery of the black neighborhoods: in a section bounded by Conant and Woodward Avenues, McNichols Street, and Seven Mile Road, just west of the Sojourner Truth Homes; and in the area bounded by Livernois, Wyoming, and Davidson Avenues and Fenkell Road. The methods of intimidation ranged from block associations buying back property to mobs of 1,500–2,000 persons protesting and vandalizing black-owned property. In one instance, an African American seamstress bought a home on a white block. Within a few days after she moved in, vandals broke windows and delivered a bomb threat, and a mob ranging up to 200 persons appeared at the home every night for several weeks. Detroit police patrolled the area and arrested several demonstrators for disturbing the peace. After the arrests, protests subsided.[26]

Activity by improvement associations in Detroit also increased during the early 1950s. In 1943, fifty-three property associations operated in the city. That number skyrocketed to 143 by 1953. Two years later, it had dwindled to eighty-eight, but the organizations continued to protest and to get realtors not to sell to African Americans. Many groups were large and representative of their neighborhoods. The Schaefer-Hubbell Property Owners Association, for example, numbered 800 of the 1,100 eligible families. According to the Detroit Urban League, meetings followed a regular pattern. They began legitimately with a guest speaker who might talk about zoning matters. When the guest left, debate would turn to concerns that members had about blacks moving into the area. They would discuss ways of keeping "undesirables" out of the district. At a meeting in 1955, a woman asked what was meant by "undesirables." Several members answered, "Niggers," and began harassing the questioner. A witness to a meeting in October 1956 had a cross burned on her lawn when she reported the group's activities to the *Detroit News*. At a board meeting of the Ruritan Park Civic Association in 1957, a resident inquired as to the purpose of the association and what methods it intended to use to meet its goal. The board told him that it was formed to keep blacks out of the area and that it would use any method available that was "not specifically illegal." But not all groups proved to be so law-abiding. Some created restrictive covenants based on membership, the association deciding who could and could not join. Others intimidated potential opponents by burning crosses on their lawns.[27]

Miami—a city in the South but not of it—saw significant upheaval when blacks tried to find homes beyond the ghettos of Overtown, Brownsville, and Liberty City in the 1950s. The city's African American community grew by 25,000 persons (nearly 61 percent) during the decade and increased from about 16 percent to more than 22 percent of the city's total population. Segregation had been practiced from the city's inception. In 1940, according to Taeuber and Taeuber, Miami had the dubious honor of being the nation's most racially segregated city. It remained so in 1950 and again in 1960.[28]

Envisioned as the jewel in Henry M. Flagler's Gold Coast, Miami had grown up almost overnight when the rail line tying it to Fort Lauderdale and points north was completed in April 1896. Many of the original 3,000 occupants of Dade County were blacks from the southeastern United States and the Bahamas who had built the Florida East Coast Railroad. African Americans comprised nearly half the persons who voted in the town's incorporation election in June 1896. Despite their importance to the local economy and the supposedly progressive racial attitudes of the northern whites who inhabited the city, blacks were forced by deed restrictions and covenants into a small enclave, first called Colored Town and then Overtown. "Residential segregation," according to Florida historian Paul S. George, "[represented] the cornerstone of racial separation [and] was from the beginning the rule in Miami."[29]

Housing posed a persistent problem for African Americans in Miami. A building boom during the 1920s trickled over into the community, bringing prosperity to some, but the growing black middle class remained hemmed in by restrictive covenants, discrimination, and the Klan. Some blacks attempted to move into Highland Park, the white section bordering Colored Town to the north, but were met with bombs. A near riot ensued when a mob of fifty whites began roaming the black section, shooting off guns indiscriminately. A devastating hurricane in 1926 destroyed many of the fragile shotgun shacks in which African Americans dwelled, exacerbating the housing crisis. No significant relief came until the PWA Housing Division built the 243-unit Liberty Square, northwest of Colored Town, in 1937. The USHA added another 730 units to the project in 1941, and the section became known as Liberty City. It directly abutted the white enclave of Edison Center, which many regarded as "among the worst white slums in the South," according to the *Miami Herald*. Even at that, the city built a wall to separate Liberty City from the shabby homes of Edison Center.[30]

White supremacist activities after the war increased racial tensions. In 1945, Klansmen burned a cross in front of a home in the Brownsville section after the Northwest Property Owners League objected to the presence of two black families. But the Klan challenge of 1945 paled in comparison to the conflict of 1951. Throughout the fall and winter of 1951, Klansmen carried out a campaign of terror against synagogues and Catholic schools. A separate group of white terrorists, the denizens of Edison Center, undertook a contemporaneous crusade to intimidate African Americans into staying away from white neighborhoods.[31]

The violence of 1951 centered on the Carver Village project in Edison Center. Although whites lived around the project, few chose to move into Carver Village because of its proximity to Liberty City. As a result, the developer, John A. Bouvier, began admitting African Americans to get some return on his investment. Blacks remained guarded about moving beyond the ghetto; by September 1951, only 115 people lived in the complex. Their migration, however, threatened to grow significantly because Miami had initiated a slum clearance project early in the year that had forced many to seek other shelter. Blacks moved into Edison Center when it became clear that no alternatives existed.[32]

The tension over Carver Village grew more volatile as African Americans prepared to move into the project in the late summer of 1951. *Miami Life* magazine declared that the city was "sitting on a keg of dynamite." Whites in the area organized the Edison Center Civic Association and Dade County Property Owners Association to lobby the city commission to take over the project and to force the blacks out. The groups stated that the city did not realize the degree of tension in the district. "Tempers [are] at a peak," they warned, requesting that the city move the African Americans "for their [own] protection." The commission responded by voting to condemn everything west of Tenth Avenue and to replace the housing with police and fire department substations and a sewage treatment plant. Mayor William M. Wolgarth first voted against the plan but then accepted it in the hope that it might restore peace. Commissioner Louis Bandel proclaimed that the plan "should help stop an explosive situation." It did not.[33]

Shortly after two o'clock on the morning of September 22, 1951, bombers attacked an unoccupied, sixteen-unit complex in the black section at Carver Village. The explosion was so big that its concussion rocked buildings fifty blocks away. Early estimates placed its size at about 100 pounds of dynamite, but investigators revised the bomb down to about twenty sticks. No one was hurt by the explosion, but it caused some $200,000 worth of damage to property.[34]

Many theories were raised to explain the bombing. Miami's police chief alleged that communists had bombed Carver Village and had paid African Americans to move into the project to incite racial tension. The NAACP's Walter White answered the charge when he visited South Florida shortly after Christmas. "Communists didn't have to create such incidents," he remarked, "loyal Americans furnished [them]." Police took two African American men into custody, questioned them, and detained them for perpetrating the bombing. They had apparently stopped at a tavern in the area while en route to deliver dynamite to a construction site but were innocent of the charges. Others suspected the Klan, but Grand Dragon William Hendrix denied involvement and suggested that "if [police] looked in the White neighborhood, they [would] probably find the guilty party." Despite the investigation and a subsequent study by state and federal investigators, Miami police did not find the bombers.[35]

The city and county moved slowly to devise a solution to the conflict. Mayor Wolgarth announced that the commission was "giving the situation a lot of thought," insisting that it required "calm and considered judgment." Whites clamored for the removal of the African Americans, but the city could not move until condemnation proceedings were completed. In early October, the county commission met to discuss the general housing issue and to try to reach a settlement. The commission placed on the ballot for the November election a proposal to make a contract with the federal government to undertake public housing projects. The move was a diversion. The county did, however, create a biracial committee to work out a countywide plan to make more land available to blacks and to construct public and private housing that blacks could afford.[36]

In late November 1951, the conflict in Edison Center grew worse, and a sense of panic started to spread across metropolitan Miami. The city began proceedings to condemn Carver Village on November 21. Opponents of the plan sued to enjoin the condemnation. As the proceedings stalled in the courts, whites again took the law into their own hands. They set off three more bombs, two at Carver Village and a third at a home not far away. A fourth explosion in northwest Miami occurred on Christmas Eve. The *Miami Herald* declared that the racial and religious violence left the city "afraid, disgraced, and ashamed."[37]

This latest rash of violence prompted several positive responses but still did not ease the tension. The city council created a coordinating committee to investigate further the causes of the violence. The Dade County Commission passed an antidynamite ordinance. It established an eleven-member panel, with seven African

American nonmember consultants, to select new sites for black housing. Most of the committee's effort would be put into collecting data on public opinion and whether whites were willing to have an African American enclave in their midst. Peter McCabe of the Miami Housing Authority pointed out the redundancy of the new planning board's mandate, saying that he could provide the data to the committee "in fifteen minutes" from existing sources. Most significantly, the county also established the Dade County Community Relations Council. The council, chaired by Hollis Rinehart, a lawyer, would include academics, state representatives, and community leaders and aimed to prevent more bombings. The Dade County Community Relations Council helped restore relative peace, but, as in other cities, flight replaced bombs as the tactic by which white Miamians maintained the racial homogeneity of neighborhoods.[38]

The black population of Los Angeles experienced tremendous growth throughout the 1950s. By 1960, more than 330,000 African Americans lived in the Los Angeles Standard Metropolitan Statistical Area, some 270,000 more than had lived there in 1940. Meanwhile, housing deteriorated, and housing opportunities remained limited. The three islands of African American settlement in downtown Los Angeles merged to form a larger black belt. A desperately poor African American slum also existed in Pacoima, in the city's northwest. During a visit in January 1950, the housing expert Charles Abrams called the housing situation in Los Angeles worse than that in New York City. The city's slum dwellings were "more substandard than New York's were twenty years ago," he declared.[39]

Whites employed a series of tactics to exclude blacks from their neighborhoods. They ranged from buy-out schemes by improvement organizations to denial of mortgage funds by lending institutions. White home owners and realtors even fought to restore the effectiveness of race-restrictive covenants. In 1951, Leola Jackson's neighbors sued for damages when she sold her covenanted property to African Americans. The plaintiffs, led by Olive Barrows, argued that *Shelly* v. *Kraemer* (1948) did not prevent them from pursuing compensation for presumed damages caused by the breach of a deed indenture. The prospect of paying damages, they hoped, would keep whites from selling to blacks and keep blacks from buying in formerly restricted neighborhoods. After losing in the state court system, Barrows appealed to the U.S. Supreme Court in 1953. The Vinson Court understood the plaintiffs' motives and ruled unanimously in favor of Jackson.[40]

Home owners in Los Angeles also used violence and intimidation. The *California Eagle*, with Loren Miller at the helm, described numerous incidents of terrorism in 1949 and throughout the 1950s. In late August 1949, Lonnie Williams tried to move his family into a house on East 70th Street. For five days, whites demonstrated around the house. The largest mob assembled on the night of August 29. Williams held them off with a gun, while his wife notified the police. Five carloads of police arrived at the scene, but instead of controlling the demonstrators, one policeman disarmed Williams, and the rest stood by idly watching. The demonstrations subsided when the police, at the request of the NAACP, placed an around-the-clock detail at the house to protect Williams and his family.[41]

Situations like that involving Williams were common. On more than a dozen occasions, terrorists burned crosses on front lawns, into lawns, or into doorways to intimidate home owners. When the widow of an African American veteran of the Great War rented an apartment to a "mixed" couple, she received many threats. "The people of 41st Place," one letter notified her, were "disgusted . . . for having mixed races in [her] home." They warned her that if she did not get rid of the tenants, they would damage her property just as they believed she had damaged theirs. In another incident, after more than a month of harassment by whites, a black woman moved out of her home. Another African American family gave up and moved out of their home on West Forty-Second Street after receiving a fifth threatening note and finding that bullets had been shot into the side of their house.[42]

The most destructive incident occurred in the Wilshire District in 1952. As early as August 1951, the owner of 2130 South Dunsmuir had received threats that his home would be blown up if he tried to sell to African Americans. One note menaced, "sell to colored we bomb your home . . . if you that crazy for $ we make you sorry . . . we have bombs ready and eye on you." But he refused to bow and sold to the home to William Bailey, the head of the science department at Carver Junior High School. Bailey moved into the home around the beginning of March, and early on Sunday morning, March 16, terrorists bombed the home. The bombing raised tremendous protest from the city's black community. According to the *Eagle*, 2,000 people attended a demonstration and rally the following week. The gathering collected $3,750 as a reward to help police find the bombers. Loren Miller acted as master of ceremonies at the event. In his speech, Miller blamed the Los Angeles Realty Board for the incident. He insisted that the board's persistent opposition to integration and its support of the plaintiffs in the 1953 *Barrows* v. *Jackson* case had created an atmosphere in which African Americans had become desperate for housing and whites remained paranoid about protecting property values. Despite the reward and a probe by a grand jury into the way police were running their investigation, no one was ever arrested for the crime.[43]

As the new population continued to press against the walls of the Los Angeles ghetto, Compton, a suburb situated southeast of the city in Los Angeles County, became the next venue for violence. Settled in 1888 by a group of Methodists led by Griffith Dickeson Compton, the town remained small until after World War II. With the return of veterans and the creation of VA-guaranteed home mortgages, the suburb grew. The white, working-class inhabitants of Compton tended to work in the defense plants and shipyards of Long Beach. Like their counterparts in Cicero, they feared that any black presence in the neighborhood would lead to complete racial transition, and they held tight to their property rights. "We fought all the way from Normandy to the Battle of the Bulge," a group of white home owners told an *Eagle* reporter: "we have a right to these homes." Furthermore, they claimed that they had bought the houses knowing that the area was under a gentlemen's agreement that African Americans would not be admitted. "'Highly Restricted'—that's the way we bought and that's the way it's going to stay," they declared.[44]

African Americans began moving into Compton in the early 1950s. One realtor likened the in-migration to "a creeping fire." Clashes between students at the local junior high school marked the beginning of the tension. It then grew into what the *Eagle* called a "reign of terror." In February 1953, a white mob beat a white home owner for selling to blacks. A group of angry white home owners, meanwhile, organized the Northwest Compton Civic Association to discuss other ways of keeping African Americans out of their neighborhood, and the Longfellow Homeowners' Association dredged up a dormant antipeddler law and brought a suit against realtors who sold the homes to blacks.[45]

During the spring and summer of 1953, the Compton Crest Improvement Association tried to intimidate blacks into leaving the area. When William Whittaker and his wife moved into a home in early April, they received a warning letter which read, "I hate you, you black bastard. Get out and Stay Out." When Whittaker did not heed that advice, vandals attacked the property, smashing flowerpots, breaking windows, and slashing screens. Members of the association, led by Joe Williams, a shop steward at the Long Beach Douglas Aircraft plant, then began to picket the homes of African Americans in the area. On May 12, the protesters turned violent. They stoned the car and the home of Alfred Jackson, a shipyard worker. The vandalism prompted the Los Angeles NAACP to wire State Attorney General Edmund G. Brown, asking him to begin an investigation. The protest ended with the increased presence of police and state troopers. Williams's union membership also played a role in quelling the violence. The UAW-CIO local to which Williams belonged put him on trial for "conduct unbecoming to a union member." It eventually sanctioned Williams with a suspension.[46]

For a month after the bombing, an "uneasy truce" prevailed in Compton, but it was broken by several incidents beginning in mid-June. On June 13, persons purporting to be the Klan burned a cross on the lawn of a black-owned home on Dwight Street. And over the next week, hoodlums circled the block honking their car horns and yelling epithets. On the evening of June 18, a rock crashed through the window of Herman White's home. Attached to it was a simple note: "You're not wanted. [signed] K.K.K." African Americans who had lived quietly in Compton for several years started facing intimidation. George Sengler, a three-year resident of the suburb, came home from work one night to find his house flooded. Vandals had set a hose through the mail slot in his side door, turned on the water, and soaked the kitchen, destroying its hardwood floor and flooding the basement. Sengler sued the city for damages but did not win. Another African American resident had windows in her Aprilla Street home smashed by bricks and had her front lawn littered with heaps of garbage. She was not intimidated, however. "We're not going to move," she told the *Eagle* adding, "they can't frighten us, we're from Illinois."[47]

The conflict in Compton finally subsided when local, state, and federal government leaders became involved. The South East Interracial Council increased its efforts to dissuade whites from responding violently to black in-migration. According to Loren Miller, the efforts of Attorney General Brown's Bureau of Criminal Investigation and Identification were redoubled to eliminate the likelihood of further violence. And another less direct sign that governments no longer would defend or ignore the white supremacists came as the strife in Compton was reaching its zenith: the Vinson Court gave its final word on restrictive covenants in *Barrows* (1953). In response, many whites in Compton chose flight over violence.[48]

Although the situation cooled somewhat in Compton after 1954, tensions continued to run high in the San Fernando Valley communities and in the suburbs of Orange County for the rest of the decade. Asian Americans and Hispanic Americans faced discrimination from white home owners and institutions. By far, however, African Americans bore the brunt of the hostility. In most instances, the conflict remained nonviolent. Property associations met to discuss ways to "preserve harmony" in the neighborhood, realtors refused to show African Americans all available properties for sale, and lending institutions refused to grant a mortgage loan. Petty violence and intimidation, however, did remain a possibility. In the 1960 hearings, Loren Miller told the U.S. Commission on Civil Rights that some twenty-five or thirty incidents had occurred "in the past couple of years." A doctor in Long Beach, for example, had $10,000 worth of damage done to his home, and in more than two dozen instances, terrorists burned crosses.[49]

The increased prospect of racial tensions and violence over housing became an issue in other West Coast cities. *The New Leader* described the West as the "New Frontier" of racial tension. "Patterns of residential segregation," it insisted, were "becoming rigid. . . . The few breaks in once-solid Caucasian areas," it added, were "made only by wealthy Negroes, usually in the entertainment fields, who [could] afford a home costing $50,000 or more." In an otherwise glowing feature story on race relations in Seattle, *The Crisis* reported that African Americans there faced the same discrimination from white realtors, lenders, block associations, and individual home owners as they did elsewhere in the country. In Portland, Oregon, the African American population actually shrank during the decade after the war. But blacks there still faced discrimination in housing. Restriction of housing opportunities combined with white flight to the suburbs to bring about an increase in segregation. The *Oregonian* noted, for example, that between 1945 and early 1957 the ratio of African American to white students at the Eliot school had changed from one in three to four in five; and where blacks numbered less than 10 percent of students at the Boise school in 1945, they now comprised half the student body.[50]

Contrary to *The New Leader's* comment regarding the housing opportunities for wealthy blacks, even the most celebrated African Americans of the era met opposition when they ventured into white districts. The baseball hero Willie Mays encountered difficulties when he tried to find a home in a white section of San Francisco.[51]

In 1957, the New York Giants moved west. Mays was the team's greatest star. In November, while in San Francisco for an All-Star exhibition game, Mays told reporters that he would buy a house in the city. San Francisco, he confirmed, "is gonna be my town." Mays and his wife found a home that they liked in the Monterey Hills section of the city. But when they made an offer on it, the house was taken off the market. Undaunted, they found another one. The asking price for the house on Miraloma Drive was $37,500. Its owner, Walter A. Gnesdiloff, insisted that he had no problem with the idea of selling it to blacks. Mays offered $37,500 cash. When neighbors heard that Mays was to buy the house, Gnesdiloff received numerous telephone calls telling him not to sell. A builder for whom Gnesdiloff often worked voiced his adamant opposition to the sale, as did another employer. Gnesdiloff's realtor also informed him that he would "have nothing to do with a sale to a Negro." Worried that he would lose business building homes on speculation if he sold the house to Mays, Gnesdiloff rejected the offer. "I'm just a union working man," he explained. "I [would] never get another job if I sold this house to that baseball player."

When the incident came to the attention of the San Francisco Council for Civic Unity (CCU), the organization applied pressure to induce Gnesdiloff to sell to Mays. A group of civic leaders had established the CCU in 1944, after the race riots in Detroit, to work to avoid similar occurrences in San Francisco. They had succeeded in limiting violence but did not achieve racial harmony. As had happened elsewhere in the country, whites fled to the suburbs: to San Mateo, Marin, Santa Clara, and Sonoma Counties. The CCU appealed to Gnesdiloff's sense of civic pride and patriotism. It pointed out that rejecting Mays would "unquestionably produce a headline news story around the world, to America's and the city's detriment." It refuted local fears about the likely decline of property values and contended that other San Francisco Bay area districts had made "easy, friendly adjustments" when the first nonwhite family came on to a block. The CCU also brought in the mayor's office to pressure Gnesdiloff. Mayor George Christopher declared that blacks had a right to live where they wanted, but he added that he could not force Gnesdiloff to sell his property. Instead, he used moral suasion to try to shame Gnesdiloff into selling to Mays. The mayor also offered the Mayses a room in his own house until they could find another home. "I'd like you and your wife to be [my] guests," he simplistically proposed, adding that they would "be portraying the kind of brotherhood the world needs." Mays declined the offer because he was staying with friends and did not want to insult them.[52]

The CCU wanted to keep the incident contained so as not to cause embarrassment to the city. When a reporter for the San Francisco Chronicle learned of the Giant's difficulties, the CCU asked him not to print the story. He agreed to delay his scoop but gave the council a deadline of November 13, 1957. As the deadline approached, supporters and opponents of the move increased their pressure. Gnesdiloff's sometime employer stormed into Gnesdiloff's house and verbally assaulted him, charging that Gnesdiloff was destroying himself and the neighborhood. Marguerite Mays, meanwhile, gave voice to her bitterness. "Down in Alabama where we come from," she said, "you know your place, and that's something, at least. But up here it's all a lot of camouflage. They grin in your face and then deceive you." Her stinging indictment of race relations in San Francisco promised to embarrass the city. The *Chronicle's* deadline passed without a resolution and, on November 14, the newspaper ran the story. It was carried by media across the country and around the world. In a letter to the *Chronicle*, a San Franciscan living in Paris reported that the foreign edition of the *New York Herald-Tribune* had run the story.[53]

The publicity finally caused movement in the deadlock. Mayor Christopher, having received calls from officials around the country, pressured Gnesdiloff to sell. The CCU continued to lobby. Opponents of the move also made a final push to persuade Gnesdiloff not to sell. Two offers came to buy the house at the asking price. But "after a hectic morning, in which some neighbors kept unrelenting pressure on him to turn down the deal . . . Gnesdiloff made his decision." He telephoned Mays, telling him, "I am very happy to have you buy my home. The majority of the people of San Francisco want it that way, and I want it too." Gnesdiloff's conversation with Mays did not end the issue. Throughout the afternoon, he tried to contact his real estate agent, Peter Morgan. He left messages giving Morgan an ultimatum to meet him with Mays, Mays's lawyer, and CCU director Edward Howden to sign documents, or he would forgo his commission. The parties met at the assigned time but without Morgan. Finally, about a half hour late, Morgan arrived. He returned the contract. He refused to take part in the sale and gave up a commission of $1,125. He claimed that in the long run he would lose more money and potential clients if he took part in the transaction. Morgan departed, and the papers were signed. Mays declared that he was glad the episode was over. "All I wanted," he declared, "was a nice house in this town where I'll be playing ball." A week after Willie and Marguerite Mays moved into their new home, someone smashed the front window with a rock. Even the great baseball Giant was not safe at home in San Francisco.[54]

The incident forced many San Franciscans to reevaluate race relations in the city. The CCU called it "shocking [and] typical of practices . . . of the private housing market." The NAACP greeted the resolution "with tempered enthusiasm" but insisted that such cases were "dramatically enacted daily by hapless Negro families whose lack of prominence does not command the attention of the press and official San Francisco." The *Chronicle* suspected that the outcome might have been "less comforting to the city's self-esteem had the house-hunter been an obscure [black] whose rebuffs drew no public notice and aroused no public outcry." The incident, it insisted, offered "irrefutable evidence that some intolerance, some racial bigotry still reside in cosmopolitan, enlightened, understanding San Francisco." Responding to Marguerite Mays's criticism, the *Chronicle* noted that the appearance of discrimination in the city could not "help but blunt the sharp edge of local indignation against citizens of the South who have been exciting little sympathy with their complaints that integration is a vexing problem." A vexing problem it was for San Franciscans. According to an informal poll of 200 whites by a local citizen, every individual polled agreed with the statement, "I'd give aid and comfort to any Negro just as quickly as I would to any white person, but I don't want Negroes in my neighborhood." Willie and Marghuerite Mays sold the house in December 1960 and moved back to New York.[55]

From 1949 through the 1950s, massive resistance to integration defined the residential conflict. Cities struggled to maintain racial peace but often could do so only by letting their communities become more racially segregated. The years of racial conflict offer considerable insight into race relations. They prove that conclusions drawn by studies contending that conflict over space was short-lived or did not recur are erroneous. There was nothing sporadic about the violence and intimidation; rather, it was calculated, systematic, and persistent. Public opinion did start to turn against the vandals and rioters over the course of the decade, but the acts of terrorism often had broad support among officials, including peace officers and others charged to protect citizens. Furthermore, demonstrations tended to be organized, revealing the participation of real estate interests, block improvement associations, and white supremacist groups. But protesters were not duped into resistance by block-busting realtors or individual racist zealots. They were numerous. They believed in what they were doing. And they seemed willing to go to extremes to keep their neighborhoods white.

Even as housing conditions seemed to get worse for African Americans during the 1950s, many more positive developments occurred in race relations generally and in the race and housing issue specifically. Politically, urban black communities in the North gained strength as their spatial concentration made them an electoral force. The Cold War and the ideological battle with the Soviets for the Third World, as already played out in Cicero and Calumet, Illinois, made some Americans aware of the unfavorable image racial violence gave the country internationally. Legally, the Supreme Court's renunciation of the "separate but equal" doctrine forced a wholesale reevaluation of race relations in the United States. Finally, and at least as importantly, civil rights organizations—notably the NAACP and the National Committee Against Discrimination in Housing—took on the issue of housing discrimination with renewed vigor. The next chapter begins the discussion of these improvements.

8

CIVIL RIGHTS

Housing . . . is the one commodity where the race, religion or national origin of the purchaser determines what he may buy and where he may buy it, regardless of his ability to pay. . . . The free enterprise system has broken down and private prejudice has determined public policy.[1]

The 1950s, as *U.S. News & World Report* put it in 1957, was "a decade of miracles." The United States was "a nation on the move" and growing faster than ever before. There were "millions of babies," "millions of pupils," "millions of jobs," "millions of pensions," "millions of households," and for them "millions [of] new homes in new cities." Americans were "the world's most prosperous people." Technological innovations made travel easier and faster, whether by air, rail, or road. They also made it easier and more entertaining to stay home with television, better and more numerous telephone links, and "energy-saving" household appliances. The decade was also an era of great anxiety over America's place in the world. The communist threat in the Far East and in Europe left many citizens uncertain about the nation's security. The struggle for hegemony and capitalist domination in the Third World caused some people to take a closer look at how the rest of the world viewed the United States.[2]

Old prejudices, as the previous chapter showed, merged with the complex of growth and fear to create a decade of upheaval and violence in American neighborhoods. But other developments during the "10 Amazing Years" illustrate the progress made in race relations during the Truman-Eisenhower era. African American migration out of the South continued unabated, forcing whites throughout the country to adapt to a new demographic condition. In northern cities, especially Chicago and Detroit, African Americans started to gain political power as a result of their spatial concentration and their consequent ability to influence elections. Many blacks also found greater employment opportunities amid the nation's economic expansion. In the most far-reaching Supreme Court decision of the period, *Brown* v.

Board of Education (1954), blacks won reversal of the nearly sixty-year-old doctrine of "separate but equal." And, in the South, a full-fledged, grassroots civil rights movement rose up to challenge all forms of institutional and private discrimination.[3]

The advance in race relations came about as academic and civic leaders redefined the rules of social interaction and the responsibilities of government, particularly those of the federal government, in the protection of democratic rights. This re-evaluation grew out of the merger of new foreign policy interests with new theories of biology and culture. The Cold War dominated U.S. foreign policy during the era. The contest with international communism for the hearts and minds of the peoples of the Third World forced many Americans to pay greater attention to world opinion. Instances of racial violence became international incidents. The Soviet Union exploited the episodes for propaganda purposes. In a war of ideologies, the "American dilemma" opened the country to devastating charges of hypocrisy and insincerity in its dealings with nonwhite peoples. Many in the media, church, and government condemned the violence not only for its immorality but also because of the effect that it had on America's reputation. The experience of the Nazi Holocaust also engendered new theories of race and social contact, leading many academics to stress tolerance of cultural and religious differences and to redefine race as a concept.

The campaign against residential segregation grew during the era. Civil rights organizations took advantage of ideological and political developments to formulate new tactics to combat housing discrimination. The NAACP worked on many fronts. It fought in the courts, collected data on housing across the nation, lobbied legislators, and began a housing locator service. Other civil rights activist groups, such as the Congress of Racial Equality and the National Association of Interracial Relations Officials (NAIRO), joined the NAACP in the campaign. A new force, the National Committee Against Discrimination in Housing (NCDH), also entered the fray. The NCDH and the NAACP grew quite adept in their campaign. They succeeded in the courts, increased their lobbying of public officials, and produced a steady stream of propaganda through films and through the publication of pamphlets and monographs. And they provided aid when possible, finding suitable dwellings for individual African Americans. In so doing, they created an open-housing movement.

Advancement in the housing campaign came slowly, however. Most whites, reluctantly or otherwise, seemed prepared to grant a degree of equality to blacks in schools and on jobs, but they refused to offer African Americans greater access to better housing. In every region of the country and irrespective of class or celebrity, blacks faced obstructions to residential integration. Whites were prepared to keep their neighborhoods white by almost any means necessary. Financial institutions remained reluctant to lend money to African Americans seeking homes in white areas. The National Association of Real Estate Boards bowed to pressure from agencies of the federal government and eliminated discriminatory language from real estate instruction manuals, but agents employed new strategies to preserve the racial integrity of neighborhoods. Home builders and developers also continued to construct exclusively white subdivisions.

The postwar period witnessed a profound development in social-scientific theories of race prejudice as academics tried to gain an understanding of the Holocaust. The horror of more than 6 million deaths at the hands of racist ideologues haunted psychologists and sociologists. They sought answers to what many deemed an incomprehensible atrocity. The American Jewish Committee sponsored probes into anti-Semitism. One study, made by a team of psychologists led by T. W. Adorno, questioned college students to determine relationships between personality and formation of prejudice. The authors concluded that prejudice comprised one part of a larger psychological matrix that they called "the authoritarian personality." They discovered a strong correlation among individuals inclined toward anti-Semitism, ethnocentrism, and fascism.[4]

In 1954, Gordon W. Allport published a synthesis on the "nature of prejudice." Accepting the thesis of an "authoritarian personality," Allport posited that society can eliminate prejudice by creating in people what he calls a "tolerant personality." The tolerant personality—in part the reverse of the authoritarian personality—is open, intelligent, self-controlled, reflective, relativistic, artistic, and devoid of "infantile, repressed, defensive, aggressive, projective portions of unconscious mental life." Allport offered a plan by which to create a polity of tolerant personalities: educate the young, paying attention to the "meaning of race" and cultural relativism; counter the folkways created by Jim Crow laws through contact and acquaintance programs; create mass media "pro-tolerance propaganda" campaigns; and provide individual therapy for the truly hard cases. An assumption that laws form attitudes and control actions buttressed Allport's modest proposal. He contended that because "we can be entirely sure that discriminative laws *increase* prejudice; . . . why, then, should not legislation of the reverse order *diminish* prejudice."[5]

The psychologist Kenneth B. Clark studied the effect that prejudice and a white supremacist society had on African American children. His doll studies formed an important element of the NAACP Legal Defense and Education Fund's complaint in the *Brown* v. *Board of Education* cases. Clark used white and black dolls to demonstrate that segregated education, equal or not, negatively affected African American children. When asked to give Clark the "doll you like best" or the "nice" doll, the black children regularly pointed to the white doll. When requested to identify the doll "that looks bad," they picked the black doll. The majority of African American children tested, whether in Philadelphia or Boston or Arkansas, indicated "an unmistakable preference for the white doll and a rejection of the black doll." The sense of inferiority evinced by the children, Clark and the LDF lawyers insisted, represented a badge of slavery, the stigma of segregation.[6]

The new psychological theories converged with new opinions about race, culture, and biology. The new principle found its clearest enunciation in the United Nations' statement on the issue. The United Nations Educational, Scientific, and Cultural Organization (UNESCO) asserted that "the myth of race" had created human and social damage, taking "a heavy toll in human lives and caus[ing] untold suffering." The UNESCO *Statement on Race* argued that "for all practical social purposes race is not so much a biological phenomenon as a social myth."[7]

The tolerance taught by "cultural relativism" provided intellectual foundation for civil rights developments in the 1950s. It did not, however, stay in the ivory towers of academia. In 1956, the National Opinion Research Center polled the white public on attitudes about African Americans. A similar poll had been made in 1942, and a comparison of the two reveals a growing tolerance of diversity. The results, cited by the Commission on Race and Housing (CRH), showed an interesting development in white opinion of African Americans. Pollsters asked whites, "Do you think Negroes are as intelligent as white people?" Eighty percent of whites polled in the North in 1956 believed blacks to be as intelligent as whites. Only half of those polled in 1942 had believed the same. Among southerners asked the same question, 60 percent answered in the affirmative in 1956. Barely 20 percent had done so fourteen years earlier. Whites were also asked if "it would make any difference" to them if an African American moved next door. In 1942, only 42 percent of northerners said that it would not, but by 1956 that group had grown to 58 percent. Even southerners seemed less concerned about the race of their neighbors: 38 percent answered the question in the negative in 1956, up from 12 percent in 1942.[8]

The Cold War and America's new international status lent urgency to the search for improved race relations. The country was locked in competition with the Soviet Union for influence over the nations forged out of the demise of colonial rule. As the new nations sent delegations to the United States, institutional racism became a greater burden on relations. Many so-called dark-skinned diplomats, representatives from sub-Saharan African and South Asian nations, experienced American racism firsthand as they traveled through the South or even in the corridor between New York City and Washington, D.C. The segregation of foreign emissaries in certain facilities or restaurants threatened to cause an international incident. Vice President Richard Nixon made the point explicitly in an article for *Jet Magazine*. "A vital factor in the conflict between international communism and the forces of democracy in Asia," Nixon contended, "is the struggle of the minds of men. . . . To practice tolerance and respect for human rights each day is not only morally right, but it [also] takes away from the Communists a weapon that they have been using so effectively against us." Housing advocates echoed the view, contending that "in the global struggle between the forces of democracy and those of tyranny, the world's eyes rest on the United States."[9]

Concern over the nation's image abroad and the likelihood that the Soviets would use incidents for propaganda heightened awareness of and opposition to mob violence over housing. Reaction to the riot in Cicero in 1951 offers evidence of this apprehension. The NAACP's Walter White called the riot a "most valuable assist to *Pravda* because the news won't have to be distorted." One might expect that White would hold that view, but seemingly more objective swayers of public opinion added their voices. Popular radio personality and commentator Walter Winchell chimed, "the bigoted idiots [of Cicero] . . . did as much for Stalin as though they had enlisted in the Red Army." New York Governor Thomas E. Dewey had firsthand knowledge of how the rest of the world saw the riot. While on a mission to Singapore, Dewey observed that the riot had been front-page news in the Asian city-state. Reports even included photographs. The violence in Trumbull Park Homes in 1953 and 1954 provided the Soviets with a similar opportunity. A black soldier stationed in Korea reported to Senator Paul Douglas that stories of the battle for Trumbull Park held "top billing on the Communist Hit Parade."[10]

The Cold War also colored the response that opponents of integration had to racial conflict. Segregationists accused civil rights activists of being communists. They alleged that the groups were under the control of Soviet operatives who conspired against the United States and who purposely fomented violence against minority groups to bring down the undemocratic, capitalist regime. The president of the South Deering Improvement Association, the group leading the opposition to integration of Trumbull Park, informed the *Daily Calumet* that communists were responsible for the black presence in the project. Insisting that he was not "anti-Negro," he declared, "I feel sorry for the Negroes here. They are being used as fools by the Communists and by the Human Relations Commission."[11]

Less openly ideological policymakers used the threat of communism as a ploy to win votes for housing legislation in Congress. During hearings regarding the 1949 Housing Act, occurring even as Mao Zedong was taking over China, HHFA Administrator Raymond Foley testified, "this legislation would provide a most effective bulwark against the inroads of socialism or communism, . . . [by eliminating] the very conditions under which socialistic or communistic systems of government may falsely appear to be acceptable." During Senate debates, Louisiana Senator Allen Ellender insisted that passage of the Housing Act was "the most realistic way to defeat Communism, Fascism, and in fact any other 'ism.'" In his capacity as the president of the National Conference of Mayors, Mayor Cooper Green of Birmingham, no friend to integration, told the Banking and Currency Committee, "from the slum areas of the cities we know crime, communism and disease thrive and prosper."[12]

Radicals did engage in housing protests, but their motives were not always clear. Their allegiances, while arguably outside the American consensus politics, did not necessarily make them communists. A bombing in Louisville offers the likeliest example of an incident that involved communists, or at least communist-sympathizers, fomenting racial tension. In 1954, Anne and Carl Braden purchased a house in Shively, an all-white suburb of Louisville and then transferred the deed to Andrew

Wade, a black businessman. Shortly after Wade moved into the house, trouble began. The Klan burned a cross on the lawn. Later, an unidentified group bombed the house. Many residents of Louisville believed that the Bradens and Wade had bombed the house themselves and then blamed it on white supremacists. The Bradens, according to Aldon Morris, were "radical newspaper people." Carl Braden, when not working for the *Courier-Journal,* was editor of the *Southern Patriot,* a labor and civil rights newspaper. Anne Braden had been an early member of the Southern Conference for Human Welfare and eventually became a field secretary of the allegedly communist Southern Conference Educational Fund. The three had been members of the Progressive Party in the 1940s, but Carl Braden swore that he did not know Wade at that time. Although many elements of the story seemed suspicious, prosecutors failed to produce any direct evidence of a communist plot. A Louisville grand jury investigation of the bombing likewise turned up nothing. Despite that, the grand jury indicted Carl and Anne Braden and four others for sedition. Vernon Bown, a white man who had lived with Wade, was indicted for the bombing. Wade himself was not indicted but received a patronizing lecture from the court about not trusting communists.[13]

Communist conspiracies rarely lay behind the housing conflict, but the rhetoric of anticommunism regularly, and at times ridiculously, surfaced during the debates. During the demonstrations at Trumbull Park Homes, for example, one white woman recounted a confrontation that she had with Donald Howard. When Howard saw the neighborhood women demonstrating, he called out to them, "Well, how does it feel being a Red?" "We're not the Reds," the women retorted, "you're the Red for moving into our neighborhood." In the words of Jackie Robinson, blacks "were stirred up long before there was a Communist Party, and they will stay stirred up long after the party has disappeared—unless Jim Crow has disappeared by then as well."[14]

The budding civil rights movement blossomed in the post-Holocaust, Cold War environment. Universities and civil rights organizations generated numerous studies on race relations, providing the data with which to influence lawmakers, and the social scientists themselves became more directly involved in the movement. Gordon Allport, for instance, sat on the CRH board. Furthermore, starting in the late 1940s, southern church leaders began coordinating grassroots efforts to challenge the status quo, such as the 1949 Baton Rouge bus boycott. As Aldon Morris has demonstrated, movement leaders developed a highly organized educational program at the Highlander Folk School in Tennessee through which to teach the tactics and strategies of civil rights activism. Very little was left to chance. Even the most famous incident in the early years of the movement was orchestrated. Rosa Parks may well have been tired when she sat down in the white section of a Montgomery bus, but she was also learned in the methods of resistance and civil disobedience. And perhaps most important, the civil rights movement found a charismatic leader and a single tactic around which to coalesce. Martin Luther King Jr. created a goal on which the movement could focus, and his philosophy of nonviolent direct action enabled the civil rights activists to obtain and keep the moral high ground. In the face of police beatings that outraged northern moderates and embarrassed the nation overseas, the passivity of activists, particularly of the children, won increasing support for the movement.[15]

Over the years, other organizations joined the NAACP in the fight against residential segregation. The groups represented labor and religious interests as well as the civil rights establishment. They included the American Civil Liberties Union; the Anti-Defamation League of B'nai B'rith; CORE; NAIRO; the National Urban League; the Brotherhood of Sleeping-Car Porters; the United Auto Workers (UAW); and a Philadelphia-based Quaker philanthropic organization, the American Friends Service Committee (AFSC). By 1950, it had become obvious that the open-housing movement needed greater coordination. The advocacy groups therefore formed a directing body: the National Committee Against Discrimination in Housing. The NCDH leadership included the foremost experts on and advocates of better housing: Robert Weaver and Charles Abrams; the UAW's Walter Reuther; and Roy Wilkins, Loren Miller, and Madison Jones of the NAACP.[16]

The NCDH member groups employed several tactics to eliminate discrimination in housing. The various chapters of the National Urban League worked in the local community, establishing employment networks and working with city planners to design low-income housing projects. The UAW coordinated the construction of integrated subdivisions for union members. CORE, another NCDH affiliate, specialized in grassroots, nonviolent demonstrations. The Los Angeles chapter, for example, protested when a builder in Gardena, a local suburb, refused to sell a home to a black high school teacher. CORE also led demonstrations in Grand Rapids and Ann Arbor, Michigan; New York City; and throughout the northeast. CORE's Brooklyn branch led tests of whether apartment houses in the borough discriminated against African Americans. It sent whites and blacks to inquire about the same advertised apartment to see if landlords gave different responses to one or the other group. Testing became a common technique for rooting out discrimination by the late 1960s. CORE branches also started a program called "Operation Windowshop." It involved taking middle-class African Americans on tours through suburban developments to look at model homes. The AFSC, led by William Moyer, a white housing expert in Chicago, worked quietly on a small scale to educate whites and erase their fears of integration. The AFSC also challenged government officials to uphold the law, protect African American home owners, and bring vandals to justice.[17]

A principal activity of all NCDH groups was lobbying public officials. In answer to the unsatisfactory response of the Cook County grand jury after the riot in Cicero in 1951, for example, the NCDH undertook a letter-writing campaign to President Truman and to Attorney General J. Howard McGrath requesting federal action against the rioters and local officials. Robert Weaver also requested that they write demanding that government undertake "an immediate attack on the underlying causes of the Cicero riots—[the] untenable housing conditions for minorities in the entire Chicago area." The greater Chicago area, he alleged, "has perhaps the strictest segregation in the country and the forces which contribute towards this pattern are still on the march." Finally, Weaver asked them to write to Administrator Foley at HHFA to urge the government to develop programs to end racial discrimination and to make more public housing available. The HHFA Race Relations Office files contain numerous letters from persons lobbying the government on behalf of NCDH member groups. "It is our belief," August Meier wrote on behalf of the Newark NAACP, for example, "that there were many causes for these incidents. . . . Prejudice and the instigation of professional hate-mongers played their part," he observed, "but of equal importance was the existence of untenable housing conditions for minorities in the entire Chicago area." Letters from members of the Women's International League for Peace and Freedom beseeched Foley "to work immediately to expand throughout the country as well as Greater Chicago the supply of standard housing." The lobbying may have had some effect. In mid-October, Foley met with Chicago officials to compel the city to work with the HHFA to correct the housing problem. And on another front, shortly after the letter campaign began, Attorney General McGrath established the federal grand jury that handed down the indictments of Cicero police chief Ervin Konovsky and six others for conspiracy to prevent Harvey E. Clark from inhabiting the apartment.[18]

Education and propaganda formed another large part of the NCDH open-housing strategy. The committee sponsored research and led educational workshops. NCDH leaders believed that changing white opinion as to integration's effect on property values or neighborhood character was a priority. Employing the methods of advocacy journalism, the committee urged publishers of popular periodicals, such as *Redbook*, *McCall's*, and *House and Home*, to place favorable stories of cooperation or defiance in their magazines. It also published a bimonthly newspaper, *Trends in Housing*. The NCDH announced that *Trends* would "give factual, objective accounts of events, . . . emphasizing information that individuals and organizations can use in their own communities" to combat discrimination in housing. The first issue attacked the federal government's "segregation policies" for delaying the correction of minority housing problems, but more commonly *Trends* accentuated the positive, offering anecdotal evidence of races cohabitating harmoniously.[19]

Exemplifying its objective to relate positive stories of organizations working to overcome prejudice, a story in the October 1956 issue of *Trends in Housing* proclaimed, "Open Occupancy Grows in Private Housing." The article recounted how the UAW built Sunnyhills, an integrated subdivision in Milpitas, California. When the Ford Motor Company moved part of its production to the Santa Clara Valley, the local union's housing committee surveyed the housing market and found inflated costs for white housing and no houses for the union's black members. The union decided to construct its own housing. The housing committee talked to builders and received several offers. *Trends* noted, however, that initially no developer was willing to construct integrated housing. When one builder finally agreed to open occupancy, he could not obtain land. When another contractor got the land, he could not get financing. When union leaders convinced the Metropolitan Life Insurance Company to agree to take the mortgages, the local government raised the costs of water and sewage facilities. Another developer in the area, meanwhile, organized protests and filed for an injunction to prevent the county from approving the UAW's plans. Yet, the union's housing committee persevered. It found a new firm willing to develop the project. To eliminate opposition, the UAW bought the adjoining subdivision. Sunnyhills opened in the winter of 1956. Blacks comprised about 10 percent of the subdivision's residents and were spread throughout the development. The initial accounts reported no racial hostility.[20]

The NCDH also cooperated with researchers studying housing discrimination. To ensure the appearance of independence of the studies, many of the investigations were funded through CRH by an organization called the Fund for the Republic. Such longtime proponents of minority housing and racial tolerance as Robert Taylor, Charles Johnson, and Gordon Allport sat on the commission. Perhaps protesting too much, CRH declared its autonomy in its publications. "The Commission," reads the foreword of Luigi M. Laurenti's *Property Values and Race*, "is an independent, private citizens' group, not part of any other organization." In case the reader missed the point, in listing CRH members, the book adds that the members of CRH served "in their individual capacities and not as representing any organization or group." Although that was true as regards the legal establishment of CRH, the overlapping of personnel exposes its ties to the NCDH and other civil rights groups. Robert Weaver acted as an adviser. Madison Jones remained in regular contact with CRH's research director, Davis McEntire. Noting these connections is not meant to impugn the commission's motives, but it points to the propagandist nature of many of the commission's studies. Highly selective in the use of data, NCDH- and CRH-sponsored studies often amounted to advocacy.[21]

The NAACP represented the most active of the NCDH affiliates and housing became its focus. In 1953, the NAACP composed a new statement on housing. "Residential segregation," the association resolved, "is the crux of the whole question of segregation. . . . [T]he eradication of any type of segregated housing that has any form of public financial support must be our first goal." After the victory in the *Brown* cases, Robert Weaver called housing the nation's "number one civil rights problem" and observed: "Since the Supreme Court decisions outlawing segregation in the schools, certain groups, fearful that the next step [would] be to end segregation in housing, [had] intensified their campaign for racially defined neighborhoods." Weaver worried that if they succeeded in "establishing this 'shiny new ghetto' pattern throughout the country," they would nullify the significance of the *Brown* ruling.[22]

Buoyed by the new environment for reform, the NAACP's Legal Defense and

Education Fund led a court challenge against segregated public housing. In 1942, the San Francisco Housing Authority (SFHA) had adopted a "neighborhood pattern policy." It resolved that when allocating public housing, it would "maintain and preserve the same racial composition which exists in the neighborhood where a project is located." In 1950, the SFHA revised its procedure regarding what it called the "commingling of races." The new policy obligated the SFHA to "avoid or refrain from any policy or practice which result[ed] . . . in discrimination or any form of segregation by reason of race." Under the new resolution, the SFHA would allocate housing based on "proportionate need." The order applied only to new housing, that is, projects built after July 1949.[23]

In spite of the resolution, San Francisco's public housing projects remained segregated in 1952. No African Americans resided in the new North Beach Place project; nor did any occupy five other city facilities. Instead, 136 black families occupied the one remaining complex, Westside Courts Apartments. The only nonblack occupant of that project was a Chinese man named Ping Yuen. Since no vacancies existed in Westside Courts, Mattie Banks and James Charley Jr. applied for an apartment in North Beach Place. Although there were vacancies, Banks and Charley were rejected. The SFHA claimed that it had to hold the openings to meet the "proportionate need" of other races. It added that pursuant to the "neighborhood pattern policy," it could not admit African Americans. Banks and Charley sued SFHA with the help of Loren Miller and the LDF.[24]

Banks v. *Housing Authority of San Francisco* reached the California Court of Appeals in 1953. The NAACP demanded that the SFHA apply the same standards in determining eligibility to all applicants for public housing, disregarding race, color, or religion. It contended that anything less contradicted the equal protection clause of the Fourteenth Amendment. The SFHA countered that its housing policy met the "separate but equal" requirements of judicial precedent. It added that segregation per se was not illegal in California or in San Francisco. The court ruled, however, that the Supreme Court in recent decisions had weakened the precedent set in *Plessy* v. *Ferguson* (1896), demanding of it stricter scrutiny. It further ruled, citing *Buchanan* v. *Warley* (1917) and *Shelley* v. *Kraemer* (1948), that the Supreme Court had made clear its position against residential segregation. Upon losing the case, the SFHA appealed to the California Supreme Court. When that body refused the petition, the SFHA pursued the question to the U.S. Supreme Court. The Warren Court also denied the SFHA a writ of certiorari, thereby upholding the lower court's ruling.[25]

The *Banks* case carried greater significance than just getting an apartment for Banks and Charley. The NAACP had entered as a copetitioner, representing all African Americans. The SFHA argued that the NAACP had no legal standing as a petitioner because the organization was not eligible for public housing. The court overruled the motion. It granted the case standing as a class action suit, thereby relieving the NAACP of having to fight the case repeatedly in different jurisdictions.

When the Supreme Court upheld the decision, it effectively set a precedent banning discrimination in public housing nationwide.[26]

The importance of the Court's decision quickly became apparent. Barely a week after the judgment, as the Senate debated a new omnibus housing bill, Senator Burnet Rhett Maybank of South Carolina declared, "I regret that [the ruling] makes it impossible for me, believing in local government, to support any public housing." The senator had been instrumental in the passage of the 1949 Housing Act in his role as chairman of the Senate Committee on Banking and Currency. He accused the Court of reversing an "acceptable and working pattern." He announced that he would oppose any public housing program and would "abandon a fight to which [his] energies and devotion [had] been dedicated for a quarter of a century." He then offered an amendment deleting the bill's public housing provision and blocking any housing construction starts. The Senate defeated the amendment on a voice vote.[27]

New conditions caused the NAACP to develop new tactics in its fight against residential segregation. It created branch housing advisory committees that focused on attacking discrimination on the grassroots level. Centered in New York City and headed by Madison S. Jones, a former race relations officer for the FHA, the national housing committee held workshops and educational programs for NAACP branches across the country. It also gathered significant housing data and acted as a clearinghouse for information on housing issues. The branch housing advisory committees worked in concert with local organizations, such as local Urban League affiliates and the various municipal committees on intergroup relations. They studied local population, home ownership and occupancy rates, land availability, and price and market statistics. They lobbied legislators to enact anti-discrimination laws, met with local mortgage lenders and real estate boards to inform them about the issue of housing discrimination, and arranged public speaking engagements and forums for housing advocates.[28]

The most radical development in the NAACP's tactics occurred when, as part of their mandate, the housing committees became quasi-realtors. According to the "Manual for Branches," each committee was to select one member to find private rentals and private homes for purchase available to African Americans and "outside of the traditionally Negro area." That person would contact renters or realtors to investigate the details concerning price and type of accommodation and then pass that information on to members seeking housing. The departments recorded any transactions that occurred—paying particular attention to "any statement made in denying housing because of race and color." The annual data would be organized to inform and lobby local officials about the housing conditions of blacks and other minorities. Jones and his staff, for example, scanned newspapers for rental and purchase advertisements and received numerous letters from landlords advertising space for rent. They also received hundreds (perhaps thousands) of requests for aid in finding suitable housing from members and African Americans in general.[29]

The NAACP branch files reveal much about the discrimination that African

Americans faced in their search for housing. They teem with stories like the one that follows. As the evidence in the last chapter demonstrates, whites often used violence and intimidation to keep blacks out of white neighborhoods, but this story represents the more common type of discrimination that blacks met. The poignancy of Esther Barr's predicament, moreover, offers insight into the injustices even the seemingly most placid of African Americans experienced in getting housing.[30]

Esther Barr worked as a supervisor in charge of casework in the Social Service Department of Montefiore Hospital's Westchester Division in Bedford Hills, New York. She lived in the hospital's staff quarters. When the department was closed in 1956, Barr lost both her job and her home. She quickly found other employment at the New York Tuberculosis and Health Association and started to look for accommodations in New York City. She reportedly sought a three-room apartment located in a less congested area of the city for which she would pay no more than $110 per month. She soon learned the extravagance of her wishes. In exasperation, Barr wrote to Thurgood Marshall to relate her story. She told Marshall that such apartments did exist, but "in the policy of those who control rentals hangs a 'White's Only' sign that is adhered to as rigidly as if it were openly [and] publicly displayed."[31]

Barr blamed herself for part of her trouble in finding suitable housing. "My difficulty," she told Marshall in her eloquent letter, "can probably be attributed partly to some of my own limitations." From her earlier visits to the city, she knew only Manhattan's business and theater districts; she felt handicapped by her "lack of knowledge as to which districts (except Harlem) . . . permit residence to Negroes." "The degree of acceptance one achieved" at Montefiore Hospital, she insisted, "was not related to his nationality, race, etc." That, coupled with her small-town, Midwestern background, caused Barr to "lose sight of . . . the restrictions still being imposed in most . . . communities." She understood, however, that racial discrimination caused most of her problem. "Many suitable apartments," she explained to Marshall, were "available up to the point that the agent learned that [she] was a Negro."[32]

Barr began her search by telephoning rental agencies that advertised apartments. She looked in the Jackson Heights, Kew Gardens, Elmhurst, and Astoria sections in Queens. She talked with realtors in the Bronx and Manhattan who listed "interracial" apartments. As the number of persons rejecting her request increased, she decided to visit agencies in person. She hoped that by seeing her and getting to know her, attitudes toward accepting her as a tenant might be changed. One agent sympathized with Barr's plight, but she had only one building that accepted minorities. She told Barr that it was accepting Spanish-speaking tenants and had in the past accepted two Chinese and one Japanese couple. But, she declared, the residents would not accept African Americans as tenants. The agent apparently was relieved that Barr did not pursue the apartment. Barr confessed that she "really did not wish to create a problem."[33]

Having failed to find an apartment on her own, Barr sought help from African

American support groups. She contacted ministers of several large churches for aid. She wrote to the Urban League, the State Committee on Civil Rights, and the State Committee Against Discrimination. She advertised in the newspaper for a place and received an offer to sublet an apartment. When she went to transfer the lease, the agent told her that she would have to fill out an application if she wanted the apartment. He had to check her references and credit standing. Three days later she was denied the apartment. Barr disclosed to Marshall that she "verified the fact that neither [her] credit nor personal references were checked."[34]

This latest defeat was what prompted Barr to write to Marshall. In addition to requesting his aid in finding her a home, she also wanted to inform the NAACP of her trouble and to express concern over the discrimination that blacks routinely faced. Barr told Marshall that as a social worker, she insisted on finding the "real worth of people." She refused to have her confidence in people shaken and felt compelled to continue her efforts "in spite of personal sacrifices in time, energy, and money." "I am unwilling to believe," she insisted, "that the majority of tenants in these large sections of New York would deny other persons residence on the single factor of their racial origin." She blamed rental agents for relying on what she considered to be outdated beliefs of whether white tenants would accept black neighbors. She acknowledged, however, that it was "true that on occasions when Negroes and other minorities do move in some tenants move out . . . and that this eventually [might] result in a devaluation of property and finally of the neighborhood." Barr understood the importance of economics, but she held out hope that if groups could have more interaction, then fear and negative stereotypes would lessen.[35]

Marshall sent Barr's letter to Madison Jones so that the housing director could take action. Jones tried to notify Barr that he had taken up her case. When he could not locate her, he contacted the Tuberculosis and Health Association. Barr's employer informed Jones that she had left the city. Exhausted and frustrated, she had put her belongings in storage and gone home to Indiana to visit her family and to rest and recuperate. Her employer was keeping the job open until she returned. It is not known whether she did return. That is where the story ends.[36]

Despite its ambiguity, Barr's story still offers several lessons about the condition of housing for African Americans in the mid-1950s. It demonstrates how even the mildest characters experienced tremendous difficulty in finding a proper place to live. On a more positive note, the tale shows the NAACP housing department's effort in serving its constituents. The number of letters requesting the department's aid demonstrate that it was taking on new responsibilities in the community, adding to its litigation a grassroots constituency service. And it reveals how futile many of the NAACP housing department's efforts ended up being in the absence of a suitable legal remedy against instances of discrimination.

Along with its workshops and constituency service, the NAACP also learned that film offered an innovative and compelling way of getting the message against discrimination to the public. An NAACP assault on stereotypical screen images caused Hollywood to present more diverse and sympathetic depictions of African Americans during the late 1940s and early 1950s. The association also engaged in film production.[37]

Dynamic Films produced several docudramas relating to housing issues for the NAACP. Nathan Zucker, a filmmaker and writer, formed the company in 1948 to make movies on provocative themes and with a social conscience. "Our object," Zucker noted in the company's promotional literature, "is not a blatant propaganda piece haranguing one extreme point of view." He wanted to portray people "as they [really] are, beset by conflicts that affect their way of thinking and acting, motivated for good or bad by pressures under which we all live, and no one either *all* right or *all* wrong." He insisted, however, that the films would "still assume a 'clear position.'"[38]

In 1958, Dynamic Films produced a fictional account of the tension set off when a black family comes to look at a home for sale in an all-white neighborhood. It focuses not on the African Americans, but on the issue from the white home owners' point of view. The man selling his home, Ira Cantey, in many ways recalls Walter Gnesdiloff, the man who sold his home to Willie Mays. He wants to sell his home and has no particular personal prejudice against blacks, but he also feels loyalty to his neighbors and does not want to upset them.[39]

All the Way Home includes the essential elements of housing conflict. The film opens with a black couple stopping at Cantey's home when they see the "For Sale" sign. A woman who spies them while hanging out her laundry is disturbed by what she sees. She makes a telephone call. "They're here right now," she tells the other end of the line, "Bold as Brass!" Later, a neighbor approaches Cantey while he does lawn work. "Nobody is going to get away with the stuff you're trying to hand out," he tells Cantey. "Nobody's threatening you," he promises, "we just want to know what you think you're doing to us?" A realtor, not too subtly named Moats, suggests that Cantey take the sign down. "That sign is a terrible thing," Moats declares, "sort of an open invitation." A local mechanic notes his opposition when Mrs. Cantey takes her car in for work. "Why do they go where they're not wanted?" he asks. Later, Ira Cantey overhears two men talking about the situation. "As I see it, school's one thing," the one man tells the other. "But your home. Your home's your private right!" Terrorism and intimidation also occur. The Canteys receive threatening phone calls. A vandal sprays black paint all over the front lawn, covering the Cantey's young daughter with it as she plays. After the violence occurs, cooler heads prevail. The neighbors organize a meeting with Cantey to discuss the situation. Not everyone is hostile. Few seem genuinely happy about the prospect of having a black neighbor, but they realize that African Americans need homes. The Cantey's pastor makes the argument against discrimination, but knowing his congregation, he does not simply follow the moral line. When asked about the church's position on integration, the best he can come up with is, "The Church sees it as a challenge." The meeting also discusses legal restrictions on discrimination, tolerance, and prejudice.

"Can't force tolerance by law," an unidentified neighbor proclaims. "This is not about tolerance," the minister responds, "but about practice. You can, by law, prevent men from committing crimes against others. . . . This is what law is for." The meeting and the film end with no clear resolution. Cantey walks home, mulling over what the neighbors have said.[40]

A voice-over narration ties the film together and provides perspective. It enables the characters to remain conflicted and saves them from having to make unnatural speeches, following Zucker's intent to show people "as they are." The narration's point of view, however, is clear and decidedly integrationist. "Even through the outbursts, the rancid questions, the outright lies," the narration asserts, "the truth has been there for us to see[:] wherever [integration] has been given an honest chance it works." People "live and grow and play and work side by side with people of other races," it continues, "and together a way of life emerges that is good for everybody." Placing the responsibility for improving housing conditions for African Americans on the shoulders of white home owners, the narration concludes that "the decision is Cantey's and no one can force him to do the right thing."[41]

The filmmakers recognized the potential for violence to occur in these situations. An early treatment of the film was called "The Rock," referring to a rock thrown through Cantey's window to intimidate him. But the producers changed the story. "Everyone is sure of one thing," the new narration asserts, "there will be no violence. No murder, no burning, no rocks thrown through windows here."[42]

The scarcity of real violence in the movie demonstrates how the filmmakers accepted the counsel of housing advocates. Madison Jones made several suggestions to the filmmakers. Early in the preproduction stage, he advised that if they intended to show blacks and whites living together, then they had to emphasize this to be "an exception to the established rule of segregation." The producers chose not to offer any scenes of integrated living. Instead, they included a montage of well-groomed African Americans at church and at work. Jones also insisted that "an extensive treatment of negative industry attitude, brokers, bankers, builders, should be made." Dynamic Films complied, at least partly. Moats is the villain of the film. A banker named Yates, however, deems the realtor's views to be extreme. In one scene, Yates argues with Moats, contending that integration need not lead to reduced property values.[43]

Upon its completion, Madison Jones reviewed *All the Way Home*. The film, he remarked, "provides a medium which will enable people to make a realistic appraisal of themselves, their friends, neighbors and colleagues relative to their attitude concerning the free housing market." He commended the producers for portraying "the usual trend of thought which mushrooms through a community when the question of open occupancy housing comes up." The film, he concluded, "points out the realities when such a solution comes from the people in the community."[44]

Another Dynamic Films production dramatized real events. *Crisis in Levittown, Pa.*, which premiered at Philadelphia City Hall in April 1958, recounts the violence that rocked the suburban community in Bucks County, Pennsylvania. Levitt and Sons had revolutionized construction and tract design, becoming perhaps the world's largest builders of private homes. In the 1920s, Abraham Levitt, the patriarch, had moved his family from the Bedford-Stuyvesant section of Brooklyn when an African American attorney bought a home in the neighborhood. As late as 1956, William Levitt, the son who took over the business, unapologetically continued a policy of racial segregation. He claimed that as a Jew he had "no room in [his] mind or heart for racial prejudice." He added, however, that he had come to know that if he sold to black families, "then 90 or 95 percent of [his] white customers [would] not buy into the community." Levitt concluded: "We can solve a housing problem, or we can try to solve a racial problem, but we cannot combine the two."[45]

In August 1957, William Myers and his family moved into a three-bedroom, ranch-style bungalow in Levittown, Pennsylvania. A veteran of the Army Quartermaster Corps during World War II, Myers worked at a refrigeration plant in Trenton, New Jersey, while pursuing a degree in electrical engineering. Bill Myers and his wife, Daisy, were active in the local Democratic Party and the League of Women Voters. They had lived with their two toddlers in a small, two-bedroom home in an adjacent Bucks County community. They paid $12,150 for the house in Levittown, which the white owner had been trying to sell for more than two years. They moved because they wanted more living space. On the night of the move, a crowd of white neighbors gathered to taunt and terrorize the family. Late on Saturday evening, the crowd grew increasingly violent, throwing stones and smashing windows. Bucks County police arrived to try to quell the violence. They blocked off access routes to the neighborhood, but the scene overwhelmed the local police, and Pennsylvania state troopers had to intervene.[46]

For more than a week, whites protested outside the Myers's home. At times the mobs numbered as many as 400 persons. Unlike their counterparts in many of the instances of mob violence elsewhere, the police in this situation made concerted efforts to disperse the crowd. On three different nights, police pressed into the mob wielding riot clubs and arresting the terrorists. During the fifth night of protest, the crowd hailed the police with stones. The whites formed the Levittown Betterment Committee to orchestrate demonstrations. They burned a cross on the Myers's lawn. They intimidated neighbors whom they believed had acted "openly friendly" to the newcomers, in one instance smearing "KKK" in eighteen-inch-high red letters on a white neighbor's house. They tried to buy Myers out, offering him $15,000 to sell the house. The tensions at Levittown continued into the autumn of 1957, finally dying out after the county court imposed a temporary injunction against the rioters. Seven of the white protesters were indicted in November and later convicted of disturbing the peace and other minor crimes.[47]

Racial violence raged in the older neighborhoods of Chicago, Miami, Los Angeles, Atlanta, Birmingham, and many other cities in the United States during the "decade of miracles." It also exploded in new communities. Levittown has come to epitomize the suburb. It should surprise no one that racial terrorism also occurred in the "ticky-tacky" developments of Levitt and Sons. Even when violence did not occur, blacks like Esther Barr commonly faced prejudice and discrimination when trying to locate suitable housing.

Race relations also went through a significant positive transformation during the 1950s. Issues far beyond the shores of North America and as close as the local schoolyard coalesced to begin to change the way white Americans viewed their black neighbors or their potential neighbors. The civil rights movement gained force, particularly after the *Brown* decision. The philosophy of nonviolence gave the civil rights activists an advantage in the struggle. The rioting and bombing outraged and embarrassed Americans of all colors. Racial incidents threatened American prestige worldwide, and the Soviets, if not actually instigating tensions, took advantage of violent events. White supremacists and segregationists were put on the defensive.

Slowly, the rhetoric of anti-discrimination started to be heard in housing debates. As the next chapter shows, through the concerted efforts of the NCDH and its constituents, lawmakers on the state and local level began to reverse generations of discriminatory policy. The complexity of national politics caused the federal government to move more hesitantly to end discrimination. But even in Washington, D.C., the persistence of open-housing activists and the reevaluation of constitutional principles would pay dividends eventually.

9

"A NEW EPOCH"

The Federal Government has become the single most important factor in the real estate market. . . . But the housing programs and policies of the Federal Government have actually intensified the trend toward further racial residential segregation.[1]

Race relations and civil rights underwent an accelerated transformation during the 1950s, and the advance would continue and grow even stronger during the Kennedy years. White supremacy and racial discrimination were fought on all fronts. The Supreme Court had ruled that governments, "with all deliberate speed," must desegregate public schools. African Americans in the South had refused to ride in the back of buses. They demonstrated that they would rather walk miles to work than continue to be treated as second-class citizens. In 1960, in Greensboro, North Carolina, student activists protested segregated lunch counters. Soon the challenge to white prejudice was taken to hotels, amusement parks, and public recreational facilities.

The civil rights movement found a leader during these years. Many blacks had worked for decades to try to improve the lot of their people. The lawyers of the Legal Defense and Education Fund, such as Charles Houston, Thurgood Marshall, and Loren Miller, had carried on the battle in the nation's courtrooms since the Great War. NAACP leaders James Weldon Johnson, Walter White, and Roy Wilkins had fought segregation and violence for two generations. A. Philip Randolph had campaigned on behalf of black laborers since the 1920s. Mary McLeod Bethune, Robert Weaver, Frank Horne, and others worked within government to bring a black voice to the halls of power. And many others had carried the torch over the years. But in Martin Luther King Jr. blacks found a focus, a single force, who had the charisma, the energy, the determination, and the tactics to carry the movement to a new level.[2]

To sustain the movement, activists depended on the support of whites. They therefore concentrated their assault on the clear constitutional injustices of restricted voting rights and unequal public education. They played on the sympathy of northerners. King's militant, nonviolent, direct action placed blacks on the moral high ground to face the dogs and firehoses of white supremacists. When public officials such as Bull Connor in Birmingham, Jim Clark in Selma, George Wallace in Tuscaloosa, Orval Faubus in Little Rock, or Ross Barnett in Oxford, chose to use force to break up nonviolent demonstrations, the images of white police beating black children created moral outrage in the hearts of many northern whites.[3]

By focusing on the state-sanctioned segregation of the South, the civil rights movement enjoyed considerable support in the rest of the nation. This strategy, however, forced most civil rights leaders to overlook the de facto segregation of the urban North and West. The right to housing, moreover, was a much more complicated issue than voting rights or access to public education. The question of whether government could regulate an individual home owner's property rights, whether it could force him to sell his home to someone to whom he did not wish to sell, was constitutionally less clear than whether the government had the authority, let alone the obligation, to ensure that a tax-paying citizen had the ability to cast a vote. Housing rights tended therefore to stand on the periphery, outside the focus of the civil rights movement during what have come to be known as "the King Years, 1954–1963."

While the South's massive resistance to the civil rights movement drew the nation's attention, open housing quietly made significant gains. The persistence of activists such as Weaver, Horne, Madison Jones, and Charles Abrams started to pay dividends. As the debate focused on segregation in public schools in the early 1950s, governments in the North and West enacted laws prohibiting racial discrimination in public housing. During the decade following the first *Brown* v. *Board of Education* decision in 1954, several cities and states enacted stronger open-housing legislation, passing laws to end discrimination even in private housing and the sale of single-family homes. The federal government, except for the judiciary, moved more hesitantly and more cautiously. Congress refused to address interracial housing, leaving the issue to the agencies of the executive. The Eisenhower administration, meanwhile, saw much peril to the nation's security and no political advantage in taking actions that would destabilize the country by imposing its will on recalcitrant states. At first, it tried to quell tensions in race relations by ignoring them. After the *Brown* ruling, however, the administration slowly abandoned its laissez-faire view of race relations in housing, as it did on civil rights issues generally.

In assessing the *Shelley* v. *Kraemer* decision, back in 1948, Justice Frank Murphy had opined that the ruling would prove to be "epoch marking." In a sense, the judge was correct. The decision marked the beginning of the slow reversal of governmental support for racial segregation. The violence of the late 1940s and 1950s heightened awareness of the housing problem facing African Americans. The lobbying efforts and information gathering of the NAACP and other groups focused attention further. As knowledge of the issue grew, some attitudes began to change. Fair and open housing slowly became part of the rhetoric of reform. By 1960, ending discrimination in housing was a national issue. During the presidential campaign that year, John F. Kennedy promised to take action to end discrimination. In 1962, he finally did. He issued an executive order prohibiting discrimination in federally assisted private housing.

The advocates of open housing did more than try to influence public opinion with reports, studies, and movies. To reform generations of discriminatory housing policy, they focused their activities on government. They hoped that well-placed operatives in the federal housing bureaucracy would move anti-discrimination policies forward on the national level.

The years following 1949 saw the federal government take on an expanded role in housing. The Housing Act of 1949 had asserted the goal of "a decent home . . . for every American family," and it had pledged to assist in slum clearance and construction of low-cost housing. The 1950 law extended and liberalized mortgage loans insured by the Federal Housing Administration and Veterans Administration and gave the VA authority to make direct loans. Federal housing officials, reacting to the increase in racial violence in the country's neighborhoods and the lobbying of activists, grew more responsive to minority housing needs. Raymond Foley and his vigorous race relations staff at the Housing and Home Finance Administration, including Frank Horne and B. T. McGraw, supported minority housing. Foley joined the National Committee Against Discrimination in Housing in blaming the federal government for the persistence of discrimination and housing blight. During hearings in January 1952, he called Washington "the chief force now contributing to the maintenance and extension of Negro ghettos." He entreated Congress to restore 35,000 public housing units cut from housing appropriations. The HHFA also imitated the NCDH in its efforts to reform public opinion. In a speech before the NCDH, Foley proudly noted that his department made a point of airing "detailed 'success stories' of the accomplishments of private enterprise in the production of private housing available to minorities."[4]

Foley's constituent agencies underwent substantial reform during the late Truman years. In February 1950, the FHA took an active step toward eliminating racial categories from its appraisal policy. Reversing more than a decade of discriminatory policies, it insisted that no application for mortgage insurance would be rejected solely on the grounds that the occupant of a dwelling might affect the stability of the neighborhood's housing market. "Homogeneity or heterogeneity of neighborhoods as to race, creed, color or nationality," Foley claimed, "is [no longer] a consideration in establishing eligibility for FHA mortgage insurance." The FHA also made other changes. The bureau hired a minority group housing adviser in its Washington headquarters. It undertook specific housing market studies to gather data related to minority groups. It expanded the race relations staff to number more than thirty researchers, advisers, and service personnel. And it introduced a statistical reporting system to record monthly listings of applications categorized to keep track of minority applicants. The FHA and the VA also stipulated that housing that they repossessed and offered for resale would be available for purchase by any person, regardless of race.[5]

Although many persons within the federal housing apparatus had the will and the energy to make major advances in gaining better housing for African Americans, they remained hamstrung by the inability to win support in Congress for an activist agenda. The FHA could change its policies on paper and could publicly proclaim the change, but it had no power to enforce its will in the face of local opposition. The Committee on Race and Housing complained, as late as 1958, that the FHA "officially encourages open occupancy, . . . but it does not attempt to control the discriminatory practices of private builders or lenders." As late as 1961, the NAACP Housing Department would still report that blacks had been "excluded from 98 percent of all [FHA] homes built since 1946." The lack of a clearcut federal legislative policy was interpreted by lenders, builders, and officials on the state and municipal level as sanctioning segregated housing. Anti-discrimination legislation from Congress remained beyond the reach of housing activists.[6]

By 1952, the Democrats had controlled the White House for twenty years. Republicans argued that the continued expansion of government proposed by the Democratic presidential candidate, Adlai Stevenson, would bankrupt the nation. Some of them also regularly pretended to confuse the name "Adlai" with "Alger," the name of the notorious communist, Alger Hiss. Even more troubling for the Democrats was the fact that foreign affairs, most notably the police action in Korea, dominated the campaign, and Stevenson lacked the martial reputation that preceded the republican candidate, the former supreme commander in the European theater during World War II. The voters, moreover, apparently preferred the "farm boy from Kansas," the self-proclaimed "simple soldier," to the reedy and intellectual Stevenson. In short, the voters liked Ike. Dwight D. Eisenhower captured more than 63 percent of the popular vote and swept forty-one states, including the southern Democratic strongholds of Florida, Virginia, Texas, and Tennessee. The Republicans rode Eisenhower's coattails into control of the House of Representatives and, with Vice President Richard M. Nixon's tie-breaking votes, control of the Senate.[7]

Civil rights did not play a large role in the campaign of 1952. Both candidates talked about equal rights and equal opportunity, but mostly in general terms. "We seek in America a true equality of opportunity for all men," Eisenhower told a crowd in West Virginia. He supported the anti–poll tax constitutional amendment and antilynching legislation, both of which enjoyed broad appeal even in the South, but he opposed legislation founding the Fair Employment Practices Commission, believing that such concerns were better left to the states. Stevenson, however, supported an active role for the federal government in civil rights, including the FEPC.

"The fight for equal rights," he declared at New York state's Democratic Convention, "must go on everyday in our souls and our consciences, in our schools and our churches and our homes, in our factories and our offices as well as our city councils, our state legislatures, *and our national Congress*." But Stevenson insisted on not making appeals to specific interest groups for their votes. "Let us work for results," he declared, "not just empty political advantage." Stevenson had another reason for not pursuing a debate on civil rights: he hoped to achieve a reconciliation with the southern wing of the party. African Americans, however, apparently did hear enough to distinguish between the two candidates. Stevenson received 76 percent of the black vote, almost equaling the tally for Harry Truman in 1948.[8]

President Eisenhower had little interest in and less knowledge of the living conditions of African Americans. According to his biographer, Robert Frederick Burk, Eisenhower confessed to aides that he opposed "social mingling" and the notion "that a Negro should court [his] daughter." But the president did recognize social injustice, and although he refused to impose the federal will on the states, he would take action within the federal government's jurisdiction. He proposed to end segregation of public facilities in the District of Columbia, including the federal government, and to continue the integration of the armed forces. He also appointed the first African American to an executive position on the White House staff. E. Frederick Morrow, a lawyer from Hackensack, New Jersey, had joined the campaign as the "bright young man" who could help the candidate appeal to black voters. After Eisenhower's victory, Morrow became the commonly ostracized and seldom listened to token of his race in the White House. Beyond these steps, according to Stephen E. Ambrose, the president went "to great lengths to divorce himself from the problem of race relations."[9]

Despite Eisenhower's efforts to keep the problem of race relations at arm's length, the issue would not go away. Only five months into his presidency, the *Brown* cases were scheduled for reargument before the Supreme Court. Eisenhower did not know where he stood on the issue of desegregation of schools. When the Court invited the administration to present a brief, the prevailing sentiment among the president's advisers, according to Richard Kluger, was "Jesus, do we really *have* to?" Several of them apparently hoped that they could solve the problem by improving the quality of racially segregated schools. Attorney General Herbert Brownell Jr., however, convinced the president of the importance of filing its position with the court. To give him time to prepare a brief, Brownell asked the Court to postpone the hearing. In September 1953, Chief Justice Fred Vinson died of a heart attack, delaying the hearings further. The delay ironically caused Eisenhower to make what Kluger called his "principal contribution" to civil rights. He selected Earl Warren as the new chief justice. The Warren Court accepted the LDF's argument that separate but equal was inherently unequal.[10]

The transition to an Eisenhower presidency brought new people and a different ideology to public housing. For those who hoped that the administration would advance minority housing, the first eighteen months of Republican governance proved distressing. Unlike public education, housing incorporated a perplexing mix of public and private interests made more complex by the Republican laissez-faire bias. Worse yet, Albert M. Cole, the president's choice to replace Raymond Foley as HHFA administrator, opposed the expansion of public housing programs. The former congressman from Kansas also resisted pressure from open-housing advocates. In 1958, responding to the Committee on Race and Housing's report, *Where Shall We Live?* he told a gathering of the National Association of Real Estate Boards that it was "not incumbent upon the Federal Government to impose integration on any form of housing that received Government aid." He insisted that the free market should decide such issues.[11]

Cole began his term at the HHFA by threatening to cut thirty race relations service jobs from the civil service rolls. He intended to make them patronage appointments. Among the HHFA employees threatened with dismissal was Frank Horne, who had worked in the race relations offices of the federal housing bureaucracy since the late 1930s. A contingent of black Republicans from Kentucky demanded that Cole replace Horne with a black realtor from Louisville named Joseph R. Ray. In September 1953, Cole broke down and requested Horne's resignation. He claimed "so much pressure" was being put on him that he had to ask Horne to quit. Within a week, nine civil rights organizations met to protest. They formed the Committee to Maintain the Integrity of the Racial Relations Service and lobbied the president to save Horne's job. The black press also imposed pressure on the administration. The NCDH insisted that it "would be a mischievous step backward" to dismiss Horne. "Weakening the service by removing the man who is generally recognized as the nation's foremost expert on race relations in housing," it suggested, "would be an act of folly." By early October, Horne's defenders succeeded in compelling the White House to intervene. The administration broke the impasse by appointing Joseph Ray to Horne's position of racial relations adviser and making Horne assistant to the HHFA administrator. Horne, however, would fare less well when Republicans tried to force him out in 1955. Horne left the federal government and went to work for New York City Mayor Robert Wagner, the father of the federal housing program during the New Deal, at the Mayor's Commission on Intergroup Relations.[12]

After the Democrats' defeat in 1952, the housing debate turned on whether a Republican administration would, in Virginia Democrat Howard W. Smith's words, "hitch-hik[e] on the New Deal bandwagon" or reduce the federal government's role. Fiscally conservative Republicans held fast to a policy of deficit reduction, whereas liberal Democrats played political games by proposing extravagantly large increases in public housing. Political posturing and gridlock kept legislators from passing significant housing legislation during the first year of the 83rd Congress. The only housing laws enacted in 1953 continued existing programs and extended to Korean War veterans the housing and lending privileges that World

War II veterans enjoyed, but offered no specific provisions for minority group housing.[13]

Although the Republicans generally opposed the expansion of government, preferred voluntary to regulatory action, and were reluctant to spend more tax dollars on building public housing, the Eisenhower administration still advanced the cause of minority housing. During a press conference two months after his inauguration, Eisenhower pledged to create a commission to seek ways to reform and streamline policies to improve the condition of housing in the United States. In September 1953, Eisenhower issued Executive Order 10486, establishing the Advisory Committee on Government Housing Policies and Programs. The committee's December 1953 report recommended several initiatives to make credit more readily available to low-income families. It also singled out minority housing as an area where government could improve living standards. Betraying its Republican majority, the committee emphasized changing the attitudes of private investors. "Legislation alone," the committee insisted, "cannot provide [the] needed sites, a flow of mortgage funds, needed new construction, nor a solution of neighborhood and related problems."[14]

Eisenhower accepted many of the committee's recommendations. He adopted the rhetoric of opportunity and anti-discrimination, but he still insisted on a spirit of voluntarism. "It must be frankly and honestly acknowledged," he told Congress in January 1954, "that many members of minority groups, regardless of their income or their economic status, have had the least opportunity of all our citizens to acquire good homes." "The administrative policies governing the operation of the several housing agencies," he insisted, "must be, and they will be materially strengthened and augmented in order to assure equal opportunity for all of our citizens to acquire within their means good and well located homes." The president, however, chose to make appeals to developers and to manipulate fiscal policy to bolster the whole housing industry rather that to pursue pinpoint legislation directed specifically at minority access to housing.[15]

Republicans expected that an unfettered political and economic environment would enable the private sector to produce enough housing to meet the country's needs. Under Eisenhower, the FHA tried to induce builders to risk building more low-cost housing by lowering the permissible vacancy rate for rental housing and by allowing investors a higher percent capitalization rate, thereby decreasing the amount of rental income necessary for the developer to make a profit. The HHFA influenced the National Association of Home Builders and the Mortgage Bankers Association into creating minority housing committees. Congress, meanwhile, enacted the first substantive federal housing legislation since 1949, proposing to construct 35,000 public housing units in each of the next four years. The numbers reflected a compromise brokered by the president between pro–public housing Democrats and budget-cutting Republican conservatives.[16]

The cardinal advance in the government's housing policy was the creation, in 1954, of the Voluntary Home Mortgage Credit Program (VHMCP) to help minority home buyers and persons in less populated regions of the country find private lenders willing to make loans. The VHMCP was the brainchild of representatives of the Life Insurance Association of America, NAREB, NAHB, and other private housing and financial interests. The program provided no mortgage money and closed no loans. To control inflation, administrators did not even intend for the VHMCP to increase the overall supply of mortgage money. "Its sole function," in the words of the HHFA administrator, "[was] to get a borrower's loan application into the hands of a private lending institution." Legislative supporters of the program represented a coalition of legislators from urban and semirural areas.[17]

In its "declaration of policy," the VHMCP proclaimed that the program was designed "to encourage and facilitate the flow of funds for housing credit into remote areas and small communities where such funds [were] not available in adequate supply." The chief target of the legislation, therefore, was inhabitants of towns of fewer than 25,000 people who suffered from too few lenders and too little available credit. The program, however, also addressed the interests of minorities. Members of minority groups were eligible for assistance regardless of geographical considerations. To qualify for VHMCP assistance, applicants had to certify that they had made at least two attempts to receive FHA- or VA-insured credit from private lending institutions but had been turned down.[18]

The VHMCP did little to cure the larger malady of discrimination that plagued America's minority housing, but it did give solace to some African Americans. It remained a small program, created as a last resort for those persons unable to find mortgage credit without its aid. In its first five years of operation, the VHMCP helped place a total of 8,458 loans, amounting to approximately $85 million, for individual members of minority groups. The program also had arranged financing for three housing projects involving 546 rental units. The first two years of the program saw more than 3,000 loans secured through VA applications, reflecting the African American community's role in the Korean War. After 1956, approximately 3,700 of the loans went under the FHA's auspices. For the 9,000 families helped by the program, the VHMCP obviously was a success.[19]

Many observers regarded the VHMCP as disappointing or worse. HHFA officials claimed that the terms of VHMCP loans were "at least as favorable as the terms prevailing in the regular mortgage market." But CRH observed that the cost of credit available through the VHMCP was so high that it limited the demand for assistance. The president of the Michigan Association of Real Estate Brokers took an even harsher view of the program. George H. Hutchinson charged that the VHMCP was "virtually a complete failure in the Detroit area." He gave examples of instances where blacks had paid too much for homes: one house would have sold to a white veteran for "$6,000 with $550 down and monthly payments [of] approximately $40," but "it was sold to a Negro veteran for $9750 with $750 down, monthly payments [of] $98"; another house that should have sold "for $11,500 with $750 down, sold to a Negro for $16,000 with a down payment of $3500," according to

Hutchinson. "It is clearly established," he declared, "that Negro home-buyers are being victimized by these arbitrary lending standards."[20]

Advocates of public housing harshly criticized the Eisenhower administration for pursuing inadequate or even wrongheaded policies. They contended that the proposed 35,000 units per year were insufficient to meet the needs of the nation. James G. Thimmes, the chairman of the Congress of Industrial Organizations (CIO) Housing Committee and a member of the President's Housing Committee, insisted that government involvement in the housing field ought to "be used to cure and not neglect or aggravate the undemocratic housing practices which are all too common in our communities." "Without assistance from the federal government," the activists argued, "the only open supply [would continue to be] old, hand-me-down housing in slum neighborhoods."[21]

NCDH groups castigated HHFA Administrator Cole, in particular, for neglecting the needs of African Americans. In 1954, Cole met with leaders of the construction industry to negotiate an increase in private low-cost housing. Acceding to HHFA requests, the NAHB adopted a plan whereby its members would allocate 10 percent of the housing they built in 1955 to African Americans. Upon learning about the proposal, NCDH leaders denounced the plan because the builders intended to provide only segregated housing. They met with Cole, but according to NCDH Executive Director Frances Levenson, it became apparent to them that "the period of negotiation with HHFA had been exhausted." Cole answered their charges, proclaiming that integration was "the problem of people of the locality: If they don't want it, they don't have it." Levenson called Cole's response an "abdication of federal responsibility." The question of integration in the new NAHB housing, however, turned out to be moot. According to Levenson, "Nothing like ten per cent of new building [was] available to minority groups, even on a segregated basis." The loss of Frank Horne from the HHFA race relations staff and Cole's unwillingness to take action against housing discrimination left open-housing advocates disheartened about advancing the issue on the federal level. Levenson reported, "the fight concerning federal housing programs [would have] to be waged in relation to specific programs in specific localities since nationwide policy was not forthcoming from Washington."[22]

The unwieldy nature of federal procedures made bold legislative or executive action against housing discrimination unlikely. The staunch southern opposition to racial integration and the conservative Republican ideology of limited government and free enterprise, moreover, rendered the enactment of open-housing legislation almost impossible on the federal level. Consequently, housing advocates turned their attention to state and local government.

Many organizations affiliated with the NCDH had apprenticed by challenging housing discrimination in New York during the 1940s. The New York State Assembly had enacted the nation's first anti-discrimination law in 1938, banning discrimination in all public housing. Although powerful on its face, the law exempted many types of dwellings and was so indifferently enforced that it had little effect in winning blacks better access to housing. In the 1940s, the State Committee Against Discrimination (SCAD) and the City Commission on Intergroup Relations gave minorities a stronger voice in the halls of power. By the end of the decade, they had become a formidable force in the housing lobby and had won significant victories for open housing. In 1944, New York City refused to give tax-exempt status to any project that denied housing to any person on account of race. Four years later, the city forbade discrimination in urban redevelopment projects and in 1949 extended the statute to include "any deed entered into by city or agency thereof." In 1946, the state legislature banned discrimination in veterans' housing.[23]

New York's statutes of the early 1950s took the issue of open housing to a new level. Responding to NAACP and SCAD lobbying and to the strengthened electoral position of African Americans, the state extended the reach of anti-discrimination policies. The Wicks-Austin law banned discrimination in public and publicly assisted housing, defining assistance to include aid from the state's condemnation power, tax exemption, and abatement. It defined segregation as discrimination. New York City enacted similar legislation in 1951, passing the Brown-Isaacs housing law. Brown-Isaacs extended the ban on discrimination to include the city's largest apartment complex, Stuyvesant Town. Built by the Metropolitan Life Insurance Company in Manhattan, Stuyvesant Town had been a target of activists from its planning stage in 1943. The project represented the worst example of urban renewal in the eyes of minority housing interests. It was tax-exempt, and its construction displaced hundreds of African American families. Metropolitan Life, however, steadfastly refused to integrate the project and tied up enforcement of the law in the courts for several years. New York's laws represented substantial advancement in relation to past practice, but they offered little enforcement power or remedy for violations. In addition, they excluded small apartment houses and all private housing.[24]

Open-housing activists copied their New York strategy throughout the North and West. During the late 1940s and early 1950s, numerous cities and states moved to ban racial and religious discrimination. By 1954, twenty-one cities had joined New York in passing some form of anti-discrimination ordinance or resolution; they ranged in size from Pasco, a town of 4,500 people in eastern Washington, to Los Angeles, and they represented every region of the country except the South. Omaha, Nebraska, and St. Paul, Minnesota, went as far as New York City had in outlawing racial segregation in public housing. St. Paul's law decreed that the city was "unequivocally opposed to segregation" and that no racial segregation would be countenanced in the city's urban renewal sites. The capital of Minnesota, along with Colorado's seat of government, also outlawed race-restrictive covenants. Eight states matched New York in banning discrimination in public housing. But as with New York's statute, most of the state laws, although not quite toothless, did not take much of a bite out of the housing problem.[25]

Not accepting moderate success, the NAACP increased its lobbying activities on the branch level. The association asked its local housing committees to meet with representatives of trade groups and the housing industry "to acquaint them with [its] position." Madison Jones recommended that the branches outline "the evils of segregation, slums, delinquency, poverty, crime, rent gouging, etc.," as well as "point up the fact that Negroes [were] better-off economically . . . than ever before." The new middle-class African American, Jones noted, could "pay his way and [was] looking for value for his dollar but [did] not move in a free housing market." Jones told his affiliates to impress upon builders and lenders that a steady market of black home buyers and renters existed from which private industry could profit if it would take the step to build integrated housing.[26]

The renewed campaign enabled the NCDH and its member organizations to advance toward their goal of open-housing legislation. The most significant progress again occurred in New York. In New York City, Mayor Robert Wagner continued to lead the crusade. In 1954, the Sharkey-Brown-Isaacs law extended the prohibition against racial discrimination to all multiple dwellings that received loans guaranteed by federal mortgage insurance. The state legislature followed suit, enacting the Metcalf-Baker law, which forbade discrimination in multiple dwellings and in developments of ten or more homes receiving government mortgage insurance through the FHA and VA. The state law did not offer an adequate enforcement procedure, however, and was revised in 1955. In a dramatic advance for open housing, two new Metcalf-Baker codes expanded the jurisdiction of the State Committee Against Discrimination, headed by Charles Abrams. To execute its duties, SCAD established a Housing Advisory Council. "This total body of pioneer[ing] law," council chairman and member of the NCDH advisory board James H. Scheuer concluded in his report to Governor Averell Harriman, "placed SCAD far in the forefront of similar efforts throughout the country to promote integrated living patterns in government-assisted housing."[27]

The Housing Advisory Council endeavored to extend the reach of the open-housing movement throughout the state. Scheuer insisted on the "most widespread possible participation by local community leaders." With a small staff, he undertook "an intensive and carefully conceived educational effort" to teach persons directly involved in the housing industry and "the multitude of citizens who comprise the market for [units covered by the laws] and who will live in them together" that integration did not need to cause property values to decline and that if whites would accept living with blacks, it would be better for both communities. The program, according to Scheuer, would necessitate "innumerable informal conversations and group conferences" and would "not bring concrete results until a long period of fermentation [had] elapsed." But it did mark an important next step in the fight against residential segregation.[28]

Between 1955 and 1957, New York pushed the advance of open housing further. On the state level, the Metcalf-Baker law of 1955 extended SCAD's reach to include publicly insured housing. The law covered multiple-unit dwellings that received FHA- or VA-insured loans after July 1, 1955, and banned discrimination by developers who owned ten or more homes in the same subdivision and who received FHA- or VA-insured loans or state loans. New York City's Commission on Intergroup Relations, headed by Frank Horne, began a project to help disperse the minority population. It provided a "centralized and systematic machinery" through which to negotiate with owners and managers of property, to establish vacancy listings, and to provide a variety of services to resolve problems or conflicts in transitional housing. The plan called for the commission to seek out accommodations outside traditionally black neighborhoods.[29]

Even more dramatically, New York City enacted the Sharkey-Brown-Isaacs law of 1957. The statute made it illegal to discriminate in the rental of units in multiple dwellings or in apartments and apartment houses with more than three units, as well as in the sale of "1- and 2-family homes in developments of 10 or more." The law authorized the Commission on Intergroup Relations to hear complaints of discrimination. It passed, in part, because African American city council members threatened publicly to embarrass Mayor Wagner if he did not agree to it.[30]

The Sharkey-Brown-Isaacs law represented the most significant advance yet toward open housing in any jurisdiction. It extended restrictions to include almost all new private housing. It was not clear whether the statute would meet constitutional muster, especially given the place of private property rights in American law, but the law had the support of the most prominent figures in the civil rights establishment. Eleanor Roosevelt heralded it as a great victory. "Friends of civil rights throughout the country," the former first lady noted, "have been heartened by passage of the Sharkey-Brown-Isaacs Law." Moreover, Mrs. Roosevelt saw the new law as a possible springboard to additional legislation. The law, she told the NAACP's Roy Wilkins, "offers the greatest opportunity to change the trend toward increasing residential segregation, which is our number one civil rights problem in the North."[31]

From New York, the renewed campaign to legislate against residential segregation spread across the North and West. The NCDH coordinated the preparation of fair-housing bills in twelve states in early 1957. "A drive to outlaw housing discrimination is in full swing throughout the country," Trends in Housing reported. In March, Washington became the second state in the nation to enact legislation outlawing discrimination in private housing receiving government mortgage insurance aid. By the end of June, two more states—Massachusetts and Oregon—had enacted similar restrictions. In 1959, Oregon went a step further and banned racial discrimination in the sale of some private housing not receiving government aid. As part of the enforcement mechanism, the state enacted a separate statute providing for the revocation of licenses for realtors who violated the ban. On the municipal level, Pittsburgh, Pennsylvania, followed New York City's lead, enacting a broad restriction on discrimination and creating a strong enforcement mechanism in December 1958. Other cities worked to eliminate irresponsible actions on the part of realtors. In 1960, Baltimore enacted anti–block-busting legislation, making realtors liable to revocation or suspension of their licenses if they were found guilty of "panic peddling."[32]

Although the fair-housing campaign succeeded on numerous fronts across the nation, the debate on civil rights versus property rights remained heated. The open-occupancy movement faced significant opposition and lost many battles. In St. Paul, Minnesota, for example, the NAACP and NCDH increased their lobbying efforts after their legislative victories of the early 1950s. In 1956, they convinced the members of the St. Paul City Council to draft an ordinance outlawing discrimination in the sale or rental of all housing and creating a commission specifically designated to enforce the regulations. With African Americans representing barely 2 percent of the city's total population, however, the housing measure lay dormant until 1958, when the construction of the St. Anthony Expressway forced the relocation of nearly 200 black families. The city council renewed its interest in the open housing ordinance, but the issue dragged on unresolved into the spring of 1959.[33]

Near the end of May, the St. Paul City Council held a public hearing on the open occupancy law. An overflow crowd attended the hearing, and many foes of the plan lined up to voice their opposition. According to the *St. Paul Dispatch*, the speakers who opposed the ordinance tended to represent home owners and builders. Shirley A. Rehnwall of Minnesota Homeowners, Inc., for example, argued that under the U.S. Constitution, "no group of individuals, regardless of race, . . . should either force entry into a community or be rejected from any community through legislation." "We do not believe in legislating either morals or human relations," Rehnwall declared. "It is every American's right to sell, rent, or lease to whomever he chooses." The executive director of the St. Paul Home Builders Association argued that the measure "would give colored persons a greater right to acquire property than property owners have to dispose of property." Persons outside the housing industry also opposed the law. The city's legal counsel, Louis P. Sheahan, announced his disapproval of the proposal and later prepared a report outlining his reasons. He claimed that the city could not create a commission on housing discrimination without an enabling state statute. His main quarrel with the ordinance, however, was that the city did not have the authority to force a private citizen to sell his home to someone that he did not want to. "It is my opinion," he declared, "that the proposed Ordinance is unconstitutional on its face."[34]

The NAACP and NCDH also had spokespeople at the hearing. George Holland, a middle-class black resident, told the crowd that he could have qualified to live in any section of the city, "except on the point of [his] color." Discrimination was rampant in St. Paul. The only reason the commissioners did not know about it, he averred, was because they did not "happen to be black. . . . I want the right to live on St. Dennis, on Summit, or on any other street in St. Paul," he declared. Several real estate representatives also urged adoption of the ordinance. They tried to counter the arguments of the law's opponents, noting the problem of overcrowding and blight in the inner city. They pointed to the recent studies of property values in transitional neighborhoods to quell the concerns of the council members. But their argument failed to convince the legislators. In August, Mayor Joseph A. Dillon and the city council accepted Sheahan's conclusion that the city did not have the authority to enact such legislation. They decided that open housing was a matter for the state, not the city, to decide. The ordinance failed.[35]

Open-housing legislation advanced on the state and local level during the late 1950s, but the federal government continued its more cautious approach. No major housing legislation was enacted. Other issues, such as the Suez Crisis, the Cold War, a declining economy, and his own health occupied President Eisenhower's time. As he began his second term, Eisenhower still hoped to keep the issue of race relations at arm's length. He had won the 1956 election by holding to the middle ground between segregationists in the South and liberal integrationists. "What [was] needed," he reasoned, was "calmness and sanity." But explosive events forced him to take dramatic action on civil rights.[36]

Southern resistance to school integration grew violent after 1955. Bombs rocked the homes and businesses of advocates of desegregation, including Arthur Shores, in Birmingham in 1956. One year later, Little Rock, Arkansas, became the scene of the largest federal intervention in a state since Reconstruction. In September 1957, white mobs tried to block black youths from entering Little Rock Central High School. The demonstrations directly violated a federal appeals court order to desegregate the school. Eisenhower had considered education to be primarily a local issue. He had hoped to let states and cities work out their own plans to satisfy the Supreme Court's desegregation order. Persistent opposition to integration on the part of white Arkansans, including Governor Orval Faubus, however, forced the president to send the 101st Airborne to keep the peace and carry out the court's demand.[37]

The Eisenhower administration also pursued a less drastic civil rights program. In January 1957, the president proposed the first civil rights legislation since Reconstruction. He had presented a bill in 1956, but election-year politics and his lukewarm support for the legislation caused it to be dead-on-arrival in Congress. Vice President Richard Nixon and Attorney General Brownell were the new bill's leading advocates in the cabinet. And although they did not belong to Eisenhower's inner circle of advisers, they convinced him that the legislation was needed. Voting rights lay at the center of the Republican plan. Many in the administration assumed that if the government guaranteed southern blacks the right to participate freely and fairly in the democratic process, then African Americans would possess sufficient power to ensure their own protection. Brownell, however, wanted to put some force behind the bill. He wanted to grant the Justice Department the authority to sue for the enforcement of not just voting rights but school desegregation. In Part III of the bill, Brownell also included language from the 1866 statute, giving the president the authority to use troops to enforce civil rights laws. When the Democrats, led by

Georgia Senator Richard Russell, blocked passage of the measures and threatened to scuttle the entire legislation, Eisenhower backed down. The Congress passed the bill and on September 9, ironically just weeks before he would send troops to Arkansas, the president signed the weakened act into law.[38]

The Civil Rights Act of 1957 did not meet the best hopes of advocates of racial justice, but it did advance the cause. Part I of the act created the Civil Rights Commission (CRC). The CRC would sit for an undetermined tenure, hold public hearings, and investigate allegations of voting discrimination and other trespasses against the constitutional guarantee of equal protection under the laws. From the perspective of open housing, the creation of the CRC represented the most significant element of the act. The commissioners traveled to four cities and requested advisory reports from the forty-eight state housing committees to get what they hoped would represent "the most complete and accurate picture possible of the obstacles to freedom of choice and equal opportunity in housing."[39]

Supporters of open housing jumped at the opportunity to convince the CRC of the need for government action to ensure better access to better homes. Charles Abrams, as chairman of SCAD, testified before the commission during its visit to New York City in 1959. He retraced the by then well-known story of African Americans' migration, their concentration in older sections of cities, and their inability to find adequate housing in the discriminatory marketplace. As housing advocates had done for two decades, he recommended that the federal government build more housing, deemphasize slum clearance, and concentrate on new construction on vacant land. But Abrams also added a new request in his lobbying. "It should be a basic tenet of American life," he asserted, "that where public aid is extended . . . the benefits of that aid or subsidization should inure to the whole population and not simply to a single class." Abrams suggested that the president "should enter an Executive order outlawing discrimination in all FHA- and VA-aided housing."[40]

After hearings in Chicago, Washington, D.C., and Atlanta, as well as New York City, the CRC issued its first report on housing in September 1959. "Discrimination in housing," the commission declared, "exist[s] to some extent in all parts of the country." The CRC reviewed the causes and effects of segregation, slums, and blight, noting the role that all levels of government played in perpetuating the problem. It also remarked on the circularity of the problem of prejudice. "The final tragedy," the commission despaired, "[is] that the effect of slums, discrimination and inequalities is more slums." It concluded that ghettoization, both economic and physical, produced "demoralized human beings" and that this condition of "demoralization then [became] a reason for 'keeping them in their place.'" "Prejudice," the commissioners insisted, "feeds on the conditions caused by prejudice."[41]

The commission offered six recommendations. It suggested that every city and state with "a substantial nonwhite population" establish an interracial or housing committee to study the local conditions, propose solutions to problems, and provide enforcement of the remedies. The CRC, however, paid more attention to the failings of the federal government on the housing issue. It suggested reforms of the federal housing bureaucracy to make each agency more responsive to the needs of African Americans and more sensitive to discriminatory policies. Most significantly, the CRC recommended that the president issue an executive order "stating the constitutional objective of equal opportunity in housing" and charging federal agencies and the CRC to "prepare and propose plans to bring about the end of discrimination in all Federally-assisted housing." The commission's report would have direct consequences on the federal political landscape within a year.[42]

The 1960 presidential election marked a dramatic advance in the politics of race relations. Blacks had started leaving the party of Lincoln during the New Deal, and the exodus increased during the Truman years. In 1952 and in 1956, neither candidate said much in regard to civil rights in their clashes. Eisenhower did slow the movement out of the Republican Party in 1956, thanks to his leadership in foreign affairs and the Democrats' issuance of the "Southern Manifesto," a pledge signed by nearly all of the southern Democrats in Congress in which they promised to defy court-ordered integration. Not until the election of 1960 did the civil rights struggle move to the center of the national dialogue. According to the election's chronicler, Theodore H. White, "the Negroes of the Northern cities meant to exercise their leverage on the Presidential election," to compel the parties to meet the movement's demands, and never before "had any group, under leadership of such talent, presented its specific community demands in such blunt and forceful terms." Vice President Nixon and Senator John F. Kennedy struggled to formulate policies that would satisfy the northern black constituency while not alienating southern white voters and vice versa. The platforms of both parties contained rhetorically strong civil rights planks. Kennedy also promised to use the power of the executive to implement changes that Congress would not enact.[43]

With little differentiating the presidential candidates on the policy level, a single act by the Democratic candidate may have turned the tide of African American support in his favor. Less than a month before the election, Martin Luther King Jr. and several other demonstrators were arrested during a sit-in at the dining room of Rich's Department Store in Atlanta. After a few days, a Fulton County court released all the protesters but King. The civil rights leader was transferred to DeKalb County, where he had earlier been convicted of driving without a proper driver's permit and had received a suspended sentence. The DeKalb County judge, Oscar Mitchell, ruled that King's part in the protest had violated the terms of his parole and ordered him to serve four months in the Reidsville maximum-security prison. Many persons close to King thought that the court had actually passed a death sentence, fearing that King would not get out of the rural prison alive. Because of King's notoriety, his conviction quickly became a national issue. Both of the presidential candidates tried to find a way to reverse the ruling. Nixon worked through back channels, asking Attorney General William Rogers to look into the matter. Kennedy took a more direct approach. On the recommendation of Harris Wofford and other advisers on civil rights, Kennedy telephoned Coretta Scott King to express his concern. Robert Kennedy, meanwhile, telephoned Judge Mitchell and secured King's release.[44]

The news of the telephone calls spread through the African American community and enriched Kennedy's stock among blacks. Martin Luther King Sr., who had declared that he intended to vote for Nixon, made a statement expressing his thanks to Kennedy. He announced that he had "a suitcase of votes" and that because Kennedy "was willing to wipe the tears from my daughter's eyes, [he would take them] to Mr. Kennedy and dump them in his lap." The Democrats worked to capitalize on the episode by printing some 2 million handbills recounting the story. They distributed them at black churches across the country on the Sunday before the election. They passed out some 500,000 of the flyers in Chicago alone. Many observers credit the telephone calls and the resulting campaign with tipping the balance toward Kennedy. The Democratic candidate took about 80 percent of the black vote in the general election and won the presidency.[45]

Housing discrimination was one of the issues addressed during the campaign. The Republican Party platform contained an anti-discrimination plank. "We pledge," the statement read, to take "action to prohibit discrimination in housing constructed with the aid of Federal subsidies." The Democrats made an even stronger statement. "The new Democratic Administration," the platform promised, "will take action to end discrimination in Federal housing programs, including federally-assisted housing." The Democrats insisted that it would take an executive order to achieve that aim. In an August press release, Kennedy promised that he would use his authority to push open housing. He observed that the executive branch could do a great deal to remedy the poor housing of blacks. Kennedy also suggested that if Eisenhower wanted to, Eisenhower "could sign an executive order ending discrimination in housing tomorrow," implying that if he were president he would be willing to sign such an order. A month before the election, Kennedy made his position even clearer. Again criticizing Eisenhower's inaction, he told voters, "one stroke of the pen would have worked wonders for millions of Negroes who want their children to grow up in decency."[46]

Having given their support to Kennedy, the African American leadership pressed the new president for the kind of vigorous and innovative action that he had promised. Blacks had played a significant role in Kennedy's election, and they knew it. They insisted that the Kennedy administration accommodate them. The NAACP, NCDH, the Urban League, NAIRO, and the National Association of Real Estate Brokers (an African American organization not to be confused with the National Association of Real Estate Boards) lobbied the administration to keep its promise. The NAACP urged members to write Kennedy to demand action. It issued a brochure entitled "The Need for an Executive Order," in which it insisted that the president "exercise his moral and legal responsibility with firm and inventive leadership by issuing an Executive Order guaranteeing that all American citizens enjoy equally all [federally assisted] housing units."[47]

Because of its singular mandate, the NCDH was able to undertake an even more focused pursuit of open housing. In September 1961, the committee requested a meeting with the president. Kennedy was unavailable, but the administration scheduled a conference between NCDH leaders and Justice Department officials, including Attorney General Robert Kennedy, for early November. In the interim, the NCDH found more ammunition to use in its lobbying effort. The Civil Rights Commission issued its report for 1961 in October. In the housing section of the report, the CRC again recommended an executive order calling for fair housing. The report advised that the order "should apply to all federally assisted housing, including housing constructed with the assistance of Federal mortgage insurance or loan guaranty, as well as federally aided public housing, elderly housing, and urban renewal projects."[48]

Emboldened by the CRC's recommendations and its own success in advancing housing legislation on the state level, the NCDH put forth "A Call on the President" to issue an executive order. The paper pursued several arguments designed to convince the administration. "Of first importance," it suggested, is that an order would enunciate "a national ethic" and provide a framework "for the realization of the goal of the National Housing Act of 1949 of 'a decent home in a suitable living environment for every American family.'" The NCDH noted the futility of the government's program of "pleading and exhortation to local agencies and the [housing] industry to 'do the right thing' and build on an open occupancy basis." Advising Kennedy to ignore the "probability of Southern opposition," it insisted that federal policy "must be the same throughout the country, and must be enforced everywhere with equal firmness." The "Call" contended that open housing was "feasible, practical and inevitable." "It can be stated categorically," the NCDH asserted, "where it has been tried, . . . open occupancy in housing works [and it] has succeeded whether conceived voluntarily or brought about by legal mandate." The white paper included a model executive order and an extended legal brief tracing the authority of the president to take the action. And finally, in case reason did not sway the president, the NCDH offered a moralistic argument. "What is more basic to the whole democratic process," the authors asked, "than man's right to seek shelter for his family, without the artificial restrictions of race, creed or national origin?"[49]

The committee followed up in its November meeting with officials from the Justice Department. Abrams led the group, which included housing experts and industry and labor leaders such as Victor Reuther of the United Auto Workers and James Luchs of Shannon and Luchs, Washington's largest real estate firm. They met with Robert Kennedy, Assistant Attorney General of the Civil Rights Division Burke Marshall, and Deputy Attorney General Nicholas Katzenbach. The conference discussed numerous aspects of the housing issue but dwelt on the social costs of discrimination and the economic opportunities that a clear statement by the administration supporting open housing would offer the real estate industry.[50]

After the meeting, the delegates concluded that the administration sympathized with the idea of ending discrimination. Jack E. Wood Jr., Madison Jones's replacement in the NAACP Housing Division, observed that the attorney general seemed "vitally interested in and support[ive of their] position." Wood added, however, that Kennedy was "reluctant to discuss any specific aspects of the problem." "The attorney general," according to Algernon Black, the chairman of the NCDH Board of Directors, "listened to us very carefully." He noted that the government was particularly interested in "the statements by the builders concerning the practical aspects and finances, and their sense of the importance of an Executive Order from their own business point of view." Abrams, the NCDH president, likewise thought that the meeting had gone well. He commented, "We are reasonably sure we're going to get an order, [but] we still don't know if it will be a Thanksgiving present or a Christmas gift." The Yuletide passed, however, and the new year began with no sign of an executive order.[51]

Politics and other priorities kept the Kennedy administration from acting on housing. Kennedy, as with Truman and Eisenhower before him, tended to view civil rights through the prism of foreign relations. The Cold War and the struggle for influence in the new nations of Africa made the president wary of taking actions that might incite incidents such as the riot in Cicero in 1951 or the Little Rock crisis in 1957. According to one biographer, Kennedy did not want episodes of open racial conflict to "give the country a bad name abroad." The Bay of Pigs fiasco so early in his term had also made Kennedy more vulnerable to criticism as a manager of foreign policy and had weakened his resolve to push forward on civil rights and housing issues.[52]

Domestic politics further restricted Kennedy's actions. As Hugh Davis Graham notes, the election had failed to give Kennedy a "working program majority." Conservative Democrats dominated committees in Congress. The president feared that they would block his other initiatives, such as a foreign trade bill and Medicare, to halt the advance of civil rights. His main proposal on housing, moving it into the cabinet by creating a Department of Urban Affairs and Housing, was likely to face particularly strong opposition just on fiscal terms. The fact that he intended to appoint Robert Weaver to the post of secretary, making Weaver the first black to hold such high office in the executive branch, made the proposal even more controversial. He could ill afford to push the anti-discrimination initiative. Just after Christmas, David Lawrence of the *New York Herald Tribune* reported that "highly placed administration sources" had told him that signing an executive order would be like "waving a red flag in front of the southern opponents of civil rights." "The White House," they insisted, "just isn't in a position to alienate anybody." Kennedy's desire to strike a balance between civil rights on the one hand and broader national and foreign policy interests on the other therefore caused him, as it had Eisenhower, to turn to the extension of voting rights as the administration's first priority. Lawrence reported that the executive order might have to wait until after the 1962 congressional session and even the November elections.[53]

Kennedy's inaction on housing distressed the NCDH leadership. To increase pressure on the president, the NCDH began the "Stroke of the Pen" campaign. It urged the press to write columns to raise the public's awareness of the issue. It also asked members to write the president advocating the signing of the order and even suggested that they send pens with which to sign it. The "Ink for Jack" crusade, according to Taylor Branch, left Harris Wofford the custodian of thousands of pens, but it failed to achieve an executive order. The housing initiatives that the Kennedy administration did pursue also came up short. The bill to create the department failed even to make it out of the House Rules Committee, and the president's second attempt at forming the cabinet post, Reorganization Plan No. 1, was killed in both houses in February. In the wake of the defeats, no relief from housing discrimination was forthcoming from the White House.[54]

The campaign for an executive order grew more vocal after the close of the legislative session in August 1962. "The patience of Negroes and other enlightened Americans . . . is not inexhaustible," Jack Wood warned. He suggested that the delays might cost the Democrats votes in the African American community. "The alarming prospect that equality of opportunity in federally assisted housing might be prolonged another year," he threatened, "could be translated in the November elections." The NAACP leader also suggested a way branch housing committees could help increase the pressure on the president. He recommended that they write Kennedy and present him with affidavits recording incidents of discrimination. Wood hoped that these would further demonstrate to the White House the "broad pattern of federal partnership in racial discrimination [and] reinforce NAACP demands that President Kennedy end [the] Federal partnership in housing discrimination by issuing an executive order."[55]

Despite the increased effort, the administration did not move on housing discrimination before the election. The results of the off-year elections were ambiguous for Kennedy. The Democrats took 53 percent of the vote, netted a four-seat increase in the Senate, and lost only four seats in the House, but the balance of power between conservatives and liberals in Congress changed little. The president, however, had put off issuance of an executive order long enough.[56]

Two weeks after the November 1962 election, Kennedy signed Executive Order 11063 on Equal Opportunity in Housing. It directed housing and law enforcement departments and agencies in the federal government "to take all action necessary and appropriate to prevent discrimination" in the sale or rental of property owned or operated by the federal government, provided with the aid of federal loans or grants, or provided by loans insured by the federal government. It outlawed discrimination by lenders who received federal loan or deposit insurance. And it established the Committee on Equal Opportunity in Housing (CEOH) to oversee the execution of the directive and make annual reports back to the president regarding the progress of open housing. The initiative excluded one- and two-family dwellings that were occupied by the seller because the administration believed broader inclusion would strain its ability to enforce the ban. Regarding properties covered by federal mortgage insurance and lenders similarly insured, moreover, the order incorporated only future transactions, thus limiting its scope to less than 20 percent of all dwellings in some states.[57]

Housing advocates hailed the executive order as a hard-won victory, but many of them were disappointed by its limited scope. "The order," HHFA Administrator Weaver declared, "makes clear the policy of our government in an area which has suffered from fear and uncertainty as well as from prejudice." He added that the order should alert "all Americans to their responsibilities toward their neighbors." The overall effect of the order, Weaver insisted, would be "to help achieve freedom of choice in housing for all Americans." Jack Wood of the NAACP acknowledged the order's symbolic importance as a statement of federal policy, noting also that it had boosted the morale of the African American community. The NCDH, however, clearly would have preferred a more inclusive directive. Its leaders suggested that the policy was too narrow to accomplish its stated goal. Disappointed, they still hoped that "if energetically and imaginatively implemented," the order could "aid considerably in modifying the widespread patterns of residential segregation for which past Government policies bear so much of the responsibility."[58]

Kennedy's issuance of Executive Order 11063 occurred a dozen years after the NAACP and other groups had formed the NCDH to direct the campaign against residential segregation. It had taken stamina, luck, and a clever, persistent strategy to achieve even this limited result. It also had taken the work of scroes of experts and activitists. Over the years, advocates of open housing refined and expanded lobbying efforts and penetrated increasingly important positions in government bureaucracies. In so doing, they helped win groundbreaking legislation on the state and municipal levels, as well as to advance the movement nationally. Whether governments could affirmatively act to end discrimination remained in question, however. Did the U.S. Constitution allow the government to force private property owners to sell their homes to persons to whom they did not wish to sell? Moreover, which was constitutionaly more important given the willingness of whites to use force to block integration of their neighborhoods, maintaining domestic tranquility or correcting the problem of discrimination? As government involvement in the housing industry increased, as African Americans gained more economic and political power, and as the discrepancies between the American creed of liberty and justice and the reality of American race relations grew more stark, the answer became clearer: where government politically had the will to act, it seemed that constitutionally it had the right to act.

Executive Order 11063 represented a major accomplishment despite its weaknesses. It did not cover existing housing receiving federally insured loans, and its execution depended on vigorous action on the part of housing agencies and the CEOH, a vigor that did not materialize. But the order marked the first time that the federal executive had declared its support for the philosophy of open housing and shown itself to be willing to take affirmative action to correct the problems of discrimination.[59]

Many obstacles remained for open-housing advocates. On the state level, home owners and realtors were developing new tactics to keep neighborhoods white. Moreover, the branch of the federal government closest to the people continued to resist integration. As the next chapter demonstrates, more violence would occur before Congress would join the campaign against residential segregation.

10

HOUSING IN A GREAT SOCIETY

Part I

There is no turning back. I don't think we're going to abandon a right goal because of a few people yelling and throwing Molotov cocktails.[1]

From World War II to the mid-1960s, the fight for racial justice slowly advanced. The developments occurred first in the Supreme Court and then in the White House. But Congress, the branch that most closely represents the views and interests of the people, had hesitated in embracing the civil rights crusade. Then, in 1964, because of the changing political climate, the ongoing effort of the civil rights movement, and the shock of President John F. Kennedy's assassination, Congress became engaged in the struggle. The Civil Rights Act of 1964 represented the boldest step yet in the "march to freedom." The Voting Rights Act of 1965 further confirmed the congressional rejection of discrimination in many American institutions. These gains, however, were made against bigotry in the South. They did not, by and large, significantly affect race relations in the North.

The central civil rights issue in the North and West involved gaining access to housing. The fair-housing movement had made headway. Numerous states and cities had enacted laws banning discrimination in public housing. In addition, President Kennedy's Executive Order 11063 had marked an important milestone in the campaign. As the movement pressed harder against the walls that kept blacks out of white neighborhoods, home owners and the housing industry pushed back. Real estate brokers and home owners' associations fought the anti-discrimination laws. They questioned the authority of government to say to whom a private property owner must sell his or her home. Opponents called the decrees "forced housing." They demanded protective legislation, constitutional amendments, and a home owners' bill of rights. The property rights movement found success in 1963 and early 1964, particularly in Detroit. In 1964, property rights advocates in California rose up to repeal the state's anti-discrimination law.

Worse than the legal resistance was the opposition that resulted when African Americans demonstrated for better access to housing. In 1966, Chicago became the new focus of Martin Luther King Jr. and other movement leaders. They formed the Chicago Freedom Movement, marching and holding rallies to protest the dual real estate market, ghettoization, and inadequate public housing. Each march met with violent backlash. A year later, a Catholic priest and local NAACP youth led similar demonstrations in Milwaukee and found similar resistance.

Much changed in the United States and the civil rights movement in 1963. African Americans sensed that significant advancement was near at hand, but many were impatient for its coming. The community began to fracture, with growing numbers joining the ranks of the black nationalists and calling for violent retaliation against police brutality. Civil rights leaders pushed harder to force the federal government to act, and white segregationists became increasingly desperate in their attempt to maintain the status quo. When the Southern Christian Leadership Conference (SCLC) organized desegregation rallies in Birmingham in April, Bull Connor had officers turn on the firehoses and use police dogs to break up the children's crusade. The scenes of police brutality shocked the nation. Martin Luther King Jr. was arrested and while incarcerated penned the "Letter from a Birmingham Jail," a testament to hope and a call to nonviolent action. In mid-June, Mississippi civil rights leader Medgar Evers was gunned down outside his home, creating more calls for retribution.[2]

The South remained the focus of civil rights action in 1963, but demonstrations started to occur across the country. In early June, activists rallied against discrimination in Philadelphia and other cities. In Los Angeles, some 75,000 African Americans greeted King in a mass rally and contributed nearly $100,000 to help the SCLC and other groups maintain the pressure against segregation in the South. An even larger rally was scheduled for Detroit at the end of the month. It was to be called the Walk to Freedom and in several ways would anticipate the March on Washington two months later.[3]

The Walk to Freedom was organized by the Trade Union Leadership Council and the Detroit Council for Human Rights (DCHR). The NAACP, American Federation of Labor–Congress of Industrial Organizations (AFL-CIO), and the local Democratic Party soon endorsed the plan. The walk's chairman, Willie Baxter of the Detroit Commission on Community Relations, explained the purpose of the demonstration. "We are marching," he declared, "to show the world we support Dr. King and the thousands of courageous Negro youngsters and their elders who are willing to die, if necessary, to end second class citizenship in America." Organizers also wanted to raise money to help pay for bonds to get civil rights workers out of jail and to pay for legal counsel and court costs. "Make no mistake about it," Baxter announced, "there is a revolution sweeping the country—the winds of freedom are blowing everywhere." Local discrimination represented the DCHR's primary reason for holding the march, although it would also be useful for the national movement.[4]

The Walk to Freedom was a tremendous success. It was held on Sunday, June 23, 1963. Some 125,000 peaceful demonstrators took part and raised more than $40,000 for the cause. State and local officials, including Mayor Jerome C. Cavanaugh, took part. Governor George Romney did not march because he did not engage in politics on the Sabbath, but he did declare Sunday "Freedom March Day." King led the procession and gave a rousing oration at its climax. He spoke of the Emancipation Proclamation and black struggle, of segregation and violence in Birmingham, and of "a magnificent new militancy within the Negro community all across the nation." He also called for nonviolent effort and denounced Black nationalists, insisting: "Black supremacy is as dangerous as white supremacy." He ended on a theme that he would perfect on the steps of the Lincoln Memorial in August. "I have a dream this afternoon," he exclaimed, "it is a dream deeply-rooted in the American dream. This afternoon I have a dream, right now down in Georgia, Mississippi and Alabama, the sons of former slaves and the sons of former slave owners will be able to live together as brothers. . . . I have a dream this afternoon," he continued, "there will be a day we will no longer face the atrocities Emmett Till and Medgar Evers had to face." For the local audience, King added, "I have a dream this afternoon—right here in Detroit a Negro will be able to buy a house or rent a house anywhere that their money will carry them." He concluded, "Yes, I have a dream this afternoon. One day that in this world of ours, the words of Amos will become real. Justice will roll down like water and righteousness like a mighty stream. . . . Yes, I have a dream this afternoon."[5]

Local activists celebrated the moment but knew that they had to follow it up with direct action if they were to achieve real gains. The head of the local NAACP, Arthur L. Johnson, concluded that the rally proved that "a genuine feeling of good will" existed between the races in Detroit. He added, however, that public officials would "still have to be pushed and prodded" into executing their pledges of action. More demonstrations were promised, demonstrations that the Detroit Urban League's Francis A. Kornegay reported would be smaller "but more intense [and] aimed at specific targets in specific areas."[6]

After the march, civil rights groups drew up plans to attack discrimination in Detroit. The DCHR had three pressing demands. It insisted that pupils should be assigned to schools according to race. Integration of public schools must occur, the council declared, even if it meant "changing the policy of enrolling pupils at neighborhood schools and transporting them to other buildings." The council also called for assurances that African Americans would have access to employment opportunities. "Union practices and rules that tend to limit or deny apprenticeship training to Negroes," the DCHR proclaimed in its press release, "must be eliminated." The third demand involved housing. DCHR Director James Del Rio, a black realtor, called on the city to find some way "to break down the pattern of exclusively white neighborhoods."[7]

The NAACP also increased its activities to focus public attention on housing discrimination. The branch employed nonviolent direct action, leading "freedom marches" through the white suburbs. Three hundred demonstrators protested segregation in Dearborn, the site of the Ford Motor Company plant. According to the 1960 census, Dearborn's population of 112,007 included only fifteen African Americans. Unlike during the rally in Detroit, however, a mob gathered to jeer the demonstrators. Some 2,000 whites taunted the protesters, throwing firecrackers into the path of the march. No one was hurt in the clash, in part because a large police presence seems to have kept the tensions from escalating. A week later, an open-occupancy march in the Redford area of northwest Detroit met a similar fate. Sixty police officers kept a small crowd of heckling whites in check. Some 300 local whites, however, welcomed an August rally in Oak Park that included the widow of Medgar Evers, and according to the *Michigan Chronicle*, the demonstrators saw "no open signs of criticism of the march or its purposes."[8]

On the legislative front, there was new movement as well. Fair-housing advocates had succeeded in getting an anti–block-busting law enacted by the city in 1962, but the Michigan legislature had rejected a statewide open-occupancy law in early 1963. The movement's leaders therefore turned their hopes back to Detroit. A week after the Walk to Freedom, Councilmen William T. Patrick and Mel J. Ravitz proposed a ban on racial bias in all real estate transactions within the city. The councilmen recognized the inadequacy of an open-occupancy law that only covered the city and not the suburbs, but they insisted that some kind of fair-housing ordinance was "urgently needed." A resolution calling for the state to enact statewide fair housing accompanied the Patrick-Ravitz proposal.[9]

Several civil rights interests lobbied for passage of the Patrick-Ravitz ordinance. The NAACP sponsored a petition drive and a "write-in" campaign with the help of the *Michigan Chronicle*. Detroiters were given a form letter to follow that concisely pressed councilmen to pass the proposal. "Equality of opportunity in housing," the letter proclaimed, "is the moral and democratic right of every citizen." "However," it continued, "nearly one-third of the citizens of Detroit are prevented from exercising this basic right because of their race and color." The letter then asked the specific legislator to use his full influence to ensure the passage of the open-occupancy ordinance.[10]

Despite the lobbying and, more significant in Detroit, the support of the United Auto Workers, a majority of the Detroit Common Council opposed the Patrick-Ravitz bill. Moderates on the council held that open-housing legislation was necessary but questioned the enforceability of the bill proposed. They did not believe that the city could enforce an antibias rule in the case of individual home owners because of the difficulty in proving discrimination. "You can observe a pattern of behavior by a businessman," one councilman observed, "but how often does a man sell his home?" Three other council members opposed any fair-housing ordinance. The hard-line segregationist, Billy Rogell, was joined in opposition by Philip J. Van Antwerp and Anthony J. Wierzbicki. Van Antwerp objected to the bill because he believed that it threatened "another basic right, that of holding property." To relieve itself of the question, the city council referred the Patrick-Ravitz bill to the Detroit Commission on Community Relations for study.[11]

An alliance of home owners and block improvement associations, meanwhile, had risen in opposition to the housing plan. The Greater Detroit Homeowners' Council (GDHC), representing some 200 groups with a potential membership of more than 250,000 people, called the proposal "the Negro master plan for domination of Detroit." It insisted that the entire civil rights movement in Detroit was destabilizing and excessive. It sponsored a second bill that reflected the influence of the National Association of Real Estate Boards. Following the wording of NAREB's "Homeowners' Bill of Rights," the proposal declared that a property owner enjoyed certain rights, including "the right of privacy, the right to choose his own friends and associates and to own, occupy and enjoy his property in any lawful fashion according to his own dictates." It guaranteed sellers the right to instruct realtors regarding who would be an acceptable buyer of a property. And it gave home owners the right "to rent or sell—or refuse to rent or sell—to any person for [their] own reasons." To ensure a hearing for its ordinance and to block the open-housing proposal, the GDHC presented the council with some 44,000 signatures on a petition. "I want to join the fight to protect my civil rights," the appeal read, embracing the rhetoric of rights and freedom. In response to the bill, Councilman Patrick declared that it "appear[ed] designed to subvert all the civil rights progress that [had been] achieved in the City of Detroit." Billy Rogell, however, asserted that "it [was] a man's right to sell his house to whoever he wishes." The moderates on council, meanwhile, called discrimination "immoral" and insisted that they "could not be a party to granting such authority."[12]

Thomas D. L. Poindexter led the charge for the home owners' rights law. A graduate of Wayne State University, Poindexter had a checkered legal and political career. He bounced around in general practice, specializing in tax law, before joining the conservative firm of Berris, Poindexter, and Berris in 1953. The *Detroit Free Press* reported that David I. Berris, his law partner, was a leader in the local John Birch Society. Poindexter ran for the Democratic congressional nomination in the 17th District in 1954 and for Common Pleas Court in 1960, losing both times. He led a court fight against a proposed increase in the local property tax and lost that, too. But the tax fight led to the creation of the GDHC and put Poindexter at the head of the movement. Poindexter railed against the Patrick-Ravitz bill, calling it "completely unsatisfactory" and contending that the "fund of good will" was being wasted and that "race relations in Detroit [were] being set back 50 years." Evincing his strong support for racial segregation, he suggested dividing Detroit into two cities: a black inner city and an independent white outer city.[13]

The Detroit council rejected the home owners' rights bill. Under council rules, however, since the bill did not pass, the petition required that the issue go to public ballot. A coalition of civil rights groups sued to enjoin the city from holding the referendum. Citizens for a United Detroit, encompassing members of the Metropolitan Detroit Council of Churches, the NAACP, and the Urban League among other groups, argued that the bill was unconstitutional because it equated a basic human right, that of access to shelter, with property rights. The challenge won in lower court. Judge Joseph A. Moynihan held that the bill tried "to appeal to the innate desire of every American citizen for independence." But its "real intention," in the court's view, was "to advance the cause of racial bigotry." Judge Moynihan insisted that it was his duty to stop any movement that sought "to advance its cause at the expense of the constitutional rights and privileges of any other group." The city, not very enthusiastic about the petition's aims in the first place, did not appeal the ruling. The GDHC, however, pressed on and won in the state Supreme Court.[14]

With the plebiscite scheduled for September 1, 1964, Citizens for a United Detroit took the fight to the public. The NAACP, while rejecting the validity of having the plebiscite at all, campaigned strongly to try to ensure its defeat. Referring to it as the "Poindexter Ordinance," the association maintained that it was "a vicious attempt, through unconstitutional means, to deprive some citizens of equal housing opportunities." "It deceives the voters," declared the Right Rev. Richard S. Emrich, Episcopal Bishop of Michigan, "it should not be called a 'Bill of Rights,' but 'The Ghetto Petition.'" "The proposed ordinance," the Detroit Bar Association advanced, was "so vague and indefinite as to violate the Fourteenth Amendment of the Federal Constitution." In its pre-election editorial, the *Michigan Chronicle* called the ordinance "notorious" and an "attempt of the reactionary element in our community to inject a note of bigotry and racism into the election." The paper insisted that the "decision of the community must be clearly in opposition to this attempt." It told its readers, "Be Sure to Vote NO for [the] Initiatory Ordinance" and even made sure to tell them repeatedly that it was the question "in the extreme right hand corner of the ballot."[15]

The African American community, however, was split over the importance of the vote. Many blacks were beginning to see the issue as irrelevant to their needs. Fair housing represented a middle-class concern, one less important to working-class and unemployed blacks. Gloster B. Current, the NAACP's director of branches, began noting the split as early as mid-1962. Working-class blacks, Current observed, seemed to be dropping away from the NAACP, many of them becoming more radical. Indeed, between 1963 and 1965, the branch lost 56 percent of its members. The DCHR, meanwhile, reflected the city's invigorated civil rights leadership and claimed that the NAACP and Urban League had become calcified special interests that had ceased to represent the city's blacks. James Del Rio, the DCHR housing director, called the NAACP leaders "a bunch of Uncle Toms" and even alleged that they were not trusted by other black Detroiters. "It couldn't be [trusted]," Del Rio argued, "bound hand and foot as it is to labor groups and the Democratic Party."[16]

More damaging to the fair-housing interests than the divisions within the African American community was growing concern about the movement's goals among hitherto moderate whites. Many of the white participants in and supporters of the Walk to Freedom had focused on Jim Crow laws in the South and the murder of Medgar Evers rather than problems in Detroit. When housing discrimination in Detroit became the focus, many whites jumped off the bandwagon or made excuses about the pace of reform. According to the *Free Press*, a "sizable majority" of whites in the metropolitan area "had little objection" to laws prohibiting discrimination in public accommodations, restaurants, and theaters. "Most [whites]," the paper suggested, "supported job retraining and apprentice-training programs and equal education opportunities for Negroes." But they balked when it came to open occupancy in housing. "A man's house is supposed to be his castle," one representative white suburbanite asserted.[17]

On primary day, Detroit voters not only approved the Home Owners' Rights Ordinance, but they also nominated Poindexter to a runoff election for a seat on the Common Council. The vote on the rights bill was close. The ordinance passed by just over 25,000 votes out of nearly 250,000 ballots cast. More striking, however, was Poindexter's triumph. He received 64,000 votes for the nomination, more than twice the number won by his closest competitor. Many observers ascribed the outcome to "white backlash," but other election returns complicate that assessment. Representative John Lesinski, the only Democrat outside the South to vote against the Civil Rights Act of 1964, was defeated in his primary. Some opponents of the bill, such as Mayor Cavanaugh, held that a newspaper strike that had been going on since mid-July kept the populace from really understanding the measure. But the fact that the voters distinguished between civil rights on the national level and housing in their neighborhood demonstrates that they understood their interests. An unwillingness to integrate their neighborhoods constitutes a more likely reason for Poindexter's and the bill's success.[18]

As white home owners and open-occupancy activists fought it out on the municipal level in Detroit, the same battle occurred on the state level in California. During the late 1950s and early 1960s, the fair-housing movement had made significant gains in the Golden State. In 1959, the California legislature enacted two major civil rights protections. The Unruh Act spoke to anti-discrimination generally, and the Hawkins Act banned discrimination in publicly assisted housing. In 1961, the state added the purely symbolic gesture of outlawing race-restrictive covenants.[19]

Events would show that support for the fair-housing movement in the Golden State was fairly soft. In early 1963, the bastion of California liberalism—Berkeley—

held a referendum on a local ordinance banning discrimination in all real estate sales and rentals. According to W. J. Rorabaugh, the liberal-dominated Berkeley city council had raised the issue with the intent of knocking out the last vestiges of conservatism in the city's administration. As Rorabaugh tells it, the purpose of the proposed ordinance was "largely symbolic . . . [because Berkeley's blacks] needed good schools and high-paying jobs a lot more than the theoretical right to buy expensive homes in the all white [neighborhoods in the] hills." The move backfired. The ordinance was blocked by a vote of 22,750 to 20,456, with 83 percent of registered voters going to the polls. One of the council's liberal, African American members, Bernice Hubbard May, summed up the process, explaining that it had shown only one thing: Berkeley's whites had said, "'It's all right to have a brother of any color, but I don't want him on my block.'"[20]

Advocates of fair housing pressed on. In the fall of 1963, William Byron Rumford, Berkeley's African American state assemblyman, sponsored a bill to expand the scope of and give teeth to the earlier state laws. The Rumford Fair Housing Act prohibited racial discrimination in the sale or rental of any private dwelling consisting of more than four units and created a specific enforcement procedure. It placed the authority for enforcement of the act in the State Fair Employment Practices Commission (SFEPC).[21]

The California Real Estate Association (CREA) and California Apartment Owners' Association opposed the Rumford Act and lobbied to kill it. When the law passed, they formed the Committee for Home Protection and spearheaded a petition drive to force a statewide plebiscite on the Rumford Act. The anti-Rumford group needed to amass 468,259 valid signatures to place the proposition on the ballot. It gathered some 600,000 in eighteen days in February 1964. "Prop. 14," as it became known, proposed to amend the state constitution to guarantee a home owner's right to sell only to whom he or she wished to sell. "Neither the State nor any subdivision or agency thereof," the amendment decreed, "shall deny, limit or abridge . . . the right of any person, [desiring to sell or rent property], to decline to sell, lease or rent such property to such person or persons as he, in his absolute discretion, chooses."[22]

As with the opponents of open occupancy in Detroit, the Committee for Home Protection spoke in terms of home owners' rights, freedom from intrusive government, and opposition to "forced housing." CREA and its affiliated members took particular aim at the SFEPC as the arbiter of housing disputes. "How is the Rumford Forced Housing Act enforced?" the realtors asked in a handbill. "Through an administrative tribunal," it replied, "not through our usual court system." The SFEPC, one opponent of the Rumford Act contended, "is the investigator, prosecutor, judge, and jury rolled into one," and that, CREA noted, ran counter to the Seventh Amendment's guarantee of trial by jury. "The primary purpose of Proposition 14 [was] not to discriminate," the president of the San Fernando Valley Board of Realtors insisted, "but to provide a safeguard for the rights of the people of California."

Under the Rumford Act, according to the realtors, "the state [was] maintaining . . . that the [property] owner may retain his freedom of choice [only] as long as his choice agrees with that of the State."[23]

California's government leaders spoke out against Proposition 14. Governor Edmund G. Brown led the opposition. Republican U.S. Senator Thomas H. Kuchel, high-level state officials, the California Bar Association, labor leaders, and the federal housing bureaucracy joined him. Brown condemned Proposition 14 as a grave step backward and challenged the legality of the proposition, suggesting that it represented an "abuse" of the initiative process. Senator Kuchel, the minority whip who had played a key role in the Senate debates on the Civil Rights Act of 1964, predicted that a "yes" vote on Proposition 14 would "create tremendous confusion with respect to real estate transactions." He called the question of open occupancy "a solemn issue of morality" and contended that the proposition "mock[ed] the American conscience." Assemblyman Rumford, meanwhile, warned that housing issues "would have to be settled in the streets" if his legislation were repealed by the proposition. HHFA Director Robert Weaver traveled from Washington to lobby against the measure. He threatened that a "yes" vote would likely cost the state millions of dollars in federal housing and urban renewal funds. If local agencies could not prove that no discrimination would occur in renewal areas, Weaver warned, "the federal government [might not] contract to make planning or other funds commitments for renewal projects."[24]

The state's religious leaders divided over the proposal, reflecting the regional split that existed throughout the population. In northern California, church leaders such as Archbishop Joseph T. McGucken of the San Francisco Archdiocese denounced the initiative. McGucken wrote from Rome to request that priests make a special statement against the proposition during mass on the Sunday before the vote. "Inequality in the opportunity to enjoy decent housing, based solely on race," the archbishop pronounced, "is an insult to human dignity." In southern California, however, James Francis Cardinal McIntyre of Los Angeles remained conspicuously silent. Catholic priests were forbidden to speak on the subject. A Carmelite priest in the Pomona area was threatened with transfer out of the state if he carried out his plan to speak before a "no" vote seminar. Another priest was forbidden to say mass after he railed against the proposition during a Sunday service. The church reprimanded the priest, asserting that he had violated the integrity of his parishioners' consciences.[25]

The fair-housing movement fought Proposition 14 at every turn. The NAACP's West Coast Regional Legal Committee, headed by Loren Miller and Nathaniel Cooley, tried to enjoin the vote, challenging the validity of the signatures on the initiative petitions. Superior Court Judge Purliss ruled that enough signatures were valid to allow a vote, but he did agree to delay the balloting from June until the general election in November, giving opponents more time to organize. Over the next months, civil rights groups worked to turn public opinion. As they had in Detroit, opponents insisted that the object of the initiative was to "make discrimination and segregation part of the public policy of the state." They contended, moreover, that the constitutional amendment would tie the hands of government "by preventing any future legislation in the field of fair housing." The NAACP organized a door-to-door campaign, working among African Americans to ensure a high voter turnout and then expanding into the white and Hispanic populations to "educate the voter[s], find out which ones will vote NO, and make sure that they get to the polls." Martin Luther King Jr. waded in, calling the initiative "sinful" and contending that a "yes" vote "would be a great blow to the cause of freedom." Bayard Rustin, a cofounder of CORE, worried that the psychological effect of passage on the African American community and the nation would be tremendous. "All over the United States," he declared at a San Francisco news conference, Proposition 14 "has become a symbol for segregation in schools and housing." If this initiative passes, Rustin warned, "there will be a spate of them introduced over the country." And Nat King Cole, a man with an intimate knowledge of the lengths whites could go to intimidate blacks who tried to move in next door, helped raise money for the "no" campaign.[26]

Despite the work of state and community leaders, polls evinced growing support for the measure. A poll in January showed opinion evenly divided: 41 percent ready to vote "yes," 40 percent "no," and 19 percent undecided. On the eve of the election, a Field Research Corporation poll showed support had risen to 49 percent, but many voters remained undecided. In northern California, polls showed opinion equally split. In the south, where the *Los Angeles Times* supported the initiative, opinion on the measure ran two-to-one in favor of the proposition. Opponents of the initiative blamed voter support on CREA's distortions and claims that the Rumford Act "was communist-inspired." They suggested that voters were confused about the real objectives and consequences of the initiative. A Field Research Corporation poll showed, however, that when pollsters had voters read a summary of the arguments for and against the measure, the "yes" vote actually increased.[27]

On November 3, 1964, the same day that they rejected the conservative Republican presidential candidate Barry Goldwater, Californians approved Proposition 14 by a vote of nearly two to one. Southern Californians voted overwhelmingly to support home owners' rights. Voters in Orange County, for example, voted "yes" at a ratio of more than three to one. With 90 percent of the precincts having reported, nearly 1,000,000 Los Angelenos had voted "yes," as compared to fewer than 400,000 "no" ballots. Rural counties across the state championed the initiative. San Joaquin County, the heart of the conservative farmbelt, polled more than thirteen to one in favor of the measure. The only support for the "no" campaign came from the San Francisco area. But even there, a majority of voters backed the amendment. With eight precincts left to report, the "yes" vote in San Francisco counted nearly 160,000 "yes" votes to 133,000 "no" votes. Marin and Santa Clara Counties had tight races, but San Mateo, Alameda, and Sonoma Counties more closely mirrored the statewide trend.[28]

After the election, fair-housing advocates vowed to take their campaign to federal court, and CREA pledged to "fight any attempt to kill Proposition 14," but the vote had exposed a nasty secret—one that once divulged would have explosive results. To paraphrase the journalist Milton Viorst, the vote showed that in California, "with its liberal governor and state legislature, where Jim Crow never lived and the exercise of the right to vote was encouraged," whites could and would still put limits on civil rights for and opportunities of African Americans.[29]

For a young activist from the Watts section of Los Angeles, the battle over Proposition 14 was a revelation. Richard Townsend, a cofounder of the Student Committee for the Improvement of Watts (SCIFW—pronounced "skee-foo"), observed that the civil rights movement in Alabama and Mississippi in 1963 and 1964 had largely been an abstraction to the African American youth in Watts, who were preoccupied dealing with gangs, police brutality, poverty, and unemployment. The fight against Proposition 14, however, brought the issues of freedom and opportunity closer and made them more real. The campaign, according to Townsend, marked "the first time [that he had] ever heard of anything political going on in the churches." He observed that "very few [blacks] got out and knocked on doors [to enlist votes against the proposition], but it was [still] really important to people. . . . Even the [poorer] blacks who couldn't move anywhere discussed it." Townsend further noted that "everyone was angry that [the issue] even came up," but they were angrier still about how the vote came out. "Everybody in Watts," he insisted, "was aware that they were being rejected by somebody, by somebody white."[30]

The sense of rejection was a significant source of the disaffection that exploded into the Watts riot in August 1965. As Viorst noted, it merged with the new consciousness growing out of the Black Muslim movement. Blacks in Watts already had access to restaurants, theaters, hotels, and schools, and they faced no restrictions on voting, except perhaps for an overwhelming sense of apathy. But they lacked economic opportunity and the defeat of fair housing, for many, exposed the reason why they still lacked opportunity. It was as Malcolm X had told them a year before the riot: "The white Southerner . . . tells the black man, to his face, that Southern whites will never accept phony 'integration.' . . . But the Northern white man, he grins with his teeth, and his mouth has always been full of tricks and lies of 'equality' and 'integration.'" Blacks in Watts were still not willing to adopt the separatism of the Black Muslims, but by August 11 they were certainly willing to accept the call to fight back against injustice with their fists and with fire. This is not meant to suggest that had Proposition 14 not succeeded, there would have been no Watts riot. It is entirely possible that the secret would have been exposed in another way. What it is meant to suggest is that the defeat of the fair-housing movement in California was a central underlying cause of the violence.[31]

Prospects for the fair-housing movement continued to get worse after Watts. In just over a year, *Trends in Housing* reported, the drive for referenda to block passage of new fair-housing legislation or to revoke existing laws had spread "from California to Michigan to Illinois to the State of Washington, and rumblings are being heard in other areas." In 1965, while Congress enacted the most sweeping and significant voting rights legislation since Reconstruction, support for open-occupancy laws eroded more. NCDH affiliates lobbied strongly for an extension of Kennedy's executive order. "At this crucial period in history," the NCDH declared, "a restricted housing market [divided the] nation, crippling the effort of responsible government and private leadership to achieve the goal of equal opportunity." "The racial ghetto," it insisted in a letter to President Johnson, "stands as an almost impenetrable barrier to meaningful gains in integrated education, equal job opportunities, normal family and community life, and the future health of the American metropolis." Johnson, however, refused to budge. He insisted that only congressional approval would give fair housing the "moral force" necessary to ensure the people's acceptance. And Congress had no plan to hear anti-discrimination legislation regarding housing during 1966.[32]

If 1964 and 1965 were bad years for the fair housing movement, then the next two years constituted a near apocalypse. For years, the leaders of the civil rights movement had made forays into the North, such as the Walk to Freedom in Detroit in 1963. Two years later, after the success of the Alabama voting rights march from Selma to Montgomery, Martin Luther King Jr. and the SCLC began searching for a northern city in which to begin a new campaign of nonviolent direct action. Given the propensity toward housing and employment discrimination in the North, the movement could have taken its challenge to any number of cities. Cleveland, New York City, Philadelphia, and Washington, D.C., were among the sites considered. The city of Chicago, however, had all the essential ingredients for a major civil rights initiative. Housing segregation was nearly absolute. Inner-city schools crumbled under the weight of overcrowding and a depleted tax base. The city had a highly concentrated political structure in the grip of Mayor Richard J. Daley. And the African American community was organized and determined to challenge the ghetto structure. The Coordinated Council of Community Organizations (CCCO), a coalition of thirty-five civil rights groups, had been fighting segregation in schools for two years and had created Operation Breadbasket to combat employment discrimination. The history of Cicero and Trumbull Park, moreover, exposed the potential volatility of the white citizenry, an important factor considering the SCLC's tactics. "If we can break the backbone of discrimination in Chicago," King assured his followers, "we can do it in all the cities in the country."[33]

At the beginning of September 1965, Andrew Young, King's close colleague from Atlanta, announced that the SCLC and CCCO would mount "a massive nonviolent movement." The Chicago Freedom Movement would unfold in three stages. Early in 1966, according to the coalition's draft plan, activists would undertake to "awaken the people" and recruit troops for the "nonviolent army" by canvassing the ghetto and educating its inhabitants. Phase two of the action, beginning in March, would consist of demonstrations to "reveal the agents of exploitation and paint a portrait of the evils" that beset Chicago's African American community. Then, as spring arrived, the third stage would begin, promising "massive action" that would establish a "coalition of conscience" and create a confrontation between "the power of the existing social order and the newly acquired power of the combined forces of good-will and the under-privileged." Initially, the coalition had no clear target other than "economic exploitation." But as winter turned into spring and then into summer without the movement having made an impact and with its nonviolent tactics coming under increasing criticism from advocates of Black Power, the coalition finally agreed to make fair housing its focus.[34]

The new plan was called Operation Open City. It was conceived by Bernard Lafayette of the American Friends Service Committee. It called for a "domestic Marshall Plan" to end poverty and blight in the inner city. "To wipe out slums, ghettos, and racism," the program declared, Chicagoans "must create an *open* city with equal opportunities and equal results." But the movement also made several specific demands. With housing its "primary target," it demanded that real estate listings and mortgage loans be "immediately available on a non-discriminatory basis." It insisted that realtors endorse and support open occupancy in theory and comply with Chicago's fair housing ordinance already on the books. It required that the city and state governments enforce existing fair practices laws and demanded that authorities revoke the licenses of real estate brokers who discriminate. It also requested programs to build new housing outside the ghetto and to rehabilitate dilapidated apartments inside the ghetto. The coalition made two demands of the federal government: issuance of an executive order that would place lending institutions under federal supervision to ensure nondiscriminatory granting of loans and passage of the proposed civil rights act with its fair-housing title intact. To achieve its goals and expose the discrimination that blacks routinely faced, the Chicago Freedom Movement planned to lead nonviolent marches through white neighborhoods, focusing on the Italian and Polish Belmont-Cragin section on the northwest side and on the Central European Gage Park-Chicago Lawn area on the southwest.[35]

The redirected movement got off to an inauspicious beginning. It had planned to begin with a big rally at Soldier Field followed by a march to City Hall, where King, imitating his namesake Martin Luther, would affix the movement's demands to the door. Poor organization and searing heat caused turnout for the rally to be a fraction of what leaders had expected. They had hoped for 100,000 supporters, but estimates of actual turnout ran closer to 30,000. Ralph David Abernathy, King's right hand in the SCLC, blamed the poor showing on divisions in the black community—a split among the more moderate Baptists, the radical and growing Black Muslim groups, and the entrenched municipal employees who were "afraid to disobey the explicit orders [to stay away] handed down by . . . Daley's straw bosses." According to Abernathy, however, general apathy among African Americans "in [the] vast, anonymous city" really caused the particularly poor turnout.[36]

King was "still the favorite" among blacks, according to a Louis Harris poll, but many civil rights groups were questioning whether the tactic of nonviolence could succeed. Two days after the rally, the heat and racial tension on the city's West Side exploded into a riot after police tried to turn off a flowing fire hydrant. The sixty-four-square-block section was home to about 80,000 people, nearly all of them African American and most of them living on welfare. Teen unemployment in the area ran upwards of 50 percent, and adult male unemployment ran at around 40 percent. For more than three days, blacks fought with police, first on the West Side and then on the South Side. Order was restored only after Governor Otto Kerner mobilized the National Guard. Not only did the riot divert attention from the movement, but it also further alienated moderate whites. Mayor Daley blamed the coalition for the riot. The SCLC, he claimed, had been threatening revolution for a year and made a business of "showing pictures and instructing people in how to conduct violence." King denied the accusations and countered that had the SCLC leadership not been in Chicago, the riot "would have been worse than Watts." He and Abernathy had met with gang leaders during the riot in an attempt, according to Abernathy, to "explain nonviolence as a positive strategy rather than a failure to fight at all." The gang members listened to the ministers. "They listened, argued, listened some more, and," Abernathy recalled, "finally said they understood . . . and would cooperate."[37]

With the city reeling from the riots and preoccupied by the news of the grisly murder by Richard Speck of eight student nurses, the Chicago Freedom Movement tentatively began small demonstrations in white sections. On the weekend of July 16, 1966, the activists held an interracial picnic in Marquette Park in the Chicago Lawn area. African American women, meanwhile, spent their Saturday shopping for groceries in Gage Park stores, comparing prices and quality. At first, local whites greeted the action more with curiosity than hostility. A vigil in Gage Park on Sunday, however, met a jeering crowd. The next weekend, the movement traveled to the Belmont-Cragin district. After a morning of testing discriminatory practices at the offices of real estate brokers, the demonstrators had a picnic in Riis Park. The day passed without incident.[38]

The mild response to the movement from white Chicagoans ended on July 29. A planned all-night vigil at a realty office in Gage Park was called off when a crowd began threatening the demonstrators. The next day, whites hurled bottles and rocks at the pickets as they marched in Gage Park. On July 31, while parading from Marquette Park to a Chicago Lawn Methodist church, the marchers faced a swelling white mob that threw cherry-bombs in their path as they neared the church. The marchers beat a hasty retreat to Marquette Park, hoping to get back to safety. But when they arrived at the park they discovered that the mob had vandalized their cars. Despite the presence of police, whites had set cars on fire, overturned them, and slashed their tires. The marchers therefore had to walk back to the South Side, the mob taunting and threatening them all the way.[39]

King did not take part in the July marches because of commitments elsewhere, but he returned to Chicago in August. He met with religious leaders and addressed a rally at the New Friendship Baptist Church. If the activists had any doubt as to King's or their own commitment to the movement, the great orator washed it away. In his famous rhetorical style, he convinced his followers to press on in the struggle. "My place is in the sunlight of opportunity," he began his refrain. "My place is in the dignity of a good job and livable wages; my place is in the security of an adequate quality education," he added. "My place," he roared, now joined by the audience, "is in the comfort and the convenience and in the nobility of good, solitary living conditions and in a good house. . . . My place is in Gage Park."[40]

On August 5, King led 800 marchers in the largest demonstration to date. It began in Marquette Park and went through Gage Park to a real estate office. Hundreds of local whites met the parade. Knowing his importance to the movement, counterdemonstrators took aim at King with rocks and bottles. A rock the size of a fist struck King in the head, knocking him to his knees, but King rose and marched onward. One of the counterdemonstrators flung a knife at King, narrowly missing him but hitting a white marcher. At their destination, the marchers knelt to pray and then began their return trek. The demonstrators arrived back at Marquette Park only to face some 4,000 hostile whites. The mob assailed the nonviolent activists with rocks and fists. A one-sided battle raged. Only the vigorous response of about 1,200 police, it seems, kept the violence from escalating to lethal proportions. The hostility stunned even the most experienced activists. Andrew Young noted that he had faced mobs in the South, "but it would be a couple of hundred or even fifty or seventy-five [and it] always came from a rabble element." In Marquette Park, however, the attackers "were women and children and husbands and wives coming out of their homes, becoming a mob." King admitted, "I have never seen such hostility and hatred anywhere in my life, even in Selma." "This," he summarized simply, "is a terrible thing."[41]

The violent response to the marches gave Operation Open City the attention that the CCCO and SCLC had wanted. They pledged to hold more demonstrations in neighborhoods across the city. That prospect frightened and disturbed city leaders. They pressured the movement to call off future marches. Chicagoans had gotten the point, they contended, and were willing to negotiate a settlement. The Commission on Human Relations recommended that coalition leaders meet face-to-face with Mayor Daley, the Chicago Real Estate Board, and other interested parties. The CCCO and SCLC expressed a willingness to meet but insisted on keeping up the pressure. Jesse Jackson, the leader of Operation Breadbasket, announced that the movement planned to march in South Deering, the site of Trumbull Park Homes, and in Cicero.[42]

Despite Daley's demand that the marches stop, the Chicago Freedom Movement continued to protest during the fortnight following the Marquette Park melee. The movement picketed the Chicago Real Estate Board offices, several banks, and the Chicago Housing Authority. It organized what Jackson called "educational tours" through white neighborhoods to show blacks "the homes they [would] be living in soon." A strengthened police presence kept the demonstrations from devolving into violence.[43]

On August 17, coalition leaders met with Mayor Daley and other civic leaders to try to end the crisis. They repeated the demands that they had been making throughout the conflict. Daley acknowledged that he might agree to the demands if the marches stopped, but many of the requests were not his to decide. The real estate industry's delegation argued that the mayor did not have the authority to speak for the realty board. They announced that they were willing to stop resisting fair housing as an idea, but they refused to budge on their opposition to the proposed statewide bill as it stood. The bill did not include regulations on property owners who sold their homes privately, and the realtors believed that the oversight put the professional sellers at a disadvantage. They suggested that they would abide by the Chicago fair housing ordinance already in existence but refused to end their court appeal against the statute. The industry's position did not satisfy the activists. After more debate, the conference ended, the two sides agreeing to meet in subcommittees for further negotiations.[44]

As the deliberations continued, the coalition proceeded with its plan to march in South Deering, while Mayor Daley moved to block future protests. "We have to keep on marching," King announced to a rally at the Greater Mount Hope Baptist Church and its radio audience. He had admitted to the conference that he was tired of demonstrating. "I am tired of the threat of death," he had told them, "tired of getting hit, tired of being beaten, tired of going to jail. . . . I do not want to be a martyr," he confessed. But he insisted that the marches would continue because they had "revealed a cancer" and they could not stop until the cancer had been cut out. Daley, meanwhile, pursued a court order enjoining the movement from marching. Although he did not get that, Daley did get an injunction restricting the size of the demonstrations and their timing. The continued marches and the injunction forced the two sides closer, but Daley had taken the upper hand. That became even more evident when the Chicago City Council endorsed the injunction by a vote of forty-five to one.[45]

On August 26, the conference subcommittee issued its report. Despite the extra week of negotiations, the settlement did not differ from that recommended before the conference adjourned on August 17. In return for the Chicago Freedom Movement's ending its protests, city and county agencies pledged to strengthen the enforcement of the fair-housing ordinance, to improve the quality and security of inner-city housing projects, and to scatter housing for the elderly across the city. The churches agreed to sponsor programs to teach their congregations about the need for open housing. Mortgage lenders affirmed a policy to provide equal service and to grant loans to all qualified persons regardless of race. The Chicago Real Estate Board, however, did not budge from its earlier position. It declared its belief in "the fundamental principle that freedom of choice in housing is the right of every citizen." It promised to withdraw its opposition to "the philosophy of open occupancy legislation at the state level," but only if the law applied to home owners as well as brokers.[46]

Backed into a corner by the injunction and with public opinion turning against them, movement leaders accepted the proposal. Local activists wanted to continue negotiations until they had won specific assurances from the city, but King prevailed. The movement had been negotiating from a position of weakness. Despite the hostility of the mobs, the tactic of nonviolent direct action had failed to sway moderate whites. According to James R. Ralph Jr., a close observer of the Chicago movement, King "recognized the limits of the size of the Chicago nonviolent army." King put the best face on the settlement. Although it represented only "a first step in a thousand mile journey," he called it "the most significant and far reaching victory that [had] ever come about in a northern community on the whole question of open housing." "The whole power structure," he proclaimed, "was forced . . . to sit down and negotiate and capitulate and make concessions that have never been made before."[47]

During the year following the Chicago Freedom Movement, urban conditions and race relations across the nation continued to deteriorate. According to a count by the Legislative Reference Service of the Library of Congress, the number of incidents of civil disorder had quadrupled from 1965 to 1966, from eleven to forty-three. This figure more than doubled again in 1967. Tensions between blacks and police rose so much that any seemingly insignificant incident could set off a firestorm of retaliatory or anarchic violence, each one more destructive than the one before. In early April, a minor riot broke out in Nashville after police, at the request of the property's owner, tried to remove an intoxicated soldier from a restaurant. Local students rained rocks and bottles down on the police and their reinforcements until officers fired shots over the heads of the demonstrators and the crowd slowly dispersed. In May, students clashed with police on the campus of Jackson State College. Three of the protesters were shot by police, one of them fatally. It took the Mississippi National Guard to restore order. And then the campus of Texas Southern University in Houston erupted. For several hours, police and demonstrators exchanged gunfire. A policeman was killed by a ricocheting bullet.[48]

With each successive week, it seemed, the conflicts grew in number and intensity. In the 94-degree heat of Tampa in June, the police shooting of a black youth fleeing a robbery erupted into a riot. For six hours, African Americans trashed, looted, and set fire to the Central Avenue commercial district. First the police, then the Florida National Guard, and finally a youth patrol made up of young blacks from the Central Park Village Housing project, some of whom had participated in the rioting, worked to restore and keep the peace. Similar disturbances occurred in June in Cincinnati, Buffalo and Niagara Falls, Atlanta, Boston and Cambridge, Philadelphia, and several other cities. In July, ninety-five cities witnessed civil disorders ranging from minor skirmishes to full-scale and deadly riots. The worst riots occurred in Newark and Detroit. When the week of rioting in Newark ended, it had caused $15 million in damage, twenty-five persons were dead, at least 725 were injured, and nearly 1,500 had been arrested. Federal troops needed to be called in to quell the violence in Detroit in late July. After six days of burning and looting, forty-three lay dead, more than 1,000 were injured, and 7,231 had been arrested. The Detroit riot caused an estimated $500 million in property damage. Despite the rhetoric of revolution, in most of the 103 cases of civil disorder in 1967, the violence had been unfocused and reactionary, and it achieved little more than to alienate the country from the civil rights movement.[49]

Along with the riots, the rhetoric of black nationalism grew in intensity. In January 1965, *Jet* magazine had published an article praising assimilation, by which it meant the amalgamation of racial and cultural differences into a single new culture, as the "explosive new concept for coming decades." In it, Dr. Ira De A. Reid, still one of the leading African American sociologists, foresaw assimilation as an objective of the Great Society. "If society continues to move ahead," he reasoned, then "biological and social assimilation will take place and [America could] be the first truly assimilated society in the modern world." Such an idea had become anathema to many in the civil rights movement by 1967, however. Many African Americans instead called for Black Power, separation from hostile whites, and for celebration of African-ness. "Black," it was proclaimed in defiance of generations of degradation, "is beautiful." Groups such as the Student Nonviolent Coordinating Committee (SNCC, pronounced snick), and CORE first pushed whites out of leadership positions and then pushed them right out of their organizations. In July 1967, the first National Conference on Black Power was held in Newark, New Jersey. According to the *New York Amsterdam News*, nearly 1,000 African Americans attended and passed a resolution calling for "paramilitary training of youth as a black militia to train black families in all aspects of self-defense and racial survival." The group also rejected the use of the term "Negro," replacing it with "black," and called for the "castigation of Christianity as 'a white religion.'" Delegates declared: "The question now is not of integrating into a white restaurant but of owning a black restaurant, not of running a liberal white candidate but a black candidate." Black power had its critics. The NAACP's Roy Wilkins, for example, considered separatism a destructive notion, calling its advocates "blind" and contending that a separate black economy ran "against the whole international trend of mankind." But the black nationalists rejected such claims. The doctrine of nonviolence was dead, having been killed in Selma. By 1967, as CORE cofounder James Farmer suggested, it seemed that "the interracialism that had been the trademark of the movement [shared its tomb]."[50]

Amid the anarchy and growing racial hostility, one prolonged demonstration differed from the rest. Milwaukee, Wisconsin, had not escaped the urban and racial problems that plagued the nation's cities. In early August, the city's African American community erupted in riot, and Governor Warren P. Knowles called in the Wisconsin National Guard to restore order. But by the end of the month, African Americans redirected their rage and turned it into a disciplined, productive force from which to draw during a major act of civil disobedience and protest. Throughout the late summer and autumn of 1967, a white priest and the NAACP's Youth Council led nightly demonstrations into the white sections of the city to pressure the government into enacting a comprehensive open-housing law.

Wisconsin, a state with a long history of progressivism, had been among the first states after New York to prohibit racial discrimination in public housing. In the early 1960s, it established an office in the state industrial commission to review claims of racial bias in "housing, recreation, education, employment, health and social welfare." According to then Governor John W. Reynolds, however, the act's reference to housing pertained only to employment of construction workers. In 1964, the state legislature failed to pass a bill that would have banned discrimination in the sale, rental, or financing of private housing. In 1965, it did enact an open-housing law, but the law covered only buildings with five or more dwelling units, or about 30 percent of the housing units in the state. With state legislators unwilling to go any farther than the 1965 law, open-housing advocates turned their attention to the cities. They requested an opinion on the legality of municipal and local ordinances from the state attorney general's office. In October 1966, Wisconsin Attorney General Bronson La Follette declared that "even though regulation of nondiscrimination in housing is a matter of statewide concern," cities and towns did have the power to pass their own housing laws. To further facilitate local action, La Follette's office issued a model open-housing ordinance to mayors around the state.[51]

By the summer of 1967, the state's abdication created tensions between the city of Milwaukee and its suburbs like those that existed in Detroit. Milwaukee's mayor, Henry W. Maier, was a national leader in urban reform efforts, and he understood the condition of blacks in the nation's cities. "In every metropolitan area," he noted, "we see apartheid on a scale to thrill the heart of every true South African." But fearing further loss of the city's tax base, he insisted that Milwaukee could not enact anti-discrimination legislation unless suburban communities and the county followed suit. "How in hell are we going to finance a city," Maier asked, "when the middle class moves out and the needs are here?" When attacked by advocates who accused him of dragging his feet on open housing and who insisted that they were focusing on the city because that was where most African Americans lived, Maier suggested that it was discrimination that was keeping African Americans in the city and keeping them out of the suburbs. "Shouldn't they have open housing where there are no Negroes?" he asked. "Wouldn't it be logical to have open housing in the suburbs to absorb some of the poor?" "I would be delighted to have central city open housing," he explained, "if [the suburbs] would build 50,000 low income units to help break this up and help these people." What would really benefit African Americans in Milwaukee, according to Maier, was state and federal money to stem the financial crisis and not just in Milwaukee, but in cities across the nation.[52]

Over the mayor's objections, fair-housing advocates began demonstrations to force the city to end housing discrimination. In late August, a group of black youths called "the commandos" and their spiritual and political adviser, Father James E. Groppi, undertook a series of marches through the mostly Polish neighborhoods on the South Side to protest segregation. The youths numbered about fifty. All but one of them was African American; they ranged in age from eighteen to twenty-six and represented a cross-section of the urban core youth population. They had been organized mainly to protect children and teens in the Youth Council, but under the influence of the thirty-six-year-old assistant pastor at St. Boniface Catholic Church, the commandos developed into a disciplined team of civil rights activists. They represented the new breed of protester; they preferred nonviolent demonstrations, but they refused to rule out violent retaliation if provoked.[53]

From the first march and rally, it was clear that the demonstrations would bring pitted battles between marchers and residents of the South Side that would throw the city into turmoil. On August 28, 1967, Groppi and the commandos amassed a throng of just over 200 persons for a march into the South Side and a picnic at Kosciuszko Park. As they crossed the Menomonee River Valley, locally referred to as "Milwaukee's Mason-Dixon line" because, as the *Milwaukee Sentinel* pointed out, it formed "a natural boundary that has unnaturally kept most minority groups out of south side neighborhoods," some 3,000 south-siders lined the march path. The local whites carried signs that proclaimed "Polish Power" and hurled epithets like "Nigger Go Home" and "Go Back to Africa." Some shouted "Sieg Heil" at the marchers; some threw stones, bottles, garbage, or chunks of wood. Several times the police escort for the marchers had to form a wedge to force a passage through the white mob. Then as they reached Kosciuszko Park, the marchers were met by some 5,000 more angry whites. Minor scuffles occurred, and the police made a few arrests, but no large-scale violence resulted. As he departed, Father Groppi pledged that the marchers would return the next night.[54]

The second night of marching brought more tension and more violence. About 13,000 south-siders mobbed the marchers, showering them with bottles and rocks and this time chanting a refrain: "kill . . . kill . . . kill . . . kill . . . kill." Terrified but not panicky, the marchers continued forward. Father Groppi directed them to close ranks and keep their heads down. "Keep cool, walk fast, girls in the middle," he advised. "Don't be afraid. If we were afraid to die," he admonished, "we wouldn't be good Christians." Police fired tear gas into the crowd, breaking it up. In all, twenty-two people were injured, none of them seriously, and forty-five were arrested. But the violence did not cease with the marchers' retreat to Freedom House, the NAACP Youth Council headquarters. As the marchers returned to base, gunshots rang out from a building across the street. Police on the scene fired a barrage into the house, but when they entered they found nobody inside. The marchers, still riled from their confrontation with racism on the South Side, turned on the police, hurling bottles and smashing the window of a squad car. As they fought, a white Chevrolet passed in front of Freedom House, and one of the car's passengers flung a firebomb at the building. It went up in flames.[55]

The violence shocked the city, but opinion leaders differed on who was responsible for it. "If the civil rights demonstrators led by Father James Groppi were trying to show that our community is poisoned by hate," the *Milwaukee Journal* asserted in an editorial condemning the white response to the demonstrations, "the point has been made." It added: "The shameful bigotry shown by whites" "was a rejection of everything Americans and Christians should stand for. The sight of children with their parents joining in chants of hate was enough to sicken decent people." The *Milwaukee Sentinel* concurred. "There's no minimizing the shame that Milwaukee should feel at the events of two recent nights," it exclaimed, "the city has been disgraced by the show of naked hatred, which must shock those who believe in the innate tolerance of all men." Most of the city's churches agreed, and a significant majority of those polled by the *Milwaukee Journal* disapproved of the white resistance to the marchers. But Mayor Maier focused on the role of the marchers in instigating the violence with their protests. To restore order, he declared a thirty-day moratorium on night demonstrations.[56]

Calling the ban on marches unconstitutional, Groppi and the commandos turned their attention to the mayor. They led civil disobedience marches through the downtown core to city hall and Maier's home and held a large rally at the gutted Freedom House to protest the lack of police protection for the demonstrators. Each demonstration brought confrontations with police. Because of the mayor's proclamation, police were ordered to arrest the marchers, including Father Groppi. The marchers resisted arrest and fought openly with police. They hailed police with rocks and other missiles, calling them "Nazis" and "Gestapo." Father Groppi complained of a double standard, insisting that the mayor was more willing to use excessive force against African Americans than against white counterdemonstrators. The NAACP and American Civil Liberties Union, meanwhile, undertook to challenge the mayor's edict in court. That battle never occurred, however, because the city rescinded the order.[57]

As the week of protests progressed, the open housing demonstrators won new supporters. Numerous local, state, and national organizations and churches voiced their sympathy for the marches and called for an open housing law. The League of Women Voters, the Human Relations Coordinating Council, and the Metropolitan Builders of Greater Milwaukee passed resolutions of support. The city's most important antipoverty planning agency, the Community Relations–Social Development Commission, also adopted a resolution supporting the movement. The press even speculated that Martin Luther King Jr. and black nationalist leader H. Rap Brown would take part in some marches. They did not appear, however.[58]

On Sunday, September 10, 1967, the cycle of housing marches and resistance began again. Some 2,300 marchers, including the comedian Dick Gregory and NAACP officials from Chicago, returned to the South Side. The march ended without serious incident. On Monday evening, 650 marchers took part in the demonstration. As they crossed the 16th Street viaduct, they were met by a mob of about 1,000 white counterdemonstrators, carrying signs reading "White Power," "Black

Slaves Forever," "Open Housing in Africa," and "Block Them Off, Nobody Goes South." They jeered and taunted the marchers, chanting "Ee-yi-ee-yi-ee-yi-o, Father Groppi's gotta go" and "We want slaves." Some of the whites began throwing bottles and rocks. The marchers fired rocks and bottles back. The two sides battled for only about fifteen minutes before police broke up the melee, and the marchers retreated to St. Boniface Church. "If we had gone any farther," Groppi remarked, "they would have slaughtered us."[59]

For the next few days, as Father Groppi, Dick Gregory, and the commandos continued their marches through other sections of the city without incident, white south-siders held counterdemonstrations. On Tuesday night, now calling themselves the "White Power Rangers" and forming into groups such as the Milwaukee Organization for Closed Housing and Milwaukee Citizens Civic Voice, the whites intended to march on St. Boniface Church. When police blocked them from crossing Wisconsin Avenue, however, they went to the home of Archbishop William E. Cousins. Toting signs that read "God Is White," and "Father Groppi Rest in Hell," the 650 demonstrators called on the archbishop to discipline the priest. After the archbishop notified the mob that he would consider its demands, the marchers headed back to the South Side, where they congregated to taunt police and caused minor disturbances.[60]

On Wednesday night, September 13, 1967, some 2,000 whites joined in the counterdemonstrations. Early in the evening, with Groppi and his marchers peacefully demonstrating in the mostly African American Near North Side, about 200 protesters held a rally in Kosciuszko Park. They then headed for the 16th Street viaduct. Along the way to the bridge, two members of the American Nazi Party from Chicago gave out signs emblazoned with swastikas and bearing the words "Symbol of White Power." Now numbering about 450, they marched on to the archbishop's residence. This time Archbishop Cousins addressed the crowd. He called for cooperation and condemned all violence. He refused to take measures against Father Groppi, saying that the crowd was being "diverted by emotion and mob psychology into fighting a straw figure while the real enemy goes unscathed." Agreeing that Groppi alone was not to blame for the open-housing marches, the crowd applauded the prelate and returned to the South Side. By the time they reached the viaduct, however, their mood had changed. They chanted white power slogans and took up the refrain, "Father Groppi's gotta go." As they reached the intersection of National and Washington, their numbers swelled to 1,500. Continuing homeward, the mob encountered an African American driving north on 16th Street. They surged at the car, shouting, "Let's get the nigger." The black man escaped as police fired tear gas and smoke bombs into the crowd, but the mob grew more enraged and began to riot. The whites smashed windows and scuffled with police until after midnight.[61]

A few days of calm reigned in the city after the Wednesday night riot. Father Groppi appeared on the CBS-TV Sunday talk show, "Face the Nation," and raised the visibility of the movement nationally. The National Board of Directors of the NAACP sent telegrams of support to the Youth Council and condemnation to the city council for its refusal to enact legislation. As they planned to march again, Father Groppi and the commandos were joined by more than 200 clergy members and hundreds of laypersons from throughout the Midwest, East Coast, and South, including representatives from the Unitarian-Universalist Commission on Religion and Race, the National Council of Churches, Jewish groups, and numerous Protestant churches.[62]

On the weekend of September 16, the marchers again ventured into the South Side. Father Groppi, suffering from a cold and exhaustion, did not take part. Instead, Dick Gregory led the protest. On Saturday evening, about 650 marchers walked through the contested area escorted by a heavily armed police brigade. It was the twentieth consecutive night of protest. Although they saw groups of whites milling about on their route and although numerous houses had signs denouncing the marchers, no violence occurred. On Sunday, 1,000 demonstrators, again protected by police, marched through the area chanting, "We're gonna be your neighbors." As they marched down 16th Street, crowds of whites started to gather. They taunted the marchers with catcalls; one youth who threw a bottle at the marchers was arrested. Signs in windows read "Niggers and Clergy! Pray for Forgiveness for Destroying Property"; and "Niggers Don't Waste Your Time Marching—Fix Up Your Homes and Yards." Again there was no violence, but as Dick Gregory warned at a rally after the march, "Don't think those south side crackers aren't mean or that they're backing down. They knew the police meant business today."[63]

As the marches continued through September and into October, city officials moved to address the conflict. Mayor Maier stuck to his position, rejecting open housing in the city if the surrounding municipalities did not follow suit. Instead, he pushed the city council to enact a law prohibiting the marches. The council refused Maier's request and instead looked into enacting a suitable open-housing ordinance. Vel R. Phillips, the only African American on the council, had been among the marchers and was arrested along with Father Groppi in early September. She had offered four open-housing proposals since 1962. All of them covered only the city and placed enforcement authority in the Community Relations–Social Development Commission. All of them had been rejected, with Phillips casting the only vote in their favor. After the riots, Phillips offered a new proposal that called on the city attorney's office and the courts to enforce the regulations. Numerous Milwaukee suburbs and bedroom communities, such as Brookfield, Germantown, and Wauwatosa, also offered statements in support of open housing. On the issue of anti-discrimination legislation, however, neither the city nor the suburbs went farther than voicing support for a stronger statewide law.[64]

The conflict continued into October. Groppi and the commandos continued marching and clashing with police and counterdemonstrators. "We will struggle," the priest declared; "we will not stop our marches; we will not stop our direct action until we get a law." The mayor also held firm. He sent a proposal for a stronger statewide statute and more money for urban development to the state legislature, but the government in Madison rejected the extra funding and watered down the housing recommendation. Members of the city council, however, finally seemed more willing to pursue a compromise even though a majority of them still opposed a statute. Business leaders had started complaining that the demonstrations were hurting them economically, and others complained that the violence was giving the city a black eye. On October 17, the council held a six-hour hearing and debate on the issue. More than 600 members of the public attended and gave voice to the full spectrum of views. At the end of the meeting, the various groups agreed to form a special committee of citizens and legislators that would hammer out an agreement. A local public relations expert offered the idea of a special committee. He suggested that it could serve the dual purpose of improving the city's image as well as potentially ending the crisis. Although neither the mayor nor the marchers were impressed, Phillips called it the "first ray of hope" in nearly two months of conflict.[65]

The eleven-member panel included five council members, Phillips among them, and six private citizens, including the leader of the commandos. Among the church, social agency, labor, and business leaders on the panel, most of whom supported a city anti-discrimination ordinance, was the president of the Milwaukee Board of Realtors. The state real estate industry had remained fairly quiet during the weeks of conflict as members carried on an internal debate over what position to take. They finally came out against a new law at the public hearing, insisting that the current laws sufficiently protected African Americans from discrimination.[66]

The panel met during the weekend of October 21, the fifty-sixth and fifty-seventh days of marching. In an endurance-testing, nineteen-hour session held in the Presidential Suite of the Pfister Hotel, the nine men and two women failed to reached a compromise. Instead, they offered three separate proposals. One, supported by seven members of the committee, called for a citywide law that covered all sales of property but would exempt the rental of owner-occupied duplexes, small rooming houses, and religious- and fraternal-affiliated institutions. A second idea, supported by Lawrence Friend of the commandos and Phillips, proposed unrestricted coverage. The third was Maier's initial proposal, supported by the realty industry, which called for a local law that would mirror the state's coverage but that placed the enforcement apparatus in the city attorney's office. The housing committee's offerings failed to impress either the mayor or the marchers. "We want that bill, not proposals," Father Groppi proclaimed at a press conference. Mayor Maier's response, meanwhile, showed his growing frustration with the entire situation. "Milwaukee," he complained, "should have never, never allowed this matter to be placed this high on the city's agenda."[67]

The housing committee, the council, the mayor, the marchers, and counterdemonstrators continued to haggle for six more weeks before finding a compromise in mid-December. The mayor's steadfast opposition to a strong open-housing law that covered only the city of Milwaukee won out. The bill did not go beyond the state's coverage, exempting the sale of owner-occupied single-family homes and the rental of owner-occupied and small apartment or rooming houses. It passed by a vote of thirteen to six. Phillips voted against it, telling the council "Thanks for nothing. . . . It is not what we want." Father Groppi and the commandos vowed to continue marching, even if it took five more years.[68]

The critical shift in the council position that enabled passage of an ordinance did not come about because of the marches. It occurred because the Milwaukee Citizens Civic Voice, one of the groups opposing legislation, presented the council with a petition demanding a referendum on the issue. The petition was meant to block the advance of open housing. It called for a two-year ban on enactment of any such statute. But for the short term, according to the *Milwaukee Journal*, it actually sped the issue along and enabled the city council to duck a hard vote. For along with its passage of the weak bill, the council announced that a referendum would be held the following April. As it turned out, no referendum was ever held. The ACLU fought it in court, and a month after its victory the issue became moot: Congress enacted a national fair-housing law.[69]

Despite their unsatisfactory outcome for local open-housing advocates, the Milwaukee marches were not a total waste of effort. Father Groppi received recognition for his work. The national NAACP honored him for "his success in arousing the conscience of the nation to the evil of segregated housing." The marches also had kept the issue before a national audience for four months. But more importantly, they showed that a concerted and sustained protest could occur in the urban North. Even without victory, as Dick Gregory noted, the campaign was important as a "testing ground for similar activities around the country." The Milwaukee movement showed that northern blacks, like their southern counterparts, could carry out a campaign of civil disobedience without it turning into an anarchic and destructive riot.[70]

As the United States left 1967 behind, race relations were nearing their nadir. The civil rights movement was spinning out of control. Tremendous advances had occurred against institutional racism in the South during the preceding decade, but the pendulum was swinging back. Many in the African American community were rejecting integration. Moderate whites were abandoning the movement as the demands of African Americans cut closer to home. The open-housing movement had struggled through five years of backsliding.

It was impossible to see for sure what was on the horizon. The war in Vietnam was taking more and more resources, both economic and human, and making it nearly impossible for Washington to continue to pursue a Great Society. Amid the fear of race war and anarchy, however, advocates continued to push for civil and constitutional rights for all Americans. Whether one more victory could be pulled out in an era of such disarray remained in question.

II

HOUSING IN A GREAT SOCIETY

Part II

The year 1968 will pinpoint the period in history that white America began in earnest to eradicate the remaining vestiges of a dual racial society.[1]

Nineteen hundred and sixty-eight has been seen as the pivotal year in recent American history. Varyingly called "the turning point" and "the most turbulent year," it
was the year that public opinion about the Vietnam War reversed. According to a
Gallup poll, in January 1968 public approval of President Lyndon Johnson's handling of the war ran about 40 percent. Two months later, after February's Tet offen-
sive, support had dwindled to about 25 percent, and outright disapproval had risen
to nearly two-thirds of those polled. Most Americans, as Walter Cronkite put it, had
thought the United States was "winning this war." After Tet, however, many Americans started to view the war as unwinnable. "To say that we are mired in stalemate,"
the influential Cronkite asserted, "seems the only realistic, yet unsatisfactory, conclusion." Tet knocked Johnson out of the race for the presidency and gave new
strength to the antiwar movement.[2]

Nineteen sixty-eight marked the demise of the New Deal coalition of northern
liberal Democrats and conservative southern Democrats. It had been hemorrhaging
for years over the question of race, but divisions over how to fight the war in Vietnam and whether to fight a war on poverty, along with the rise of a populist, white
supremacist backlash led by Governor George Wallace of Alabama, finally killed it.
In addition, the economy seemed out of control. The U.S. dollar collapsed. Europeans began purchasing gold at alarming rates, causing the United States to tap its
reserves. On March 14, the United States lost $372 million in gold trading, and
many feared even greater losses for the next day. The Federal Reserve Board scrambled,
raising interest rates a full point to 5.5 percent. "The nation," board chairman

William McChesney Martin declared, was "in the midst of the worst financial crisis since 1931." The Great Society crumbled. A summer and autumn of turmoil and shock would bring what Allen J. Matusow called "the rout of the Liberals."[3]

Nineteen sixty-eight also marked the unraveling of the civil rights movement. It was the year that the movement lost its strategic focus: political and economic participation through integration. The legislative successes of the preceding decade forced the movement to set new priorities. The anarchic urban racial violence of the preceding three years removed elements of the movement from the moral high ground and alienated much of its moderate white support. The movement's old guard, as represented by the Southern Christian Leadership Conference, moved toward the high-minded but less specific or practically achievable goal of eradication of poverty. The resulting Poor People's March on Washington was a fiasco. The more radical organizations—the Student Nonviolent Coordinating Committee, the Congress of Racial Equality, and the Black Panthers—grew increasingly demoralized and disorganized. And, of course, 1968 was the year that the civil rights movement lost its unifying leader, when James Earl Ray murdered Martin Luther King Jr. in Memphis on April 4.[4]

Few expected any good news on the open-occupancy front as 1968 began. There was strong sentiment in the country that the African American rioters should not be rewarded for their violent behavior. The 1966 elections had brought a forty-seven-seat swing in the House of Representatives in favor of the presumably fiscally conservative, law-and-order Republicans. In the Senate, one of the strongest voices for civil rights and housing legislation, Paul Douglas of Illinois, had gone down in defeat. But circumstances shifted in the spring, and by the end of May 1968, two of the most significant events in the fair-housing movement occurred. First, a combination of opportunism in Congress, presidential politics, and the shocking murder of King and the ensuing riots brought a surprise victory on the legislative front. Some six weeks later, the Supreme Court capped its affirmative rulings for fair housing. It found that the property rights of African Americans had been protected against discrimination all along. The Civil Rights Act of 1866, the Court declared, had guaranteed that "all citizens of the United States shall have the same right, in every State and territory, as is enjoyed by white citizens thereof to inherit, purchase, lease, sell, hold, and convey real and personal property."[5]

Amid the darkness and trials of the fair-housing movement during the mid-1960s, there was at least one glimmer of light. It came from an unlikely source. It came from where the fight against race-restrictive zoning and this story of it began: in Baltimore, Maryland.

Reflecting its location below the Mason-Dixon Line, Maryland had long been a one-party state run by the Democrats. With the growth of Baltimore and suburban Washington, D.C., however, the Democrats became divided. A liberal urban wing controlled Montgomery and Prince George's Counties. A conservative wing dominated the rest of the state, particularly the Eastern Shore. The division grew deeper when the civil rights movement radicalized after 1963, as the Democratic presidential primary in 1964 revealed. Lyndon Johnson's candidate, Daniel Brewster, eventually won the primary by carrying the Washington suburban counties and 53 percent of the state. But Alabama Governor George C. Wallace swept through the state with his message of segregation and populism, whipping up racial and class rivalries and exposing a reactionary sentiment against the civil rights movement similar to what had been seen in Detroit the previous year. Wallace won 90 percent of the white vote in the Eastern Shore and 60 percent of the white vote in Baltimore and Baltimore County.[6]

During the gubernatorial race of 1966, the Democratic Party broke in two. The radicalization of the civil rights movement, ghetto riots, demonstrations in Baltimore, and particularly the demand for fair housing created a strong white backlash. George P. Mahoney had run for the party's nomination in each primary since the early 1950s, never coming close to victory. But in 1966, he capitalized on the fracture, founding his campaign on opposition to open occupancy in housing. "Your Home Is Your Castle—Protect It" became his campaign slogan and the focus of the gubernatorial contest.[7]

Maryland's Republicans picked Spiro T. Agnew, the president of the Baltimore County Commission, as their candidate. Agnew, remembered best as Richard Nixon's shamed vice president, began his political career on the Baltimore County Board of Appeals. A protégé of Mayor Theodore McKeldin, he knew how to take advantage of divisions among the Democrats. In 1962, he capitalized on such a split to become the first Republican president of the county since 1895. Agnew often alienated civil rights activists with his gradualistic approach to desegregation, but he enjoyed support among African American moderates and boasted numerous civil rights achievements. He had forced the county to establish a human relations commission for the purpose of improving race relations, and he headed negotiations that led to the integration of a local amusement park. In 1963, he supported a federal urban renewal program despite the advice from colleagues that the federal government's directive requiring open occupancy in the projects would cost him politically. Adapting to the political atmosphere, Agnew recommended that the county commission stick to increasing access to jobs and schools. Explaining his moderation, he insisted that liberals went too far in expecting the social equality of the races, contending that "social acceptance could never be legislated because it is voluntary."[8]

Initially, Agnew opposed fair-housing legislation. Open-occupancy laws, he had declared in 1963, "violated the civil rights of others just as clearly as segregation violates the civil rights of the Negro." He asserted that civil rights did not just mean ending racial discrimination but included "the right of privacy, the right to own and enjoy property without government interference, the right to do business for profit and the right to seek out and prefer the company of one man to another." Reflecting on his own ethnicity, Agnew argued that if a home owner "dislikes Greeks he should not have to deal with Greeks, and the government that infringes upon his discretion in this respect abrogates his freedom of selection and disregards the intent of the Constitution." In place of anti-discrimination laws, he prescribed "educating the general public so that changes from a segregated to an integrated neighborhood [would] not affect property values."[9]

Continued attacks from activists and persistent discrimination by builders and landlords caused Agnew to alter his position. In 1965, he hinted that he might accept legislation requiring developers of large tracts to open new subdivisions to minorities, but he refused to include individual home owners under the regulation. In 1966, bowing to the demands of the human relations commission, Agnew went a step further and instructed the county solicitor to draft a law prohibiting discrimination in the sale or rental of new houses and new apartments. Conscious of the concerns of the construction and real estate industries, however, he insisted that the bill not compel a property owner to sell his home to someone to whom he did not wish to sell and required that the city of Baltimore enact a similar bill lest it put the county at a disadvantage. Agnew included only new construction under the proposal so that, as he observed, African Americans would not be accused of "running down neighborhoods which were run-down when they got there." As a sort of lab experiment, Agnew insisted that he wanted to "put the best image on integrated housing possible." But the test did not come to pass. To no one's surprise, the Maryland's House of Delegates blocked the open-occupancy bill. Despite the defeat, Agnew benefited from the exercise. His restraint enabled him to maintain his popularity among white moderates, but his push for even limited fair-housing legislation also won him increasing support in the black community. The state Republican Party therefore advanced Agnew as its candidate for governor in 1966.[10]

The split in Maryland's Democratic Party gave Agnew an unprecedented opportunity for victory. When George Mahoney won the nomination and placed his home owners' rights slogan in the platform, moderates and liberals bolted the party and tried to develop an independent campaign by Carlton R. Sickles. When Sickles refused to run, they had to settle for the ultraliberal Hyman A. Pressman, who favored unrestricted open-occupancy legislation. Agnew, meanwhile, started his campaign by espousing his limited fair-housing plan. He intended to draw a clear distinction between his position and Mahoney's but was careful not to appear too liberal for Maryland voters. He told reporters in September, "If an open-housing bill affecting the right of the individual homeowner to sell to whomever he wishes is passed [by the legislature], I would veto it." But as the chance of winning the votes of liberal Democrats increased, Agnew tried to close off Pressman's support in Baltimore's black community. He announced that he would accept open-housing legislation applying to existing private homes "if it were passed by a strong vote and if there were public sentiment for it." The strategy worked. Agnew became the anti-Mahoney candidate.[11]

Agnew's support for fair housing made the difference in the election. He won the state with a plurality of the vote, becoming only the fifth Republican governor in the state's history. He won overwhelming majorities in Montgomery and Prince George's Counties, as well as small majorities in Frederick and the western counties. Mahoney won majorities in the conservative Eastern Shore counties, in Baltimore County, and in Annapolis. The *Baltimore Sun* called the outcome "a display of eminent good sense" by the voters. It also explained that Mahoney's stand on open occupancy had cost him the election. "Mr. Mahoney, once again, is a loser," the paper declared in its lead editorial. "For a while he looked like a possible or even a probable victor, but as the campaign drew toward its end his manufactured banner with its single slogan grew increasingly tattered."[12]

As Maryland's new government convened in January 1967, an important change in the makeup of the legislature and the administration became clear. Because of reapportionment, for the first time in the state's history, urban areas held a majority of seats in the General Assembly. Agnew had received most of his support from urban areas, and so in his inaugural address, he focused on urban issues. He stressed crime prevention and eradication of overcrowding in schools, urban blight, and pollution. "A new day has come [to Maryland]," Agnew declared, "bringing with it a new alliance." "This new alliance," he explained "is not labeled conservative or liberal, rich or poor, white or black, Christian or Jew, Republican or Democrat. This new alliance should be called people . . . principle . . . progress."[13]

Shortly after the new Republican governor arrived in Annapolis, the Democratic Senate took up fair housing. The measure's staunchest support came from representatives of suburban Washington and urban Baltimore. As introduced, the plan proposed to prohibit discrimination in sales of new houses and rental in new and existing buildings with five or more apartments. But as it wended its way through both chambers of the legislature, it was watered down considerably. Ultimately, it covered only dwellings built after May 31, 1967, and it excluded owner-occupied apartment buildings containing fewer than twelve units; individually owned homes; developments of four or fewer houses; and at the behest of State Delegate W. Dale Hess, who was also a developer, any project completed before June 1968 for which a building permit had been obtained before June 1, 1967. Despite its shortcomings, the bill still represented a quantum leap forward for Maryland, for, as the *Washington Evening Star* observed, the issue of civil rights in the state had hitherto been "impenetrable."[14]

Maryland's new fair-housing act could only be characterized as moderate, but it raised the ire of many white property owners. Two groups, the Maryland Petition Committee and the Maryland Taxpayers Association, organized to block the law by forcing the state to hold a referendum on the subject. Under the state's loose referendum procedure, sponsors of a vote needed signatures equal to 3 percent of the number of persons who had voted in the previous statewide election. In this case, the petitioners needed only 27,593 signatures to force a referendum. Easing the way of petitioners even more was a stipulation that only half of those signatures had to be presented at the time the petition was filed; the remaining names could be gathered over the succeeding thirty days and then submitted. The day before the law was to take effect, the petitioners delivered more than 20,000 signatures to the capitol.[15]

In an audacious display of support for the law, the Agnew administration rejected the petition on a technicality. The state attorney general ruled that the Maryland Petition Committee had failed to provide proper documentation accounting for a donation of $13.50 that the organization had received. The committee, it seems, had not shown how the money was spent or what its source was. Because of the accounting discrepancy, the attorney general disqualified nearly three-quarters of the petitioner's signatures. "That $13.50 is a pretty flimsy peg on which to base a ruling," the president of the taxpayers association, Arthur B. Lego, asserted. "We can easily account for the donations," petition committee leader Zelher Albritton added, "and will do so when we file the rest of our petitions by the June 30 deadline." The administration, however, stuck by the decision. Maryland's secretary of state announced that the petition had failed. The opponents vowed to continue their fight, but the court battle dragged on for nearly a year before they won the right to hold a referendum. When that vote finally came in November 1968, the Maryland law had been rendered moot by legislation on the federal level, and Governor Agnew was on his way along Route 50 to the vice presidency.[16]

Maryland's legislation signaled broadening support for the principle of fair housing, but the question of the constitutionality of the laws remained. In 1967, the issue came before the Supreme Court. The case of *Reitman* v. *Mulkey* actually approached the question in reverse. It grew out of a challenge to California voters' passage of Proposition 14 and asked whether a guarantee of home owners' rights contravened the Fourteenth Amendment. The case involved a suit by Lincoln W. Mulkey and his wife against Neil Reitman. When Reitman refused to rent them an apartment, the Mulkeys sued, claiming that Reitman had violated their rights under the Rumford Act. An Orange County court ruled in favor of Reitman, accepting the defense's assertion that the new state constitutional provision had rendered Rumford null and void. The state Supreme Court, however, reversed the decision, declaring that the home owners protection contravened the equal protection clause of the Fourteenth Amendment.[17]

The issue came to the High Court in March 1967. Thurgood Marshall, now the solicitor general of the United States, argued the case in support of Mulkey. He asserted that the intent of the home owners clause was "to create a constitutional right to discriminate on racial grounds." He held that because it was a constitutional and not a statutory provision, the clause would be unreasonably difficult to repeal or amend. African Americans in California, he insisted, would face discrimination in perpetuity.[18]

In May, a divided Court ruled in favor of Mulkey. Basing its opinion on the equal protection clause of the Fourteenth Amendment, the five-member majority accepted the respondents' case. It ruled that "the state constitutional provision was invalid as embodying in the state's basic charter, immune from legislative, executive, or judicial regulation, . . . [the] right to discriminate on racial grounds." In a concurring opinion, Justice William O. Douglas went farther in defense of the decision. He based his opinion on a broad definition of "state action" that not only brought private housing under the rubric of the Fourteen Amendment but also hinted at how the commerce clause might be used to justify fair-housing laws. Zoning, he insisted, was the mandate of the state or municipality. Under Proposition 14, however, according to Douglas, private institutions, such as the realty industry, had taken over that zoning function, and since these institutions "practice[d] racial discrimination and zone[d] our cities into white and black belts or white and black ghettos," Douglas contended that they were fulfilling a governmental function in a way forbidden under the Fourteenth Amendment. Douglas further claimed that the question before the Court was not purely private. Rather, "urban housing [was] in the public domain." The growth of "vast schemes of public financing with which the States and the Nation have been extensively involved in recent years," he observed, made housing "like restaurants, inns, and carriers." "The real estate brokerage business," he concluded, "must be dedicated, like the telephone companies and the carriers and the hotels and motels, to the requirements of service to all without discrimination."[19]

In 1965, President Johnson had contended that it was up to Congress to make the next move on fair housing. Housing had occupied a place in the Great Society reforms, but only in the area of urban renewal and public housing. In September 1965, Congress raised housing and urban development to a cabinet position. The reorganization plan had been under consideration since the Kennedy administration. It had stalled, in part, because legislators expected Kennedy to nominate Robert Weaver as the Department of Housing and Urban Development's first secretary. Supporters of the reorganization feared that the appointment of an African American to the cabinet would have so alienated southern conservatives that they would have killed the whole plan.[20]

Weaver was still the prime candidate for the job when Johnson signed the bill into law. After two more years of advance and with African Americans rioting in the streets, the symbolic gesture of appointing a black to a cabinet position was imperative, and Johnson had insisted that the job would go to the "best informed man in the field." Even arch-segregationists in the Senate approved of a Weaver nomination. Republican Senator Strom Thurmond of South Carolina, one-time Dixiecrat candidate for president, considered him to be an able administrator and "objective in racial matters." Senators A. Willis Robertson of Virginia and John Sparkman of Alabama agreed. "When people asked me what I was going to do about the nomination," Robertson recounted, "I said I was going to support it."[21]

Johnson, however, delayed the nomination. The HHFA administrator, nicknamed somewhat derogatorily "the brains," was considered "colorless and drab."

According to Johnson's adviser Joseph A. Califano, Weaver was "not personally popular on [Capitol] Hill and Senate Majority Leader Mike Mansfield of Montana didn't think well of him." Furthermore, Weaver was in the president's doghouse for making public a draft of a rent supplement plan, one that promised to subsidize persons with incomes that Republicans considered to be too high. When the House defeated the proposal, Johnson blamed Weaver. Before he would risk any of his political capital on a Weaver nomination, the president told Califano, he had to be sure that he had Weaver's "pecker in [his] drawer." After some arm-twisting to bring both Mansfield and Weaver into line, Johnson appointed the HHFA director to the position of secretary. Weaver, the son of a postman, thus became the first African American to hold such high office in the executive branch.[22]

In 1966, President Johnson again called on Congress to act against housing discrimination. In very strong rhetorical terms, he presented Congress with a plan in his State of the Union address. "We must give the Negro the right to live in freedom among his fellow Americans," Johnson insisted. He called for "Congress to declare resoundingly that discrimination in housing and all the evils it breeds are a denial of justice and a threat to the development of our growing urban areas." "The time has come," he asserted, "to combat unreasoning restrictions on any family's freedom to live in the home and the neighborhood of its choice."[23]

By 1966, Congress had enacted every piece of civil rights legislation introduced since 1957, but it was immediately evident that the mood of the legislators had changed. Senator Everett M. Dirksen of Illinois, the minority leader, called the fair-housing provision unconstitutional and an invasion of property rights. He vowed to defeat it. In August, the House passed a watered-down version of the fair-housing title, but when the Senate took it up in September, the bill met southern opposition. For two weeks, North Carolina Democrat Sam J. Ervin led a filibuster that blocked the bill's advance. Johnson's ally, Mike Mansfield, filed two cloture votes to end the filibuster, but they failed by substantial margins. The rejection of cloture ended consideration of fair housing for 1966. Already stung by the disappointment faced by the Chicago Freedom Movement, Martin Luther King Jr. declared that the demise of the civil rights Act of 1966 "surely herald[ed] darker days for this social era of discontent."[24]

As urban riots tore up the United States during the spring and summer of 1967, activists again demanded that the federal government take steps to improve housing opportunities for African Americans. "One of the burning frustrations Negro residents carry with them in city ghettos," the NAACP's Roy Wilkins observed, is "the knowledge that even if they want to and have the means to do so, very often they cannot get out." The NAACP therefore called on Congress to enact fair-housing legislation. The racial tensions, the National Committee Against Discrimination in Housing suggested, grew out of unemployment, "deprivation and squalor." It urged government to relieve the pressure on the ghetto by improving housing and job-creating industries in the urban core. But, the organization contended, equally important was opening access to the suburbs. With jobs moving outside the urban core, NCDH leaders reasoned, "we must empower ghetto residents to bid for housing opportunities in the suburbs at the same time that they bid for employment opportunities." Since "state and local fair housing laws [had] not given Negro Americans this power," the NCDH insisted, "obviously Federal fair housing legislation . . . is essential."[25]

Failing congressional action, the American Friends Service Committee called for President Johnson to expand the coverage and improve the enforcement of Executive Order 11063. The organization drafted a report to the president reviewing its experiences on the front line of fair-housing activity and offering the administration its recommendations. The report alleged that the executive order was "being widely and flagrantly violated by builders, brokers and lenders." It also claimed that the implementation of the order by the Federal Housing Administration and the Veterans Administration was "at best ineffective, and at worst subversive of the goal of equal opportunity in housing." "Typical of reactions encountered by our staff," the AFSC reported, was "the statement by a FHA office director[:] 'I see no utility in Executive Orders.'" Housing agencies, according to the report, had not lived up to their obligation to establish guidelines for compliance by the realty and building industries, nor had they offered counseling programs or established an enforcement machinery to prosecute violators. Indeed, the report insisted, they had not even sufficiently assessed conditions to determine whether discrimination was occurring. The AFSC therefore called for "major changes in the basic approach and procedures of FHA and VA" and asked, in particular, that "top administrators . . . make clear . . . that among the criteria of adequate job performance [of staff] will be the extent of observance of agency procedures implementing nondiscrimination."[26]

The Johnson administration rejected the idea of expanding the executive order and instead again called on Congress to pass fair-housing legislation. Legislators must act, the president maintained, because "it is decent and right [and because] injustice must be opposed, however difficult or unpopular the issue." The administration even changed its tactics to facilitate the legislative process. After the failure of the 1966 omnibus bill, the civil rights faction in Congress split the bill's six titles into individual legislation. The tactic succeeded only in winning enactment of the least controversial bill: a five-year extension of the Commission on Civil Rights. The House did pass a bill to protect civil rights workers, but the bill stalled in the Senate Judiciary Committee until after it was too late for the whole Senate to take it up before the end of the session. An open-housing bill was offered by Senator Walter F. Mondale of Minnesota, and the Senate Housing and Urban Affairs Subcommittee held hearings on it in August, but nothing came of it before the session ended.[27]

In January 1968, the second session of the 90th Congress began with the Senate considering the resolution protecting civil rights workers, H.R. 2516, that had passed in the House the previous year. Senator Mondale hoped to add his fair-housing provision to the bill as an amendment. His legislative assistant recalled, however, that the judiciary committee's civil rights leadership, Senators Philip A. Hart, the Michigan Democrat, and Jacob K. Javits, the New York Republican, recommended that Mondale wait to "see how the stage set itself for a more far-reaching civil rights measure."[28]

Debate on H.R. 2516 began in late January. Southern senators, led by Ervin, had promised another filibuster, but they also offered a substitute bill. The proposal kept the House provisions outlawing the injury of, intimidation of, or interference with persons exercising their civil rights but eliminated the central phrase, "because of his race, color, religion or national origin" from the bill. It also excluded from the legislation coverage of activities that involved only state or local benefits, such as voting in state or local elections, attending public school, state jury service, and other activities. The Senate voted to table the Ervin amendment in early February by a vote of fifty-four to twenty-nine. There was still no indication that the civil rights faction in the Senate could muster enough votes to impose cloture on a southern filibuster. Senate liberals, however, had polled members and determined that there was enough support for the basic bill to ensure that it could be the fallback position if compromise were necessary.[29]

After the Senate tabled the Ervin amendment, the civil rights faction decided to ratchet up their demands. Senators Edward W. Brooke of Massachusetts, the only African American in the chamber, and Mondale introduced an open-occupancy amendment to the bill. The amendment had the full support of the Johnson administration and replicated the administration's 1967 proposal, except that it contained a "Mrs. Murphy" exemption. The exemption, named for a mythical landlady on Social Security who rented out rooms in her house to boarders to make ends meet, was needed to win the support of moderate Republicans.[30]

Southern Democrats railed against the Mondale proposal. Ervin regarded it as an outrageous infringement on private property. If the bill passed, he fumed, a person's right to sell his home would be "dependent upon the unbridled will of one Cabinet officer sitting on the banks of the Potomac." Ervin undertook to filibuster the bill, and on February 16, Majority Leader Mansfield filed a cloture motion. The motion failed. From the margin of defeat, fifty-five to thirty-seven, it seemed that the civil rights forces had made no headway. Of the eight senators not voting, however, five had announced their support for limiting debate. Had they voted, it would have brought the total to sixty in favor of cloture. Sixty votes was still short of the two-thirds that would be needed if all senators were present and voting, but it would have been six votes closer than Mansfield had gotten in 1966.[31]

Senate Minority Leader Everett Dirksen voted against cloture, but he soon saw an opportunity to save the legislation and win the issue for the Republican Party. Over the weekend of February 21, he indicated to the civil rights faction that he was prepared to work out a compromise. During the next week, Dirksen, along with his son-in-law, Senator Howard Baker of Tennessee, met with Attorney General Ramsey Clark and Assistant Attorney General Stephen Pollack to iron out the specifics of the deal. The Senate's civil rights leadership, including Mondale and Brooke, also sat in on the meetings. Dirksen recommended that the fair-housing clause of the bill extend the exemption to include not only the Mrs. Murphys but also to owners who sold or rented their homes themselves rather than through a realtor. The distinction seemed slight, amounting to only about 10 percent of properties, and it was less than what the liberals expected to have to give up, but the exemption played directly to the Republican position on home owners' rights. Because an individual home owner might sell his or her home only once in his or her lifetime, Dirksen believed that any discriminatory behavior on the home owner's part would have so small an effect on the overall market as to make such a significant encroachment on individual liberty as open-occupancy regulations excessive. Realtors, however, had a greater effect and could legitimately be regulated by government. The Dirksen compromise gave the advocates of open housing the votes needed for passage.[32]

A conjunction of factors explained Dirksen's switch. The riots of 1967 had concerned him. The violence, he argued, "put this whole matter in a different frame." He did not want to worsen "the restive condition" in the cities; neither did he want to have a situation develop for which the country had no cure and that would lead to more violence. And from a different angle, Dirksen reasoned that open housing was needed to serve the veterans, particularly the black veterans, returning from Vietnam to an inadequate housing supply. Others offered a political explanation for the shift, although Dirksen denied it. Numerous Republicans, most notably Baker, had advised the minority leader that a Republican-drawn compromise could help the party in the fall elections, a point not lost on the presidential candidates, Nelson Rockefeller and Richard Nixon.[33]

Dirksen's switch was only one part of the story, however. Other senators had to be swayed. That work was undertaken by the NAACP, the NCDH, and the Leadership Conference on Civil Rights (LCCR). After their failure earlier, the organizations had stepped up the campaign, denouncing the government as "builders of ghettos." Lyndon Johnson, who had kept up a steady effort to ensure passage of the bill, gave special credit for the success to his adviser, the LCCR's chief lobbyist and director of the Washington NAACP, Clarence M. Mitchell. According to the president, Mitchell toiled tirelessly for months lobbying on the issue. "Clarence Mitchell's endless hours of work" began to show results, Johnson recalled in his memoirs. "Dirksen could sense the shifting tide [and] he chose to master that tide." A major gaffe by the opponents of the housing plan also facilitated the bill's passage. Housing industry lobbyists were caught off guard by the advance of the bill. The National Association of Real Estate Boards did not mount an opposition campaign until after the bill had passed the Senate.[34]

Yet one more element worked to the open-housing advocates' advantage. The National Advisory Commission on Civil Disorders issued its report on the first day of March. The Kerner Commission declared that the closed housing market was a core reason behind the ghetto riots and the sense of desperation among urban blacks.[35]

On March 11, the Senate passed the civil rights bill with the fair-housing title intact, and it was taken up again by the House. Supporters of the legislation pushed to have the House adopt the amended bill without lengthy debate. But conservatives, perhaps responding to the flood of personal letters and phone calls from NAREB members and individual home owners, wanted the bill to be sent to a conference committee. "We should follow the time-tested principles of parliamentary procedure," Minority Leader Gerald R. Ford declared. Events in late March, however, squelched the intentions of many House Republicans to obstruct the bill. On March 31, Lyndon Johnson announced that he would not seek the nomination of his party for president because he intended to focus his efforts on the war in Vietnam. Johnson's withdrawal left the presidential race wide open. Nixon and Rockefeller moved to capitalize on the vacuum, pressing hard to get the House Republicans to pass the bill.[36]

A second event, the assassination of Martin Luther King Jr. on April 4, raised passions over the bill even higher. For a week following the killing, African Americans across the country went on a rampage. Remembering the riots of 1967, many Americans feared that the King riots portended all-out race war. Opponents of the bill tried to capitalize on the furor by claiming that the "present climate [was] too charged with emotion [to produce] well-reasoned legislation." Representative William M. Tuck, a southern Virginia Democrat, for example, asserted that "legislation of an emotional nature should never be acted upon . . . at a time when we are faced with tensions such as those which now exist." "Laws," Tuck insisted, "should be considered and acted upon only in an atmosphere of careful and thoughtful deliberation." "I resent threats of force and duress in anything," Omar Burleson of Texas declared, "and if I had to legislate under such conditions I would walk out of this Chamber and not return." Representative William L. Hungate, a Republican from Missouri, suggested that the House merely look back to the Gulf of Tonkin Resolution and the Vietnam quagmire for an example of the consequences of legislative action hastily taken.[37]

Some of the supporters of the bill, meanwhile, used the violence that resulted from the assassination of King to convince the House that the legislation was long past due. "Every man has a choice," California Republican James C. Corman told the House; "we can sit and deplore, for whatever reason is most comfortable, the havoc that is shaking this Nation . . . or we can stand up and furnish the leadership necessary to end the vicious and deep-rooted causes of racial hatred and fear." Others tried to convince legislators to take action despite the riots. Charles E. Goodell, a Republican from Jamestown, New York, for example, counseled House members against letting the current atmosphere alter their vote. He observed that it would be wrong "to vote for bad legislation because of the cruel pathos of the assassination" and that it would be equally wrong "to vote against good legislation because of the senseless rioting in our streets." Instead, he implored his colleagues "to resist the temptation to react to the passion of the moment" and to vote for the bill because it "should be passed." "In fairness," he admitted, "it is long overdue."

"Fair housing legislation," Republican representative Robert McClory of Illinois remarked, "is far more than a nostrum hastily concocted to cure racial strife. It is an integral part of the congressional attempt to help the Negro enter the mainstream of American life." "I have no illusions that the passage of this bill will in some way stop the riots," Hervey G. Mechan, a Maryland Democrat, added, "[but] this legislation is an important step toward assuring all our citizens the opportunity to fully participate in the life of our country."[38]

One week to the day after the assassination, Lyndon Johnson signed the first federal fair-housing law. It covered nearly 80 percent of dwellings in the United States, and it marked the end of governmental support for residential segregation.

Just over a month after the enactment of the Civil Rights Act of 1968, the U.S. Supreme Court added a postscript to the fair-housing movement's victory. The case involved a three-year-old conflict over whether a realtor was obliged to sell an African American a home in suburban St. Louis. In 1965, Joseph Lee Jones had tried to buy a home in Paddock Woods from the Alfred H. Mayer Company but was refused. He sued, claiming that the discrimination was illegal based on the Civil Rights Act of 1866, which stipulated that "all citizens shall have the same right as is enjoyed by white citizens to purchase real property." Thus, unlike most of the earlier cases, *Jones* v. *Mayer* did not turn on the Court's reading of the equal protection clause of the Fourteenth Amendment but on a congressional statute.[39]

In a controversial seven-to-two decision, the High Court ruled in favor of Jones. The majority found that the statute forbade racial discrimination in the sale or rental of housing by private individuals receiving no public funds. To make this discovery, the majority relied on a very broad reading of the statute itself and of the debates surrounding its passage. It carried the arguments made against segregation in the second *Brown* v. *Board of Education* case to the extreme. Whereas the Court in 1955 had found the evidence contradictory and inconclusive, in *Jones* it insisted that Congress had intended to eliminate all forms of discrimination, including those perpetrated by private individuals. Relying on a contemporary report offered in the *Congressional Record* to counter arguments that the 1866 law was meant merely to repeal state Black Codes, the Court determined that "history leaves no doubt . . . we must accord [the law] a sweep as broad as its language."[40]

The *Jones* decision marked a final major victory for the fair-housing movement. The ruling expanded the status of fair housing even beyond what Congress had just passed. Whereas the 1968 law was not to become fully effective until 1970, the *Jones* decision took effect immediately. Moreover, the Court's reading of the 1866 law left no exceptions to coverage, meaning no "Mrs. Murphy" or any other exemption. As the *New York Times* noted, "all racial discrimination in houses and apartments becomes a violation of law and those subjected to racial exclusion have the right to court relief and damages." "The law is now unequivocal," the *Times* announced, "what remains is for white communities to remove the fences of racism that still segment the lives of too many Americans."[41]

With the passage of the Civil Rights Act of 1968, better known as the Fair Housing Act, and the *Jones* decision, the campaign against residential segregation finally succeeded in its aim. It won legislative guarantees that minorities would have access to housing and not face discrimination from realtors or lenders based on their race or religion. The struggle had been intense. Many whites had believed that the movement was "trying to go too fast." They commiserated with the plight of the black community but maintained that the activists had to give the voting and desegregation laws time to take effect before moving on to housing. They still objected to the demand that blacks win social equality, not just legal equality. Some contended that the ghetto riots demonstrated that blacks were savages. Home owners, meanwhile, proved that they could fight savagely to keep their neighborhoods white.[42]

In the face of continued white violence, the civil rights community split over the right tactical approach to advancing the movement. The divisions, ironically, created a synergism that brought victory for fair housing. Each element was needed to end the congressional silence on housing discrimination. Many civil rights activists viewed nonviolence as anachronistic, but without the exposure of white resistance by the militant, nonviolent direct action of Operation Open City in Chicago or Father Groppi's marches in Milwaukee, many northern whites would have continued to believe that racism existed only in the South. The extreme rhetoric of the Black Power element jeopardized the high moral ground won by the nonviolent activists, but without it, it is unlikely that the degree of fear necessary to push legislators away from the status quo could have been generated. Congress did not want to reward the rioters, but neither did it want to see more rioting. And although the NCDH-NAACP-LCCR approach made the lobbyists and lawyers seem out of touch with the grass roots, without their ability to speak the language of Congress, the White House, and the courts, the movement would not have been able to come up with remedies for the injustices in housing. Demanding equality and threatening revolution otherwise or employing moral suasion to win the sympathy of the public at large were invaluable, but having legal and constitutional arguments for changing generations of law was essential to bringing about that change.

The Fair Housing Act, director of the NAACP's Housing Program William R. Morris contended, promised "vast social and economic returns to black Americans." They included "the elimination of slums and blight, the development of a rewarding environment in communities and the relief of racial tensions." Morris's comments show how important access to better housing was to many blacks. Whether his words would reflect reality remained to be seen.[43]

Ironically, in the year that brought so much bad news, the fair-housing movement saw its greatest achievement. After nearly six decades of effort, it had reversed the legal supports for residential segregation, replacing race-based housing ordinances with anti-discrimination laws. Next it would be up to the people to follow the law, to reverse centuries of cultural practice, to change their attitudes about race, and to accept integration in their neighborhoods as they had elsewhere in their lives.

AFTERWORD

Keeping the Neighborhood White

What is required is a recognition by society that it has been guilty of crimes and that it is prepared to atone. With that beginning, there need be no doubt about the end.[1]

Since the enactment of the Civil Rights Act of 1968, urban geographers and sociologists have executed study after study measuring residential segregation. In one, Scott McKinney and Ann B. Schnare assessed the trends in racial separation from 1960 to 1980. They developed a formula that measured what they call "exposure rates." These reflect the degree of racial contact occurring in sixty-four standard metropolitan statistical areas (SMSAs) grouped into four regions: Northeast, North-Central, South, and West. McKinney and Schnare's research indicated a decrease in black exposure to whites during the 1960s in all four regions, which they explain as a reflection of the ongoing white flight to segregated suburbs that resulted in monochromatic inner cities. Between 1970 and 1980, the authors found that black exposure to whites increased in all four regions. This, they insisted, reflected increased suburbanization of African Americans. The study showed, moreover, that the Northeast and South experienced a net increase in black exposure to whites, and therefore integration, between 1960 and 1980. When the authors took the incomes of African Americans into consideration, however, their data showed that the exposure of poorer blacks to whites actually decreased in all four regions, indicating an increase in racial segregation for poorer blacks. The authors therefore concluded that class was becoming more important than race as a factor in determining levels of residential segregation. They contended that fair housing laws were the most important factor explaining their findings.[2]

Nancy Denton and Douglas Massey, meanwhile, have employed the Taeuber

and Taeuber block-by-block analysis to study the character of American neighborhoods, considering data of class and income to create more subtle indices of dissimilarity. The authors noted that the economic progress that African Americans enjoyed in the late 1960s subsided about the time of the Arab oil embargo in 1973.
Stagflation increased African American unemployment and caused middle-class black
families to experience "downward mobility," leaving fewer households with "the
socioeconomic resources necessary to sustain residential mobility and, hence, integration." But Denton and Massey contend that race so dominates the issue of mobility and spatial distribution that questions of "what would have happened if black
economic progress had continued become moot." Their data show that indices of
dissimilarity in neighborhoods where family incomes are more than $50,000 do
not differ significantly from those where incomes are less than $2,500 per year. In
second-tier SMSAs, with populations between about 1,000,000 and 2.5 million
(such as Boston, Buffalo, Pittsburgh, and New Orleans), the indices actually show
higher rates of segregation in the wealthiest neighborhoods. "Even if black incomes
had continued to rise through the 1970s," the authors insist, "segregation would
not have declined. . . . In 1980, as in the past, money did not buy entry into white
neighborhoods of American cities." Massey concludes: "Not only are blacks much
less likely than other groups to achieve suburban residence, but once within suburbs, they are subject to much higher levels of segregation."[3]

Reynolds Farley's measurement of segregation in the 1980s, using the same indices of dissimilarity approach, reaches quite different, more hopeful conclusions. He
acknowledges that the open housing movement "was bolstered by subsequent developments in residential finance." He notes, for example, that the Community
Reinvestment Act of 1977, which required federally chartered lenders to "meet the
credit needs of the *entire* metropolis," including low-income areas, brought new
sources of credit to African Americans. Farley avers that these bureaucratic developments and changes in attitudes of whites toward open housing caused "a 'quiet
revolution' [to occur] as the anti-redlining movement grew into a more powerful
community development movement." "There is no confusion about what happened," he alleges; "there was a pervasive pattern of modest declines [in segrega-
tion], the average index of dissimilarity dropping from sixty-nine to sixty-five" between 1980 and 1990.[4]

Although Farley is correct about the declining rates in indices of dissimilarity in
most metropolitan areas, other measures of segregation point to persistent separation or even an increasing separation of the races. John R. Logan and Mark Schneider
have brought new analytical tools to the study of residential segregation. They use
the "correlation ratio" as a basis of analysis. Without going into the mathematical
details of the approach, correlation ratios, according to Logan and Schneider, measure "the differences among communities in the percentage of their own population
which is black. It takes high values when some communities approach an all-white
racial composition while others approach an all black racial composition." Logan

and Schneider's research has observed an increase in the correlation ratios even as values in the indices of dissimilarity have dropped. They conclude, therefore, that American suburban communities became increasingly racially polarized.[5]

In yet other studies, sociologists and urban geographers have concluded that despite improvements in indices of dissimilarity and exposure rates, the degree of improvement has remained small and the actual block-by-block integration short-lived. Barrett A. Lee and Peter B. Wood, for example, have shown that racial succession remains the most common result of African American migration into a white area. But "even in the absence of succession," they noted, "stability sometimes proved temporary, with the percentage of blacks decreasing instead of increasing." In these areas, the authors observed, the "residential invasion" was overtaken by "non-Anglo minority groups[:] Hispanics, Asians, etc." Lee and Wood conclude that the issue of residential segregation has become more complex as the United States becomes more multiracial. John M. Goering, a sociologist specializing in the study of the dynamics of neighborhood and racial transition in New York City, has taken an even more pessimistic view of the issue. "None of the research or modeling of racial succession," he contends, "provides any reason for optimism about the future of neighborhood racial integration in American cities."[6]

No matter their nuances and contradictions, the important question suggested by these studies remains: why does residential segregation persist? Some observers of the issue blame the government's weak enforcement of fair-housing legislation. Under the Fair Housing Act, the Department of Housing and Urban Development (HUD) was responsible for enforcement of the nondiscrimination provisions. During the summer hearings in 1968, HUD Secretary Robert Weaver requested $11.1 million from Congress so that the department could hire 850 new investigators. The House Appropriations Committee, however, recommended allocating just $2.1 million. Even that amount was denied HUD by the House and Senate conferees in the fiscal year 1969 appropriations bill. Weaver decried the decision. "We simply cannot implement the fair housing law without more personnel," he exclaimed, and "[w]ithout manpower, the fair housing law [was] meaningless." By the early 1970s, the HUD's staffing inadequacies were apparent. A field staff of forty-two people handled Title VIII complaints for the entire country—more than 2,500 complaints in 1972 alone. Even if Weaver had obtained more manpower, the Fair Housing Act gave HUD little prosecutorial authority with which to compel compliance. As part of the Dirksen compromise, the department had been empowered only to engage in "conference, conciliation and persuasion." In the worst case, HUD could employ the executive power of the Justice Department, but only if the attorney general deemed that the bias represented a "pattern or practice" or that the incident had "general public importance." Thus, the responsibility for enforcement often fell on private individuals, those who could least afford it, who sued offenders of the law.[7]

Since the enactment of the Fair Housing Act, thousands of cases involving equal opportunity in housing have come before the courts despite the critic's fears. They have been based not only on Title VIII, but also on state statutes, the Thirteenth and Fourteenth Amendments, and the anti-discrimination provisions of the Civil Rights Act of 1866, following the *Jones* v. *Mayer* precedent. In every major decision, the courts have made clear the law's ban on discrimination and unreasonable practices.[8]

Federal courts have been very active in extending the reach of the federal fair housing laws by expanding the definition of who could file a suit. Lower courts have granted standing to nonprofit corporations intending to build low-income housing, to block improvement associations, and to the NAACP. This has alleviated some of the law's enforcement weaknesses because suits no longer were reliant solely on the individual victim's ability to finance litigation.[9]

The broadest expansion of standing came with regard to housing testers. The tactic of testing for discrimination had been used by the Congress of Racial Equality in the 1960s, but it was first systematically pursued by Housing Opportunities Made Equal (HOME) in the 1970s. To test for discrimination, HOME would send two teams of investigators—one white and the other black, but both having similar economic status—to inquire about buying a home or renting an apartment. After the inquiry, the teams would compare notes on how each was treated by the broker or landlord. If they found that the African American team was shown different properties, given inadequate service, or turned away altogether, then HOME would bring forth a complaint. After years of legal wrangling, in 1982 the Supreme Court conferred standing on housing testers not directly affected by discrimination and thereby enhanced the government's investigative powers by enabling private fair-housing interests to pick up the slack.[10]

Along with the courts, certain elements in the real estate industry have undertaken to abolish discriminatory practices and even pursue fair housing. In the 1970s, the National Association of Realtors (formerly the National Association of Real Estate Boards) not only changed its official policy toward fair housing, for example, passing an "Equal Rights Resolution" in 1975, but it also adopted an affirmative action marketing policy to open areas to blacks. From the appraisers' perspective, industry literature suggests that race became a more positive factor in their valuation of property. Whereas prior to 1950 appraisers assumed that the infiltration of a white neighborhood by African Americans automatically reduced property values, numerous studies in the late 1950s suggested that the relationship between race and property value was more complicated. In the short term, prices often fell as whites abandoned a neighborhood after the first black moved in. Then because of the short supply of suitable housing opportunities for African Americans, as more blacks learned that the housing was available, values could actually increase. NAREB's efforts hve not significantly altered housing patterns, however.[11]

The weaknesses in the Fair Housing Act's enforcement elements were a topic of concern in Congress throughout the 1970s and early 1980s. Both chambers held numerous hearings into the issue, but no legislation made it out of committee until 1980. Representative Don Edwards, a Democrat from Santa Clara County, California, who was chairman of the Judiciary Subcommittee on Civil and Constitutional Rights, was chief sponsor of the bill. Referred to by his Republican colleagues as "relentlessly liberal," Edwards had come to Congress in 1962 and for the full length of his eventual thirty-two-year career as a legislator had been a strong advocate of all civil rights legislation. The Edwards bill carried two major provisions. It expanded coverage of the law to prohibit discrimination against the disabled and other groups, and it extended the act's reach by prohibiting discrimination by mortgage insurance companies. The bill also provided stronger enforcement provisions by codifying much of what the courts had already established. It would continue to enable private individuals to sue, but new provisions would allow HUD to investigate complaints itself or to hire independent testers to investigate. To adjudicate disputes, the bill established a panel of "administrative law judges" that could issue cease-and-desist orders or provide other appropriate action against the offending party. To expedite matters, the bill empowered the HUD secretary to determine whether the case would be better concluded in an administrative hearing or by referral to the attorney general.[12]

Numerous interests organized to press for the enactment of the bill. In his State of the Union address, President Jimmy Carter had called it "the most critical civil rights legislation before the Congress in years." He dispatched cabinet officials and housing personnel to Capitol Hill to lobby for the bill. In testimony before the Edwards subcommittee, HUD Secretary Patricia Roberts Harris called the 1968 law "less than half a loaf." "It defined and prohibited discriminatory housing practices," she admitted, "but failed to include the enforcement tools necessary to prevent such practices and provide relief to victims of discrimination." The civil rights coalition that had been central in the enactment of the 1968 act, the Leadership Conference on Civil Rights, also pressured lawmakers. NAREB, meanwhile, staunchly opposed the reforms. According to *Congressional Quarterly*, NAREB particularly objected to the HUD enforcement mechanism, calling it an inappropriate expansion of HUD's regulatory power and insisting that the administrative law judge approach was unconstitutional because it ran afoul of the Seventh Amendment—guaranteeing jury trials for civil cases involving more than $20. Despite the opposition, a bipartisan coalition, headed by Edwards and Representative Hamilton Fish Jr., a Republican from New York, passed the bill in the House by a vote of 310 to 95 in June. The Senate did not take up the bill until after the November elections that swept Ronald Reagan into the White House and a Republican majority into the Senate. During the lame-duck session in December 1980, the legislation stalled when conservative Republicans, led by Senators Strom Thurmond of South Carolina and Orrin G. Hatch of Utah, joined to filibuster the bill.[13]

The fair-housing movement did not mass a sufficient attack for reform again until the last year of the Reagan administration. When Representative Don Edwards again offered a bill, the Fair Housing Amendments Act of 1988, neither the friends nor the foes of the issue had changed their position since 1980. The bill had one very well-placed friend in the House, however. In 1983, Hamilton Fish Jr. became the ranking member on the House Judiciary Committee. A fourth-generation legislator, he was a strong supporter of civil rights and many other liberal social policies. The bill also had a well-placed but more discreet friend in the administration. Vice President George Bush, who as a representative from Texas had voted for the 1968 law, wanted civil rights legislation to help him along the presidential campaign trail. Throughout May and early June 1988, Fish sought a compromise between civil rights leaders and NAREB. Finally, on June 14, the parties hammered out a deal. The compromise entailed creating a panel of administrative law judges, but it offered either party the right to have the dispute heard in federal court instead. With the Seventh Amendment question taken away, opposition from the White House and from NAREB evaporated, and the bill sailed through the House. It passed by a vote of 376 to 23. [14]

The critical compromise between civil rights groups, NAREB, and the White House all but assured passage of the Fair Housing Amendments Act in the Senate. Senator Edward M. Kennedy, the bill's chief Democratic sponsor, and Pennsylvania's Arlen Specter, the Republican cosponsor of the bill, with the help of Majority Leader Robert C. Byrd of West Virginia, pushed the final bill through. Evincing the breadth of support for the compromise, Orrin Hatch, a leader of the 1980 filibuster, even asked to be named as a cosponsor of the bill. "This is a historic day," Hatch declared, "this is a historic bill." President Reagan, meanwhile, called on the Senate to pass "the landmark civil rights bill for which we have worked so long and hard." The final bill passed by a vote of ninety-four to three. In celebration, Kennedy called the new law "the most important expansion of civil rights in the last 25 years." "This moment has been many years in the making," he chimed, "and what a beautiful moment it is." [15]

Despite the rhetoric, more emphatic laws have not significantly altered residential racial patterns. A 1993 study of suburban Chicago, for example, demonstrated the tenacity of segregation. Only 423 African Americans were among the 183,000 denizens of McHenry County. In Kane County, according to Lowell Culver, nearly 92 percent of the 19,000 black residents lived in two communities, Aurora and Elgin. And although African Americans comprised more than 10 percent of the population of Will County, three out of every four African Americans in the county lived in either Joliet, Bolingbrook, or University Park. Similar conditions exist in the Washington, D.C., suburbs in Prince George's County and elsewhere in the country. Ten years after the enactment of the amendments, it was still possible for a *New York Times* headline to declare, "Segregation Persists Despite Fair Housing Act." [16]

The voluminous academic and legal literature regarding violations of fair-housing legislation and discrimination by realtors and the scores of suits brought against realtors and landlords illustrate the persistence of prejudice. Block busting and racial steering have been the two most common discriminatory practices employed by the realty industry. The urban economist George Galster has demonstrated, for example, that in Memphis and Cincinnati, although real estate agents have not absolutely refused to show African Americans properties in all-white sections, they have tended to show blacks fewer homes than they would show whites in those neighborhoods. In addition, the homes that they do show blacks tend to be closer to blocks that already have African American residents. Robert W. Lake adds that African Americans "spend on average half again as much time as whites" when looking for a home or apartment, and they tend to have to spend more money for less housing.[17]

Mortgage lenders and municipal governments have also discriminated against African American home buyers. Lenders often employ the tactic of redlining when considering loans to blacks. They may refuse to grant a mortgage to an African American intending to move into a certain neighborhood, or they may impose financial obstacles on the applicant, such as forcing him or her to make a larger down payment, offering a shorter loan repayment period or a higher interest rate, or assessing higher closing costs on the purchase. In this way, they discourage blacks from seeking loans in white areas. Governments, meanwhile, have also tried to maintain residential segregation. They have avoided racially specific zoning restrictions by imposing dwelling height and size requirements for construction or by concentrating low-income housing in the inner city rather than dispersing it throughout metropolitan areas.[18]

More telling still than the discrimination by realtors, lenders, and local governments is evidence regarding racial attitudes. According to a 1978 poll, although 86 percent of whites responded that they would not move if a single black family moved in next door, only 46 percent of them said that they would not move if "black people came to live in large numbers," and barely a quarter of the respondents would willingly remain in a neighborhood whose population was 50 percent black. That attitude has persisted. A 1996 poll showed that nearly 40 percent of white Americans supported laws permitting property owners to discriminate on the basis of race when selling or renting their homes or apartments. Nearly 45 percent of white southerners, according to the poll, said that they would support such a law. Most African Americans, meanwhile, prefer areas that are racially mixed but that already have substantial numbers of other blacks.[19]

Even relatively minor public resistance to residential integration will have a significant effect on whether neighborhoods remain segregated. According to Nathan Glazer, "only a little preference or prejudice leads to people moving into or out of a neighborhood at such rates as to create high concentrations which hardly anyone individually wants." In an article written as a Festschrift to Charles Abrams, Glazer presents a disturbingly simple experiment that illustrates the difficulty of overcoming "relatively mild preferences for one's own group." Glazer tells readers to picture a sheet of paper divided in one-inch squares. Supposing that a collection of dimes and one of pennies represent members of two homogeneous groups, in this case whites and African Americans, spread them at random on the grid. Postulate that "every dime wants at least half its neighbors to be dimes, every penny wants a third of its neighbors to be pennies, and any dime or penny whose immediate neighbor does not meet these conditions gets up and moves." Then observe the result. "The result in every case," Glazer shows, "is 'segregation'—all the pennies [are] in one area of the board."[20]

But not all opposition is minor. Not since the large-scale riots of the 1960s have entire communities taken part in violent resistance to residential integration, yet violence persists. The Klanwatch Project, a unit of the Southern Poverty Law Center in Montgomery, Alabama, counted forty-five instances of arson or cross burning and "hundreds of acts of vandalism, intimidation and other incidents" nationwide in 1985 and 1986 "directed at members of minority groups who had moved into mostly white areas." In its 1989 survey, Klanwatch reported 289 cases of racially motivated vandalism and violence; of those, 130 involved conflict arising from minorities moving into predominantly white neighborhoods. Between 1985 and 1990, according to the Chicago Commission on Human Rights, 1,129 racial "hate crimes" were reported, and half of them occurred within neighborhoods undergoing racial transition. In Los Angeles, the city commission on human relations reported that 167 racially motivated "hate crimes" occurred during 1989 alone. The U.S. Department of Justice investigated twenty-six incidents of cross burning in 1996.[21]

Such acts of intimidation have occurred nationwide, from Maine to Florida, from suburban Washington, D.C., to California, and numerous places in between. In the late 1970s, Nassau County, Westchester County, Queens, Brooklyn, and Staten Island, New York, all witnessed disturbances after blacks moved onto formerly all-white blocks. In one instance, terrorists torched a Deer Park, Long Island, home one day after they had burned a cross into the front lawn. In 1982, several weeks of protest culminated in three nights of firebombing after three African American families moved into a predominantly white apartment building in the Dorchester section of Boston. In 1986, tiny Tilghman Island, Maryland, was the site of a cross burning after Miles Gray Jr. and his family became the only black residents of the Chesapeake Bay island. Gray, a hotel executive, had been transferred from a job in Virginia Beach to Easton, Maryland. In February, he found what the *Washington Post* described as "the secluded bayfront house with its large trees and beautiful sunsets." Gray apparently felt the stares of the islanders from the moment he moved in. Then, less than two months after their arrival, the Grays found a blackened 8-foot cross smoldering at the edge of their front lawn. A trial of the culprits led to jail terms for two of the accused: one man was given forty-five days, the other was given sixty days, and a woman accomplice was sentenced to community service. The incident prompted attention throughout the region. A contingent of the Baltimore County chapter of the Ku Klux Klan demonstrated to protest what it called "the strict sentences" handed down to the perpetrators; the Grays received moral support from groups in Easton and Talbot County. But in early 1987, Gray accepted a transfer to Miami, observing "I can't say Tilghman Island was a bad place. . . . The property was beautiful, and some of the people were very nice. The only thing I could figure out," he suggested, "was that there are some people who just don't understand that it's 1987. It's like the twilight zone out there."[22]

Incidents in New York, New Jersey, Ohio, and Mississippi in the 1990s wrought more damage to both property and psyches. In Ridgewood, New Jersey, a wealthy Bergen County enclave, a black couple awoke to find that vandals had spread excrement on their mailbox, piled feces on their "welcome mat," and written them a crude, misspelled note, reading "Nigers Go Home." A black family in Brooklyn had their $265,000 home destroyed by a firebomb in early February 1990. That incident caught the attention of New York Mayor David Dinkins, who called it a "reprehensible assault [designed to] keep an African American family from moving into a home they [had] bought on the open market." In 1991, Dorothy and J. R. Jorden moved into a mobile home in Eudora, Mississippi. Starting in the spring of 1992, they became the victims of several incidents of intimidation. On May 3, they found a smoldering cross on their front lawn. Two weeks later, they were awakened in the night when a couple of white vandals stoned their home. A few days later, they were the victims of a second cross burning. Police captured the culprits, and the Jordens eventually received a $2,000 settlement, but they refused to live in Eudora, moving instead to Tennessee. In October 1994, a group of white teenagers in Cleveland made a Molotov cocktail for the purpose of intimidating a middle-aged black couple, Eddie and Grace Byrd. The Byrds had faced prior vandalism and abuse, but the firebombing so traumatized Mrs. Byrd that she had to be hospitalized on several occasions after the incident. It also caused them to feel the need to keep a family member standing guard at their home twenty-four hours a day. In 1996, the perpetrators of the violence were ordered to pay $10,000 in damages to the Byrds.[23]

And when bombs do not actually fly, there are still threats and intimidation. Any of a thousand examples could be used to show the persistent resistance to integration of neighborhoods, but one reported in *Time* magazine will do. In 1987, Edwina Barron, an attractive, middle-aged, African American research librarian, rented a condominium in the mostly white Cleveland suburb of Euclid, Ohio. The night after her arrival, she was visited by one of the white residents. The man knocked on her door, and when she cracked it open he pushed his way into her home, saying "I have to talk to you." Barron described the man's attitude as "We don't want you here." According to Barron, the man informed her that he had discussed her presence with some of his neighbors and that if she decided to stay, then he would not be responsible for the consequences. She would be "taking her chances." Barron admitted that the incident caused a mixture of hostility, hatred, anger, and fear to well up in her. She had not expected to be welcomed by her neighbors. She half expected to be ignored, her neighbors acting as if she "didn't exist." "That would not have disturbed me one bit," she suggested, "because I've been black all my life and run into situations like this." She knew that the man had no right to say these things, but she moved out anyway. One month after the incident, she took a bungalow in a racially mixed section of Cleveland.[24]

This conflict, or just the threat of it, results in African Americans being unwilling to make the first move toward integration. Even the optimist Reynolds Farley has had to recognize this fact. "Most Detroit area blacks," he relates in one study, "are reluctant to be the first of their race in a white neighborhood." Fewer than one-third of the respondents to his 1992 poll were willing to risk moving into an all-white neighborhood. More significant still than the 1992 result is the fact that it showed a decrease of more than 5 percent over a similar 1976 inquiry, suggesting a greater inclination toward self-segregation. A *Chicago Sun-Times* poll taken in 1993 confirms the point. Nearly three-quarters of African American respondents who lived in the city believed that black families who move into all-white neighborhoods were "harassed and attacked."[25]

All racial and ethnic groups desire to live in comfortable surroundings that provide relevant services and conjure up a sense of community. Therefore, not all of the unwillingness to integrate derives from fear of conflict. Some African Americans have voluntarily segregated themselves, as is their right, for political and cultural reasons. And complete integration is not necessarily the final objective anyway. "The test," as Charles Abrams put it, "is not whether a group is segregated but whether there are elements of compulsion which keep its members in place when they are ready, willing, and able to live elsewhere."[26]

The history of almost continuous racial conflict over housing in the twentieth century evinces not so much a problem of inadequate enforcement by government agencies or the inadequacy of the laws themselves as a determined effort on the part of white home owners, landlords, and tenants to keep their neighborhoods white, which has resulted in most blacks being disinclined to alter that condition. Realty companies, lending institutions, and governments have engaged in activities that sustain the community's segregationist wishes. In so doing, however, they represent the will of their constituencies. If neighborhood improvement associations and individual home owners demonstrated a ready acceptance of, or even just indifference to, black in-migration, then realtors and government officials would have neither the will nor the need to pursue segregationist policies. Instead, the conflict over residential space demonstrates that laws and institutional discrimination followed the violence and resistance to integration. They were remedial actions taken to restore peace, order, and stability to neighborhoods.

The campaign against residential segregation, meanwhile, remains a significant and instructive achievement for the NAACP, the NCDH, and the civil rights movement. From its first battles in Baltimore, St. Louis, and Louisville through the extreme violence of the 1920s and the subsequent brief and inadequate truce, the expansion of governmental activity in housing during the Depression and World

War II, and the explosion in violent resistance during the 1950s and 1960s, the campaign represented a stubborn resolve to end second-class citizenship for African Americans. In its principal objective, the campaign succeeded. It reversed all legal supports for segregation. It won legal protection against discrimination in housing.

But the campaign has not achieved its broader aims. Blacks still do not enjoy equal access to housing, and American neighborhoods remain racially segregated. It may be too early to fairly assess the full effects of legislation. Legislated change, after all, seems to occur as an evolutionary, not a revolutionary, process. But without the sanction of popular opinion, laws have little force, and none of these laws enjoyed sweeping democratic support. Whether by legal means or extralegal means, many white home owners have proven that they will fight to protect their property from what they perceive as a threat. Only when the prospect of integration ceases to be seen as a threat will racial relations in the United States really improve. Until then, most white Americans will likely continue to support programs, maybe even affirmative action programs, that increase the opportunities of blacks to progress in education and employment. And African Americans will continue their slow advance to opportunity and equality, as long as they don't move next door.

THE REASON

How The Crisis *explained the Great Migration in 1919. ("The Reason" by Allen A. Smith, Courtesy of the NAACP,* The Crisis)

Dr. Ossian Sweet (left), Clarence Darrow (right), and other members of the Sweet defense team, 1926. (Courtesy of the NAACP, The Crisis, photographer unknown)

James Weldon Johnson, executive secretary of the NAACP, 1920–1930. (NAACP Collection, Prints and Photographs Division, Library of Congress)

Walter F. White, executive secretary of the NAACP from 1931–1954, during a speech in Oakland, California, in 1954. The topic reportedly involved the violence over housing in Miami, Florida. (NAACP Collection, Prints and Photographs Division, Library of Congress—photograph by E.F. Joseph)

Thurgood Marshall, special counsel of the NAACP Legal Defense and Education Fund. Among his many other accomplishments, his leadership in the fight against race-restrictive convenants during the 1940s inspired African American communities across the country and brought about a major advance in civil rights law. (NAACP Collection, Prints and Photographs Division, Library of Congress)

Robert C. Weaver, first secretary of the U.S. Department of Housing and Urban Development. From the 1930s through the 1960s, Weaver was foremost in the campaign for better housing for African Americans (HUD Collection, National Archives)

Substandard housing in Washington, D.C., circa 1950. (NAACP Collection, Prints and Photographs Division, Library of Congress)

Substandard housing in Baltimore, Maryland, circa 1950. (NAACP Collection, Prints and Photographs Division, Library of Congress)

Girls playing jacks in Sunnyhills, an integrated UAW development in Milpitas, California. This was a propaganda photo taken for the National Committee Against Discrimination in Housing, 1956. (NAACP Collection, Prints and Photographs Division, Library of Congress; photo by Dandelet)

Donald and Bettye Ann Howard checking the security of the plywood covering their living-room window. The Howards underwent nearly a year of constant terrorism and bombardment after moving into Trumbull Park Homes in a Chicago suburb in 1953. (Chicago Historical Society, Claude Barnett Collection, Negative ICHi-15102)

HELP STOP

Negro Encroachment into White Areas

Unscrupulous White and Negro Real Estate Agents
From Exploiting Negro Home Buyers

Spreading of Communism

ALSO HELP US TO

Better Our Race Relations

Better Our City Government

The Eagle will stand for the rights of Southern people—in opposition to the effort being made by propaganda groups sponsored by communism, and other
subversive groups.

EITHER DONATE OR SUBSCRIBE

1 Year $3.00
6 Months $1.50
2 Years $5.00

Date_____ 1949

Name_____

Address_____

City_____

State_____

WEST END EAGLE

839 Park St., S. W.   Phone AM. 1000

Advertisement for the Atlanta-based West Side Cooperative Corporation's West Side Eagle, 1949. (Ralph McGill Papers, Emory University Special Collections)

Picketers at the home of an African American in Miami, 1957. (Courtesy of United Press International)

White counterdemonstrators opposing the nightly marches of Father James Groppi and the NAACP Youth Council in Milwaukee, Wisconsin, 1967. (Courtesy of AP/Wide World Photo)

APPENDIX

Table A.1 Population by Color, Selected Cities (1900–1970)

	Total Black Population	Percentage of Total Population
Atlanta, Ga.		
1900	35,912	39.8
1910	51,902	33.5
1920	62,796	31.3
1930	90,075	33.3
1940	104,533	34.6
1950	121,416	36.6
1960	186,464	38.3
1970	255,051	51.3
Baltimore, Md.		
1900	79,258	15.6
1910	84,749	15.2
1920	108,322	14.8
1930	142,106	17.7
1940	165,843	19.3
1950	226,053	23.8
1960	326,589	34.8
1970	420,210	46.4
Birmingham, Ala.		
1900	16,575	43.1
1910	52,305	39.4
1920	70,230	39.3
1930	99,077	38.2
1940	108,938	40.7
1950	130,115	39.9
1960	135,113	39.6
1970	126,388	42.0

(table continues)

Table A.1 (continued)

	Total Black Population	Percentage of Total Population
Chicago, Ill.		
1900	30,150	1.8
1910	44,103	2.8
1920	109,458	4.1
1930	233,903	6.9
1940	277,731	8.2
1950	509,437	14.1
1960	812,637	22.9
1970	1,102,620	32.7
Dallas, Tx.		
1900	9,035	21.2
1910	18,024	19.6
1920	24,023	15.1
1930	38,742	14.9
1940	50,488	17.1
1950	56,958	13.1
1960	129,242	19.0
1970	210,238	24.9
Detroit, Mich.		
1900	4,111	1.4
1910	5,741	1.2
1920	40,838	4.1
1930	120,066	7.7
1940	149,119	9.2
1950	303,721	16.4
1960	482,223	28.9
1970	660,428	43.7
Los Angeles, Calif.		
1900	2,131	2.1
1910	7,599	2.4
1920	15,579	2.7
1930	38,894	3.1
1940	63,774	4.2
1950	211,585	10.7
1960	334,916	13.5
1970	503,606	17.9

(table continues)

Table A.1 (continued)

	Total Black Population	Percentage of Total Population
Louisville, Ky.		
1900	39,139	19.1
1910	40,522	18.1
1920	40,087	17.1
1930	47,354	15.4
1940	47,158	14.8
1950	57,772	15.7
1960	70,075	38.8
1970	86,040	32.8
Miami, Fla.		
1900	not reported	
1910	2,258	41.3
1920	9,270	31.3
1930	25,116	22.7
1940	36,857	21.3
1950	40,262	16.3
1960	65,213	22.4
1970	76,156	22.7
New York City		
1900	60,666	1.8
1910	91,709	1.9
1920	152,467	2.7
1930	327,706	4.7
1940	458,444	6.1
1950	775,516	9.8
1960	1,087,931	14.0
1970	1,666,636	21.2
St. Louis, Mo.		
1900	35,516	6.2
1910	43,960	6.4
1920	69,854	9.0
1930	93,580	11.4
1940	108,765	13.3
1950	154,448	18.0
1960	214,377	28.6
1970	254,191	40.9

Source: Hollis R. Lynch, *The Black Urban Condition: A Documentary History, 1866–1971* (New York: Crowell, 1973), 425–432; Bureau of the Census, *Census Reports: Twelfth Census, 1900* (Washington, D.C.: GPO, 1901), 441; *Thirteenth Census, 1910: Population I: General Report and Analysis* (Washington, D.C.: GPO, 1913), 208–209, 223; *Fourteenth Census, 1920: Population III: Composition and Characteristics of the Population by States* (Washington, D.C.: GPO, 1922), 118.

Table A.2 Population by Color, Metropolitan Birmingham, Alabama, by Selected Census Tract (1950 and 1960)

Tract	Population, 1950		Population, 1960	
	Black	White	Black	White
Graymont-Border				
29	7,499	198	7,931	68
30	190	10,078	214	8,710
40	209	10,345	152	8,894
41	2,664	1,633	2,929	1,267
Graymont-Interior				
39	1,619	1,663	1,739	2,401
52	1,004	2,877	969	4,999
Homewood				
A-107	1,244	10,622	2,274	18,077
Mountain Brook				
A-109	280	8,079	146	12,532
Vestavia Hills				
C-129	no data	no data	59	9,238
C-144	no data	no data	25	6,272

Source: Bureau of the Census, *Seventeenth Census, 1950: Population II: Characteristics of the Population, Alabama* (Washington, D.C.: GPO, 1952), 2 — 65, 2 — 66; *Seventeenth Census, 1950: Population III: Census Tract Statistics: Birmingham, Ala.* (Washington, D.C.: GPO, 1952), 7 — 10; *Eighteenth Census, 1960: Censuses of Population and Housing: Birmingham, Ala.* (Washington, D.C.: GPO, 1961), 16 — 22.

Table A.3 Population by Color, City of Dallas, Texas, by Selected South Dallas Census Tract (1940 to 1960)

	Population					
	1940		1950		1960	
Tract	Black	White	Black	White	Black	White
35	0	2,404	186	2,397	2,372	150
36	0	3,262	287	2,722	3,041	73
37	0	2,121	6,840	648	6,880	62
38	0	3,912	699	3,734	5,559	49
39	0	2,933	5,555	2,091	9,290	131

Source: Bureau of the Census, *Seventeenth Census, 1950: Population III: Dallas, Texas,* 9; *Eighteenth Census, 1960: Census of Population and Housing: Dallas, Texas* (Washington, D.C.: GPO, 1961), 18.

Table A.4 Population by Color, City of Chicago, by Selected South Chicago Census Tract (1940 to 1960)

Tract	Population					
	1940		1950		1960	
	Black	White	Black	White	Black	White
558	6	1,179	1,553	220	1,865	0
560	760	2,834	5,218	341	4,818	0
561	162	3,014	3,069	1,615	5,197	0
562	3	3,756	3,478	2,129	7,429	0
593	84	4,969	493	4,740	5,977	0
594	12	5,087	541	5,161	7,341	0
595	5	4,717	212	5,361	8,217	0
624	3	3,279	4,261	69	4,008	0
877	388	12,635	3,363	10,693	12,964	0
886	3	2,655	251	2,304	2,198	0
877	13	1,026	0	1,003	1,368	0
895	122	1,653	317	1,559	707	0
896/7	77	724	837	61	2,988	0

Source: Bureau of the Census, *Sixteenth Census, 1940: Population and Housing Statistics for Census Tract and Community Areas, Chicago, Ill.* (Washington, D.C.: GPO, 1943), 56–58; *Seventeenth Census, 1950: Population III: Chicago, Ill.* (Washington, D.C.: GPO, 1952), 38, 57; *Census of Population and Housing, 1960: Chicago, Ill.* (Washington, D.C.: GPO, 1961), 59, 61, 63, 79–81.

Table A.5 Population by Color, Metropolitan Chicago–Cook County by Selected
Subcommunity (1950 to 1955/1956)

Subcommunity	Population, 1950		Population, 1955/1956	
	White	Nonwhite	White	Nonwhite
Arlington Hts[a]	8,768	12	19,149	2
Hinsdale[b]	8,602	74	11,246	78
Lombard[c]	9,807	10	16,276	8
La Grange Park	6,170	6	10,317	5
Melrose	13,264	102	15,944	70
Merrionette Pk	1,101	0	2,330	0
Morton Grove	3,917	9	11.521	17
Niles	3,583	4	10,183	16
Oak Lawn[a]	8,744	2	17,875	20
Oak Park[a]	63,382	147	61,187	139
Park Forest[d]	8,126	12	23,618	97
Skokie	14,812	20	33,364	41
Skokie[a]			43,889	98
Westchester[a]	4,306	2	12,710	0
Winnetka	11,796	309	12,763	295
Worth	1,471	1	4,493	0

Notes: a. 1956. b. Includes Du Page County section. c. In Du Page County. d. Includes Will County section.

Source: Bureau of the Census, Series P-28, *Special Census Series* (Washington, D.C.: GPO, 1955–1957).

Table A.6 Population Change by Color, Metropolitan Detroit, City of Detroit by Selected Subcommunity, Plus Hamtramck and Highland Park (1940 to 1950)

| | Change in Population, 1940 to 1950 | | | |
| | Number | | Percent | |
Subcommunity	White	Nonwhite	White	Nonwhite
Cadillac 1A	−11,459	+16,102	−43	+60
John R. 1B	−13,474	+16,834	−55	+30
Mt. Elliott 1C	−15,597	+11,913	−27	+312
Oakland 1D	−21,464	+25,731	−78	+139
Center 1E	−13,145	+8,115	−21	+1,887
Cass 2A	−7,923	+2,430	−12	+271
Fort 2B	−1,059	+1,480	−5	+167
Michigan 2C	−5,425	+5,008	−14	+745
Delray 2D	−4,848	+1,964	−18	+18
Vernor 2E	−4,579	+1,032	−9	+200
McNichols 3A	−4,307	+3,284	−18	+479
Lawton 3B	−5,878	+1,967	−11	+155
Boulevard 3C	−6,957	+3,427	−14	+4,427
Tireman 3D	−9,550	+8,259	−31	+39
Ford 3E	−11,405	+7,995	−35	+427
Hamtramck 4A	−7,854	+1,370	−17	+41
Highland Pk 4B	−7,072	+2,655	−14	+199
Indian Vlge 5A	−6,027	+6,517	−15	+1,137
Algonquin 5B	−3,215	+1,657	−7	+427
Riverside 5C	−5,105	+1,387	−9	+196
Harper 5D	−3,598	+1,433	−14	+470
Pingree 5E	−3,522	+2,403	−11	+424
Mack 5F	−4,160	+2,202	−13	+610
Chandler 6A	+11,670	+47	+23	+300
Connor 6B	+5,138	−6	+16	−24
Denby 6C	+16,546	+6	+145	+300
Burbank 6D	+14,438	−4	+78	−18
Mt. Olivet 6E	+30,981	+65	+143	+929
Wyoming 7A	−229	+14	−1	+280
Livernois 7B	−2,009	+66	−5	+80
Warren 7C	−2,290	+851	−13	+80
Springwells 7D	−8,970	+96	−18	+18
Baby Creek 7E	−3,490	+30	−11	+23

(table continues)

Table A.6 (continued)

| | Change in Population, 1940 to 1950 | | | |
| | Number | | Percent | |
Subcommunity	White	Nonwhite	White	Nonwhite
MacKenzie 8A	+7,082	+6	+32	+24
Warrendale 8B	+26,157	+15	+165	+300
Park 8C	+33,658	+28	+451	+280
Schoolcraft 8D	+2,810	−1	+22	−7
Redford 9A	+22,315	−11	+138	−22
Cooley 9B	+8,769	+4	+25	+20
Couzens 9C	+32,820	+96	+495	+1,100
Marygrove 9D	+2,424	−13	+8	−19
Palmer 9E	+12,172	+196	+48	+51
Northlawn 9F	+1,642	+5,184	+104	+275
Lodge 10A	−2,946	+371	−8	+63
Forest Ln 10B	−794	+4	−7	+100
Davison 10C	−6,828	+7,439	−36	+133
Cleveland 10D	+1,292	+1,017	+7	+203
Pershing 10E	+13,070	+1,398	+163	+105
State Fair 10F	+3,878	+2,589	+8	+312

Source: Detroit Commission of Community Relations–Human Rights Department, Part 3, Series I, Box 17, "Population Studies," Detroit, 11–15.

Table A.7 Population by Color, Metropolitan Miami by Municipality and Selected
Census Tract (1950 to 1970)

	Population					
	1950		1960		1970	
	Black	White	Black	White	Black	White
Municipality						
Miami	40,262	208,700	65,213	225,888	76,156	256,377
C. Gables	1,734	12,677	2,164	32,605	2,173	40,089
Hialeah	488	19,186	872	66,025	1,157	100,696
Miami Beach	605	45,644	493	62,577	319	86,311
N. Miami	13	10.717	29	28,657	69	34,592
Tract						
A-10	2,192	12,905	5,538	18,343	18,719	9,567
10-A/10.01			2	4,990	1,365	4,540
10-B/10.02			3	5,581	5,224	1,925
10-C/10.03			4	5,124	4,599	2,088
10-D/10.04			5,529	2,648	7,531	1,014
A-15	7,019	1,260	14,850	118	13,607	33
15-A/15.01			16,739	33	5,748	11
15-B/15.02			8,111	85	7,859	12
A-17	2,207	7,301	7,077	6,636	8,118	5,716
17-A/17.01			2,822	2,422	4,378	1,303
17-B/17.02			4,255	506	3,709	385
17-C/17.03			0	3,708	31	4,028
A-18	2,681	9,287	8,172	3,842	17,613	1,362
18-A/18.01			4,622	652	5,986	60
18-B/18.02			6	1,799	5,922	740
18-C/18.03			3,544	1,391	5,705	562
A-19	4	7,045	11,677	3,016	16,909	219
19-A/19.01			5,487	322	5,793	37
19-B/19.02			6,190	2,694	11,116	182
A-23/23/0023	1	5,713	0	5,185	7,773	562

Source: Bureau of the Census, *Seventeenth Census of the U.S., 1950: Population II: Characteristics of the Population, Part 10, Fla.* (Washington, D.C.: GPO, 1952), 57–58; *Seventeenth Census of the U.S., 1950: Population III: Census Tract Statistics, P-D31: Miami, Fla.* (Washington, D.C.: GPO, 1952), 6–10; *Eighteenth Census of the U.S., 1960: Censuses of Population and Housing, Census Tracts, PHC(1)-90: Miami, Fla., S.M.S.A.* (Washington, D.C.: GPO, 1961), 15–16, 25–26; *Nineteenth Census of the U.S., 1970: Censuses of Population and Housing, Census Tracts, PHC(1)–129: Miami, Fla., S.M.S.A.* (Washington, D.C.: GPO, 1973), 1, 6–7, 13–14, 20–21.

NOTES

NOTES TO THE PREFACE (PAGES vii TO viii)

1. "Love Me I'm a Liberal," Phil Ochs. Copyright 1965. Renewed 1993, Barricade Music, Inc. (ASCAP). All Rights Reserved. Used By Permission.

2. Derrick Bell, *Faces at the Bottom of the Well: The Permanence of Racism* (New York: Basic Books, 1992). The idea of "truthful remembering" I first heard about in a sermon from my pastor at Old Presbyterian Meeting House, Rev. Gary Charles. The notion has since been supported and elaborated upon by a discussion on the purpose of history and "What Is a Nation?" presented in John Ralston Saul, *Reflection of a Siamese Twin: Canada at the End of the Twentieth Century* (Toronto: Viking, 1997), 30.

NOTES TO INTRODUCTION (PAGES 1 TO 12)

1. Gunnar Myrdal, with the assistance of Richard Sterner and Arnold Rose, *An American Dilemma: The Negro Problem and Modern Democracy* (New York: Harper & Brothers, 1944), 622–23.

2. Regarding the social and cultural importance of home ownership, see, to begin with, Charles Abrams, *The Future of Housing* (New York: Harper & Bros., 1946); Kenneth T. Jackson, *Crabgrass Frontier: The Suburbanization of the United States* (New York: Oxford University Press, 1985); Kenneth Fox, *Metropolitan America: Urban Life and Urban Policy in the United States, 1940–1980* (Jackson: University of Mississippi Press, 1986); Gwendolyn Wright, *Building the Dream: A Social History of Housing in America* (New York: Pantheon, 1981).

3. *Porter* v. *Johnson*, cited in Elmer M. McMillion, "Racial Restrictive Covenants Revisited," in Alfred Avins, ed., *Open Occupancy vs. Forced Housing Under the Fourteenth Amendment: A Symposium on Anti-Discrimination Legislation, Freedom of Choice, and Property Rights in Housing* (New York: Bookmailer, 1963), 93. Franklin D. Roosevelt is cited in Ronald Tobey, Charles Wetherall, and Jay Brigham, "Moving Out and Settling In: Residential Mobility, Home Owning, and the Public Enframing of Citizenship, 1921–1950," *American Historical Review* 95 (1990), 1417, 1395–1422.

4. Robert N. Bellah, Richard Madsen, William M. Sullivan, Ann Swidler, and Steven M. Tipton, *Habits of the Heart: Individualism and Commitment in American Life* (New York: Perennial Library,

1985), 35–41; and Robert N. Bellah, Richard Madsen, William M. Sullivan, Ann Swidler, and Steven M. Tipton, *The Good Society* (New York: Vintage, 1991), 85–88.

5. For a full discussion of the development of a constitutional right of privacy, see Darien A. McWhirter and Jon D. Bible, *Privacy as a Constitutional Right: Sex, Drugs, and the Right to Life* (New York: Quorum, 1992), 91–105. On the use of violence to protect one's home, see Monica D. Blumenthal, Robert L. Kahn, Frank M. Andrews, and Kendra B. Head, *Justifying Violence: Attitudes of American Men* (Ann Arbor: Institute for Social Research, University of Michigan, 1971), 108–9. Richard Maxwell Brown traces the development of this peculiarly American legal right to stand one's ground in *No Duty to Retreat: Violence and Values in American History and Society* (New York: Oxford University Press, 1991). For a discussion of Colorado's law see William Wilbanks, *The Make My Day Law: Colorado's Experiment in Home Protection* (Lanham: University Press of America, 1990).

6. John R. Feagin and Melvin P. Sikes, *Living with Racism: The Black Middle-Class Experience* (Boston: Beacon, 1994), 224.

7. W. E. B. Du Bois, *The Souls of Black Folk* (New York: Bantam Classics, 1989; originally published in 1903), 115.

8. This has proven to be a provocative analysis, becoming the central debate in the historiography of race relations in the "New South." According to the Woodward thesis, blacks who had enjoyed political and civil access during Reconstruction gradually lost it in the Black Codes that came with Redemption. Total subjugation did not occur until the 1890s, when political and economic elites imposed racial segregation on the region as a way of ending the Populist revolt by inhibiting unity among the working classes of both races. C. Vann Woodward, *The Strange Career of Jim Crow*, 3d rev. ed. (New York: Oxford University Press, 1974), 3–8, 31–109; and Woodward, "*Strange Career* Critics: Long May They Persevere," *Journal of American History* 75 (December 1988), 857–68.

9. The sociological and psychological literature of race relations proceeds in two strands: the personality approach and the social contact or social conflict/cognitive approach. In the wake of World War II, social scientists rushed to study the cause of the Holocaust. The American Jewish Committee sponsored probes into anti-Semitism that established an approach based on personality, a "psychodynamic approach." Though somewhat dated, the conclusions of the "personality theorists" hold strength in some circles of research. They include T. W. Adorno, Else Frenkel-Brunswik, Daniel J. Levinson, and R. Nevitt Sanford, *The Authoritarian Personality* (New York: Harper & Row, 1950); Gordon W. Allport, *The Nature of Prejudice* (Reading: Addison-Wesley, 1954); and Kenneth B. Clark, *Prejudice and Your Child* (Boston: Beacon Press, 1955). The sociologist Thomas Pettigrew questions the importance of personality in the formation of racist and segregationist attitudes. He argues instead that separatist attitudes often form "*after* the harsh facts of racial discrimination and segregation in housing." He asserts, "Behavior change typically precedes, rather than follows from, attitude change." See Thomas F. Pettigrew, *Racial Discrimination in the United States* (New York: Harper & Row, 1975), 11–34, 92–126. Others root their studies in "rational cognitive motivation theory" to challenge personality theory. See Henri Tajfel, "The Roots of Prejudice: Cognitive Aspects," in Peter Watson, ed., *Psychology and Race* (Chicago: Aldine, (1974, 1973), 76–95; Wolfgang Stroebe and Chester A. Insko, "Stereotype, Prejudice, and Discrimination: Changing Conceptions in Theory and Research," in Daniel Bar-Tel, Carl F. Graumann, Arie W. Kruglanski, and Wolfgang Stroebe, eds., *Stereotyping and Prejudice: Changing Conceptions* (New York: Springer-Verlag, 1989), 3–36; Marshall H. Segall, Donald T. Campbell, and Melville J. Herskovits, *The Influence of Culture on Visual Perception* (Indianapolis: Bobbs-Merrill, 1966). See also Robin M. Williams Jr., *Strangers Next Door: Ethnic Relations in American Communities* (Englewood Cliffs: Prentice-Hall, 1964), and the discussion below and in Chapter 8 herein.

10. John W. Cell, *The Highest Stage of White Supremacy: The Origins of Segregation in South Africa and the American South* (Cambridge: Cambridge University Press, 1982), 3; Charles S. Johnson, *Backgrounds to Patterns of Negro Segregation* (New York: Crowell, 1943), 158–63. Also see Joel Williamson, *After Slavery: The Negro in South Carolina During Reconstruction, 1861–1877* (New York: Norton, 1975); *The Crucible of Race: Black-White Relations in the American South Since Emancipation* (New York: Oxford University Press, 1984); Harold N. Rabinowitz, "More Than the Woodward Thesis: Assessing *The Strange Career of Jim Crow*," in *Journal of American History* 75 (1988), 842–56, and in *The First New South, 1865–1920* (Arlington Heights: Harlan Davidson,

1992); Bell, *Faces at the Bottom of the Well*, passim.; and Leon F. Litwack, *North of Slavery: The Negro in the Free States, 1790–1860* (Chicago: University of Chicago Press, 1961). A historiographical discussion of race relations in urban America occurs in Kenneth L. Kusmer, "The Black Urban Experience in American History," in *The State of Afro-American History: Past, Present, and Future*, ed. Darlene Clark Hine (Baton Rouge: Louisiana State University Press, 1986), 91–122.

11. On the Progressive argument for segregation, see, for example, Don H. Doyle, *Nashville in the New South, 1880–1930* (Knoxville: University of Tennessee Press, 1985).

12. T. J. Woofter Jr., *Negro Problems in Cities* (New York: Doubleday, 1928), 39; Ray Stannard Baker, cited in Florette Henri, *Black Migration: Movement North, 1900–1920* (Garden City: Anchor/ Doubleday, 1975), 82.

13. Woofter, *Negro Problems in Cities*; Douglas S. Massey and Nancy A. Denton, *American Apartheid: Segregation and the Making of the Underclass* (Cambridge and London: Harvard University Press, 1993), 35; Abrams, *Forbidden Neighbors: A Study of Prejudice in Housing* (New York: Harper & Bros., 1955), 81–136, 150–190, 279–305. The exceptions to this tendency are the studies of specific cities, such as: Arnold R. Hirsch, *Making the Second Ghetto: Race and Housing in Chicago, 1940–1960* (Cambridge: Cambridge University Press, 1983); Peter H. Rossi and Robert A. Dentler, *The Politics of Urban Renewal: The Chicago Findings* (New York: Glencoe, 1961); and B. J. Widick, *Detroit: City of Race and Class Violence* (Detroit: Wayne State University Press, 1989).

14. See Abrams, *Forbidden Neighbors*, 150–190; Karl Taeuber, "The Contemporary Context of Housing Discrimination," *Yale Law and Policy Review* 6 (1988), 340–342, 345. See also the impressive literature on racial discrimination in housing and real estate, including Musa Bish, Jean Bullock, and Jean Milgram, *Racial Steering: The Dual Housing Market and Multiracial Neighborhoods* (Philadelphia: National Neighbors, 1973); Margery R. Boichel, Herbert A. Auerbach, Theodore Bakerman, and David H. Elliott, "Exposure, Experience and Attitudes: Realtors and Open Occupancy," *Phylon* 30 (1969), 325–337; William H. Brown Jr., "Access to Housing: The Role of the Real Estate Industry," reprinted in Paul Finkelman, ed., *The Era of Integration and Civil Rights, 1930–1990*, 74–86; George C. Galster, "More Than Skin Deep: The Effect of Housing Discrimination on the Extent and Pattern of Racial Residential Segregation in the United States," in John M. Goering, ed., *Housing Desegregation and Federal Policy* (Chapel Hill: University of North Carolina Press, 1986), 119–138; Galster, "Residential Segregation in American Cities: A Contrary Review," *Population Research and Policy Review* 7 (1988), 93–112; Galster, "Racial Steering in Housing Markets: A Review of the Audit Evidence," *Review of Black Political Economy* 18 (1990), 105–129; Galster, "Racial Steering by Real Estate Agents: Mechanisms and Motives," *Review of Black Political Economy* 19 (1990), 39–63; Galster, "Racial Discrimination in Housing Markets During the 1980s: A Review of the Audit Evidence," *Journal of Planning Education and Research* 9 (1990), 165–175; Julia L. Hansen and Franklin J. James, "Housing Discrimination in Small Cities and Nonmetropolitan Areas," in Gary A. Tobin, ed. *Divided Neighborhoods: Changing Patterns of Racial Segregation, Urban Affairs Annual Reviews* 32 (Newbury Park: Sage, 1987), 181–207; Rose Helper, "Success and Resistance Factors in the Maintenance of Racially Mixed Neighborhoods," in Goering, *Housing Desegregation*, 170–194; John F. Kain, "Housing Market Discrimination and Black Suburbanization in the 1980s," in Tobin, *Divided Neighborhoods*, 68–94; James A. Kushner, *Fair Housing: Discrimination in Real Estate Community Development and Revitalization* (Colorado Springs and New York: Shepard's and McGraw-Hill, 1983); Robert W. Lake, *The New Suburbanites: Race and Housing in the Suburbs* (New Brunswick, N.J.: Rutgers University Press, 1981); Peter J. Leahy, "Are Racial Factors Important for the Allocation of Mortgage Money?" *American Journal of Economics and Sociology* 44 (1985), 183–196; Diana Pearce, "Gatekeepers and Homeseekers: Institutional Patterns of Racial Steering," *Social Problems* 26 (1979), 325–342; Marc A. Weiss, *The Rise of the Community Builders: The American Real Estate Industry and Urban Land Planning* (New York: Columbia University Press, 1987); John Yinger, *Prejudice and Discrimination in the Urban Housing Market* (Cambridge: Department of City and Regional Planning, Harvard University, 1977); Yinger, "The Racial Dimension of Urban Housing Markets in the 1980s," in Tobin, *Divided Neighborhoods*, 43–67.

15. NAREB Code of Ethics, cited in Gregory D. Squires, Larry Bennett, Kathleen McCourt, and Philip Nyden, *Chicago: Race, Class, and the Response to Urban Decline* (Philadelphia: Temple University Press, 1987), 9, and elsewhere; Ernest M. Fisher, *Principles of Real Estate Practice*, cited in Luigi

Laurenti, *Property Values and Race: Studies in Seven Cities* (Berkeley: University of California Press, 1960), 9; Rose Helper, *Racial Policies and Practices of Real Estate Brokers* (Minneapolis: University of Minnesota Press, 1969), 32–36. Frederick M. Babcock, Maurice R. Massey Jr., and Walter L. Greene, "Techniques of Residential Location Rating," *Appraisal Journal* 6 (1938), 137; NAREB teaching manual, cited in letter from J. Francis Pohlhaus, Counsel, Washington Bureau of NAACP to Nathaniel Colley, President, Central Valley Area, Sacramento, January 22, 1957, in Papers of the NAACP, Group III, Box A-162, "Housing, NAREB," Manuscript Collection, Library of Congress, Washington, D.C. (hereinafter cited as NAACP Papers . . . LOC, Manuscript Division). Charles Abrams offers a history of NAREB's racial policy up to the 1950s in *Forbidden Neighbors*, 150–68. An assessment, focusing on the business aspects of NAREB, occurs in Weiss, *Rise of the Community Builders*, 22–52.

16. Weaver, *The Negro Ghetto* (New York: Russell and Russell, 1967, 1948), 158; Thomas F. Pettigrew, *Racially Separate or Together?* (New York: McGraw-Hill, 1971), 20; Myrdal, *An American Dilemma*, 625; Oscar I. Stern, "The End of the Restrictive Covenant," *Appraisal Journal* 16 (1948), 435; Lee F. Johnson, "Housing: A 1950 Tragedy," *The Survey* 86 (1950), 551–55; Harry Conn, "Housing: A Vanishing Vision," *New Republic*, July 16, 1951, 12–14; Abrams, *Forbidden Neighbors*, 151–54. The FHA's opposition to the anti-discrimination clause is cited in "Memorandum, Prepared by the NAACP concerning the Present Discriminatory Policies of the FHA," October 28, 1944, 4, Papers of the NAACP, Part 5, The Campaign Against Residential Segregation, Group II, Box A-268, "Federal Housing Administration, General, 1947–1948," Reel 5 at 0555, Microfilm Collection, Amelia Gayle Gorgas Library, Tuscaloosa, Alabama (hereinafter cited as NAACP Papers, Part 5, Group no., etc.)

17. Robert C. Weaver, "The Negro as Tenant and Neighbor," *Public Housing Weekly News* 1 (May 21, 1940), 3.

18. George W. Lee, *Beale Street* (New York: Ballou, 1934), excerpted in Hollis R. Lynch, *The Black Urban Condition: A Documentary History, 1866–1971* (New York: Crowell, 1973), 212; "fecundmellow," Faulkner's term, indicates a sultry licentiousness supposedly pervading black communities, see William Faulkner, *Light in August* (New York: Random House, 1932), 385. The quotation regarding race mixing occurs in Alice J. Reilly to Mayor James H. Preston, File 106, "Segregation Ordinance," James H. Preston Mayoral Papers, Baltimore City Archives, Baltimore, Maryland.

19. Robert C. Weaver, *The Negro Ghetto* (New York: Russell and Russell, 1967, 1948), 231–56.

20. Clement E. Vose, *Caucasians Only: The Supreme Court, the NAACP, and the Restrictive Covenant Cases* (Berkeley: University of California Press, 1967); Mark V. Tushnet, *Making Civil Rights Law: Thurgood Marshall and the Supreme Court, 1936–1961* (New York: Oxford University Press, 1994), 81–98.

21. As regards the evolution of civil rights and housing law, this trend is a central thesis of this work and has been gleaned, in part, from research in the Papers of the NAACP, "The Campaign Against Residential Segregation, 1914–1955." Some other discussions include the following: U.S. Senate Committee on Banking and Currency, *Federal Housing Programs: A Chronology and Brief Summary of Congressional and Executive Action Affecting Housing from 1892 to October 25, 1949, and a Description of Present Federal Housing Programs* (Washington, D.C.: GPO, 1950); Housing and Home Finance Agency, *State Statutes and Local Ordinances Prohibiting Discrimination in Housing and Urban Renewal Operations* (Washington, D.C.: GPO, 1961); Housing and Home Finance Agency, *Fair Housing Laws: Summaries and Text of State and Municipal Laws* (Washington, D.C.: GPO, 1964); Wilhelmina A. Leigh, "Civil Rights Legislation and the Housing Status of Black Americans: An Overview," *Review of Black Political Economy* 20 (1991), 5–28; Kenneth Pearlman, "The Closing Door: The Supreme Court and Residential Segregation," *Journal of the American Institute of Planners*, 44 (1978), 160–69; Veronica M. Reed, "Civil Rights Legislation and the Housing Status of Black Americans: Evidence from Fair Housing Audits and Segregation Indices," *Review of Black Political Economy* 20 (1991), 29–42. See also Tushnet, *Making Civil Rights Law*; Vose, *Caucasians Only*; and Leland B. Ware, "Invisible Walls: An Examination of the Legal Strategy of the Restrictive Covenant Cases, *Washington University Law Quarterly* 67 (Fall 1989), 737–772.

22. William Julius Wilson, *The Declining Significance of Race: Blacks and Changing American Institutions* (Chicago: University of Chicago Press, 1978); Wilson, "The Declining Significance of

Race," *Society* 15 (Jan.–Feb. 1978), 56–62; and Wilson, "The Declining Significance of Race: Revisited but Not Revised," *Society* 15 (July–Aug.), 11, 15–21.

Charles Willie posits an interesting counterhypothesis that I will develop in greater detail below. It focuses on middle-class blacks. He believes "the significance of race is increasing . . for middle-class blacks who, because of school desegregation, and affirmative action, . . are coming into direct contact with whites for the first time for extended interaction." Middle-class blacks become symbols and role models for their people. "Try as hard as they may," Willie suggests, "middle class blacks . . are almost obsessed with race" (15): Charles V. Willie, "The Inclining Significance of Race," *Society* 15 (July–Aug. 1978), 10, 12–15.

A new hypothesis, presented by Charles Washington, posits that over the last two generations race relations have moved from a caste system to a class system and back to caste. Washington delineates five characteristics of a caste system: affiliation by descent with some endogamy expected; normative forces that justify and legitimate the status quo; institutionalized inequality; few socioeconomic mobility mechanisms; and skepticism about the efficacy of programs to stimulate upward mobility (238). A class system, meanwhile, is based on egalitarianism where "individual talent and efforts are the primary delimiting factors" (237).

Few could contest the merits of Washington's observation that the economic and social egalitarian spirit of the Great Society has declined, but his emphasis on the underclass causes him to exaggerate the degree of declension in race relations. Legal developments, particularly fair and open housing laws, have reduced institutional inequalities. Like Wilson, Washington does not take sufficient account of the black middle class, but he does successfully identify the changes that occurred and believes that racism still permeates much of society. Charles Washington, "From Caste to Class to Caste: The Changing Nature of Race Relations in America," in George C. Galster and Edward W. Hill, *The Metropolis in Black and White: Place, Power, and Polarization* (New Brunswick: Center for Urban Policy Research), 236–57.

For background and the ongoing debate about the importance of race in the United States, also see Doris Y. Wilkinson, "Gender and Social Inequality: The Prevailing Significance of Race," *Daedalus* 124 (Winter 1995), 167–78; Feagin and Sikes, *Living with Racism*; Charles T. Banner-Haley, *The Fruits of Integration: Black Middle-Class Ideology and Culture, 1960–1990* (Jackson: University of Mississippi Press, 1994); Rose L. H. Finkenstaedt, *Face-to-Face: Blacks in America, White Perceptions and Black Realities* (New York: Morrow, 1994); Cornel West, *Race Matters* (New York: Vintage, 1994); Andrew Hacker, *Two Nations: Black and White, Separate, Hostile, Unequal* (New York: Scribner's, 1992); Shelby Steele, *The Content of Our Character: A New Vision of Race in America* (New York: St. Martin's Press, 1990); Harold Cruse, *Plural but Equal: A Critical Study of Blacks and Minorities and America's Plural Society* (New York: Morrow, 1987); Bart Landry, *The New Black Middle Class* (Berkeley: University of California Press, 1987); Thomas J. Durant Jr. and Joyce S. Louden, "The Black Middle-Class in America: Historical and Contemporary Perspectives," *Phylon* 47 (1986), 253–63; E. Franklin Frazier, *Black Bourgeoisie* (New York: Free Press, 1957).

On the making and growth of the underclass, see Nicholas Lemann, *The Promised Land: The Great Black Migration and How It Changed America* (New York: Vintage, 1992). See also Massey and Denton, *American Apartheid*.

23. Helper, *Racial Policies and Practices*, 35; David L. Hamilton and George D. Bishop, "Attitudinal and Behavioral Effects of Initial Integration of White Suburban Neighborhoods," *Journal of Social Issues* 32 (1976), 60. Regarding the idea of "occupational elites," see Adelaide M. Cromwell, *The Other Brahmins: Boston's Upper Class, 1750–1950* (Fayetteville: University of Arkansas Press, 1994); and W. Ashbie Hawkins, "A Year of Segregation in Baltimore," *The Crisis* 3 (1911), 27–28.

24. Nathan Glazer, "Race and the Suburbs," in O. H. Koenigsberger, S. Groak, and B. Bernstein, eds., *The Work of Charles Abrams* (Oxford: Pergamon, 1980), 175–80; James R. Grossman, *Land of Hope: Chicago, Black Southerners, and the Great Migration* (Chicago: University of Chicago Press, 1989), 264–65.

25. W. E. B. Du Bois, "The Dilemma of the Negro," in Julius Lester, ed., *The Seventh Son: The Thought and Writings of W. E. B. Du Bois* (New York: Random House, 1971), 537; Du Bois, ed., *The Negro in Business* (New York: AMS Press, 1971, reprint of 1899 edition, Atlanta). Also see Du Bois, "The Black North: A Social Study," in Richard J. Meister, ed., *The Black Ghetto: Promised Land or*

Colony? (Lexington: D. C. Heath, 1972), 3–19; James Borchert, *Alley Life in Washington: Family, Community, Religion, and Folklife in the City, 1850–1970* (Urbana: University of Illinois Press, 1980); Albert S. Broussard, "Organizing the Black Community in the San Francisco Bay Area, 1915–1930," *Arizona and the West* 23 (1981), 335–354; John Sibley Butler, "Myrdal Revisited: The Negro in Business," *Daedalus* 124 (Winter 1995), 199–221; St. Clair Drake and Horace R. Cayton, *Black Metropolis: A Study of Negro Life in a Northern City* (New York: Harcourt, Brace, 1945), 99–128, 379–97, 658–754; Harold X. Connolly, *A Ghetto Grows in Brooklyn* (New York: New York University Press, 1977), 79–125; Cromwell, *The Other Brahmins*, passim.; Leon Forrest, *Relocations of the Spirit* (Wakefield: Asphodel Press, 1994), 49–65; E. Franklin Frazier, *Black Bourgeoisie* (Glencoe: Free Press, 1957), and "Human, All Too Human: The Negro's Vested Interest in Segregation," in G. Franklin Edwards, ed., *E. Franklin Frazier on Race Relations: Selected Writings* (Chicago: University of Chicago Press, 1968), 283–91; Grossman, *Land of Hope*, 98–132; James Weldon Johnson, *Black Manhattan* (New York: Arno Press reprint, 1968); David M. Katzman, *Before the Ghetto: Black Detroit in the Nineteenth Century* (Urbana: University of Illinois Press, 1973); Sidney Kronus, *The Black Middle Class* (Columbus: Merrill, 1971), 2–39; Kenneth L. Kusmer, *A Ghetto Takes Shape: Black Cleveland, 1870–1930* (Urbana: University of Illinois Press, 1976), 91–154; Kusmer, "Black Urban Experience"; Landry, *New Black Middle Class*, 36–66; Douglas K. Meyer, "Evolution of a Permanent Negro Community in Lansing," *Michigan History* 55 (1971), 141–54; Roi Ottley, *"New World A-Coming": Inside Black America* (Boston: Houghton-Mifflin, 1943), 59–121; Seth M. Scheiner, *Negro Mecca: A History of the Negro in New York City, 1865–1920* (New York: New York University Press, 1965); Allan H. Spear, *Black Chicago: The Making of a Negro Ghetto* (Urbana: University of Illinois Press, 1967), 29–126; Henry Louis Taylor Jr. and Vicky Dula, "The Black Residential Experience and Community Formation in Antebellum Cincinnati," in Henry Louis Taylor Jr., ed., *Race and the City: Work, Community, and Protest in Cincinnati, 1820–1970* (Urbana: University of Illinois Press, 1993); Quintard Taylor, "The Emergence of Black Communities in the Pacific Northwest: 1865–1910," *Journal of Negro History* 64 (1979), 342–54; Lillian S. Williams, "Afro-Americans in Buffalo, 1900–1930: A Study in Community Formation," *Afro-Americans in New York Life and History* 8 (1984), 7–35.

26. Du Bois, "Dilemma," in Lester, *Seventh Son*, 534–545. Du Bois spoke on that topic on several occasions. These ideas appear in less well-thought-out forms in "The Conservation of Races," "Is Race Separation Practicable," and "The Race Problem," all collected in Philip S. Foner, ed., *W. E. B. Du Bois Speaks: Speeches and Addresses, 1890–1919* (New York: Pathfinder, 1970). See also James Weldon Johnson, *Along This Way: The Autobiography of James Weldon Johnson* (New York: Penguin, 1933), 412.

Racial integration does not have to mean cultural assimilation. The Canadian psychologist J. W. Berry has offered a fruitful contemporary discussion of the distinction between the two ideas of integration and assimilation. Berry has inquired as to the impact of the governmental policy of multiculturalism on Canadians. Two issues faced the people under the policy: maintaining and developing their group's ethnic distinctiveness and deciding whether and how intergroup contact should be maintained. Berry asked his subjects two questions: (1) "Are cultural identity and customs of value, and to be retained?" and (2) "Are positive relations with the larger society of value, and to be sought?" From the responses, Berry draws four categories of cultural relations: integration, assimilation, segregation-separation, and deculturation. He categorizes relations that held both cultural identity and positive relations with the larger society of value as integration. Integration therefore involves not just entry into society, but entry with the maintenance of one's cultural identity. Assimilation differs from integration. It involves the negation of cultural identity to facilitate positive relations with the larger society. Those of Berry's subjects who answered "yes" to the question about identity and "no" to the question of contact are categorized as segregationist or separatist. The final group, an apparently uninspired and misanthropic lot, answered "no" to both questions and were categorized as preferring deculturation. Table I displays Berry's findings:

In Canada, the dominant response favored integration—positive interaction with the maintenance of ethnic diversity. Berry recognized, however, that the policy of multiculturalism led to ethnocentrism, encouraging "positive own group evaluation" and resulting in a "widely present" pattern of ethnocentric opinion. Berry concedes that ethnic parochialism threatens social harmony, but the

Table 1   A Model of Possible Forms of Cultural Relations in Plural Societies

		QUESTION 1: Are cultural identity and customs of value, and to be retained?	
		YES	NO
QUESTION 2: Are positive relations with the larger society of value, and to be sought?	YES	Integration	Assimiliation
	NO	Segregation/separation	Deculturation

government, believing that "only when a person has confidence in his own cultural foundations canhe have respect for other groups," pursued the program anyway because it hoped it could reach an important first stage in resolving national tensions. See: J. W. Berry, "Cultural Relations in Plural Societies: Alternatives to Segregation and Their Socio-psychological Implications," in Norman Miller and Marilynn B. Brewer, eds., *Groups in Contact: The Psychology of Desegregation* (Orlando: Academic Press, 1984), 11–27.

27. On the development and distinctiveness of black culture, see Lawrence W. Levine, *Black Culture and Black Consciousness: Afro-American Folk Thought From Slavery to Freedom* (New York: Oxford University Press, 1977), passim. Rather more provocative but still insightful discussions of the role of the "dilemma of the Negro" and black culture in the twentieth century include Derrick Bell, *And We Are Not Saved: The Elusive Quest for Racial Justice* (New York: Basic Books, 1987), 222; Fred R. Harris and Roger W. Wilkins, eds., *Quiet Riots: Race and Poverty in the United States, the Kerner Report Twenty Years Later* (New York: Pantheon, 1988); Lewis M. Killian, *The Impossible Revolution, Phase II: Black Power and the American Dream*, 2d ed. (New York: Random House, 1975), 119; and Addison Gayle, ed., *The Black Aesthetic* (Garden City, N.Y.: 1971). See also Finkenstaedt, *Face-to-Face*, 222–254.

NOTES TO CHAPTER I (PAGES 13 TO 29)

1. A folk axiom cited in Philip A. Johnson, *Call Me Neighbor, Call Me Friend: The Case History of the Integration of a Neighborhood on Chicago's South Side* (Garden City: Doubleday, 1965), 17.

2. Poverty and peonage defined life for many, but 3 percent of blacks held white-collar jobs. See Landry, *The New Black Middle Class*, 19–20; and Pete Daniel, *The Shadow of Slavery: Peonage in the South, 1901–1969* (Urbana: University of Illinois Press, 1972), 19–42. See also George M. Fredrickson, *Black Image in the White Mind: The Debate on Afro-American Character and Destiny, 1817–1914* (New York: Harper Torchbooks, 1972), 228–319; J. Morgan Kousser, *The Shaping of Southern Politics: Suffrage Restriction and Establishment of the One-Party System, 1880–1910* (New Haven: Yale University Press, 1974), 182–237; Joel Williamson, *The Rage for Order: Black/White Relations in the American South Since Emancipation* (New York: Oxford University Press, 1988), 78–116; George C. Wright, *Racial Violence in Kentucky, 1865–1940: Lynchings, Mob Rule, and "Legal Lynchings"* (Baton Rouge: Louisiana State University Press, 1990).

3. George A. Levesque, *Black Boston: African American Life and Culture in Urban America, 1750–1860* (New York: Garland, 1994), 32–37; Johnson, *Black Manhattan*, 58–59; Litwack, *North of Slavery*, 168; Scheiner, *Negro Mecca*, 15–38.

4. Richard C. Wade, *Slavery in the Cities: The South 1820–1860* (New York: Oxford University Press, 1964), 56–57, 65–70.

5. Ira Berlin, *Slaves Without Masters: The Free Negro in the Antebellum South* (New York: Pantheon, 1974), 252–55; Leonard P. Curry, *The Free Black in Urban America 1800–1850: The Shadow of the Dream* (Chicago: University of Chicago Press, 1981), 55–57, 79. Curry develops indices of racial dissimilarity for antebellum cities just as the demographers Karl E. Taeuber and Alma F. Taeuber had

done in their investigation of residential segregation in the twentieth century. The Taeubers performed a block-by-block study of 206 cities to evaluate the degree of racial separation in each of them. They then established an "index of dissimilarity" with which to compare the cities. A rating of 100 on the index represented complete racial segregation within blocks. A rating of zero reflected complete racial balance. Although the index of dissimilarity is very useful in measuring segregation at a point in time, it does not assess changes in levels of segregation over time as accurately as the correlation ratio developed by Otis D. Duncan and Beverly Duncan. This is noted in John R. Logan and Mark Schneider, "Racial Segregation and Racial Change in American Suburbs, 1970–1980," *American Journal of Sociology* 89 (1984), 879–81. The significance of the different measurements will be revisited in the Afterword herein. See also Karl E. Taeuber and Alma F. Taeuber, *Negroes in Cities: Residential Segregation and Neighborhood Change* (Chicago: Aldine, 1965); Otis D. Duncan and Beverly Duncan, "A Methodological Analysis of Segregation Indices," *American Sociological Review* 20 (1955), 210–17; and Stanley Lieberson and Donna K. Carter, "Temporal Changes and Urban Differences in Residential Segregation: A Reconsideration," *American Journal of Sociology* 88 (1982), 296–310.

6. Howard N. Rabinowitz, *Race Relations in the Urban South, 1865–1890* (Urbana: University of Illinois Press, 1980), 98–100, 106. See also Don H. Doyle, *New Men, New Cities, New South: Atlanta, Nashville, Charleston, Mobile, 1860–1910* (Chapel Hill: University of North Carolina Press, 1990); and Garrett Power, "Apartheid Baltimore Style: The Residential Segregation Ordinance of 1910–1913," in *Maryland Law Review* 42 (1983), 289–93.

7. Rabinowitz, *Race Relations in the Urban South*, 98, 100, 102–4; Leavy W. Oliver, "Zoning Ordinances in Relation to Segregated Negro Housing in Birmingham, Alabama," master's thesis, Indiana University, 1951, Southern Collection, Birmingham Public Library, Birmingham, Alabama, 7.

8. Hollis R. Lynch, ed., *The Black Urban Condition: A Documentary History, 1866–1971* (New York: Crowell, 1973), 424–26; Johnson, *Black Manhattan*, 59; Scheiner, *Negro Mecca*, 15–35; Elizabeth Hafkin Pleck, *Black Migration and Poverty: Boston, 1865–1900* (New York: Academic Press, 1979), 77; and D. Randall Beirne, "The Impact of Black Labor on European Immigration into Baltimore's Oldtown, 1790–1910," *Maryland Historical Magazine* 83 (1988), 332; Roger Lane, *Roots of Violence in Black Philadelphia, 1860–1900* (Cambridge: Harvard University Press, 1986), 7–8, 20–21, 33; T. Lynn Smith, "The Redistribution of the Negro Population of the United States, 1910–1960," *Journal of Negro History*, 51 (July 1966), 157. Philadelphia's total population was 1,293,647 in 1900 and 1,684,000 in 1910. See Russell Weigley, editor, *Philadelphia: A 300-Year History* (New York: Norton, 1982), 488, 491–92, 526–27, 531–32.

9. Lynch, *Black Urban Condition*, 424–27; Beirne, "Baltimore's Oldtown," 332; Power, "Apartheid Baltimore Style," 289–93; Joseph Garonzik, "The Racial and Ethnic Make-up of Baltimore Neighborhoods, 1850–1870," *Maryland Historical Magazine* 71 (1976), 394–95.

10. Harold A. McDougall, *Black Baltimore: A New Theory of Community* (Philadelphia: Temple University Press, 1993), 36–37. Also see Suzanne Ellery Greene, "Black Republicans on the Baltimore City Council," *Maryland Historical Magazine* 74 (1979), 203–22.

11. W. Ashbie Hawkins, "A Year of Segregation in Baltimore," *The Crisis* 3 (1911), 27; *Baltimore News*, September 20, 1892, cited in Garrett Power, "Apartheid Baltimore Style: The Residential Segregation Ordinance of 1910–1913," *Maryland Law Review* 42 (1983), 290.

12. Power, "Apartheid Baltimore Style," 291; Hawkins, "A Year of Segregation," 27; W. Theodore Durr, "People of the Peninsula," *Maryland Historical Magazine* 77 (1982), 38.

13. Hawkins, "A Year of Segregation," 27. Also see Roderick N. Ryon, "Old West Baltimore," *Maryland Historical Magazine* 77 (1982), 59.

14. Ryon, "Old West Baltimore," 56–58; Power, "Apartheid Baltimore Style," 298, 308; Hawkins, "A Year of Segregation," 27–28.

15. Hawkins, "A Year of Segregation," 28; Power, "Apartheid Baltimore Style," 298.

16. Hawkins, "A Year of Segregation," 28–29; Power, "Apartheid Baltimore Style," 299–300; Greene, "Black Republicans," 210.

17. S. S. Field, "The Constitutionality of Segregation Ordinances," *Virginia Law Review* 5 (November 1917), 88–89.

18. Hawkins, "A Year of Segregation," 29; Power, "Apartheid Baltimore Style," 302–3.

19. Power, "Apartheid Baltimore Style," 304–5.

20. *The Crisis* 6 (1913), 323; 7 (1913–1914), 63, 140.

21. The most complete listing of cities with segregation laws occurs in *The Crisis*. See *The Crisis* 3 (1912), 227; *The Crisis* 4 (1912), 115–16; *The Crisis* 7 (1913), 63; *The Crisis* 10 (1915), 290; *The Crisis* 15 (December 1917), 69; and a survey of journal volumes 6–15. See also Monroe N. Work, ed., *Negro Year Book: An Annual Encyclopedia of the Negro, 1918–1919* (Tuskegee: Negro Year Book Publishing, 1919), 114; Gilbert Osofsky, *Harlem: The Making of a Ghetto, 1890–1930,* 2d ed. (New York: Harper Torchbooks, 1971), 106–8; "New York Property Owners Adopt a Restrictive Covenant," in Richard B. Sherman, ed., *The Negro and the City* (Englewood Cliffs: Prentice-Hall, 1970), 23–24; Roger L. Rice, "Residential Segregation by Law, 1910–1917," *Journal of Southern History* 34 (1968), 180–81; Daniel T. Kelleher, "St. Louis' 1916 Residential Segregation Ordinance," *The Bulletin* 26 (1970), 239–48; and Charles S. Johnson, for the Committee on Negro Housing, *Negro Housing*, President's Conference on Home Building and Home Ownership, vol. 6 (Washington, D.C.: National Capital Press, 1932) 37–40.

22. *The Crisis* 3 (1912), 99, 145, 227; *The Crisis* 4 (1912), 273.

23. Work, *Negro Year Book, 1914–1915* (Tuskegee: Negro Year Book Publishing, 1913), 55; "Dynamite in Kansas City," in *The Crisis* 3 (1912), 160–62; *The Crisis* 13 (1917), 246; Larry Grothaus, "Kansas City Blacks, Harry Truman and the Pendergast Machine," *Missouri Historical Review* 69 (1974), 68–70 (65–82); Donald B. Oster, "Reformers, Factionalists, and Kansas City's 1925 City Manager Charter," *Missouri Historical Review* 72 (1978), 304–5; Lyle W. Dorsett, *The Pendergast Machine* (New York: Oxford University Press, 1968), 23–49.

24. Free blacks and slaves comprised 2 percent of the city's total population in 1860; Lynch, *Black Urban Condition,* 421–26; see also Lawrence O. Christensen, "Race Relations in St. Louis, 1865–1916," *Missouri Historical Review* 78 (1984), 123–24.

25. Christensen, "Race Relations in St. Louis," 128–29.

26. *The Crisis* 4 (1912), 64; *The Crisis* 4 (1912), 272; Kelleher, "St. Louis' 1916 Residential Segregation Ordinance," 239.

27. Kelleher, "St. Louis' 1916 Residential Segregation Ordinance," 241–44; see also *The Crisis* 11 and 12, March–June 1916; and Christensen, "Race Relations," passim. See also George Everett Slavens, "The Missouri Negro Press, 1875–1920," *Missouri Historical Review* 64 (1970), 425.

28. *The Crisis* 11 (1916), 260, 307–8; *The Crisis* 12 (1916), 15, 37, 87.

29. Booker T. Washington, "My View of Segregation Laws," in Robert B. Sherman, ed., *The Negro and the City* (Englewood Cliffs: Prentice-Hall, 1970), 21–22. William B. Hartsfield, cited in Ronald H. Bayor, "The Civil Rights Movement as Urban Reform: Atlanta's Black Neighborhoods and a New 'Progressivism,'" *Georgia Historical Quarterly* 77 (1993), 289.

30. Power, "Apartheid Baltimore Style," 305–6; *State of Maryland* v. *Gurry,* 3 Baltimore City CT. 262 (1913); *State of Maryland* v. *Gurry,* 121 Md. 534 (1913); *State of North Carolina* v. *Darnell,* 81 S.E. 338, 166 N.C. 300 (1914); *Carey* v. *City of Atlanta,* 143 Ga. 192 (1915); memo, Mr. Brinsmade to Miss Nerney, June 11, 1914, Papers of the NAACP, Part 5, Group I, Box C-276, "Housing, 1914–1922," Reel 1 at 461. The federal Circuit Court's injunction against the St. Louis law is cited in *The Crisis* 12 (1916), 87.

31. NAACP Sixth Annual Report, 1915, in *The Crisis* 11 (1916), 245, 249. For discussions similar to what follows, also see Vose, *Caucasians Only;* and Mark V. Tushnet, *The NAACP's Legal Strategy Against Segregated Education, 1925–1950* (Chapel Hill: University of North Carolina Press, 1987).

32. George C. Wright, *Life Behind a Veil: Blacks in Louisville, Kentucky, 1865–1930* (Baton Rouge: Louisiana State University Press, 1985), 103–7, 111–18; table 2, 46. On the Colored Branch of the Louisville Free Public Library, a second eastern branch established in 1909, and the Louisville commercial enclave, see *Official Souvenir Program* of the National Negro Business League Convention, Louisville, Kentucky, August 18–20, 1909, 36, 48, at University of Louisville Archives, William F. Ekstrom Library, Louisville, Kentucky.

33. Wright, *Life Behind a Veil,* 118–19; Binford cited in *Louisville Courier-Journal,* November 15, 1913, 4; see also Rice, "Residential Segregation by Law," 182.

34. The brief for the appeal in *Buchanan* v. *Warley* offers the single incident reported above: "Brief for the Plaintiff in Error on Rehearing," October Term Su CT. no. 231, Clayton B. Blakey and Moorfield Storey, Counsel, 19, NAACP Papers, Part 12, Group I, Box G-76, "Louisville, Kentucky, 1916–1917," Reel 11 at 343 (hereinafter cited as NAACP Papers, Part 12, Group no., etc.).

The report of the Committee on Negro Housing of the President's Conference on Home Building and Home Ownership alludes to a bombing in Louisville but offers no specific date or location: Johnson, *Negro Housing*, 47. A survey of the *Louisville Courier-Journal* and the *Louisville Times*, *The Crisis*, *The Negro Year Book*, and secondary sources has turned up only two reports of violence over housing prior to the 1950s. The lack of reports of such incidents in the papers does not prove that no violence occurred. The title of the ordinance—"An ordinance to prevent conflict and ill-feeling between the white and colored races in the city of Louisville, and preserve the public peace and promote the general welfare by making reasonable provisions requiring as far as practicable, the use of separate blocks for residences, places of abode, and places of assembly by white and colored people respectively"—suggests the city's concern over potential conflict. See also "Brief for the Plaintiff," 18.

35. Cited in Pennington, "Ordinance of May 11, 1914," 8.

36. *Louisville Courier-Journal*, November 15, 1913, 4; see also the unpublished seminar paper by Margaret B. Pennington, "What Was the Ordinance of May 11, 1914 Adopted by the City of Louisville?" 9, College of Arts and Sciences, 542 Student Papers, 1980–1982, at University of Louisville Archives, William F. Ekstrom Library, Louisville, Kentucky.

37. C. H. Parrish, A. E. Meyzeek, and J. R. Colbert, "History of the Louisville Segregation Case and the Decision of the Supreme Court," Legal Committee of the Louisville Branch of the NAACP, 1917, 6–8, in NAACP Papers, Part 12, Group I, Box G-76, "Louisville, Kentucky, 1916–1917," Reel 11 at 343; Blakey and Storey, "Brief for the Plaintiff," 19, 22; Pennington, "Ordinance of May 11, 1914," 7. See also Loren Miller, "Louisville's Housing Anniversary," *The Crisis* (1967), 255–58.

38. Blakey, cited in Parrish, Meyzeek, and Colbert, "History," 11.

39. *Buchanan* v. *Warley*, 245 U.S. 60; Blakey's advice to Warley is cited in Parrish, Meyzeek, and Colbert, "History," 12. The importance of the collusion charge has been suggested in Benno C. Schmidt Jr., "Principle and Prejudice: The Supreme Court and Race in the Progressive Era: Part 1: The Heyday of Jim Crow," *Columbia Law Review* 82 (1982), 511–14.

40. *Buchanan* v. *Warley*; Blakey, cited in Parrish, Meyzeek, and Colbert, "History," 12; Rice, "Residential Segregation by Law," 189. Storey, cited in Schmidt, "Principle and Prejudice," 504.

41. *Buchanan* v. *Warley*; Stuart Chevalier and Pendleton Beckley, *Charles H. Buchanan, Plaintiff in Error*, versus *William Warley, Defendant in Error* (Louisville, n.d.; filed in U.S. Supreme Court, October term, 1915, on April 1, 1916), 47–48, cited in Rice, "Residential Segregation by Law," 191.

42. *Buchanan* v. *Warley*.

43. Ibid.

44. Schmidt, "Principle and Prejudice," 505–23.

45. NAACP Papers, Part 5, Group I, Box G-81, "Kentucky, Louisville, 1916–1917," Reel 4 at 752; Group II, Box B-130, "Restrictive Covenants, California, 1940–1946," Reel 20 at 265; *Louisville Leader*, November 10, 1917, 2; Clipping, *Louisville Leader*, November 17, 1917, 1, NAACP Papers, Part 12, Group I, Box G-76, "Louisville, Kentucky, 1916–1917," Reel 11 at 343; *Baltimore Afro-American Ledger*, November 10, 1917, 4. Storey, cited in Schmidt, "Principle and Prejudice," 511. See also Rice, "Residential Segregation By Law," 186.

46. Eugene P. Conser, editor of NAREB's *Headlines*, cited in John H. Denton, *Apartheid American Style* (Berkeley: Diablo Press, 1967), 45–46.

47. On Birmingham's zoning statutes, see new zoning ordinance, August 9, 1949, Police Surveillance Files, File 6.4, "Green, S. L." Archives, Birmingham Public Library, Birmingham, Alabama. On the prolonged battle over the ordinance, see Chapter 6 herein and George R. Byrum to James W. Morgan, July 15, 1949, James W. Morgan Mayoral Papers, Archives, Birmingham Public Library, Birmingham, Alabama (hereinafter cited as Morgan Papers). See also *City of Richmond* v. *Deans*, 218 U.S. 704 (1930); *Allen* v. *Oklahoma City*, 175 Okl. 421, 52 P 2d. 1054 (1936); *Clinard* v. *City of Winston-Salem*, 217 N.C. 119 (1940). Regarding Atlanta and Birmingham, see *City of Birmingham* v. *Mary Means Monk*, 185 F 2d. 859 (1951); regarding New Orleans, see *Harmon* v. *Tyler*, 273 U.S. 668 (1926).

48. Citations come from Alice J. Reilly to James H. Preston, July 22, 1918; Reilly to Preston, July 2, 1918; Preston to Reilly, June 24, 1918; Real Estate Board of Baltimore to Preston, July 20, 1918;

and Preston to Allen J. Graham, September 19, 1918, in Preston Mayoral Papers, File 106, "Segrega-
tion Ordinance." See also other letters and petitions in Preston Mayoral Papers, File 106; *Baltimore
Afro-American Ledger*, November 10, 1917, 1; Garrett Power, "Pyrrhic Victory: Daniel Goldman's
Defeat of Zoning in the Maryland Court of Appeals," *Maryland Historical Magazine* 82 (1987), 277;
Power, "Apartheid Baltimore Style," 314–15; McDougall, *Black Baltimore*, 40. Regarding the other
cities, see *The Crisis*, 12 (1917), 29; clipping, *St. Louis Argus*, August 9, 1918, NAACP Papers, Part 5,
Group I, Box C-276, "Discrimination, Housing, 1914–1922," Reel 1 at 461; exchange of letters
between J. W. Johnson and Pierce Atwater, assistant secretary of the Minneapolis Civic and Commerce Association, December 1920, NAACP Papers as above.

49. McDougall, *Black Baltimore*, 40–41.

NOTES TO CHAPTER 2 (PAGES 30 TO 47)

1. From an editorial in *Philadelphia Public Journal*, October 10, 1925, reprinted in NAACP
Papers, Part 5, Group I, Box D-86, "Sweet Case, October 9–21, 1925," Reel 2 at 1164.

2. John Higham, *Strangers in the Land: Patterns of American Nativism 1860–1925*, college edition
(New York: Atheneum, 1963), 194–234, 300–30, and passim. On the Great Migration, see Chicago
Commission on Race Relations, *The Negro in Chicago: A Study of Race Relations and a Race Riot* (New
York: Arno Press and *New York Times*, 1968, reprint), 80–92; William Cohen, "The Great Migration
as a Lever for Social Change," in Alfredteen Harrison, ed., *Black Exodus: The Great Migration from the
American South* (Jackson: University Press of Mississippi), 72–82; Connolly, *A Ghetto Grows in Brooklyn*,
52–75; Peter Gottlieb, *Making Their Own Way: Southern Blacks' Migration to Pittsburgh, 1916–30*
(Urbana: University of Illinois Press, 1987); Gottlieb, "Rethinking the Great Migration: A Perspec-
tive from Pittsburgh," in Joe William Trotter Jr., ed., *The Great Migration in Historical Perspective:
New Dimensions of Race, Class, and Gender* (Bloomington: Indiana University Press, 1991), 68–82;
Grossman, *Land of Hope*, passim.; Florette Henri, *Black Migration: Movement North, 1900–1920*
(Garden City: Anchor-Doubleday, 1975); Kusmer, *A Ghetto Takes Shape*, 38–40; Osofsky, *Harlem*,
127–49; Smith, "The Redistribution of the Negro Population"; Spear, *Black Chicago*, 129–222;
Stewart E. Tolnay and E. M. Beck, "Rethinking the Role of Racial Violence in the Great Migration,"
in Harrison, ed., *Black Exodus*, 20–35; Joe William Trotter Jr., "Introduction: Black Migration in
Historical Perspective," in Trotter, ed., *Great Migration*, 1–21; Weaver, *The Negro Ghetto*, 25–37.

3. Chicago Commission on Race Relations, *The Negro in Chicago*, 80–86.

4. "The Reason," in *The Crisis* 19 (1920), 264; Grossman, *Land of Hope*, 35.

5. Population figures are from decennial census records gathered in Lynch, *Black Urban Condition*, 426–28.

6. Osofsky, *Harlem*, 92, 105–9, 127–28.

7. Roi Ottley and William J. Weatherby, eds., *The Negro in New York: An Informal Social History*
(New York: New York Public Library and Oceana, 1967), 229–64; Ottley, *"New World A-Coming,"*
1, 59–99; Osofsky, *Harlem*, 117–23, 179–87; Cheryl Lynn Greenberg, *"Or Does It Explode?" Black
Harlem in the Great Depression* (New York: Oxford University Press, 1991), 13–41. See also sections
on Harlem in Edmund David Cronon, *Black Moses: The Story of Marcus Garvey and the Universal
Negro Improvement Association* (Madison: University of Wisconsin Press, 1968, 1955); Tony Martin,
Marcus Garvey, Hero: A First Biography (Dover: Majority Press, 1983); and Judith Stein, *The World of
Marcus Garvey: Race and Class in Modern Society* (Baton Rouge: Louisiana State University Press,
1986), 38–60, 128–52. On the arts in Harlem, see James Haskins, *The Cotton Club* (New York:
Random House, 1977); Nathan Irvin Huggins, *Harlem Renaissance* (New York: Oxford University
Press, 1971); David L. Lewis, *When Harlem Was in Vogue* (New York: Knopf, 1981).

8. The black population of Queens grew even more dramatically, from 5,120 (1 percent of the
total in 1920) to nearly 19,000 (1.8 percent) in 1930: Rosenwaike, *Population History of New York
City*, 133–34. Greenberg, *"Or Does it Explode?"* 14; Osofsky, *Harlem*, 135.

9. Mrs. Robert Waddell to James Weldon Johnson, May 1921, NAACP Papers, Part 5, Group I,
Box C-276, "Housing, 1914–1922," Reel 1 at 461; Walter White to Lt. James F. Gegan, NYC Police
Dept., December 1924, NAACP Papers, as above, "Housing, 1923–1929," Reel 1 at 525. See

Connolly, *A Ghetto Grows in Brooklyn*, 58–60; Ernest Quimby, "Bedford-Stuyvesant," in Rita Seiden Miller, *Brooklyn USA: The Fourth Largest City in America* (New York: Brooklyn College Press, 1979), 230–31.

10. Palatine Insurance Co., Ltd., to Glens Falls Fire Insurance Co., August 20, 1924, NAACP Papers, Part 5, Group I, Box D-48, "Browne, Samuel A., 1924," Reel 2 at 292.

11. General report, NAACP Papers, Part 5, Group I, Box D-48, "Browne, Samuel A., 1925–1926," Reel 2 at 355.

12. NAACP Annual Report, 1925, NAACP Papers, Part 5, Group I, Box C-404, "Residential, General, January 1925–October 1937," Reel 1 at 948.

13. Chicago Commission on Race Relations, *The Negro in Chicago*, 4–52, 106–230; Drake and Cayton, *Black Metropolis*, 58–76; Hirsch, *Making the Second Ghetto*, 40–44, 68–69; Thomas Lee Philpott, *The Slum and the Ghetto: Neighborhood Deterioration and Middle-Class Reform, Chicago, 1880–1930* (New York: Oxford University Press, 1978), 113–227; Spear, *Black Chicago*, 147–66, 208–22. Regarding the informal agreement between the city, realtors, and property owners, see Real Estate Board of Baltimore to Mayor James H. Preston, July 20, 1918; Preston to Anthony K. Warner of Chicago, July 17, 1918; and Preston to Real Estate Board of Baltimore, July 17, 1918; in Preston Mayoral Papers, File no. 106, "Segregation Ordinance." See also Power, "Apartheid Baltimore Style," 314–15.

14. Chicago Commission on Human Rights, *The Negro in Chicago*, 109–15, 124.

15. Herman H. Long and Charles S. Johnson, *People vs. Property: Race Restrictive Covenants in Housing* (Nashville: Fisk University Press, 1947), 117–23.

16. "Clean Blocks—Good Citizens," *The Crisis* 51 (1944), 312; Long and Johnson, *People vs. Property*, 12–14, 51; Otis Dudley Duncan and Beverly Duncan, *The Negro Population of Chicago: A Study of Residential Succession* (Chicago: University of Chicago Press, 1957), 95–96; Chicago Commission on Race Relations, *The Negro in Chicago*, 612–21, 643–47; Philpott, *The Slum and the Ghetto*, 209–69; Spear, *Black Chicago*, 223–29.

17. Work, ed., *Negro Year Book, 1918–1919*, 50–51; *Chicago Defender*, August 3, 1918, 1, 3; *New York Times*, July 29, 1918, 7 (hereinafter cited as *NYT*). On Cleveland, see Kusmer, *A Ghetto Takes Shape*, 161–67, 174–77, 206–7, 215–22, 251–74.

18. Olivier Zunz, *The Changing Face of Inequality: Urbanization, Industrial Development, and Immigrants in Detroit, 1880–1920* (Chicago: University of Chicago Press, 1982), 139–41, 327, 373–75; Katzman, *Before the Ghetto*, 69–75; Lynch, *Black Urban Condition*, 427–28.

19. Katzman, *Before the Ghetto*, 126–33, 207; David Allan Levine, *Internal Combustion: The Races in Detroit, 1915–1926* (Westport: Greenwood, 1976), 6, 71–93, 118–24; August Meier and Elliott Rudwick, *Black Detroit and the Rise of the UAW* (New York: Oxford University Press, 1979), 8–11, 16–22. A brief history of the Detroit branch of the NAACP is found in a letter from Lucille Black of the Michigan State Conference to Eugene Hall, branch publicist, March 7, 1939, NAACP Papers, Part 12, Series C: The Midwest, Group I, Box G-97, "Detroit Branch, January–March 1939," Reel 14 at 208.

20. Levine, *Internal Combustion*, 137–41.

21. Robert W. Bagnall to Maud S. Henderson, Secretary, Detroit Branch, March 12, 1923, NAACP Papers, Part 5, Group I, Box G-95, "Detroit Branch, 1923," Reel 11 at 852; NAACP press release, March 6, 1925, NAACP Papers, as above, "Detroit Branch, January–June 1925," Reel 12 at 001.

22. *A. B. Parmalee et al.* v. *Charles Morris*, Cal. No. 30,062, Michigan Supreme Court (1922); and *Porter* v. *Barrett*, 233 Mich. 373, 206 N.W. 532 (1925). White's response occurs in White to Johnson, September 16, 1925, NAACP Papers, Part 5, Group I, Box D-85, "Sweet Case, March–September 16, 1925," Reel 2 at 923; 1925 Annual Report, NAACP Papers, Part 5, Group I Box C-404, "Residential, General, January 1925–October 1937," Reel 1 at 948; Levine, *Internal Combustion*, 153–54; Sidney Fine, *Frank Murphy: The Detroit Years* (Ann Arbor: University of Michigan Press, 1975), vol. 1, 146–47.

23. White to Johnson, September 16, 1925, NAACP Papers, Part 5, Group I, Box D-85, "Cases Supported, Sweet Case, March–Sept. 16, 1925," Reel 2 at 0923; "Opening to Jury, November 16, 1925," NAACP Papers, Part 5, Group I, Box D-87, "Sweet Case, 1925," Reel 3 at 920; NAACP

Field Secretary William Pickens to Rev. R. L. Bradby, July 31, 1925, NAACP Papers, Part 5, Group I, Box D-87, "Sweet Case, 1925," Reel 3 at 920; Levine, *Internal Combustion*, 156–57.

24. The most thorough narrative on the Sweet case occurs in Kenneth G. Weinberg, *A Man's Home, a Man's Castle* (New York: McCall, 1971). See also Arthur Garfield Hays, *Let Freedom Ring* (New York: Boni and Liveright, 1928), 195–233; Clarence Darrow, *The Story of My Life* (New York: Scribner's, 1932), 301–11; Fine, *Frank Murphy*; Levine, *Internal Combustion*.

25. Weinberg, *A Man's Home*, 6–7; Walter White, "The Sweet Trial," in *The Crisis* 31 (1926), 126; and Arthur G. Hays, Address to NAACP Annual Meeting, January 3, 1926, NAACP Papers, Part 5, Group I, Box D-86, "Sweet Case, January–February, 1926," Reel 3 at 400.

26. Undated memo, NAACP Papers, Part 5, Group I, Box D-86, "Sweet Case, Dec. 9–16," Reel 3 at 254; Levine, *Internal Combustion*, 158, 174–75; "Argument of Clarence Darrow in the Case of Henry Sweet," 27–28, NAACP Papers as above, Box D-87, "Sweet Case, May 5–28, 1926," Reel 3 at 560. On the threats against the previous owner, see Irving Stone, *Clarence Darrow for the Defense* (Garden City: Doubleday, 1941), 473.

27. "Annual Report, 1925," NAACP Papers, Part 5, Group I, Box C-404, "Residential, General. January 1925–October 1937," Reel 1 at 948; White to Johnson, Sept. 16, 1925, NAACP Papers as above, Box D-85, "Sweet Case, March–Sept. 16, 1925," Reel 2 at 923; "*People* v. *Sweet*, Recorder's Court of Detroit, Michigan; Partial Transcript of Hearing, November 5, 1925," 5, 10–13, NAACP Papers as above, Box D-87, "Sweet Case, 1925," Reel 3 at 919; undated memo, NAACP Papers as above, Box D-86, "Sweet Case, Dec. 9–16, 1925," Reel 3 at 254; *Detroit Free Press*, September 10, 1925, 1. See also Levine, *Internal Combustion*, 158–65.

28. "Argument of Clarence Darrow," 27–28, NAACP Papers, Part 5, Group I, Box D-86, "Sweet Case, Dec. 9–16," Reel 3 at 254; "*People* v. *Sweet*," 15–17, 32–36; White, "The Sweet Trial," 128.

29. Patrolman Frank Lee Gill's statement was reported in *Detroit News*, September 18, 1925. It was refuted by later testimony when other witnesses claimed that only two shots emanated from the house. Both are cited in NAACP Papers, Part 5, Group I, Box D-85, "Sweet Case, March–Sept. 16, 1925," Reel 2 at 0923.

30. Bradby to Johnson, July 27, 1925, NAACP Papers, Part 5, Group I, Box G-95, "Detroit Branch, June–December 1925," Reel 12 at 058; Mayor Smith's statement printed in *Detroit Free Press*, September 12, 1925, 1; Assistant District Attorney Moll's comments cited in *Detroit Free Press*, September 11, 1925, 1; police statements taken from testimony in *People* v. *Sweet* Transcript, NAACP Papers, Part 5, Group I, Box D-87, "Sweet Case, 1925," Reel 3 at 940. See also Report from White to Johnson, Sept. 16, 1925, NAACP Papers as above, Box D-85, "Sweet Case, March–Sept. 16, 1925," Reel 2 at 923.

31. The Interracial Committee issued its report at the end of 1926. Smith cited in *Detroit Free Press*, September 12, 1925, 1; see also White to Johnson, September 16, 1925, NAACP Papers, Part 5, Group I, Box D-85, "Sweet Case, March–September 16, 1925," Reel 2 at 923; Levine, *Internal Combustion*, 166; Fine, *Frank Murphy*, vol. 1, 169–70.

32. James Weldon Johnson to Clarence Darrow, October 7, 1925, NAACP Papers, Part 5, Group I, Box D-86, "Sweet Case, October 1–8, 1925," Reel 2 at 1096.

33. James Weldon Johnson, press release, October 29, 1925; White to Seligmann, October 22, 1925, NAACP Papers, Part 5, Group I, Box D-86, "Sweet Case, October 22–31, 1925," Reel 3 at 001; 1925 Annual Report, NAACP Papers, Part 5, Group I, Box C-404, "Residential, General, January 1925–October 1937," Reel 1 at 948; White to Ossian Sweet, October 6, 1925, NAACP Papers as above, Box D-86, "Sweet Case, October 1–8, 1925," Reel 2 at 1096. See also Darrow, *The Story of My Life*, 301–2.

34. Survey of clippings, and *Philadelphia Public Journal*, October 10, 1925, NAACP Papers, Part 5, Group I, Box D-86, "Sweet Case, October 9–21, 1925," Reel 2 at 1164; *Philadelphia Public Journal* reprint of *Amsterdam News* editorial, December 27, 1925; *Houston Informer*, November 28, 1925, NAACP Papers as above, Box D-88, "Sweet Case, Clippings, November 21–29, 1925," Reel 4 at 076, and "Sweet Case, Clippings, December 1925," Reel 4 at 154.

35. James Weldon Johnson, press release, October 29, 1925, NAACP Papers, Part 5, Group I, Box D-86, "Sweet Case, October 22–31, 1925," Reel 3 at 001; Walter White, report of trip March

21–24, 1926, NAACP Papers as above, "Sweet Case, March 5–30, 1926," Reel 3 at 456. Fine, *Frank Murphy*, vol. 1, 154–55.

36. On Murphy's political ambitions, see Moses L. Walker to Walter White, NAACP Papers, Part 5, Group I, Box D-86, "Sweet Case, October 22–31, 1925," Reel 3 at 001. See also speech by Murphy before Survey Associates, Inc., in 1937, cited in *The Survey* 85 (1949), 410; Fine, *Frank Murphy*, vol. 1, 146, 154–55, 166–68. Murphy's comment about liberalism is cited in Weinberg, *A Man's Home*, 41. On White's activities, see White to Johnson, October 31, 1925, and November 7, 1925, NAACP Papers, Part 5, Group I, Box D-86, "Sweet Case, November 2–16, 1925," Reel 3 at 050; White to Johnson, November 20, 1925, NAACP Papers as above, "Sweet Case, November 17–30, 1925," Reel 3 at 127.

37. On Toms's alleged Klan membership, see Moses L. Walker to Walter White, October 8, 1925, NAACP Papers, Part 5, Group I, Box D-86, "Sweet Case, 1925," Reel 3 at 940. See also *People v. Sweet*, November 5, 1925, in NAACP Papers, as above.

38. White to Johnson, November 13, 1925, and NAACP press release, November 13, 1925, NAACP Papers, Part 5, Group I, Box D-86, "Sweet Case, November 2–16, 1925," Reel 3 at 050; *People v. Sweet*, November 5, 1925, and "Argument of Clarence Darrow in the case of Henry Sweet, May 11, 1926," NAACP Papers as above, Box D-87, "Sweet Case, 1925," Reel 3 at 940, and "Sweet Case, May 5–28, 1926," Reel 3 at 552; David E. Lilienthal, "Has the Negro the Right of Self-Defense?" *The Nation* 121, December 23, 1925, 724–25. Morrow, cited in White, "The Sweet Trial," 127.

39. *People v. Sweet*; White to Johnson, November 20, 1925, NAACP Papers, Part 5, Group I, Box D-86, "Sweet Case, November 17–30, 1925," Reel 3 at 127; Stone, *Clarence Darrow*, 482; Arthur Garfield Hays, *Trial by Prejudice* (New York: Covici-Friede, 1933), 352–54; and Hays, Address before the NAACP, January 3, 1926, NAACP Papers as above, "Sweet Case, January–February, 1926," Reel 3 at 400.

40. NAACP press release and *Detroit Times* reprint, November 27, 1925, NAACP Papers, Part 5, Group I, Box D-86, "Sweet Case, November 17–30, 1925," Reel 3 at 127; Stone, *Clarence Darrow*, 482; and White, "The Sweet Trial," 125.

41. White, "The Sweet Trial," 125; press release, Walter White, November 28, 1925, NAACP Papers, Part 5, Group I, Box D-86, "Sweet Case, November 17–30," Reel 3 at 127; Fine, *Frank Murphy*, vol. 1, 161–62, 164.

42. White, "The Sweet Trial," 126; NAACP press release, January 15, 1926, and Hays, "Address before NAACP," January 3, 1926, NAACP Papers, Part 5, Group I, Box D-86, "Sweet Case, January–February, 1926," Reel 3 at 398 and 400; *Washington Daily American*, December 19, 1925; *Boston Chronicle*, November 28, 1925; *California Eagle*, December 18, 1925; *Cleveland Call*, November 28, 1925, NAACP Papers, Part 5, Group I, Box D-88, "Sweet Case, Clippings, December 1925," Reel 4 at 154, and "Sweet Case, Clippings, 1926–1927," Reel 4 at 209.

43. Walter White, press release, November 28, 1925, NAACP Papers, Part 5, Group I, Box D-86, "Sweet Case, November 17–30," Reel 3 at 127; NAACP memo, March 1926, NAACP Papers as above, "Sweet Case, March, 5–30, 1926," Reel 3 at 456; NAACP press release, April 23, 1926, NAACP Papers as above, "Sweet Case, April 1–30," Reel 3 at 490; Fine, *Frank Murphy*, vol. 1, 166; Darrow, *Story of My Life*, 311.

44. James Weldon Johnson, "Detroit," in *The Crisis* 32 (1926), 117–19; Clarence Darrow, "Closing Argument in the Case of Henry Sweet," 87–88, NAACP Papers, Part 5, Group I, Box D-86, "Sweet Case, May 5–28, 1926," Reel 3 at 560.

45. Johnson, "Detroit," 119; Robert M. Toms, "Prosecutor's Address," reprinted in *Detroit Free Press*, May 14, 1926, 1.

46. Johnson, "Detroit," 120.

47. The article in *Current History Magazine*, is cited in White to Judge Ira Jayne, September 28, 1926; Moses Walker, NAACP Papers, Part 5, Group I, Box D-87, "Sweet Case, September–October, 1926," Reel 3 at 725. For meeting of Toms and Moll with Darrow, see Darrow, *Story of My Life*, 311.

48. Mayor's Committee on Race Relations, "Report," 4, 7–8; Bruno Lasker, "The Negro in Detroit," in *The Survey* 58, April 15, 1927, 72–73, 123; Levine, *Internal Combustion*, 205–7; Fine, *Frank Murphy*, vol. 1, 169–70.

49. Weinberg, *A Man's Home*, 124; Levine, *Internal Combustion*, 204; Work, ed., *Negro Year Book, 1931–1932* (Tuskegee: Negro Year Book Publishing, 1931), 70.

50. Darrow, *Story of My Life*, 313. Letter from Leonard C. Morse to Frank Murphy, April 21, 1926, and letter from Walter White to Frank Murphy, May 21, 1926, Frank Murphy Papers, Series I, Box 1, "Correspondence, April–May, 1926," Bentley Historical Library, University of Michigan, Ann Arbor. See also Fine, *Frank Murphy*, vol. 1, 166–67.

51. Weinberg, *A Man's Home*, 124; Fine, *Frank Murphy*, vol. 1, 168–69; Levine, *Internal Combustion*, 202–3; NAACP Papers, Part 5, Group I, Box G-94, "Michigan State Conference, 1937–1939," Reel 11 at 404.

52. *Corrigan* v. *Buckley*; Marshall cited in Vose, *Caucasians Only*, 52–54; see also Long and Johnson, *People vs. Property*, 88, 92–93.

53. Long and Johnson, *People vs. Property*, 12–14, 51; see also Thomas H. Wright, *Human Relations in Chicago: Report of Mayor's Commission on Human Relations [MCHR] for 1946* (Chicago: MCHR, 1946), 82; and Robert C. Weaver, "Chicago: A City of Covenants," *The Crisis* 53 (1946), 75–78, 93. Vose enumerates the covenant cases across the nation in *Caucasians Only*, 19, 257 at notes 116–21, 123. See also Jack Greenberg, *Race Relations and American Law* (New York: Columbia University Press, 1959), 276–79; and Charlotta A. Bass, *Forty Years: Memoirs from the Pages of a Newspaper* (Los Angeles: Bass, 1960), 97–102.

NOTES TO CHAPTER 3 (PAGES 48 TO 63)

1. President Herbert Hoover, Address to the President's Conference on Home Building and Home Ownership, December 2, 1931, *Housing Objectives and Programs*, John M. Gries and James Ford, eds., President's Conference on Home Building and Home Ownership, vol. 11 (Washington, D.C.: Federal Capital Press, 1932), 2.

2. Federal Emergency Relief Administration, "The Negro and Relief," by Alfred Edgar Smith, *FERA Monthly Report, March 1936* (Washington, D.C.: GPO, 1936), 13–14; Ire De A. Reid, "Black Wages for Black Men," in Philip S. Foner and Ronald L. Lewis, eds., *The Black Worker: A Documentary History from Colonial Times to the Present*, vol. 6: *The Era of Post-War Prosperity and the Great Depression, 1920–1936*, 99–103; Greenberg, *"Or Does It Explode?"* 42–44; Joseph H. Willits, "Some Impacts of the Depression upon the Negro in Philadelphia," in Foner and Lewis, *Black Worker: Era of Post-War Prosperity and the Great Depression*, 90–91.

3. The value of real property owned by blacks as assessed in tax records is reported in Work, ed., *Negro Year Book, 1916–1917*, 2; *Negro Year Book, 1925–1926*, 2; *Negro Year Book, 1931–1932*, 118; *Negro Year Book, 1937–1938*, 1, 90–92, 257–59; Myrdal *An American Dilemma*, 196–97, 295–303. For accounts of the Depression's impact on blacks, also see Leslie H. Fishel Jr., "The Negro in the New Deal," in Bernard Sternsher, ed., *The Negro in Depression and War: Prelude to Revolution, 1930–1945* (Chicago: Quadrangle, 1969), 7–28; E. Franklin Frazier, "Some Effects of the Depression on the Negro in Northern Cities," in Richard J. Meister, ed., *The Black Ghetto: Promised Land or Colony?* (Lexington: D.C. Heath, 1972), 119–27; Harvard Sitkoff, *A New Deal For Blacks: The Emergence of Civil Rights as a National Issue*, vol. 1: *The Depression Decade* (New York: Oxford University Press, 1978); Raymond Wolters, "The New Deal and the Negro," in John Braeman, Robert H. Bremner, and David Brody, eds., *The New Deal: The National Level* (Columbus: Ohio State University Press, 1975), 170–217.

4. Smith, "The Negro and Relief," 10–11, 14. The Urban League study is cited in *Atlanta Daily World*, January 12, 1937, 1 (*Atlanta Daily World* hereinafter cited as *ADW*). See also U.S. Federal Emergency Relief Administration, "Work Relief Wage Policies, 1930–1936," by Arthur E. Burns, *FERA Monthly Report, June 1936*, 29–31; Robert F. Hunter, "Virginia and the New Deal," in John Braeman, Robert H. Bremner, and David Brody, eds., *The New Deal: The State and Local Levels* (Columbus: Ohio State University Press, 1975), 109–14; David J. Maurer, "Relief Problems and Politics in Ohio," in Braeman, Bremner, and Brody, *The New Deal: The State and Local Levels*, 83–93;

John Robert Moore, "The New Deal in Louisiana," in Braeman, Bremner, and Brody, *The New Deal: The State and Local Levels*, 145–50; Sitkoff, *A New Deal for Blacks*, 34–38; Douglas L. Smith, *The New Deal in the Urban South* (Baton Rouge: Louisiana State University Press, 1988), 62–85.

5. Lynch, *Black Urban Condition*, 428–29; Robert C. Weaver, "The Negro and Low-Rent Housing," an address delivered October 7, 1938, before the Eastern Regional Conference of the National Negro Congress, printed as USHA Document no. 40746 H, 1941, 2.

6. State and local governments had dabbled in slum clearance, urban renewal, and housing issues during the Progressive era, mostly from the perspective of sanitation and hygiene. In 1892, the federal government undertook the study of slums in cities of 200,000 or more population. It then ignored the question for twenty-five years, except for a study of slums in the District of Columbia in 1908. The Wilson administration created the United States Housing Corporation (USHC) in 1918 to provide "housing, local transportation and other general utilities" for war workers. After the war, USHC's activities diminished, and in the early 1920s, Congress authorized the sale of publicly owned facilities. See U.S. Senate Committee on Banking and Currency, *Federal Housing Programs*, 2; Housing and Home Finance Agency, *A Summary of the Evolution of Housing Activities in the Federal Government* (Washington, D.C.: GPO, 1950), 4–5; A. Gram Robinson, "The Controversy over a Long-Range Federal Housing Program," *Congressional Digest* 27 (1948), 167; Robert Moore Fisher, *Twenty Years of Public Housing: Economic Aspects of the Federal Program* (New York: Harper & Bros., 1959), 73–79; Robert K. Brown, *The Development of the Public Housing Program in the United States* (Atlanta: Bureau of Business and Economic Research, School of Business Administration, Georgia State College of Business Administration, 1960), 1–2; Jewel Bellush and Murray Hausknecht, "Urban Renewal: An Historical Overview," in Jewel Bellush and Murray Hausknecht, eds., *Urban Renewal: People, Politics, and Planning* (Garden City: Anchor-Doubleday, 1967), 3–16.

7. Roscoe Conkling Bruce, *The Idea of Cooperative Housing as Exemplified by the Paul Laurence Dunbar Apartments in New York City*, prepared for the Committee on Negro Housing, in Johnson, *Negro Housing*, 245–48. See also Carol Aronovici and Elizabeth McCalmont, *Catching Up with Housing* (Newark: Beneficial Management Corp., 1936); and photographs in Carol Aronovici, *Housing the Masses* (New York: Wiley and Sons, 1939), 183; Osofsky, *Harlem*, 155–58. On Chicago, see "The Negro Coming into His Own," *Housing* 18 (1929), reprinted in Johnson, ed., *Negro Housing*, 239–41; "Modern Housing for Negroes Brings Gratifying Results," *American City* 43 (1930), cited in Johnson, ed., *Negro Housing*, 241–42.

8. Herbert Hoover, *The Memoirs of Herbert Hoover: The Cabinet and the Presidency, 1920–1933* (New York: Macmillan, 1952), 92–95, 256–58.

9. Hoover, cited in *Housing Objectives and Programs*, Gries and Ford, eds., xv.

10. *Housing Objectives and Programs*, Gries and Ford, eds., xiii, 102–5, 253–61; Senate Committee on Banking and Currency, *Federal Housing Programs*, 2.

11. Johnson, *Negro Housing*, v–xii, 1–3, 79–91.

12. Ibid., 102–4, 114–18.

13. Franklin D. Roosevelt, "The Governor Approves a New Multiple Dwellings Law, April 18, 1929"; and "An Address on Better Housing Conditions (Excerpts), New York City, February 28, 1930," in Franklin D. Roosevelt, *The Public Papers and Addresses of Franklin D. Roosevelt*, vol. 1, *The Genesis of the New Deal, 1928–1932* (New York: Random House, 1938), 309–13.

14. Franklin D. Roosevelt, Inaugural Address, March 4, 1933, in Franklin D. Roosevelt, *The Public Papers and Addresses of Franklin D. Roosevelt*, vol. 2, *The Year of Crisis* (New York: Random House, 1938), 13; Roosevelt, "The Home Owners Loan Act Is Signed—the President Urges Delay in Foreclosures," June 13, 1933, in Roosevelt, *Public Papers: The Year of Crisis*, 233–34; John H. Fahey, "Functions and Objectives of the Federal Home Loan Bank Board," in Coleman Woodbury, ed., *Housing Officials' Year Book, 1935* (Chicago: National Association of Housing Officials, 1935), 9–15; Charles Abrams, *The Future of Housing* (New York: Harper & Bros., 1946), 239–48; Ronald Tobey, Charles Wetherall, and Jay Brigham, "Moving Out and Settling In: Residential Mobility, Home Owning, and the Public Enframing of Citizenship, 1921–1950," *American Historical Review* 95 (1990), 1417.

15. Roosevelt, notes to "The Functions, Powers and Regulations of the Public Works Administration, Executive Order No. 6252," in Roosevelt, *Public Papers: The Year of Crisis*, 332–36; Abrams, *The Future of Housing*, 210–20, 249–58; Fisher, *Twenty Years of Public Housing*, 79–91; Mabel L.

Walker, *Urban Blight and Slums: Economic and Legal Factors in Their Origin, Reclamation, and Prevention* (Cambridge: Harvard University Press, 1938); J. Joseph Huthmacher, *Senator Robert F. Wagner and the Rise of Urban Liberalism* (New York: Atheneum, 1968), 89.

16. Horatio B. Hackett, "Problems and Policies of the Housing Division of P.W.A.," in Woodbury, ed., *Housing Officials' Year Book, 1935*, 1–5; Federal Emergency Administration of Public Works, *Urban Housing: The Story of the PWA Housing Division, 1933–1936, PWA Bulletin no. 2* (Washington, D.C.: GPO, 1936), 27–37 (hereinafter cited as PWA); U.S. Public Works Administration, *America Builds: The Record of PWA* (Washington, D.C.: GPO, 1939), 208–17; Abrams, *The Future of Housing*, 224–38; Fisher, *Twenty Years of Public Housing*, 82–85.

17. Harold Ickes, cited in "Housing," in *Opportunity* 12 (1934), 327; Frank S. Horne and B. T. McGraw, "Minority Group Considerations in Administration of Governmental Housing Programs," (1947), 1, in U.S. Department of Housing and Urban Development, Program Files, Race Relations Program, 1946–1958, "Speeches, 1944–1953," Record Group 207, Archives II, College Park, Maryland (hereinafter cited as RG 207, Program Files).

18. PWA, *Urban Housing*, 82–83; Florence Fleming Corey, "Atlanta's Techwood and University Homes Projects: The Nation's Laboratory for Public Housing," *Atlanta History* 31 Chinter 1987–1988), 18–22. Dana F. White, "The Black Sides of Atlanta: A Geography of Expansion and Containment, 1970–1870," *Atlanta Historical Journal* 26 (1982), 218.

19. Leslie S. Perry, NAACP, Statement before the House Banking and Currency Committee, April 26, 1949, U.S. House of Representatives, Committee on Banking and Currency, *Housing Act of 1949: Hearings Before the Committee on Banking and Currency, House of Representatives, 81st Cong., 1st Sess. on H.R. 4009* (Washington, D.C.: GPO, 1949), 218–20.

20. FHA *Underwriter's Manual* cited in NAACP memo, October 20, 1944, NAACP Papers, Part 5, Group II, Box A-268, "FHA, General, 1947–1948," Reel 5 at 555. See also NAACP Conference Resolutions, Richmond Conference, July 1, 1939, in *The Crisis* 46 (1939), 280.

21. Abrams, *The Future of Housing*, 224–38; Brown, *Development of the Public Housing Program*, 10–11; Senate Banking and Currency Committee, *Federal Housing Programs*, 4; Fisher, *Twenty Years of Public Housing*, 8–12, 79–125; Loula D. Lasker, "Three Years of Public Housing," *Survey Graphic* 26 (1937), 81, 116; Robert C. Weaver, "The Negro in a Program of Public Housing," *Opportunity* 16 (1938), 199–200.

22. "Summary of the Wagner-Steagall Housing Bill," February 25, 1937, NAACP Papers, Part 5, Group I, Box C-257, "Wagner-Steagall Bill, February 25–July 20, 1937," Reel 1 at 403; Fisher, *Twenty Years of Public Housing*, 8–12, 124–28; Senate Banking and Currency Committee, *Federal Housing Programs*, 5; Abrams, *The Future of Housing*, 259–280; Richard O. Davies, *Housing Reform During the Truman Administration* (Columbia: University of Missouri Press, 1966), 12. Morgenthau, cited in Richard Polenberg, "The Decline of the New Deal," in Braeman, Bremner, and Brody, eds., *The New Deal: The National Level*, 251–53. See also *S. 4424, . . . A [Housing] Bill . . . Senator Robert F. Wagner*, February 24, 1936, NAACP Papers, Part 5, Group I, Box C-257, "Wagner-Ellenbogen Bill, April 3–June 9, 1936," Reel 1 at 285; and Huthmacher, *Senator Robert F. Wagner and the Rise of Urban Liberalism*, 205–16.

23. Horne and McGraw, "Minority Group Considerations," 2; "The Negro in the Nation," *Survey Graphic* 36 (1947), 95; *The Crisis* 48 (1941), 298. On Weaver's career, see "National Defense Labor Problems: The Weaver Appointment," *The Crisis* 47 (1940), 319; "Cities: Hope for the Heart," *Time Magazine*, March 4, 1966, 29–33; Fishel, "The Negro in the New Deal," 9; Ralph J. Bunche, *The Political Status of the Negro in the Age of FDR*, ed. Dewey W. Grantham (Chicago: University of Chicago Press, 1973), 618–20; and "Robert C. Weaver—New Cabinet Member," *The Crisis* (1966), 120–21, 129. See also Weaver, *The Negro Ghetto;* and Lemann, *Promised Land*, 71–72. On the Black Cabinet, see B. Joyce Ross, "Mary McLeod Bethune and the National Youth Administration: A Case Study of Power Relationships in the Black Cabinet of Franklin Delano Roosevelt," in John Hope Franklin and August Meier, eds., *Black Leaders of the Twentieth Century* (Urbana: University of Chicago Press, 1982), 191–220.

24. See Frances Murray, ed., *The Negro Handbook, 1949* (New York: Macmillan, 1949), 99. See also Sitkoff, *A New Deal for Blacks*, 268–97. NAACP Statement, April 30, 1937, NAACP Papers, Part 5, Group I, Box C-307, "Housing, January–May 1937," Reel 1 at 584; Walter White, "Statement

Before the Senate Committee on Education and Labor," April 24, 1936, NAACP Papers, Part 5, Group I, Box C-257, "Wagner-Ellenbogen Bill, April 3–June 9, 1936," Reel 1 at 395.

25. See, for example, a policy statement of the New York City Land Usage Committee in *Land Usage*, April–May 1936, cited in Walker, *Urban Blight and Slums*, 213: the committee argued that it was "not necessarily essential to rehouse all low-rent tenants upon the identical property where they now live[d]." See also Robert C. Weaver, "Negroes Need Housing," *The Crisis* 47 (1940), 139; Raphael Knight, "Stage Spotlights Harlem Housing," *The Crisis* 45 (1938), 143–44; and Hartman, "The Housing of Relocated Families," in Wilson, ed., *Urban Renewal*, 293–335.

26. The quotation occurs in an unidentified, undated, handwritten letter, NAACP Papers, Part 5, Group I, Box C-257, "Wagner-Steagall Bill, February 25–July 20, 1937," Reel 1 at 403. See also Horne and McGraw, "Minority Group Considerations," 2–3.

27. "Resolutions at Detroit Conference," *The Crisis* 44 (1937), 242, 247; "Conference Resolutions, Richmond Conference," July 1, *The Crisis* 46 (1939), 280"; "Conference Resolutions, Philadelphia," June 18–23, *The Crisis* 47 (1940), 295, 298.

28. Tushnet, *Making Civil Rights' Law*, 27; many of the Los Angeles cases are related in Bass, *Forty Years*, 97–102. Other cases include *Du Ross* v. *Trainer*, 122 Cal. A 732 (1932); *Foster* v. *Stewart*, 134 Cal. A 482 (1933). See also NAACP Papers, Part 5, Group I, Box C-404, "Segregation, Residential, Los Angeles, January 16–March 28, 1930," Reel 2 at 001. On West Virginia, see *White* v. *White*, 108 W.Va. 128, 150 S.E. 531 (1929); NAACP News Release, November 15, 1929; and NAACP News Release, December 20, 1929, NAACP Papers, Part 5, Group I, Box D-60, "Huntington, W.Va., Restrictive Covenant Case, 1929," Reel 2 at 469.

29. "Iron Ring in Housing," *The Crisis* 47 (1940), 205; A. C. MacNeal, "Southsiders to Fight Residential Segregation," NAACP Papers, Part 5, Group I, Box C-404, "Segregation, Residential, Chicago, November 1, 1936–November 23, 1937," Reel 1 at 1121.

30. *Hansberry* v. *Lee*; also see "Complaint in Equity, Circuit Court of Cook County, *Lee* v. *Hansberry*," NAACP Papers, Part 5, Group I, Box C-404, "Residential, Chicago, Illinois, Legal Documents, 1937," Reel 1 at 1207.

31. NAHO, an organization composed of government administrators and housing experts, was established in 1935 to work as a clearinghouse of information and an advisory panel for its local membership. NAHO manual cited in Robert C. Weaver, "Racial Policy in Public Housing," *Phylon* 1 (1940), 151–52. See also National Association of Housing Officials, *Housing Officials' Yearbooks (1935–1941)* (Chicago: NAHO, 1935–1941).

32. The term "federal bulldozer" comes from Martin Anderson, *The Federal Bulldozer: A Critical Analysis of Urban Renewal, 1949–1962* (Cambridge: MIT Press, 1964).

33. *ADW*, February 10, 1937, 1; *ADW*, February 13, 1937, 1; *ADW*, November 10, 1; *ADW*, November 24, 1; Corley, "Atlanta's Techwood and University Homes Projects," 17–36; Samuel L. Adams, "Blueprint for Segregation: A Survey of Atlanta Housing," *New South* 22 (1967), 76; Robert A. Thompson, Hylan Lewis, and Davis McEntire, "Atlanta and Birmingham: A Comparative Study in Negro Housing," in Nathan Glazer and Davis McEntire, eds., *Studies in Housing and Minority Groups* (Berkeley: University of California Press, 1960), 27.

34. *Liberty Annex Corp.* v. *City of Dallas*, 289 S.W. 1067 (1927), 295 S.W. 591 (1933); *Dallas Express*, January 29, 1927, NAACP Papers, Part 5, Group I, Box C-404, "Residential, Dallas, Texas, December 10, 1926–March 31, 1927," Reel 1 at 1341.

35. Memo by Legal Research Assistant, Frank Reeves, October 24, 1940, NAACP Papers, Part 5, Group II, Box A-310, "Dallas, Texas, 1940," Reel 6 at 815; memo by Reeves, November 22, 1940, NAACP Papers, as above, Reel 6 at 907.

36. Memo by Reeves, "Dallas Housing Situation," November 22, 1940, NAACP Papers, Part 5, Group II, Box A-310, "Dallas, Texas, 1940," Reel 6 at 907; G. F. Porter, Executive Secretary, Dallas NAACP to Franklin Roosevelt, July 9, 1941, NAACP Papers as above, "Dallas, Texas, 1941," Reel 6 at 923. Dr. Bush Jones, cited in *Dallas Express*, August 1940, NAACP Papers, Part 5, Group II, Box A-310, "Dallas, Texas, 1940," Reel 6 at 815.

37. *Dallas Express*, August 1940, NAACP Papers, Part 5, Group II, Box A-310, "Dallas, Texas, 1940," Reel 6 at 815; see also NAACP Papers as above, "Dallas, Texas, 1941," Reel 6 at 1018.

38. Porter to Thurgood Marshall, August 12, 1940; *Dallas Express,* week of August 19, 1940; Dallas *Journal,* August 19, 1940, NAACP Papers, Part 5, Group II, Box A-310, "Dallas, Texas, 1940," Reel 6 at 815.

39. Reeves to Marshall, October 18, 1940, NAACP Papers, Part 5, Group II, Box A-310, "Dallas, Texas, 1940," Reel 6 at 815.

40. Reeves to Marshall, October 22, 1940; Earl Jones's statement to police, October 1940, NAACP Papers, Part 5, Group II, Box A-310, "Dallas, Texas, 1940," Reel 6 at 815.

41. Porter to Marshall, September 7, 1940; C. F. O'Donnell to Porter, September 19, 1940; Mayor Woodall Rodgers to Anna B. Wright, September 27, 1940; Reeves to Marshall, October 22, 1940; NAACP Papers, Part 5, Group II, Box A-310, "Dallas, Texas, 1940," Reel 6 at 815.

42. White to W. Lee O'Daniel, October 5, 1940; O'Daniel to White, October 7, 1940; Porter to Marshall, Sept. 25, 1940; Marshall to O. John Rogge, October 5, 1940; Reeves to Marshall, October 22, 1940; Marshall to Harold Young, October 10, 1940; NAACP Papers, Part 5, Group II, Box A-310, "Dallas, Texas, 1940," Reel 6 at 815.

43. Porter to White, October 6, 1940; Reeves to Marshall, October 22, 1940; Porter to Marshall, October 15, 1940, NAACP Papers, Part 5, Group II, Box A-310, "Dallas, Texas, 1940," Reel 6 at 815.

44. Minutes from council meeting, NAACP Papers, Part 5, Group II, Box A-310, "Dallas, Texas, 1940," Reel 6 at 815; Reeves to Marshall, July 16, 1941, NAACP Papers as above, "Dallas, Texas, 1941," Reel 6 at 943.

45. Porter to Marshall, October 17, 1940, NAACP Papers, Part 5, Group II, Box A-310, "Dallas, Texas, 1940," Reel 6 at 815.

46. Porter to Marshall, December 23, 1940, NAACP Papers, Part 5, Group II, Box A-310, "Dallas, Texas, 1940," Reel 6 at 916; Porter to Marshall, January 6, 1941, and January 13, 1941, NAACP Papers as above, "Dallas, Texas, 1941," Reel 6 at 924.

47. Reeves to Marshall, July 16, 1941; NAACP to Attorney General Robert H. Jackson, January 17, 1941; NAACP Papers, Part 5, Group II, Box A-310, "Dallas, Texas, 1941," Reel 6 at 943; *Dallas Morning News,* May 9, 1941, II 1 (*Dallas Morning News* cited hereinafter as *DMN*).

48. Marshall to ACLU, July 28, 1941, NAACP Papers, Part 5, Group II, Box A-310, "Dallas, Texas, 1941," Reel 6 at 951; *DMN,* May 10, 1941, II 2; *DMN,* May 11, 1941, II 1; *DMN,* May 13, 1941, II 4; *DMN,* May 16, 1941, II 1; *Dallas Express,* November 29, 1941, NAACP Papers, Part 5, Group II, Box A-310, "Dallas, Texas, 1941," Reel 6 at 980. See also Jim Schutze, *The Accommodation: The Politics of Race in an American City* (Secaucus: Citadel Press, 1986), 5–6.

NOTES TO CHAPTER 4 (PAGES 64 TO 78)

1. Franklin D. Roosevelt to the National Public Housing Conference, February 6, 1942, cited in Herbert Emmerich, FPHA, "Statement of the National Housing Agency, FPHA, Office of Racial Relations," May 1942, 2, NAACP Papers, Part 5, Group II, Box B-80, "USHA, 1941–1942," Reel 18 at 583.

2. *Chicago Defender,* December 20, 1941, 1.

3. Bureau of the Census, Population Division, *Population Special Reports, Civilian Migration in the United States, December 1940 to March 1945,* Series P-S 5, 1; Bureau of the Census, Population Division, *Current Population Reports, Population Characteristics, Internal Migration in the United States: April 1940 to April 1947,* Series P-20 14, 1–2, 5–6, 13; WPA study cited in Daniel M. Johnson and Rex R. Campbell, *Black Migration in America: A Social Demographic History* (Durham, N.C.: Duke University Press, 1981), 102–3; Ira De A. Reid, "Special Problems of Negro Migration During the War," in Frank G. Boudreau and Clyde V. Kiser, eds., *Postwar Problems of Migration* (New York: Milbank Memorial Fund, 1947), 153; Richard Polenberg, *One Nation Divisible: Class, Race, and Ethnicity in the United States Since 1938* (New York: Viking Press, 1980), 72–73.

4. Harold B. Myers, "Defense Migration and Labor Supply," cited in Johnson and Campbell, *Black Migration in America,* 101. See also Dominic J. Capeci, *Race Relations in Wartime Detroit: The*

Sojourner Truth Housing Controversy of 1942 (Philadelphia: Temple University Press, 1984), 28–99, 150–62; Daniel, *Shadow of Slavery*, 174–186; Johnson and Campbell, *Black Migration in America*, 105–110; Lemann, *Promised Land*, 40–58; Polenberg, *One Nation Divisible*, 70–74; and discussion in Chapter 7 herein.

5. See Table A.1 herein; Reid, "Special Problems of Negro Migration," 153; *Baltimore Afro-American*, January 1, 1944, 15; Arthur C. Verge, "The Impact of the Second World War on Los Angeles," *Pacific Historical Review* 63 (1994), 303; Marylynn S. Johnson, "War as Watershed: The East Bay and World War II," *Pacific Historical Review* 63 (1994), 319; Dominic J. Capeci, *The Harlem Riot of 1943* (Philadelphia: Temple University Press, 1977), 58. See also L. D. Reddick, ed., "The Negro in the North During Wartime," *Journal of Educational Sociology* 17 (1943–1944), 257–320; and L. D. Reddick, ed., "The New Race-Relations Frontier," *Journal of Educational Sociology* 19 (1945), 129–206.

6. Philip J. Funigiello, *The Challenge to Urban Liberalism: Federal-City Relations During World War II* (Knoxville: University of Tennessee Press, 1978), 81.

7. National Housing Agency, *Housing for War and the Job Ahead: A Common Goal for Communities . . . for Industry, Labor and Government* (Washington, D.C.: GPO, 1944), 5–6 (hereinafter referred to as NHA); Senate Committee on Banking and Currency, *Federal Housing Programs*, 6–7; Funigiello, *Challenge to Urban Liberalism*, 88; Brown, *Development of the Public Housing Program*, 43–44.

8. Roosevelt quotation occurs in notes to "Coordination of National Defense Housing; Executive Order No. 8632," January 11, 1940, in Franklin Delano Roosevelt, *Public Papers and Addresses of Franklin D. Roosevelt*, 1940 vol.: *War—and Aid to Democracies* (New York: Macmillan, 1941), 709; Senate Committee on Banking and Currency, *Federal Housing Programs*, 6–7; Housing and Home Finance Agency, *A Summary of the Evolution of Housing Activities*, 8–9; Funigiello, *Challenge to Urban Liberalism*, 89–91.

9. NHA, *Housing for War and the Job Ahead*, 5, 7–9; Senate Committee on Banking and Currency, *Federal Housing Programs*, 6–7; Funigiello, *Challenge to Urban Liberalism*, 88; Brown, *Development of the Public Housing Program*, 43–44.

10. Congress had authorized $300,000,000 for NHA in the 1943 budget. The House, however, had appropriated only $100,000,000 before the summer recess. On Blandford, see Administrator's Order no. 9 cited in Horne and McGraw, "Minority Group Considerations," 4; *Chicago Defender*, February 20, 1943, 9; *Chicago Defender*, April 17, 1943, 8; *Chicago Defender*, May 1, 1943, 9; *Chicago Defender*, September 18, 1943, 5. See also "jellyfish" citation in Hirsch, *Making the Second Ghetto*, 12. Ferguson is cited in "Memorandum . . concerning the Present Discriminatory Policies of the FHA," October 28, 1944, 4, NAACP Papers, Part 5, Group II, Box A-268, "Federal Housing Administration, General, 1947–1948," Reel 5 at 555. On the FWA, see *The Negro Handbook, 1942*, ed. Frances Murray (New York: Malliet, 1942), 1; Emmerich, "The Negro in Public War Housing," 2, NAACP Papers, Group II, Box B-80, "USHA, 1941–1942," Reel 18 at 583.

11. *A Monthly Summary of Events and Trends in Race Relations* 1 (August 1943), 2, 10, reprinted by Negro Universities Press, 1969 (hereinafter cited as *Race Relations*).

12. Memo from Detroit NAACP to Marshall, January 1942, NAACP Papers, Part 5, Group II, Box A-234, "Housing, General, January–February 1942," Reel 5 at 012; "A Factual Exposé of the Nevada-Fenelon Defense Housing Project Controversy," a speech by the Hon. Rudolph G. Tenerowicz, in House of Representatives, February 27, 1942, 4–5, NAACP Papers as above, Box A-235, "Housing, Press Releases and Clippings, 1940–1942," Reel 5 at 505. See also Capeci, *Race Relations in Wartime Detroit*, 28–99, 150–162; and Dominic J. Capeci and Martha Wilkerson, *Layered Violence: The Detroit Rioters of 1943* (Jackson: University of Mississippi Press, 1991).

13. Elaine Latzman Moon, *Untold Lives, Unsung Heroes: An Oral History of Detroit's African American Community, 1918–1967* (Detroit: Wayne State University Press, 1994), 203; Capeci, *Race Relations in Wartime Detroit*, 79; "A Factual Exposé," 5, 8, 14; NAACP press release, January 1942, NAACP Papers, Part 5, Group II, Box A-235, "Housing, Press Releases and Clippings, 1940–1942," Reel 5 at 446. Capeci, *Race Relations in Wartime Detroit*, 78.

14. Detroit NAACP to White, January 1942; Philip M. Klutznick to White, January 17, 1942; Klutznick to White, January 24, 1942; DDHC press release, January 15, 1942, NAACP Papers, Part 5, Group II, Box A-234, "Housing, General, January–February 1942," Reel 5 at 012; "Summary of Sojourner Truth Homes, Detroit, Michigan, March 6, 1942," NAACP Papers as above, "Housing, General, March 2–10, 1942," Reel 5 at 120.

15. Detroit NAACP to White, January 1942; "Summary," March 6, 1942; and Gloster B. Current to Marshall, January 19, 1942, NAACP Papers, Part 5, Group II, Box A-234, "Housing, General, January–February 1942," Reel 5 at 012; Arthur W. Mitchell to White, January 21, 1942, NAACP Papers as above, "Housing, General, January–February 1942," Reel 5 at 012; *Official Congressional Directory,* 1941 (Washington, D.C.: GPO, 1941), 25, 206.

16. Roy Wilkins to Reeves, March 4, 1942; Wilkins to Franklin Roosevelt, February 28, 1942, NAACP Papers, Part 5, Group II, Box A-234, "Housing, General, March 2–10, 1942," Reel 5 at 070; "Detroit Has a Race Riot," *Life,* March 16, 1942, 40–41.

17. "Summary," March 6, 1942; Wilkins to Reeves, March 4, 1942; Wilkins to Roosevelt, February 28, 1942; NAACP Papers, Part 5, Group II, Box A-234, "Housing, General, March 2–10, 1942," Reel 5 at 070; "Detroit Has a Race Riot," 40–41.

18. "Detroit Has a Race Riot," 40; Frank B. Woodford, "Storm over Housing in Detroit," *NYT,* March 15, 1942, IV, 7; "Summary," March 6, 1942, NAACP Papers, Part 5, Group II, Box A-234, "Housing, General, March 2–10, 1942," Reel 5 at 120; Current to Wilkins, March 18, 1942, NAACP Papers as above, "Housing, General, March 11–30, 1942," Reel 5 at 159.

19. Clipping, *Detroit Free Press,* March 7, 1942; handbill, "How You Can Speed Federal Action," March 1942; NAACP press release, March 6, 1942, NAACP Papers, Part 5, Group II, Box A-235, "Housing, Press Releases and Clippings, 1940–1942," Reel 5 at 446.

20. *Detroit Free Press,* March 6, 1942, 1; "Axis Utilizing Housing Dispute," *Detroit Free Press,* March 7, 1942; and *NYT,* March 10, 1942, NAACP Papers, Part 5, Group II, Box 235, "Housing, Press Releases and Clippings, 1940–1942," Reel 5 at 446.

21. *Detroit News,* April 15, 1942; and *Detroit Free Press,* April 16, 1942, NAACP Papers, Part 5, Group II, Box A-235, "Detroit Michigan, Housing, Press Releases, 1940–1942," Reel 5 at 446; *The Crisis* 49 (1942), 199.

22. "3 Truth Housing Foes Indicted by U.S. Jury," *Detroit Times,* April 16, 1942, NAACP Papers, Part 5, Group II, Box A-235, "Housing, Press Releases and Clippings, 1940–1942," Reel 5 at 446. Tenerowicz no longer represented the district after the November elections because the Democrats ran George G. Sadowski. See *The Crisis* 48 (1942), 311.

23. Current to White, April 30 1943, NAACP Papers, Part 5, Group II, Box A-235, "Housing, General, December 1942–1943," Reel 5 at 301.

24. Loring Moore, Office of Civilian Defense, "Report of Survey of Race Relations in Detroit, August 26–September 3, 1943," 13–14, NAACP Papers, Part 5, Group II, Box A-496, "Racial Tension, Detroit, Mich., 1943–44," Reel 13 at 040; Thurgood Marshall, "Report Concerning Activities of Police During Riots, June 21–22, 1943," NAACP Papers, as above, "Detroit, Michigan, 1943–1944," Reel 13 at 007; Walter White, "What Caused the Detroit, Michigan, Riots," July 1943, 24, NAACP Papers, as above, Reel 13 at 093. See also National Advisory Commission on Civil Disorders, *The Kerner Report,* 224; Capeci and Wilkerson, *Layered Violence,* 179–85; and Richard Polenberg, *War and Society: The United States, 1941–1945* (New York: Lippincott, 1972), 140–43.

25. Conflict arose again in the winter of 1944–1945, when whites opposed the construction of 1,000 temporary dwellings for black defense workers in the Oakwood area. Moore, "Survey of Race Relations in Detroit," 14, NAACP Papers, Part 5, Group II, Box A-496, "Detroit, Michigan, 1943–1944," Reel 13 at 040; William E. Hill, American Council on Race Relations, "Field Report to Robert C. Weaver, to Ascertain the Major Causes of Racial Tension, 1945," 11, and Hill, "Summary of Facts," 3, NAACP Papers, as above, "Racial Tension, Detroit, Mich., 1945–46," Reel 13 at 140. For examples of MCIR advertisement, see Papers of Detroit Commission on Community Relations—Human Rights Department, Part I, Series I, Box 15, "Advertising Against Discrimination, Clippings," Wayne State University Archives of Labor and Urban Affairs and University Archives, Walter P. Reuther Library, Wayne State University, Detroit, Michigan (hereinafter cited as CCR-HRD Papers). The Oakwood incident is cited in Hill, "Major Causes of Racial Tension," 6–7, NAACP

Papers, as above; George Schermer, "Preliminary Report of the Detroit Interracial Committee, March 1, 1945–June 30, 1945," 1, NAACP Papers, as above, Reel 13 at 164.

26. Mrs. C. W. Barnett and T. J. S. Waxter, "Negro Housing" (Baltimore: Citizen's Planning and Housing Association [CPHA] and Emergency Home Service, Department of Welfare, June 6, 1942), 2, 6; CPHA, "Memorandum on Negro Housing in Metropolitan Baltimore," August 1944, 1; *Baltimore Afro-American,* January 1, 1944, 15. See also Edward S. Lewis, "Profiles: Baltimore," *Journal of Educational Sociology* 17 (1944), 288–90. "Baltimore Housing Authority Yields to Racial Opposition," *Baltimore Afro-American Ledger,* April 3, 1943, 16.

27. *Baltimore Afro-American Ledger,* May 1, 1943, 4; *Race Relations* 1 (August 1943), 11; "The Story of Herring Run," *Race Relations* 1 (September 1943), 7–8; "Whites Hit Baltimore U.S. Homes," *Chicago Defender,* April 24, 1943, 4; *Baltimore Afro-American Ledger,* April 24, 6.

28. *Baltimore Afro-American Ledger,* September 4, 1943, 3; *Baltimore Afro-American Ledger,* November 6, 1943, 10; *Baltimore Afro-American Ledger,* May 1, 6, and "War Housing Is Held Up as Agencies Play Game of Hide-Seek," May 1, 10; *Chicago Defender,* May 22, 1943, 4; *Chicago Defender,* August 7, 1943, 3.

29. *Baltimore Afro-American Ledger,* May 29, 1943, 12; *Baltimore Afro-American Ledger,* July 17, 1943, 21.

30. *Baltimore Afro-American Ledger,* July 24, 1943, 6; "The Story of Herring Run," 7–8.

31. *Baltimore Afro-American Ledger,* July 24, 1943, 6. A discussion of McKeldin's rise to political power occurs in George H. Callcott, *Maryland and America: 1940–1980* (Baltimore: Johns Hopkins University Press, 1985), 131–33.

32. "Housing Is Delayed Again; City Council to Pass on Sites" and "State Official, Congressman Protest Site; 100 Urge Action," *Baltimore Afro-American Ledger,* July 31, 1943, 6.

33. "FPHA Puts Housing Issue Up to Mayor," *Baltimore Afro-American Ledger,* August 14, 1943, 11.

34. "Permanent Housing Out After Mayor Fails to Approve Site," *Baltimore Afro-American Ledger,* August 28, 1943, 15; "5,000 Turn Out for Unity-for-Victory Rally; Mayor Dodges Housing Issue," *Baltimore Afro-American Ledger,* August 28, 1943, 20; "4 War Homes Sites Dubbed Undesirable," *Baltimore Afro-American Ledger,* November 6, 1943, 10; *Baltimore Afro-American Ledger,* November 13, 1943, 9.

35. Verge, "Impact of the Second World War on Los Angeles," 293, 298–99. See also Keith E. Collins, *Black Los Angeles: The Maturing of the Ghetto, 1940–1970* (Saratoga: Century Twenty One, 1980), 26–31, 38–46, 69–74. See also J. Gregg Layne, "Annals of Los Angeles," *California Historical Society Quarterly* 13 (1974), 195–234 and 301–54; and Carl I. Wheat, ed., "California's Bantam Cock: The Journals of Charles E. DeLong, 1854–1863," *California Historical Society Quarterly* 256–58, 281–82.

36. Los Angeles's black population in 1940 numbered 63,774 (4.2 percent); in 1944 it numbered 118,888; and in 1950 the black population of the city and adjacent area numbered 211,585 (10.7 percent). The black population of the SMSA of Los Angeles in 1950 was 171,209. See Table A.1 and Bureau of the Census, *Seventeenth Census of the United States, 1950: Population II: Characteristics of the Population, Part 5, California* (Washington, D.C.: GPO, 1952), 100. See also Collins, *Black Los Angeles,* 18–29, 38–46; Verge, "Impact of the Second World War on Los Angeles," 303–307; Bass, *Forty Years,* 1–6; Bessie Averne McClenahan, *The Changing Urban Neighborhood: From Neighbor to Nigh-Dweller* (Los Angeles: University of Southern California, 1929), 83–96; Robert M. Fogelson, *The Fragmented Metropolis: Los Angeles, 1850–1930* (Cambridge: Harvard University Press, 1967) 147, 200–2.

37. Dorothy W. Baruch, "Sleep Comes Hard," *Nation* (January 1945), 96; Weaver, *Negro Ghetto,* 88. See also Charles B. Spaulding, "Housing Problems of Minority Groups in Los Angeles County," *Annals of the American Academy of Political and Social Science* 248 (1946), 222–23; Raphael F. Sonenshein, *Politics in Black and White: Race and Power in Los Angeles* (Princeton: Princeton University Press, 1993), 29.

38. Lawrence de Graaf, cited in Mike Davis, *City of Quartz: Excavating the Future in Los Angeles* (New York: Verso, 1990), 163. See also Bass, *Forty Years,* 101–10; Lawrence B. de Graaf, "The City of Black Angels: Emergence of the Los Angeles Ghetto, 1890–1930," *Pacific Historical Review* 33 (1970), 328–50; Verge, "Impact of the Second World War on Los Angeles," 305–5.

39. Bass, *Forty Years*, 104–5; *Chicago Defender,* October 7, 1944, 1; *Chicago Defender,* July 28, 1945, 1; *Race Relations* 3 (January 1946), 181. Judge Thurmond Clarke is cited in "The Architectural Forum," Southern Regional Council Papers, Series I, Reel 2 at 31, Special Collections, Robert W. Woodruff Library, Atlanta University Center, Atlanta, Georgia (hereinafter cited as SRC Papers). See also Collins, *Black Los Angeles*, 30.

40. *California Eagle* cited in Bass, *Forty Years,* 102–5; Baruch, "Sleep Comes Hard," 96.

41. Eddie Salitor, the *Maywood-Bell Southwest Herald,* and *California Eagle* cited in Bass, *Forty Years,* 102–3.

42. Bass, *Forty Years,* 103–104.

43. The incident is recounted in Davis, *City of Quartz,* 399–401; Verge, "Impact of the Second World War on Los Angeles," 303–4, 310.

44. Polenberg, *War and Society*, 4.

NOTES TO CHAPTER 5 (PAGES 79 TO 97)

1. Abrams, *The Future of Housing*, 17.

2. Census reviewed in Lynch, *Black Urban Condition*, 430–31.

3. National Association of Housing Officials, "Housing for the United States After the War" (Chicago: NAHO, 1944), iv, xvii–xviii, 49–51; Richard O. Davies, *Housing Reform During the Truman Administration* (Columbia: University of Missouri Press, 1966), 11; National Housing Agency, *Fifth Annual Report, January 1, to December 31, 1946,* 1; Robert K. Brown, "The Development of the Public Housing Program in the United States" (Atlanta: Bureau of Business and Economic Research, School of Business Administration, Georgia State College of Business Administration, 1960), 49.

4. Davies, *Housing Reform During the Truman Administration,* 15–26, 126–29.

5. Ibid., 29–33.

6. Senate Committee on Banking and Currency, *Federal Housing Programs,* 8; Davies, *Housing Reform During the Truman Administration,* 25–27, 33–34; Huthmacher, *Wagner and the Rise of Urban Liberalism,* 299–302.

7. Senate Committee on Banking and Currency, *Federal Housing Programs,* 8–9; Housing and Home Finance Agency, *A Summary of the Evolution of Housing Activities,* 10–11.

8. Memo concerning "Present Discriminatory Policies of the FHA," October 28, 1944, 1–2, NAACP Papers, Part 5, Group II, Box A-268, "FHA, General, 1947–1948," Reel 5 at 555; Thurgood Marshall, *Memorandum to the President . . Racial Discrimination by the FHA,* April 1949, in U.S. House of Representatives, Committee on Banking and Currency, *Housing Act of 1949: Hearings,* 223–29; *Chicago Defender,* March 10, 1944, 6.

9. NAREB spokesman, cited in *Race Relations* 1, no. 11 (July 1944), 7. *Pittsburgh Courier,* October 9, 1943, cited in *Race Relations,* 1, no. 3 (October 1943), 10.

10. William C. Berman, *Politics of Civil Rights in the Truman Administration* (Columbus: Ohio State University Press, 1970), 9–12, 23–24, 55.

11. Michael Carter, "Senator Taft Talks for AFRO," *Baltimore Afro-American Ledger,* May 6, 1944, 1, 15.

12. Horne and McGraw, "Minority Group Considerations," 7; *Chicago Defender,* February 16, 1946, 12; *Chicago Defender,* February 23, 1946, 1; *Chicago Defender,* June 22, 1946, 1; *Chicago Defender,* July 20, 1946, 5; *Chicago Defender,* July 27, 1946, 1; *Chicago Defender,* May 17, 1947, 1, 4; *ADW,* November 13, 1947, 1, 4; *ADW,* November 18, 1947, 2. See also Davies, *Housing Reform During the Truman Administration,* 43–44.

13. Horne and McGraw, "Minority Group Considerations," 7–13, 27; Davies, *Housing Reform During the Truman Administration,* 57–60; Ross, "Mary McLeod Bethune," 191–93.

14. Berman, *Politics of Civil Rights in the Truman Administration,* 79–135; Harry S. Truman, "Speech Before the Ministerial Alliance, Harlem, October 29, 1948," in Gregory Bush, ed., *Campaign Speeches of American Presidential Candidates, 1948–1984* (New York: Ungar, 1985), 12.

15. Harvard Sitkoff, "Harry Truman and the Election of 1948: The Coming of Age of Civil Rights in American Politics," *Journal of Southern History* 37 (1971), 601–5, 612–13.

16. Harry S. Truman, "State of the Union Address, January 5, 1949," reprinted in *Congressional Digest* 28 (1949), 64; Senate Committee on Banking and Currency, *Federal Housing Programs,* 13. Statement of Raymond M. Foley, April 7, 1949, House Committee on Banking and Currency, *Housing Act of 1949: Hearings,* 42.

17. Statement of Leslie S. Perry, April 26, 1949, House Committee on Banking and Currency, *Housing Act of 1949, Hearings,* 220.

18. U.S. Senate, *Housing Act of 1949, Summary of Provisions of the National Housing Act of 1949,* July 14, 1949, in *Senate Documents, 81st Cong., 1st Sess., Miscellaneous IX, Doc. no. 99* (Washington, D.C.: GPO, 1949); *Congressional Record, 81st Cong., 1st Sess., 1949,* 48, 4791–804. Congressional Quarterly Service, *Housing a Nation* (Washington, D.C.: CQS, 1966), 28.

19. *Congressional Record, 81st Cong., 1st Sess., 1949,* 4798; Edgar G. Brown cited in *Congressional Record, 81st Cong., 1st. Sess., 1949,* 4791; and Statement by Edgar H. Brown before the House of Representatives Committee on Banking and Currency, April 26, 1949, House Committee on Banking and Currency, *Housing Act of 1949: Hearings,* 235–42.

20. *Congressional Record, 81st Cong., 1st Sess., 1949,* 4797.

21. *Congressional Record, 81st Cong., 1st Sess., 1949,* 4856–857.

22. Statement by Robert P. Gerholz, May 4, 1949, House Committee on Banking and Currency, *Housing Act of 1949, Hearings,* 587; Harry S. Truman, "Address to the United States Conference of Mayors, March 21, 1949," in Harry S. Truman, *Public Papers of the President, Harry S. Truman, 1949* (Washington, D.C.: GPO, 1964), 176. Davies, *Housing Reform During the Truman Administration,* 110.

23. *Congressional Record, 81st Cong., 1st Sess., 1949,* 8138, 12186–189.

24. *ADW,* July 1, 1949, 1; *ADW,* July 3, 1949, 1; *ADW,* July 13, 1949, 1.

25. Brown, *Development of the Public Housing Program in the United States,* 65.

26. FHA Race Relations Office report cited in *ADW,* July 24, 1949, 1.

27. CHA chairman cited in J. G. St. Clair Drake, "Profiles: Chicago," *Journal of Educational Sociology* 17 (1944), 264; see also Hirsch, *Making the Second Ghetto,* 9–12, 16–18; Wright, *Human Relations in Chicago,* 80, 83.

28. Statistics are for census tracts 558 and 560–62: Bureau of the Census, *Sixteenth Census, 1940: Population and Housing Statistics for Census Tract and Community Areas, Chicago, Ill.* (Washington, D.C.: GPO, 1943), 56–58; *Seventeenth Census, 1950: Population III: Chicago, Ill.* (Washington, D.C.: GPO, 1952), 38, 57. See Table A.4. See also Duncan and Duncan, *The Negro Population of Chicago,* 96–97. Hirsch, *Making the Second Ghetto,* 5.

29. *Chicago Defender,* February 24, 1945, 9.

30. *Race Relations* 1 (1944), 5–6, 126; *Chicago Defender,* October 21, 1944, 6; *Chicago Defender,* May 19, 1945, 1; *Chicago Defender,* July 6, 1946, 1, 6.

31. "Landlords Plot Reign of Terror," by Ernest Lilienstein, *Chicago Defender,* February 16, 1946, 5.

32. Johnson, *Call Me Neighbor, Call Me Friend,* 42, 44–45. The Park Manor violence is also recounted in Hirsch, *Making the Second Ghetto,* 56–59. See also *Chicago Defender,* March 23, 1946, 5; *Chicago Defender,* July 6, 1946, 1, 6.

33. Wright, *Human Relations in Chicago,* 89–90, 119–155; Hirsch, *Making the Second Ghetto,* 54–56, 60, 90–95.

34. Velie, "Housing: Detroit's Time Bomb," 14; Joe T. Darden, Richard Child Hill, June Thomas, and Richard Thomas, *Detroit: Race and Uneven Development* (Philadelphia: Temple University Press, 1987), 113.

35. Velie, "Housing: Detroit's Time Bomb," 78; Darden et al., *Detroit: Race and Uneven Development,* 122; Abrams, *Forbidden Neighbors,* 100–1.

36. "Population Change by Color, Metropolitan Detroit Area by District and Civil Division: 1940 and 1950," and "Population Change by Color, City of Detroit by Subcommunity: 1940 to 1950," CCR-HRD Papers, Part 3, Box 17, "Population Studies." See Table A.6.

37. George Schermer, "Summary Report to City of Detroit Interracial Committee," 2, CCR-HRD Papers, Part I, Series I, Box 3, "Demonstrations Protesting Negro Occupancy of Houses, 9/1/45–9/1/46"; "Second Annual Report: City of Detroit Interracial Committee, 1945," CCR-HRD Papers, Part III, Series I, Box 2, "Annual Reports."

38. "Chronological Table of Demonstrations Protesting Negro Occupancy of Houses, September 1, 1945 to September 1, 1946," in "Housing Incident Reports, 1946," 5–8, CCR-HRD Papers, Part 1, Series I, Box 3, "Demonstrations Protesting Negro Occupancy of Houses"; and Thomas H. Kleene to Schermer, January 17, 1946, CCR-HRD Papers, Part 3, Series IV, Box 27, "Incidents, 1945–1946"; Kleene and Schermer to Interracial Committee, December 27, 1945, CCR-HRD Papers, as above. Women had played a key role in the violence at Chicago's Airport Homes. According to Wright, "a great many women were in the front ranks of the mob and began to fight with the policemen, kicking and scratching and slapping at them." See Wright, *Human Relations in Chicago*, 129. See also Hirsch, *Making the Second Ghetto*, 76–78.

39. John Field and Joseph Coles, "Report of Incident, August 23, 1948," 1–3, CCR-HRD Papers, Part III, Series IV, Box 26, "Interracial Committee, Housing Discrimination"; George Schermer, "Report of Incident, August 24, 1948," 1–5; "Three Families Move into Homes on Harrison As Police Stand By to Prevent Violence," *Michigan Chronicle*, August 28, 1948, 1; "Negro Families Terrorized: Jeering Whites Parading," *Michigan Chronicle*, September 18, 1948, 1, 8; "A Northern City 'Sitting on Lid' of Racial Trouble," *U.S. News and World Report*, May 11, 1956, 35 (*U.S. News and World Report* hereinafter cited as *USNWR*).

40. "McGhee Case to Be Heard This Week," *Michigan Chronicle*, January 17, 1948, 1, 19; Vose, *Caucasians Only*, 80–121.

41. On *Shelley* v. *Kraemer*, see Vose, *Caucasians Only*, 100–21, 151–210. The most reliable source for the specifics of the case remains Chief Justice Fred M. Vinson's decision of May 3, 1948: *Shelley* v. *Kraemer*, 334 U.S. 1.

42. *Hurd* v. *Hodge*, 334 U.S. 24 (1948). See Berman, *Politics of Civil Rights in the Truman Administration*, 5. See also Tushnet, *Making Civil Rights Law*, 92–96; Vose, *Caucasians Only*, 156–57, 190; and Sidney Fine, *Frank Murphy: The Washington Years*, vol. 3 (Ann Arbor: University of Michigan Press, 1984), 565.

43. Robert E. Cushman, "The Laws of the Land," *Survey Graphic* 36 (1947), 17; Long and Johnson, *People vs. Property*, 88, 91; Abrams, *Forbidden Neighbors*, 220–21; Tushnet, *Making Civil Rights Law*, 81; Stern, "The End of the Restrictive Covenant," *Appraisal Journal* 16 (October 1948), 438.

44. Vose, *Caucasians Only*, 168–74, 191–93; "Committee on Civil Rights: Agenda for Policy, Committee Meetings, June 30–July 1, 1947," 11, Dorothy Rogers Tilly Papers, Box 3, Special Collections, Robert W. Woodruff Library, Emory University, Atlanta, Georgia; Berman, *Politics of Civil Rights in the Truman Administration*, 74; Abrams, *Forbidden Neighbors*, 220.

45. "See 50–50 Chance Cases Won, Covenants Ruled Out," *Michigan Chronicle*, January 25, 1948, 1, 19; *NYT*, January 16, 1948, 30; *NYT*, January 17, 1948, 3.

46. "See 50–50 Chance Cases Won, Covenants Ruled Out," *Michigan Chronicle*, January 25, 1948, 1, 19.

47. *Shelley* v. *Kraemer*, 334 U.S. 1; Vose, *Caucasians Only*, 205–10. Murphy cited in Fine, *Frank Murphy: The Washington Years*, 565.

48. "Due Process of Law and Racial Restrictive Covenants," *Appraisal Journal* 16 (January 1948), 83; "The Outlawry of Racial Restrictive Covenants," *Appraisal Journal* 16 (July 1948), 370–75; Stern, "The End of the Restrictive Covenant," *Appraisal Journal*, October 1948, 434, 441–42.

49. "Constitutional Property Ban Requested," *Los Angeles Times*, August 11, 1948, 1, 8; "Realty Board Asks Change in Constitution," *California Eagle*, August 12, 1948, 1, 5; "Property Race Curb," *Los Angeles Herald-Express*, August 11, 1948, A17.

50. *Michigan Chronicle*, May 8, 1948, 1, 7–8; *Michigan Chronicle*, May 15, 1948, 1, 3, 8.

51. "King Cole Determined to Move into Newly Purchased Home," *California Eagle*, August 5, 1948, 1, 5.

52. "King Cole Determined to Move into Newly Purchased Home," *California Eagle*, August 5, 1948, 1, 5; James Haskins with Kathleen Benson, *Nat King Cole: A Personal and Professional Biography* (Chelsea, Mich.: Scarborough House, 1990), 81–82; MPI Home Entertainment, Inc., *Unforgettable: Nat "King" Cole* (1989).

53. Haskins, *Nat King Cole*, 82; MPI Home Entertainment, Inc., *Unforgettable: Nat "King" Cole* (1989).

NOTES TO CHAPTER 6 (PAGES 98 TO 114)

1. T. Eugene "Bull" Connor cited in Harrison E. Salisbury, "Fear and Hatred Grip Birmingham," *NYT,* April 12, 1960, 1.

2. Pete Daniel, "Going Among Strangers: Southern Reactions to World War II," *Journal of American History* 77 (1990), 886–911.

3. Michael James O'Connor, "The Measurement and Significance of Racial Residential Barriers in Atlanta, 1890–1970," doctoral diss., University of Georgia, 1977, 24, 28; Thompson, Lewis, and McEntire, "Atlanta and Birmingham," 17. See also Doyle, *New Men, New Cities, New South,* 136–58; Ronal H. Bayor, "Roads to Racial Segregation: Atlanta in the Twentieth Century," *Journal of Urban History* 15 (1988), 3–21; Dan Durett and Dana F. White, *An-Other Atlanta: The Black Heritage* (Atlanta: Atlanta Bicentennial Commission/The History Group, 1975), "Sweet Auburn" section; Clifford M. Kuhn, Harlon E. Joye, and E. Bernard West, *Living Atlanta: An Oral History of the City, 1914–1948* (Atlanta and Athens: Atlanta Historical Society/University of Georgia Press, 1990), 37–40.

Note also Adams, "Blueprint for Segregation," 75–77; O'Connor, "Measurement and Significance of Racial Residential Barriers," 92–117; and David Andrew Harmon, "Beneath the Image: The Civil Rights Movement and Race Relations in Atlanta, 1946–1981," doctoral diss., Emory University, 1993, 128–36, all of which rely on Thompson, Lewis, and McEntire, extensively.

4. "Zoning Ordinance, May 1929," NAACP Papers, Part 5, Group I, Box C-404, "Residential, Atlanta, Georgia, May 22, 1929–April 16, 1931," Reel 1 at 1059; and Copy of Petition, *Shackter* v. *City of Atlanta,* Superior Court of Fulton County, Georgia, February 13, 1931, NAACP Papers as above, Reel 1 at 1081; "An Ordinance, March 19, 1931," NAACP Papers, as above, Reel 1 at 1089.

5. Floyd J. Calvin, "Heman Perry Started Atlanta on Its Home Building Program," *Pittsburgh Courier,* October 31, 1931, cited in Johnson, *Negro Housing,* 237; Andrew M. Ambrose, "Redrawing the Color Line: The History and Patterns of Black Housing in Atlanta, 1940–1973," doctoral diss., Emory University, 1992, 96–97. See also Durett and White, *An-Other Atlanta,* Cascade Heights Section; and Kuhn, Joye, and West, *Living Atlanta,* 40, 42.

6. *Atlanta Journal,* October 23, 1947, 1, 12; Kuhn, Joye, and West, *Living Atlanta,* 42, 44–45; Adams, "Blueprint for Segregation," 74–75; Ambrose, "Redrawing the Color Line," 79.

7. A more critical look at Mayor Hartsfield exposes the mayor's manipulation of black voters, as evinced by his comment that "he knew how to 'use' the Negro, but was able successfully to avoid letting the Negro 'use' him." See Harold H. Martin, *William Berry Hartsfield: Mayor of Atlanta* (Athens: University of Georgia Press, 1978), 68, 99, 172. On the development of black political strength in the 1930s and 1940s, see Harmon, "Beneath the Image," chap. 1.

8. Citizens of Buckhead accepted annexation in a referendum in 1950; see Bradley R. Rice, "The Battle of Buckhead: The Plan of Improvement and Atlanta's Last Big Annexation," *The Atlanta Historical Journal* 25 (Winter 1985), 9–16. Martin, *William Berry Hartsfield,* 47–52; Harmon, "Beneath the Image," 49–55, 59–67.

9. *Chicago Defender,* July 1, 1944, 11; *New York Amsterdam News,* November 9, 1946, 1. *Chicago Defender,* July 1, 1944, 11; *Chicago Defender,* May 10, 1947, 1. Memo, September 3, 1946, and Memo, November 8, 1946, Ralph E. McGill Papers, Series V, Box 51, "Columbians," at Special Collections, Emory University, Atlanta, Georgia (hereinafter cited as McGill Papers). See Michael Newton and Judy Ann Newton, *Racial and Religious Violence in America: A Chronology* (New York: Garland, 1991), 422; Martin, *William Berry Hartsfield,* 52.

10. Memo for file, December 16, 1946, McGill Papers, Series V, Box 51, "Columbians"; Newton and Newton, *Racial and Religious Violence,* 422. Murray, *Negro Handbook, 1949,* 191; *Atlanta Journal,* October 23, 1947, 1, 12; *ADW,* October 25, 1947, 1; *ADW,* October 28, 1947, 1; *ADW,* October 29, 1947, 1, 6; *ADW,* October 30, 1947, 1, 3, 6; *ADW,* November 1, 1947, 1.

11. *ADW,* October 30, 1947, 3. Walter Aiken was also founder of the National Association of Real Estate Brokers. See "He Died Tuesday: 'Chief' Aiken's Funeral Today," *ADW,* December 15, 1965, 1, 8.

12. *ADW,* October 29, 1947, 1, 6; *ADW,* October 31, 1947, 1; Ambrose, "Redrawing the Color Line," 98–99; Thompson, Lewis, and McEntire, "Atlanta and Birmingham," 23.

13. *ADW,* January 13, 1948, 1; *ADW,* May 7, 1948, 1; *ADW,* March 6, 1949; and Harold C. Fleming to Monroe Berger, December 21, 1949, SRC Papers, "Housing," Reel 30 at 993. Atlanta Housing Council, cited in Thompson, Lewis, and McEntire, "Atlanta and Birmingham," 23.

14. *ADW,* February 15, 1949, 1; *ADW,* February 16, 1949, 1; *ADW,* February 17, 1949, 1; *ADW,* February 18, 1949, 1; *ADW,* March 6, 1949, 1; *ADW,* March 19, 1949, 1.

15. *ADW,* March 18, 1949; *ADW,* March 24, 1949, 1. See also *The West End Eagle,* April 1, 1949, 1; and Joseph M. Wallace, *The West End Eagle,* April 8, 1949, McGill Papers, Series V, File 51–1, "Columbians." See also O'Connor, "Racial Residential Barriers in Atlanta," 104.

16. "A Round-Up of Bomb Violence," *New South* (1952), 6; Thompson, Lewis, and McEntire, "Atlanta and Birmingham," 29. Bureau of the Census, *Eighteenth Census of the United States, 1960: Censuses of Population and Housing, PHC(1)–8: Atlanta, Ga., Standard Metropolitan Statistical Area,* 21. U.S. Commission on Civil Rights, *Report of the United States Commission on Civil Rights, 1959* (Washington, D.C.: GPO, 1959), 1595; "Negro Home in White Atlanta Area Dynamited," *Jet,* September 16, 1954, 5; "Blast Negro Home in White Atlanta Area," *Jet,* July 19, 1956, 5.

17. Adams, "Blueprint for Segregation," x. Taeuber and Taeuber, *Negroes in Cities,* 40. Harmon, "Beneath the Image," 74; Thompson, Lewis, and McEntire, "Atlanta and Birmingham, 13–83. "Fate of Housing Project Seen as Failing to Pass," *ADW,* December 4, 1959, 1, 6; "Aldermanic Board Fails to Approve Site for Project," *ADW,* December 8, 1959, 1, 8; Executive Committee of Voters' League Schedules Special Meet to Probe Denial of Project Site," *ADW,* December 10, 1959, 1; "Let No Thoughtful Citizen Be Unconcerned on Housing," *ADW,* December 10, 1959, 1.

According to "Bombings List" of the Birmingham Police Department, fourteen race bombings occurred between 1955 and 1963. Nine more incidents happened between 1945 and 1955, totaling twenty-three. Admittedly, Birmingham's honor in having fewer bombings is dubious. See, Police Surveillance Files, File 3.1 (a), "Bombings."

18. Carl T. Rowan, *South of Freedom* (New York: Knopf, 1952), excerpted in Lynch, ed., *Black Urban Condition,* 296. Salisbury, "Fear and Hatred Grip Birmingham," 28. The Birmingham Chamber of Commerce suit contended that Salisbury distorted and telescoped incidents "covering many prior years in an effort to provide a picture of the moment—a picture that is not true, even reasonably true." Salisbury's claims were quite accurate for the period in question, however. A disturbing example of this white supremacy and black subservience occurred shortly after Birmingham annexed Zion City, near East Lake. The Civil League of Zion City wrote the City Commission to request sewers, fire plugs, a fire station, and other improvements. The rhetoric of the letter as well as its content illustrate the condition of race relations. The Civil League reported that the area was "without water half of the time" because of inadequate pipes. The district had no traffic signs, paved roads, or sidewalks. When the city provided garbage removal, the Civil League wrote thanking them "from [their] deepest heart for having extended garbage service to [the] community." See Birmingham Chamber of Commerce to *NYT,* May 2, 1960, Morgan Papers, File 24.31, "*New York Times* Suit, 1960"; and C. L. Burns to Morgan, January 21, 1952, Morgan Papers, File 18.37, "Negroes, 1952."

19. "Zoning Ordinance of Birmingham, Alabama," August 4, 1926, in Sara Griffith, "Birmingham: The Magic City," B.S., Sociology Notebook, Northwestern University, Spring 1938; and Horace C. Wilkinson, "Petition for Writ of Certiorari, *City of Birmingham* v. *Mary Means Monk,* 1951," Morgan Papers, Monk File. Carl V. Harris, "Reforms in Government Control of Negroes in Birmingham, Alabama, 1890–1920," *Journal of Southern History* 38 (1972), 571, 600. For discussions of race relations in early Birmingham, see Feldman, "A Sense of Place," passim.; Griffith, "Birmingham: The Magic City"; Robert J. Norrell and Otis Dismuke, *The Other Side: The Story of Birmingham's Black Community* (Birmingham: n.p., 1981); Oliver, "Zoning Ordinances," passim. Population data are also in Oliver, "Zoning Ordinances," 7; and spatial data appears in *NYT,* August 11, 1949, 26.

20. Shores to Marshall, November 16, 1939, NAACP Papers, Group I, Box C-404, "Residential, General, January 6–November 19, 1939," Reel 1 at 1001. On the zoning board's policy, see Survey of Zoning Board of Adjustment Minutes, 1926–1952, City of Birmingham Department of Urban Planning, Records, Files 1135.7.1–1135.10.1, Archives, Birmingham Public Library, Birmingham, Alabama. Discussion of the LDF program appears in Vose, *Caucasians Only,* 45–47, 262 at note 81. Also see Lynda Dempsey Cochran, "Arthur D. Shores: Advocate for Freedom," master's thesis, Georgia Southern University, 1977," 29–30, 42–43, 45–47, 52–53; and Glenn T. Eskew, "The Alabama Christian Movement for Human Rights and the Birmingham Struggle for Civil Rights," in David

J. Garrow, ed., *Birmingham, Alabama, 1956–1963: The Black Struggle for Civil Rights* (Brooklyn: Carlson, 1989), 17; Robert J. Norrell, "Caste in Steel: Jim Crow Careers in Birmingham, Alabama," *Journal of American History* 73 (1986)," 680–81.

NAACP challenges proved victorious against race-restrictive zoning ordinances. The U.S. Supreme Court, of course, had ruled against residential segregation laws, but cities and states continued to try to use them despite their unconstitutionality. In February 1929, the Council of the City of Richmond, Virginia, approved an ordinance that prohibited any person from occupying a residence on a street where the majority of residences were "occupied by those with whom said person [was] forbidden to intermarry." The NAACP sued to enjoin the city from enforcing the statute, and in the fall of 1929 the case came before Judge D. Lawrence Groner of the U.S. District Court. To support their case, Richmond's attorneys used the same arguments that cities had in the cases of the 1910s, saying property rights were not absolute, zoning for the protection of morals and racial integrity was a legitimate use of the police power, blacks and whites were treated equally under the law, and integration would cause racial conflict. Judge Groner held the law invalid. In January 1930, the U.S. Circuit Court upheld the ruling. In May, the Supreme Court denied a hearing to the city's final appeal in a terse decision: "PER CURIAM: Decree affirmed. *Buchanan* v. *Warley*, . . . *Harmon* v. *Tyler.*" See *City of Richmond* v. *Deans*, 218 U.S. 704 (1930); NAACP News Release, February 14, 1929; Council of the City of Richmond, *An Ordinance*, February 15, 1929, NAACP Papers, Part 5, Group I, Box D-68, "Cases Supported. Richmond, Virginia. Residential Segregation, February–May 1929," Reel 2 at 801; *Richmond News Leader,* January 14, 1930; Alfred E. Cohen (attorney for the NAACP), Letter to the Editor, *The St. Luke Herald,* May 31, 1930, NAACP Papers as above, "Cases Supported. Richmond, Virginia. Residential Segregation Case, 1930," Reel 2 at 895.

The NAACP defeated the Richmond law, but other cities forced the NAACP to continue fighting zoning ordinances. In 1929, Atlanta imposed a zoning law that used language similar to that in the Richmond restriction. The Atlanta City Council unanimously passed the new restriction over Mayor Isaac Ragsdale's veto. When that law fell, the city passed another one in 1931. This statute tried to use the precedent of segregated schools, which the courts had accepted. The Fulton County Superior Court negated the ordinance. In January 1933, numerous demonstrations arose when blacks tried to move onto a white block in Oklahoma City. When fear of a riot surfaced, Governor of Oklahoma William H. Murray issued an executive military order establishing segregated residential zones for each race, separated by a "neutral Non-Trespass Zone." The City Council subsequently fixed the zoning order through an ordinance. The NAACP fought the new order several times in 1935 before finally defeating it in the case of *Allen* v. *Oklahoma City* in 1936. Blacks defeated a zoning ordinance in Winston-Salem, North Carolina, in 1940. By the beginning of World War II, therefore, only a few staunchly resistant cities, most notably Birmingham, Alabama, used zoning laws to separate the races. On Atlanta, see "Zoning Ordinance, May 1929," NAACP Papers, Part 5, Group I, Box C-404, "Residential, Atlanta, Georgia, May 22, 1929–April 16, 1931," Reel 1 at 1059; and Copy of Petition, *Shackter* v. *City of Atlanta*, Superior Court of Fulton County, Georgia, February 13, 1931, NAACP Papers as above, Reel 1 at 1081; "An Ordinance, March 19, 1931," NAACP Papers, as above, Reel 1 at 1089. See also *Allen* v. *City of Oklahoma,* 175 Okl. 421, 52 P 2d. 1054 (1936); *Clinard* v. *City of Winston-Salem,* 217 N.C. 119 (1940); Gov. William H. Murray, *Executive Military Order,* May 1, 1933; *In Re: Habeus Corpus of Sidney Hawkins,* No. 26,597, Supreme Court of the State of Oklahoma; *F. C. Scott* v. *John Watt, Chief of Police of the City of Oklahoma City,* No. 26,571, District Court of Oklahoma County, Oklahoma, NAACP Papers, Part 5, Group I, Box C-405, "Segregation, Residential, Oklahoma City, Oklahoma, April 11, 1933–December 9, 1935," Reel 2 at 060.

21. Oliver, "Zoning Ordinances," 7. Norrell, "Caste in Steel," 681; Norrell and Dismuke, "The Other Side," 24. Glenn Thomas Eskew, "But for Birmingham: The Local and National Movements in the Civil Rights Struggle," doctoral diss., University of Georgia, 1993, Southern Collection, Birmingham Public Library, Birmingham, Alabama, 81. See also Carl Grafton, "James E. Folsom's 1946 Campaign," *Alabama Review* 35 (1982), 172–99.

22. *Birmingham World,* June 1, 1949, 1. Birmingham District Housing Authority, *Social and Economic Survey of the Birmingham District for 1940* (Washington, D.C.: WPA. GPO, 1943), 30. Jefferson County, Alabama, Board of Health, *Health as an Indication of Housing Needs in Birmingham, Alabama* (Birmingham: n.p., 1950), 6.

23. *Allen* v. *City of Birmingham,* U.S. District Court for the Northern District of Alabama, Complaint, NAACP Papers, Part 5, Group II, Box B-129, "Alabama, *Allen* v. *City of Birmingham,* 1946," Reel 19 at 0096; and Robert L. Carter to Shores, October 21, 1946, NAACP Papers, as above, Box B-130, "Alabama, 1946–1947," Reel 20 at 0134.

24. Letter, Shores to Marshall, June 11, 1947, NAACP Papers, Part 5, Group II Box B-130, "Restrictive Covenants," Reel 20 and 0134. *Birmingham News,* August 19, 1947, 1. *Matthews* v. *City of Birmingham,* Civic action no. 6046, unreported, NAACP Papers, Part 5, Group II, Box B-130, "Alabama, 1946–1947," Reel 20 at 134.

25. *Birmingham World,* March 4, 1949, 6.

26. *Birmingham News,* March 27, 1949, 1.

27. *Birmingham News,* March 27, 1949, 1–2; *News,* August 9, 1949, 1, 4.

28. Telegram, Shores to John J. Hill, April 5, 1949, NAACP Papers, Part 5, Group II, Box B-129, "Residential Segregation," Reel 19 at 108. *Birmingham World,* March 29, 1949, 6. William A. Nunnelley, *Bull Connor* (Tuscaloosa: University of Alabama Press, 1991), 37.

29. *Birmingham World,* August 29, 1949, 8; *Birmingham World,* June 7, 1949, 6. Statement by C. E. Henderson to Birmingham Police, April 18, 1949, Police Surveillance Files, File 6.4 (a), "S. L. Green."

30. *Birmingham World,* March 29,1949, 6. Statement of E. E. Campbell to Birmingham Police, April 28, 1950, Police Surveillance Files, File 6.13, "Henderson Residence." Letter to Emory O. Jackson, June 25, 1949; and letter, Robert L. Carter to James Castor, 5 July 1949, NAACP Papers, Part 5, Group II, Box B-141, "Birmingham, Alabama, Correspondence, 1949–1950," Reel 20 at 157. Letter, A. C. Maclin to Police Chief Floyd Eddins, 20 July 1949, NAACP Papers, as above.

31. Map of area, Police Surveillance Files, File 6.4 (b), "Green, S. L."; George R. Byrum Jr. to Morgan, July 15, 1949, Morgan Papers, File 33.7, "Zoning Board, Smithfield, 1949–1950."

They included Arthur Shores; Bishop Greene; Rev. J. L. Ware, president of the Baptist Ministers Conference; Rev. H. B. Wilson, president of the Methodist Ministers Council; W. C. Patton of the Negro Business League; C. W. Hayes, superintendent of Schools; Robert Williams, the owner of Bob's Savoy Cafe; Ruth Jackson, president of Birmingham Beauty College; Mrs. L. S. Gaillard, president of the Negro Women's Clubs; E. W. Raggart, a dentist; Charles V. Henley, grand master of the Masons; A. G. Gaston, president of the Booker T. Washington Insurance Co.; and Gertrude Anderson, a housewife. Robert L. Coar, president of the Property Owners' Association, was added later. The whites were Ben Ray; George R. Byrum, chairman of the City Zoning Commission; Rev. W. Nelson Guthrie; A. Key Foster of the First National Bank; and William Mitch of the United Mine Workers. Letter from Morgan to Robert Williams, July 14, 1949, Morgan Papers, "Smithfield Zoning File"; *Birmingham World,* July 22, 1949, 1.

32. *Birmingham World,* July 29, 1949, 8. *Birmingham News,* August 9, 1949, 1; *Birmingham News,* August 15, 1949, 1.

33. A. C. Maclin to James H. Morgan, June 6, 1949; Maclin to Holt McDowell, and Maclin to Floyd Eddins, June 2, 1949; Emory O. Jackson to Thurgood Marshall, received July 25, 1949, NAACP Papers, Part 5, Group II, Box B-141, "Birmingham, Alabama, Correspondence, 1949–1950," Reel 20 at 0157. *Birmingham World,* March 29, 1949, 6; July 22, 1949, 1.

34. Connor cited in Shores to Marshall, August 1, 1949, NAACP Papers, Part 5, Group II, Box B-130, "Birmingham Alabama, Correspondence, 1949–1950," Reel 20 at 157. *NYT,* September 7, 1949, 35. Regarding Connor's states' rights views, see the announcement of his intention to run for governor: *Birmingham Post,* December 6, 1949, 1. *Birmingham News,* August 9, 1949, 4; Willis to Green, July 19, 1949, Morgan Papers, "Smithfield Zoning File." *NYT,* August 11, 1949, 26. Ordinance 709-F cited in *Monk et al.* v. *City of Birmingham et al.,* 87 F. Su 538. See also Nunnelley, *Bull Connor,* 1, 4, 36–37.

35. "Smithfield Court Resolutions," *Birmingham World,* August 19, 1949, 1. Statement of Benjamin W. Henderson to Birmingham Police, August 22, 1949, Police Surveillance Files, File 6.4 (a), "Green, S. L. Bombing, 1949." See also *Birmingham News,* August 13, 1949, 1, 2; *Birmingham World,* August 9, 1949, 1; *Birmingham World,* August 12, 1949, 1; *Birmingham World,* August 16, 1949, 1; *NYT,* August 1949, 14, 48.

36. *Birmingham World,* August 23, 1949, 1; see also Thurgood Marshall, "Memo to the President of the United States concerning Racial Discrimination by the Federal Housing Administration," in

U.S. House of Representatives, Committee on Banking and Currency, *Housing Act of 1949: Hearings,* 223–29.

37. Emory O. Jackson to Roy Wilkins, September 29, 1949, NAACP Papers, Group II, Box B-129, "Residential Segregation," Reel 19 at 0108; Horace C. Wilkinson et al., Petition for Writ of Certiorari to the Supreme Court of the United States, February 26, 1951, Morgan Papers, Monk File.

38. Thurgood Marshall, NAACP Press release dated December 15, 1949, NAACP Papers, Group II, Box B-130, "Restrictive Covenants," Reel 20 at 0157. *Monk v. City; Birmingham News,* December 13, 1949, 10.

39. *Birmingham News,* 14 April 1950, 1, 10; *Birmingham World,* 25 April 1950, 1. Emory Jackson to Roy Wilkins, 9 June 1950, NAACP Papers, Group II, Box B-130, "Restrictive Covenants," Reel 20 at 0157.

40. *Birmingham World,* April 21, 1950, 1; *Birmingham News,* April 25, 1950, 14.

41. *City of Birmingham et al.* v. *Mary Means Monk et al.,* 185 F. 2d. 859.

42. United Press, 14 December 1950, NAACP Papers, Group II, Box B-130, "Restrictive Covenants," Reel 20 at 0212. *Birmingham World,* 26 December 1950, 8.

43. City of Birmingham Zoning Ordinance, December 2, 1954, 16–18, Morgan Papers, File 33.12, "City Records, Zoning Board, 1954." Bureau of the Census, *Seventeenth Census of the United States, 1950: Population III: Census Tract Statistics, P-D5: Birmingham, Ala.* (Washington, D.C.: GPO, 1952), 7–10; *Eighteenth Census of the United States, 1960: Censuses of Population and Housing, PHC (1) 17: Birmingham, Ala., Standard Metropolitan Statistical Area* (Washington, D.C.: GPO, 1961), 16–22. See Table A.2. On the other bombings, see Bombings List, Birmingham Police Surveillance Files, File 3.1 (a), "Bombings."

44. *Richmond Afro-American,* January 29, 1949, 1–2; *Richmond Afro-American,* April 16, 1949, 6; *Richmond Times-Dispatch,* April 20, 1949, 1, 16; *Richmond Afro-American,* April 23, 1949, 7; *Richmond Afro-American,* April 30, 1B; *Richmond Times-Dispatch,* May 8, 1949, 6-B; *NYT,* January 8, 1950, 19. *NYT,* May 22, 1952, 21; "Second Home Bombed in Norfolk Housing Violence," *Jet,* September 30, 1954, 7; "Bomb Blast Rocks Negro Home in Chattanooga," *Jet,* October 17, 1957, 4; "Statement Regarding Practices of Federal and State Housing Authorities," 4–5, NAACP Papers, Group II, Box A-308, "Housing Bills, General, 1949–1951," Reel 5 at 885. On the political and social environment in Richmond, see Christopher Silver, *Twentieth-Century Richmond: Planning, Politics, and Race* (Knoxville: University of Tennessee Press, 1984), 179–80, 184–85.

45. Bureau of the Census, *Seventeenth Census of the United States, 1950: Population III: Census Tract Statistics, P-14: Dallas, Texas* (Washington, D.C.: GPO, 1952), 7. On the Trinity River Industrial District and Love Field, see Schutze, *The Accommodation,* 10–12, 61–65.

46. *DMN,* July 12, 1951, III-1; *DMN,* July 13, 1951, 1, 3; *DMN,* July 16, 1951, 1; *DMN,* August 4, 1951, III 1; *DMN,* August 10, 1951, 1; *DMN,* August 14, 1951, III-1; *DMN,* August 31, 1951, III-1; and *DMN,* September 22, 1951, 1, 4. On the grand jury report see Schutze, *The Accommodation,* 1, 67–74. For Dallas census data, see Bureau of the Census, *Seventeenth Census, 1950: Population III: Dallas, Texas,* 9; *Eighteenth Census, 1960: Census of Population and Housing: Dallas, Texas* (Washington, D.C.: GPO, 1961), 18. See Table A.3.

NOTES TO CHAPTER 7 (PAGES 115 TO 132)

1. Reprinted by permission from Lorraine Hansberry, *A Raisin in the Sun* (New York: Vintage, 1994), 100.

2. Quotations are from "The Race Problem Moves North," 70. See also "Race Trouble in the North . . Chicago: Where Whites and Negroes Battle Again," *USNWR,* August 9, 1957, 31–33; Morley Cassidy, "Northern Negro's Advice: 'Talk Out Loud' About Race Troubles," *USNWR,* August 23, 1957, 74; "When a Negro Moves into a Northern Town," *USNWR,* August 30, 1957, 29–32; Loren Miller, "Statement of Loren Miller," *Hearings Before the United States Commission on Civil Rights: Hearings Held in Los Angeles, January 25–26, 1960* (Washington, D.C.: GPO, 1960), 257;

incidents cited in Los Angeles Urban League, "Minority Housing in Metropolitan Los Angeles," in *Hearings Held in Los Angeles, January 25–26, 1960*, 157–59.

3. Housing and Home Finance Agency, *Our Nonwhite Population and Its Housing: The Changes Between 1950 and 1960* (Washington, D.C.: GPO, 1963), 2. See Table A.1.

4. See Jackson, *Crabgrass Frontier*, 231–45; Fox, *Metropolitan America*, 52–54, 60–65; Elaine Tyler May, *Homeward Bound: American Families in the Cold War Era* (New York: Basic Books, 1988), 162–82; David Halberstam, *The Fifties* (New York: Villard, 1993), 132–43. For the situation in Philadelphia, see Dorothy Sutherland Jayne, "'First Families': A Study of Twenty Pioneering Families and Their Experience as the First Blacks in All-White Neighborhoods, between 1946 and 1959" (Philadelphia: Commission on Human Relations, 1960), in NAACP Papers, Group III, Box A-167, "Housing Pennsylvania, Philadelphia, 1956–1965," LOC, Manuscript Division.

5. *House and Home*, April 1953, 47. National Urban League, Inc., "The National Housing Situation As It Affects the Non-White Population . . . A Statement Submitted to the President of the United States," June 18, 1954, in NAACP Papers, Part 5, Group II, Box A-312, "Housing, General, 1954, July–December," LOC, Manuscript Division. Emphasis in original. The remark regarding New York City comes from "The Race Problem Moves North," *USNWR*, August 23, 1957, 70.

6. See Table A.4. Bureau of the Census, *Sixteenth Census, 1940: Population and Housing Statistics for Census Tract and Community Areas, Chicago, Ill.* (Washington, D.C.: GPO, 1943), 56–58; *Seventeenth Census, 1950: Population III: Chicago, Ill.* (Washington, D.C.: GPO, 1952), 38, 57; *Census of Population and Housing, 1960: Chicago, Ill.* (Washington, D.C.: GPO, 1961), 59, 61, 63, 79–81.

7. Rossi and Dentler, *The Politics of Urban Renewal*, 19–22; regarding white flight to the suburbs, see Table A.5. Bureau of the Census, Series P-28, *Special Census Series* (Washington, D.C.: GPO, 1955–1957).

8. Thomas H. Wright, *Report of the Anti-Racial Demonstrations and Violence Against the Home and Persons of Mr. and Mrs. Roscoe Johnson, 7153 St. Lawrence Avenue, July 25, 1949*, 2–3, 11, 30, 80, and Appendix B, 1–5, NAACP Papers, Part 5, Group II, Box B-121, "Racial Tension, General, 1949," Reel 19 at 002. The chant is cited in Johnson, *Call Me Neighbor, Call Me Friend*, 2.

9. *Chicago Defender*, March 3, 1945, 6; Hirsch, *Making the Second Ghetto*, 54–56.

10. NAACP to Thomas Wright, June 14, 1951, NAACP Papers, Part 5, Group II, Box B-130, "Residential Segregation, Cicero, Ill., July 1951," Reel 19 at 492.

11. Homer A. Jack, "Cicero Nightmare," *The Nation*, July 20, 1951, 54–56; Byron S. Miller, "Cicero's Covenants," *New Republic*, August 6, 1951, 11–13. Walter White, "Disgrace in Cicero," *New York Herald-Tribune*, July 23, 1951, NAACP Papers, Part 5, Group II, Box B-130, "Residential Segregation, Cicero, Ill., July 1951," Reel 19 at 492.

12. *NYT*, July 13, 1951, 38; *NYT*, July 15, 1951, 34, D 2; "Cicero Nightmare," 64–65.

13. *NYT*, July 13, 1951, 38; *NYT*, July 14, 1951, 28; "Terror in Cicero," *Newsweek Magazine*, July 23, 1951, 17; "Ugly Nights in Cicero," *Time Magazine*, July 23, 1951, 11. The Clark quotation comes from Harvey Clark Jr., "A Cicero Postscript," *Interracial Review* article, NAACP Papers, Part 5, Group II, Box B-130, "Residential Segregation, Cicero, Ill., 1952–1953," Reel 19 at 739.

14. *NYT*, July 13, 1951, 38; *NYT*, July 14, 1951, 28; White, "Disgrace in Cicero."

15. NAACP News Release, October 11, 1951; *Chicago Daily Sun-Times*, September 6, 1951; NAACP News Release, September 20, 1951; NAACP News Release, December 13, 1951, in NAACP Papers, Part 5, Group II, Box B-130, "Cicero, Ill., September–December, 1951," Reel 19 at 661. Walter White, *New York Herald-Tribune*, October 3, 1951, 1, 5, NAACP Papers as above, Box A-313, "Illinois, 1953–55," Reel 9 at 078; NAACP News Release, June 5, 1952; Clipping, *NYT*, March 1953, NAACP Papers as above, "Cicero, Ill., 1952–1953," Reel 19 at 739. Regarding the Clarks' move to Connecticut, see *NYT*, August 11, 1951, 28.

16. From a transcript of a radio interview by CBS, *The World Today*, Sunday, April 25, 1954, 9, in NAACP Papers, Part 5, Group II, Box A-313, "Housing, Illinois, 1953–1955," Reel 9 at 157; see also CCHR, "'The Trumbull Park Homes Disturbances,' Documentary Report no. 1, August 1953–March 1954," May 14, 1954, NAACP Papers as above, Reel 9 at 131.

17. Aerial bombs are fireworks that "when exploded, propel a second charge that explodes with a brilliant flash" and is accompanied by a loud explosive noise: CCHR, "'The Trumbull Park Homes Disturbances,' Documentary Report no. 1, August 1953–March 1954," May 14, 1954, 5, NAACP Papers, Group II, Box A-313, "Illinois, 1953–1955," Reel 9 at 131. Chicago Negro Chamber of

Commerce, "Report to the People on Chicago Citizens Mobilization for Law Enforcement," 2, NAACP Papers, as above, Reel 9 at 127.

18. Transcript from *The World Today,* 5, NAACP Papers, Part 5, Group II, Box A-313, "Housing, Illinois, 1953–1955," Reel 9 at 157.

19. Ibid.

20. Martin H. Kennelly, cited in *Council Against Discrimination News* 2 (1954), 3, NAACP Papers, Part 5, Group II, Box A-313, "Housing, Illinois, 1953–1955," Reel 9 at 143. Transcript from *The World Today,* 4, and "The Herald," September 16, 1954, NAACP Papers, as above, Reel 9 at 157 and 180; "'Too Much Sacrifice' Forces Family From Chicago Riot Site," *Jet,* May 13, 1954, 4–5.

21. NAACP Press Release, May 11, 1954, NAACP Papers, Part 5, Group II, Box A-313, "Housing, Illinois, 1953–1955," Reel 9 at 180; Assistant Attorney General Olney to White, July 3, 1954; and statement by Trumbull Park blacks through the NAACP, September 6, 1954, NAACP Papers, Part 5, Group II, Box A-313, "Housing, Illinois, 1953–1955," Reel 9 at 185; *Housing Authority of San Francisco* v. *Banks,* 98 L. Ed. 1114 (1954).

22. "Race Trouble Moves North," *USNWR,* March 8, 1957, 27–32; United States Commission on Civil Rights, *Report of the United States Commission on Civil Rights, 1959* (Washington, D.C.: GPO, 1959), 431, 434–35.

23. "Race Trouble Moves North," 29; "Chicago: Where Whites and Negroes Battle Again," 32; U.S. Commission on Civil Rights, *Report, 1959,* 431, 443–44.

24. Darden et al., *Detroit: Race and Uneven Development,* 77–80, 120; Lynch, *Black Urban Condition,* 428–30; Virginius Delaney, "A Frank Talk to North and South About Integration," *USNWR,* March 15, 1957, 114.

25. "A Brief Analysis of Housing Incidents, 2/21/55," CCR-HRD Papers, Part I, Series III, Box 2, "Housing Incident Reports, 1955, 1961, 1966"; Darden et al., *Detroit,* 126–27. "A Northern City 'Sitting on Lid,' of Racial Trouble," 38.

26. "A Brief Analysis of Housing Incidents, 2/21/55," and an unidentified, hand-written chart of incidents in CCR-HRD Papers, Part I, Series III, Box 2, "Housing Incident Reports, 1955, 1961, 1966"; "A Northern City 'Sitting on Lid' of Racial Trouble," 38; *Trends in Housing* 1, no. 4 Feb.–March, 1957, 1, in NAACP Papers, Part 5, Group III, Box A-162, "Housing, NCDH, 1956–1957," LOC, Manuscript Division.

27. Clipping, *Detroit News,* July 14, 1963, CCR-HRD Papers, Part I, Series I, Box 15, "*Detroit News,* November 1963–October 1964"; Richard J. Peck, Detroit Urban League, "Summary of Known Improvement Association Activities in the Past Two Years, 1955–1957," CCR-HRD Papers, Part 3, Series IV, Box 25, "Improvement Associations General List"; Detroit NAACP Branch, Executive Secretary's Report, November 11, 1956, in NAACP Papers, Part 5, Group III, Box A-160, "Housing Michigan, Detroit 1956–1964," LOC, Manuscript Division.

28. Miami had an index of racial dissimilarity ratings of 97.9 in 1940, 97.8 in 1950, and 97.9 in 1960: Taeuber and Taeuber, *Negroes in Cities,* 41; Table A.1, below.

29. David Leon Chandler, *Henry Flagler: The Astonishing Life and Times of the Visionary Robber Baron Who Founded Florida* (New York: Macmillan, 1986), 149–57, 173–86, 231; Paul S. George, "Colored Town: Miami's Black Community, 1896–1930," *Florida Historical Quarterly* 56 (1978), 432–37; Bruce Porter and Marvin Dunn, *The Miami Riot of 1980: Crossing the Bounds* (Lexington: Lexington Books, 1984), 1–9.

30. Murray, *Negro Handbook, 1942,* 184–85; Porter and Dunn, *Miami Riot of 1980,* 7–9; Frank B. Sessa, "Miami in 1926," *Tequesta* 16 (1956), 30–36; *Miami Herald,* September 25, 1951, B1 (*Miami Herald* hereinafter cited as *MH*).

31. *Race Relations* 3 (August–September 1945), 8; Murray, ed., *Negro Handbook 1949,* 189; Abrams, *Forbidden Neighbors,* 120–35; and discussion in text below.

32. *MH,* September 24, 1951, 6; *MH,* September 25, 1951, B1.

33. *MH,* September 24, 1951, B1; *MH,* September 23, 1951, 8; *MH,* September 19, 1951, B1, and September 20, 1951, 10. *Miami Life* cited in Abrams, *Forbidden Neighbors,* 124.

34. *MH,* September 23, 1951, 1, 8; *MH,* September 25, 1951, B1; *Florida Times-Union,* September 23, 1951, 23 (*Florida Times-Union* hereinafter cited as *FTU*); *FTU,* December 1, 1951, 17.

35. White cited in *FTU,* December 29, 1951, 2; *MH,* September 23, 1951, 12; see also Abrams, *Forbidden Neighbors,* 125–26.

36. *MH,* October 27, 1951, B1; *MH,* October 30, 1951, B1; *MH,* November 9, 1951, C1; *MH,* November 17, 1951, B1; *MH,* November 21, 1951, 1.

37. *MH,* November 22, 1951, B1; *MH,* November 29, 1951, B1; *MH,* December 25, 1951, 4; *FTU,* December 3, 1951, 18; *FTU,* December 28, 1951, 14; Abrams, *Forbidden Neighbors,* 129.

38. The total population of Metropolitan Miami grew during the decade from about 495,000 to over 935,000. The population of the suburb of Hialeah, for example, increased by nearly three and one-half times to total almost 67,000, of whom only 872 were African American. Between 1950 and 1960, Liberty City expanded eastward into Edison Center. According to an analysis of census tracts, only four blacks lived in tract A-19, the tract that had included Edison Center, in 1950. More than 7,000 whites lived in the tract. In 1960, with the section now divided into two census tracts, the black community numbered 11,677 persons, whereas whites counted barely 3,000. By 1970, only 219 white persons remained. See Bureau of the Census, *Seventeenth Census of the United States, 1950: Population II: Characteristics of the Population, Part 10, Florida* (Washington, D.C.: GPO, 1952), 57–58; *Seventeenth Census of the United States, 1950: Population III: Census Tract Statistics, P-D31: Miami, Fla.* (Washington, D.C.: GPO, 1952), 6–10; *Eighteenth Census of the United States, 1960: Censuses of Population and Housing, Census Tracts, PHC(1)-90: Miami, Fla., SMSA* (Washington, D.C.: GPO, 1961), 15–16, 25–26; *Nineteenth Census of the United States, 1970: Censuses of Population and Housing, Census Tracts, PHC(1)–129: Miami, Fla., Standard Metropolitan Statistical Area* (Washington, D.C.: GPO, 1973), 1, 6–7, 13–14, 20–21.

On the county's response to the violence, see *MH,* December 11, 1951, B1; *MH,* January 10, 1952, B1; *MH,* January 18, 1952, 20; *MH,* January 23, 1952, C1; *FTU,* December 6, 1951, 13; *FTU,* December 27, 1951, 6.

39. Loren Miller, "Statement of Loren Miller," *Hearings Before the United States Commission on Civil Rights: Hearings Held in Los Angeles, January 25–26, 1960* (Washington, D.C.: GPO, 1960), 257; Los Angeles Urban League, "Minority Housing in Metropolitan Los Angeles," *Hearings Held in Los Angeles, January 25–26, 1960,* 156–59; Donald J. Hager (Los Angeles Urban League), "Statement of Donald J. Hager," *Hearings Held in Los Angeles, January 25–26, 1960,* 139–40; *California Eagle,* January 5, 1950, 1; *California Eagle,* February 7, 1952, 1; *California Eagle,* February 14, 1952, 1.

40. *Barrows v. Jackson,* 73 S.Ct. 1031 (1953). Similar suits had been brought in Missouri (1949), Oklahoma (1951), and Michigan (1952). Missouri's Supreme Court ruled that such suits were permissible. Oklahoma's Supreme Court concluded that both whites and blacks were liable for damages, but Michigan's court decided that damages could not be collected. See "What the Branches Are Doing" section, *The Crisis* 59 (1952), 590–91; see also Fred C. Ash, "The Last of the Restrictive Covenants," *Appraisal Journal* 21 (1953), 595–97.

41. *California Eagle,* September 8, 1949, 1, 3; *California Eagle,* September 15, 1949, 1.

42. These incidents and others are recounted in the *California Eagle,* from 1949 to 1953. See August 18, 1949, 1; August 25, 1949, 1; September 15, 1949, 1; February 2, 1950, 1; June 5, 1950, 1; June 16, 1950, 4; June 30, 1950, 1, 4; August 4, 1950, 3; January 3, 1952, 1; March 20, 1952, 1–2; April 3, 1942, 1–2; April 24, 1952, 1; May 1, 1952, 1; May 29, 1952, 1; June 19, 1; September 11, 1952, 1; October 9, 1952, 1; October 16, 1952, 1. See also Health and Welfare Dept., Los Angeles Urban League, "Minority Housing in Metropolitan Los Angeles," Summer 1959, in *Hearings Before the United States Commission on Civil Rights, Los Angeles, San Francisco, 1960* (Washington, D.C.: GPO, 1960), 144–57.

43. See weekly front-page coverage in the *California Eagle,* March 20, 1952, through April 17, 1952, and June 12, 1952, through July 3, 1952; see also *California Eagle,* May 22, 1952, 1.

44. The Compton story has been pieced together from reports in the *California Eagle,* from February 19, 1953, through July 23, 1953. An *Eagle* reporter, Bob Ellis, wrote a series of articles reviewing events, entitled "The Compton Story." They appeared in the *Eagle* during May and June 1953.

45. See front-page coverage: *California Eagle,* February 19, 1953, through June 18, 1953.

46. See front-page coverage in the *California Eagle,* April 16, 1953, through July 23, 1953; see also Bob Ellis, "The Compton Story," in *California Eagle,* May 14, 1953, 1, 8.

47. *California Eagle,* June 25, 1953 1; *California Eagle,* July 2, 1953, 1.

48. NAACP Papers, Part 5, Group II, Box A-309, "Housing, California, 1953–1955," Reel 6 at 201.

49. Of the ninety-five incidents of exclusion reported to the Los Angeles County Commission on Human Relations between July 1950 and June 26, 1959, seventy incidents occurred to blacks. And note that none of the incidents occurring in Compton in 1953 was recorded by the commission. See Los Angeles Urban League, "Minority Housing in Metropolitan Los Angeles," in *Hearings Held in Los Angeles, January 25–26, 1960*, 158–59; "Statement of Loren Miller," *Hearings Held in Los Angeles, January 25–26, 1960*, 251–52, 260.

50. Frank Mankiewicz, "Jim Crow Housing on the West Coast," *The New Leader*, May 3, 1954, reprinted in U.S. Commission on Civil Rights, *Hearings Before the United States Commission on Civil Rights, Los Angeles, San Francisco, 1960* (Washington, D.C.: GPO, 1960); Lewis G. Watts, "Racial Trends in Seattle, Washington, 1958," *The Crisis* 65 (1958), 333–38. Lorna Marple, president of Portland branch of the NAACP to Madison Jones, special assistant for housing, January 12, 1956; and *The Oregonian*, April 18, 1957, in NAACP Papers, Part 5, Group III, Box A-167, "Housing, Oregon, Portland, 1956–1964," LOC, Manuscript Division.

51. The great Brooklyn Dodger, Jackie Robinson, also experienced difficulties. In 1953, Robinson resided in Jamaica, Long Island, but wanted to find a home in the "exclusive backcountry" in North Stamford, Connecticut. On several occasions, however, when he and his wife voiced interest in a property, they found it inexplicably removed from the market. Rachel Robinson blamed the difficulties on realtors and "the 'gentlemen's agreement' that binds brokers to an unwritten law among themselves." She told a reporter that when she asked some of the brokers why she was having so much trouble, they insisted that they were not discriminating but that neighbors would object. The constitution of the Greenwich real estate board prevented members from selling or renting to "any race or nationality that would tend to bring down real estate values."

Robinson's plight slowly caught the public's attention. The *Bridgeport Herald* reported his difficulty at the end of October, but the public did not take notice until December, when a group of Stamford ministers, along with some business people, circulated a letter in support of the Robinsons. The circular declared that excluding people solely because of their race "could lessen the spiritual, economic and social development" of the area. Some of their parishioners, however, believed that the ministers had "blown up the issue," and they feared the admission of blacks to the area would "jeopardize investments." The story's notoriety proved enough to prompt the developer to ignore a gentlemen's agreement. He sold the Robinsons a home on a 5-acre lakeside lot for $65,000.

In a follow-up article in 1955, the *New York Herald-Tribune* noted that the Robinsons felt "at home" in the new neighborhood and that, according to Rachel Robinson, the neighbors had "accepted [them] as just another family." One white neighbor did move out because of the Robinsons. Answering some criticism that the Robinsons were abandoning the black community, Rachel Robinson insisted that "we feel . . that our children will have most of their social contacts with Negro children. We are proud of our race," she declared. "We do feel, however, that Negroes and whites and other peoples should learn to live together in friendship." See reprint of *Bridgeport Herald* article, October 25, 1953, NAACP Papers, Part 5, Group II, Box A-309, "Housing, Connecticut, 1953–1955," Reel 6 at 670; *NYT*, December 12, 1953, 21; and *NYT*, December 18, 1953, 20; Don Ross, "Jackie Robinsons Feel At Home in Stamford," *New York Herald Tribune*, June 13, 1955, in NAACP Papers, as above, Reel 6 at 210.

A similar fate also awaited Cleveland Indian Larry Doby, the first African American to play in the American League, when he tried to find a house in his hometown of Paterson, New Jersey, in 1949; the jazz pianist and composer Erroll Garner met resistance that left him homeless for months in Los Angeles in 1957; prizefighter and one-time heavyweight champion Sonny Liston was forced to back out of a rental agreement (valued at $3,500 for a month) in Coral Gables, Florida, where he intended to train for his first bout with Cassius Clay in 1964 because whites in the neighborhood objected. See *Richmond Afro-American*, January 8, 1949, 5; NAACP Papers, Group III, Box A-157, "Housing, 'G,'" LOC Manuscript Division; "Sonny Liston Hit by Housing J'Crow," *ADW*, January 25, 1964, 1.

52. "Willie Mays Is Denied S.F. House—Race Issue," *San Francisco Chronicle* (hereinafter *SFC*), November 14, 1957, 1, 22; David Perlman, "Willie Mays Buys S.F. Home After Race Dispute,"

SFC, November 15, 1957, 1–2; "Housing a Giant," 2–5. See also statement by CCU Executive Director, Frank Quinn, in U.S. Commission on Civil Rights, *Hearings Before the United States Commission on Civil Rights, Los Angeles and San Francisco, 1960* (Washington, D.C.: GPO, 1960), 546–48; statement by Mayor Christopher George in U.S. Commission on Civil Rights, *Hearings*, 474.

53. "Willie Mays Is Denied S.F. House—Race Issue," *SFC*, November 14, 1957, 1, 22; Perlman, "Willie Mays Buys S.F. Home After Race Dispute," *SFC*, November 15, 1957, 1–2; Letter to the Editor, *SFC*, November 19, 1957, 24; "Housing a Giant," 4, 7.

54. "Housing a Giant," 6; Perlman, "Willie Mays Buys S.F. Home After Race Dispute," *SFC*, November 15, 1957, 1–2. The stoning is reported in Willie Mays with Lou Sahadi, *Say Hey: The Autobiography of Willie Mays* (New York: Pocket Books, 1988), 151.

55. "Housing a Giant," 5, 7; "NAACP Says Home Bias Occurs Daily," *SFC*, November 15, 1957, 2; "Ban on Bias In S.F. Home Sales Sought," *SFC*, November 17, 1957, 1; "San Francisco's Welcome to Mays," *SFC*, November 15, 1957, 20; Letter, *SFC*, November 2, 1957, 20; "Willie Mays Buys N.Y. Home," *Chicago Defender*, June 4, 1960, 1.

NOTES TO CHAPTER 8 (PAGES 133 TO 149)

1. National Committee Against Discrimination in Housing (NCDH), "A Call on the President of the United States for the Issuance of an Executive Order Ending Discrimination in All Federal Housing Programs," September 1961, 3, NAACP Papers, 1993 Edition, Box 21, "Housing, NCDH, Miscellaneous, 1961–1965," Library of Congress, Manuscript Division, Washington, D.C. (hereinafter NAACP Papers, 1993 Edition, . . . LOC, Manuscript Division).

2. "10 Amazing Years: 1947–1957, a Decade of Miracles," *USNWR*, December 27, 1957, 42–53.

3. "10 Amazing Years," 42; *Brown* v. *Board of Education of Topeka*, 347 U.S. 483 (1954), 349 U.S 483 (1955).

4. Adorno et al., *The Authoritarian Personality*, 6, 152–55, 385, and passim.

5. Allport, *The Nature of Prejudice*, xv, 73, 130, 359–63, 426–32, 469.

6. See Richard Kluger, *Simple Justice: The History of* Brown *v.* Board of Education *and Black America's Struggle for Equality* (New York: Vintage, 1975), 314–45; Tushnet, *Making Civil Rights Law*, 158–61, 179–81, 348; Mark Chesler, Joseph Sanders, and Debra Kalmuss, *Social Science in Court: Mobilizing Experts in the School Desegregation Cases* (Madison: University of Wisconsin Press, 1988), passim.

7. Kluger, *Simple Justice*, 308–9; Clifford Orwin, "All Quiet on the (Post) Western Front?" *The Public Interest* 123 (Spring 1996), 4–6. UNESCO *Statement on Race* is cited in Howard Shorr, "'Race Prejudice Is Not Inborn—It Is Learned': The Exhibit Controversy at the Los Angeles Museum of History, Science and Art, 1950–1952," *California History* 69 (1990), 278–79.

8. The whole question reads, "In general, do you think Negroes are as intelligent as white people—that is can they learn things just as well if they are given the same education and training?" Cited in Commission on Race and Housing (CRH), *Where Shall We Live? Report of the Commission on Race and Housing* (Berkeley: University of California Press, 1958), 16.

9. Vice President Richard Nixon, "Nixon Says Racial Integration Offsets Communist Propaganda," *Jet*, February 4, 1954, 6–7; NCDH, "A Call on the President," 18; Carl M. Brauer, *John F. Kennedy and the Second Reconstruction* (New York: Columbia University Press, 1977), 77–78; the phrase "dark-skinned diplomats" comes from Richard Reeves, *President Kennedy: Profile of Power* (New York: Touchstone, 1993), 60; see also Mary L. Dudziak, "Desegregation as a Cold War Imperative," in Paul Finkelman, ed., *The Era of Integration and Civil Rights, 1930–1990* (New York: Garland, 1992), 152–70; Dennis Clark, "Urban Renewal and Intergroup Relations," NAACP Papers, Part III, Box A-167, "Housing Pennsylvania, Philadelphia, 1956–1965," LOC, Manuscript Division.

10. Walter White is cited in Camille De Rose, *The Camille De Rose Story* (Chicago: Camille De Rose, 1953), 191. Walter Winchell is cited in John T. Madigan, ABC News Director, to White, July

25, 1951, NAACP Papers, Part 5, Group II, Box B-130, "Residential Segregation, Cicero Illinois, 1952–1953," Reel 19 at 739; Governor Dewey is cited in *NYT*, August 1, 1951, 3; Corp. Allen W. Lyons to Sen. Paul Douglas, March 8, 1954, NAACP Papers, Part 5, Group II, Box A-313, "Illinois, 1953–1955," Reel 9 at 125.

11. "Transcript of *The World Today*," 5.

12. Foley and Green statements occur in Committee on Banking and Currency, *Housing Act of 1949: Hearings*, 23 and 538. Senator Ellender is cited in CQS, *Housing a Nation*, 25.

13. See Harvey Klehr, John Earl Haynes, and Fridrikh Igorevich Frisov, *The Secret World of American Communism* (New Haven: Yale University Press, 1995), 12. The story from the Bradens' perspective occurs in Anne Braden, *The Wall Between* (New York: Monthly Review, 1958).

It is difficult to pin down communist activity in this case because the Bradens undeniably shared a labor-oriented ideology. But it has not been proved categorically that they were members of the Communist Party, let alone allied to a Soviet cell. A confessed communist, Alberta Ahearn, told the court that she had known the Bradens as members of the Communist Party between 1951 and 1954. Carl Braden, however, continued to deny the allegation, even before the House Un-American Activities Committee. In 1959, Braden was convicted of contempt of Congress for failing to answer HUAC's questions and sentenced to one year in prison. See Braden, *The Wall Between*, 182–214; Aldon Morris, *The Origins of the Civil Rights Movement: Black Communities Organizing for Change* (New York: Free Press, 1984), 166–73; Kenneth O'Reilly, *Racial Matters: The F.B.I.'s Secret File on Black America, 1960–1972* (New York: Free Press, 1989), 43–44, 120, 128. On Braden's conviction, see Michael Friedly with David Gallen, *Martin Luther King Jr.: The FBI File* (New York: Carroll and Graf, 1993), 117. See also David J. Garrow, *The FBI and Martin Luther King Jr.: From "Solo" to Memphis* (New York: Norton, 1981), 25.

On the NAACP's position on communism, see Tushnet, *Making Civil Rights Law*, 295, 366; on Reuther's actions, see Klehr, Haynes, and Frisov, *Secret World of American Communism*, 12. My search of the *Guide to the Records of the Subversive Activities Control Board, 1950–1972*, ed. Paul L. Kesaris, Library of Congress, Microform Division, Washington, D.C.; a search of U.S. Department of Justice, *General Index, 1928–1951*, RG 60, Archives II, College Park, Maryland (courtesy of Archivist Fred J. Romanski, June 1996); and of White House Office, Office of the Special Assistant for National Security Affairs (Robert Cutler, Dillon Anderson, and Gordon Gray), *Records, 1952–1961*, FBI Series, including *The Communist Party, USA, and Radical Organizations, 1953–1960*, Robert E. Lester, coordinator, Dwight D. Eisenhower Library, Abilene, Kansas (courtesy of Archivist David J. Haight, June 1996), turned up nothing incriminating against NCDH affiliates.

14. "Transcript of *The World Today*," 5. Jackie Robinson cited in Dudziak, "Desegregation as a Cold War Imperative," 108.

15. For Allport's role in the CRH, see *Where Shall We Live?* v; Morris, *The Origins of the Civil Rights Movement*, passim.

16. NCDH's founding members were Amalgamated Clothing Workers of America-CIO; American Baptist Convention; Council on Christian Social Progress; ACLU; American Council on Human Rights; American Ethical Union; American Friends Service Committee; American Jewish Committee; American Jewish Congress; American Newspaper Guild; American Veterans Committee; Americans for Democratic Action; Anti-Defamation League of B'nai B'rith; Brotherhood of Sleeping Car Porters; committees of the Congregational Christian Churches; CORE; Cooperative League of the USA; Friendship House; Jewish Labor Committee; League for Industrial Democracy; NAACP; NAIRO; National Council of Churches of Christ; National Council of Negro Women; National Urban League; Protestant Episcopal Church–Department of Christian Social Relations; United Presbyterian Church–Office of Church and Society; United Auto Workers–CIO; United Steel Workers–CIO.

17. On the Urban League, see, for example, Atlanta Urban League, *A Report of the Housing Activities of the Atlanta Urban League* (Atlanta: n.p., 1951); and *Factors Influencing and Restraining the Housing Mobility of Negroes in Metropolitan Detroit*, in Papers of the Detroit Urban League, Bentley Historical Library, University of Michigan, Ann Arbor, Michigan. The UAW's efforts are exemplified by its work in Milpitas, California, discussed below, *Trends in Housing* 1, no. 2 (October 1956). On CORE, see *Trends in Housing* 6, no. 6 (November–December 1962); NAACP Papers, Part III, Box A-163, "Housing, New York—Brooklyn, 1956–1957"; August Meier and Elliott M. Rudwick, *CORE:*

A Study in the Civil Rights Movement, 1942–1968 (Urbana: University of Illinois Press, 1975), 183–86. On the American Friends, see James R. Ralph Jr., *Northern Protest: Martin Luther King Jr., Chicago, and the Civil Rights Movement* (Cambridge: Harvard University Press, 1993), 99–100.

18. Robert C. Weaver, "Cicero Demands Immediate Action by All Responsible Americans," RG 207, HUD Program Files, Box 751, "National Committee Against Discrimination in Housing," Archives II; August Maier (NAACP Newark Branch) to Raymond Foley, October 25, 1951. Members of these other groups also lobbied Foley at HHFA: the Human Relations Council of Nutley, N.J.; the Newark Teachers Union; the Frontiers Club of Dayton, Ohio; the Allegheny County (Pa.) Council on Civil Rights; and the Essex County (N.J.) Intergroup Council. See RG 207, HUD Program Files, Box 53, "Racial Relations 650, 1951." On Foley's meeting with the Chicago officials, see B. T. McGraw to Raymond Foley, October 20, 1951, RG 207, HUD, Program Files, Box 751, "Cicero," Archives II.

19. Charles Abrams, "Letter to the President, November 1, 1961, Detailing NCDH's Position Advocating the Coverage by the Executive Order of All Federally-aided and Supervised Financial Institutions," in NCDH, "A Call on the President," Section III; *Trends in Housing*, 1956–1957, and Frances Levenson, Press Release, July 23, 1956, in NAACP Papers, Part III, Box-164, "General Office Files, NCDH," LOC, Manuscript Division; Juliet Z. Saltman, *Open Housing as a Social Movement: Challenge, Conflict and Change* (Lexington: Heath, 1971), 29–31, 131.

20. *Trends in Housing* 1, no. 2 (October 1956), 1–3, 8. Evidence shows that *Trends* was read by people in power: HHFA race relations adviser Joseph R. Ray, cited the Milpitas example of voluntarism at work during a speech before the American Missionary Association at Fisk University in 1957. See Joseph R. Ray, "Federal Policies and Programs for the Elimination of Housing Discrimination," 5, RG 207, HUD Program Files, Box 749, "Speeches–1954," Archives II.

21. On the close ties between the NAACP Housing Committee and CRH and on Madison Jones's correspondence with Davis McEntire, see NAACP Papers, Part 5, Group II, Box A-313, "Housing, Madison Jones, 1955," LOC, Manuscript Division. See also Laurenti, *Property Values and Race*, v, 30–33, 41–43, 47–65.

A sample bibliography of NCDH- and CRH-sponsored studies includes NCDH, *How the Federal Government Builds Ghettos* (New York: NCDH, 1967); NCDH—Brotherhood-in-Action Conference, New York, 1965, *Affirmative Action to Achieve Integration: A Report Based on the NCDH Brotherhood-in-Action Conference*, New York: NCDH, 1966); CRH, *Where Shall We Live?*; Charles Abrams, *Forbidden Neighbors*; Luigi M. Laurenti, "Effects of Nonwhite Purchases on Market Prices of Residences," *Appraisal Monthly*, July 1952; Belden Morgan, "Values in Transition Areas: Some New Concepts," *The Review of the Society of Residential Appraisers*, March 1952; E. F. Schietinger, "Race and Residential Market Values in Chicago," *Land Economics*, November 1954; John McDermott and Dennis Clark, "Helping the Panic Neighborhood: A Philadelphia Approach," *Interracial Review*, August 1955; Glazer and McEntire, *Studies in Housing and Minority Groups*; George Grier and Eunice Grier, *Privately Developed Interracial Housing* (Berkeley: University of California Press, 1960).

22. Tushnet offers the most complete analysis of the LDF's activities during the early 1950s in Tushnet, *Making Civil Rights Law*, 137–68. For the NAACP housing statement, see NAACP Report to NCDH, 1953, from 1953 St. Louis Annual Meeting, June 23–28, "Statement on Housing," in NAACP Papers, Part 5, Group II, Box A-311, "Housing, General, 1950–1952," Reel 7 at 672. Robert C. Weaver cited at NCDH Conference, March 14, 1955, in RG 207, HUD Program Files, Box 745, "Conferences," Archive II.

23. *Banks et al. v. Housing Authority of San Francisco et al.*, 120 Cal A 2d 1 (1953).

24. Ibid.

25. The cases to which the California court referred were the University of Texas Law School case, *Sweatt v. Painter*, 339 U.S. 629 (1950); *McLaurin v. Oklahoma State Regents for Higher Education*, 339 U.S. 637 (1950); and the Southern Railway segregated dining car case, *Henderson v. United States*, 339 U.S. 816 (1950). See *Banks v. Housing Authority*; see also *Housing Authority of San Francisco v. Banks*, 98 L.Ed 1114 (1954).

26. *Banks v. Housing Authority*; and *Housing Authority v. Banks*.

27. Maybank, cited in CQS, *Housing a Nation*, 32. See also Maybank, cited in a telegram, Clarence Mitchell of the D.C. branch of the NAACP to Walter White, June 4, 1954, in NAACP Papers, Part 5, Group II, Box A-311, "Housing, General, February–September, 1953," Reel 7 at 800.

28. Madison S. Jones, "An NAACP Branch Housing Committee: How It Functions—What It Does," in NAACP Papers, Part 5, Group II, Box A-313, "Housing, Manuals for Branches, 1953," Reel 9 at 584; see also Jack Wood to Madison Jones, June 21, 1963, NAACP Papers, Part III, Box A-164, "Housing, New York City, 1960–1965," LOC, Manuscript Division.

29. Jones, "An NAACP Branch Housing Committee," 4.

30. Files of other housing groups, such as the Race Relations Service of HHFA, are filled with similar stories. See Record Group 207, General Records of the Department of Housing and Urban Development, Housing and Home Finance Agency, Subject Files 1947–1960, "Race Relations," Archives II, College Park, MD (hereinafter HUD, HHFA Subject Files).

31. Mrs. Esther Barr to Thurgood Marshall, March 29, 1956, in NAACP Papers, Part III, Box A-165, "Housing, NYC, 1956–1959," LOC, Manuscript Division.

32. Ibid.

33. Ibid.

34. Ibid.

35. Ibid.

36. Memo by Madison S. Jones, April 5, 1956, in NAACP Papers, Part III, Box A-165, "Housing, New York City, 1956–1959," LOC, Manuscript Division.

37. For a discussion of the NAACP's campaign in Hollywood, see Thomas Cripps, *Black Film as Genre* (Bloomington: Indiana University Press, 1978).

38. Nathan Zucker, "Dynamic Films: A Presentation on a Motion Picture on the Subject of Minority Housing," "Structure and Format," 1, in NAACP Papers, Part III, Box A-157, "Housing, Films, 1956–1958," LOC, Manuscript Division.

39. Dynamic Films, Screenplay of "All the Way Home," in NAACP Papers, Part III, Box A-157, "Housing, Films, 1956–1958," LOC, Manuscript Division.

40. Ibid.

41. Ibid.

42. "The Rock," a film treatment by Muriel Rukeyser (Dynamic Films), in NAACP Papers, Part III, Box A-157, "Housing, Films, 1956–1958," LOC, Manuscript Division.

43. Helen Ruth Kristt (Dynamic Films) to Madison Jones, June 14, 1957, in NAACP Papers, Part III, Box A-157, "Housing, Films, 1956–1958," LOC, Manuscript Division.

44. Jones is cited in a promotional bill contained in a letter, Dynamic Films to Madison Jones, February 27, 1958, NAACP Papers, Part III, Box A-157, "Housing, Films, 1956–1958," LOC, Manuscript Division.

45. In 1955, the NAACP sued Levitt and Sons to force the company to admit blacks, but the court ruled that it had no authority to regulate private housing. Levitt did open some sections of his subdivisions to qualified blacks. "Levitt Hailed [sic] into Federal Court," *The Crisis* 62 (1955), 158–59, 190; *NYT*, August 15, 1957, 14; Lee R. Bobker (Dynamic Films) to Madison Jones, February 10, 1958, NAACP Papers, Part III, Box A-157, "Housing Films, 1956–1958," LOC, Manuscript Division. On Levitt and Sons, see also Halberstam, *The Fifties*, 137–38, 141; and Herbert J. Gans, *The Levittowners: Ways of Life and Politics in a New Suburban Community* (New York: Columbia University Press, 1982, 1967).

46. *NYT*, August 15, 1957, 14; *NYT*, August 16, 1957, 10; *NYT*, August 17, 1957, 7; *NYT*, August 22, 1957, 16; NAACP Summary Report, August 23, 1957, NAACP Papers, Part III, Box A-167, "Pennsylvania, Levittown, 1956–1959," LOC, Manuscript Division.

47. *NYT*, August 15, 1957, 14; *NYT*, August 16, 1957, 10; *NYT*, August 17, 1957, 7; *NYT*, August 18, 1957, 73; *NYT*, August 20, 1957, 29; *NYT*, August 21, 1957, 29; *NYT*, August 22, 1957, 16; *NYT*, September 26, 1957, 13; *NYT*, December 15, 1957, 78; *NYT*, December 15, 1957, 78; *NYT*, February 27, 1958, 29, 55; *NYT*, August 16, 1958, 20; *NYT*, August 24, 1958, 62.

NOTES TO CHAPTER 9 (PAGES 150 TO 171)

1. NCDH, "Statement to Political Parties for Conventions, 1956," NAACP Papers, Part III, Box A-162, "Housing, NCDH, 1956–1957," LOC, Manuscript Division.

2. This statement is not intended to dismiss as insignificant other black leaders—Ralph Abernathy, Fred Shuttlesworth, Fannie Lou Hamer, Robert Moses, James Farmer, Andrew Young, or Malcolm X, for example. It merely recognizes that had Martin Luther King Jr., not existed, the movement would have had to invent him.

3. David J. Garrow, *Bearing the Cross: Martin Luther King Jr., and the Southern Christian Leadership Conference* (New York: Vintage, 1988), 173–230.

4. Foley's testimony is cited in "NAACP Report on Housing Program to [NCDH]," NAACP Papers, Part 5, Group II, Box A-311, "Housing, General, 1950–1952," Reel 7 at 672; Raymond M. Foley, "Statement before the NCDH, May 20, 1952," 2, RG 207, HUD, Program Files, Box 749, "Speeches, 1944–1953," Archives II.

5. FHA had eliminated the references to race from its "Appraisal Manual" in 1947 but had not actually changed its policy. Foley, "Statement before the NCDH, May 20, 1952," 2, RG 207, Program Files, Box 749, "Speeches, 1944–1953," Archives II; George W. Snowden, "Role of Racial Relations Service in the Federal Housing Administration," Speech before FHA Directors, August 1954, 12, RG 207, Program Files, Box 749, "Speeches, 1954"; NCDH, "A Call on the President," Archives II, 5.

6. CRH, *Where Shall We Live?* 30; Robert C. Wood (NAACP housing director), memo dated April 22, 1961, NAACP Papers, Part III, Box A-157, "Housing, FHA, 1958–1963," LOC, Manuscript Division.

7. Stephen E. Ambrose, *Eisenhower: The President* (New York: Simon and Schuster, 1984), 9–10, 13–35, 406–11; Ambrose, *Nixon: The Education of a Politician, 1913–1962* (New York: Simon and Schuster, 1987), 298; Robert F. Burk, *Dwight D. Eisenhower: Hero and Politician* (Boston: Twayne, 1986), 159–64; Porter McKeever, *Adlai Stevenson: His Life and Legacy* (New York: Morrow, 1989), 173–223.

8. The idea that the antilynching and anti–poll tax stances were not radical derives from Stevenson's letter to Virginia governor John S. Battles, August 23, 1952, in which he notes, "Dick Russell is confident that the South will support a poll tax constitutional amendment and that an anti-lynching law . . . could readily be enacted." The American Institute of Public Opinion estimated that 76 percent of blacks voted for Stevenson, 1 percent fewer than had voted for Truman in 1948. *The Crisis* marked Stevenson's black support at 73 percent, 4 percent more than they estimated had voted for Truman. See Adlai Stevenson, *The Papers of Adlai E. Stevenson:* vol. 4: *"Let's Talk Sense to the American People," 1952–1955* (Boston: Little, Brown, 1974), 47–48, 57. See also Robert Frederick Burk, *The Eisenhower Administration and Black Civil Rights* (Knoxville: University of Tennessee Press, 1984), 17–18, 20.

9. E. Frederick Morrow has written several books of observations on his place as a pioneering black in the Republican Party. See, in particular, E. Frederick Morrow, *Black Man in the White House* (New York: Coward-McCann, 1963); and *Forty Years a Guinea Pig* (New York: Pilgrim Press, 1980). See also Burk, *Dwight D. Eisenhower: Hero and Politician*, 159; Ambrose, *Eisenhower: The President*, 304–5; and Burk, *Eisenhower Administration and Black Civil Rights*, 77–88. Eisenhower promised to desegregate the District of Columbia in many campaign speeches and his State of the Union address, February 2, 1953: Dwight D. Eisenhower, *Public Papers of the Presidents of the United States: Dwight D. Eisenhower, 1953* (Washington, D.C.: GPO, 1960), 30.

10. Ambrose, *Eisenhower: The President*, 190; Tushnet, *Making Civil Rights Law*, 201–3, 223; Kluger, *Simple Justice*, 650–52, 656, 664–65.

11. Walter White, "Implications of the Ouster of the Head of the Racial Relations Service, HHFA," in *Chicago Defender,* July 30, 1953, NAACP Papers, Part 5, Group II, Box A-313, "Housing, Horne, Frank S., 1952–1954," Reel 8 at 599; on Cole's background in Congress, see Burk, *Eisenhower Administration and Black Civil Rights,* 113–14. Cole's comment before the NAREB Convention was reported in *NYT,* November 14, 1958, 46; *SFC,* Nov. 14, 1958.

12. White, "Implications of the Ouster of [Horne]"; Roy Wilkins to Walter White, September 3, 1953; NCDH press release, September 10, 1953; Maxwell M. Rabb, Assistant to President Roy Wilkins, October 20, 1953, NAACP Papers, Part 5, Group II, Box A-313, "Housing, Horne, Frank S., 1952–1954," Reel 8 at 0576; and NCDH, "The Facts in the Dismissal of Dr. Frank Horne and Mrs. Corienne R. Morrow from the Office of the Administrator, HHFA, December 29, 1955"; "Analysis of HHFA Administrator Albert M. Cole's Response to Protest Regarding His Dismissal of

Frank S. Horne and Corienne R. Morrow," September 22, 1955, NAACP Papers, Part 5, Group II, Box A-313, "Housing, Frank Horne, 1955," Reel 8 at 758.

13. Howard W. Smith, cited in CQS, *Housing a Nation*, 32; see also *Housing a Nation*, 31.

14. Eisenhower, *Public Papers . . . 1953*, 128–29; President's Advisory Committee on Government Housing Policies and Programs, *Report of the Committee*, 2, in NAACP Papers, Part 5, Group II, Box A-312, "Housing, General, January–June 1955," Reel 8 at 144; CQS, *Housing a Nation*, 32.

15. Dwight D. Eisenhower, "Housing Message to Congress," January 25, 1954.

16. "Non-White Housing," *House and Home*, April 1953; CQS, *Housing a Nation*, 32–34; Ambrose, *Eisenhower: The President*, 158; Burk, *Eisenhower Administration and Black Civil Rights*, 114–16.

17. The other groups included the American Life Insurance Convention, the National Retail Lumber Dealers Association, and mortgage lending organizations: HHFA, VHMCP, "Operating Policy Statement No. 1," September 24, 1954; HHFA, VHMCP, "Operating Policy Statement No. 2," November 30, 1954, in RG 207, General Records of the Housing and Home Finance Administration, Records of the Voluntary Home Mortgage Credit Program, 1954–1965, Files of the National Committee Correspondence, Box 2, Archives II, College Park, MD (hereinafter cited as VHMCP Papers).

18. HHFA, "The Voluntary Home Mortgage Credit Program," March 14, 1960; HHFA, Divisions of Plans and Programs, "A Study of the Voluntary Home Mortgage Credit Program, January 3, 1957"; and Arthur W. Viner, "The Voluntary Home Mortgage Credit Program," (1956), in RG 207, VHMCP Papers, Box 1.

19. HHFA, "The Voluntary Home Mortgage Credit Program," March 14, 1960.

20. NAACP Housing Department. "The Voluntary Home Mortgage Credit Program: What It Is and How It Works," NAACP Papers, Part 5, Group II, Box A-312, "Housing, General, January–June 1955," Reel 8 at 173; George H. Hutchinson to Roy Wilkins, n.d.; and Detroit Real Estate Brokers Association, press release, n.d., NAACP Papers, Part III, Box A-160, "Housing, Michigan, Detroit," LOC, Manuscript Division. See also CQS, *Housing A Nation*, 30, 34–41.

21. *Housing for America*, statement by James G. Thimmes (Washington, D.C.: CIO Housing Committee, 1954), NAACP Papers, Part 5, Group II, Box A-312, "Housing, General, January–June 1954," Reel 7 at 1028.

22. Madison Jones, "Suggestions for Integration in Private Housing, March 10, 1955," NAACP Papers, Part 5, Group II, Box A-312, "Housing, General, January–June, 1955," Reel 8 at 162; NAACP, "Outline of Basic NAACP Housing Policy and Program," and NAACP Housing Division, "Resolution on Housing Passed at the 46th NAACP Annual Conference, June 1955," NAACP Papers, as above, Reel 8 at 171; NCDH, "Executive Director's Report, May 1956," and Frances Levenson to Sen. Prescott Bush, July 23, 1956, in NAACP Papers, Part III, Box A-162, "Housing, NCDH, 1956–1957," LOC, Manuscript Division; "Resolution 47th Annual Conference, June 26–July 1, 1956," RG 207, HUD Program Files, Box 745, "Conferences–NAACP," Archives II; NAACP, "Memorandum to the Fund for the Republic's Commission on Race and Housing, Sept 1, 1955," NAACP Papers, Part 5, Group II, Box A-313, "Housing, Madison Jones, 1955," Reel 9 at 280.

23. HHFA, "Non-Discriminatory Clauses in Regard to Public Housing and Urban Redevelopment Undertakings," Prepared by the Division of Law and the Racial Relations Service, June 1953, 21–22, in NAACP Papers, Part 5, Group II, Box A-316, "Housing, States—General, 1952–1954," Reel 11 at 005.

24. Saltman, *Open Housing as a Social Movement*, 29; NAACP, "Racial Discrimination in Housing," undated, NAACP Papers, Part 5, Group II, Box A-312, "Housing, General, January–June 1955," Reel 8 at 123; "Local Laws of the City of New York for the Year 1951, No. 41," NAACP Papers, as above, Box A-315, "Housing, New York City, 1951–1955," Reel 9 at 1201.

25. The cities are Boston; Cincinnati, Cleveland, and Toledo; Denver; Fresno and Richmond, California; Hartford; Los Angeles; Minneapolis and St. Paul; Newark; Omaha; Pasco, Washington; Philadelphia and Pittsburgh; Pontiac, Michigan; Providence; St. Louis; San Francisco; and Washington, D.C. The states include Connecticut, Massachusetts, Michigan, Minnesota, New Jersey, Pennsylvania, Rhode Island, and Wisconsin. For the St. Paul law, see HHFA, "Non-Discriminatory Clauses in Regard to Public Housing and Urban Redevelopment Undertakings," June 1953, 32. See also Joseph B. Robison, "Housing—the Northern Civil Rights Frontier," *Western Reserve Law Review* 13 (1961), 112–27.

26. Madison Jones, "Suggestions for Integration in Private Housing," NAACP Papers, Part 5, Group II, Box A-312, "Housing, General, January–June, 1955," Reel 8 at 162.

27. State of New York, Executive Department, State Commission Against Discrimination, "Law Against Discrimination"; James H. Scheuer, "First Annual Report of the Housing Advisory Council to the New York State Commission Against Discrimination, 1956," 1–3, in NAACP Papers, Part III, Box A-165, "Housing, New York, SCAD, 1956–1957," LOC, Manuscript Division; Charles Abrams, "Statement," in U.S. Commission on Civil Rights, *Housing Hearings, 1959* (Washington, D.C.: GPO, 1959), 147, 152–55, 181–88, 191–93.

28. Scheuer, "First Annual Report," 6–8.

29. City of New York Commission on Intergroup Relations began a "Minority Dispersion into the Total Housing Supply, Prospectus on a Action-Study Project, September 1956," NAACP Papers, Part III, Box A-166, "Housing, New York State, 1956–1965," LOC, Manuscript Division.

30. Charles Abrams, "Prepared Statement of Charles Abrams," *Housing Hearings, 1959*, 192–93. On the role of black city councilmen, see Duane Lockard, *Toward Equal Opportunity: A Study of State and Local Antidiscrimination Laws* (New York: Macmillan, 1968), 33, 59.

31. Eleanor Roosevelt to Roy Wilkins, December 30, 1957, NAACP Papers, Part III, Box A-165, "Housing, New York SCAD, 1956–1963," LOC, Manuscript Division.

32. By the end of 1960, sixteen states and dozens of cities had enacted fair-housing legislation, ranging from narrow guarantees banning discrimination in government-owned housing to the broad restrictions in New York, Pittsburgh, and Oregon. See "Fair Housing Bills Readied in 12 States," *Trends in Housing* 1, no. 4 February–March 1957, 1; *Trends in Housing* 6, no. 6, Nov–Dec, 1962; HHFA, *Nondiscrimination Clauses in Regard to Public Housing, Private Housing and Urban Redevelopment Undertakings,* October 1957; HHFA, *Fair Housing Laws . . . Summaries and Test of State and Municipal Laws, September 1964* (Washington, D.C.: GPO, 1964); NCDH, "The Fair Housing Statutes and Ordinances, as of October 1, 1965," in NAACP Papers, 1993 Edition, Box A-162, "Housing, NCDH Reports, 1964–1965," LOC, Manuscript Division. An excellent case study on the issue of legislation occurs in W. Edward Orser, *Blockbusting in Baltimore: The Edmondson Village Story* (Lexington: University of Kentucky Press, 1994).

33. Draft ordinance: "To prohibit Discriminatory Practices in the Sale, Lease, Mortgage and Use of Housing Accommodation Based upon Race"; Housing and Redevelopment Authority, "Report on Survey of Residents to Be Displaced by St. Anthony Expressway, May, 1958"; clippings, *St. Paul Pioneer Press*, May 23, 1959, and *St. Paul Dispatch*, May 22, 1959, NAACP Papers, Part III, Box A-161, "Housing, Minnesota, St. Paul, 1956–1960," LOC, Manuscript Division.

34. Clippings, *St. Paul Dispatch*, May 22, 1959; *St. Paul Dispatch*, August 5, 1959; and Louis H. Sheahan, "Report on Proposed Housing Ordinance, August 3, 1959," 7, 12, 34, in NAACP Papers, Part III, Box A-161, "Housing, Minnesota, St. Paul, 1956–1960," LOC, Manuscript Division.

35. Clippings, *St. Paul Dispatch*, May 22, 1959; *St. Paul Dispatch*, August 5, 1959; and Louis H. Sheahan, "Report on Proposed Housing Ordinance, August 3, 1959," 7, 12, 34, in NAACP Papers, Part III, Box A-161, "Housing, Minnesota, St. Paul, 1956–1960," LOC, Manuscript Division.

36. Eisenhower's steady leadership in foreign affairs, notably the Hungarian crisis in the fall of 1956, doubtless also contributed to his success in November. See Taylor Branch, *Parting the Waters: America in the King Years, 1954–1963* (New York: Touchstone, 1988), 182–83, 191–92; Ambrose, *Eisenhower: The President*, 287–375, 387.

37. Tony Freyer, *The Little Rock Crisis: A Constitutional Interpretation* (Westport: Greenwood Press, 1984), passim.; Burk, *The Eisenhower Administration and Black Civil Rights*, 174–203; Branch, *Parting the Waters*, 222–25; Tushnet, *Making Civil Rights Law*, 257–66; Ambrose, *Eisenhower: The President*, 414–26.

38. Burk, *The Eisenhower Administration and Black Civil Rights*, 204–26; Congressional Quarterly Service, *Congressional Quarterly Almanac, 1957* (Washington, D.C.: CQS, 1958), 553–69; Branch, *Parting the Waters*, 222–24; Ambrose, *Eisenhower: The President*, 406–10.

39. U.S. Commission on Civil Rights, *With Liberty and Justice for All* (Washington, D.C.: GPO, 1959), 140–41.

40. Abrams, "Statement," *Housing Hearings, 1959*, 151, 153, 158–59.

41. U.S. Commission on Civil Rights, *With Liberty and Justice for All*, 140–67.

42. Ibid., 180–89.

43. Accurate data regarding the African American vote in the 1950s is hard to obtain. Branch, citing Kennedy biographer Theodore Sorenson, claims that Eisenhower received 60 percent of the black vote in 1956. Ambrose, citing Kennedy biographer Herbert S. Parmet, writes that Stevenson won 60 percent of the black vote. According to Warren E. Miller and Santa Traugott, the "Democratic Percentage of 2-Party Presidential Vote" for blacks was 64 percent. For 1952, it was 80 percent and for 1960, it was 71 percent. Given the concentration of the researchers, it is safe to assume that their numbers are fairly accurate. But even if these numbers are not precisely accurate, one can conclude that in 1956, Eisenhower slowed the exodus of blacks from the Republican Party. See Warren E. Miller and Santa Traugott, *American National Election Studies Data Sourcebook, 1952–1986* (Cambridge: Harvard University Press, 1989), 316; Branch, *Parting the Waters*, 192–93; Ambrose, *Nixon: Education of a Politician*, 596–97; Theodore H. White, *Making of the President, 1960* (New York: Book-of-the-Month Club ed., 1988; originally published Atheneum, 1961), 234–37; Harold C. Fleming, "The Federal Executive and Civil Rights: 1961–1965," *Daedalus* 94 (Fall 1965), 921–22.

44. Ambrose, *Nixon*, vol. 1, 596; Branch, *Parting the Waters*, 356–57, 360–68, 373–74; White, *Making of the President, 1960*, 321–23; Fleming, "Federal Executive and Civil Rights," 91–92.

45. Ambrose, *Nixon*, vol. 1, 597; Branch, *Parting the Waters*, 373–74, 378; White, *Making of the President, 1960*, 323.

46. Party platforms and Kennedy statements cited in NCDH, "A Call on the President," 7.

47. Memo, Jack Wood to Roy Wilkins, November 17, 1961, NAACP Papers, Part III, Box A-158, "Housing, 'F'"; NAACP Newsletter, November 1961, NAACP Papers, as above, "Housing, Newsletters," LOC, Manuscript Division; "Calloway Reports Progress at NAREB Directors' Meet," *ADW,* March 11, 1962, 1, 8.

48. Commission on Civil Rights, *Housing: 1961,* cited in Abrams, "Letter to the President, November 1, 1961," in NCDH, "A Call on the President," Section III.

49. NCDH, "A Call on the President," 5, 8–10, 13–38.

50. The delegation included Charles Abrams, NCDH president; Algernon Black of the Society for Ethical Culture and the chairman of the NCDH Board of Directors; Robert Dowling, director of First National City Bank; Marvin Gilman, a member of the NCDH Board and a building contractor in Baltimore and Washington; Crane Hausseman, cochairman of the NCDH Advisory Council; Marjorie Lawson, Frances Levenson, and Joseph Robinson, members of the NCDH Board; James Luchs of Shannon and Luchs; James Scheuer and John Tishman, both members of the NCDH Advisory Council; Victor Reuther, UAW, and Roland Sawyer of the United Steelworkers Union; and Jack E. Wood Jr., NAACP housing director and member of the NCDH Board of Directors. See Memo, Jack E. Wood Jr., to Roy Wilkins, November 17, 1961, NAACP Papers, Part III, Box A-162, "Housing, NCDH, 1957–1961," LOC, Manuscript Division.

51. Wood to Wilkins, November 17, 1961; Algernon Black to Roy Wilkins, November 22, 1961, NAACP Papers, Part III, Box A-162, "Housing, NCDH, 1957–1961," LOC, Manuscript Division.

52. Reeves, *President Kennedy*, 60, 127, 132–33, 499–500, 517.

53. Hugh Davis Graham, *The Civil Rights Era: Origins and Development of National Policy* (New York: Oxford University Press, 1990), 28; clipping, David Lawrence, "Are Principles Obsolete?" *New York Herald Tribune*, December 27, 1961, NAACP Papers, Part III, Box A-162, "Housing, NCDH, 1957–1961," LOC, Manuscript Division; Fleming, "Federal Executive and Civil Rights," 922–23, 931; Reeves, *President Kennedy*, 62–64.

54. Frances Levenson, Memo, "Stroke of the Pen" campaign, December 29, 1961, and Jack Wood to James Hicks, editor of *Amsterdam News*, October 6, 1961, NAACP Papers, Part III, Box A-162, "Housing, NCDH, 1957–1961," LOC, Manuscript Division; Branch, *Parting the Waters*, 586–87; CQS, *Housing a Nation*, 46–47.

55. NAACP Newsletter, August 1962, NAACP Papers, Part III, Box A-158, "Housing, Newsletters," LOC, Manuscript Division; Jack Wood to Branch Presidents and Housing Committee Chairmen, August 1962, NAACP Papers, Part III, Box A-165, "Housing, NYC, 1960–1965," LOC, Manuscript Division.

56. Reeves, *President Kennedy,* 429–31.

57. Executive Order 11063, November 20, 1962, printed in HHFA, *Fair Housing Laws,* 355–359; NCDH, *Report of the National Conference on Equal Opportunity in Housing: Challenge to American Communities* (New York: NCDH, 1963), 7–8, 45.

58. Robert C. Weaver, HHFA Summation and Comment, November 20, 1962, NAACP Papers, Part III, Box A-158, "Housing 'H,'" LOC, Manuscript Division; Jack Wood, Open Memo, April 1963, NAACP Papers, Part III, Box A-160, "Housing 'Mc,'" LOC, Manuscript Division; NCDH, *Equal Opportunity in Housing,* 1.

59. NCDH, *Equal Opportunity in Housing,* 1–3.

NOTES TO CHAPTER 10 (PAGES 172 TO 196)

1. Nicholas Katzenbach, cited in the *Baltimore Sun,* October 3, 1966, 1.

2. These events are recounted in Branch, *Parting the Waters,* 756–845, and many other places.

3. "'Full Equality Can Stop Us,'" *Michigan Chronicle,* June 8, 1963, 1, 4; "Outline March Plans," *Michigan Chronicle,* June 8, 1963, 1, 4.

4. It was originally called a "march," but for some reason (perhaps because it is less threatening), it was finally called a "walk." "Outline March Plans," *Michigan Chronicle,* June 8, 1963, 1, 4; "City Mobilizes in Support of Demonstration," *Michigan Chronicle,* June 15, 1963, 1, 2; Michael Parks, "City Negroes Aim for Full Integration," *Detroit News,* June 25, 1963, 1, 4; *Detroit News,* July 3, 1963, 6.

5. "We March for Freedom Now!" *Michigan Chronicle,* June 22, 1963, 1, 3; "$50,000 Collection Reported: Donations Fail to Equal Record Demonstration," *Michigan Chronicle,* June 29, 1963, 1, 2; "Parade Highlights: Walk for Freedom Drew Many Types," *Michigan Chronicle,* June 29, 1963, 1; "Partial Text of Speech by Rev. M. L. King," *Michigan Chronicle,* June 29, 1963, 3, 11; "125,000 Rally in Detroit to Protest Discrimination," *NYT,* June 24, 1963, 20; *The Detroit Free-Press,* June 23, 1963, 1–2; *Detroit Free Press,* June 24, 1; *Detroit News,* June 24, 1963, 1–2, 4, 19–20.

6. Broadus N. Butler, "After Marches, What Then?" *Michigan Chronicle,* June 29, 1963, 8; *Detroit Free Press,* June 24, 1963, 1; *Detroit News,* June 24, 1963, 1–2, 4, 19–20. Arthur L. Johnson, cited in Jack Mann, "Negroes Here Pledge More Demonstrations," *Detroit Free Press,* June 25, 1963, 1–2. Francis A. Kornegay, cited in Parks, "City Negroes Aim for Full Integration," *Detroit News,* June 25, 1963, 1–4. See also Jack L. Walker, "Fair Housing in Michigan," in Lynn W. Eley and Thomas W. Casstevens, eds., *The Politics of Fair-Housing Legislation: State and Local Case Studies* (San Francisco: Chandler, 1968), 364–67.

7. Parks, "City Negroes Aim for Full Integration," *Detroit News,* June 25, 1963, 1, 4; *Detroit News,* July 3, 1963, 6.

8. *Detroit Free Press,* June 23, 1963, 1, 10; "In Dearborn: You Had to Be There to Believe It Happened," *Michigan Chronicle,* June 29, 1963, 2; "Redford Next for NAACP Housing Walk," *Michigan Chronicle,* July 6, 1963, 1; Don Myers, "Negroes March in Redford Area," *Detroit Free Press,* July 7, 1963, 1; "A Welcomed Rally: No Signs Carried in Oak Park Walk," *Michigan Chronicle,* August 3, 1963, A3.

9. Tom McPhail, "Housing Bias Ban Proposed," *Detroit Free Press,* July 2, 1963, 1; "Rival Housing Plans Vie for Approval of Council," *Detroit News,* July 14, 1963, in NAACP Papers, Group III, Box A-160, "Housing, Michigan, Detroit 1956–1964," LOC, Manuscript Division.

10. "Sponsor 'Write-In' for Open Occupancy," *Michigan Chronicle,* July 27, 1963, A5.

11. Jo Ann Hardee, "Homeowners' Inclusion in Bill on Bias Opposed," *Detroit News,* July 2, 1963, 3.

12. Ordinance cited in *NAACP et al.* v. *City of Detroit et al.* (Dec. 21, 1964), in NAACP Papers, Group III, Box A-160, "Housing, Michigan, Detroit, 1956–1964," LOC, Manuscript Division; see also "Rival Housing Plans," *Detroit News,* July 14, 1963. Council members are cited in Tom McPhail, "43,000 Demand City Vote to Block Open Housing," *Detroit Free Press,* July 13, 1963, 1. *Detroit News* reported the total number of votes as 44,027, "Rival Housing Plans," July 14, 1963, in NAACP

Papers, Group III, Box A-160, "Housing, Michigan, Detroit 1956–1964," LOC, Manuscript Division; see also Tom McPhail, "City Homeowners Group to Fight Open Occupancy," *Detroit Free Press,* July 6, 1963, 5.

13. "Statement of Thomas L. Poindexter, Attorney, Detroit, Mich.," *Civil Rights—Public Accommodations: Hearings Before the Committee on Commerce, United States Senate, 88th Congress, First Sess. on S.1732, Part 2, August 1, 1963,* 1087; Hardee, "Homeowners' Inclusion Opposed," 3; see also John Millhone, "Thomas Poindexter, Spokesman for the White Counter-Revolt," *Detroit Free Press,* November 3, 1963, in NAACP Papers, Group III, Box A-160, "Housing, Michigan, Detroit, 1956–1964," LOC, Manuscript Division; and "Rival Housing Plans."

14. The coalition included the NAACP, the Detroit Urban League, the American Jewish Committee, the UAW, the Detroit Bar Association, the Anti-Defamation League of B'nai B'rith, the Detroit Archdiocesan Council of Catholic Men, the Council of Metropolitan Detroit, the Catholic Lawyers Guild, the Wolverine Bar Association, and the Detroit Coordinated Council on Human Relations. See NAACP Press Release, NAACP Papers, Group III, Box C-66, "Geographical, Detroit January–July 1964," LOC, Manuscript Division; and Detroit Urban League, "Greater Detroit Homeowners' Association v. NAACP et al.," Papers of the Detroit Urban League, Box 54, "Greater Detroit Homeowners' Association Petition, 1964," Bentley Historical Library, University of Michigan, Ann Arbor. Judge Moynihan's decision cited in *Trends in Housing,* January–February, 1964, in NAACP Papers, Group III, Box A-160, "Housing, Michigan, Detroit, 1956–1964," LOC, Manuscript Division; "Property Rights and Equal Opportunity to Housing: A Brief on an Apparent Conflict of Rights," CCR-HRD Papers, Part III, Box 25, "Housing Discrimination, 1959–1963." See also *Michigan Chronicle,* June 27, 1964, A5; *Michigan Chronicle,* July 4, 1964, A10. And see Denton, *Apartheid American Style,* 131–32.

15. "NAACP to Oppose Local Politicians," NAACP News Release, July 8, 1964, NAACP Papers, Group III, Box C-66, "Geographical, Detroit, January–July 1964," LOC, Manuscript Division; Detroit Urban League, "Why Every Detroit Citizen Should Vote 'No' on the Homeowner's Ordinance," June 22, 1964, Detroit Urban League, Box 54, "Greater Detroit Homeowners' Association Petition, 1964," Bentley Historical Library, University of Michigan, Ann Arbor; *Michigan Chronicle,* August 29, 1964, A1, A3, B9, D16; David R. Jones, "Romney Swamps Rival in Primary," *NYT,* September 2, 1964, 26.

16. Gloster B. Current to H. R. McCrary, June 28, 1962, NAACP Papers, Group III, BOX C-64, "Geographical, Detroit, January–September, 1962," LOC, Manuscript Division. Branch membership numbered 29,402 in 1963 but dropped to less than 13,000 in 1965: Gloster B. Current to Dr. and Mrs. W. A. Thompson, November 8, 1965, NAACP Papers as above, "Geographical, Detroit, 1965," LOC, Manuscript Division. James Del Rio cited in Parks, "City Negroes Aim for Full Integration," *Detroit News,* June 25, 1963, 4.

17. Tom Shawver, John Mueller, and Robert Cotter, "Push for Rights May Hurt Kennedy in the Suburbs," *Detroit Free Press,* July 14, 1963, 1–2.

18. "'People Taken In': Home Ordinance Passes Despite Tough Opposition," *Michigan Chronicle,* September 12, 1964, A3; David R. Jones, "Lesinski, Rights Bill Opponent, Defeated in Michigan Primary," *NYT,* September 3, 1964, 14.

19. *Neil Reitman et al.* v. *Lincoln W. Mulkey et al.,* 387 U.S. 369, 87 S.Ct. 1627, L.Ed. 2d 830 (1967). See also Denton, *Apartheid American Style,* 8.

20. W. J. Rorabaugh, *Berkeley at War: The 1960s* (New York: Oxford University Press, 1989), 56–60.

21. *Reitman* v. *Mulkey;* Rorabaugh, *Berkeley at War,* 59–60; Denton, *Apartheid American Style,* 8; and Thomas W. Casstevens, "California's Rumford Act and Proposition 14," in Eley and Casstevens, eds., *Politics of Fair-Housing Legislation,* 238–58.

22. Art. I, para. 26 of the California Constitution, cited in *Reitman* at 370; the petition count is cited in Casstevens, "California's Rumford Act," 262.

23. Don Hood, President, San Fernando Valley Board of Realtors, Van Nuys, California, Letter to the Editor, *Los Angeles Times,* October 20, 1964, II 4; Letter to the Editor, *Los Angeles Times,* October 27, 1964, II 4; Denton, *Apartheid American Style,* 13–15.

24. Governor Brown's views are recorded in Daryl E. Lembke, "Brown Demands End to Initiative 'Abuses,'" *Los Angeles Times,* October 21, 1964, 5; and Charles Greenberg, "Prop 14 Passage Seen

by Brown and Cranston," *Los Angeles Times,* October 28, 1964, 16; Senator Kuchel is cited in *SFC,* October 25, 1964, 1, 23, and *Los Angeles Times,* October 25, 1964, 16; Rumford is cited in *SFC,* October 20, 1964, 6, and see Donovan Bess, "Realtor vs. Rumford on Prop 14," *SFC,* October 17, 1964, 2; Weaver is cited in Paul Beck, "Prop 14 Called Peril to Urban Renewal Fund," *Los Angeles Times,* October 20, 1964, 26. On Kuchel's role in the Civil Rights Act debate, see Congressional Quarterly Service, *Congressional Quarterly Almanac, 1964* (Washington, D.C.: CQS, 1965), 355.

25. "McGucken Denounces Prop 14," *SFC,* October 23, 1964, 1, 19; Michael Harris, "Realtors' Measure Now Is Law," *SFC,* November 4, 1964, 19; Paul Beck, "Priest Ordered to Keep Silent on Prop 14," *Los Angeles Times,* October 21, 1964, 5; "Priest's Ban Reported After Prop 14 Sermon," *Los Angeles Times,* October 26, 1964, 14.

26. Tarea Hall Pittman to Roy Wilkins, "Short Summary of NAACP Activity in Fight Against Segregation Initiative Proposition 14," and NCDH Californians Against Proposition 14, "Campaign Manual: Section VII—Precinct Work and Get-Out-the-Vote," September 1964, NAACP Papers, Group III, Box A-164, "Housing, Proposition 14 (California), 1963–1965," LOC, Manuscript Division. Martin Luther King Jr. cited in Paul Weeks, "Dr. King Sees Tragedy If Prop 14 Is Approved," *Los Angeles Times,* October 28, 1964, 16; Bayard Rustin cited in J. Campbell Bruce, "Eyes of the Nation on Prop 14 Vote," *SFC,* October 26, 1964, 5; "Nat Helped Raise $130,000 to Attack Housing Bids," *Jet* 27 (March 4, 1965), 20; How Movie Stars Aid Fight for Fair Housing: Millions of Dollars Flood Calif. in Rights Tug-of-War," *Jet,* October 22, 1964, 58–62. See also Casstevens, "California's Rumford Act," 263–64.

27. Mervin D. Field, "49 Pct. of Voters Now Favor Prop 14," *Los Angeles Times,* October 16, 1964, 3, and the same article under the banner, "Proposition 14 Well in Lead," *SFC,* October 16, 1964, 2; Paul Beck, "Prop 14 Backers Claim Red Plot, Foes Charge," *Los Angeles Times,* October 30, 1964, 14; Melvin D. Field, "Prop 14 Running Far Ahead," *SFC,* November 1, 1964, 1, 26.

28. "Prop 14 Vote," *SFC,* November 4, 1964, 1C.

29. The president of CREA is cited in "Fight Against Housing [Bias] Is Declared," *ADW,* January 11, 1965, 1, 4. The court battle occurred in the case of *Reitman* v. *Mulkey,* 387 U.S. 369, 87 S.Ct. 1627, L.Ed. 2d 830 (1967). See discussion in text below. Milton Viorst, *Fire in the Streets: America in the 1960s* (New York: Simon and Schuster, 1979), 323.

30. Viorst, *Fire in the Streets,* 317–25, 326–27.

31. Malcolm X is cited in Viorst, *Fire in the Streets,* 317–25.

32. *Trends in Housing,* November–December 1963, 37; Al Black to Roy Wilkins, December 22, 1964; NCDH, "Statement and Recommendations on Executive Order No. 11063," November 19, 1964; NCDH to Lyndon B. Johnson, December 16, 1965, NAACP Papers, Group III, Box A-162, "Housing, NCDH," LOC, Manuscript Division. On Johnson's position, see Lyndon Baines Johnson, *The Vantage Point: Perspectives of the Presidency, 1963–1969* (New York: Holt, Rinehart and Winston, 1971), 176–77.

33. Martin Luther King cited in Ralph, *Northern Protest,* 43. See also the erroneously titled article, "10,000 Participate in King's First Northern March," *ADW,* July 27, 1965, 1; CCCO-SCLC, "Program of the Chicago Freedom Movement, July 1966," in David J. Garrow, ed., *Chicago 1966: Open Housing Marches, Summit Negotiations, and Operation Breadbasket* (Brooklyn: Carlson, 1989), 147–54; Ralph, *Northern Protest,* 7–42; Garrow, *Bearing the Cross,* 431–34, 447–56.

34. Garrow, *Bearing the Cross,* 456–66; Ralph, *Northern Protest,* 38–102.

35. Kathleen Connolly, "The Chicago Open Housing Conference," in Garrow, *Chicago 1966,* 62–63; Garrow, *Bearing the Cross,* 472, 492; Ralph, *Northern Protest,* 105–7; CCCO-SCLC, "Program of the Chicago Freedom Movement," 100–6.

36. King and Daley cited in Ralph, *Northern Protest,* 109–12; Abernathy's views are cited in Ralph David Abernathy, *And the Walls Came Tumbling Down* (New York: Harper & Row, 1989), 373.

37. Louis Harris poll, cited in *Newsweek,* August 22, 1966, 32. Abernathy, *And the Walls Came Tumbling Down,* 376–77; see also Chester Higgins, "Chicago Rioting Leaves Deaths, Injuries: National Guard Called," *Jet,* July 28, 1966, 6–13; Ralph, *Northern Protest,* 105–6; "Crisis of Color '66," *Newsweek,* August 22, 1966, 20–38; Garrow, *Bearing the Cross,* 492–98; Mary Lou Finley, "The Open Housing Marches, Chicago, Summer 1966," in Garrow, ed., *Chicago 1966,* 18–20.

38. Finley, "The Open Housing Marches," 21–22; Ralph, *Northern Protest,* 119–21.

39. Ralph, *Northern Protest,* 118–21; Connolly, "Chicago Open Housing Conference," 63–65; Finley, "Open Housing Marches," 20–22.

40. King cited in Ralph, *Northern Protest,* 122.

41. Accounts differ regarding the narrative details about when King was struck by the rock. I have used Ralph, *Northern Protest,* 122–23, and Charles Higgins, "Inside Report: Anatomy of Race Hate in Chicago Rights Marches in Lily-White Areas Trigger Hate Violence," *Jet,* August 25, 1966, 14–21. See also Garrow, *Bearing the Cross,* 499–500; Connolly, "Chicago Open-Housing Conference," 65.

42. Ralph, *Northern Protest,* 142–45; Connolly, "Chicago Open-Housing Conference," 66–67; Finley, "Open Housing Marches," 23; Garrow, *Bearing the Cross,* 500–2.

43. Ralph, *Northern Protest,* 148–49; Finley, "Open Housing Marches," 23.

44. Ross Beatty of the Chicago Real Estate Board cited in Connolly, "Chicago Open-Housing Conference," 78. See also Garrow, *Bearing the Cross,* 502–14; Ralph, *Northern Protest,* 152–58.

45. King's admission to the conference is cited at length in Garrow, *Bearing the Cross,* 512–13; his radio address is cited in Connolly, "Chicago Open-Housing Conference," 80. See also Garrow, *Bearing the Cross,* 514–17; Connolly, "Chicago Open-Housing Conference," 80–82; Ralph, *Northern Protest,* 158–65.

46. Thomas G. Ayers, "Report of the Subcommittee to the Conference on Fair Housing Convened by the Chicago Conference on Religion and Race," under the title, "The 'Summit Agreement,'" in Garrow, *Chicago, 1966,* 147–54.

47. Ralph, *Northern Protest,* 169–70; Garrow, *Bearing the Cross,* 524–25.

48. U.S. National Advisory Commission on Civil Disorders, *The Kerner Report,* 40–41.

49. U.S. National Advisory Commission on Civil Disorders, *The Kerner Report,* 42–108, 114, 158–60; Congressional Quarterly Service, *Congressional Quarterly Almanac, 1967* (Washington, D.C.: CQS, 1968), 795–99; "Newark Racial Outbreak Worst in Recent Years," *ADW,* July 15, 1967, 1; "Riots Roundup, *New York Amsterdam News,* July 15, 1967, 2; "4,700 Troops Arrive to Stop Detroit Riot," *ADW,* July 25, 1967, 1, 4; "Riots Must Not Become Fixture of Summer Life, NAACP Director Warns at National Convention," *ADW,* July 12, 1967, 1; "And Now, Detroit," *ADW,* July 25, 1967, 6; "Roundup of the 'Hot Summer,'" *New York Amsterdam News,* July 29, 1967, 42.

50. "What's Ahead for Negroes in 1965 Assimilation: Explosive New Concept for Coming Decades," *Jet,* January 14, 1965, 14–16; George Barner, "What Was Accomplished at the Black Power Conference," *New York Amsterdam News,* July 29, 1967, 1, 41; Gertrude Wilson, "White-On-White a Measure of Desperation," *New York Amsterdam News,* August 5, 1967, 15; "Black Power Won't Aid Negro—Wilkins," *ADW,* September 20, 1967, 2; James Farmer, *Lay Bare the Heart: An Autobiography of the Civil Rights Movement* (New York: Plume, 1986), 306–8. A concise and compelling telling of the growth and development of "Black Power" as "the newest slogan of the revolution" occurs in Lewis M. Killian, *The Impossible Revolution Phase 2: Black Power and the American Dream,* 2d ed. (New York: Random House, 1972), 57–128.

51. "State to Fight Housing Bias," *Milwaukee Journal,* February 13, 1964, 1 (hereinafter cited as *MJ*); "Open Housing Model Sent to State Mayors," *MJ,* September 18, 1967, 12.

52. "Maier Urges Shift in Urban Attitudes," *MJ,* September 16, 1967, 1, 5; "Maier Fears Lone Action, '2nd Core,'" *MJ,* early edition, September 13, 1967, 1, 2.

53. "Youth Commandos Go All Out for Priest," *MJ,* September 18, 1967, 1, 4.

54. "March Set Tonight on South Side," *MJ,* August 28, 1967, 1, 2; "Negro Picnic OK'd for South Side Park Tonight; No Talks," *MJ,* August 28, 1967, 1 Final Edition; "8,000 Taunt Rights Marchers on S. Side," *Milwaukee Sentinel,* August 29, 1967, 1, 16 (hereinafter cited as *MS*); "Opposition on South Side More Intense Than in Tosa," *MS,* August 29, 1967, 5; "Crowds Harass Groppi Marchers," *MJ,* August 29, 1967, 1, 12; "'Let Them Stay on the North Side,'" *MS,* August 30, 1967, 5; "White Children Chant Hate Cries at Marchers," *MS,* August 30, 1967, 5.

55. "22 Hurt in South Side Melee; Tear Gas Used, 45 Arrested," *MS,* August 30, 1967, 1, 6; "White Children Chant Hate Cries at Marchers," *MS,* August 30, 1967, 5; "Freedom House Fire Bombed, Gutted," *MS,* August 30, 1967, 1, 12; "Shots Heard as Freedom House Burns," *MJ,* Au-

gust 30, 1967, 1, 27; "Maier Orders 30 Day Ban on Night Demonstrations . . . Edict Goes to Aldermen for Approval," *MJ*, August 30, 1967, 1, 14.

56. "Groppi Proves His Case," *MJ*, August 30, 1967, 22; "A City Shamed," *MS*, August 31, 1967, 14; "Cousins Attacks Hate Campaign," *MJ*, September 13, 1967, 1, 25; "Clergy Group 'Ashamed of Bigotry,'" *MS*, August 31, 1967, 5, 12; "Methodist Bishop Asks City to Act on Housing," *MJ*, September 13, 1967, II: 2; "80% Denounce White Hecklers," *MJ*, August 31, 1967, 1, 9; "Maier Orders 30 Day Ban on Night Demonstrations . . . Edict Goes to Aldermen for Approval," *MJ*, August 30, 1967, 1, 14.

57. "New NAACP Rally Set After 58 Arrests," *MJ*, August 31, 1967, 1, 12; "Police Break Up Core Rally, Arrest 53 at Freedom House," *MS*, August 31, 1967, 1, 8; "Marching to S. Side Postponed," *MS*, August 31, 1967, 1, 12; "Demonstration Ban Challenged," *MS*, August 31, 1967, 5, 9; "Police Arrest Vel Phillips, Groppi as March Is Foiled," *MS*, September 1, 1967, 1, 6; "Groppi Arrested, 13 Hurt in 5th Night of Violence," *MS*, September 2, 1967, 1, 18; "Father Groppi 'Won't Cool' Holy War on Housing," *MS*, September 4, 1967, II: 15.

58. "Civil Rights Group Stages Night March," *MS*, September 4, 1967, 1, 6; "Methodist Bishop Asks City to Act on Housing," *MJ*, September 13, 1967, II: 2; "League Aid Set in Open Housing," *MS*, August 29, 1967, 6; "2 Suburbs Approve Open Housing Goal," *MJ*, September 19, 1967, 1, 16; "Anti-poverty Group Endorses Open Housing and Marches," *MJ*, September 15, 1967, II: 1.

59. "South Siders, Marchers Clash," *MJ*, September 12, 1967, 1, 4; "Housing Opponents Take to Streets," *MJ*, September 12, 1967, photo page.

60. "Whites March to Chancery, Ask Action Against Groppi," *MJ*, September 13, 1967, 1, 18; "Cousins Attacks Hate Campaign," *MJ*, September 13, 1967, 1, 25; "March Stirs Violence," *MS*, October 9, 1967, 1, 9.

61. "Gas Halts Whites on Rampage," *MJ*, September 14, 1967, 1, 8; "Cousins Attacks Hate Campaign," *MJ*, September 13, 1967, 1, 25.

62. "NAACP Affirms Support on Housing Demonstrations," *ADW*, September 17, 1967, 1, 5; "Core Marchers Go South Again," *MJ*, September 17, 1967, 1, 18; "Ministers Call for City Open Housing," *MJ*, September 17, 1967, II: 1; "Groppi Would Quit 'If It Helped Goal,'" *MJ*, September 18, 1967, II: 1–2.

63. "Core Marchers Go South Again," *MJ*, September 17, 1967, 1, 18; "Chanting Marchers Vow to Live on South Side," *MJ*, September 18, 1967, II: 1–2.

64. "Groppi Would Quit 'If It Helped Goal,'" *MJ*, September 18, 1967, II: 1–2; "Council Group Puts Off Plan to Curtail Marches," *MJ*, September 19, 1967, II: 1–2; "Groppi Gives Speech, Then Sits Out March," *MJ*, September 19, 1967, II: 1–2; "Ald. Phillips Offers Law on Housing, 1 Big Change," *MJ*, September 19, 1967, 1, 5; "2 Suburbs Approve Open Housing Goal," *MJ*, September 19, 1967, 1, 16; "Tosa Council Votes to Back Any Statewide Housing Law," *MJ*, September 20, 1967, II: 1; "Brookfield Warm to Groppi Speech," *MJ*, September 20, 1967, II: 1–2.

65. "Strong State Housing Law Eyed by Meier," *MS*, October 9, 1967, 1, 14; "March Stirs Violence . . . 30 Injured; Gregory Arrested," *MS*, October 9, 1967, 1, 9; "Maier's Proposals Suffer in Committee," *MS*, October 10, 1967, 1, 12; "Marchers, Police Clash Again; 22 Are Injured," *MS*, October 10, 1967, 1, 2; "Maier Firm on Open Housing," *MS*, October 14, 1967, 5; "625 Jam Council Chambers for Debate," *MS*, October 17, 1967, 1, 8; "Ald. Phillips Hails Action At Hearing," *MS*, October 17, 1967, 1, 9; "Housing Talks Seen Result of Behind the Scene Efforts," *MS*, October 18, 1967, 1, 8.

66. "Realtors Study Silent Stand on Open Housing Law," *MS*, October 7, 1967, III: 1–2; "7 Named to Housing Subcommittee," *MS*, October 18, 1967, 1, 8; "10 Now on Open Housing Unit," *MS*, October 19, 1967, 5; "Maier Has No Comment; Marches Continue," *MS*, October 23, 1967, 12; "Realtor Sees No Need for Bias Laws," *MJ*, December 13, 1967, II: 2.

67. "Housing Law Needed: Panel . . . Maier's Support Essential," *MS*, October 23, 1967, 1, 12; "Housing Meeting 'Down to Earth,'" *MS*, October 23, 1967, 5; "Maier Has No Comment; Marches Continue," *MS*, October 23, 1967, 12.

68. "Limited Housing Law Approved by Council," *MJ*, December 13, 1967, 1, 4; "Years of Marching Promised, If Needed," *MJ*, December 13, 1967, 4; "Many Homes Exempt in City Housing Law," *MJ*, December 13, 1967, 5.

69. "City Will Not Defend Referendum Legality," *MJ*, December 11, 1967; "Limited Housing Law Approved by Council," *MJ*, December 13, 1967, 1, 4; "U.S. Judge Bars Vote in Milwaukee on Open Housing," *NYT*, March 6, 1968, 93.

70. "NAACP Honors Father Groppi, White Priest," *NYT*, January 8, 1968, 29; "City Called Rights Testing Ground," *MS*, October 10, 1967, II: 8.

NOTES TO CHAPTER 11 (PAGES 197 TO 211)

1. William R. Morris, "The 1968 Housing Act: New Hope for Negroes," *The Crisis* (1968), 169–70.

2. Irwin Unger and Debi Unger, *Turning Point: 1968* (New York: Scribner's, 1988); "the most turbulent year" is a chapter title in James T. Patterson, *Grand Expectations: The United States, 1945–1974* (New York: Oxford University Press, 1996). The Gallup Poll is cited in Paul Joseph, *Cracks in the Empire: State Politics in the Vietnam War* (New York: Columbia University Press, 1987), 166. Walter Cronkite is cited in Larry Berman, *Lyndon Johnson's War* (New York: Norton, 1989), 174–75.

3. A detailed discussion of the economic crisis of March 1968 occurs in Joseph, *Cracks in the Empire*, 262–64; William McChesney Martin is cited in Allen J. Matusow, *The Unraveling of America: A History of Liberalism in the 1960s* (New York: Harper Torchbooks, 1984), 396. See also Matusow, *The Unraveling of America*, 395–439; Alonzo J. Hamby, *Liberalism and Its Challengers: From F.D.R. to Bush*, 2d ed. (New York: Oxford University Press, 1992), 277–81.

4. Patterson, *Grand Expectations*, 697.

5. Cited in *Jones v. Alfred H. Mayer Co.*, 392 U.S. 409, 20 L.Ed 2d 1189, 88 S.Ct. 2186 (1968).

6. Jules Witcover, *White Knight: The Rise of Spiro Agnew* (New York: Random House, 1972), 88–102; Dan T. Carter, *The Politics of Rage: George Wallace, the Origins of the New Conservatism, and the Transformation of American Politics* (New York: Simon and Schuster, 1995), 212–15; Joseph Albright, *What Makes Spiro Run: The Life and Times of Spiro Agnew* (New York: Dodd, 1971), 113.

7. Alan L. Dessoff, "Party Backs Mahoney on Occupancy," *Washington Post*, October 14, 1966, 1, 7; *The Baltimore Afro-American*, October 22, 1966, 1.

8. Agnew cited in Witcover, *White Knight*, 92–93. See also Witcover, *White Knight*, 86–105; Albright, *What Makes Spiro Run*, 6, 101–13.

9. Witcover, *White Knight*, 88, 92–93.

10. Ibid., 109–10.

11. "Mahoney Rivals Oppose His Stand on Housing," *Washington Post*, October 3, 1966, 1, 12; "Md. GOP Opens Its Doors," *Washington Post*, October 8, 1966, B1; "Agnew Changes Position on Open Occupancy Law," *Washington Post*, October 13, 1966, B1; *Washington Post*, October 14, 1966, B1; "Campaign Begun in Baltimore to Capture Negro Vote for Agnew," *Washington Post*, October 16, 1966; Dessoff, "Party Backs Mahoney on Occupancy"; "Democrats Adopting Sickles Rights Plank," *Washington Post*, October 4, 1966, B3; "Sickles Seeks Unity For Party Conclave," *Washington Post*, October 12, 1966, 1, 23; *Baltimore Sun*, November 9, 1966, 1; Witcover, *White Knight*, 138–47.

12. *Baltimore Sun*, November 9, 1966, 1, 14.

13. "Tawes' Address Opens Legislature," *Annapolis Evening Capital*, January 18, 1967, 1, 6; "Agnew Vows 'Pursuit of Excellence,'" *Annapolis Evening Capital*, January 25, 1967, 1, 5; "Maryland's Advance," *Washington Evening Star*, March 30, 1967, A-16.

14. "NAACP Meeting to Pressure Legislature for Housing Law," *Annapolis Evening Capital*, February 8, 1967, 2; "Housing Bills Would Prohibit Discrimination in Sales, Rent," *Annapolis Evening Capital*, February 9, 1967, 3; "House of Delegates Enacts Open Occupancy Law," *Annapolis Evening Capital*, March 28, 1967, 1, 5; "Maryland's Senate Passes Measure on Open Housing," *NYT*, March 29, 1967, 27; "Fair Housing Bill Gets Assembly Push," *Washington Evening Star*, March 27, 1967, 31; "Open Housing Bill OK'd, Legislature Adjourns," *Washington Evening Star*, March 29, 1967, 1, C-2; "Maryland's Advance," *Washington Evening Star*, March 30, 1967, A-16.

15. "Petitions Hit Housing, Tax," *Annapolis Evening Capital*, June 1, 1967, 2, 8; "Maryland Balks Effort to Force a Referendum on Fair Housing," *NYT*, June 11, 1967, 81; "Maryland Law in Doubt,"

NYT, June 17, 1967, 15; "Maryland Fair Housing Foes to Seek Vote Despite Ruling," *Washington Evening Star,* June 11, 1967, D1.

16. "Open Housing Bill: Burch Says Petitions Invalid, Pending Ruling," *Annapolis Evening Capital,* June 10, 1967, 1, 3; "Maryland Balks Effort to Force a Referendum on Fair Housing," *NYT,* June 11, 1967, 81; "Maryland Fair Housing Foes to Seek Vote Despite Ruling," *Washington Evening Star,* June 11, 1967, D1; "Referendum Ordered on Open Housing Law," *NYT,* March 8, 1968; "Tax Plan Loses in Michigan," *NYT,* November 7, 1968, 36.

17. *Reitman* v. *Mulkey.*

18. Ibid.

19. Ibid. A detailed analysis of the legal and juridical importance of *Reitman* occurs in Black, "'State Action,' Equal Protection, and California's Proposition 14," 69–109.

20. "Robert C. Weaver—New Cabinet Member," *The Crisis* (1966), 120–21, 129; Joseph A. Califano Jr., *The Triumph and Tragedy of Lyndon Johnson: The White House Years* (New York: Simon and Schuster, 1991), 126–27; Robert C. Weaver, "Housing for Minority Families," *The Crisis* (1966), 421–26, 431.

21. "Ex-NAACPer First Negro to Get Cabinet Post," *Jet,* January 27, 1966, 3–5; Simeon Booker, "'Proud Moment for America,' Says LBJ of 1st Negro in Cabinet," *Jet,* January 25, 1966, 8–10.

22. Califano, *Triumph and Tragedy,* 127–30; "Ex-NAACPer First Negro to Get Cabinet Post," 3–5.

23. Johnson's State of the Union Address cited in *Fair Housing—Fair Lending* (Englewood Cliffs: Prentice Hall Law and Business, 1994), 2311.

24. Congressional Quarterly Service, *Congressional Quarterly Almanac, 1966* (Washington, D.C.: CQS, 1967), 450–72; see also Roy Wilkins, "The Civil Rights Bill of 1966," *The Crisis* (1966), 302–06, 330.

25. "Roy Wilkins Urges Fair Housing Bill in Senate Testimony," *ADW,* August 31, 1967, 2; "Ghetto Tensions Can Be Stopped by Good Housing," *ADW,* August 30, 1967, 2.

26. American Friends Service Committee, *A Report to the President: AFSC Experience and Recommendations re: Executive Order 11063 on Equal Opportunity in Housing* (Philadelphia: AFSC, 1967), 1–8.

27. Lyndon Johnson, cited in Congressional Quarterly Service, *Congressional Quarterly Almanac, 1968* (Washington, D.C.: CQS, 1969), 153. See also Congressional Quarterly Service, *Congressional Quarterly Almanac, 1967* (Washington, D.C.: CQS, 1968), 772, 773–75, 792; Jean Eberhart Dubofsky, "Fair Housing: A Legislative History and a Perspective," *Washburn Law Journal* 8, 1969, 149; Graham, *Civil Rights Era,* 267.

28. Dubofsky, "Fair Housing," 150.

29. Dubofsky, "Fair Housing," 151; CQS, *Almanac, 1968,* 155–56; Graham, *Civil Rights Era,* 270–71.

30. Mrs. Murphy is explained in CQS, *Almanac, 1966,* 456. See also Dubofsky, "Fair Housing," 152.

31. See also CQS, *Almanac, 1966,* 471; CQS, *Almanac, 1968,* 157; Graham, *Civil Rights Era,* 270–71.

32. Dubofsky, "Fair Housing," 156–57; CQS, *Almanac, 1968,* 158–59; Graham, *Civil Rights Era,* 271–72; Witcover, *White Knight,* 175–76.

33. CQS, *Almanac, 1968,* 159–60, 167.

34. NCDH, *How the Federal Government Builds Ghettos,* 15, 19; Johnson, *Vantage Point,* 176–77; CQS, *Almanac, 1968,* 166–68; Graham, *Civil Rights Era,* 272–73.

35. National Advisory Commission on Civil Disorders, *The Kerner Commission,* 203–6, 243–50.

36. CQS, *Almanac, 1968,* 164–65, 167–68; Johnson, *Vantage Point,* 178–79.

37. *Congressional Record,* 90th Congress, Second Session, Volume 114, April 10, 1968, 9530–36.

38. Ibid., 9531, 9552, 9564–76.

39. *Joseph Lee Jones, et ux.* v. *Alfred H. Mayer Co., et al.,* 392 U.S. 409 (1968).

40. In the dissenting opinion, Justice John Harlan, joined by Justice Byron White, offered several essential points. He called the decision "most ill-considered and ill-advised." First, it was unnecessary for the Court to make such a bold claim, in Harlan's opinion, because the Fair Housing Act had so diminished the public importance of the *Jones* petition that the "writ of certiorari should be dismissed

as improvidently granted." The minority also questioned why no other court had seen such a power in the law. "The precedents," it noted, "are distinctly opposed to the Court's view of the statute." Harlan also made an extended and very powerful argument against the majority's reading of the debates of the Thirty-Ninth Congress, showing that the original intent of the legislation was more limited and was directed only to "state-authorized discrimination." In "the individualistic ethic of their time, which emphasized freedom and embodied a distaste for governmental interference which was soon to culminate in the era of laissez-faire," Harlan concluded, "most of these men would have regarded it as a great intrusion on individual liberty for the Government to take from a man the power to refuse to enter into a purely private transaction involving the disposition of property, albeit those personal reasons might reflect racial bias." See *Jones* v. *Mayer;* see also Del Menge and George Ramey, "Constitutional Law: The End of Private Racial Discrimination in Housing Through Revival of the Civil Rights Act of 1866," *Tulsa Law Journal* 6 (1970), 146–63.

41. "No 'Badges of Slavery,'" *NYT,* June 22, 1968, 32. In October 1968, Jones and the Alfred H. Mayer Co. settled their grievance out of court. Jones agreed that the housing company had not acted out of racial prejudice, and the company agreed to pay all legal costs and to pay Jones $2,000. See "Couple Reaches Settlement in Landmark Housing Case," *NYT,* October 29, 1968, 52.

42. These opinions are presented in the Harris poll: "White Consensus: They're Trying to Go Too Fast," *Newsweek,* August 22, 1966, 24–26.

43. Morris, "The 1968 Housing Act," *The Crisis* (1968), 169–70.

NOTES TO AFTERWORD (PAGES 212 TO 222)

1. Martin Luther King Jr., cited in Alan B. Anderson and George W. Pickering, *Confronting the Color Line: The Broken Promise of the Civil Rights Movement in Chicago* (Athens: University of Georgia Press, 1986), 172.

2. Scott McKinney and Ann B. Schnare, *Trends in Residential Segregation by Race: 1960–1980* (Washington, D.C.: Urban Institute, 1986), 3–11. See also Reynolds Farley, "The Changing Distribution of Negroes Within Metropolitan Areas: The Emergence of Black Suburbs," *American Journal of Sociology* 75 (1970), 512–29; Lake, *The New Suburbanites,* 77–137; Wilhelmina A. Leigh, "Trends in the Housing Status of Black Americans Across Selected Metropolitan Areas," *Review of Black Political Economy* 19 (1991), 43–64; Wilhelmina A. Leigh and James D. McGhee, "A Minority Perspective on Residential Racial Integration," in Goering, ed., *Housing Desegregation,* 31–42; Gary Orfield, "Separate Societies: Have the Kerner Warnings Come True?" in Fred R. Harris and Roger W. Wilkins, eds., *Quiet Riots: Race and Poverty in the United States, The Kerner Report Twenty Years Later* (New York: Pantheon, 1988), 100–22.

3. Denton and Massey, *American Apartheid,* 84–88; Douglas S. Massey, "Residential Segregation in American Cities," in Fred L. Pincus and Howard J. Erlich, eds., *Race and Ethnic Conflict: Contending Views on Prejudice, Discrimination, and Ethnoviolence* (Boulder: Westview, 1994), 126.

4. Reynolds Farley, "Black-White Residential Segregation: The Views of Myrdal in the 1940s and Trends in the 1980s," in Obie Clayton Jr., ed., *An American Dilemma Revisited: Race Relations in a Changing World* (New York: Russell Sage, 1996), 51–55.

5. For a detailed explanation of the differences between correlation ratios and indices of dissimilarity, see Logan and Schneider, "Racial Segregation and Racial Change in American Suburbs," 334–35. See also Stanley Lieberson and Donna K. Carter, "Temporal Changes and Urban Differences in Residential Segregation: A Reconsideration," *American Journal of Sociology* 88 (1982), 296–310.

6. Barrett A. Lee and Peter B. Wood, "The Fate of Residential Integration in American Cities: Evidence from Racially Mixed Neighborhoods, 1970–1980," *Journal of Urban Affairs* 12 (1990), 425–26, 433–34; John H. Goering, "Neighborhood Tipping and Racial Transition: A Review of Social Science Evidence," *Journal of the American Institute of Planners* 44 (January 1978), 76.

7. CQS, *Congressional Quarterly Almanac, 1968,* 471, 609; U.S. Commission on Civil Rights, *Equal Opportunity in Suburbia: A Report of the United States Commission on Civil Rights* (Washington, D.C.: GPO, 1974), 41–42; House of Representatives Report No. 865, 96th Congress, Second Session, cited in James A. Kushner, "An Unfinished Agenda: The Federal Fair Housing Enforcement

Effort," *Yale Law and Policy Review* 6 (1988), 354. The weak character of HUD's enforcement powers is also made clear in George R. Metcalf, *Fair Housing Comes of Age* (New York: Greenwood,
1988), 4–5, 83–85.

8. *Equal Opportunity in Housing Cases* (Englewood Cliffs: Prentice-Hall, 1983); James A. Kushner,
Fair Housing: Discrimination in Real Estate Community Development and Revitalization, 2d ed. (New
York: McGraw-Hill, 1995), 1039–1157.

9. *Park View Heights Corp. v. City of Black Jack*, 467 F.2d 1208 (1972); *Broadmoor Improvement
Association v. Stan Weber and Associates, Inc.*, 597 F.2d 568 (1979); *Southern Burlington County NAACP
v. Mount Laurel*, EOH 16,654, 67 N.J. 191, 336 A 2d 713 (1975).

10. The Supreme Court decision occurred in the Richmond, Virginia, case in *Havens Realty Corp.
v. Coleman*. On the establishment of Housing Opportunities Made Equal, Inc., see Metcalf, *Fair
Housing Comes of Age*, 92–93, 197–204; Galster, "Racial Steering in Housing Markets," 105–29;
Teresa L. McRae, "*Havens Realty Corp. v. Coleman*: Extending Standing in Racial Steering Cases to
Housing Associations and Testers," *Urban Law Annual* 22 (1981), 107–34; and *Havens Realty Corp.
v. Coleman*, 455 U.S. 363 (1982).

11. National Association of Realtors, *Affirmative Marketing Handbook* (Chicago: National Association of Realtors, 1975); "Notes and Comments," *Appraisal Journal* 44 (1976), 593; National
Association of Realtors, *Equal Opportunity Committee Handbook: A Handbook to Assist in Adoption
and Implementation of the Affirmative Marketing Agreement and in Conducting Educational and Outreach Programs* (Chicago: National Association of Realtors, 1978); W. M. Ladd, "Effect of Integration
on Property Values," cited in Alfred N. Page, "Race and Property Values," *Appraisal Journal* 36 (1968),
335–41.

12. The issue of discrimination in the mortgage insurance industry was taken up in *Dunn v. The
Mid-Western Indemnity Mid-American Fire and Casualty Co.*, 472 F. Su 1106, EOH 15,297 (1979),
wherein the Ohio Federal Court held that discriminatory denial of mortgage insurance constituted a
violation of the Fair Housing Act of 1968. See "Fair Housing Amendments Act of 1980," *Congressional Record*, 96th Congress, Second Session, vol. 126–Part 24, December 3, 1980, 31686–99;
Congressional Quarterly Service, *Congressional Quarterly Almanac, 1979* (Washington, D.C.: CQS,
1980), 390–91; Congressional Quarterly Service, *Congressional Quarterly Almanac, 1988* (Washington, D.C.: CQS, 1989), 68–69. On Don Edwards, see also Robert Pear, "Conversations/Don Edwards:
A Champion of Civil Liberties Lays Down His Lance," *NYT*, April 3, 1994, IV: 7.

13. "Fair Housing Amendments Act of 1980," *Congressional Record*, 96th Congress, Second Session, vol. 126–Part 24, December 3, 1980, 31686–99; "Fair Housing Amendments Act of 1980,"
Congressional Record, 96th Congress, Second Session, vol. 126–Part 24, December 9, 1980, 32988–
96. See also "Senate Filibuster Kills Fair Housing Bill," *Congressional Quarterly Almanac: 1980*, 373;
Fair Housing—Fair Lending (Englewood Cliffs: Prentice Hall Law and Business, 1993), 2319;
Schwemm, *Housing Discrimination: Law and Litigation* (Deerfield: Clark Boardman Callaghan, 1997),
5–11.

14. "Floor Fight Likely over Amendments: Fair-Housing Bill Approved By House Judiciary Committee," *Congressional Quarterly Weekly Report*, April 30, 1988, 1159–60; "Fish Plays Pivotal but
Difficult Judiciary Role," *Congressional Quarterly Weekly Report*, April 30, 1988, 1160; "Citing Cancer, Fish Declares He Will Retire from Congress," *NYT*, March 16, 1994, B5; "Clear Sailing Forecast
for Fair-Housing Bill," *Congressional Quarterly Weekly Report*, June 25, 1988, 1729–30; "House Backs
Move to Strengthen Enforcement of Housing Rights," *NYT*, June 30, 1988; Floor Action Expected
This Month: Fair-Housing Protagonists May Have a Deal," *Congressional Quarterly Weekly Report*,
June 18, 1988, 1682; Tom Kenworthy, "House Approves Sanctions Against Violators of Fair Hous-
ing Law," *Washington Post*, June 30, 1988, A4; Don Phillips, "Senate Votes to Toughen Housing Act,"
Washington Post, August 3, 1988, 1, 11.

15. "Backed by Reagan, Senate OKs Fair-Housing Law," 2203–4; Irvin Molotsky, "Senate Acts to
Enforce Housing Law," *NYT*, August 3, 1988, B5; Don Phillips, "Senate Votes to Toughen Housing
Act," *Washington Post*, August 3, 1988, 1; "Compromise Fair-Housing Bill Is Cleared," *Congressional
Quarterly Almanac, 1988*, 73–74.

16. "The Great Divide: Racial Attitudes in Chicago," *Chicago Sun-Times* special reprint (January
1993), 8, Chicago Collection, Chicago Public Library; *NYT*, February 13, 1999, A15.

17. Galster, "Racial Steering in Housing Markets," 105–29; Galster, "Racial Steering by Real Estate Agents," 39–63; Galster, "Racial Discrimination in Housing Markets During the 1980s," 165–75; Galster, "Neighborhood Racial Change," 35–39; Lake, *The New Suburbanites*, 147–51, 180–203; *Zuch v. Hussey*, 394 F.Su 1028 (1975); see also Bish, Bullock, and Milgram, *Racial Steering*; Kain, "Housing Market Discrimination," 68–94; Wayne J. Villenez, "Race, Class and Neighborhood: Differences in the Residential Return on Individual Resources," *Social Forces* 59 (1978), 414–30.

18. Metcalf, *Fair Housing Comes of Age*, 103–14, 116–24; Lake, *The New Suburbanites*, 165–203, 29–35; Commission on Civil Rights, *Equal Opportunity in Suburbia*, 29–35; *Laufman v. Oakley Building. and Loan Co.*, 408 F. Su 489 (1976); *Dunn v. Mid-Western Indemnity*; *Park View Heights Corp. v. City of Black Jack*, 467 F.2d 1208 (1972); *City of Black Jack v. U.S.*, 422 U.S. 1042 (1975).

19. The 1978 poll is cited in Massey and Denton, *American Apartheid*, 90–93; Eugene Robinson, "In Search of the South: A Small Town Looks to the Future," *Washington Post*, July 15, 1996; Farley, "Black-White Residential Segregation," 73.

20. The experiment is borrowed from Thomas Schelling, "On the Ecology of Micromotives," *The Public Interest* 25 (Fall 1971), 82; see Glazer, "Race and the Suburbs," in Koenigsberger, Groak, and Bernstein, *Work of Charles Abrams*, 177–78.

21. *NYT*, February 15, 1987, 29; *NYT*, April 28, 1990, 26; *Washington Post*, February 2, 1987, E1, E5; Newton and Newton, *Racial and Religious Violence in America*, 430–35; "Justice Department Investigates 26 Cross-Burnings Nationwide in 1996," *The Advocate*, NFHA, January 1997. In 1990, in response to the Hate Crime Statistics Act, the federal government began collecting data from police forces nationwide for the purpose of tracking hate crimes. Unfortunately, the data are not broken down precisely enough to facilitate conclusions based on racial conflict over residential space. See, for example, U.S. Department of Justice, Federal Bureau of Investigation, Criminal Justice Information Services, *Hate Crime Statistics: 1995* (Washington, D.C.: GPO, 1997), 1, 7–9.

22. Pat Williams with Wista Johnson, "L.I. Couple to Rebuild Fire Damaged Home," *New York Amsterdam News*, March 10, 1979, 1, 10; G. Davis Brown, "Cross Burnings," *The Black American* 18, no. 41 (1979), 22; Mark Schneider, "Racists Force Three Black Families Out of Homes," *The Black American* 21, no. 31 (1982), 29; Sue Anne Pressley, "Tilghman Residents Hope Cross Burning Chapter Is History," *Washington Post*, February 2, 1987, E1, E5. See also "Federal Judge Awards Damages," *The Advocate*, NFHA, October 1995; "Maryland Cross-Burner Sent to Prison," *The Advocate*, NFHA, June 1996; "Justice Department Investigates 26 Cross-Burnings Nationwide in 1996."

23. J. Zamgba Browne, "Racist Bombings Won't Scare Us, Couple Vows," *New York Amsterdam News*, February 17, 1990, 3; Jesse H. Walker, "Racism Also Called on Black N.J. Family," *New York Amsterdam News*, February 17, 1990, 3, 49; "Damages Awarded to Victims in Ohio and Mississippi Racial Intimidation Cases," *The Advocate*, NFHA, September 1996.

24. Walter Shapiro, "Unfinished Business," *Time Magazine*, August 7, 1989, 25. See also "Boston Housing Authority Told to Pay $100,000," *The Advocate*, NFHA, December 1996; "Florida Man Faces Jail Term," *The Advocate*, NFHA, February 1997; "Jury Awards $40,000," *The Advocate*, NFHA, May 1998.

25. Farley, "Black-White Residential Segregation," 73; "The Great Divide: Racial Attitudes in Chicago," *Chicago Sun-Times*, 18.

26. Charles Abrams, *The City Is the Frontier* (New York: Harper Colophon, 1965), 64.

BIBLIOGRAPHY

UNPUBLISHED PRIVATE MANUSCRIPTS AND GOVERNMENT PAPERS

African American Collection, University of Louisville Archives, William F. Ekstrom Library, Louisville, Kentucky.

City of Birmingham, Department of Urban Planning, Records 1926–1960, Archives, Birmingham Public Library, Birmingham, Alabama.

City of Birmingham, Police Department Surveillance Files, 1947–1980, Archives, Birmingham Public Library, Birmingham, Alabama.

College of Arts and Sciences, 542 Student Papers, 1980–1982, University of Louisville Archives, William F. Ekstrom Library, Louisville, Kentucky.

Detroit Commission on Community Relations—Human Rights Department Collection, Wayne State University Archives of Labor and Urban Affairs and University Archives, Walter P. Reuther Library, Wayne State University, Detroit, Michigan.

George Edwards Collection, Wayne State University Archives of Labor and Urban Affairs and University Archives, Walter P. Reuther Library, Wayne State University, Detroit, Michigan.

Guide to the Records of the Subversive Activities Control Board, 1950–1972, Paul L. Kesaris, ed., Library of Congress, Microform Division, Washington, D.C.

William B. Hartsfield Papers, Special Collections, Robert W. Woodruff Library, Emory University, Atlanta, Georgia.

Ralph E. McGill Papers, Special Collections, Robert W. Woodruff Library, Emory University, Atlanta, Georgia.

James W. Morgan, Mayoral Papers, Archives, Birmingham Public Library, Birmingham, Alabama.

Frank Murphy Papers, Bentley Historical Library, University of Michigan, Ann Arbor, Michigan.

Papers of the Detroit Urban League, Bentley Historical Library, University of Michigan, Ann Arbor, Michigan.

Papers of the NAACP, Group III, Series C, and Group IV, Series A, Manuscript Collection, Library of Congress, Washington, D.C.

Papers of the NAACP, 1993 Edition, Manuscript Collection, Library of Congress, Washington, D.C.

Papers of the NAACP, Part 5, "The Campaign Against Residential Segregation, 1914–1955," Microfilm Collection, Amelia Gayle Gorgas Library, Tuscaloosa, Alabama.

Papers of the NAACP, Part 12, "Selected Branch Files, 1913–1939," Microfilm Collection, Amelia Gayle Gorgas Library, Tuscaloosa, Alabama.

James H. Preston, Mayoral Papers, Baltimore City Archives, Baltimore, Maryland.

Records of the White House Office, Office of the Special Assistant for National Security Affairs (Robert Cutler, Dillon Anderson, and Gordon Gray): 1952–1961, FBI Series, including *The Communist Party, USA, and Radical Organizations, 1953–1960*, Robert E. Lester, coordinator, Dwight D. Eisenhower Library, Abilene, Kansas (courtesy of Archivist David J. Haight).

Southern Regional Council Papers, Special Collections, Robert W. Woodruff Library, Atlanta University Center, Atlanta, Georgia.

Dorothy Rogers Tilly Papers, Special Collections, Robert W. Woodruff Library, Emory University, Atlanta, Georgia.

U.S. Department of Housing and Urban Development, General Records . . . Records of the Voluntary Home Mortgage Credit Program, 1954–1965, Files of the National Committee Correspondence, Record Group 207, National Archives II, College Park, Maryland.

U.S. Department of Housing and Urban Development, Program Files, Race Relations Program, 1946–1958, Record Group 207, National Archives II, College Park, Maryland.

U.S. Department of Justice, "General Index," 1928–1951, RG 60, Archives II, College Park, Maryland (courtesy of Archivist Fred J. Romanski, June 1996).

Vertical Files, Historic Maryland Collection, Enoch Pratt Free Library, Baltimore, Maryland.

GOVERNMENT DOCUMENTS

Birmingham District Housing Authority, *Social and Economic Survey of the Birmingham District for 1940* (Washington, D.C.: WPA/GPO, 1943).

Burns, Arthur E., "Work Relief Wage Policies, 1930–1936," Federal Emergency Relief Administration, *Monthly Report, June 1 Through June 30, 1936*, 22–55.

Chicago Commission on Race Relations, *The Negro in Chicago: A Study of Race Relations and a Race Riot* (Chicago: University of Chicago Press, 1922; Arno Press and the New York Times, 1968).

[Chicago] Mayor's Commission on Human Relations, *Human Relations in Chicago: Report of Mayor's Commission on Human Relations for 1946*, by Thomas H. Wright (Chicago: Mayor's Commission on Human Relations, 1946).

Congressional Directory (Washington, D.C.: GPO). (See notes for citations.)

Congressional Record (Washington, D.C.: GPO). (See notes for citations.)

Connecticut Commission on Civil Rights, *Racial Integration in Private Residential Neighborhoods in Connecticut* (Hartford: Connecticut Commission on Civil Rights, 1957).

Gries, John M., and James Ford, eds., *Housing Objectives and Programs*, President's Conference on Home Building and Home Ownership, vol. 11 (Washington, D.C.: National Capital Press, 1932).

Jefferson County, Alabama, Board of Health, *Health as an Indication of Housing Needs in Birmingham, Alabama* (Birmingham: n.p., 1950).

Johnson, Charles S., for the Committee on Negro Housing, *Negro Housing*, President's Conference on Home Building and Home Ownership, vol. 6 (Washington, D.C.: National Capital Press, 1932).

Maryland Community Development Administration, *Minority Housing Enclaves in Maryland* (Annapolis: Department of Economic and Community Development, Community Development Administration, 1974).

Philadelphia Housing Association, *Philadelphia's Negro Population: Facts on Housing* (Philadelphia: Commission on Human Relations, 1953).

President's Committee on Civil Rights, *To Secure These Rights* (Washington, D.C.: GPO, 1947).

Roosevelt, Franklin D., "Statements of Franklin D. Roosevelt on Housing," United States Housing Authority, Document 30446H (Washington, D.C.: n.p., 1941).

Scott, Barbara W., *The Status of Housing of Negroes in Pittsburgh* (Pittsburgh: Commission on Human Relations, 1962).

U.S. Bureau of the Census, *Census Reports: Twelfth Census of the United States, 1900* (Washington, D.C.: GPO, 1901).

———, *Thirteenth Census of the United States, 1910: Population I: General Report and Analysis* (Washington, D.C.: GPO, 1913).

———, *Fourteenth Census of the United States, 1920: Population III: Composition and Characteristics of the Population by States* (Washington, D.C.: GPO, 1922).

———, *Sixteenth Census of the United States, 1940: Population I: Number of Inhabitants* (Washington, D.C.: GPO, 1942).

———, *Sixteenth Census of the United States, 1940: Population II: Characteristics of the Population* (Washington, D.C.: GPO, 1943).

———, *Seventeenth Census of the United States, 1950: Housing V: Block Statistics, Part 20, Birmingham, Ala.* (Washington, D.C.: GPO, 1952).

———, *Seventeenth Census of the United States, 1950: Population II: Characteristics of the Population, Part 5, California; Part 10, Florida* (Washington, D.C.: GPO, 1952).

———, *Seventeenth Census of the United States, 1950: Population III: Census Tract Statistics, P–D2: Atlanta, Ga.; P–D5: Birmingham, Ala.; P–D10: Chicago, Ill.; P–D14: Dallas, Texas; P–D31: Miami, Fla.* (Washington, D.C.: GPO, 1952).

———, *Eighteenth Census of the United States, 1960: Population I: Characteristics of the Population, PC (1)–11D: Florida* (Washington, D.C.: GPO, 1961).

———, *Eighteenth Census of the United States, 1960: Censuses of Population and Housing, Census Tracts, PHC(1)–8: Atlanta, Ga., Standard Metropolitan Statistical Area; PHC(1)–17: Birmingham, Ala., S.M.S.A.; PHC(1)–26: Chicago, Ill., S.M.S.A.; PHC(1)–34: Dallas, Texas; PHC(1)–90: Miami, Fla., S.M.S.A.* (Washington, D.C.: GPO, 1961).

————, *Eighteenth Census of the United States, 1960: Housing III, City Blocks: HC(3)–118, Atlanta, Ga.* (Washington, D.C.: GPO, 1961).

————, *Nineteenth Census of the United States, 1970: Population I: Characteristics of the Population, Part 11, Section 1: Florida* (Washington, D.C.: GPO, 1973).

————, *Nineteenth Census of the United States, 1970: Censuses of Population and Housing, Census Tracts, PHC(1)–129: Miami, Fla., Standard Metropolitan Statistical Area* (Washington, D.C.: GPO, 1973).

————, Population Division, *Current Population Reports*, Series P–S; Series NP; Series P–20 (Washington, D.C.: GPO, 1947).

————, Population Division, *Current Population Reports*, Series P–28; Series P–46 (Washington, D.C.: GPO, 1957).

U.S. Commission on Civil Rights, *Hearings Before the United States Commission on Civil Rights, Housing, New York City, Atlanta, Chicago, 1959* (Washington, D.C.: GPO, 1959).

————, *Report of the United States Commission on Civil Rights, 1959* (Washington, D.C.: GPO, 1959).

————, *With Liberty and Justice for All* (Washington, D.C.: GPO, 1959).

————, *Hearings Before the United States Commission on Civil Rights, Los Angeles, San Francisco, 1960* (Washington, D.C.: GPO, 1960).

————, *1961 United States Commission on Civil Rights Report, Part 4: Housing* (Washington, D.C.: GPO, 1961).

————, *The 50 States Report Submitted to the Commission on Civil Rights by the State Advisory Committees, 1961* (Washington, D.C.: GPO, 1961).

————, *Civil Rights '63: 1963 Report of the United States Commission on Civil Rights* (Washington, D.C.: GPO, 1963).

————, Florida Advisory Committee, *Constitutional Principle vs. Community Practice: A Survey of the Gap in Florida* (Washington, D.C.: GPO, 1963).

————, *Above Property Rights*, Clearinghouse Publication 38 (Washington, D.C.: GPO, 1972).

————, *Understanding Fair Housing*, Clearinghouse Publication 42 (Washington, D.C.: GPO, 1973).

————, *Equal Opportunity in Suburbia: A Report of the United States Commission on Civil Rights* (Washington, D.C.: GPO, 1974).

————, *Statement on Metropolitan School Desegregation* (Washington, D.C.: GPO, 1977).

————, *Confronting Racial Isolation in Miami* (Washington, D.C.: GPO, 1982).

————, *State of Civil Rights, 1957–1983: The Final Report of the U.S. Commission on Civil Rights* (Washington, D.C.: GPO, 1983).

————, *A Sheltered Crisis: The State of Fair Housing in the Eighties* (Washington, D.C.: GPO, 1983).

————, *Issues in Housing Discrimination* (Washington, D.C.: GPO, 1985).

————, *The Fair Housing Amendments Act of 1988: The Enforcement Report* (Washington, D.C.: GPO, 1994).

U.S. Department of Justice, Federal Bureau of Investigation, Criminal Justice Information Services, *Hate Crime Statistics: 1995* (Washington, D.C.: GPO, 1997).

U.S. Federal Emergency Administration of Public Works, *Slums and Blighted Areas in the United States*, by Edith Elmer Wood, *PWA Housing Division Bulletin 1* (Washington, D.C.: GPO, 1935).

————, *Urban Housing: The Story of the PWA Housing Division* (Washington, D.C.: GPO, 1936).

————, *Harlem River Houses* (Washington, D.C.: GPO, 1937).

————, *America Builds: The Record of PWA* (Washington, D.C.: GPO, 1939).

U.S. Federal Emergency Relief Administration, "The Negro and Relief," by Alfred Edgar Smith, in *FERA Monthly Report, March 1936* (Washington, D.C.: GPO, 1936), 10–17.

————, "Work Relief Wage Policies, 1930–1936," by Arthur E. Burns, in *FERA Monthly Report, June 1936* (Washington, D.C.: GPO, 1936), 22–87.

U.S. Federal Housing Administration, *Proceedings of the Realtors' Housing Conference Discussing the National Housing Act (as Amended February 3, 1938)* (Washington, D.C.: GPO, 1938).

————, *Annual Reports, 1935–1950* (Washington, D.C.: GPO, 1935–1954).

————, *The FHA Story in Summary* (Washington, D.C.: GPO, 1959).

U.S. House of Representatives, Committee on Banking and Currency, *Housing Act of 1949: Hearing Before the Committee on Banking and Currency, House of Representatives, 81st Cong., 1st Sess. on H.R. 4009* (Washington, D.C.: GPO, 1949).

————, *Housing Act of 1952: Hearing Before the Committee on Banking and Currency, House of Representatives, 82d Cong., 2d Sess. on S. 3066* (Washington, D.C.: GPO, 1952).

————, *Hearing Before the Committee on Banking and Currency, House of Representatives, 83d Cong., 2d Sess. on H.R. 7839* (Washington, D.C.: GPO, 1954).

U.S. House of Representatives, Committee on the Judiciary, *Hearings Before Subcommittee No. 5 of the Committee on the Judiciary, House of Representatives, 86th Cong. 1st Sess.* (Washington, D.C.: GPO, 1959).

————, *Federal Government's Role in the Achievement of Equal Opportunity in Housing: Hearings Before the Civil Rights Oversight Subcommittee (Subcommittee No. 4)* (Washington, D.C.: GPO, 1972).

U.S. Housing and Home Finance Agency, *Annual Reports, 1950–1958* (Washington, D.C.: GPO, 1950–1958).

————, *A Summary of the Evolution of Housing Activities in the Federal Government* (Washington, D.C.: GPO, 1951).

————, *Open Occupancy in Public Housing* (Washington, D.C.: GPO, 1953).

————, *State Statutes and Local Ordinances Prohibiting Discrimination in Housing and Urban Renewal Operations* (Washington, D.C.: GPO, 1961).

————, *Our Nonwhite Population and Its Housing: The Changes Between 1950 and 1960* (Washington, D.C.: GPO, 1963).

————, *Fair Housing Laws: Summaries and Text of State and Municipal Laws* (Washington, D.C.: GPO, 1964).

U.S. Housing Authority, *Housing and Delinquency*, by Robert C. Weaver, USHA Document 24463 (Washington, D.C.: n.p., 1941).

————, *The Negro and Low-Rent Housing*, by Robert C. Weaver, Document 40746 H (Washington, D.C.: n.p., 1941).

————, *New Cities, New Citizens: The Program of the United States Housing Authority* (Washington, D.C.: GPO, 1941).

U.S. National Advisory Commission on Civil Disorders, *Report of the National Advisory Commission on Civil Disorders* (Washington, D.C.: GPO, 1969; reprinted as *The Kerner Report*, New York: Pantheon, 1988).

U.S. National Housing Agency, *Annual Reports, 1–5* (Washington, D.C.: GPO, 1942–1946).

————, *Housing for War and the Job Ahead* (Washington, D.C.: GPO, 1944).

U.S. Public Housing Administration, *Trends Toward Open Occupancy in Housing Programs, Numbers 3–8 and 12* (Washington, D.C.: GPO, 1954–1959, 1963).

U.S. Senate, Committee on Banking and Currency, *Housing Act of 1949: Report from the Committee on Banking and Currency on S. 1070*, February 25, 1949, with *Supplemental Report, 84, Part 2*, March 11, 1949, in *Senate Reports, 81st Cong., 1st Sess., Miscellaneous I, Calendar 71* (Washington, D.C.: GPO, 1949).

————, *Housing Act of 1949, Summary of Provisions of the National Housing Act of 1949*, July 14, 1949, in *Senate Documents, 81st Cong., 1st Sess., Miscellaneous IX, Doc. #99* (Washington, D.C.: GPO, 1949).

————, *Federal Housing Programs: A Chronology and Brief Summary of Congressional and Executive Action Affecting Housing from 1892 to October 25, 1949, and a description of Present Federal Housing Programs* (Washington, D.C.: GPO, 1950).

————, *Nominations of Robert C. Weaver and Robert C. Wood, Hearing . . . January 17, 1966* (Washington, D.C.: GPO, 1966).

U.S. Senate, Committee on the Judiciary, *Civil Rights—1959, Hearings Before the Subcommittee on Constitutional Rights of the Committee on the Judiciary, United States Senate, 86th Cong., 1st Session, Volumes 1–4* (Washington, D.C.: GPO, 1960).

————, *Fair Housing Amendments Act of 1987: Hearings Before the Subcommittee on the Constitution . . . on S. 558* (Washington, D.C.: GPO, 1988).

COURT CASES

A. B. Parmalee et al. v. *Charles Morris*, Cal. No. 30,062, Michigan Supreme Court (1922)

Allen v. *Oklahoma City*, 175 Okl. 421, 52 P 2d. 1054 (1936)

Austin Dunn v. *The Mid-Western Indemnity Mid-American Fire and Casualty Co.*, 472 F. Su 1106, EOH 15,297 (1979)

Banks v. *Housing Authority of San Francisco*, 120 Cal. A 2d 1 (1953)

Barrows v. *Jackson*, 73 S.Ct. 1031, 346 U.S. 249 (1953)

Berman v. *Parker*, 348 U.S. 26 (1954)

Broadmoor Improvement Association v. *Stan Weber and Associates, Inc.*, 597 F.2d 568 (1979)

Brown v. *Board of Education of Topeka*, 347 U.S. 483 (1954), 349 U.S 294 (1955)

Bryan v. *PA Human Relations Commission*, EOH 16,564 (1979)

Buchanan v. *Warley*, 245 U.S. 60 (1917)

Carey v. *City of Atlanta*, 143 Ga. 192 (1915)

Cherry v. *Amoco Oil Co.*, EOH 15,320 (1979)

City of Birmingham v. *Monk*, 185 F.2d 859 (1951)

City of Black Jack v. *United States*, 422 U.S. 1042 (1975)

City of Dallas v. *Liberty Annex Corp.* (Tex. Civ. A) 19 S.W. 2d 845 (1929)

City of Richmond v. *Deans*, 37 F.2d 712,713 (1930)

Clinard v. *City of Winston-Salem*, 217 N.C. 119 (1940)

Corrigan v. *Buckley*, 271 U.S. 323 (1926)

Dorsey v. *Stuyvesant Town Corp.*, 229 N.Y. 512 (1955)

Dred Scott v. *Sandford*, 60 U.S. 393 (1857)

Du Ross v. *Trainer*, 122 Cal. A 732 (1932)

Dunn v. *The Mid-Western Indemnity Mid-American Fire and Casualty Co.*, 472 F. Su 1106, EOH 15,297 (1979)

Foster v. *Stewart*, 134 Cal. A 482 (1933)

Gladstone Realtors v. *Village of Bellwood [IL]*, EOH 15,284 (1979)

Hall v. *DeCuir*, 95 U.S. 485 (1877)

Hansberry v. *Lee*, 311 U.S. 32 (1940)

Harmon v. *Tyler*, 273 U.S. 668 (1927)

Havens Realty Corp. v. *Coleman*, 455 U.S. 363 (1982)

Henderson v. *United States*, 339 U.S. 816 (1950)

Holmes and Bivens v. *Ledbetter and the City of Detroit*, 294 F.Su 991 (1968)

Housing Authority of San Francisco v. *Banks*, 98 L.Ed. 1114 (1954)

Hurd v. *Hodge*, 334 U.S. 24 (1948)

Johnson v. *Levitt and Sons, Inc.*, 131 F. Su 114 (E.D. Pa. 1955)

Jones v. *Alfred H. Mayer Co.*, 392 U.S. 409 (1968)

Jones v. *Oklahoma City*, 78 F. 2d 860 (1935)

Laufman v. *Oakley Building and Loan Co.*, 408 F. Su 489 (1976)

Liberty Annex Corp. v. *City of Dallas*, 289 S.W. 1067 (1926)

Mays v. *Burgess*, 79 U.S. App. D.C. 343; 80 U.S. App. D.C. 236

McGhee v. *Sipes*, 334 U.S. 1 (1948)

McLaurin v. *Oklahoma State Regents for Higher Education*, 339 U.S. 637 (1950)

Monk v. *City of Birmingham*, 87 F. Su 538 (1950)

New York State Commission Against Discrimination v. *Pelham Hall Apartments, Inc.*, 10 Misc.2d 334, 170 N.Y.S.2d 750 (1958)

Northside Realty Associates v. *United States*, EOH 15,312 (1979)

Park View Heights Corp. v. *City of Black Jack*, 467 F.2d 1208 (1972)

Plessy v. *Ferguson*, 163 U.S. 537 (1896)

Porter v. *Barrett*, 233 Mich. 373, 206 N.W. 532 (1925)

Porter v. *Johnson*, 232 Mo. A 1150, 115 S.W. 2d 529 (1938)

Reitman v. *Mulkey*, 387 U.S. 369, 87 S.Ct. 1627, L.Ed. 2d 830 (1967)

Scott v. *Watt*, 175 Okla. 426 (1935)

Shelley v. *Kraemer*, 334 U.S. 1 (1948)

Skold v. *Johnson*, EOH 16,617 (1981)

Southern Burlington County NAACP v. *Mount Laurel*, EOH 16,654, 67 N.J. 191 (1975)

Spaulding v. *Blair, Sec. of State, Maryland*, 403 F.2d 862 (1968)

State of Maryland v. *Gurry*, 3 Balt. City Ct. 262 (1913)

State of Maryland v. *Gurry*, 121 Md. 534 (1913)

State of North Carolina v. *Darnell*, 81 S.E. 338, 166 N.C. 300 (1914)

Sweatt v. *Painter*, 339 U.S. 629 (1950)

United States v. *AIREA*, EOH 15,306 (1979)

United States v. *City of Birmingham, MI*, EOH 15,427 (1982)

Village of Euclid, Ohio v. *Ambler Realty Co.*, 272 U.S. 365 (1926)
White v. *White*, 108 W.Va. 128, 150 S.E. 531 (1929)
Zuch v. *Hussey*, 394 F. Su at 1028 (1975)

NEWSLETTERS, NEWSPAPERS, AND PERIODICALS

Advocate, National Fair Housing Advocate Online News Archive at www.fairhousing.com
Annapolis Evening Capital
Appraisal Journal
Atlanta Constitution
Atlanta Daily World
Atlanta Journal
Baltimore Afro-American
Baltimore Afro-American Ledger
Baltimore Sun
Bergen Evening Record
Birmingham News
Birmingham Post
Birmingham Post-Herald
Birmingham World
Black American (New York)
Buffalo Evening News
California Eagle (Los Angeles)
Chicago Defender
Chicago Sun-Times
Chicago Tribune
Civil Rights Digest
Cleveland Plain Dealer
Collier's
Congressional Quarterly Weekly Report
Crisis
Dallas Morning News
Detroit Free Press
Detroit News
Detroit Tribune
Florida Times-Union (Jacksonville)
Harvard Law Review
House and Home
Jet Magazine
Life Magazine
Look Magazine
Long Island Daily Press
Los Angeles Herald-Express
Los Angeles Times
Louisville Courier-Journal

Louisville Leader
Louisville Times
Miami Herald
Michigan Chronicle
Michigan Law Review
Milwaukee Journal
Milwaukee Sentinel
Monthly Summary of Trends and Events in Race Relations
Nation
National Review
New Republic
New South (SRC)
Newsweek Magazine
New York Amsterdam News
New York Times
Opportunity: Journal of Negro Life
Paterson (NJ) *Evening News*
Pittsburgh Courier
Providence Journal
Public Housing (USHA)
Realtors' Headlines (NAREB)
Richmond Afro-American
Richmond Times-Dispatch
San Francisco Chronicle
San Francisco Examiner
Survey
Time Magazine
Trends in Housing (NCDH)
Tulsa Daily World
U.S. News & World Report
Washington Afro-American
Washington Post
Washington Post and Times Herald
Washington Evening Star

BOOKS, PAMPHLETS, ADDRESSES, AND REPORTS

Abernathy, Ralph David, *And the Walls Came Tumbling Down* (New York: Harper & Row, 1989).
Abrams, Charles, *The Future of Housing* (New York: Harper & Brothers, 1946).
———, *Race Bias in Housing* (New York: ACLU, NAACP, American Council on Race Relations, 1947).
———, *Forbidden Neighbors: A Study of Prejudice in Housing* (New York: Harper & Bros., 1955).
———, *The City Is the Frontier* (New York: Harper Colophon, 1965).

Adams, Carolyn, David Bartelt, David Elesh, Ira Goldstein, Nancy Kleniewski, and William Yancey, *Philadelphia: Neighborhoods, Division, and Conflict in a Postindustrial City* (Philadelphia: Temple University Press, 1991).

Adorno, T. W., Else Frenkel-Brunswik, Daniel J. Levinson, and R. Nevitt Sanford, *The Authoritarian Personality* (New York: Harper & Row, 1950).

Agnew, Spiro T., *Addresses and State Papers of Spiro T. Agnew, Governor of Maryland, 1967–1969*, ed. Franklin L. Burdette (Annapolis: State of Maryland, 1975).

Albright, Joseph, *What Makes Spiro Run: The Life and Times of Spiro Agnew* (New York: Dodd, 1971).

Allport, Gordon W., *The Nature of Prejudice* (Reading: Addison-Wesley, 1954).

Ambrose, Stephen E., *Eisenhower: The President* (New York: Simon and Schuster, 1984).

———, *Nixon: The Education of a Politician, 1913–1962* (New York: Simon and Schuster, 1987).

———, *Nixon: The Triumph of a Politician, 1962–1972* (New York: Simon and Schuster, 1989).

American Friends Service Committee, *A Report to the President: AFSC Experience and Recommendations re: Executive Order 11063 on Equal Opportunity in Housing* (Philadelphia: AFSC, 1967).

Anderson, Alan B., and George Pickering, *Confronting the Color Line: The Broken Promise of the Civil Rights Movement in Chicago* (Athens: University of Georgia Press, 1986).

Anderson, E. Frederick, *The Development of Leadership and Organization Building in the Black Community of Los Angeles from 1900 Through World War II* (Saratoga: Century Twenty One, 1980).

Anderson, Martin, *The Federal Bulldozer: A Critical Analysis of Urban Renewal, 1949–1962* (Cambridge: MIT Press, 1964).

Aronovici, Carol, and Elizabeth McCalmont, *Catching Up with Housing* (Newark: Beneficial Management Corp., 1936).

———, *Housing the Masses* (New York: Wiley, 1939).

Atlanta Committee for Cooperative Action, *A Second Look: The Negro Citizen in Atlanta* (Atlanta: n.p., 1960).

Atlanta Urban League, *A Report of the Housing Activities of the Atlanta Urban League* (Atlanta: n.p., 1951).

Banner-Haley, Charles T., *The Fruits of Integration: Black Middle-Class Ideology and Culture, 1960–1990* (Jackson: University of Mississippi Press, 1994).

Barnard, Harry, *Independent Man: The Life of Senator James Couzens* (New York: Scribner's, 1958).

Barnes, Annie S., *The Black Middle Class Family: A Study of Black Subsociety, Neighborhood, and Home in Interaction* (Bristol: Wyndham Press, 1985).

Barr, Alwyn, *Black Texans: A History of Negroes in Texas, 1528–1971* (Austin: University of Texas Press, 1973 and 1982).

Bass, Charlotta A., *Forty Years: Memoirs from the Pages of a Newspaper* (Los Angeles: Bass, 1960).

Baum, Daniel Jay, with Karen Orloff Kaplan, *Toward a Free Housing Market* (Coral Gables: University of Miami Press, 1971).

Bauman, John F., *Public Housing, Race, and Renewal: Urban Planning in Philadelphia, 1920–1974* (Philadelphia: Temple University Press, 1987).

Beadle, Muriel, *The Hyde Park–Kenwood Urban Renewal Years* (Chicago: n.p., 1967).

Belknap, Michael, *Federal Law and Southern Order: Racial Violence and Constitutional Conflict in the Post-Brown South* (Athens: University of Georgia Press, 1987).

Bell, Derrick, *And We Are Not Saved: The Elusive Quest for Racial Justice* (New York: Basic Books, 1987).

———, *Faces at the Bottom of the Well: The Permanence of Racism* (New York: Basic Books, 1992).

Bellah, Robert N., Richard Madsen, William M. Sullivan, Ann Swidler, and Steven M. Tipton, *Habits of the Heart: Individualism and Commitment in American Life* (New York: Perennial Library, 1985).

———, *The Good Society* (New York: Vintage, 1992).

Berlin, Ira, *Slaves Without Masters: The Free Negro in the Antebellum South* (New York: Pantheon, 1974).

Berman, Larry, *Lyndon Johnson's War* (New York: Norton, 1989).

Berman, William C., *The Politics of Civil Rights in the Truman Administration* (Columbus: Ohio State University Press, 1970).

Bish, Musa, Jean Bullock, and Jean Milgram, *Racial Steering: The Dual Housing Market and Multiracial Neighborhoods* (Philadelphia: National Neighbors, 1973).

Blair, Thomas L., *Retreat to the Ghetto: The End of a Dream?* (New York: 1977).

Blau, Peter M., *Inequality and Heterogeneity: A Primitive Theory of Social Structure* (New York: Free Press, 1977).

Blauner, Bob, *Black Lives, White Lives: Three Decades of Race Relations in America* (Berkeley: University of California Press, 1989).

Blumenthal, Monica D., Robert L. Kahn, Frank M. Andrews, and Kendra B. Head, *Justifying Violence: Attitudes of American Men* (Ann Arbor: Institute for Social Research, University of Michigan, 1972).

Bogle, Donald, *Toms, Coons, Mulattoes, Mammies and Bucks: An Interpretive History of Blacks in American Films* (New York: Continuum, 1973, 1989).

Borchert, James, *Alley Life in Washington, D.C.: Family, Community, Religion, and Folklife in the City, 1850–1970* (Urbana: University of Illinois Press, 1980).

Braden, Anne, *The Wall Between* (New York: Monthly Review, 1958).

Bradford, Amory, *Oakland's Not for Burning* (New York: McKay, 1968).

Branch, Taylor, *Parting the Waters: America in the King Years, 1954–63* (New York: Touchstone, 1988).

Brauer, Carl M., *John F. Kennedy and the Second Reconstruction* (New York: Columbia University Press, 1977).

Brink, William, and Louis Harris, *Black and White: A Study of U.S. Racial Attitudes Today* (New York: Simon and Schuster, 1967).

Broussard, Albert S., *Black San Francisco: The Struggle for Racial Equality in the West, 1900–1954* (Lawrence: University of Kansas Press, 1993).

Brown, Richard Maxwell, *No Duty to Retreat: Violence and Values in American History and Society* (New York: Oxford University Press, 1991).

Brown, Robert K., *The Development of the Public Housing Program in the United States* (Atlanta: Bureau of Business and Economic Research, Georgia State College of Business Administration, 1960).

Brownell, Blaine A., *The Urban Ethos in the South, 1920–1930* (Baton Rouge: Louisiana State University Press, 1975).

Brundage, W. Fitzhugh, *Lynching in the New South: Georgia and Virginia, 1880–1930* (Urbana: University of Illinois Press, 1993).

Buell, Emmett H., Jr. and Richard A. Brisbin Jr., *School Desegregation and Defended Neighborhoods: The Boston Controversy* (Lexington: Heath, 1982).

Bunche, Ralph J., *The Political Status of the Negro in the Age of FDR*, ed. Dewey W. Grantham (Chicago: University of Chicago Press, 1973).

Burk, Robert Frederick, *Eisenhower Administration and Black Civil Rights* (Knoxville: University of Tennessee Press, 1984).

———, *Dwight D. Eisenhower: Hero and Politician* (Boston: Twayne, 1986).

Burkey, Richard M., *Racial Discrimination and Public Policy in the United States* (Lexington: Heath, 1971).

Button, James W., *Blacks and Social Change: Impact of the Civil Rights Movement in Southern Communities* (Princeton: Princeton University Press, 1989).

Callcott, George H., *Maryland and America: 1940–1980* (Baltimore: Johns Hopkins University Press, 1985).

Capeci, Dominic J., Jr., *The Harlem Riot of 1943* (Philadelphia: Temple University Press, 1977).

———, *Race Relations in Wartime Detroit: The Sojourner Truth Housing Controversy of 1942* (Philadelphia: Temple University Press, 1984).

Capeci, Dominic J., Jr., and Martha Wilkerson, *Layered Violence: The Detroit Rioters of 1943* (Jackson: University of Mississippi Press, 1991).

Carson, Clayborne, *In Struggle: SNCC and the Black Awakening of the 1960s* (Cambridge: Harvard University Press, 1981).

Carter, Dan T., *Scottsboro: A Tragedy of the American South*, rev. ed. (Baton Rouge: Louisiana State University Press, 1979).

———, *The Politics of Rage: George Wallace, the Origins of the New Conservatism, and the Transformation of American Politics* (New York: Simon and Schuster, 1995).

Cashman, Sean Dennis, *African-Americans and the Quest for Civil Rights, 1900–1990* (New York: New York University Press, 1991).

Cell, John W., *The Highest Stage of White Supremacy: The Origins of Segregation in South Africa and the American South* (Cambridge: Cambridge University Press, 1982).

Chafe, William H., *Civilities and Civil Rights: Greensboro, North Carolina, and the Black Struggle for Freedom* (New York: Oxford University Press, 1980).

Chandler, David Leon, *Henry Flagler: The Astonishing Life and Times of the Visionary Robber Baron Who Founded Florida* (New York: Macmillan, 1986).

Chesler, Mark, Joseph Sanders, and Debra Kalmuss, *Social Science in Court: Mobilizing Experts in the School Desegregation Cases* (Madison: University of Wisconsin Press, 1988).

Clark, Henry, *The Church and Residential Segregation: A Case Study on an Open Housing Covenant Campaign* (New Haven: Yale University Press, 1965).

Clark, Kenneth B., *Dark Ghetto: Dilemmas of Social Power* (New York: 1965).

Clark, Thomas A., *Blacks in Suburbs: A National Perspective* (New Brunswick: Center for Urban Policy Research, 1979).

Cohen, Richard M., and Jules Witcover, *A Heartbeat Away: The Investigation and Resignation of Vice President Spiro T. Agnew* (New York: Viking, 1974).

Cohodas, Nadine, *Strom Thurmond and the Politics of Southern Change* (New York: Simon and Schuster, 1993).

Colburn, David R., *Racial Change and Community Crisis: St. Augustine, Florida, 1877–1980* (Gainesville: University of Florida Press, 1991).

Collins, Keith E., *Black Los Angeles: The Maturing of the Ghetto, 1940–1950* (Saratoga: Century Twenty One, 1980).

Commission on Race and Housing, *Where Shall We Live?: Report of the Commission on Race and Housing* (Berkeley: University of California Press, 1958).

Congressional Quarterly Service, *Congressional Quarterly Almanac, 1954* (Washington, D.C.: CQ Service, 1955).

———, *Congressional Quarterly Almanac, 1957* (Washington, D.C.: CQ Service, 1958).

———, *Congressional Quarterly Almanac, 1964* (Washington, D.C.: CQ Service, 1965).

———, *Congressional Quarterly Almanac, 1965* (Washington, D.C.: CQ Service, 1966).

———, *Congressional Quarterly Almanac, 1966* (Washington, D.C.: CQ Service, 1967).

———, *Congressional Quarterly Almanac, 1967* (Washington, D.C.: CQ Service, 1968).

———, *Congressional Quarterly Almanac, 1968* (Washington, D.C.: CQ Service, 1969).

———, *Congressional Quarterly Almanac, 1980* (Washington, D.C.: CQ Service, 1981).

———, *Congressional Quarterly Almanac, 1988* (Washington, D.C.: CQ Service, 1989).

———, *Housing a Nation* (Washington, D.C.: CQ Service, 1966).

Connolly, Harold X., *A Ghetto Grows in Brooklyn* (New York: New York University Press, 1977).

Cripps, Thomas, *Black Film as Genre* (Bloomington: Indiana University Press, 1978).

Cortner, Richard C., *A Mob Intent on Death: The NAACP and the Arkansas Riot Cases* (Middletown: Wesleyan University Press, 1988).

Cromwell, Adelaide M., *The Other Brahmins: Boston's Upper Class, 1750–1950* (Fayetteville: University of Arkansas Press, 1994).

Cruse, Harold, *Plural but Equal: A Critical Study of Blacks and Minorities and America's Plural Society* (New York: Morrow, 1987).

Curry, Leonard P., *The Free Black in Urban America 1800–1850: The Shadow of the Dream* (Chicago: University of Chicago Press, 1981).

Curtis, Lynn A., *Violence, Race, and Culture* (Lexington: Heath, 1975).

Damerill, Reginald G., *Triumph in a White Suburb: The Dramatic Story of Teaneck, N.J., The First Town in the Nation to Vote for Integrated Schools* (New York: Morrow, 1968).

Daniel, Pete, *The Shadow of Slavery: Peonage in the South, 1901–1969* (Urbana: University of Illinois Press, 1972).

———, *Breaking the Land: The Transformation of Cotton, Tobacco, and Rice Cultures Since 1880* (Urbana: University of Illinois Press, 1985).

Darden, Joe T., Richard Child Hill, June Thomas, and Richard Thomas, *Detroit: Race and Uneven Development* (Philadelphia: Temple University Press, 1987).

Darrow, Clarence, *The Story of My Life* (New York: Scribner's, 1932).

Davies, Richard O., *Housing Reform During the Truman Administration* (Columbia: University of Missouri Press, 1966).

Davis, Mike, *City of Quartz: Excavating the Future in Los Angeles* (New York: Verso, 1990).

Dennis, Sam Joseph, *African-American Exodus and White Migration, 1950–1970: A Comparative Analysis of Population Movements and Their Relations to Labor and Race Relations* (New York: Garland, 1989).

Denton, John H., *Apartheid American Style* (Berkeley: Diablo, 1967).

Deskins, Donald Richard, Jr., *Residential Mobility of Negroes in Detroit, 1837–1965*, Michigan Geographical Publication 5 (Ann Arbor: University of Michigan, Department of Geography, 1972).

de Vise, Pierre, *Chicago's Widening Color Gap* (Chicago: Interuniversity Social Research Committee, 1967).

Dollard, John, *Caste and Class in a Southern Town* (New York: Harper & Bros., 2d ed., 1949).

Dorsett, Lyle W., *The Pendergast Machine* (New York: Oxford University Press, 1968).

Dorsey, James, *Up South: Blacks in Chicago's Suburbs, 1719–1983* (Bristol: Wyndham Hall, 1986).

Doucet, Michael, and John Weaver, *Housing the North American City* (Montreal and Kingston: McGill-Queen's University Press, 1991).

Doyle, Don H., *Nashville in the New South, 1880–1930* (Knoxville: University of Tennessee Press, 1985).

———, *New Men, New Cities, New South: Atlanta, Nashville, Charleston, Mobile, 1860–1910* (Chapel Hill: University of North Carolina Press, 1990).

Drake, St. Clair, and Horace Cayton, *Black Metropolis: A Study of Negro Life in a Northern City*, rev. and enlarged ed. (New York: Harcourt, Brace, 1970).

Du Bois, W. E. B., ed., *The Negro in Business* (New York: AMS Press, 1971, a reprint of the 1899 ed., Atlanta).

———, *The Souls of Black Folk* (New York: Bantam Classics, 1989, originally published 1903).

Duncan, Otis Dudley, and Beverly Duncan, *The Negro Population of Chicago: A Study in Residential Succession* (Chicago: University of Chicago Press, 1957).

Durett, Dan, and Dana F. White, *An-Other Atlanta: The Black Heritage* (Atlanta: Atlanta Bicentennial Commission, History Group, 1975).

Dye, Thomas R., *The Politics of Equality* (Indianapolis: Bobbs-Merrill, 1971).

Eisenhower, Dwight D., *Public Papers of the Presidents of the United States: Dwight D. Eisenhower, 1953* (Washington, D.C.: GPO, 1960).

Eley, Lynn W., and Thomas W. Casstevens, eds., *The Politics of Fair-Housing Legislation: State and Local Case Studies* (San Francisco: Chandler, 1968).

Equal Opportunity in Housing Cases, vol. 3 (Englewood Cliffs, N.J.: Prentice-Hall, 1983).

Essien-Udom, E. U., *Black Nationalism: A Search for Identity in America* (Chicago: University of Chicago Press, 1962).

Evans, Arthur S., Jr., and David Lee, *Pearl City, Florida: A Black Community Remembers* (Boca Raton: Florida Atlantic University Press, 1990).

Farmer, James, *Lay Bare My Heart: An Autobiography of the Civil Rights Movement* (New York: Plume, 1985).

Feagin, Joe R., *Ghetto Social Structure: A Survey of Black Bostonians* (San Francisco: R and E Research Associates, 1974).

Feagin, Joe R., and Michael P. Sikes, *Living with Racism: the Black Middle-Class Experience* (Boston: Beacon, 1994).

Fine, Sidney, *Frank Murphy: The Detroit Years* (Ann Arbor: University of Michigan Press, 1975).

———, *Frank Murphy: The New Deal Years* (Chicago: University of Chicago Press, 1979).

———, *Frank Murphy: The Washington Years* (Ann Arbor: University of Michigan Press, 1984).

Finkenstaedt, Rose L. H., *Face-to-Face: Blacks in America, White Perceptions and Black Realities* (New York: Morrow, 1994).

Fisher, Margaret, and Frances Levinson, *Federal, State, and Local Action Affecting Race and Housing* (Washington, D.C.: n.p., 1962).

Fisher, Robert Moore, *Twenty Years of Public Housing: Economic Aspects of the Federal Program* (New York: Harper & Bros., 1959).

Fleischman, Stanley, and Sam Rosenwein, *The New Civil Rights Act—What It Means to You* (Los Angeles: Blackstone, 1964).

Fogelson, Robert M., *The Fragmented Metropolis: Los Angeles, 1850–1930* (Cambridge: Harvard University Press, 1967).

Foner, Philip S., *W. E. B. Du Bois Speaks: Speeches and Addresses, 1890–1919* (New York: Pathfinder, 1970).

Formisano, Ronald P., *Boston Against Busing: Race, Class, and Ethnicity in the 1960s and 1970s* (Chapel Hill: University of North Carolina Press, 1991).

Franklin, John Hope, and Isidore Starr, eds., *The Negro in Twentieth Century America: A Reader on the Struggle for Civil Rights* (New York: Vintage, 1967).

Frazier, E. Franklin, *The Negro Family in the United States* (Chicago: University of Chicago Press, 1939).

———, *Black Bourgeoisie* (New York: Free Press, 1957).

Fredrickson, George M., *The Black Image in the White Mind: The Debate on Afro-American Character and Destiny, 1817–1914* (New York: Harper Torchbooks, 1972).

Freyer, Tony, *The Little Rock Crisis: A Constitutional Interpretation* (Westport: Greenwood Press, 1984).

Funigiello, Philip J., *The Challenge to Urban Liberalism: Federal-City Relations during World War II* (Knoxville: University of Tennessee Press, 1978).

Galster, George C., *Federal Fair Housing Policy in the 1980s: The Great Misapprehension* (Cambridge: 1988).

Galster, George C., and Edward W. Hill, eds., *The Metropolis in Black and White* (New Brunswick: Center for Urban Policy Research, 1992).

Gans, Herbert J., *The Levittowners: Ways of Life and Politics in a New Suburban Community* (New York: Columbia University Press, 1982, 1967).

Garrow, David J., *Bearing the Cross: Martin Luther King, Jr., and the Southern Christian Leadership Conference* (New York: Vintage, 1988).

Gayle, Addison, ed., *The Black Aesthetic* (Garden City: Doubleday, 1971).

Glazer, Nathan, *We Are All Multiculturalists Now* (Cambridge: Harvard University Press, 1997).

Goldfield, David R., *Cotton Fields and Skyscrapers: Southern City and Region, 1607–1980* (Baton Rouge: Louisiana State University Press, 1982).

Goodman, James, *Stories of Scottsboro* (New York: Pantheon, 1994).

Gottlieb, Peter, *Making Their Own Way: Southern Blacks' Migration to Pittsburgh, 1916–30* (Urbana: University of Illinois Press, 1987).

Graham, Hugh Davis, *The Civil Rights Era: Origins and Development of National Policy, 1960–1972* (New York: Oxford University Press, 1990).

Grant, Nancy L., *TVA and Black Americans: Planning for the Status Quo* (Philadelphia: Temple University Press, 1990).

Green, Constance McLaughlin, *The Secret City: A History of Race Relations in the Nation's Capital* (Princeton: Princeton University Press, 1967).

Greenberg, Cheryl Lynn, *"Or Does It Explode?" Black Harlem in the Great Depression* (New York: Oxford University Press, 1991).

Greenberg, Jack, *Race Relations and American Law* (New York: Columbia University Press, 1959).

Gregory, Dick, with James R. McGraw, *Up from Nigger* (New York: Stein and Day, 1976).

Grier, George, and Eunice Grier, *Privately Developed Interracial Housing* (Berkeley: University of California Press, 1960).

———, *Equality and Beyond: Housing Segregation and the Goals of the Great Society* (Chicago: Quadrangle, 1966).

———, *20 Years of Suburban Fair Housing, Inc.: A Pioneer Nondiscriminatory Real Estate Firm in Philadelphia's White Suburbia* (Bethesda: Grier Partnership, 1980).

Grimshaw, Allen D., ed., *Racial Violence in the United States* (Chicago: Aldine, 1969).

Grodzins, Morton, *The Metropolitan Area as a Racial Problem* (Pittsburgh: University of Pittsburgh Press, 1962).

Grossman, James R., *Land of Hope: Chicago, Black Southerners, and the Great Migration* (Chicago: University of Chicago Press, 1989).

Hacker, Andrew, *Two Nations: Black and White, Separate, Hostile, Unequal* (New York: Scribner's, 1992).

Halberstam, David, *The Fifties* (New York: Villard, 1993).

Hall, Raymond L., *Black Separatism and Social Reality: Rhetoric and Reason* (New York: Pergamon, 1977).

Hamby, Alonzo L., *Beyond the New Deal: Harry S. Truman and American Liberalism* (New York: Columbia University Press, 1973).

———, *Liberalism and Its Challengers: From F.D.R. to Bush*, 2d ed. (New York: Oxford University Press, 1992).

Hansberry, Lorraine, *A Raisin in the Sun* (New York: Vintage reprint, 1994).

———, *To Be Young, Gifted and Black: A Portrait of Lorraine Hansberry in Her Own Words*, adapted by Robert Nemiroff (New York: Samuel French, 1971).

Harris, Fred R., and Roger W. Wilkins, eds., *Quiet Riots: Race and Poverty in the United States* (New York: Pantheon, 1988).

Haskins, James, with Kathleen Benson, *Nat King Cole: A Personal and Professional Biography* (Chelsea, Mich.: Scarborough House, 1990).

Hays, Arthur Garfield, *Let Freedom Ring* (New York: Boni and Liveright, 1928).

———, *Trial by Prejudice* (New York: Covici-Friede, 1933).

Hays, R. Allen, *The Federal Government and Urban Housing: Ideology and Change in Public Policy*, 2d ed. (Albany: State University of New York Press, 1995).

Hecht, James L., *Because It Is Right: Integration in Housing* (Boston: Little, Brown, 1970).

Helper, Rose, *Racial Policies and Practices of Real Estate Brokers* (Minneapolis: University of Minnesota Press, 1969).

Henri, Florette, *Black Migration: Movement North, 1900–1920* (Garden City: Anchor/Doubleday, 1975).

Hesslink, George K., *Black Neighbors: Negroes in a Northern Rural Community* (Indianapolis: Bobbs-Merrill, 1974).

Higham, John, *Strangers in the Land: Patterns of American Nativism 1860–1925,* college ed. (New York: Atheneum, 1963).

Himes, Joseph S., *Racial Conflict in American Society* (Columbus: Merrill, 1973).

Hirsch, Arnold R., *Making the Second Ghetto: Race and Housing in Chicago, 1940–1960* (Cambridge: Cambridge University Press, 1983).

Hoover, Herbert, *The Memoirs of Herbert Hoover: The Cabinet and the Presidency, 1920–1933* (New York: Macmillan, 1952).

———, *The Memoirs of Herbert Hoover: The Great Depression, 1929–1941* (New York: Macmillan, 1952).

Housing Opportunities Made Equal, *Racial Steering by Real Estate Sales Agents in Metropolitan Richmond* (Richmond: HOME, 1980).

Hunsberger, Willard D., *Clarence Darrow: A Bibliography* (Metuchen: Scarecrow, 1981).

Huthmacher, J. Joseph, *Senator Robert F. Wagner and the Rise of Urban Liberalism* (New York: Atheneum, 1968).

Jackson, Kenneth T., *The Ku Klux Klan in the City, 1915–1930* (New York: Oxford University Press, 1967).

———, *Crabgrass Frontier: The Suburbanization of the United States* (New York: Oxford University Press, 1985).

Jacobs, Jane, *The Death and Life of Great American Cities* (New York: Vintage, 1961).

Jacoway, Elizabeth, and David R. Colburn, eds., *Southern Businessmen and Desegregation* (Baton Rouge: Louisiana State University Press, 1982).

Jennings, M. Kent, *Community Influentials: The Elites of Atlanta* (London: Free Press of Glencoe Collier-Macmillan, 1964).

Jensen, Richard J., *Clarence Darrow: The Creation of an American Myth* (New York: Greenwood, 1992).

Johnson, Charles S., *Backgrounds to Patterns of Negro Segregation* (New York: Crowell, 1943).

Johnson, Daniel M., and Rex R. Campbell, *Black Migration in America: A Social Demographic History* (Durham, N.C.: Duke University Press, 1981).

Johnson, James Weldon, *Along This Way: The Autobiography of James Weldon Johnson* (New York: Penguin, 1933).

———, *Black Manhattan* (New York: Knopf, 1940; Arno Press and the New York Times reprint, 1968).

Johnson, Lyndon Baines, *The Vantage Point: Perspectives of the Presidency, 1963–1969* (New York: Holt, Rinehart and Winston, 1971).

Johnson, Philip A., *Call Me Neighbor, Call Me Friend: The Case History of the Integration of a Neighborhood on Chicago's South Side* (Garden City: Doubleday, 1965).

Johnston, R. J., *Residential Segregation, the State and Constitutional Conflict in American Urban Areas* (London: Academic Press, 1984).

Joseph, Paul, *Cracks in the Empire: State Politics in the Vietnam War* (New York: Columbia University Press, 1987).

Karl, Barry D., *The Uneasy State: The United States from 1915 to 1945* (Chicago: University of Chicago Press, 1983).

Katzman, David, *Before the Ghetto: Black Detroit in the Nineteenth Century* (Urbana: University of Illinois Press, 1973).

Keating, W. Dennis, *The Suburban Racial Dilemma: Housing and Neighborhoods* (Philadelphia: Temple University Press, 1994).

Kennedy, Lawrence W., *Planning the City upon a Hill: Boston Since 1630* (Amherst: University of Massachusetts Press, 1992).

Killian, Lewis M., *The Impossible Revolution, Phase II: Black Power and the American Dream*, 2d ed. (New York: Random House, 1975).

King, Richard H., *Civil Rights and the Idea of Freedom* (New York: Oxford University Press, 1992).

Kirby, J. T., *Rural Worlds Lost: The American South, 1920–1960* (Baton Rouge: Louisiana State University Press, 1987).

Klehr, Harvey, John Earl Haynes, and Fridrikh Igorevich Frisov, *The Secret World of American Communism* (New Haven: Yale University Press, 1995).

Kluger, Richard, *Simple Justice: The History of Brown v. Board of Education and Black America's Struggle for Equality* (New York: Vintage, 1975).

Kronus, Sidney, *The Black Middle Class* (Columbus: Merrill, 1971).

Kuhn, Clifford M., Harlon E. Joye, and E. Bernard West, *Living Atlanta: An Oral History of the City* (Atlanta and Athens: Atlanta Historical Society and University of Georgia Press, 1990).

Kushner, James A., *Fair Housing: Discrimination in Real Estate Community Development and Revitalization* (Colorado Springs and New York: Shepard's, McGraw-Hill, 1983).

———, *Fair Housing: Discrimination in Real Estate Community Development and Revitalization*, 2d ed. (New York: McGraw-Hill, 1995).

Kusmer, Kenneth L., *A Ghetto Takes Shape: Black Cleveland, 1870–1930* (Urbana: University of Illinois Press, 1976).

Lake, Robert W., *The New Suburbanites: Race and Housing in the Suburbs* (New Brunswick: Rutgers University Press, 1981).

Landry, Bart, *The New Black Middle Class* (Berkeley: University of California Press, 1987).

Lane, Roger, *Roots of Violence in Black Philadelphia, 1860–1900* (Cambridge: Harvard University Press, 1986).

Larsen, Lawrence H., *The Urban South: A History* (Lexington: University of Kentucky Press, 1990).

Laurenti, Luigi, *Property Values and Race: Studies in Seven Cities* (Berkeley: University of California Press, 1960).

Leavell, R. H., T. R. Snavely, T. J. Woofter Jr., W. T. B. Williams, and Francis D. Tyson, *Negro Migration in 1916–1917* (Washington, D.C.: GPO; reprint New York: Negro Universities Press, 1969).

Lee, Douglass B., *Analysis and Description of Residential Segregation: An Application of Centrographic Technique to the Study of the Spatial Distribution of Ethnic Groups in Cities* (Ithaca: Cornell University Press, 1967, 1966).

Lee, Frank F., *Negro and White in Connecticut Town* (New York: Bookman, 1961).

Leigh, Wilhelmina A., *Shelter Affordability for Blacks: Crisis or Clamor?* (New Brunswick: Transaction Press, 1982).

Lemann, Nicholas, *The Promised Land: The Great Black Migration and How It Changed America* (New York: Vintage, 1991).

Lester, Julius, ed., *The Seventh Son: The Thought and Writings of W. E. B. Du Bois* (New York: Random House, 1971), two vols.

Levesque, George A., *Black Boston: African American Life and Culture in Urban America, 1750–1860* (New York: Garland, 1994).

Levine, David, *Internal Combustion: The Races in Detroit, 1915–1926* (Westport: Greenwood, 1976).

Levine, Lawrence W., *Black Culture and Black Consciousness: Afro-American Folk Thought from Slavery to Freedom* (New York: Oxford University Press, 1977).

Lewis, David L., *King: A Critical Biography* (New York: Praeger, 1970).

Litwack, Leon F., *North of Slavery: The Negro in the Free States, 1790–1860* (Chicago: University of Chicago Press, 1961).

Lockard, Duane, *Toward Equal Opportunity: A Study of State and Local Antidiscrimination Laws* (New York: Macmillan, 1968).

Logan, John R., and Harvey L. Molotch, *Urban Fortunes: The Political Economy of Place* (Berkeley: University of California Press, 1987).

Long, Herman H., and Charles S. Johnson, *People vs. Property: Race Restrictive Covenants in Housing* (Nashville: Fisk University Press, 1947).

Mahoney, Richard D., *JFK: Ordeal in Africa* (New York: Oxford University Press, 1983).

Marable, Manning, *Race, Reform and Rebellion: The Second Reconstruction in Black America, 1945–1982* (Jackson: University Press of Mississippi, 1984).

Marchand, B., *The Emergence of Los Angeles: Population and Housing in the City of Dreams, 1940–1970* (London: Pion, 1986).

Marsh, Robert, *Agnew The Unexamined Man: A Political Profile* (New York: Evans, 1971).

Martin, Elizabeth Anne, *Detroit and the Great Migration* (Ann Arbor: Bentley Historical Library/University of Michigan, 1993).

Martin, Harold H., *William Berry Hartsfield: Mayor of Atlanta* (Athens: University of Georgia Press, 1978).

———, *Atlanta and Environs: A Chronicle of Its People and Events: Years of Change and Challenge, 1940–1976*, vol. 3 (Atlanta and Athens: Atlanta Historical Society and University of Georgia Press, 1987).

Martin, James J., *American Liberalism and World Politics, 1931–1941*, vol. 2 (New York: Devin-Adair, 1964).

Massey, Douglas S., and Nancy A. Denton, *American Apartheid: Segregation and the Making of the Underclass* (Cambridge: Harvard University Press, 1993).

Matusow, Allen J., *The Unraveling of America: A History of Liberalism in the 1960s* (New York: Harper Torchbooks, 1984).

Mayhew, Leon H., *Law and Equal Opportunity: A Study of the Massachusetts Commission Against Discrimination* (Cambridge: Harvard University Press, 1968).

McClenahan, Bessie Averne, *The Changing Urban Neighborhood: From Neighbor to Nigh-Dweller* (Los Angeles: University of Southern California, 1929).

McCoy, Donald R., *The Presidency of Harry S. Truman* (Lawrence: University of Kansas Press, 1984).

McCullough, David, *Truman* (New York: Simon and Schuster, 1992).

McDougall, Harold A., *Black Baltimore: A New Theory of Community* (Philadelphia: Temple University Press, 1993).

McGovern, James R., *Anatomy of a Lynching: The Killing of Claude Neal* (Baton Rouge: Louisiana State University Press, 1982).

McKeever, Porter, *Adlai Stevenson: His Life and Legacy* (New York: Morrow, 1989).

McKinney, Scott, and Ann B. Schnare, *Trends in Residential Segregation by Race: 1960–1980* (Washington, D.C.: Urban Institute, 1986).

McMahan, C. A., *The People of Atlanta: A Demographic Study of Georgia's Capital City* (Athens: University of Georgia Press, 1950).

McMillen, Neil R., *The Citizen's Council: Organized Resistance to the Second Reconstruction, 1954–1964* (Urbana: University of Illinois Press, 1971).

McWhirter, Darien A., and Jon D. Bible, *Privacy as a Constitutional Right: Sex, Drugs, and the Right to Life* (New York: Quorum, 1992).

Meier, August, and Elliott M. Rudwick, *From Plantation to Ghetto: An Interpretive History of American Negroes* (New York: Hill and Wang, 1966).

———, *CORE: A Study in the Civil Rights Movement, 1942–1962* (Urbana: University of Illinois Press, 1975).

Metcalf, George R., *Fair Housing Comes of Age* (New York: Greenwood, 1988).

Milgram, Morris, *Good Neighborhood: The Challenge of Open Housing* (New York: Norton, 1977).

Miller, Warren E., and Santa Traugott, *American National Election Studies Data Sourcebook, 1952–1986* (Cambridge: Harvard University Press, 1989).

Mitchell, J. Paul, *Federal Housing Policy and Programs: Past and Present* (New Brunswick: Center for Urban Policy Research Rutgers University, 1985).

Molotch, Harvey Luskin, *Managed Integration: Dilemmas of Doing Good in the City* (Berkeley: University of California Press, 1972).

Moon, Elaine Latzman, *Untold Lives, Unsung Heroes: An Oral History of Detroit's African American Community, 1918–1967* (Detroit: Wayne State University Press, 1994).

Moore, Alfred Stevenson, *Public Housing Administration in the Birmingham District* (Birmingham: n.p., 1949).

Morris, Aldon, *The Origins of the Civil Rights Movement: Black Communities Organizing for Change* (New York: Free Press, 1984).

Morrow, E. Frederick, *Black Man in the White House: A Diary of the Eisenhower Years by the Administrative Officer for Special Projects* (New York: Coward-McCann, 1963).

Mowitz, Robert J., and Deil S. Wright, *Profile of a Metropolis: A Case Book* (Detroit: Wayne State University Press, 1962).

Murray, Frances, ed., *The Negro Handbook, 1942* (New York: Malliet, 1942).

———, *The Negro Handbook, 1949* (New York: Macmillan, 1949).

Myers, William Starr, and Walter H. Newton, *The Hoover Administration: A Documented Narrative* (New York: Scribner's, 1936).

Myrdal, Gunnar, with the assistance of Richard Sterner and Arnold Rose, *An American Dilemma: The Negro Problem and Modern Democracy* (New York: Harper & Brothers, 1944).

National Association of Housing Officials, *Housing Officials' Yearbooks (1935–1941)* (Chicago: NAHO, 1935–1941).

———, *Housing for the United States After the War* (Chicago: NAHO, 1944).

National Association of Realtors, *Affirmative Marketing Handbook* (Chicago: National Association of Realtors, 1975).

———, *Equal Opportunity Committee Handbook: A Handbook to Assist in Adoption and Implementation of the Affirmative Marking Agreement and in Conducting Educational and Outreach Programs* (Chicago: National Association of Realtors, 1978).

National Committee Against Discrimination in Housing, *Report of the National Conference on Equal Opportunity in Housing: Challenge to American Communities, Washington, D.C., April 25 and 26, 1963* (New York: NCDH, 1963).

———, Brotherhood-in-Action Conference, New York, 1965, *Affirmative Action to Achieve Integration: A Report Based on the NCDH Brotherhood-in-Action Conference*, New York: NCDH, 1966).

———, *How the Federal Government Builds Ghettos* (New York: NCDH, 1967).

National Urban League, *The State of Black America* (New York: National Urban League, 1977–1981).

Nesteby, James R., *Black Images in American Films, 1896–1954: The Interplay Between Civil Rights and Film Culture* (Washington, D.C.: University Press of America, 1982).

Newman, Dorothy K., Nancy J. Amidei, Barbara L. Carter, Dawn Day, William J. Kruvant, and Jack S. Russell, *Protest, Politics, and Prosperity: Black Americans and White Institutions, 1940–1975* (New York: Pantheon, 1978).

Newton, Michael, and Judy Ann Newton, *Racial and Religious Violence in America: A Chronology* (New York: Garland, 1991).

———, *The Ku Klux Klan: An Encyclopedia* (New York: Garland, 1991).

Norrell, Robert J., and Otis Dismuke, *The Other Side: The Story of Birmingham's Black Community* (Birmingham: n.p., 1981).

Northwood, L. K., and Ernest A. T. Barth, *Urban Desegregation: Negro Pioneers and Their White Neighbors* (Seattle: University of Washington Press, 1965).

Nunnelley, William A., *Bull Connor* (Tuscaloosa: University of Alabama Press, 1991).

Oldenquist, Andrew, *The Non-Suicidal Society* (Bloomington: Indiana University Press, 1986).

Olson, Sherry H., *Baltimore: The Building of an American City* (Baltimore: Johns Hopkins University Press, 1980).

O'Reilly, Kenneth, *"Racial Matters": The F.B.I.'s Secret File on Black America, 1960–1972* (New York: Free Press, 1989).

Orfield, Gary, and Carol Ashkinaze, *The Closing Door: Conservative Policy and Black Opportunity* (Chicago: University of Chicago Press, 1991).

Orfield, Gary, Albert Woolbright, and Helene Kim, *Neighborhood Change and Integration in Metropolitan Chicago: A Report of the Leadership Council for Metropolitan Open Communities* (Chicago: n.p., 1984).

Orser, W. Edward, *Blockbusting in Baltimore: The Edmondson Village Story* (Lexington: University of Kentucky Press, 1994).

Osofsky, Gilbert, *Harlem: The Making of a Ghetto, 1890–1930*, 2d ed. (New York: Harper Torchbooks, 1971).

Ottley, Roi, *"New World A-Coming": Inside Black America* (Boston: Houghton-Mifflin, 1943).

Ottley, Roi, and William J. Weatherby, eds., *The Negro in New York: An Informal Social History* (New York: New York Public Library and Oceana, 1967).

Parris, Guichard, and Lester Brooks, *Blacks in the City: A History of the National Urban League* (Boston: Little, Brown, 1971).

Patterson, James T., *Mr. Republican: A Biography of Robert A. Taft* (Boston: Houghton-Mifflin, 1972).

———, *Grand Expectations: The United States, 1945–1974* (New York: Oxford University Press, 1996).

Pemberton, William E., *Harry S. Truman: Fair Dealer and Cold Warrior* (Boston: Twayne, 1989).

Pettigrew, Thomas F., *Racially Separate or Together?* (New York: McGraw-Hill 1971).

———, *Racial Discrimination in the United States* (New York: Harper & Row, 1975).

Phillips, Cabell, *The Truman Presidency: The History of a Triumphant Succession* (New York: Macmillan, 1966).

Philpott, Thomas, *The Slum and the Ghetto: Neighborhood Deterioration and Middle-Class Reform, Chicago, 1880–1930* (New York: Oxford University Press, 1978).

Pinkney, Alphonso, *The Myth of Black Progress* (Cambridge: Cambridge University Press, 1984).

Pleck, Elizabeth Hafkin, *Black Migration and Poverty: Boston, 1865–1900* (New York: Academic Press, 1979).

Polenberg, Richard, *War and Society: The United States, 1941–1945* (New York: Lippincott, 1972).

———, *One Nation Divisible: Class, Race, and Ethnicity in the United States Since 1938* (New York: Viking Press, 1980).

Porter, Bruce, and Marvin Dunn, *The Miami Riot of 1980: Crossing the Bounds* (Lexington: Lexington Books, 1984).

Portes, Alejandro, and Alex Stepick, *City on the Edge: The Transformation of Miami* (Berkeley: University of California Press, 1993).

Potomac Institute, *The Federal Role in Equal Housing Opportunity: An Affirmative Program to Implement Executive Order 11063* (Washington, D.C.: Potomac Institute, 1964).

Rabinovitz, Francine F., with William J. Siembieda, *Minorities in Suburbs: The Los Angeles Experience* (Lexington: Heath, 1976).

Rabinowitz, Howard N., *Race Relations in the Urban South, 1865–1890* (Chicago: University of Illinois Press, 1980).

Raines, Howell, *My Soul Is Rested: Movement Days in the Deep South Remembered* (New York: Putman, 1977).

Rainwater, Lee, and William L. Yancey, *The Moynihan Report and the Politics of Controversy* (Cambridge: Harvard University Press, 1967).

Ralph, James R., Jr., *Northern Protest: Martin Luther King, Jr., Chicago, and the Civil Rights Movement* (Cambridge: Harvard University Press, 1993).

Reeves, Richard, *President Kennedy: Profile of Power* (New York: Touchstone, 1993).

Reid, Ira De A., *The Negro Community of Baltimore* (Baltimore: National Urban League, 1935).

———, *In a Minor Key: Negro Youth in Story and Fact* (Washington, D.C.: American Council on Education, 1940).

Revesz, Etta, *Hate Don't Make No Noise: Anatomy of a New Ghetto* (New York: Viking Press, 1978).

Roosevelt, Franklin Delano, *The Public Papers and Addresses of Franklin D. Roosevelt*, vol. 1: *The Genesis of the New Deal* (New York: Random House, 1938).

———, *The Public Papers and Addresses of Franklin D. Roosevelt*, vol. 2: *The Year of Crisis, 1933* (New York: Random House, 1938).

———, *The Public Papers and Addresses of Franklin D. Roosevelt*, vol. 3: *The Advance of Recovery and Reform, 1934* (New York: Random House, 1938).

———, *The Public Papers and Addresses of Franklin D. Roosevelt*, 1938 vol.: *The Continuing Struggle for Liberalism* (New York: Macmillan, 1941).

———, *The Public Papers and Addresses of Franklin D. Roosevelt*, 1940 vol.: *War—and Aid to Democracies* (New York: Macmillan, 1941).

Rorabaugh, W. J., *Berkeley at War: The 1960s* (New York: Oxford University Press, 1989).

Rose, Harold M., *Social Processes in the City: Race and Urban Residential Choice* (Washington, D.C.: Association of American Geographers, 1969).

Rose, Jerome G., *After Mount Laurel: The New Suburban Zoning* (New Brunswick: Center for Urban Planning Research, 1977).

Rosengarten, Theodore, *All God's Dangers: The Life of Nate Shaw* (New York: Avon, 1974).

Rosenwaike, Ira, *Population History of New York City* (Syracuse: Syracuse University Press, 1972).

Rossi, Peter H., and Robert A. Dentler, *The Politics of Urban Renewal: The Chicago Findings* (New York: Glencoe, 1961).

St. James, Warren D., *The National Association for the Advancement of Colored People: A Case Study in Pressure Groups* (New York: Exposition, 1958).

Saltman, Juliet Z., *Open Housing as a Social Movement: Challenge, Conflict and Change* (Lexington: Heath, 1971).

Scheiner, Seth M., *Negro Mecca: A History of the Negro in New York City, 1865–1920* (New York: New York University Press, 1965).

Schnare, Ann B., *The Persistence of Racial Segregation in Housing* (Washington, D.C.: Urban Institute, 1978).

Schnore, Leo F., *Class and Race in Cities and Suburbs* (Chicago: Markham, 1972).

Schuchter, Arnold, *White Power/Black Freedom: Planning the Future of Urban America* (Boston: Beacon, 1968).

Schulman, Bruce J., *Lyndon B. Johnson and American Liberalism: A Brief Biography with Documents* (Boston: St. Martin's Press, 1995).

Schuman, Howard, Charlotte Steeh, and Lawrence Bobo, *Racial Attitudes in America: Trends and Interpretations* (Cambridge: Harvard University Press, 1985).

Schutze, Jim, *The Accommodation: The Politics of Race in an American City* (Secaucus: Citadel Press, 1986).

Schwemm, Robert G., ed., *The Fair Housing Act After Twenty Years: A Conference at Yale Law School, March 1988* (New Haven: Yale University Press, 1989).

———, *Housing Discrimination: Law and Litigation* (Deerfield: Clark Boardman Callaghan, 1997.

Sheil, Most Reverend Bernard J., and Loren Miller, *Racial Restrictive Covenants* (Chicago: Chicago Council Against Racial and Religious Discrimination, 1946).

Shull, Steven A., *A Kinder, Gentler Racism? The Reagan-Bush Civil Rights Legacy* (Armonk: M. E. Sharpe, 1993).

Silver, Christopher, *Twentieth-Century Richmond: Planning, Politics, and Race* (Knoxville: University of Tennessee Press, 1984).

Silver, Christopher, and John V. Moeser, *A Separate City: Black Communities in the Urban South, 1940–1968* (Lexington: University of Kentucky Press, 1995).

Sims, Edward, *Black Nomads in the Urban Centers: The Effects of Racism and Urbanism on the Black Family* (Washington, D.C.: University Press of America, 1978).

Sitkoff, Harvard, *A New Deal for Blacks: The Emergence of Civil Rights as a National Issue,* vol. 1: *The Depression Decade* (New York: Oxford University Press, 1978).

———, *The Struggle for Black Equality* (New York: Hill and Wang, 1981).

Smith, David M., *Inequality in an American City: Atlanta, Georgia, 1960–1970* (London: Department of Geography, Queen Mary College, University of London, 1981).

Smith, Douglas L., *The New Deal in the Urban South* (Baton Rouge: Louisiana State University Press, 1988).

Sonenshein, Raphael F., *Politics in Black and White: Race and Power in Los Angeles* (Princeton: Princeton University Press, 1993).

Sorenson, Theodore C., *Kennedy* (New York: Harper & Row, 1965).

Southern Regional Council, *Housing for Negroes in Atlanta, Georgia* (Atlanta: n.p., 1959).

Spear, Allan H., *Black Chicago: The Making of a Negro Ghetto* (Urbana: University of Illinois Press, 1967).

Squires, Gregory D., Larry Bennett, Kathleen McCourt, and Philip Nyden, *Chicago: Race, Class, and the Response to Urban Decline* (Philadelphia: Temple University Press, 1987).

Stacey, William A., *Black Home Ownership: A Sociological Case Study of Metropolitan Jacksonville* (New York: Praeger, 1972).

Steele, Shelby, *The Content of Our Character: A New Vision of Race in America* (New York: St. Martin's Press, 1990).

Stein, Judith, *The World of Marcus Garvey: Race and Class in Modern Society* (Baton Rouge: Louisiana State University Press, 1986).

Stevenson, Adlai E., *The Papers of Adlai E. Stevenson:* vol. 4, *"Let's Talk Sense to the American People," 1952–1955* (Boston: Little, Brown, 1974).

Stone, Clarence N., *Regime Politics: Governing Atlanta, 1946–1988* (Lawrence: University of Kansas Press, 1989).

Stone, Irving, *Clarence Darrow for the Defense* (Garden City: Doubleday, 1941).

Taeuber, Karl E., and Alma F. Taeuber, *Negroes in Cities: Residential Segregation and Neighborhood Change* (Chicago: Aldine, 1965).

Taub, Richard P., D. Garth Taylor, and Jan D. Dunham, *Paths of Neighborhood Change: Race and Crime in Urban America* (Chicago: University of Chicago Press, 1984).

Tindall, George B., *The Emergence of the New South, 1913–1945* (Baton Rouge: Louisiana State University Press, 1967).

Truman, Harry S., *Speech Before the Harlem Ministerial Alliance*, October 29, 1948, reprinted in Gregory Bush, ed., *Campaign Speeches of American Presidential Candidates, 1948–1984* (New York: Ungar, 1985), 10–2.

———, *State of the Union Address*, January 5, 1949, reprinted in *Congressional Digest* 28 (1949), 41–3, 64.

———, *Memoirs: Volume One: Years of Decisions* (New York: Doubleday, 1955).

———, *Public Papers of the President, Harry S. Truman, 1949* (Washington, D.C.: GPO, 1964).

Tucker, William, *The Excluded Americans: Homelessness and Housing Policies* (Washington, D.C.: Regnery Gateway, 1990).

Tushnet, Mark V., *The NAACP's Legal Strategy Against Segregated Education, 1925–1950* (Chapel Hill: University of North Carolina Press, 1987).

———, *Making Civil Rights Law: Thurgood Marshall and the Supreme Court, 1936–1961* (New York: Oxford University Press, 1994).

Tuttle, William M., Jr., *Race Riot: Chicago in the Red Summer of 1919* (New York: Atheneum, 1970).

Unger, Irwin, and Debi Unger, *Turning Point: 1968* (New York: Scribner's, 1988).

Viorst, Milton, *Fire in the Streets: America in the 1960s* (New York: Touchstone/Simon and Schuster, 1979).

von Furstenberg, George M., Bennett Harrison, and Ann R. Horowitz, eds., *Patterns of Racial Discrimination*, vol. 1: *Housing* (Lexington: Heath, 1974).

Vose, Clement E., *Caucasians Only: The Supreme Court, the NAACP, and the Restrictive Covenant Cases* (Berkeley: University of California Press, 1967).

Wade, Richard C., *Slavery in the Cities: The South, 1820–1860* (New York: Oxford University Press, 1964).

Walker, Mabel L., *Urban Blight and Slums: Economic and Legal Factors in Their Origin, Reclamation, and Prevention* (Cambridge: Harvard University Press, 1938).

Warren, Donald I., *Black Neighborhoods: An Assessment of Community Power* (Ann Arbor: University of Michigan Press, 1975).

Washington, James M., ed., *A Testament of Hope: The Essential Writings of Martin Luther King, Jr.* (San Francisco: Harper & Row, 1986).

Watson, Frank, *Housing Problems and Possibilities in the United States* (New York: Harper & Bros., 1935).

Weaver, Robert C., *Hemmed In: ABC's of Race Restrictive Housing Covenants* (Chicago: American Council on Race Relations, 1945).

———, *The Negro Ghetto* (New York: Russell and Russell, 1967 reissue, 1948).

———, *Dilemmas of Urban America* (Cambridge: Harvard University Press, 1966).

———, *The Urban Complex* (New York: Anchor, 1966).

Weicher, John C., *Housing: Federal Policies and Programs* (Washington, D.C.: American Enterprise Institute, 1980).

Weigley, Russell, ed., *Philadelphia: A 300-Year History* (New York: Norton, 1982).

Weinberg, Kenneth G., *A Man's Home, a Man's Castle* (New York: McCall, 1971).

Weiss, Marc A., *The Rise of the Community Builders: The American Real Estate Industry and Urban Land Planning* (New York: Columbia University Press, 1987).

West, Cornel, *Race Matters* (New York: Vintage, 1994).

White, Theodore H., *The Making of the President, 1960* (New York: Book-of-the-Month Club ed., 1988; originally published Atheneum, 1961).

White, Walter, *A Man Called White: The Autobiography of Walter White* (New York: Viking, 1948).

White, William S., *The Taft Story* (New York: Harper & Bros., 1954).

Widick, B. J., *Detroit: City of Race and Class Violence* (Detroit: Wayne State University Press, 1989).

Wilbanks, William, *The Make My Day Law: Colorado's Experiment in Home Protection* (Lanham: University Press of America, 1990).

Wilcox, Roger, *The Psychological Consequences of Being a Black American: A Sourcebook of Research by Black Psychologists* (New York: Wiley, 1971).

Wilkins, Roy, with Tom Mathews, *Standing Fast: The Autobiography of Roy Wilkins* (New York: Viking, 1982).

Williams, Robin M., Jr., *Strangers Next Door: Ethnic Relations in American Communities* (Englewood Cliffs: Prentice-Hall, 1964).

Williamson, Joel, *After Slavery: The Negro in South Carolina During Reconstruction, 1861–1877* (New York: Norton, 1975).

———, *The Crucible of Race: Black-White Relations in the American South Since Emancipation* (New York: Oxford University Press, 1984).

Wilson, Franklin D., *Residential Consumption, Economic Opportunity, and Race* (New York: Academic Press, 1979).

Wilson, William Julius, *The Declining Significance of Race: Blacks and Changing American Institutions* (Chicago: University of Chicago Press, 1978).

Witcover, Jules, *White Knight: The Rise of Spiro Agnew* (New York: Random House, 1972).

Wolff, Reinhold P., and David K. Gillogly, *Negro Housing in the Miami Area: Effects of the Postwar Building Boom* (Miami: Bureau of Business and Economic Research–University of Miami, 1951).

Wolk, Allan, *The Presidency and Black Civil Rights: Eisenhower to Nixon* (Rutherford: Fairleigh Dickinson University Press, 1971).

Wolman, Harold, *Politics of Federal Housing* (New York: Dodd, Mead, 1971).

Woodward, C. Vann, *The Strange Career of Jim Crow*, 3d rev. ed. (New York: Oxford University Press, 1974).

Work, Monroe N., ed., *Negro Year Book: An Annual Encyclopedia of the Negro*, vols. 1, 3–11 (Tuskegee: Negro Year Book Publishing, 1912, 1914–1952).

Wright, George C., *Life Behind a Veil: Blacks in Louisville, Kentucky, 1865–1930* (Baton Rouge: Louisiana State University Press, 1985).

———, *Racial Violence in Kentucky, 1865–1940: Lynchings, Mob Rule, and "Legal Lynchings"* (Baton Rouge: Louisiana State University Press, 1990).

Wright, Gwendolyn, *Building the Dream: A Social History of Housing in America* (New York: Pantheon, 1981).

Wrinn, Stephen M., *Civil Rights in the Whitest State* (Lanham: University Press of America, 1995).

Yinger, John, *Prejudice and Discrimination in the Urban Housing Market* (Cambridge: Department of City and Regional Planning, Harvard University, 1977).

———, *Racial Transition and Public Policy* (Cambridge: Department of City and Regional Planning, Harvard University, 1978).

Zunz, Olivier, *The Changing Face of Inequality: Urbanization, Industrial Development, and Immigrants in Detroit, 1880–1920* (Chicago: University of Chicago Press, 1982).

ARTICLES AND BOOK CHAPTERS

Abrams, Charles, "The Housing Problem and the Negro," *Daedalus* 95 (1966), 64–76.

———, "Some Blessings of Urban Renewal," in James Q. Wilson, ed., *Urban Renewal: The Record and the Controversy* (Cambridge: MIT Press, 1966).

Adams, Samuel L., "Blueprint for Segregation: A Survey of Atlanta Housing," *New South* 22 (1967), 73–84.

Alexander, Will W., "The Negro in the Nation," *Survey Graphic* 36 (1947), 92–96.

Allen, Francis A., "Critique of 'Racial Discrimination in "Private" Housing,'" *California Law Review* 22 (1964), 46–49.

———, "Remembering *Shelley* v. *Kraemer*: Of Public and Private Worlds," *Washington University Law Quarterly* 67 (Fall 1989), 709–37.

Aloi, Frank, and Arthur Abba Goldberg, "Racial and Economic Exclusionary Zoning: The Beginning of the End?" *Urban Law Annual* 4 (1971), 9–62.

American Academy of Arts and Sciences, "Transcript of the Conference on the Negro American—May 14–15, 1965," *Daedalus* 95 (1966), 287–441.

Aronovici, Carol, "The Future of Negro Housing," *Opportunity* 18 (1940), 378–9, 389.

Ash, Fred C., "The Last of the Restrictive Covenants," *Appraisal Journal* 21 (1953), 595–7.

Ashby, William M., "No Jim Crow in Springfield Federal Housing," *Opportunity: Journal of Negro Life* 20 (1942), 170–71, 188.

Ayers, Thomas G., "The 'Summit Agreement,'" in David J. Garrow, ed., *Chicago 1966: Open Housing Marches, Summit Negotiations, and Operation Breadbasket* (Brooklyn: Carlson, 1989), 147–54.

Babcock, Frederick M., Maurice R. Massey Jr., and Walter L. Greene, "Techniques of Residential Location Rating," *Appraisal Journal* 6 (1938), 133–40.

Baker, Elmore, and William A. Occomy, "A Real Estate Program for Negroes," *Opportunity* 19 (1941), 45–46.

Baruch, Dorothy W., "Sleep Comes Hard," *Nation* 141 (January 1945), 95–96.

Bayor, Ronald H., "Roads to Racial Segregation: Atlanta in the Twentieth Century," *Journal of Urban History* 15 (1988), 3–21.

———, "Urban Renewal, Public Housing and the Racial Shaping of Atlanta," *Journal of Policy History* 1 (1989), 419–39.

———, "The Civil Rights Movement as Urban Reform: Atlanta's Black Neighborhoods and a New 'Progressivism,'" *Georgia Historical Quarterly* 77 (1993), 286–309.

Beard, Rick, "From Suburb to Defended Neighborhood: The Evolution of Inman Park and Ansley Park, 1890–1980," *Atlanta Historical Journal* 26 (Summer–Fall 1982), 113–40.

Beirne, D. Randall, "The Impact of Black Labor on European Immigration into Baltimore's Oldtown, 1790–1910," *Maryland Historical Magazine* 83 (1988), 331–45.

Bellush, Jewel, and Murray Hausknecht, "Urban Renewal: An Historical Overview," in Jewel Bellush and Murray Hausknecht, eds., *Urban Renewal: People, Politics, and Planning* (Garden City: Anchor-Doubleday, 1967), 3–16.

Benoit, M. Deborah, "Expanding Protection Against Blockbusters Through the First Amendment," *Urban Law Annual* 7 (1974), 319–28.

Betten, Neil, and Raymond A. Mohl, "The Evolution of Racism in an Industrial City, 1906–1940: A Case Study of Gary, Indiana," *Journal of Negro History* 59 (1974), 51–64.

Berry, J. W., "Cultural Relations in Plural Societies: Alternatives to Segregation and their Sociopsychological Implications," in Norman Miller and Marilyn B. Brewer, eds., *Groups in Contact: The Psychology of Desegregation* (Orlando: Academic Press, 1984), 11–27.

Black, Charles L., Jr., "'State Action,' Equal Protection, and California's Proposition 14," *Harvard Law Review* 81 (1967), 69–109.

Blauner, Bob, "Self-Segregation Should Be Accepted," in Paul A. Winters, ed., *Race Relations: Opposing Viewpoints* (San Diego: Greenhaven, 1996), 216–23.

"Blight, Bigotry, and Bombs," in Harold C. Fleming, ed., *Changing Patterns in the New South* (Atlanta: Southern Regional Council, 1953), 25–27.

Bobo, Lawrence, Howard Schuman, and Charlotte Steeh, "Changing Racial Attitudes Toward Residential Integration," in John M. Goering, ed., *Housing Desegregation and Federal Policy* (Chapel Hill: University of North Carolina Press, 1986), 152–69.

Bolling, Edward A., "A Coherent Method for Weighing the Discriminatory Effect of Exclusionary Zoning: *Huntington Branch, NAACP* v. *Town of Huntington,* 844 F.2d 926 (2d Cir. 1988)," *Washington University Journal of Urban and Contemporary Law* 37 (1990), 257–72.

Brearley, H. C., "The Negro's New Belligerency," *Phylon* 5 (1944), 339–45.

Brewer, Marilyn B., and Norman Miller, "Beyond the Contact Hypothesis: Theoretical Perspectives on Desegregation," in Miller and Brewer, eds., *Groups in Contact,* 281–302.

Brittain, John C., "Integration in a Color-Blind Society Is Not Possible," in Winters, ed., *Race Relations,* 205–8.

Bromley, David G., and Charles F. Longino Jr., "On White Racism," in David G. Bromley and Charles F. Longino Jr., eds., *White Racism and Black Americans* (Cambridge: Schenkman, 1972), 1–13.

Broussard, Albert S., "Organizing the Black Community in the San Francisco Bay Area, 1915–1930," *Arizona and the West* 23 (1981), 335–54.

Brown, William H., "Access to Housing: The Role of the Real Estate Industry," reprinted in Paul Finkelman, ed., *The Era of Integration and Civil Rights, 1930–1990* (New York: Garland, 1992), 74–86.

Brownell, Blaine A., "The Urban South Comes of Age, 1900–1940," in Blaine A. Brownell and David R. Goldfield, eds., *The City in Southern History: The Growth of Urban Civilization in the South* (Port Washington: National University Publications—Kennikat Press, 1977), 123–58.

Bullard, Robert D., "Blacks and the American Dream of Housing," in Jamshid A. Momeni, ed., *Race, Ethnicity and Minority Housing in the United States* (New York: Greenwood, 1986), 53–68.

Bullock, Henry Allen, "Urbanism and Race Relations," in Rupert B. Vance and Nicholas J. Demerath, eds., *The Urban South* (Chapel Hill: University of North Carolina Press, 1954), 207–29.

Burby, Raymond J., III, and Shirley F. Weiss, "Public Policy for Suburban Integration . . . The Case for New Communities," *Urban Law Annual* 11 (1976), 101–30.

Butler, John C., "Due Process of Law and Racial Restrictive Covenants," *Appraisal Journal* 16 (1948), 79–85.

———, "The Outlawry of Racial Restrictive Covenants," *Appraisal Journal* 16 (1948), 370–75.

Butler, John Sibley, "Myrdal Revisited: The Negro in Business," *Daedalus* 124 (Winter 1995), 199–221.

Butterfield, Fox, "The Exodus of Newark Blacks," in Louis H. Masotti and Jeffrey K. Hadden, eds., *Suburbia in Transition* (New York: New Viewpoints, 1973), 74–77.

Caldwell, Earl, "The Problems of a Black Suburb," in Masotti and Hadden, eds., *Suburbia in Transition,* 78–81.

Casey-Leininger, Charles F., "Making the Second Ghetto in Cincinnati: Avondale, 1925–1970," in Henry Louis Taylor, Jr., ed., *Race and the City: Work, Community, and Protest in Cincinnati, 1820–1970* (Urbana: University of Illinois Press, 1993), 232–57.

Casstevens, Thomas W., "The Defeat of Berkeley's Fair-Housing Ordinance," in Lynn W. Eley and Thomas W. Casstevens, eds., *The Politics of Fair-Housing Legislation: State and Local Case Studies* (San Francisco: Chandler, 1968), 187–236.

————, "California's Rumford Act and Proposition 14," in Eley and Casstevens, eds., *Politics of Fair-Housing*, 237–84.

Cayton, Horace R., "Negro Morale," *Opportunity* 19 (1941), 371–75.

Chandler, James P., "Fair Housing Laws: A Critique," *Hastings Law Journal* 24 (1973), 159–213.

Christensen, Lawrence O., "Race Relations in St. Louis, 1865–1916," *Missouri Historical Review* 78 (1984), 123–36.

Clark, Evans, "The Subsidy in Low-Rental Housing," in David T. Rowlands and Coleman Woodbury, eds., *Current Developments in Housing, The Annals of the American Academy of Political and Social Science* 190 (1937), 151–61.

Clark, Kenneth B., "The Civil Rights Movement: Momentum and Organization," *Daedalus* 95 (1966), 239–67.

Clark, William A. V., "Residential Segregation in American Cities: A Review and Interpretation," *Population Research and Policy Review* 5 (1986), 95–127.

————, "Understanding Residential Segregation in American Cities: Interpreting the Evidence," *Population Research and Policy Review* 8 (1988).

————, "Neighborhood Transitions in Multiethnic-Racial Contexts," *Journal of Urban Affairs* 15 (1993), 161–72.

Clay, Phillip L., "The Process of Black Suburbanization," *Urban Affairs Quarterly* 14 (1979), 405–24.

Cobb, James C., "Urbanization and the Changing South: A Review of Literature," *South Atlantic Urban Studies* 1 (1977), 253–66.

Cohen, William, "The Great Migration as a Lever for Social Change," in Alfredteen Harrison, ed., *Black Exodus: The Great Migration from the American South* (Jackson: University Press of Mississippi), 72–82.

Connolly, Kathleen, "The Chicago Open Housing Conference," in Garrow, *Chicago 1966*, 49–95.

Corley, Florence Fleming, "Atlanta's Techwood and University Homes Projects: The Nation's Laboratory for Public Housing," *Atlanta History* 31 (Winter 1987–1988), 17–36.

Cushman, Robert E., "The Laws of the Land," *Survey Graphic* 36 (1947), 14–18, 97–99.

Daly, Victor R., "The Housing Crisis in New York City," *The Crisis* 21 (1920), 61–62.

Daniel, Pete, "Going Among Strangers: Southern Reactions to World War II," *Journal of American History* 77 (1990), 886–911.

Darden, Joe T., "Choosing Neighbors and Neighborhoods: The Role of Race in Housing Preference," in Gary A. Tobin, ed., *Divided Neighborhoods: Changing Patterns of Racial Segregation, Urban Affairs Annual Review* 32 (Newbury Park: Sage, 1987), 15–42.

Darnton, John, "The Exodus of Newark Whites," in Masotti and Hadden, eds., *Suburbs in Transition*, 66–69.

de Graaf, Lawrence B., "The City of Black Angels: Emergence of the Los Angeles Ghetto, 1890–1930," *Pacific Historical Review* 33 (1970), 328–50.

Dorsen, Norman, "Critique of 'Racial Discrimination in 'Private' Housing,'" *California Law Review* 22 (1964), 50–55.

Downs, Anthony, "Alternative Futures for the American Ghetto," *Appraisal Journal* 36 (1968), 486–530.

———, "Residential Segregation: Its Effects on Education," *Civil Rights Digest* 3 (Fall 1970), 2–8.

———, "The Successes and Failures of Federal Housing Policy," in Eli Ginzberg and Robert M. Solow, eds., *The Great Society: Lessons for the Future* (New York: Basic Books, 1974), 124–45.

Du Bois, W. E. B., "An Essay Toward a History of the Black Man in the Great War," *The Crisis* 18 (1919), 63–87.

———, "Race Relations in the United States, 1917–1947," in Bernard Sternsher, ed., *The Negro in Depression and War: Prelude to Revolution, 1930–1945* (Chicago: Quadrangle, 1969), 29–44.

———, "The Black North: A Social Study," in Richard J. Meister, ed., *The Black Ghetto: Promised Land or Colony?* (Lexington: D. C. Heath, 1972), 1–19.

Dubofsky, Jean Eberhart, "Fair Housing: A Legislative History and a Perspective," *Washburn Law Journal* 8 (1969), 149–66.

Dudziak, Mary L., "Desegregation as a Cold War Imperative," in Finkelman, ed., *The Era of Integration and Civil Rights*, 133–92.

Duncan, Otis D., and Beverly Duncan," A Methodological Analysis of Segregation Indices," *American Sociological Review* 20 (1955), 210–17.

Durant, Thomas J., Jr. and Joyce S. Louden, "The Black Middle-Class in America: Historical and Contemporary Perspectives," *Phylon* 47 (1986), 253–63.

Durr, W. Theodore, "People of the Peninsula," *Maryland Historical Magazine* 77 (1982), 27–53.

Ellis, Ann Wells, "A Crusade Against 'Wretched Attitudes': The Commission on Interracial Cooperation's Activities in Atlanta," *Atlanta Historical Journal* 23 (Spring 1979), 21–44.

———, "'Uncle Sam Is My Shepherd': The Commission on Interracial Cooperation and the New Deal in Georgia," *Atlanta Historical Journal* 30 (Spring 1986), 47–63.

Eskew, Glenn T., "The Alabama Christian Movement for Human Rights and the Birmingham Struggle for Civil Rights, 1956–1963," in David J. Garrow, ed., *Birmingham, Alabama, 1956–1963: The Black Struggle for Civil Rights* (Brooklyn: Carlson, 1989), 3–114.

Farley, Reynolds, "The Changing Distribution of Negroes Within Metropolitan Areas: The Emergence of Black Suburbs," *American Journal of Sociology* 75 (1970), 512–29.

———, "Black-White Residential Segregation: The Views of Myrdal in the 1940s and Trends in the 1980s," in Obie Clayton Jr., ed., *An American Dilemma Revisited: Race Relations in a Changing World* (New York: Russell Sage, 1996), 45–75.

Field, S. S., "The Constitutionality of Segregation Ordinances," 5 *Virginia Law Review* (November 1917), 81–91.

Finley, Mary Lou, "The Open Housing Marches, Chicago, Summer 1966," in Garrow, ed., *Chicago 1966*, 1–47.

Fishel, Leslie H., Jr., "The Negro in the New Deal Era," in Sternsher, ed., *The Negro in Depression and War*, 7–28.

Flanders, Sen. Ralph E., "Address to the National Public Housing Conference, New York, May 4, 1948," *Congressional Digest* 27 (1948), 174, 176, 178.

Fleming, Harold C., "Housing for a New Middle Class," *The Survey* 87 (1951), 384–85.

———, "The Federal Government and Civil Rights: 1961–1965," *Daedalus* 94 (Fall 1965), 921–48.

Flowerdew, Robin, "Spatial Patterns of Residential Segregation in a Southern City," *Journal of American Studies* 13 (1979), 93–107.

Foard, Ashley A., and Hilbert Fefferman, "Federal Urban Renewal Legislation," in Wilson, ed., *Urban Renewal*, 71–125.

Foley, Donald L., "Institutional and Contextual Factors Affecting the Housing Choices of Minority Residents," in Amos H. Hawley and Vincent Rock, eds., *Segregation in Residential Areas: Papers on Racial and Socioeconomic Factors in Choice of Housing* (Washington, D.C.: National Academy of Sciences, 1973), 85–147.

Franklin, John Hope, "History of Racial Segregation in the United States," in Ira De A. Reid, ed., *Racial Desegregation and Integration, Annals of the American Academy of Political and Social Sciences* 304 (1956), 1–9.

Frazier, E. Franklin, "Human, All Too Human," *Survey Graphic* 36 (1947), 74–75, 99–100.

———, "Some Effects of the Depression on the Negro in Northern Cities," in Richard J. Meister, ed., *The Black Ghetto: Promised Land or Colony* (Lexington: D.C. Heath, 1972), 119–127.

Galster, George C., "More Than Skin Deep: The Effect of Housing Discrimination on the Extent and Pattern of Racial Residential Segregation in the United States," in Goering, ed., *Housing Desegregation*, 119–38.

———, "Residential Segregation and Interracial Discrimination in Housing," *Journal of Urban Economics* 21 (1987), 22–44.

———, "Residential Segregation in American Cities: A Contrary Review," *Population Research and Policy Review* 7 (1988), 93–112.

———, "Neighborhood Racial Change, Segregationist Sentiments, and Affirmative Marketing Policies," *Journal of Urban Economics* 27 (1990), 344–61.

———, "Racial Discrimination in Housing Markets During the 1980s: A Review of the Audit Evidence," *Journal of Planning Education and Research* 9 (1990), 165–75.

———, "Racial Steering in Housing Markets: A Review of the Audit Evidence," *Review of Black Political Economy* 18 (1990), 105–29.

———, "Racial Steering by Real Estate Agents: Mechanisms and Motives," *Review of Black Political Economy* 19 (1990), 39–63.

Galster, George C., and Donald L. Demarco, "Prointegrative Policy: Theory and Practice," *Journal of Urban Affairs* 15 (1993), 141–60.

Galster, George C., and W. Mark Keeney, "Race, Residence, Discrimination, and Economic Opportunity: Modeling the Nexus of Urban Racial Phenomena," *Urban Affairs Quarterly* 24 (1988), 87–117.

Gans, Herbert J., "The White Exodus to Suburbia Steps Up," in Masotti and Hadden, eds., *Suburbs in Transition*, 46–61.

———, "The Failure of Urban Renewal," in Wilson, ed., *Urban Renewal*, 537–57.

George, Paul S., "Colored Town: Miami's Black Community, 1896–1930," *Florida Historical Quarterly* 56 (1978), 432–47.

———, "Policing Miami's Black Community, 1896–1930," *Florida Historical Quarterly* 57 (1979), 434–50.

Glasco, Laurence, "Double Burden: The Black Experience in Pittsburgh," in Samuel P. Hays, ed., *City at the Point: Essays on the Social History of Pittsburgh* (Pittsburgh: University of Pittsburgh Press, 1989), 69–103.

Glassberg, Susan Spiegel, "Legal Control of Blockbusting," *Urban Law Annual* 5 (1972), 145–70.

Glazer, Nathan, "Race and the Suburbs," in O. H. Koenigsberger, S. Groak, and B. Bernstein, eds., *The Work of Charles Abrams* (Oxford: Pergamon, 1980), 175–80.

Goering, John M., "Neighborhood Tipping and Racial Transition: A Review of Social Science Evidence," *Journal of the American Institute of Planners* 44 (1978), 68–78.

Goodman, John L. and Mary L. Streitwieser, "Explaining Racial Differences: A Study of City-to-Suburb Residential Mobility," *Urban Affairs Quarterly* 18 (1983), 301–25.

Gorham, Thelma Thurston, "Negroes and Japanese Evacuees," *The Crisis* 52 (1945), 314–16, 330.

Gottlieb, Peter, "Rethinking the Great Migration: A Perspective from Pittsburgh," in Joe William Trotter Jr., ed., *The Great Migration in Historical Perspective: New Dimensions of Race, Class, and Gender* (Bloomington: Indiana University Press, 1991), 68–82.

Grafton, Carl, "James E. Folsom's 1946 Campaign," *Alabama Review* 35 (1982), 172–99.

Granger, Lester B., "Negroes and War Production," *Survey Graphic* 31 (1942), 469–71, 543–44.

Graubard, Stephen R., "An American Dilemma Revisited," *Daedalus* 124 (Winter 1995), v–xxxiv.

Gremley, William, "Social Control in Cicero," in Allen D. Grimshaw, ed., *Racial Violence in the United States* (Chicago: Aldine, 1969), 170–83.

Grier, George, and Eunice Grier, "Equality and Beyond: Housing Segregation in the Great Society," *Daedalus* 95 (Winter 1966), 77–106.

———, "The Negro Ghetto and Federal Housing Policy," in Robinson O. Everett and John D. Johnston Jr., eds., *Housing* (Dobbs Ferry: Oceana, 1968), 191–99.

Grimshaw, Allen D., "Relationships Among Prejudice, Discrimination, Social Tension, and Social Violence," in Grimshaw, ed., *Racial Violence in the United States*, 446–54.

———, "Negro-White Relations in the Urban North: Two Areas of High Conflict Potential," in Grimshaw, ed., *Racial Violence in the United States*, 455–65.

———, "Urban Racial Violence in the United States: Changing Ecological Considerations," in Grimshaw, ed., *Racial Violence in the United States*, 287–98.

Gross, Peter, "Still No Year of Jubilee," *Civil Rights Digest* 1 (Fall 1968), 9–12.

Grothaus, Larry, "Kansas City Blacks, Harry Truman and the Pendergast Machine," *Missouri Historical Review* 69 (1974), 65–82.

Guest, Avery M., "The Changing Racial Composition of Suburbs, 1950–1970," *Urban Affairs Quarterly* 14 (1978), 195–206.

Haas, Edward F., "The Southern Metropolis, 1940–1976," in Brownell and Goldfield, eds., *The City in Southern History*, 159–91.

Hamilton, David L., and George D. Bishop, "Attitudinal and Behavioral Effects of Initial Integration of White Suburban Neighborhoods," *Journal of Social Issues* 32 (1976), 47–67.

Hansen Julia L., and Franklin J. James, "Housing Discrimination in Small Cities and Nonmetropolitan Areas," in Tobin, ed., *Divided Neighborhoods*, 181–207.

Hare, Nathan, "The Sociological Study of Racial Conflict," *Phylon* 33 (1972), 27–31.

Harlan, Louis R., "Booker T. Washington and the Politics of Accommodation," in John Hope Franklin and August Meier, eds., *Black Leaders of the Twentieth Century* (Urbana: University of Chicago Press, 1982), 1–18.

Harris, Carl V., "Reforms in Government Control of Negroes in Birmingham, Alabama, 1890–1920," *Journal of Southern History* 38 (1972), 567–600.

Hartman, Chester, "The Housing of Relocated Families," in Wilson, ed., *Urban Renewal*, 293–335.

Hatchett, David, "Black Nationalism," *The Crisis* 95 (February 1988), 14–21.

Hauser, Philip M., "The Challenge of Metropolitan Growth," *Appraisal Journal* 27 (1959), 220–27.

Hawkins, W. Ashbie, "A Year of Segregation in Baltimore," *The Crisis* 3 (1911), 27–30.

Headrick, William Cecil, "Race Riots: Segregated Slums," *Current History* (September 1943), 30–34.

Hein, Virginia H., "The Image of 'A City Too Busy To Hate': Atlanta in the 1960's," *Phylon* 33 (1972), 205–21.

Helper, Rose, "Success and Resistance Factors in the Maintenance of Racially Mixed Neighborhoods," in Goering, ed., *Housing Desegregation*, 170–194.

Hirsch, Arnold R., "Massive Resistance in the Urban North: Trumbull Park, Chicago, 1953–1957," *Journal of American History* 82 (September 1995), 522–50.

Hirschberg, Theodore, Alan Burstein, Eugene Ericksen, Stephanie Greenberg, and William Yancey, "A Tale of Three Cities: Blacks and Immigrants in Philadelphia, 1850–1880, 1930, and 1970," in Wade Clark Roof, ed., *Race and Residence in American Cities, The Annals of the American Academy of Political and Social Science* 441 (1979), 55–81.

Hoben, Edmond H., "Administrative Problems of Government in Housing," in Rowlands and Woodbury, eds., *Current Trends in Housing*, 176–83.

Horne, Frank S., "Providing New Housing for Negroes," *Opportunity* 18 (1940), 305–8.

———, "Interracial Housing in the United States," *Phylon* 19 (1958), 13–20.

Horowitz, Harold W., "Fourteenth Amendment Aspects of Racial Discrimination in 'Private' Housing," *California Law Review* 52 (March 1964), 1–45.

Hoult, Thomas Ford, "About Detroit . . . We Told You So," *The Crisis* 74 (1967), 407–10.

Hughes, Mark Alan, and Janice Fanning Madden, "Residential Segregation and the Economic Status of Black Workers: New Evidence for an Old Debate," *Journal of Urban Economics* 29 (1991), 28–49.

Hunter, Charlayne, "On the Case of Resurrection City," in August Meier, ed., *The Transformation of Activism* (New York: Adline, 1970), 5–27.

Hunter, Robert F., "Virginia and the New Deal," in John Braeman, Robert H. Bremner, and David Brody, eds., *The New Deal: The State and Local Levels* (Columbus: Ohio State University Press, 1975), 103–36.

Hutcheson, Charles Sterling, "The Constitutionality of the President's Order Barring Discrimination in Federally Assisted Housing," in Alfred Avins, ed., *Open Occupancy vs. Forced Housing Under the Fourteenth Amendment: A Symposium on Anti-Discrimination Legislation, Freedom of Choice, and Property Rights in Housing* (New York: Bookmailer, 1963), 100–11.

Huttman, Elizabeth D., and Terry Jones, "American Suburbs: Desegregation and Resegregation," in Elizabeth D. Huttman, ed., *Urban Housing Segregation of Minorities in Western Europe and the United States* (Durham: Duke University Press, 1991).

Ink, Dwight A., "The Department of Housing and Urban Development—Building a New Federal Department," in Everett and Johnston, eds., *Housing*, 191–99.

Jacoby, Tamar, "Integration in a Color-Blind Society Should Be the Goal," in Winters, ed., *Race Relations*, 200–4.

Janowitz, Morris, "Patterns of Collective Racial Violence," in Hugh Davis Graham and Ted Robert Gurr, eds., *The History of Violence in America: Historical and Comparative Perspectives* (New York: Praeger, 1969).

Johnson, Barry V., "Housing Segregation in the Urban Population of the Midwest," in Huttman, ed., *Urban Housing Segregation*, 243–71.

Johnson, James Weldon, "Detroit," in *The Crisis* 32 (1926), 117–20.

Johnson, Lee F., "Housing: A 1950 Tragedy," *The Survey* 86 (1950), 551–55.

Johnson, Marylynn S., "War as Watershed: The East Bay and World War II," *Pacific Historical Review* 63 (1994), 315–31.

Jones, Eugene Kinckle, "The Negro in Industry and in Urban Life," from *Opportunity* 12 (May 1934), reprinted in Philip S. Foner and Ronald L. Lewis, eds., *The Black Worker: A Documentary History from Colonial Times to the Present*, vol. 6: *The Era of Post-War Prosperity and the Great Depression, 1920–1936* (Philadelphia: Temple University Press, 1981), 103–7.

Jung, Herbert, "Control of Panic Selling by Regulation of 'For Sale' Signs," *Urban Law Annual* 10 (1975), 323–33.

Kain, John F., "The Influence of Race and Income on Racial Segregation and Housing Policy," in Goering, ed., *Housing Desegregation*, 99–118.

———, "Housing Market Discrimination and Black Suburbanization in the 1980s," in Tobin, ed., *Divided Neighborhoods*, 68–94.

Kantrowitz, Nathan, "Racial and Ethnic Residential Segregation in Boston 1830–1970," in Roof, ed., *Race and Residence in American Cities*, 41–54.

Kapsis, Robert E., "Powerlessness in Racially Changing Neighborhoods," *Urban Affairs Quarterly* 14 (1979), 425–42.

Kelleher, Daniel T., "St. Louis' 1916 Residential Segregation Ordinance," *The Bulletin, Missouri Historical Society* 26 (1970), 239–48.

Kennedy, T. H., "Racial Tensions Among Negroes in the Intermountain Northwest," *Phylon* 7 (1946), 358–64.

Knight, Raphael, "Stage Spotlights Harlem Housing," *The Crisis* 45 (1938), 143–44.

Kushner, James A., "Litigation Strategies and Judicial Review Under Title I of the Housing and Community Development Act of 1974," *Urban Law Annual* 11 (1976), 37–100.

———, "An Unfinished Agenda: The Federal Fair Housing Enforcement Effort," *Yale Law and Policy Review* 6 (1988), 348–60.

Kusmer, Kenneth L., "The Black Urban Experience in American History," in Darlene Clark Hine, ed., *The State of Afro-American History: Past, Present, and Future* (Baton Rouge: Louisiana State University Press, 1986), 91–122.

Landye, Thomas M., and James J. Vanecko, "The Politics of Open Housing in Chicago and Illinois," in Eley and Casstevens, eds., *Politics of Fair Housing*, 65–104.

Lasker, Bruno, "The Negro in Detroit," *The Survey* 58 (April 15, 1927), 72–73, 123.

Lasker, Loula D., "Three Years of Public Housing," *Survey Graphic* 26 (1937), 78–82, 115–16.

Laurenti, Luigi M., "Effects of Nonwhite Purchases on Market Prices of Residences," *Appraisal Journal* 20 (1952), 314–29.

Leahy, Peter J., "Are Racial Factors Important for the Allocation of Mortgage Money?" *American Journal of Economics and Sociology* 44 (1985), 183–96.

Ledbetter, William H., "Public Housing—a Social Experiment Seeks Acceptance," in Everett and Johnston, eds., *Housing*, 306–43.

Lee, Barrett A., and Peter B. Wood, "The Fate of Residential Integration in American Cities: Evidence from Racially Mixed Neighborhoods, 1970–1980," *Journal of Urban Affairs* 12 (1990), 425–36.

Leigh, Wilhelmina A., "Civil Rights Legislation and the Housing Status of Black Americans: An Overview," *Review of Black Political Economy* 19 (1991), 5–28.

———, "Trends in the Housing Status of Black Americans Across Selected Metropolitan Areas," *Review of Black Political Economy* 19 (1991), 43–64.

Leigh, Wilhelmina A., and James D. McGhee, "A Minority Perspective on Residential Racial Integration," in Goering, ed., *Housing Desegregation*, 31–42.

Levenson, Frances, and Margaret Fisher, "The Struggle for Open Housing," *Progressive* 26 (December 1962), 25–29.

Lieberson, Stanley, and Donna K. Carter, "A Model for Inferring the Voluntary and Involuntary Causes of Residential Segregation," *Demography* 19 (1982), 511–26.

———, "Temporal Changes and Urban Differences in Residential Segregation: A Reconsideration," *American Journal of Sociology* 88 (1982), 296–310.

Lieberson, Stanley, and Arnold R. Silverman, "Precipitants and Underlying Conditions of Race Riots," in Grimshaw, ed., *Racial Violence in the United States*, 354–70.

Lilienthal, David E., "Has the Negro the Right of Self-Defense?" *Nation* 121 (1925), 724–25.

Locke, Alain, "The Unfinished Business of Democracy," *Survey Graphic* 31 (1942), 455–59.

Logan, John R., and Mark Schneider, "Racial Segregation and Racial Change in American Suburbs," *American Journal of Sociology* 89 (1984), 874–88.

Logan, John R., and Linda Brewster Stearns, "Suburban Racial Segregation as a Nonecological Process," *Social Forces* 60 (1981), 61–73.

Logan, Rayford W., "The United States Supreme Court and the Segregation Issue," in Reid, ed., *Racial Desegregation*, 10–16.

Lomax, D. A., "Valuation in an Infiltrated Neighborhood," *Appraisal Journal* 39 (1971), 247–53.

Lotchin, Roger W., "California Cities and the Hurricane of Change: World War II in the San Francisco, Los Angeles, and San Diego Metropolitan Areas," *Pacific Historical Review* 63 (1994), 393–420.

Macklin, Harriett J., and Bob Holmes, "Housing and Black Atlanta," in Bob Holmes, ed., *The Status of Black Atlanta 1993* (Atlanta: Southern Center for Studies in Public Policy, 1993), 87–104.

Marshall, Thurgood, "Equal Justice Under Law," *The Crisis* 46 (1939), 199–201.

———, "The Gestapo in Detroit," *The Crisis* 50 (1943), 232–33, 246–47.

Martin, Louis E., "The Truth About Sojourner Truth," *The Crisis* 49 (1942), 112–13, 142.

———, "Detroit—Still Dynamite," *The Crisis* 51 (1944), 8–10, 25.

Martin, Robert E., "Racial Invasion," *Opportunity* 19 (1941), 324–28.

Masotti, Louis H., and Jeffrey K. Hadden, "Introduction," in Masotti and Hadden, eds., *Suburbs in Transition*, 3–12.

Massey, Douglas S., "Residential Segregation in American Cities," in Fred L. Pincus and Howard J. Erlich, eds., *Race and Ethnic Conflict: Contending Views on Prejudice, Discrimination, and Ethnoviolence* (Boulder: Westview, 1994), 124–32.

Massey, Douglas S., Gretchen A. Condran, and Nancy A. Denton, "The Effect of Residential Segregation on Black Social and Economic Well-Being," *Social Forces* 66 (1980), 29–56.

Massey, Douglas S., and Nancy A. Denton, "Spatial Assimilation as a Socioeconomic Outcome," *American Sociological Review* 50 (1985), 94–105.

———, "Trends in the Residential Segregation of Blacks, Hispanics, and Asians, 1970–1980," *American Sociological Review* 52 (1987), 802–25.

Massey, Douglas S., and Eric Fong, "Segregation and Neighborhood Quality: Blacks, Hispanics, and Asians in the San Francisco Metropolitan Area," *Social Forces* 69 (1990), 15–32.

Maurer, David J., "Relief Problems and Politics in Ohio," in Braeman, Bremner, and Brody, *The New Deal: The State and Local Levels*, 77–102.

McDaniel, Clyde O., Jr., "Housing Segregation of Blacks in the South," in Huttman, ed., *Urban Housing Segregation*, 272–84.

McGovney, D. O., "Racial Residential Segregation by State Court Enforcement of Restrictive Covenants or Conditions in Deeds Is Unconstitutional," *California Law Review* 33 (March 1945), 5–39.

McGraw, B. T., "The Housing Act of 1954 and Implications for Minorities," *Phylon* 16 (1955), 171–82.

McMillion, Elmer M., "Racial Restrictive Covenants Revisited," in Avins, ed., *Open Occupancy*, 90–9.

McRae, Teresa L., "*Havens Realty Corp. v. Coleman*: Extending Standing in Racial Steering Cases to Housing Associations and Testers," *Urban Law Annual* 22 (1981), 107–34.

Menge, Del, and George Ramey, "Constitutional Law: The End of Private Racial Discrimination in Housing Through Revival of the Civil Rights Act of 1866," *Tulsa Law Journal* 6 (1970), 146–63.

Meyer, Douglas K., "Evolution of a Permanent Negro Community in Lansing," *Michigan History* 55 (1971), 141–54.

———, "Changing Negro Residential Patterns in Michigan's Capital, 1915–1970," *Michigan History* 56 (1972), 151–67.

Millen, James S., "Factors Affecting Racial Mixing in Residential Areas," in Hawley and Rock, eds., *Segregation in Residential Areas*, 148–71.

Miller, Loren, "Covenants in the Bear Flag State," *The Crisis* 53 (1946), 138–40, 155.

———, "Supreme Court Covenant Decision—An Analysis," *The Crisis* 55 (September 1948), 265–66, 285.

————, "The Protest Against Housing Segregation," in Arnold M. Rose, ed., *The Negro Protest*, *The Annals of the American Academy of Political and Social Science* 357 (1965), 73–79.

————, "Louisville's Housing Anniversary," *The Crisis* 74 (1967), 255–58.

Milobsky, David, "Power from the Pulpit: Baltimore's African-American Clergy, 1950–1970," *Maryland Historical Magazine* 89 (1994), 275–89.

Mohl, Raymond A., "On the Edge: Blacks and Hispanics in Metropolitan Miami Since 1959," *Florida Historical Quarterly* 69 (1990), 37–56.

Moon, Henry Lee, "Danger in Detroit," *The Crisis* 53 (1946), 12–13, 28–29.

Moore, John Robert, "The New Deal in Louisiana," in Braeman, Bremner, and Brody, *The New Deal: The State and Local Levels*, 137–66.

Moore, Shirley Ann, "Getting There, Being There: African-American Migration to Richmond, California, 1910–1945," in Trotter, ed., *Great Migration*, 106–27.

Morris, William R., "The 1968 Housing Act: New Hope for Negroes," *The Crisis* 75 (1968).

Murphy, Thomas P., "Race-Based Accounting: Assigning the Costs and Benefits of a Racially Motivated Annexation," *Urban Affairs Quarterly* 14 (1978), 169–94.

Muth, Richard, "The Causes of Housing Segregation," U.S. Commission on Civil Rights, *Issues in Housing Discrimination* (Washington, D.C.: GPO, 1986).

"The Negro in the Mid-War South—the Durham Statement by Negro Southerners," in Harold C. Fleming, ed., *Changing Patterns in the New South* (Atlanta: Southern Regional Council, 1953), 1–3.

Neverdon-Morton, Cynthia, "Black Housing Patterns in Baltimore City, 1885–1953," *The Maryland Historian* 16 (1985), 41–56.

"New York Property Owners Adopt a Restrictive Covenant," in Richard B. Sherman, ed., *The Negro and the City* (Englewood Cliffs: Prentice-Hall, 1970), 23–24.

Norrell, Robert J., "Caste in Steel: Jim Crow Careers in Birmingham, Alabama," *Journal of American History* 73 (1986), 669–94.

O'Brien, Robert W., and Lee M. Brooks, "Race Relations in the Pacific Northwest," *Phylon* 7 (1946), 21–31.

Olsen, Edgar O., "Do the Poor and the Black Pay More for Housing?" in George M. von Furstenberg, Bennett Harrison, and Ann R. Horowitz, eds., *Patterns of Racial Discrimination*, vol. 1: *Housing* (Lexington: Heath, 1974), 205–11.

"Open Housing," *Civil Rights Digest* 4 (December 1971), 17–21.

Orwin, Clifford, "All Quiet on the (Post) Western Front?" *The Public Interest* 123 (Spring 1996), 3–21.

Oster, Donald B., "Reformers, Factionalists, and Kansas City's 1925 City Manager Charter," *Missouri Historical Review* 72 (1978), 296–327.

Page, Alfred N., "Race and Property Values," *Appraisal Journal* 36 (1968), 335–52.

Palmer, Dewey H., "Moving North: Migration of Negroes During World War I," from *Phylon* 25 (1967), reprinted in Bromley and Longino, eds., *White Racism and Black Americans*, 29–43.

Parker, Elsie Smith, "Both Sides of the Color Line, Part I," *Appraisal Journal* 11 (1943), 27–34.

————, "Both Sides of the Color Line, Part II," *Appraisal Journal* 11 (1943), 231–49.

Peabody, Malcolm E., Jr., "Custom Changing: Fundamental Change Required, HUD Tells Realtors," *The Journal of Intergroup Relations* 2 (1973), 46–58.

Pearce, Diana, "Gatekeepers and Homeseekers: Institutional Patterns of Racial Steering," *Social Problems* 26 (1979), 325–42.

Pearlman, Kenneth, "The Closing Door: The Supreme Court and Residential Segregation," *Journal of the American Institute of Planners* 44 (1978), 160–69.

Pettigrew, Thomas F., "Attitudes on Race and Housing: A Social-Psychological View," in
Hawley and Rock, eds., *Segregation in Residential Areas*, 21–84.

———, "New Patterns of Prejudice: The Different Worlds of 1984 and 1964," in Pincus
and Erlich, eds., *Race and Ethnic Violence*, 53–59.

Pilkington, Charles Kirk, "The Trials of Brotherhood: The Founding of the Commission on
Interracial Cooperation," *Georgia Historical Quarterly* 69 (1985), 55–80.

Polenberg, Richard, "The Decline of the New Deal," in John Braeman, Robert H. Bremner,
and David Brody, eds., *The New Deal: The National Level* (Columbus: Ohio State University Press, 1975), 246–66.

Poston, Ted, "On Appeal in the Supreme Court," *The Survey* 85 (1949), 18–21.

Powell, Richard, "The Relationship Between Property Rights and Civil Rights," in John H.
Denton, ed., *Race and Property* (Berkeley: Diablo, 1964), 16–34.

Power, Garrett, "Apartheid Baltimore Style: The Residential Segregation Ordinance of 1910–
1913," *Maryland Law Review* 42 (1983), 289–328.

———, "Pyrrhic Victory: Daniel Goldman's Defeat of Zoning in the Maryland Court of
Appeals," *Maryland Historical Magazine* 82 (1987).

"Program of the Chicago Freedom Movement, July 1966," in Garrow, *Chicago 1966*, 97–109.

Quarles, Benjamin, "A. Philip Randolph: Labor Leader at Large," in Franklin and Meier,
eds., *Black Leaders of the Twentieth Century*, 139–65.

Quimby, Ernest, "Bedford-Stuyvesant: The Making of a Ghetto," in Rita Seiden Miller, ed.,
Brooklyn USA: The Fourth Largest City in America (New York: Brooklyn College Press,
1979), 229–38.

Rabinowitz, Howard N., "More Than the Woodward Thesis: Assessing *The Strange Career
of Jim Crow*," *Journal of American History* 75 (1988), 842–56.

Randolph, A. Philip, "The Economic Crisis on the Negro," from *Opportunity* 9 (May 1931),
reprinted in Foner and Lewis, *The Black Worker*, 71–76.

———, "Why Should We March?" *Survey Graphic* 31 (1942), 488–89.

Reddick, L. D., ed., "The Negro in the North During Wartime," *Journal of Educational
Sociology* 17 (1943–1944), 257–320.

———, ed., "The New Race-Relations Frontier," *Journal of Educational Sociology* 19 (1945–
1946), 129–206.

Reed, Veronica M., "Civil Rights Legislation and the Housing Status of Black Americans:
Evidence from Fair Housing Audits and Segregation Indices," *Review of Black Political
Economy* 19 (1991), 29–42.

Reid, Ira De A., "Southern Ways," *Survey Graphic* 36 (1947), 39–42, 107–08.

———, "Special Problems of Negro Migration During the War," in Frank G. Boudreau
and Clyde V. Kiser, eds., *Postwar Problems of Migration* (New York: Milbank Memorial
Fund, 1947), 150–58.

Reissman, Leonard, "Urbanization in the South," in John C. McKinney and Edgar T.
Thompson, eds., *The South in Continuity and Change* (Durham: Duke University Press,
1965), 79–100.

Resnick, Joel E., "Title VIII Litigation: Demise of the *Prima Facie* Case Doctrine in the
Seventh Circuit—*Metropolitan Housing Development Corp.* v. *Village of Arlington Heights*,"
Urban Law Annual 15 (1978), 325–35.

Rice, Bradley R., "Urbanization, 'Atlanta-ization,' and Suburbanization: Three Themes for the Urban History of Twentieth-Century Georgia," *Georgia Historical Quarterly* 68 (1984), 40–59.

———, "The Battle of Buckhead: The Plan of Improvement and Atlanta's Last Big Annexation," *The Atlanta Historical Journal* 25 (Winter 1985), 5–22.

Rice, Roger L., "Residential Segregation by Law, 1910–1917," *Journal of Southern History* 34 (1968), 179–99.

"Robert C. Weaver—New Cabinet Member," *The Crisis* 73 (1966), 120–21, 129.

Robinson, A. Gram, ed., "The Controversy over a Long-Range Federal Housing Program," *Congressional Digest* 27 (1948), 165–92.

Robinson, Ned, "Civil Rights and Property Rights Re-Examined," in Denton, ed., *Race and Property*, 35–41.

Robison, Joseph B., "Housing—The Northern Civil Rights Frontier," *Western Reserve Law Review* 13 (1961), 101–27.

———, "Fair-Housing Legislation in the City and State of New York," in Eley and Casstevens, eds., *Politics of Fair Housing*, 27–64.

Roof, Wade Clark, "Race and Residence: The Shifting Basis of American Race Relations," in Roof, ed., *Race and Residence in American Cities*, 1–12.

Roof, Wade Clark, Thomas L. Van Valey, and Daphne Spain, "Residential Segregation in Southern Cities: 1970," *Social Forces* 55 (1976), 56–71.

Rose, Harold M., "Metropolitan Miami's Changing Negro Population, 1950–1960," *Economic Geography* 40 (1964), 221–38.

Rosenthal, Jack, "More Blacks in the Suburbs," in Masotti and Hadden, eds., *Suburbs in Transition*, 74–77.

Ross, B. Joyce, "Mary McLeod Bethune and the National Youth Administration: A Case Study of Power Relationships in the Black Cabinet of Franklin Delano Roosevelt," in Franklin and Meier, *Black Leaders of the Twentieth Century*, 191–220.

Ryon, Roderick N., "Old West Baltimore," *Maryland Historical Magazine* 77 (1982), 54–69.

Sancton, Thomas, ed., "Segregation," *Survey Graphic* 36 (January 1947).

Schmidt, Benno C., Jr., "Principle and Prejudice: The Supreme Court and Race in the Progressive Era, Part 1: The Heyday of Jim Crow," *Columbia Law Review* 82 (1982), 444–524.

Scott, Richard R., "Blacks in Segregated and Desegregated Neighborhoods: An Exploratory Study," *Urban Affairs Quarterly* 18 (1983), 327–46.

Sessa, Frank B., "Miami in 1926," *Tequesta* 16 (1956), 15–36.

Shannon, Jasper B., "Political Obstacles to Civil Rights Legislation," in Robert K. Carr, ed., *Civil Rights in America: Annals of the American Academy of Political and Social Science* 275 (1951), 53–60.

Shorr, Howard, "'Race Prejudice Is Not Inborn—It Is Learned': The Exhibit Controversy at the Los Angeles Museum of History, Science and Art, 1950–1952," *California History* 69 (1990), 276–83, 311–12.

Showalter, J. Stuart, "Intergovernmental Conflict in the Regulation of Blockbusting Activities," *Urban Law Annual* 4 (1971), 212–15.

Sitkoff, Harvard, "The Detroit Race Riot of 1943," *Michigan History* 53 (1969), 183–206.

———, "Harry Truman and the Election of 1948: The Coming of Age of Civil Rights in American Politics," *Journal of Southern History* 37 (1971), 597–616.

————, "Racial Militancy and Interracial Violence in the Second World War," *Journal of American History* 58 (1971), 661–81.

Slavens, George Everett, "The Missouri Negro Press, 1875–1920," *Missouri Historical Review* 64 (1970), 413–31.

Sloane, Martin E., "Housing Discrimination—The Response of Law," *North Carolina Law Review* 42 (1963), 106–35.

————, "The 1968 Housing Act: Best Yet—But Is It Enough?" *Civil Rights Digest* 1 (Fall 1968), 1–8.

Sloane, Martin E., and Monroe H. Freedman, "The Executive Order on Housing: The Constitutional Basis for What It Fails To Do," *Howard Law Journal* 9 (1963), 1–19.

Smith, Richard A., "Creating Stable Racially Integrated Communities: A Review," *Journal of Urban Affairs* 15 (1993), 115–40.

Smith, T. Lynn, "The Emergence of Cities," in Vance and Demerath, eds., *The Urban South*, 24–37.

————, "The Redistribution of the Negro Population of the United States, 1910–1960," *Journal of Negro History* 51 (1966), 155–73.

Spain, Daphne, "Race Relations and Residential Segregation in New Orleans: Two Centuries of Paradox," in Roof, ed., *Race and Residence in American Cities*, 82–96.

————, "Pyrrhic Victory: Daniel Goldman's Defeat of Zoning in the Maryland Court of Appeals," *Maryland Historical Magazine* 82 (1987), 275–87.

Spaulding, Charles B., "Housing Problems of Minority Groups in Los Angeles County," *Annals of the American Academy of Political and Social Science* 284 (1946), 220–25.

Steele, Shelby, "Self-Segregation Should Be Condemned," in Winters, ed., *Race Relations*, 209–15.

Stern, Oscar I., "The End of Restrictive Covenants," *Appraisal Journal* 16 (1948), 434–42.

Stokes, Anson Phelps, "American Race Relations in War Time," *Journal of Negro Education* 14 (1945), 535–51.

Stucker, Jennifer L., "Race and Residential Mobility: The Effects of Housing Assistance Programs on Household Behavior," in Goering, ed., *Housing Desegregation*, 253–61.

Sugrue, Thomas J., "Crabgrass-Roots Politics: Race, Rights, and the Reaction Against Liberalism in the Urban North, 1940–1964," *Journal of American History* 82 (September 1995), 551–78.

"Symposium on the State Action Doctrine of *Shelley* v. *Kraemer:* Panel Discussion," *Washington University Law Quarterly* 67 (Fall 1989), 773–76.

Taeuber, Karl, "The Contemporary Context of Housing Discrimination," *Yale Law and Policy Review* 6 (1988), 339–47.

Tansill, Charles C., Alfred Avins, Sam S. Crutchfield, and Kenneth Colegrove, "The Fourteenth Amendment and Real Property Rights," in Avins, ed., *Open Occupancy*, 68–89.

Taylor, Henry Louis, Jr., and Vicky Dula, "The Black Residential Experience and Community Formation in Antebellum Cincinnati," in Taylor, ed., *Race and the City*, 96–125.

————, "City Building, Public Policy, the Rise of the Industrial City, and Black Ghetto–Slum Formation in Cincinnati, 1850–1940," in Taylor, ed., *Race and the City*, 156–92.

Taylor, Quintard, "The Emergence of Black Communities in the Pacific Northwest: 1865–1910," *Journal of Negro History* 64 (1979), 342–54.

————, "Black Urban Development—Another View: Seattle's Central District, 1910–1940," *Pacific Historical Review* 58 (1989), 429–48.

Thomas, Richard W., "The Black Urban Experience in Detroit: 1916–1967," in Kenneth
    L. Kusmer, ed., *Black Communities and Urban Race Relations in American History*, vol. 9,
    Overviews, Theory and Historiography (New York: Garland, 1991), 296–320.
Thompson, Robert A., "Social Dynamics in Demographic Trends and the Housing of Mi-
    nority Groups," *Phylon* 19 (1958), 31–43.
Thompson, Robert A., Hylan Lewis, and David McEntire, "Atlanta and Birmingham: A
    Comparative Study in Negro Housing," in Nathan Glazer and David McEntire, eds.,
    Studies in Housing and Minority Groups (Berkeley: University of California Press, 1960),
    13–83.
Tobey, Ronald, Charles Wetherall, and Jay Brigham, "Moving Out and Settling In: Resi-
    dential Mobility, Home Owning, and the Public Enframing of Citizenship, 1921–1950,"
    American Historical Review 95 (1990), 1395–422.
Tolnay, Stewart E., and E. M. Beck, "Rethinking the Role of Racial Violence in the Great
    Migration," in Harrison, ed., *Black Exodus*, 20–35.
Trotter, Joe William, Jr., "Introduction: Black Migration in Historical Perspective," in
    Trotter, ed., *Great Migration*, 1–21.
Tuck, R. D., "Behind the Zoot Suit Riots," *Survey Graphic* 32 (1943), 313–16.
Verge, Arthur C., "The Impact of the Second World War on Los Angeles," *Pacific Historical
    Review* 63 (1994), 289–314.
Villenez, Wayne J., "Race, Class and Neighborhood: Differences in the Residential Return
    on Individual Resources," *Social Forces* 59 (1978), 414–30.
Virrick, Elizabeth L., "New Housing for Negroes in Dade County, Florida," in Glazer and
    McEntire, *Studies in Housing and Minority Groups*, 135–43.
von Furstenberg, George M., and R. Jeffery Green, "The Effect of Income and Race on the
    Quality of Home Mortgages: A Case for Pittsburgh," in von Furstenberg, Harrison, and
    Horowitz, *Patterns of Racial Discrimination*, 165–79.
Walker, Jack L., "Fair Housing in Michigan," in Eley and Casstevens, eds., *Politics of Fair
    Housing*, 353–82.
Ware, Leland B., "Invisible Walls: An Examination of the Legal Strategy of the Restrictive
    Covenant Cases," *Washington University Law Quarterly* 67 (Fall 1989), 737–72.
Washington, Booker T., "My View of Segregation Law," reprinted in Sherman, *The Negro
    and the City*, 20–22.
Waters, Laughlin E., and Robert S. Thompson, "The California Housing Initiative," *Los
    Angeles Bar Bulletin*, July 1964, 328–31, 360–64.
Weaver, Robert C., "The Negro in a Program of Public Housing," *Opportunity* 16 (1938),
    198–203.
———, "Negroes Need Housing," *The Crisis* 47 (1940), 138–39, 158.
———, "The Negro as Tenant and Neighbor," *Public Housing Weekly News* 1 (May 21,
    1940), 3–4.
———, "Racial Policy in Public Housing," *Phylon* 1 (1940), 149–56, 161.
———, "Detroit and Negro Skill," *Phylon* 4 (1943), 131–43.
———, "Whither Northern Race Relations Committees?" *Phylon* 5 (1944), 205–18.
———, "Chicago: A City of Covenants," *The Crisis* 53 (1946), 75–78, 93.
———, "A Tool For Democratic Housing," *The Crisis* 54 (1947), 47–48.
———, "Northern Ways," *Survey Graphic* 36 (1947), 43–47, 123–24.

———, "Integration in Public and Private Housing," in Reid, ed., *Racial Desegregation*, 86–97.

———, "Housing for Minority Families," *The Crisis* 73 (1966), 421–26, 431.

———, "Charles Abrams as a Champion of Civil Rights in Housing," in Koenigsberger, Groak, and Bernstein, *Work of Charles Abrams*, 27–33.

Wheat, Carl I., ed., "California's Bantam Cock: The Journals of Charles E. DeLong, 1854–1863," *California Historical Society Quarterly* 256–58, 281–82.

White, Dana F., "The Black Sides of Atlanta: A Geography of Expansion and Containment, 1870–1970, "*Atlanta Historical Journal* 26 (Summer–Fall 1982), 199–225.

White, Walter, "Negro Segregation Comes North," *Nation* 121 (1925), 458–60.

———, "The Sweet Trial," *The Crisis* 31 (1926), 125–29.

———, "The Right to Fight for Democracy," *Survey Graphic* 31 (1942), 472–74.

Wiese, Andrew, "Places of Our Own: Suburban Black Towns Before 1960," *Journal of Urban History* 19 (1993), 30–54.

Wilkins, Roy, "The Civil Rights Bill of 1966," *The Crisis* 73 (1966), 302–06, 330.

Wilkinson, Doris Y., "Gender and Social Inequality: The Prevailing Significance of Race," *Daedalus* 124 (Winter 1995), 167–78.

Williams, Lee, "Concentrated Residences: The Case of Black Toledo, 1890–1930," *Phylon* 43 (1982), 167–76.

Williams, Lillian S., "Afro-Americans in Buffalo, 1900–1930: A Study in Community Formation," *Afro-Americans in New York Life and History* 8 (1984), 7–35.

Williamson, Joel, "The Oneness of Southern Life," *South Atlantic Urban Studies* 1 (1977), 78–89.

Willie, Charles V., "The Inclining Significance of Race," *Society* 15 (Jan.–Feb. 1978), 15, 63.

Willits, Joseph H., "Some Impacts of the Depression upon the Negro in Philadelphia," from *Opportunity* 11 (July 1933), reprinted in Foner and Lewis, eds., *The Black Worker*, vol. 6, 89–94.

Wilson, F. Page, "Miami: From Frontier to Metropolis: An Appraisal," *Tequesta* 14 (1954), 25–50.

Wilson, Franklin D., "Patterns of White Avoidance," in Roof, ed., *Race and Residence in American Cities*, 132–41.

Wilson, James Q., "Review of Luigi M. Laurenti, *Property Values and Race: Studies in Seven Cities* and George Grier and Eunice Grier, *Privately Developed Interracial Housing*," *Appraisal Journal* 28 (1960), 397–401.

Wilson, William Julius, "The Declining Significance of Race: Revisited but Not Revised," *Society* 15 (Jan.–Feb. 1978), 14, 62.

Winder, Alvin, "Residential Invasion and Racial Antagonism in Chicago," *Phylon* 12 (1951), 239–41.

Winger, Stewart, "Unwelcome Neighbors," *Chicago History* 21 (1992), 56–72.

Winnick, Louis, "An American Trilemma: The Persistence of Racialist Housing Patterns in the USA," in Koenigsberger, Groak, and Bernstein, *Work of Charles Abrams*, 169–74.

Wolters, Raymond, "The New Deal and the Negro," in Braeman, Bremner, and Brody, *The New Deal: The National Level*, 170–217.

Woodbury, Coleman, "Integrating Private and Public Enterprise in Housing," in Rowlands and Woodbury, eds., *Current Developments in Housing*, 162–75.

Woodward, C. Vann, "*Strange Career* Critics: Long May They Persevere," *Journal of American History* 75 (1988), 857–68.

Yinger, John, "Measuring Discrimination with Fair Housing Audits," *American Economic Review* 76 (1986), 881–93.

———, "The Racial Dimension of Urban Housing Markets in the 1980s," in Tobin, ed., *Divided Neighborhoods*, 43–67.

PAPERS, THESES, AND DISSERTATIONS

Ambrose, Andrew M., "Redrawing the Color Line: The History and Patterns of Black Housing in Atlanta, 1940–1973," doctoral diss., Emory University, 1992.

Barresi, Charles M., "Residential Invasion and Succession: A Case Study," master's thesis, University of Buffalo, 1959, Buffalo–Erie County Public Library, Special Collections.

Cassady, Kevin Anderson, "Black Leadership and the Civil Rights Struggle in Birmingham, Alabama, 1960–1964," undergraduate thesis, Georgetown University, 1986, Birmingham Public Library, Southern Collection.

Cochran, Lynda Dempsey, "Arthur D. Shores: Advocate for Freedom," master's thesis, Georgia Southern University, 1977.

Corley, Robert Gaines, "The Quest for Racial Harmony: Race Relations in Birmingham, Alabama, 1947–1963," doctoral diss., University of Virginia, 1979.

Eskew, Glenn Thomas, "But for Birmingham: The Local and National Movements in the Civil Rights Struggle," doctoral diss., University of Georgia, 1993.

Feldman, Lynne Barbara, "A Sense of Place: Homeownership and Community-Building Among African-Americans in Smithfield, 1900–1920," master's thesis, Florida State University, 1993.

Griffith, Sara, "Birmingham: The Magic City," Bachelor of Science in Sociology Notebook, Northwestern University, 1938.

Harmon, David Andrew, "Beneath the Image: The Civil Rights Movement and Race Relations in Atlanta, 1946–1981," doctoral diss., Emory University, 1993.

O'Connor, Michael James, "The Measurement and Significance of Racial Residential Barriers in Atlanta, 1890–1970," doctoral diss., University of Georgia, 1977.

Oliver, Leary W., "Zoning Ordinances in Relation to Segregated Negro Housing in Birmingham, Alabama," master's thesis, Indiana University, 1951.

Pennington, Margaret B., "What Was the Ordinance of May 11, 1914 Adopted by the City of Louisville?" College of Arts and Sciences, 542 Student Papers, 1980–1982, University of Louisville Archives, William F. Ekstrom Library.

Steeh, Charlotte Andrea Goodman, "Racial Discrimination in Alabama, 1870–1910," doctoral diss., University of Michigan, 1975.

INDEX

ABOUT
THE AUTHOR

Stephen Grant Meyer was born in Oakville, Canada. He grew up in the suburbs of Toronto and in rural southern Ontario. He earned a bachelor's degree in history and American studies from the University of Toronto where he went on to receive a master's degree in American history. Meyer was awarded a doctorate in American history from the University of Alabama in 1996. He resides in northern Virginia with his wife, Lori. This is his first book.